categories of ... outline: p. 159.

THE GLOBAL CENTURY

GLOBALIZATION AND NATIONAL SECURITY

VOLUME I

THE GLOBAL CENTURY

GLOBALIZATION AND NATIONAL SECURITY

VOLUME I

EDITED BY

RICHARD L. KUGLER
AND ELLEN L. FROST

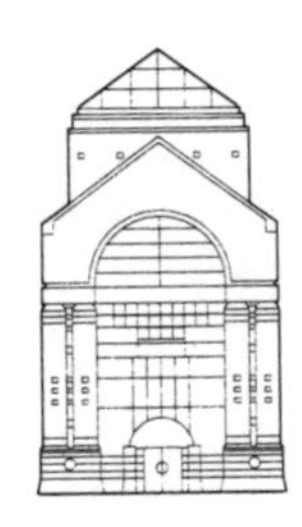

NATIONAL DEFENSE UNIVERSITY PRESS
WASHINGTON, D.C.
2001

The opinions, conclusions, and recommendations expressed or implied within are those of the contributors and do not necessarily reflect the views of the Department of Defense or any other agency of the Federal Government.

Library of Congress Cataloging-in-Publication Data

The Global Century: Globalization and National Security / edited by Richard L. Kugler and Ellen L. Frost.

p. cm.

Includes bibliographical references and index.

ISBN 1-57906-053-6 (pbk.)

1. Globalization. 2. Security, International. 3. National Security—United States. 4.United States—Foreign Relations—1993– I. Kugler, Richard L. II. Frost, Ellen L.

JZ1318.G556 2001
327.73—dc21

2001030603

First printing, June 2001

NDU Press publications are sold by the U.S. Government Printing Office. For ordering information, call (202) 512-1800 or write to the Superintendent of Documents, U.S. Government Printing Office, Washington, D.C. 20402. For GPO publications on-line, access their web site at: http://www.access.gpo.gov/su_docs/sale.html.

For current publications of the Institute for National Strategic Studies, consult the National Defense University Web site at: http://www.ndu.edu.

Contents

Part II. U.S. National Security Policy: Emerging Priorities

Part III. Military Power: The Challenges Ahead

Volume II

Part IV. Global Trends: Unity or Fragmentation?

Preface

Vice Admiral Paul G. Gaffney II, USN
President, National Defense University

The 21st century will be the first truly Global Century. Growing cross-border flows of trade, investment, finances, information, technology, cultures, values, ideas, and people are drawing the far corners of the Earth together, creating new opportunities and dangers. Decisions, events, and people anywhere in the world—no matter how distant—can now influence our safety, prosperity, and policies. Several important questions arise from accelerating globalization. How will this dynamic unfold? What are its strategic consequences? Will it draw the world closer together in a web of cooperative ties, or will it tear the world apart, creating conflict and strife? What are the implications for U.S. foreign policy and national security strategy? How can the America help *shape* the new global environment? These questions are addressed in these volumes.

Volume I of *The Global Century: Globalization and National Security* examines globalization's impact on world affairs and the task of forging responsive policies and strategies. Volume II provides additional in-depth analyses of global and regional trends, and of policies for dealing with them. Taken together they are the product of a major research project sponsored by the Department of the Navy and carried out by the Institute for National Strategic Studies at the National Defense University. The project brought together a team of more than 50 experts from a variety of disciplines. The results of their intellectual labors and collaboration are on display in these path-breaking volumes.

These volumes do not represent the views of the Department of Defense or any other governmental agency. They are scholarly inquiries aimed at stimulating new policy thinking and at driving home the urgency of coming to grips with globalization. They offer an opportunity to learn about an exciting and important worldwide trend that is affecting countries and people everywhere—a trend that U.S. strategists will need to address in the coming years.

Foreword

The Honorable Jerry MacArthur Hultin
Under Secretary of the Navy, 1997–2000

The close of the 20th century has been filled with such striking new features that few can avoid the allure and burden of seriously examining and pondering their implications. These new features are often summed up in a phenomenon called *globalization*, which can be defined as the international interaction of information, financial capital, commerce, technology, and even labor at exponentially greater speeds and volume than previously thought possible.

The global environment is in the midst of fascinating technological, economic, and political changes. The proliferation of international corporations, the great impact of government policies both at home and abroad, cultural differences, and evolving security considerations demand that we understand globalization before we can determine the optimum course to steer. This new environment is already having a dramatic effect on domestic and international businesses, as well as on military operations—especially the employment of naval forces.

Certainly this was true during the 3 years that I served as Under Secretary of the Navy. Our days and many nights were filled with planning and decisions that arose in the main from the new qualities of the 21st century. First, people issues dominated the forefront as young men and women questioned the rigors of military life, especially the life of a sailor or a marine who deploys away from his or her home and family for up to 6 months at a time. Second, the operational warfighting capabilities of both the Navy and the Marine Corps underwent fundamental changes as precision, network centric, and high-density information were fused into operations, weapon systems, and platforms. Third, business issues became more important in decisionmaking as the means and methods of the new Information Age economy offered revolutionary new approaches for departmental management. For example, significant gains will come from innovations, such as the Navy-Marine Corps Intranet, enterprise resource planning projects, knowledge management tools, and e-business strategies.

Yet as important as these innovations are, globalization poses more fundamental challenges that can best the understood by asking two fundamental questions: What significance should we attach to the new forces of globalization for the national security of the United States? And, how can we respond to and shape globalization through the use of naval power?

Although our current fighting forces are capable of powerful action "Forward . . . from the Sea," a failure to address these two new questions could put the Nation's security at risk. The burden of supporting international stability has been far more taxing than we anticipated when the Cold War ended. Furthermore, unless we can create an environment in which the global economy thrives and all people—both at home and abroad—ascend the economic ladder, we are likely to be assaulted by more asymmetrical violence in the short run and to face a phalanx of hostile, near-peer competitors in the long run. While the challenge of enabling global economic growth is a profound moral, political, and financial responsibility that requires fundamentally new knowledge and insights, the future security of our Nation will be increasingly dependent on our skills and performance in this new arena.

To develop a better understanding of the phenomenon of globalization and its implications, the Navy Secretariat commissioned the Institute for National Strategic Studies at the National Defense University to examine and debate the attributes and effects of globalization on national security and naval power. This 18-month study represents our contribution to an open discussion about the implications of globalization and the role of military force in the 21st century.

I hope that you will join in this endeavor by adding your insights and energy to our discussion. We owe to all who brought the United States to this position of global prominence the wise and judicious use our military power. We are duty bound to employ our very best thinking to meet the challenges and opportunities of this new century.

Thank you to all who contributed to this project.

Acknowledgments

The two volumes of *The Global Century: Globalization and National Security* are products of a research project on globalization and security sponsored by the Department of the Navy and carried out by the Institute for National Strategic Studies (INSS) at the National Defense University (NDU). For their support and guidance, special thanks are due to the former Under Secretary of the Navy, Jerry M. Hultin, and the Deputy Under Secretary, Charles Nemfakos, as well as their staffs.

The editors of both volumes are Richard L. Kugler and Ellen L. Frost with help from Stephen J. Flanagan and Harlan K. Ullman. The editors were greatly assisted by the INSS globalization team led by Kimberley L. Thachuk. This team included Lt Col Charles B. Shotwell, USAF, Colleen M. Herrmann, Esther A. Bacon, and Elena Beloderik.

The editors gratefully acknowledge those who contributed to the production of these volumes. Editorial Associates of Washington, DC, performed initial copyediting and indexing; the Publication Directorate at INSS and the staff of NDU Press—William R. Bode, George C. Maerz, Lisa M. Yambrick, and Jeffrey D. Smotherman—under the supervision of Robert A. Silano, Director of Publications, conducted final copyediting; Jeffrey D. Smotherman also designed and composed all text; and William A. Rawley and Nicholas C. Crawford of the Typography and Design Division of the U.S. Government Printing Office designed the cover.

The strategic assessments and policy appraisals contained in these two volumes represent the work of many scholars and analysts. The editors thank them for their participation and contributions.

THE GLOBAL CENTURY

GLOBALIZATION AND NATIONAL SECURITY

VOLUME I

Introduction: Policies for a Globalized World

For a term that entered the vernacular only a few years ago, *globalization* has come a long way. It is now a household word, spawning books, newspaper stories, public debates, and protest movements. While people argue about whether its effects are good or bad, virtually nobody doubts its importance. UN Secretary General Kofi Annan has spoken of its criticality. *A National Security Strategy for a New Century*[1] proclaimed globalization as the transforming reality of our times, one that will have a major impact on the 21st century. Because this judgment seems correct, globalization requires careful study not only to understand its properties but also to determine how best to deal with it. Like all powerful changes capable of propelling the entire world toward an uncertain destination, a dynamic this important is not something to be taken for granted.[2]

Globalization already is the subject of a burgeoning literature about its key features. Even so, its widespread consequences and policy implications are not yet well understood. To be sure, globalization is reshaping the world economy and altering how people communicate with each other. But its impact seems destined to be even broader and more strategic. In potent ways, globalization likely will affect how international security affairs unfold in the coming years. Directly or indirectly, it will help determine whether the future brings war or peace. As a result, it will influence not only American economic policies but also overall U.S. foreign policy and national security strategy, including defense strategy and military forces. For these reasons, the time has arrived for a serious examination of globalization, where it is taking the world, and how it can best be channeled in healthy directions.

The Global Century: Globalization and National Security is a two-volume work. Volume I provides an overall framework. It focuses on globalization's impact on world affairs and on the task of forging responsive U.S. policies and strategies. Volume II provides additional analyses of specific global and regional trends, and of policies for dealing with them. Scholarly in their tone and content, both volumes aim to illuminate and educate, not advocate. They do not put forth any single theory of globalization's future or a fixed policy blueprint to follow. Indeed, they present a wide range of opinions, interpretations, and recommendations from more than 50 experts drawn from multiple disciplines and specializations. They offer core themes, including a weighty sense of globalization's strategic essence and an insightful portrayal of the policy choices facing the United States and other countries. Their goal is to help inform the reader about globalization, its consequences, and its policy implications.

The stage for both volumes can best be set by briefly explaining what is meant by *globalization*. The dictionary defines the term as "the act of making something global or worldwide in scope and application." As used here, globalization is a dynamic process of change characterized by the growing cross-border flows of trade, investments, finances, technology, ideas, cultures, values, and people. It thus measures the pulse of international activity today and tomorrow. As noted in *A National Security Strategy for a New Century*, this process of accelerating interaction is drawing countries and regions closer together, creating a growing web of ties in both geographical and functional terms. In practical terms, it means that events halfway around the world can now profoundly affect our lives, including our safety and prosperity. This definition of globalization is meant to be empirical and neutral. It implies nothing about whether globalization will produce overall progress or regression, or whether it rewards one policy over another. The task of making these evaluative judgments rests with the authors.

This book begins with a chapter written by Stephen J. Flanagan that summarizes the main messages of both volumes. Part I provides 5 chapters that help put globalization into strategic and policy perspective. Part II offers 10 chapters that address emerging priorities for U.S. foreign policy and national security strategy. Part III offers 10 chapters on the challenges facing U.S. defense strategy, military forces, and naval power.

Taken together, the 26 chapters of volume I make it clear that in the coming years, the United States and many other countries will face a strong imperative to design wise, effective policies for handling globalization. The reason is clear. Globalization helps promote progress abroad by encouraging market capitalism, democracy, the free flow of information, and cooperative security affairs. But it also can contribute to economic dislocation, political turmoil, inflamed security rivalries, and even war. Globalization should be neither wholly celebrated nor wholly vilified, but instead seen for what it is worth and the complex changes that it produces. Acting in concert with other trends on the world scene, globalization can have both good and bad effects. Much depends upon the regional settings in which it occurs. Whereas the wealthy democracies are well situated to benefit from globalization, other regions present a more complicated picture. There and elsewhere, globalization is far from a purely impersonal force. Its course will be greatly influenced by how governments everywhere react to it. If governments design sound policies for handling globalization, they will greatly enhance their prospects for channeling it in directions that promote progress and minimize its damaging effects. In essence, globalization has the potential to become whatever governments, countries, and people around the world decide to make of it.

Because the United States is a global power, the policy agenda confronting it will be especially important, demanding, and different from past agendas. The United States will need to think and act globally like never before. It will need not only to see the world as a whole but also to consider the changing relationships among its parts. Clearly, the United States will need to forge sound policies for handling globalization's powerful economic dynamics. But the challenge does not end there. The United States also will need to work hard at blending its foreign economic policies with its diplomacy and its national security strategy abroad. Prospects for war or peace will be determined by how economic, political, and security affairs interact in the coming years. The United States can best safeguard its own interests, encourage progress, and lessen impending dangers by ensuring that its policies in these and other areas work together, not alone or at cross-purposes. Acting in these ways will not be easy. Indeed, the U.S. Government will face difficult challenges in harnessing its many departments and agencies to this demanding task. It will need to design new ways of making and carrying out foreign policy and national security strategy in the Global Century.

The United States also will face the challenge of forging its defense strategy and military forces to meet the new requirements being created by globalization and other trends. In the past, the Department of Defense has not viewed globalization as a major consideration in defense planning. But the reality is that globalization will have a profound impact on future international security affairs. It will lessen some security dangers, but it will magnify others. It will help give rise to new military missions, purposes, and priorities in new geographical locations. It will influence the ways in which future wars are fought. The United States will need to remain the world's strongest military power. Working in concert with allies and partners, it also will need to use its military forces to shape the strategic terrain in peacetime, to respond to crises and other situations, and to win the wars of the future. For these reasons, an agenda of change lies ahead in U.S. defense strategy. This judgment applies to the full spectrum of U.S. military forces, but it holds especially true for the Navy and maritime operations: areas where the new demands and requirements of globalization will be powerfully manifested.

Will the U.S. Government and other countries respond effectively? Only time will tell. What can be said is that the challenge of shaping the new Global Century is already upon us. The time to act is now.

Notes

[1] The White House, *A National Security Strategy for a New Century* (Washington, DC: Government Printing Office, December 1999).

[2] In a recent public opinion poll of American attitudes, fully 87 percent of respondents said that they are aware of globalization; 30 percent said it is good for the United States; 22 percent said it is bad; and 25 percent said it makes no difference. See *The Washington Post*, October 27, 2000, A13.

Chapter 1

Meeting the Challenges of the Global Century

Stephen J. Flanagan

Mastering the challenges of the 21st century will require governments and citizens everywhere to see, think, and act globally—in ways never demanded of them before. In previous centuries, the course of history was determined largely by events in only a few regions, particularly Europe and North America. The world's continents existed mostly apart, not influencing each other a great deal. No longer. During the 21st century, the struggle for progress and prosperity, as well as the questions of war and peace, will be influenced by events in many disparate places. Events at the far corners of the Earth are already starting to affect each other to a greater degree than in the past. This is happening because of a fast-growing network of ever closer ties.

This immense transformation is being propelled by globalization: a powerful, dimly understood process of worldwide change that has exploded onto the public consciousness only recently, but has major implications for international security affairs in this Global Century. The two companion volumes of this set offer a comprehensive assessment of globalization's interrelated facets and strategic impact. In order to shape the evolution of international affairs in this Global Century, the United States—as well as its allies and friends—needs a foreign policy and national security strategy that draws, in an integrated fashion, on many disparate elements of state power. In support of this strategy, military planners will be asked to maintain a full spectrum of capabilities from more nuanced peacetime engagement, to regional conflict management, to theater war fighting. No one can claim to know where the 21st century is headed. In many ways, we are staring into a dense rolling fog, seeing little clearly, yet sensing an opportunity for great progress, as well as great danger. The imperative facing us is to help guide the future in ways that will make the Global Century a period of widening prosperity and peace.

Stephen J. Flanagan is the director of the Institute for National Strategic Studies and vice president for research at the National Defense University. He has served in senior positions with the National Security Council, Department of State, National Intelligence Council, and U.S. Senate. Dr. Flanagan also has held positions at the Kennedy School of Government at Harvard University and the International Institute for Strategic Studies.

Globalization: Here to Stay

Globalization is not a passing intellectual fad. Rather, it aptly describes the new era that is emerging from the shattered glacis of the old Cold War divide. This era is built on a truly global economy that is powered by the accelerating pace of transport, telecommunications, and information technology. Globalization makes it harder for states to live in isolation from one another.

The emerging global system is rapidly eroding the old boundaries between foreign and domestic affairs, and those between economics and national security. Developments in one sphere are increasingly having rapid and sometimes surprising impacts on the other. Coming to grips with the challenges of the global era requires transforming the way we think about the world and formulate policy. It requires more synergy and dynamism in the development of economic, security, and other government policies.

Protesters at meetings of the International Monetary Fund (IMF) around the world have painted globalization as an unmitigated source of evil, with devastating consequences for the developing world. The Clinton administration's *National Security Strategy*, published in December 1999, portrayed globalization as an important and largely positive force that is fostering international integration. The contributors to the two volumes of *The Global Century* show that globalization's effects are mixed and uneven across different regions and within various countries. Globalization has many elements that are of evident benefit to all; for example, the new ease of global communication and transportation has boosted trade. But these very same innovations have facilitated the growth in transnational crime and weapons proliferation, which have negative consequences around the world. This dichotomy is reflected in the following statistics:

> Flows of U.S. trade and investment are now equivalent to more than 30 percent of U.S. GDP [gross domestic product]. But in this global economy, the United States is increasingly affected by crime originating in other countries. Almost 40 percent of the cases being handled by the U.S. Federal Bureau of Investigation today, from telemarketing fraud to car theft to money laundering, have an international dimension.[1]

In responsive, adaptive (generally democratic) countries, globalization is fostering stability and prosperity. However, most countries with weak or authoritarian governments must now struggle mightily just to keep pace in the global marketplace. The widening gap between them and the rest of the world is yielding internal turmoil and regional instability. Still others are falling further and further behind the norm, unable to compete in the global economy and buffeted by many of globalization's negative consequences. The resulting economic and social disparities have sometimes exacerbated ethnic tensions and historical intercommunal grievances, and they have helped to spawn terrorism and armed conflicts that are placing new demands on international and regional institutions. For example:

- The Asian financial crisis intensified ethnic tensions and instability in Indonesia that ultimately led to the need for a United Nations (UN) peacekeeping operation in East Timor.
- The former Yugoslavia was largely cut off from the global economy because of its lack of market reforms and its authoritarian rule. The resulting economic stagnation exacerbated ethnic and regional tensions in the country. Ethnic Albanians used the Internet to raise substantial funds for the Kosovo Liberation Army, while Serbian reformers used the Internet to skirt government censorship.
- Criminal gangs in Sierra Leone have financed their insurrection through sales of diamonds on the international market.

Welcome to the Global Century.

The challenge for the United States and other countries is to take advantage of globalization's opportunities while minimizing its dangers. But addressing this challenge requires a better understanding of globalization and its effects. It also requires new, more integrated policy approaches and mechanisms for decisionmaking that will foster sound policies. Despite official recognition of globalization as a major factor in the international system, most components of the U.S. Government have been very slow to adapt structures and processes accordingly. Security, economic, science and technology, and law enforcement policies that are essential to coping with the challenges of the global era are still developed largely in isolation from one another. These policy streams are generally integrated only at the highest levels and only when necessitated by a crisis.

Key Features of Globalization

Globalization's Hydra-Headed Manifestations

Globalization is a long-term process of change, not a static condition. It comes in many forms, of which economic globalization is only one. The central features of globalization are the rapid, growing, and uneven cross-border flow of goods, services, people, money, technology, information, ideas, culture, crime, and weapons. Owing to globalization, the pace of international activity is increasing.

Globalization's core features are addressed in a highly integrated fashion by Ellen L. Frost in volume I. These key features are also treated, in varying degrees, by many other chapters in both volumes. While the contributors offer a wide range of opinions, they also reflect a strong consensus on globalization's properties and strategic consequences.

Globalization is merely one factor in the international arena, where many other trends and dynamics are at work. The key to analyzing its impact is to understand how it is interacting with the other factors. Globalization is capable of bringing the world together, tearing it apart, or facilitating some combination of both. Much will depend on how key countries react to it.

Globalization is not entirely new. A global economy began to emerge at the end of the 19th century and continued to develop through the 1930s. The process was disrupted by the two world wars and the Cold War. It was not until the 1970s that trade as a percentage of global output reached the level that it had achieved before World War I (15 percent). This was because trade protectionism, nationalism, global conflict, and the rise of the communist bloc had slowed the effects of globalization. This could happen again. Globalization is a powerful force, but it is not unstoppable or completely impervious to governmental actions.

Alan K. Henrikson's chapter in volume I explains how the globalization of U.S. foreign policy, which actually began a century ago and is continuing today, has not been driven by ideology or a grand strategy. Rather, it has emerged as a logical response to events and to connections between and among diverse situations where U.S. interests are at stake. Yes, the world is globalizing, but equally important, U.S. foreign policy is steadily becoming more global in its thinking, its logic, and its concepts.

Globalization today does have some marked differences from that in the past. For example, from the late 1970s on, the *integration of capital and commodity markets* has surpassed all previous indicators and is still spreading.[2] This reflects a fuller realization of the institutional framework created after World War II to promote global trade and growth, and to settle disputes according to agreed-upon rules. The postwar boom in East Asian economies and improvements in transportation technology are also key drivers of economic globalization.

What is most unique about globalization in the current era is the *revolution in information technology*, accompanied by the spread of cable television, the increasing number of personal computers, and the instant availability of information. One of the key hallmarks of globalization is the emergence of the Internet, which has the effect of spreading knowledge to the far corners of the Earth.

As Frost illustrates in volume I, there are several other foundations and enablers of globalization in the current era. The success of the Western policy of democratic enlargement has yielded a larger group of states well prepared to embrace the challenges of globalization. The passing of socialism and the triumph of market-oriented economic policies in much of the world have been key drivers as well. Also influential have been the knowledge revolution, business-driven interaction of advanced telecommunications, technology transfer, and capital flows. Globalization would not be occurring in its present form were it not for the business application of the knowledge revolution—for example, computers, email, satellites, and other innovations. A related driver of globalization is *market competition*. The current phase of globalization first appeared in commercial and economic form. Beginning in the late 1970s, breakthroughs in transportation and communications technology, a general lowering of trade barriers, and a worldwide shift toward market-oriented policies transformed the structure of global business.

Globalization's Risks and Benefits

Globalization is having a number of effects—economic, political, cultural, religious, social, demographic, environmental, and military—with various attendant risks and benefits. Understanding these aspects of globalization is important because the interaction among them can be benign or destructive, and it can trigger new security problems in which the United States may be called upon to intervene. While globalization can lessen tensions, it can also increase them.

Most economists applaud economic globalization because they place a high value on *efficiency*. They argue that the more global the scale of the market, the more efficient the allocation of resources. Several major studies have concluded that nations with open, market-oriented economies have grown at least twice as fast as those with closed economies, and in the 1970s and 1980s the disparity was even higher.[3] Never before in history have so many people in so many countries experienced a rise in real income. However, other statistics in the poorer regions, including rapid population growth, environmental degradation, and disease, are far less encouraging. What is hotly debated is to what extent globalization has exacerbated poverty in various parts of the world. In the eyes of globalization's critics, there is a direct, causal relationship between globalization-fed corporate profits and global poverty.

The potential of economic globalization to wreak great turmoil rapidly is becoming more evident. The speed, volatility, and sudden withdrawal of financial flows sent a number of countries spinning into recession in 1997–1998. This was the first real "crisis" of globalization. The collapse of the Thai *baht* pulsed through most of Asia and then to much of South America, ravaging the economies of Brazil and its neighbors. The collapse of confidence associated with the Asian crisis ultimately spread to Russia, crippled what was left of the Russian economy, and brought forth a younger, technocratic leader to clean up the mess. This was not a predictable chain reaction. This experience leads David J. Rothkopf to argue in volume I that new transnational institutional and regulatory frameworks are needed to temper the potentially destructive impact on smaller states of highly volatile international financial markets.

The speed of changes in income and its distribution within and among countries can also rock political stability. As a general rule, globalization offers rising elites and the urban middle class a bigger share of the economic pie. If this share increases too rapidly, and if the rest of the pie is not made available to others because of monopolies or corruption, the government can lose its legitimacy, as it did in Indonesia. If the speed of change is glacial because the government has deliberately isolated its citizens from globalization and restricted the free flow of information, disgruntled students and merchants may complain or rebel, as they have in China and Iran. Likewise, the uneven distribution of direct foreign investment in the developing world—three-quarters goes to fewer than a dozen countries, with the Middle East accounting for only a fraction—will intensify a widening income gap *within* the developing world.

Income gaps mirror social and geographical divisions both within societies and among countries and regions. In most countries, unskilled laborers, workers in protected industries, and small farmers are increasingly at risk of rapid dislocation due to external developments. What is politically important is the perception of prosperity relative to that of other groups or states. Globalization exposes these fissures and often exacerbates them.

The digital divide, the growing divergence between those who have access to, and are capable of using, computers and the Internet, and those who are left behind is another trend of concern. Information is a critical element of political empowerment. As a recent task force concluded, the challenge is to adopt the right mix of public policies and public-private projects, possibly spearheaded by the G–8 group of world leaders, to create a "global digital opportunity" instead of a threat.[4]

Some lessons of economic globalization are clear. If a government pursues market-oriented policies that benefit the ruling elite or the middle class at the expense of the poor, if inadequate disclosure and weak supervisory organs trigger a run on the banks, and if social safety nets are weak or absent, openness to globalization can severely destabilize the political system and hurt the most vulnerable members of the population. Since people in other countries tend to assume that the United States pulls the strings of the World Bank and IMF, financial crises of the Indonesian variety not only evoke a legitimate humanitarian outcry, but they also ignite anti-Americanism.

Cultural dimensions of globalization are also being felt. The worldwide predominance of American business practices and popular culture, facilitated by the globalization of the communications and entertainment industries, has raised anxieties and backlash among elites in some countries who fear the loss of their own cultural identity and in some areas of the world where the national identity is weak or recently formed. Popular culture has fostered the learning of English, the language of international communication, which has accelerated the global flow of ideas. Cultures that are capable of borrowing and adapting foreign influences are generally faring better in the face of globalization. But globalization has also helped spawn awareness of traditional cultures that face the threat of extinction.

Globalization is facilitating the spread of religious ideas, rather than destroying religion. The strength of religious values and institutions has helped people in many regions cope with the alienation, the insecurity associated with the decline of traditional authority, and the rapid economic changes that accompany globalization. Indeed, much of the violence that is sometimes described as religious is actually political backlash associated with globalization. Douglas M. Johnston shows how globalization is accelerating the revival of religious and cultural identities once thought to be in decline. Political Islam is one example, but not the only one. Although cultural wars are unlikely, he says, communal conflict is becoming a hallmark of globalization. Moreover, a backlash is building against Western values and practices, which often are perceived as demeaning and exploitative. Religion and culture can also contribute to peace if their moral values are properly nourished. The challenge, Johnston says, is to separate the good from the bad.

Globalization is also having a profound impact on where people live and on the health and welfare of women. Global agribusiness and other changes associated with globalization are propelling urbanization. The global flow of business is being accompanied by a global flow of people, with more than 120 million migrant workers in 2000, nearly double the number in 1965. These flows bring in people with energy to work hard in building a new life or to accept menial jobs that more affluent societies have difficulty filling. But they also bring enormous social and health problems. Many women have taken advantage of the opportunities accompanying globalization to participate in the labor force.

For all these reasons, the once popular idea that globalization is an unbridled good, fostering progress everywhere, is fading. Replacing it is a recognition that globalization has positive and negative effects. The challenge is to absorb the good effects and limit the bad effects.

Democracies Cope Better with Globalization

As several contributors note, the widening income gap both within countries and between countries and regions that are adapting relatively well to globalization and those that are left behind should be a matter of growing concern to national security strategists, not just international development experts. In volume II, Laura Rozen chronicles how the global debt crisis of the 1980s exacerbated the economic crisis in the former Yugoslavia. In turn, this economic reversal polarized the richer and poorer regions of the federation and fueled the ethnic tensions that led to separatist movements and war. Sudden shifts in wealth can also cause backlash toward successful ethnic minorities. Extremist movements can often attract those uprooted or fearful of globalization. There is a real risk that these governments or substate actors within them will become more hostile to the West and more aggressive. Moreover, the countries that are falling behind in the global economy are found in regions of the world with simmering interstate and intrastate tensions; among these countries are many that support terrorism and are actively pursuing the development of weapons of mass destruction (WMDs).

Governments that want to attract global investors today know that they must strengthen the rule of law and their judicial systems, particularly with respect to commercial transactions. However, in countries where the legal and institutional structures are weak, globalization has generally intensified the problems of bribery and corruption, and facilitated the development of criminal networks. Corruption and crime not only divert resources, but they also damage public confidence in a market economy. In the area of public works, crime and corruption jeopardize public safety and can severely damage the environment. In these circumstances, "it becomes all too easy for an economically beleaguered public to confuse democratization with the corruption and criminalization of the economy—creating fertile soil for an authoritarian backlash and engendering potentially hostile international behavior by these states in turn."[5]

Kimberley L. Thachuk shows in volume II how organized crime, drug trafficking, and terrorism, aided by the Information Age, are rapidly growing, to the point where they already form a sinister underbelly of globalization that threatens the security of all countries, including the developed democracies. These criminal activities also have the potential to infect world politics on a larger scale by creating criminal states that seek economic profits through illicit activities and use their military power accordingly.

Certain societies with a flexible social structure, respect for the value of shared information, and openness to new technology are well suited for the global age. There is considerable evidence that the political cultures that adapt most successfully to economic globalization feature *accountable and adaptive institutions based on some minimal level of civic trust.* Attitudes toward work, education, entrepreneurship, and the future are important. Policy choices can help to promote the right mix.

Broadly speaking, the political cultures of North America, Western and Central Europe (not including the Balkans), most of East Asia (including Southeast Asia,

Australia, and New Zealand, but not Indonesia and North Korea), and a few South American countries (Chile and Brazil) are either adapting relatively well to globalization or have a good chance of doing so if transitional political problems can be resolved. China and India remain uncertain because they are confronting enormous internal problems and because some regions within their borders are adapting far better than others. Significantly, the successful countries are either "free" or "partly free," that is, democracies or "soft" authoritarian states with substantial democratic features. But even the most effective democratic polities are hard-pressed to cope with some of globalization's challenges and increasingly are seeking support from foreign governments and international institutions. This is another manifestation of political globalization.

By contrast, with some exceptions, nations located in a huge swath of contiguous territory ranging from the former Soviet Union through the Middle East and South Asia to sub-Saharan Africa are presently ill suited for globalization. They exhibit some combination of weak or closed political institutions, inflexible or divisive social cultures marked by vengeance and distrust, predominantly tribal or clan loyalties, and excessive regulation accompanied by a high degree of corruption. Much of the Andean region and the Balkans are also adapting poorly to globalization.

The growth of international communications has contributed to a new global political awareness. Television and the Internet have, to paraphrase the late Thomas P. "Tip" O'Neill, made all local politics global. Moreover, as Samuel Feist explains in volume II, the global village is shrinking as new technologies are making it far easier to broadcast and receive news worldwide. These communications innovations have had many positive effects. They have facilitated media exposure of abuses of official power, diffused norms of democracy and human rights, and heightened awareness of environmental problems and regional conflicts. Because markets need information to function properly, the Chinese and other authoritarian governments that also want to play in the global economy are finding it increasingly difficult to control the flow of information. Over time, these pressures toward greater openness could stimulate political liberalization. However, these developments also present new challenges for U.S. policymakers. As Feist notes, modern news organizations are international, not national actors. Their reporting can accelerate the pace of political conflicts and subject military operations to daily, and sometimes unhelpful, scrutiny.

Also, while the pervasive, instantaneous reach of the international media is creating a global living room, this awareness has not always galvanized international responses to crises. The so-called CNN effect, the notion that heightened awareness of human suffering forces government responses to crises that may be of peripheral interest, is overstated. While European and U.S. citizens pressed their governments to respond to graphic media reports of atrocities in the Balkans, there were no such demands for responses to equally horrific suffering during conflicts in Rwanda, Chechnya, and Afghanistan. These other cases were not assessed to be as important or compelling. Thus, geopolitical and other filters appear to be able to temper the CNN effect. Moreover, additional information can actually make it harder to sort out national interests in various crises.

Leslie David Simon notes in volume II that the "Net," the ever expanding global communications network linked together by the Internet, which is both a product and instigator of globalization, is spreading information, changing business and governmental institutions, creating enormous new wealth, and generally strengthening democracy. But he cautions that the Net cannot itself eliminate security problems and dangers associated with its development. Simon recommends further steps by government and business to protect critical infrastructure. Martin C. Libicki reminds us in volume II that other international networks, such as those for commodities and finance, are also vulnerable to certain faults, with disruptive ripple effects on other nodes.

Globalization's Impact on the International System

Globalization is doing more than reshaping the world economy and communications. It is also shaping international politics and security affairs. Here, too, the effects are uneven and hydra-headed. In our globalizing world, many contradictory things are happening at the same time and will be for the foreseeable future. States are losing power; states are not losing power. Some groups dream of nationhood, others have only recently won it, and members of the European Union (EU) are moving beyond it. Depending on the area, the rule of law is on the rise or breaking down. Local culture is threatened or flowering. Religion is fading away or undergoing a revival.

Shaping International Politics

Globalization does not necessarily foster integration or stability, as columnist Thomas L. Friedman and economist Dani Rodrik have suggested.[6] Actually, in the near and medium term, globalization appears to contribute to several simultaneous tensions that are shaping the current era of international politics—for example, fragmentation-integration, localization-globalization, and decentralization-centralization. Globalization is speeding up the pace at which unifying change is occurring, but it is also providing an environment conducive to many of these disintegrative trends. These simultaneous forces for integration and disintegration are aptly described by James N. Rosenau as *fragmegration*. Rosenau argues that only through such change can democracies prosper and that antidemocratic systems benefit from political stasis. He concludes that national governments are generally losing power to transnational forces.

Globalization is creating a new context for the formal and informal exercise of national power. Regional and international institutions, local governments, and nonstate actors, particularly large transnational corporations and some nongovernmental organizations (NGOs), are making use of some of the instruments of globalization and diminishing the nation-state's monopoly on power. Some power is shifting to the international arena (for example, both the spread of and fight against organized crime and terrorism); some power is shifting down to local levels (for example, citizen mobilization through email and the Internet); and new power centers are being created as NGOs and corporations use the tools of the Information Age to shape policy outcomes (for example, Seattle protests against the World Trade Organization [WTO]).

In Europe, Latin America, and Asia, regional economic agreements are becoming a dominant expression of relations among states, particularly on trade, giving regional structures such as the European Union, the Association of Southeast Asian Nations (ASEAN), and the Southern Cone Common Market (MERCOSUR) a geopolitical personality. As Charles B. Shotwell notes, globalization is leading to the writing of new international laws and to expanding roles for such organizations as the WTO and the United Nations. This development offers the promise of creating better ways to help regulate global conflict in economics, politics, and security affairs. But outside the transatlantic community, regional security arrangements are evolving more slowly and are likely to remain informal and flexible.

Changing Nature of Security

Globalization does not eliminate traditional geopolitical concerns. National governments and various substate actors are not motivated by economic gain alone. There are still many lingering political conflicts over territory, borders, military competition, resources, and ethnic and cultural differences. Such stresses and strains on geopolitics continue to coexist and interact with the emerging global system. Sometimes globalization mitigates these stresses and strains, and sometimes it exacerbates them.

Indeed, as Robert E. Hunter and Jonathan T. Howe note, while the world economy is integrating as a result of the globalization of finance, geopolitical affairs are fragmenting along regional lines. In the absence of the bipolar political confrontation, regional political and security affairs are safely unfolding independently, with little linkage to or impact on developments in other regions. While this situation reduces the risks of regional tension triggering a wider global conflict, a pattern characteristic of the Cold War period, it has exacerbated instability in key places.

Control of energy resources (both oil and gas) and access to them are re-emerging as critical issues in world politics, as Martha Caldwell Harris (volume I) and Patrick L. Clawson (volume II) explain. Globalization is increasing demands for energy in order to propel economic growth. Although the world supply seems likely to match the demand in the coming years, the United States and its industrial partners will remain dangerously dependent on oil from the Persian Gulf and other unstable places. This especially is true for Asia, whose dependence on Persian Gulf oil is growing. This dynamic has the potential to create new forms of international political conflict.

Ideas still matter in the global era, as Esther A. Bacon and Colleen M. Herrmann demonstrate in their survey in volume II of foreign policy models. These authors find a spectrum of ideologies, values, and beliefs around the world today, all animated by a mix of economics, politics, and security. One model is democratic enlargement and participation in capitalist markets. But other models include national interests, nationalism, strategic preservationism, outlaw behavior, and state survival. They argue that the main effect will be to produce a world of great diversity as globalization gains momentum.

Overall, globalization is leading to a new, largely bifurcated international structure. It is divided between those countries that are well integrated into, and committed to, the evolving norms of the global economy and those countries that are either being left behind by, or may seek to challenge the norms of, the emerging global order.

- This first group is composed of about 80 to 100 countries that share a commitment to democracy, open trade, and collaborative relations. This liberal, democratic, and peaceful *global core group* includes the countries of North America, Western and Central Europe, Japan, most of East Asia, and the southern half of Latin America. Within this group, there is an inner core of about 30 countries (EU members, Canada, Japan, and a few other Asian countries) with per capita GDPs in excess of $20,000, well above the $7,000 world average. Another 50 states in Latin America, Asia, and parts of Africa that are struggling to keep pace and make progress comprise the outer core of this group.
- The countries that are largely being left behind by the emerging global economy are in sub-Saharan Africa, the Greater Middle East, much of the former Soviet Union, the northern half of Latin America, and several states that have placed themselves outside most international norms (for example, Iraq and North Korea). This group has a per capita income well below $6,000 a year and finds it difficult to transform and adapt to keep up with the core group; these are the *global outliers*.
- The outlying group includes several powerful countries whose likely evolution is uncertain. They could emerge as even larger mainstream players in the global economy, they could suffer further internal turmoil and fragmentation because of their inability to cope with the effects of globalization, or they could choose to take advantage of some of globalization's facets while largely challenging the norms that they find objectionable or incompatible with their national interests. This group includes China, India, Russia, and Iran. In the first three countries, there are sections well integrated into the global economy. But overall, these societies and their political structures are not well suited for energetic participation in the global economy. Some of these governments and their citizens may actively resist playing by some of its rules. They could opt to become more integrated into the global system or participate in it fitfully or in ways that are advantageous to their national interests, as they focus on bolstering their regional power status. They are either ambivalent toward, or willing to actively challenge the norms of, the emerging global system.

One key variable will be the extent to which the governments on the outer core of the democratic community can strengthen their political structures and restart their economies so that they can join the inner core and fully partake of the growing prosperity and stability. Absent changed policies, most of the outliers will likely suffer from continuing political and economic stagnation and the instability that accompanies it. Most of these countries are likely to see continuing turmoil and conflict, as they are buffeted by the forces of globalization and unable to take advantage of its most positive features. This scenario could be altered for the outer core democracies and globally disadvantaged countries if they prove willing to pursue the policies and structural adjustments required to flourish in the Global Century. In this context, activist policies of engagement by the global core group could help promote prosperity, democratic development, and effective conflict prevention and management.

Where is this bifurcated international system headed? The scenario for major progress rests on the hope that democracy, market economics, and multilateral cooperation will spread outward from the democratic core, eventually encompassing most of the rest of the world in a stable global order. A less attractive scenario is that the world will remain as it is today, with much of the world outside the democratic core beset by struggle and economic hardship. The most worrisome scenario is that of a complete collapse of the emerging global system brought about by the toxic interaction of widespread economic turmoil, possibly caused by globalization, and new, polarizing geopolitical or sociocultural forces. Such a global economic collapse could trigger trade wars, widespread nationalist extremism, multiple regional conflicts, and general global disorder. Because all three of these scenarios are possible, U.S. policy should be alert to the new requirements being posed by each of them. Policymakers will need to promote progress where possible, address new risks and dangers, and act quickly and decisively to head off a descent into chaos.

Preventing and Managing Turmoil in the Developing World

Traditionally, security has been an external, cross-border concept. In the global era, security threats increasingly have transnational manifestations. This has led most of the world's democracies to place a higher emphasis on new forms of security cooperation. To be sure, protection of territory and citizens remain paramount defense priorities, particularly with respect to certain outlaw states of concern. However, economic considerations figure more prominently than in the past in national security policy. As the U.S. National Security Strategy document says, security policies should "promote the well-being and prosperity of the Nation and its people." In this context, security has been more broadly defined to allow the use of defense establishments to deal with damaging environmental disasters or destabilizing population flows. Most of the prosperous democracies are willing to use their defense establishments to help promote and safeguard democratic polities abroad, but there is a preference for doing this through multilateral mechanisms. This is a marked change from the Cold War period, when defense planning was driven by ideological hostility and worst case scenarios. Brooke Smith-Windsor outlines in volume II how Canadian security policy has tried to respond to the challenges of globalization by blending the tools of sustainable development, preventive diplomacy, and diverse military engagements in "human security" operations.

Globalization has exacerbated certain transnational security threats to all states. But the economic and other nonsecurity aspects of globalization also pose significant threats to the internal security and stability of many rigidly controlled or weak states. The collapse of internal control can also have damaging consequences for regional security, as rebel armies, drug traffickers, or extremist religious groups pursue their agendas with little respect for national borders. The developed democracies would be well served by improving the level and coordination of assistance to help these countries improve governance and battle organized crime, corruption, warlordism, and piracy.

Stability in the Cold War required the maintenance of deterrence and preservation of the political status quo. Stability in the global era means peaceful adaptation to change. In this context, the central objective of U.S. foreign and security policy in the global era should be to shape the emerging world order in ways that protect U.S. and allied interests and common values. The promotion of global norms and institutions for managing change and conflict will be an important element of an effective strategy.

Carol Lancaster shows clearly in volume II that globalization is neither an unqualified blessing nor an unqualified disaster for the developing world. It offers many benefits, but also carries many potential costs in economic volatility, recession, and increasing economic disparities among and within countries. But as Richard L. Kugler notes in volume I, these consequences are likely to lead to considerable turbulence in a wide belt of developing countries. Development assistance and other elements of regional engagement should be better coordinated with defense strategies designed to head off regional conflicts and the quest for WMDs. Similarly, regional security cooperation and the engagement of Armed Forces with a wide circle of allies and partners should be part of an integrated economic, political, and military strategy stretching from the Middle East through South Asia and into Southeast Asia. The developed democracies can react to, and cope with, this turmoil, or they can engage in more focused preventive actions.

David P.H. Denoon makes a compelling case that investment in sustainable growth should be seen as a national security goal as well as a foreign assistance priority because, in the less developed countries, stability is more likely to accompany steady, sustained economic growth. Greater stability could mean reduced demand on the prosperous democracies for military intervention. Thus, greater investment in sustainable development policies aimed at the developing countries to head off crises and help them cope with the challenges that globalization presents is a logical step.

How should this assistance be focused? Neither a global social safety net nor redistribution of the world's resources appears to be the most effective answer. As Lancaster argues, good governance and political leadership have been key factors in determining the economic performance of developing countries. These factors will also have enormous impact on their ability to cope with globalization. Thus, this is where the industrial democracies should allocate their assistance funds. The goal of such assistance should be to support the evolution of accountable, flexible domestic institutions that foster free choice, diversity, and autonomy.

Government assistance to these countries should complement the activities of nongovernmental organizations. Development assistance and other elements of regional engagement should be better coordinated with defense strategies designed to head off regional conflicts and the quest for WMDs. In addition, regional security cooperation and the engagement of Armed Forces with a wide circle of allies and partners should be part of an integrated economic, political, and military network of local and transnational nongovernmental organizations. Globalization has strengthened the effectiveness and reach of NGOs, and their efforts can be leveraged through more effective public-private partnerships. Finally, the developed world needs to give greater attention to the impact of its financial, energy, and trade policies on the developing countries.

The U.S. defense establishment can make a positive contribution to this effort through a more creative peacetime engagement of military forces. The inculcation of democratic values and effective civil-military relations in the developing world through military training and education can contribute to the management of peaceful change in developing societies. As Harlan K. Ullman, Bradd C. Hayes, and Stephen Benson argue, this kind of peacetime engagement will be an increasingly important element of a naval strategy that more and more often has emphasized influencing events ashore. This kind of engagement can have tremendous payoffs in that it can help countries avoid turmoil that might create new demands for international peacekeeping operations or other kinds of intervention. This engagement can help to build familiarity with operational practices and the patterns of cooperation that can later facilitate the development of coalition actions.

The global era demands new approaches to managing change and containing crises that draw upon and integrate the full range of tools available to the United States and other developed democracies. These approaches should include more holistic strategies that take into account the relationship between such diverse instruments as the programs of the international financial institutions, bilateral democracy promotion programs, activities of NGOs, and aspects of military engagement, particularly the Theater Engagement Plans of the major regional commanders in chief (CINCs). All these elements need to be brought to bear in efforts to manage change and shape the international security environment in positive ways.

For their part, governments of developing countries can help smooth their adaptation to globalization by pursuing such policies as strengthening the rule of law, dismantling unnecessary regulatory restrictions, promoting education, punishing corruption, fostering inclusion, guaranteeing the peaceful transfer of power, emphasizing the adaptive elements of the prevailing political culture, and, where feasible, deepening trade and investment relationships with neighboring countries. These steps are far more important than geography and natural resources. Countries that are resource-poor, have no seaports, or lack navigable rivers have to try harder, but if the policy climate is right—and if their neighbors are not waging war on them—they can often find a niche. Successful adaptation depends on the strength, flexibility, responsiveness, and openness of institutions; the cultures in which those institutions are embedded; and the ability of individual leaders to shape those institutions and cultures for the new era.

Globalization's Uneven Regional Impact

The globalized world of the early 21st century will not be a homogenous place. Great differences will still exist among the world's multiple regions. The regionally oriented chapters in volume II explore the impact of globalization on current affairs in each region, and the interplay between regional economic and security affairs, which will be key in determining patterns for the coming decade and beyond.

Richard L. Kugler portrays Europe as a showcase of globalization because it is adopting broad regional norms, unifying, and becoming peaceful. In adapting the North Atlantic Treaty Organization (NATO) and the European Union to the new era, Europe has been developing a stable post-Cold War security structure in tandem with economic and political integration. Nonetheless, he notes, Europe faces challenges in wisely guiding its internal unification, establishing cooperative relations with Russia, and dealing with still stressful security affairs in the Balkans, Turkey, and the Mediterranean. Beyond this, Europe faces the added challenge of determining how it will play a larger role in world affairs outside its own continent.

Whereas Europe is integrating, F. Stephen Larrabee writes, Russia and its neighbors are responding to globalization in the opposite way: political disintegration. Russia faces profound troubles in adopting democracy and free markets in a setting of political and economic disarray. While Russia is making some headway in establishing closer relations with Central Asian states in the former Soviet Union, Larrabee says, Ukraine and key Caucasus states have uneasy relations with Russia and seek closer relations with Europe. Because prospects in this region are not bright, the United States will face new challenges in dealing with Russia and its neighbors.

The two chapters on Latin America survey its economic affairs and security prospects. Moisés Naím and Carlos Lozada contend that the current economic situation in Latin America combines the good, the bad, and the ugly—for example, market reforms, poverty, and crime. Looking ahead, they judge that the most likely scenario is the emergence of three separate regional economies in the north, center, and south, with slow, yet steady, progress. But they prefer a "Big Bang" effort led by the United States and Brazil to upgrade the entire continent, and they fear an anti-U.S. backlash against globalization. Luis Bitencourt argues that in contrast to other continents, Latin America faces no major security threats or wars. However, it does face a mounting set of lesser problems for which it is ill prepared—for example, organized crime, drug trafficking, and local violence. He calls for U.S. leadership in overhauling the region's collective security institutions, coupled with economic and political progress to alleviate deep-seated problems.

The two chapters on the Middle East and Persian Gulf explore that region's struggle to cope with a globalizing world. Across the Middle East, with its mostly poor economies and shaky governments, as Kathleen Ridolfo notes, globalization is feared and distrusted. Islamic fundamentalism and Arab nationalism are partial backlashes to it. Yet there are signs of progress: Arab businessmen and modernizing political leaders realize that globalization can be a source of economic and political gains. In the unstable Persian Gulf, Shahram Chubin argues, globalization is creating stress on domestic affairs; furthermore, there is a perception of globalization as a Western effort to impose its political values on traditional regimes. Meanwhile, globalization is not dampening the region's treacherous security affairs, which derive from vulnerable oil fields, military imbalances, and political confrontations. Both contributors call for better tuned and far-sighted U.S. policies in the region.

Surveying Asia's economic affairs, Richard P. Cronin writes that globalization has had many positive effects in triggering market reforms, greater democracy, and faster growth. Yet, the 1997 crisis exposed Asia's vulnerability to abrupt financial shocks and its need for further reforms. Moreover, globalization is having uneven effects, uplifting elites and coastal areas, but leaving the masses and rural areas in trouble. While Cronin judges that Asia's economic progress hinges on stable security politics, Thomas W. Robinson argues that globalization is a disturbing variable, not a fundamental dynamic. Even so, he says, major change is in the winds because China, Japan, the United States, and other countries are all reevaluating their strategic priorities. The consequence, according to Robinson, may be greater instability if events are not handled properly. Although still poor and internally troubled, China is achieving big economic gains owing to globalization, and India is making progress as well. As both countries gain economic strength, they likely will pursue traditional geopolitical goals rather than integration with the U.S.-led democratic community. The effect will be to lend further complexity to the tenuous security politics of Asia and South Asia. The bottom line is that the United States will face a future of strategic challenges and opportunities there.

P. François Hugo explains that sub-Saharan Africa lies at the backwaters of the modern world economy. This vast continent remains dominated by poverty, weak governments, unstable societies, and outdated economies. At present, he says, globalization is mostly worsening Africa's plight, yet many Africans are now searching for ways to respond. Africa will need outside economic help, but its countries can cooperate in handling the region's often-troubled security affairs.

Thus, globalization's uneven dynamics are having very different regional consequences. Economics and security affairs are interacting as an engine of progress in some regions, but as a source of strain in others. Europe is moving toward peaceful unity, and Latin America is making progress on economic integration and political stability. But Russia and its neighbors are rapidly falling behind the prosperous democracies because of their less adaptive political cultures, declining infrastructures, and distorted or incomplete market reforms. Africa remains poverty-stricken, and the tradition-laden Middle East and Persian Gulf face economic struggles and a stressful security environment. Asia is key, but its economics and security affairs may be pulling in different directions. Emerging events in all these regions make clear that the actions of the United States and its democratic partners can make a big difference in determining whether the future brings promise or peril.

Implications for Security Policy and Military Affairs

Globalization is not bringing geopolitics to an end. Many traditional forms of geopolitics remain active on the world scene, and in some places, globalization is giving rise to new stresses and turbulence in the international system. Taming both the old and new geopolitical dynamics in order to allow for globalization's positive effects to advance will be a key challenge of statecraft. The intelligent use of U.S. military power and maintenance of security partnerships with cooperating countries will be key to achieving this goal.

A Flexible Global Security Architecture

International mechanisms and institutions for coping with the challenges of the global era remain asymmetrical. Just as economic globalization has outpaced other forms of globalization, international economic and financial institutions, and a number of specialized agencies of the United Nations (for example, health and telecommunications), are well developed, with established procedures and norms. In contrast, security institutions and arrangements have remained largely regional and generally anemic, with the exception of the transatlantic region. This disparity between economic and security institutions is likely to persist for some time. Development of truly global security norms has proven quite difficult, as recent debates over military action against Serbia and maintaining sanctions against Iraq have illustrated. The UN Security Council can function in certain cases, but its structure is outdated and it is frequently incapable of action. Security Council reform should be a priority of a U.S. strategy for the global era. As several contributors note, this will require a willingness to accept some limits on freedom of action so as to ensure the upholding of global principles that serve our long-term interests.

However, this lag in the development of new security structures calls for further strengthening of the instruments for regional cooperation and security in order to contain or reduce existing threats and prevent the emergence of new ones. Sir Laurence Martin (volume II) argues that alliances and alignments will remain a pervasive feature of international politics for some time, even as they must adapt to changing circumstances. Ronald D. Asmus (volume I) chronicles the success of this adaptation in Europe, where the Partnership for Peace (PFP) and the Euro-Atlantic Partnership Council have allowed NATO countries to build a web of political and military cooperation with a wide circle of states. The success of these NATO efforts has been helped tremendously by the incentive of eventual NATO membership, with the security guarantee that membership entails. Still, Asmus argues that if NATO were designed from scratch to handle today's strategic challenges, it would be a very different alliance from the one now existing. Rather than defending Europe's borders, it would focus on addressing new challenges arising outside them. While NATO has begun reforming its policies and military capabilities for such new missions, faster progress is warranted in the coming years.

This process of building coalitions can be achieved elsewhere, particularly if such efforts build on existing alliances and patterns of cooperation. In Asia, the U.S.-Japan and U.S.-Korea alliances are slowly being adapted to meet the needs of an emerging, more complicated security environment. However, as Admiral Dennis Blair has recognized, neither these alliances nor new regional structures may be well suited to new tasks and may not be optimal in certain contexts.[7] It may also be possible to develop patterns of cooperation in bilateral and limited multilateral settings that can be drawn upon in times of need to form variable geometry coalitions. New security communities, based on certain shared interests in the global era, can be developed to enable a wide group of states to work together to safeguard these interests. For the United States, this will require some adaptation of standard operating procedures. Rather than expecting a diverse array of Asia/Pacific partners to adopt U.S. or NATO standards and procedures, as has happened with PFP, the U.S. military may need "multivoltage sockets" to allow a diverse array of forces to "plug into" these coalitions.

A Military Strategy of Shaping and Crisis Management

The globalizing world requires that U.S. military forces remain strong and well prepared. But U.S. forces cannot remain static. They must adapt to new challenges and missions, even as they absorb new technologies created by the Information Age.

They will need to be prepared for new forms of warfare, while carrying out new peacetime shaping missions and responding to crises.

Richard L. Kugler and Seymour J. Deitchman point out in volume I that globalization's effects on international security require a shift in U.S. defense strategy from continental Eurasia to a greater focus on the southern and eastern regions of the Eurasian land mass, North Africa, the Middle East, and Southeast Asia and Oceania. The growing turmoil in this contiguous "southern belt" is acquiring greater strategic importance because it can have a significant detrimental impact on global economics and stability, and trigger U.S. security commitments. Significant engagements are also possible in sub-Saharan Africa and Latin America for humanitarian and certain security interests. Coping with these needs will require maintenance of military capabilities to project power rapidly, with a dominant effect, into the outlying world; continued forward presence; and the enhancement of military cooperation with allies and partners. This new strategy will also need to cope with the further proliferation of WMDs—with the attendant potential for escalation—and, as William W. Keller and Janne E. Nolan note in volume II, with enhanced conventional weapons. Challenging urban operations in littoral areas will also likely dominate military actions, for as Deitchman notes, two-thirds of the world's population is concentrated within 250 miles of the coast, mostly in urban areas.

The authors of the military chapters in these volumes broadly agree that the global era calls for a military strategy that combines peacetime regional engagement, crisis management, and maintenance of warfighting capabilities to mitigate and contain likely conflicts in the troubled outer periphery. Deitchman, Kugler, and Anthony H. Cordesman (volume I) argue that robust forces are needed in the coming decades to protect the American homeland, diverse economic interests, and allies from a widely dispersed set of actors—small and large countries and transnational groups—who are well armed and capable of mounting powerful asymmetrical threats. All agree that the main threat to U.S. forces in the coming two decades is not an emerging major peer competitor, but a more diverse set of regional challengers who can prevent the United States and its allies from achieving common goals. These challengers, both states and some nonstate actors, will have more sophisticated weapons, and will also be capable of conducting asymmetrical operations. For example, China need not defeat the U.S. 7th Fleet in actions akin to a second Battle of Midway in order to prevent the United States from executing its strategy in a Taiwan crisis. Similarly, Iran could close the Strait of Hormuz and choke Western energy supplies by simply launching a few naval missiles and mines.

Thus far, U.S. forces have been built and sized for fighting major theater wars. But the reality of the last 10 years, the opening decade of the Global Century, is that they have often operated in multiple, simultaneous lesser regional contingencies.[8] According to a study by Defense Forecasts International, the United States has engaged in 514 lesser regional contingencies during the 1990s, mostly in Asia, Central and South America, and North America (primarily disaster relief operations).

Most of the authors of these military chapters conclude that protection of U.S. interests in this rapidly changing environment is likely to require the maintenance of U.S. forces at least as large as those envisioned by the 1997 Quadrennial Defense

Review. Cordesman likens the world to Jurassic Park, with such diverse threats as regional challengers skilled in asymmetrical threats, proliferation of weapons of mass destruction (WMD) and missile technologies, and growing ethnic and religious violence exacerbated by a widening economic divide. Cordesman concludes that coping with these threats will require engagement in diverse low-level conflicts, major regional contingencies, and widespread peacetime engagement. In contrast, Kugler calls for broadening of the Two Major Theater War (two-MTW) standard in favor of a standard that embraces carrying out normal military missions in multiple theaters short of war; being fully prepared to fight and win a single MTW in various places; and maintaining a large insurance policy for more and larger military conflicts. While it may appear that the force requirements for this approach are similar to the force requirements of today, Kugler and Deitchman argue that in the future this posture must become more flexible and adaptive, and may require selective force augmentation, new overseas facilities, new CINC operational plans, and bigger defense budgets. Deitchman suggests the need for further reorientation of military operations toward expeditionary warfare, with even more dispersed pre-positioning of supplies and equipment, beyond what now exists in Europe, Asia, and in the Indian Ocean region. Deitchman and Kugler note that the Department of Defense (DOD) will need to set priorities and consolidate assets in order to maintain sufficient forces, high readiness, and steady modernization. Kugler contends that improvements to allied force capabilities and coalition arrangements could be as important as enhancing the quality of U.S. forces.

Paul K. Davis (volume I) reaches conclusions broadly similar to those of Kugler. Davis advocates more flexible force structures (including smaller, but more capable Army brigades that are better suited for coalition and expeditionary operations than a brigade is today) and a vigorous pursuit of transformation by full exploitation of the revolution in military affairs (RMA) and by adherence to the operational concepts of the *Joint Vision 2020* plan developed by the U.S. Joint Chiefs of Staff. In particular, Davis notes that the joint experimentation work being sponsored by the U.S. Joint Forces Command—which includes two large integrating concepts, Rapid Decisive Operations and Attack Operations Against Critical Mobile Targets—may offer important insights on improving military operations in the global era. Davis notes that while U.S. allies and partners will most often need forces "for peacekeeping and some moderately stressful peacemaking," they, too, will need to undertake certain restructuring and modernization to ensure the effectiveness of coalition operations.

The Armed Forces will need to be able to operate jointly, using more tailored packages with all the benefits of the larger structure that provide global reach, including lift, intelligence, and communications. The United States needs forces and command structures that are more flexible and capable of responding on short notice to dynamic situations. Solveig Spielmann (volume I) and Theodore Roosevelt Malloch (volume II) argue that these military challenges are similar to those that economic globalization has presented to business. They urge DOD and the services to learn from the experience of the corporate world in renewing and restructuring their operations. In particular, Spielman urges effective exploitation of the advanced integrated information systems and revamping of personnel practices. Two chapters in volume

II address the challenges posed by certain states of concern that are determined to challenge current international norms. Kori Schake and Justin Bernier note how current U.S. efforts to isolate these states and subject them to sanctions are eroding in the face of globalization. They argue for a new policy that would employ financial interventions with narrower, more targeted sanctions. William Miller explores how the acquisition of WMDs and effective delivery systems by these countries of concern will make them more potent adversaries. Miller notes that while U.S. nuclear and conventional superiority will still provide Washington with considerable leverage in a crisis, maintaining a full range of options will require new force employment doctrines and development of missile defenses.

Growing Demands on Naval Forces

U.S. naval forces are well suited to the challenges of the global era. Their inherent flexibility and broad range of capabilities allow them to perform the spectrum of likely missions in the Global Century, ranging from peacetime presence and engagement to crisis response and countervailing military action. Naval forces have a distinct advantage in crisis response, given the rapidity with which they can transition from peacetime presence missions to wartime operations. All the naval analysts agree that the Navy's peacetime presence and overseas engagement activities are critical and will remain so. Indeed, Stephen Benson calls for the issuance of an overarching U.S. naval engagement policy and support for engagement planning and assessment. The naval contributors also agree that operations in the littoral areas and with coalition partners will become increasingly important and that the pace of these operations will require effective exploitation of the latest information technologies. However, they offer differing perspectives on the relative priority of other traditional Navy missions and on the size and composition of naval forces.

Seymour J. Deitchman argues that a robust Navy, structured largely as it is today with carrier battle groups, amphibious ready groups, and strategic ballistic missile submarines, will be needed in the coming decades. While those naval forces will retain significant tactical and operational autonomy, he says, they will be increasingly dependent on national and other service assets for technical support, particularly in the critical areas of command, control, communications, and computers, intelligence, surveillance, and reconnaissance (C^4ISR). Deitchman calls for sustained improvements of the Navy through C^4ISR systems and smart munitions. He also calls for greater attention to countering the threats of mine warfare and of the quiet modern submarines entering service with a growing number of potentially hostile countries. In addition, Deitchman points out that in the global era, the Marine Corps will have to be prepared to achieve rapid success with minimal destruction in urban environments; with hostile populations, as well as with military or quasi-military defenders; and under the watchful eye of the international media. This requires continued training and tactical innovations such as those that have been under development in the Commandant's Battle Laboratory.

In the same spirit, Sam J. Tangredi (volume I) concludes that the Navy's traditional missions of sea control and protection of the lanes of communication in order to sustain the global economy will remain high priorities. Tangredi cites DOD studies concluding that the Navy will need 360 ships, including some new variants, and 15 carrier battle groups (CVBGs): a force larger than today's 316 ships and 12 CVBGs. Bradd C. Hayes (volume I) emphasizes the importance of the Navy's maintaining its readiness to fight regional wars and lesser conflicts that threaten vital and important U.S. national security interests. Hayes sees the need for the Navy to meet the aforementioned new and old challenges while maintaining force levels, readiness, and modernization, but worries that likely budgets will not support all these efforts. Thus, he would limit the development of conventional naval forces designed primarily to hedge against greater than expected capabilities of regional powers, WMD, and major acts of terrorism, and rely on nuclear deterrent forces for this function.

Harlan K. Ullman and Gwyn Prins (volume I) offer alternative visions of the Navy's future priorities. They both dismiss the likelihood of major regional wars and large battles at sea. Ullman says that the Navy should focus less on command of the seas and more on influencing events ashore through effective peacetime engagement. He sees future naval missions as being heavily weighted toward operations designed to reassure friends and allies, restrain adversaries, and build coalition partnerships. He calls for further study of new ways to achieve influence, including training, military-to-military contacts, and combined operations with coalition partners. Ullman concludes that in this less demanding strategic environment, the Navy should exploit "effects-based targeting," alternative deployment patterns, and both the "knowledge revolution" and the "people revolution." These steps, he argues, could allow the Navy to conduct key missions with considerably reduced force levels, by producing ships that have increased weapons lethality and require greatly reduced crews and maintenance. This would free personnel and resources for what he sees as more peacetime shaping missions ashore. Prins assumes a similar strategic context and recommends that the Navy and Marine Corps focus more on maintaining capabilities suited to the low end of the spectrum—peace operations, humanitarian interventions, and lesser regional crises—and reduce their investment in ballistic missile submarines.

Timothy L. Terriberry and Scott C. Truver (volume I) remind readers that the Coast Guard has been in the vanguard in coping with many of the challenges of the global era, including operations against narcotics and smuggling, but also the negotiation and enforcement of conventions for maritime safety and environmental protection. Globalization, with its attendant growth in legal and illegal trade and transit, is placing new demands on the Coast Guard, such as pollution monitoring for vessels at sea, immigration control, protection of fisheries, humanitarian operations, and coping with asymmetrical threats to coastal areas. They argue that these tasks require recapitalization of the Coast Guard's aging deep-water capability. So, too, the Coast Guard, as a multimission law enforcement, humanitarian, and regulatory agency, as well as a military service, is well suited to support CINC theater engagement, particularly with emerging democracies that are building limited coastal defense forces.

Policymaking and Engagement for the Global Era

The contributions to these volumes show that the U.S. Government is inadequately organized to deal with the challenges of the global era. Pursuing the goals and strategies that have been outlined calls for revamping the policymaking process and integrating the military and nonmilitary components of national power. The following broad conclusions about the U.S. Government's strategy and organization emerge from these two volumes:

> 1. Successful strategies and policies in the global era require much closer coordination between the economic, security, law enforcement, environmental, and science and technology policymaking communities in Washington.

There should be far more dialogue and structured interactions among the various elements of government than there are now, along with more coherent, high-level guidance and coordination. Because such a bureaucratic transformation would have to begin at the top, the President must set the tone. Such steps will likely require specific changes in each agency's personnel system in order to become institutionalized. These personnel systems should encourage rotational assignments and reward individuals who break down agency barriers, rather than protect them.

The Bush administration should undertake a comprehensive review of all interagency working groups in the policy areas noted above in order to assess areas of overlap and potential areas for better policy fusion. The Office of Management and Budget (OMB) might take the lead in such a process. The Bush administration should then consider unifying the National Security Council and the National Economic Council to ensure better integration of these policy streams. Another option, which merits careful review, would be to unify several major elements of the Executive Office of the President—the National Security Council, the National Economic Council, and parts of the Office of Science and Technology Policy and other White House offices involved with the effects of globalization; this body could report to the National Security Council or could become a new, integrated Executive Office of the President staff under the Special Assistant to the President for National Security Affairs. That individual would likely need two substantive Deputy National Security Advisors, one for economic and one for national security affairs.[9]

Joint meetings of the National Security Council and the National Economic Council are unusual, and their various interagency subgroups rarely communicate with one another. These separate organizational structures are unsuited to the challenges of the global era. A more integrated structure would ensure that the various elements of national policy required to respond to the challenges of the global era are given high-level guidance and formulated in relation to one another. The Department of State should consider similar measures to bridge the gap between its economic, regional, and international security bureaus.

DOD should take steps to ensure effective coordination of policy analysis and appropriate force planning by its elements with global and various regional responsibilities, including the major regional commanders in chief. The Pentagon also needs to find a workable bureaucratic mechanism to integrate economic, environmental, and cultural factors into its policy planning. These two functions might be served by a small group of senior planners with a mandate to provide direct, cross-cutting support on global security affairs to the Under Secretary for Policy. The Service secretaries might consider developing a similar group of advisors.

The Treasury Department must consult with, and be consulted by, the full range of policy players, including DOD, to a far greater degree than in the past. For their part, Congressional leaders should take corresponding steps to break down the rigid division of responsibilities in their committee structure and have more joint committee hearings on legislation. Other economic agencies need to explore how they might factor international security and law enforcement considerations into their policy development at early stages. If such organizational changes were effected, U.S. international policies could reflect a tightly coordinated blend of financial, commercial, technological, and military resources and priorities. This new commingling could lead not only to meaningful changes in policy but also to better overall performance. Such reviews could cast foreign aid and military engagement in new light, as complementary elements of an overall strategy for crisis prevention and management.

> 2. The nonmilitary instruments of foreign policy require more robust funding to achieve key policy goals and work in a better balance with military instruments.

The ability to shape globalization rather than just react to it requires adequate resources and a better balance between "hard" and "soft" security. Armed Forces will still need robust funding to remain prepared to fight wars and conduct the demanding range of global era military operations outlined in the defense sections of these volumes. But this military strength needs to be supplemented by enhanced capabilities in other areas of statecraft.

Nonmilitary instruments of U.S. foreign policy, such as foreign aid, educational exchanges and scholarships, visitors' programs, public diplomacy, and contributions to humanitarian programs and multilateral organizations, are pitifully small in comparison with U.S. military power and global reach. Spending on these nonmilitary instruments has shrunk steadily over the last 20 years, from 4 percent of the Federal budget in the 1960s to 1 percent today. Inexpensive programs to promote democracy, the rule of law, and economic reform in some of the key countries buffeted by globalization, such as Russia and the new states of Eurasia, could yield enormous dividends and help prevent future crises.[10,11] These "soft power" activities can have enormous effect over time, and they are more important than ever today because even overwhelming military power is often of limited use in dealing with the social turmoil and other consequences of globalization. Moreover, more effective use of these nonmilitary shaping and crisis prevention instruments could reduce demands on U.S. and allied armed forces for peace operations. This would have a salutary effect on military readiness and preparations for major combat operations. Without a better stocked and more diversified toolbox, U.S. military forces will be under mounting pressure to solve problems for which military power is not well suited.

At the same time, as Michael J. Dziedzic (volume I) explains, the Executive Branch has recognized that the requirement for complex contingency operations abroad and at home has continued to grow. These demand more effective interagency and international civil-military coordination. Crisis and conflict management will require better integration of all the tools of the U.S. Government, as well as leveraging of the capabilities of allies, partners, and NGOs, across a spectrum of activities, including humanitarian, economic development, law enforcement, and external security concerns.[12]

Generous educational and training programs, development assistance, credit programs, conflict prevention, and old-fashioned diplomacy should receive higher priority. Officeholders in these fields should have adequate budgets and staffs, as well as access to the White House. Their perspectives are essential to an integrated strategy.

> 3. The global era requires a streamlined, flexible, and integrated U.S. Government decisionmaking process adapted to the Internet Age and capable of responding quickly to fast-moving foreign crises.

Decisionmaking and military operations will have to become speedier, communications more direct, and organizations flatter and more streamlined. This change will be difficult because of the wide variety of perspectives that need to be built into an effective strategy. But compartmentalized activities will no longer suffice. This is as true in the Armed Forces as it is in the rest of the foreign policy community. As the former Commander in Chief of the U.S. Central Command, General Anthony C. Zinni, put it, "Napoleon could reappear today and recognize my Central Command staff organization: J–1, administration stovepipe; J–2, intelligence stovepipe—you get the idea. . . . This must be fixed."[13]

> 4. Policymakers and military planners need to be more aware of historical, technological, cultural, religious, environmental, and other aspects of world affairs than they have been to date.

More people with expertise in nonmainstream fields should be hired and utilized in mainstream positions. Nongovernment actors of all backgrounds should be consulted routinely by both diplomatic and military planners. Congressional staff visits to global trouble spots should be encouraged.

> 5. Building and maintaining coalitions with friends and allies to channel globalization in constructive directions and mitigate its harshest aspects should receive high priority.

As the military contributors uniformly agree, enlisting effective support from friends and allies warrants enhanced regional engagement activities by all branches of the Armed Forces, including the Coast Guard. Developing and sustaining such efforts may sometimes require political and/or military operational compromises, but the dividends are worth the risks.

Conclusion

Globalization holds great promise. It is broadly consistent with U.S. national security and foreign policy interests, as well as the long-term needs of most of the world's people. Over time, globalization promotes openness, encourages political and economic reforms, strengthens the demand for the rule of law, fosters integration, and reduces the likelihood of conflict and resort to military force.

From a security perspective, the worrisome phrase is "over time." In areas of the world where poverty is widespread and institutions are weak, economic globalization is outstripping the development of public and private means to help ordinary people cope with its effects. In the near term, globalization can sharpen class differences, feed rampant corruption, fortify dictators, and arm criminal elements and terrorists. Shocks associated with rapid globalization, especially short-term financial flows, can shake up the body politic, throw more people into poverty, foment riots, and force a retreat from market-oriented reforms, whipping up anti-Americanism in the process. This uncertainty about globalization's impact warrants the maintenance of robust and flexible U.S. military capabilities for peacetime engagement, conflict management, and combat operations in diverse areas of the unstable "southern arc" noted earlier.

The overarching objectives of U.S. global policies (economic, development, and defense) should be to shape the emerging world order in ways that avoid disasters and channel the wave of globalization in directions that ease adaptation to rapid change and peaceful integration. The United States should avoid policies that polarize the global community and strive to promote global norms, as well as global systems, institutions, and rules. At the same time, U.S. policymakers should place a premium on the protection of regional, national, local, group, and individual autonomy based on diversity and free choice; reflected in strong, accountable, and flexible domestic institutions; and sustained by the rule of law. Finally, the U.S. defense establishment needs to work with other agencies and NGOs to enhance its engagement in the support of sustainable development; to nurture institutions and instruments of cooperative security, founded on widely shared norms and respectful of autonomy; and to contain, reduce, or prevent conflicts and other threats to a peaceful world order.

While the Armed Forces are the world's strongest today, they cannot afford to stand pat. Globalization and other dynamics are rapidly changing the world. New military technologies, doctrines, and structures are also fast appearing. In order to remain highly effective, U.S. forces, including the Navy, will need to change in responsive ways. Moreover, they must meet two different requirements: staying prepared for major combat missions while performing such global era operations as presence, engagement, strategic shaping, peacekeeping, humanitarian missions, and crisis interventions. A demanding future thus lies ahead for DOD and the Navy. Their ability to handle it will play a major role in determining whether the United States copes effectively with the new promises and stressful dangers of the globalizing world.

Notes

[1] Louis J. Freeh, statement for the record before the United States Senate, Committee on Appropriations, Subcommittee on Foreign Operations, Washington, DC, April 21, 1998.

[2] Michael D. Bordo, Barry Eichengreen, and Douglas A. Irwin, "Is Globalization Today Really Different from Globalization a Hundred Years Ago?" *Brookings Trade Forum 1999* (Washington, DC: The Brookings Institution Press, 1999), 1–50.

[3] Anton Lukas, *WTO Report Card III: Globalization and Developing Countries*, Trade Briefing Paper No. 10, The Cato Institute, June 20, 2000, 2.

[4] World Economic Forum Task Force, "From the Global Digital Divide to the Global Digital Opportunity," statement to the G–8 Kyushu-Okinawa Summit, July 21–23, 2000, <www.weforum.org>.

[5] Patrick Glynn, Stephen J. Kobrin, and Moisés Naím, "The Globalization of Corruption," in Kimberly Ann Elliott, *Corruption and the Global Economy* (Washington, DC: Institute for International Economics, 1997), 10.

[6] Thomas L. Friedman, *The Lexus and the Olive Tree: Understanding Globalization* (New York: Farrar, Straus and Giroux, 1999) and Dani Rodrik, *Has Globalization Gone Too Far?* (Washington, DC: Institute for International Economics, 1997).

[7] Dennis C. Blair and John T. Hanley, Jr., "From Wheels to Webs: Reconstructing Asia-Pacific Security Arrangements," *Washington Quarterly* 24, no. 1 (Winter 2001), 7–17.

[8] See Barry Blechman, "Alternative Force Sizing Mechanism for the Department of Defense," unpublished interim briefing for the Department of Defense, September 2000.

[9] This approach has been advocated by former Deputy Assistant to the President for National Security Affairs, James Steinberg in an address to the National Defense University Globalization Project on October 18, 2000.

[10] Richard Gardner, "The One Percent Solution: Shirking the Cost of World Leadership," *Foreign Affairs* 79, no. 2 (July/August 2000), 3.

[11] Zbigniew Brzezinski, "Engaging Russia," *The National Interest*, no. 61 (Fall 2000), 5–16.

[12] See Presidential Decision Directive (PDD) 56, 62, and others.

[13] Anthony C. Zinni, farewell address, transcript of Robert McCormick Tribune Foundation—U.S. Naval Institute Address, March 2000, 8.

PART I.
GLOBALIZATION: STRATEGIC IMPLICATIONS FOR THE UNITED STATES

Chapter 2

Globalization and National Security: A Strategic Agenda

Ellen L. Frost

Something called *globalization* has become a surging, relentless, and irreversible force in our era. But what is it? What is new and different about it? Does it make the world safer or more dangerous? What can the United States do about the new challenges that it poses? What goals, strategies, tools, and ways of making decisions does the United States need in this new environment?

Supporters claim that globalization will eventually force all governments to pursue peaceful, democratic, rules-based, and market-oriented policies, resulting in a richer, healthier, safer, more educated, and more stable world population. Critics believe, by contrast, that globalization feeds corporate profits at the expense of workers, undermines democracy, accelerates environmental destruction, lowers health and labor standards, imposes cultural homogeneity, feeds crime, and escalates armed conflict.

From a U.S. policy perspective, globalization can be a catalyst (if not a cause) of both outcomes, depending on the specific policies and attributes of the "receiving" country. Because of its speed and reach, today's globalization can be stabilizing or destabilizing, disruptive or enriching, a tool of peacemakers or racketeers. On balance, globalization benefits the United States and other democratic and quasi-democratic countries. Sweeping arguments about whether globalization is "good" or "bad" for the rest of the world, however, shed little light on real-life situations because it can be either.[1] No government can stop it, but an important goal of U.S. foreign and defense policy should be to help channel it in benign directions. This task is urgent because at present, *economic and technological globalization is outstripping—or highlighting the total absence of—global and regional institutional means for coping with the impact of globalization on ordinary people and on the environment in which they live.*

This mixed assessment has important consequences for U.S. foreign policy and security policy. If globalization is making the world uniformly richer and safer, the United States can gradually wind down its defense spending and reorient its foreign policy away from security threats. If the world is splitting apart and becoming more violent, the United States will have to become more security-oriented and more focused on its limited vital interests, with or without allies. If the world is reacting unevenly to

---

Ellen L. Frost is a visiting fellow in the Institute for International Economics. She has served as Deputy Assistant Secretary of Defense for Economic and Technology Affairs and as Counselor to the U.S. Trade Representative. Dr. Frost is the author of Transatlantic Trade: A Strategic Agenda *and* For Richer, For Poorer: The New U.S.-Japan Relationship.

globalization, then the United States will need to remain globally engaged on more or less the same scale as it is now, but with somewhat different priorities and missions.

Globalization, far from being a media buzzword, is real, mostly new, and quite different from its pre-World War I ancestor. Coming to grips with this force calls for substantially transforming the way that U.S. leaders think about the world and adjusting their policy instruments accordingly. U.S. policymakers should forge a strategy based on cross-disciplinary analysis informed by all aspects of globalization, including not only commercial, financial, technological, military, political, environmental, and social aspects, but also cultural, religious, psychological, educational, and historical perspectives. *Holistic thinking has become a national security imperative.*

The overarching goal of such a globalization-infused strategy should be to shape the emerging world order in a way that protects U.S. interests and promotes American and allied values. The implementing goals are

- The promotion of global norms through peaceful adaptation to change and integration, accompanied by the development of viable global systems, institutions, and rules
- The protection of regional, national, local, group, and personal autonomy based on diversity and free choice, reflected in strong, accountable, and flexible domestic institutions sustained by the rule of law
- The enhancement and expansion of institutions and instruments of cooperative security to contain, reduce, or prevent conflicts and other threats to a peaceful world order

In carrying out their strategy in support of these goals, policymakers should make necessary compromises with allies and friends and construct new coalitions with nongovernmental organizations (NGOs) and private business. The strategy also requires more diversified foreign policy tools, including adequately funded nonmilitary instruments of foreign policy. If U.S. policymakers lack such diverse tools, U.S. military forces will be under pressure to cope with problems for which military power is not well suited or is even counterproductive.

Finally, U.S. policymakers urgently need a streamlined, flexible, and coordinated domestic decisionmaking process that makes full use of information technology and is capable of responding quickly to crises. This process, initiated by the White House and embedded in the goals and missions of the various departments and agencies, should

- Embody close, daily coordination of economic and security policies
- Build support for active global engagement in Congress and the public
- Seek common ground with those voicing legitimate concerns about globalization

Understanding Globalization

Globalization *Defined*

Globalization is a long-term process, not a static condition. It is the nonstop aftershock of the current explosion of knowledge. It has unleashed a rapid, ongoing, uneven, and sometimes disruptive process of expansion of cross-border networks and flows not only of goods, services, money, and technology, but also of ideas, information, culture, people, and power. It should not be seen in exclusively linear terms, but rather as a complex dynamic in which global, regional, national, local, and individual forces are all in play, often at the same time. It brings into being an elite culture shaped and colored by information, entertainment, and money—the world of cybercafes and caffé latté, Madonna and MTV, Web pages and dot-coms, hedge funds and derivatives.

Globalization comes in many forms, of which economic globalization is only one. Time lags between these different forms make the mix lumpy, uneven, and occasionally flammable. In a globalizing world, many contradictory things are true at the same time and will be for the foreseeable future. States are losing power; states are not losing power. Groups such as the Kurds and the Chechens dream of nationhood; East Timor has just won it; and Europeans are moving beyond it. Depending on the site, the rule of law is rising or breaking down. Local culture is threatened or flowering. Religion is fading away or undergoing a revival. And so on.

Despite these near-term contradictions, the definition of globalization as a long-term process implies a transition to "globality"—a more interconnected world system in which interdependent networks and flows surmount traditional boundaries (or make them irrelevant).[2] Globality can also refer to global governance, the idea that the world community should assume "greater collective responsibility in a wide range of areas, including security."[3] This notion highlights the "governance gap," the disparity between the existence of global rules governing commercial transactions and the absence or vagueness of such rules in other domains. Finally, globality suggests the basic unity of the human spirit, expressed through global awareness, a consciousness of common humanity, concern for the Earth, and a common set of basic norms.

If globalization is a transition to globality, then the defining characteristic of globalization is movement toward integration. In a popular book, Thomas Friedman defines globalization in part as a dynamic, ongoing process involving "the inexorable integration of markets, nation-states, and technologies to a degree never witnessed before."[4] Economist and globalization analyst Dani Rodrik uses a similar definition.[5] The National Security Strategy issued by the White House in December 1999 defines globalization as "the process of accelerating economic, technological, cultural, and political integration."[6] The Defense Science Board's report on globalization and security defines it as "the integration of the political, economic, and cultural activities of geographically and/or nationally separated peoples."[7]

Integration refers to the process of incorporating different elements into a whole. One meaning of integration implies intensified contact, but not necessarily common values. High levels of immigration, for example, may bring people from different cultures together, but they may clash. Recent violence against immigrants in southern

Spain is an example. Another meaning of integration implies close ties and a sense of distinct identities among members of ethnic and religious groups. Globalization has helped to link aggrieved members of a diaspora or persecuted minority, such as Jews, Kurds, and Armenians. A higher form of integration stands for tolerance, inclusion, and a common identity based on norms rather than on skin color or language. Globalization has facilitated bonding among groups that define themselves in terms of values (for example, environmentalists and human rights activists). Integration in this higher sense is the basis of a pluralistic community—the opposite of segregation, exclusion, apartheid, or "ethnic cleansing." The way that globalization fosters integration in any of the three forms—that is, intensified contact, separate identities, or a pluralistic community respecting common norms—embodies a change in the way that people organize themselves, relate to each other, and exercise power.[8]

With respect to relations among nations, integration implies movement toward a global market, a legal and regulatory framework, a sense of political community, and common standards of governance and justice. At the moment, the European Union is the only major post-World War II example of comprehensive and durable supranational integration, and many factors besides globalization contributed to this outcome (centuries of war between France and Germany, to name an obvious one). *Globalization appears to be fostering norms-based, pluralistic, institutional integration only among democracies and quasi-democratic states that have put in place a stable security framework, the rudiments of a market-oriented economy, a rules-based system of justice, and a certain minimal level of tolerance and civic trust—and only then imperfectly and after decades (if not centuries) of struggle.*

Differences in Globalization Today

Skeptics argue that globalization is not new. It certainly has historical roots. By the end of the 19th century, the global economy was marked by a high degree of interdependence. Technology had advanced dramatically. There was even a global culture of sorts. Borders were relatively more open than they are today, especially within colonial empires. In fact, it was not until the 1970s that trade as a percentage of global output reached the levels achieved before World War I.

Several economists have pointed to indicators such as these to argue that globalization today is not really new. These comparisons, however, are limited and misleading in at least two respects. First, since the late 1970s, the integration of capital and commodity markets has surpassed all previous indicators, and the process is continuing to this day.[9] A number of historical factors have contributed to this trend. After World War II, statesmen decided to fashion an institutional framework to promote global trade and growth and to create and manage the international monetary system. The post-World War II boom in East Asian economies and improvements in transportation technology (notably container ships and jet engines) also contributed greatly to global economic integration.

Second, what is most distinctive about globalization in the current era is the revolution in information technology, accompanied by the spread of personal computers and the instant availability of information. The characteristics of this explosion of communication—speed, compression, pervasiveness, global reach, and potential to touch the daily lives of every human being on this planet—are unprecedented. Skeptics may argue that the invention of the steam engine, the railway, the telegraph, the automobile, and the telephone were revolutionary as well, and indeed they were. But the story of globalization in the last quarter of the 20th century illustrates that differences in degree have added up to a significant, relentless, and irreversible difference in kind. Globalization should not be enshrined as the only cause of change. In some cases, it may be marginal, but it should not be dismissed as an intellectual fad.

Subglobal Globalization: Regions, Nations, Localities, and Individuals

Globalization is not limited to the global level as such. On the contrary, it sparks new ways of doing things at all levels and ignites opposing impulses and identities. James Rosenau sees three pervasive tensions characteristic of this era: fragmentation-integration, localization-globalization, and decentralization-centralization.[10,11]

Regions. One of the spillover effects of globalization is a trend toward regional integration. This trend often takes commercial forms, but it has strategic significance.

In some parts of the world (for example, Europe, Latin America, Asia), where there is no war and security arrangements are stable, regional economic agreements designed to promote free trade and investment are becoming the dominant geopolitical expression of relations between states. These agreements have given some regions of the world a certain "face" or geopolitical personality, reflecting emerging integration in the "higher," norms-based sense. Examples include European integration; *Mercado Común del Sur* (MERCOSUR)—the Common Market of the South, which for Brazil and other members serves as a geopolitical counterweight to U.S. domination of the area; the Association of Southeast Asian Nations (ASEAN), which was designed in part to halt the spread of communism; and the Asia-Pacific Economic Cooperation (APEC) forum, which has extended diplomatic outreach to Russia and China.

Conversely, the absence of meaningful regional economic cooperation is a signal that governments in that region are not adopting policies that will allow them to take advantage of globalization. It is no coincidence that sub-Saharan Africa and South Asia, where regional cooperation is minimal or nonexistent, record the lowest per capita income levels in the world. The conflict-prone Middle East has similarly low levels of regional economic integration.

Outside the transatlantic community, regional security arrangements are evolving more slowly and are likely to be informal and flexible. Rigid adherence to the principle of noninterference in internal affairs, often to the exclusion of mutual benefit, dies hard in a region where memories of colonial occupation are still vivid. Nevertheless, working-level dialogues and confidence-building measures are gradually taking shape in key areas of the world. In Asia, for instance, the ASEAN Regional Forum (ARF) draws in major non-ASEAN members to discuss regional security issues. Several ASEAN governments have established an antipiracy center in Kuala Lumpur, with which the U.S. Pacific Command cooperates.

Nations. Globalization is creating a new context for, and transforming the formal and informal exercise of, national power. The combination of technology, international institutions, local governments, and nonstate actors is diluting nation-states' monopoly on governance and creating new forms of power.[12] Although nation-states remain sovereign, their leaders are choosing to shift some of their power "up" to international institutions because of the need for new rules to govern global transactions and to respond to new global threats. Power is also shifting "down" to local groups and individuals as local citizens derive information from the Web, mobilize and organize each other through electronic mail (email), and become both subjects and users of the media. At all levels of authority, power is shifting "sideways," and new power is being created, as nongovernment players ranging from corporations to environmentalists shape the priorities and outcomes of national decisionmaking.[13]

These changes do not add up to a withering away of the state as such. In countries where there are functioning governments, the control of territory and the monopoly of organized force are still the dominant expressions of power. As one scholar puts it, state power is becoming unbundled into functional parts—executives, legislatures, independent agencies, and courts. These parts are networking with counterparts abroad rather than withering or disappearing.[14]

National power now stems less and less from endowed assets (for example, land and natural resources) and more and more from chosen or created assets (for example, mastery of information technology, market-friendly economic policies, a climate that supports innovation and risk, and a skilled workforce). Cities with commercial links to urban centers in other countries are an emerging part of the new global scene.[15] These are characteristics found in the United States and other industrialized democracies and associated with high-performance military capability.[16] Societies that lack these attributes will either gravitate toward the outlook and orbit of this democratic core or remain chronically malnourished.

Nonstate Actors, Localities, and Individuals. At the same time, regional and international organizations and national governments must now deal with many more nonstate actors than they have ever had to deal with before. The global economy has boosted corporate resources to record levels. Many politically active corporations wield large amounts of money; the market value of Microsoft and General Electric, for example, leaves most national gross domestic products (GDPs) in the dust. In the nonprofit world, NGOs that hitherto confined themselves to domestic politics now travel routinely to places like Geneva. Nearly a thousand nongovernmental organizations were represented at the 1999 ministerial meeting of the World Trade Organization (WTO) in Seattle, up from half a dozen or so attending trade talks in the 1940s and 1950s. Because of the nature of globalization, international cooperation now impinges on internal sovereignty and necessarily involves nonstate actors.[17]

Rebel movements and other opponents of national governments also make use of the Internet and other forms of modern communication. A good example is the Serbian opposition's radio station, which went on line in 1997–1998 even after Slobodan Milosevic had shut down its studio. Similarly, email messages from Kosovo offered the first clear evidence of Serbian intentions to crush Kosovar-Albanian leadership. The demonstrations that toppled the Milosevic regime in October 2000 were broadcast all over the world, attracting global attention and widespread support.

In many parts of the world, particularly in cities and coastal communities, the sudden availability of telecommunications products and services has enabled local communities and groups to mobilize across borders, with or without the cooperation of local governments. In some instances, this process creates or strengthens local identities, brings grievances to the fore, and gives rise to organized communal, ethnic, or religious protest movements. Email links such groups with each other and with foreign supporters, while instant media coverage raises worldwide awareness of the plight of those who are being victimized. Human rights activists in Java, for example, say that they first learned about atrocities committed by the army elsewhere in Indonesia from emails sent from the New York-based Human Rights Watch.

Finally, globalization operates at the level of individuals. Individual dissidents like Aung San Su Kyi of Burma now have a global audience. More broadly, globalization appears to intensify the process by which individuals in society become differentiated from one another and from their elders. Globalization also enables individuals to connect in new ways. Thanks in part to the global media, individuals—especially the young—are borrowing selectively from other cultures, especially American popular culture. They are also developing their own lifestyles and expressing their own convictions to an unprecedented degree. Global firms are learning to adapt their products and services not only to accommodate long-standing cultural sensitivities but also to cater to increasingly individualistic young people as they develop new cultural identities and tastes.[18] Whether these increasingly differentiated individuals watch CNN, place long-distance calls on their cellular telephones, or log onto the Web in cybercafes, they are both creating and tapping into a global community.

In sum, globalization is an uneven, relentless, and frequently disruptive process toward a more interconnected world system. It has historical roots, but it is substantially new and different. Surging through all levels of society, it stimulates alternatives and opposites. It brings many more actors into play, bringing about integration, but not always a sense of community. It is fostering regional integration and "unbundling" national power. It appears to benefit open, market-oriented democratic and quasi-democratic states more than authoritarian ones.

Foundations, Enablers, and Drivers of Globalization

Foundations

The United States laid the foundations of today's globalization in the years immediately following World War II. It did so by mobilizing and leading a democratic, market-oriented community of nations and, with its allies, establishing the institutions to support that community. The strategy encompassed security, democracy, and economics. The security component was anchored in the North Atlantic Treaty Organization (NATO) and a series of regional treaty commitments. The democratic component sought to strengthen non-communist regimes, preferably democratic ones. The economic component included recovery programs in Germany and Japan, and a cooperative, rules-based trading system (that is, the General Agreement on Tariffs and Trade, or GATT). The International Monetary Fund (IMF) and the World Bank were established at about the same time.

This three-armed strategy of building a community through economic, political, and security cooperation continued throughout the Cold War. In one form or another, it remains U.S. policy to this day. It rests on a conviction that economic growth and political freedom cannot flourish without a credible military shield. It also reflects a view that drawing other nations into the circle of market-oriented democracies is the best way to sustain world peace. (The case for China's entry into the WTO, for example, includes arguments of this kind.) Seen from that perspective, globalization is both the fruit of post-World War II U.S. and allied policies and a catalyst for further integration in the norms-based sense of the term.

Enablers

A fundamental enabler of globalization in most regions of the world is the absence of a major war or major internal strife. A stable, secure environment is often taken for granted, but it is the underpinning of growth. Since sound business decisions require a reasonable degree of stability, investments tend to be postponed when nations are at war or on the brink of war. Normal commercial protections are often suspended. Conversely, the peaceful environment sustained by alliances between the United States, Europe, and Japan has permitted reductions in defense spending, thereby easing the tax burden and freeing resources for commercial investment.

Another enabler is the post-Cold War triumph of market-friendly policies in developing countries and the strengthening of those policies in industrialized ones. Socialism is passé. Deregulation, privatization, the lowering of barriers to trade and investment, and the protection of intellectual property are in. Implementation and enforcement frequently fall short, and a few governments still have not received the message. Still, globalization would not be as widespread as it is today without a fundamental change in the global economic policy environment.

In all countries, policy enablers include sound fiscal and monetary policies, a free flow of information, some degree of accountability on the part of both governments and major economic actors, a functioning tax system, protection of private property, opportunities for the rising middle class to find jobs and to enter and exit markets, predictable rules based on some minimum standards of law and justice, and support for education and training. The extent to which governments adopt and implement this mix of policies is one of the key variables determining whether globalization as a whole is stabilizing or destabilizing.

The huge American market, with its seemingly insatiable consumers, is an enabler all by itself. For most of the last decade, American growth has far outstripped that of its major trading partners. Many global industries target first and foremost the American market. In addition, the United States contributes mightily to globalization because it is a source of innovation and creativity. Its institutions of higher learning attract tens of thousands of students from all over the world. Most of the products and networks that buzz and hum in the service of globalization originate in American brains.

Drivers

The major driver of globalization is the knowledge revolution. In the first instance, this knowledge was largely developed by and for business. The knowledge revolution takes the form of a business-driven and business-invented triad consisting of advanced telecommunications, technology transfer, and capital flows.

Globalization would not be occurring in its present form were it not for the business application of the knowledge revolution—computers, email, satellites, jet engines, and other innovations. These high-technology products and services do not flow around the world all by themselves. The world would not be "wired" to the extent that it is if telecommunications companies had not sold and installed the appropriate equipment. The popular culture of the United States would not enjoy a global audience were it not for the American entertainment industry and the hardware and software that goes with it. None of these things would be happening if financial institutions had not made arrangements to transfer funds across borders.

A related driver of globalization is market competition. The current phase of globalization first appeared in commercial and economic form. Beginning in the late 1970s, breakthroughs in transportation and communications technology, a general lowering of trade barriers, and a worldwide shift toward market-oriented policies transformed the structure of global business. Regional trade and investment agreements took on new life: roughly two-thirds of world trade now takes place within free trade areas or among countries committed to free trade and investment by a certain date. Even energy, a strategic commodity long subjected to special relationships and long-term contracts, is now traded or sold in an increasingly global and deregulated market.

The globalization of business has led to the dispersal of the phases of production of components, goods, and services around the world for local, national, regional, and global markets. This pattern of production fosters economies of scale and permits adaptation to local consumer taste. It also gives rise to world-class standards of performance, quality, and efficiency. In the 1990s, economic globalization spread well beyond major companies and banks. Thanks to personal computers, globalization has been pulled downward, as it were, into small enterprises and literally into the lap(top)s of individuals. Operating from home with a few thousand dollars worth of equipment, anyone can become a global merchant.

Global companies are not in business to feed the hungry, but to defeat their rivals. During the late 1970s and 1980s, markets in highly industrialized countries were becoming saturated. Developing countries, with their high growth rates and youthful population, seemed attractive. Meanwhile, Japanese companies led the way in improving quality and automating manufacturing, capturing major markets in the United States as well as in the developing world. Both the lure of new markets and the threat of Japanese competition spurred European and American firms to boost quality and innovation, streamline operations, build global acquisition networks, establish competitive footholds abroad, enter into strategic partnerships, and offer new services. These dynamics contributed visibly to the successful conclusion of the Uruguay Round of multilateral trade negotiations (1986–1993), which led to the establishment of the World Trade Organization.

The globalization of finance has become a hallmark of the present era. Larger banks had operated abroad for decades, but only under restraints imposed by the host government. During the 1980s, these restraints began to unravel. Providers of financial services followed their corporate clients abroad and soon acquired new customers. They invented new market instruments and offered customers better returns than they had ever had before. The liberalization of financial services has proceeded in parallel with—or even ahead of—trade and investment.[19]

Benefits and Risks of Globalization

Understanding the major faces of globalization—economic, political, cultural, religious, social, demographic, environmental, and military (and the benefits and risks associated with them)—is important because the interaction between them can be either benign or destructive. Any one or two of them can trigger security problems in which the United States may be called upon to intervene or otherwise lend assistance. Conversely, globalization presents new opportunities for expanding the democratic community of nations and promoting peace and prosperity.

Economic Globalization

Globalization, Wealth, and Poverty. Most economists are enthusiastic about economic globalization because they place a high value on efficiency. Globalization encourages market behavior, and markets demand efficiency. The more global the scale of the market, the more efficient the allocation of resources can become. Resources can be shifted from less productive to more productive use. Lower tariffs help to hold inflation down and spur competitiveness. Foreign investment brings technology, innovation, and management skills. New jobs are created to serve global markets. Job losses occur in less efficient sectors, but these are more than offset by overall gains in national employment opportunities.

According to at least three major studies, nations with open, market-oriented economies have grown at least twice as fast as those with closed economies, and in the 1970s and 1980s, the disparity was even higher.[20] Never before in history have so many people in so many countries experienced a rise in real income. In the last 10 years, the period roughly associated with the most expansive phase of globalization, the number of people living in absolute poverty has declined, albeit modestly (24 percent in 1998, down from 29 percent in 1990).[21] World health indicators such as longevity and infant mortality have steadily improved almost everywhere.

That is the good news. Other known measures are grim (for example, continuing population growth in regions unable to sustain existing communities). What is hotly debated is to what extent, if any, globalization is to blame for the ripples of suffering washing over the world's poor. Everyone agrees that globalization is efficient; the burning issue is justice.

To globalization's critics, there is a direct, causal relationship between globalization-fed corporate profits and global poverty. According to one group, the World Bank and the International Monetary Fund "have maintained most nations of the global south in poverty."[22] According to another, the "current globalization model" is not free trade, but "corporate managed trade."[23,24] Such critics believe that globalization is eroding democracy, stamping out indigenous cultures, and ravaging the environment.[25]

Specific examples cited by opponents of World Bank and IMF policies vary widely. Many involve environmental destruction caused by large-scale projects such as dams or the displacement of small farmers by agribusiness concerns. Austerity programs established by the International Monetary Fund have eliminated subsidies on commodities consumed by the poor, resulting in overnight price hikes. The United Nations (UN) Development Program's *Human Development Report, 1999* does not go as far as protesters in Seattle, but it complains that globalization is threatening "human security" and "squeezing out care, the invisible heart of human development."[26]

There is often another side to antiglobalization horror stories. But there is no doubt that the speed, volatility, and sudden withdrawal of financial flows sent a number of countries spinning into recession in 1997–1998. This was the first real "crisis" of globalization. The collapse of the Thai *baht* pulsed through most of Asia and then to much of South America, ravaging the economies of Brazil and its neighbors. The collapse of confidence associated with the Asian crisis ultimately spread to Russia, crippled what was left of the Russian economy, and brought forth a younger, technocratic leader to clean up the mess. From Thailand to Russia: not a chain one might have predicted.

In Indonesia, which was hit hardest by the crisis, growth declined by 14 percent in 1 year, and the number of people living in absolute poverty temporarily doubled, from 10 percent to almost 20 percent. The Suharto government fell, and secessionist movements gathered steam—not only in East Timor but also in Sumatra and in Irian Jaya. Attacks on religious groups intensified as well. For the first time in more than 30 years, Indonesians have a democratically elected government. But they also face economic disarray, political confusion, and local violence. The new government's leaders agree that the International Monetary Fund made mistakes, but they argue forcefully that the main cause of this turmoil is not globalization, but rather the Suharto government's failure to adopt the political and economic institutions and behavior needed to accommodate the pressures of globalization.

Some lessons of economic globalization are clear. If a government pursues market-oriented policies that benefit the ruling elite or the middle class at the expense of the poor, if inadequate disclosure and weak supervisory organs trigger a run on the banks, and if social safety nets are weak or absent, openness to globalization can severely destabilize the political system and hurt the most vulnerable members of the population. Since people in other countries tend to assume that the United States pulls the strings of the World Bank and IMF, financial crises of the Indonesian variety ignite anti-Americanism as well as evoking a legitimate humanitarian outcry.[27]

Globalization and Gaps. The widening income gap both within countries and between countries and regions that are adapting relatively well to globalization and those that are left behind is a matter of great concern to national security strategists, especially if governments in the latter group brandish weapons of mass destruction. The fear is that these governments will become more hostile to the West and possibly more aggressive.

A country's GDP divided by its population, or per capita GDP, is a widely used yardstick of national wealth. Critics of the World Bank have argued against excessive reliance on per capita GDP statistics. They prefer broader sets of measures variously known as "human development," "human security," and the like, which include standards of health, education, and quality of life. Nevertheless, per capita GDP conforms fairly closely with these other indicators of development—at a national or aggregate level.[28]

Other ways of measuring gaps besides calculating the aggregate per capita GDP might include examining the income gap between inhabitants of wealthy coastal regions and those living in more remote interior regions (as in China), between the dominant ethnic group and the entrepreneurial minority (Chinese in Southeast Asia and Indians in Africa), between high school and college graduates, and between those who are computer-literate and those who are not (the digital divide). These gaps may have more impact on a country's political stability than changes in aggregate per capita GDP.

The speed of relative changes in income can also rock stability. As a general rule, globalization offers rising elites and the urban middle class a bigger share of the pie. If this share increases too rapidly, and if the rest of the pie is not made available to others because of monopolies or corruption, the government can lose its legitimacy, as it did in Indonesia. If the speed of change is glacial because the government has deliberately isolated its subjects from globalization and restricted the free flow of information, disgruntled students and merchants may complain or rebel, as they apparently have in Iran.

International and regional comparisons are particularly relevant to U.S. foreign policy and security strategy. To revert to the standard measurement, the gap between the per capita GDP of one nation or region and that of other nations and regions has been growing. In sub-Saharan Africa, for example, per capita GDP in the 1990s is about the same as it was in the 1960s, while in every other region it has grown. African population growth has swelled the numbers of impoverished people by another 30 million. Africa's share of international trade has declined, while its indebtedness is the highest in the world.[29]

International capital flows tell a similar story. There is already a huge investment gap between the developed world and a small handful of developing countries on the one hand, and everybody else on the other. Three-quarters of all foreign direct investment in the developing world goes to fewer than a dozen countries. Of total private capital flows to developing countries from 1990 to 1996, the Middle East received only 2 percent, which is lower than all other regions. Since most countries need foreign capital to develop (including the United States in the 19th century), the investment gap will intensify a widening income gap within the developing world.

Do these income and investment gaps undermine political stability? Ordinary people do not normally spend time perusing national, regional, and international income statistics, but they are keenly aware of their own wealth or poverty. One of their questions is likely to be "Compared to what?" It matters enormously whether the poor are getting poorer in absolute terms or only relatively less rich in comparison with their own elites.[30] Pushing large numbers of people into poverty in absolute terms not only robs them of food, clothing, and shelter, but also undermines the perceived legitimacy of the government.

Income gaps reflect social and geographical divisions both within societies and among countries and regions. Depending on the country, low-skilled workers, workers in protected industries, small farmers, and landless laborers may well be at risk of losing their ability to provide for themselves and their families. Globalization exposes these fissures and imbalances and may exacerbate them.

The latest gap to receive attention in the context of globalization is the so-called digital divide, the growing divergence between those with access to, and capable of using, computers and the Internet, and those who are left behind. Access to information is a path to empowerment. The challenge is to adopt the right mix of public policies and public-private projects, possibly spearheaded by the G–8 group of world leaders, to create a global digital opportunity instead of a threat.[31]

Bribery and Corruption. In countries where there are weak legal and institutional structures, globalization has intensified the problem of bribery and corruption. Analyzing more than 30 economic, political, and social indicators from 34 countries, A.T. Kearney found that rapidly globalizing countries have experienced dramatic growth in corruption.[32] Corruption on a small scale has long served to grease the wheels of society, to provide access for marginalized groups, to guarantee the outcome of elections, and to enable the low-level official to feed his family. But in many countries, the corruption equilibrium has spun out of control, causing the downfall of governments and companies alike.[33]

Corruption siphons off resources, warps efficiency, saps the vitality of economic activity, and distorts public perceptions of how a market economy functions. In the area of public works, it jeopardizes public safety and can severely damage the environment. In these circumstances, "it becomes all too easy for economically beleaguered public to confuse democratization with the corruption and criminalization of the economy—creating fertile soil for an authoritarian backlash and engendering potentially hostile international behavior by these states in turn."[34]

Economic Globalization and Political Culture. No one has ever been able to predict whether and when rising poverty, inequality, and corruption will erupt in violence or why some states "fail" while others prosper.[35] Social and political patterns that fostered successful recovery in the early post-World War II years may not succeed so well in the more dynamic era of globalization. Conversely, certain societies turn out to have strengths well suited to the global age. For example, the lack of rigid hierarchy, respect for the value of shared information, and openness to new technology in Finnish society have allowed the Finns to embrace advanced information technology, and a Finnish company (Nokia) now dominates the worldwide mobile telephone market.[36] Moreover, cultures are not static; they are tapestries of "predispositions."[37] Gifted leaders can foster change within a cultural tradition, as Jawaharlal Nehru, Lee Kuan Yew, Kwame Nkrumah, and Mao Tse-tung did in their very different ways.

Perceptions Matter. In a stable society, people at all levels must think that they have a reasonable chance of living in peace and improving their lives or the lives of their children. They must also believe that in some way their voices will be heard, either at the ballot box or elsewhere. They must have some minimal sense that their institutions will work for them, even if the institutions are influenced by wealthy elites.

There is considerable evidence that political cultures that adapt most successfully to economic globalization feature accountable and responsive institutions based on some minimal level of civic trust, embedded in flexible and adaptive cultures. Attitudes toward work, education, entrepreneurship, and the future are important. Policy choices can help to promote the right mix.[38]

Broadly speaking, the political cultures of North America, Western and Central Europe (not including the Balkans), most of Asia (including Australia, New Zealand, and eastern and southern China, but not Myanmar and North Korea), and a few South American countries (for example, Chile and Brazil) are either adapting relatively well to globalization or have a good chance of doing so if political problems can be resolved. (India is still a question mark because some regions are adapting far better than others.) Significantly, the countries adapting successfully are either "free" or "partly free," that is, democracies or "soft" authoritarian states with substantial democratic features.[39] In many of these countries, the shock of the Asian financial crisis temporarily worsened already serious poverty, but most of them have resumed growth.

By contrast, with some exceptions, the nations located in a huge swath of contiguous territory ranging from the former Soviet Union in the north and Pakistan in the east through the Balkans, the Middle East, and sub-Saharan Africa in the south are presently ill suited for globalization. It appears that much of the Andean region is also adapting poorly to globalization. These regions exhibit some combination of weak or closed political institutions; inflexible or divisive social cultures marked by vengeance and distrust; predominantly tribal, family, or clan loyalties and/or a high degree of cronyism; and excessive regulation accompanied by a high degree of corruption.

Political Globalization

The globalization of politics has contributed to a new political awareness. Television has not merely brought other people's politics into the living room; it has also exposed abuses, revealed the face of war, and diffused certain political values, such as human rights and democracy, to more people than ever before. Prominent political leaders such as Nelson Mandela are known all around the world.

Over time, economic globalization undermines authoritarian governments because markets need information to work. The need for open information undercuts secretive regimes by creating pressure to expose the assets and liabilities of banks and corporations, including those controlled by dictators and their cronies. It also strengthens the ability of the press to conduct honest economic reporting and expose corruption. By providing more economic opportunity, globalization opens the door to new elites and fosters the growth of a middle class with a stake in stable and legitimate governments. Western investors often bring more egalitarian patterns of communication, as well as higher labor standards.

The need to attract global investment creates pressure to institute the rule of law or at least some predictable system of justice, enforced by a modern legal system and a trained, independent judiciary. Modern economies need laws governing market entry (competition), market exit (bankruptcy), contract enforcement, the protection of property, and intellectual property rights, among others. These pressures have spillover effects because the educated middle class tends to agitate for corresponding political rights.

Globalization can help to promote human rights and environmental protection. Political activists use email to communicate with their foreign counterparts and expand their networks at home. International observers monitor elections and flash their judgments around the world. Networking of this kind has brought to global attention a number of serious human and environmental problems. Among them are reliance on child labor, residual slavery and bondage, mistreatment of women and girls, arbitrary detention and torture, persecution of ethnic minorities, corruption, the destruction of the rain forest, environmental pollution, and many others. Publicity brings pressure on the governments that tolerate such practices and sometimes stimulates corrective action.[40]

Globalization can also overwhelm fragile political systems. Volatile financial flows can wreak havoc on existing power structures before alternative groups and institutions have had time to develop, leaving a temporary vacuum. (This is a problem in Indonesia, where the army indirectly ran local government until the fall of Suharto.) Criminal networks can sprout up, wielding political power of their own. Sudden changes in relative wealth can lead to the scapegoating of successful minorities, such as ethnic Chinese or Jews. Extremist movements, often aided from abroad, can attract those uprooted by globalization. Separatist movements can take root and flourish. Subsistence farmers can be forced to flock to the cities, placing new demands on officials and upsetting long-standing political arrangements between different ethnic groups. Even anarchism has made a comeback.

In these circumstances, it is hard for even the best of governments to exercise power effectively. Well-meaning governments can get the blame for dislocations beyond their control. Sometimes, they rely on outside pressure from the United States or IMF staff to provide political cover for doing what they already know needs to be done. They may receive support from friendly political organizations abroad, such as social democratic parties in Europe or American labor unions. This, too, is political globalization.

Globalization, Culture, and Religion

Culture is not something separate from globalization, to be pursued at leisure on a Sunday afternoon. Globalization is both shaping and being shaped by ways of thought, habits, values, religion, and other aspects of social life. It has both intensified old identities and fostered new ones. The cultural aspect of globalization is as relevant to U.S. policymaking as trade and financial flows.

Culture. In the social sciences, *culture* became segregated from the study of politics and economics several decades ago. But capital and technology do not sail around the world by themselves. They pass through human hands in the form of paper or through human fingers on a keyboard, and they reflect decisions made by human beings. As one scholar has written, culture includes symbols, individual experiences, biological dispositions, embodied social habits, and deliberative thought. It is a "meaning-making medium" that influences all spheres, including politics and economics.[41]

For a society to adapt well to economic globalization, cultural attitudes must permit risk and failure as well as success. Cultures must be capable of borrowing and adapting foreign influences as well as rejecting them. The talents of young people of both sexes must be put to use in the job market or in other productive activities. Opening up opportunities to women doubles the talent pool, lowers the rate of population growth, and improves public health. Trust and loyalty must extend beyond the family or kinship group, as must the sharing of spoils. For the most part, these last two conditions are absent in sub-Saharan Africa and much of the Middle East. When the king of Jordan died in 1999, for example, foreign governments sent presidents and foreign ministers to his funeral, but most Arab rulers sent their relatives.

Thanks to the globalization of the communications and entertainment industries, American popular culture is flooding the world. Most of the best known images, sounds, idols, and stars come from the United States. (An exception is Pokémon, which is from Japan, but its name is derived from the English words "pocket monster.") Even food is caught up in the trend. In 1999, McDonald's opened 1,790 restaurants, an average of 5 per day, more than 90 percent of which are outside the United States.[42]

Young people in particular flock to American films, rock music, clothing, and other icons of popular culture. Even remote villages hardly touched by globalization are likely to feature a soft drink stand selling Coca-Cola, manned by someone in an American T-shirt. Sometimes, these icons are associated with social messages (for example, rap and reggae music), but more often they are apolitical. Only in the most superficial ways do they signal "Americanization."

At the same time, the globalization of American popular culture has a liberating effect on the world's youth. Rock songs and films from the United States make young people feel empowered and "with it." While these feelings may or may not promote American values, they whet youthful appetites for more things American. "Pop" culture has fostered the spread of English, albeit in forms that sometimes seem strange to native speakers. Since English is the main language of international communication, anything that fosters an interest in learning it eventually opens doors to a wider world.

Through the entertainment industry, many forms of culture have found global audiences. Globalization has even helped to preserve some traditional cultures from extinction. For example, media attention has lent support to efforts to save indigenous people in areas of Brazil that are subject to rapid and destructive development. In many countries, however, elites fear that globalization will bring about a loss of cultural identity. They watch as their local cultures are swamped by American imports and commercialized by tourists. Their concern may be hard for U.S. citizens to understand. After all, the United States imports both foreigners and foreign cultures with abandon, without worrying about who they are. Indeed, the American identity is partly founded on such flows.

In some parts of the world, however, national identity is weak and young—only a few decades old, in some cases. Boundaries are arbitrary, left over from the days when colonial powers carved up entire continents between them. The secession of one province or another is a real threat. Elites in these countries may or may not oppose modernization of their culture, but they have an understandable concern. They see the worst of the United States washing over their heartland, not the best. They associate globalization with American materialism and self-centeredness, as opposed to loyalty, self-discipline, spirituality, and the well-being of the group. Their images of the United States, derived in part from movies and television, include promiscuity, violence, materialism, disrespect for authority, drug abuse, divorce, guns, and crime.

Fortunately, there is little likelihood that the richness and diversity of human cultures will dissolve. Living cultures have a way of thriving and adapting despite the barrage of Hollywood glitz and techno-gimmickry. But it behooves U.S. leaders, including U.S. military personnel, to be more sensitive to the threat that images of the free-wheeling American lifestyle poses to older societies. All too easily, the United States can become a "devil," as it did in the Ayatollah Khomeini's Iran.

Aside from these risks, the combination of American business culture and popular culture bestows on the United States a degree of "soft" power that its citizens never consciously sought. The result is that they find themselves in a leadership role to which they have devoted little thought, planning, and resources. As a Singaporean official concluded, "[The] softer aspect of American influence is in some ways even more profound than its hard power. Globalization must therefore be led by the U.S."[43]

Religion. The reach of religion is becoming more global than ever before. Not only is globalization compatible with most forms of religion, but it also facilitates the spread of religious ideas. In fact, the major religions are now world religions. The Dalai Lama, Pope John Paul II, and Billy Graham are world figures. Sacred texts are available on the Web. Interfaith dialogue, aided by globalization, is now well established.

To some, the popularity of religion is surprising. Beginning with the Enlightenment, modernist thinkers have equated religion with superstition and championed secular and "rational" thinking. The postmodernist perspective is similarly hostile to religion. It downplays group cohesion and modern forms of organization in favor of individual fulfillment. This form of individualism can include a spiritual dimension (for example, yoga, meditation, and the New Age movement), but it rejects traditional, organized religions as narrow and coercive. In its place, it enshrines the individual as the central focus of worship.[44]

Despite these intellectual movements, religion is flourishing. It has reappeared in the former Soviet Union, it is clearly making inroads in China, and it is a vital force in most other regions of the world. Moreover, it is pervasive in that beehive of globalization, the United States. Far from destroying religion, globalization has created conditions that allow the practice of religion to expand. Globalization ushers in a greater degree of openness to ideas from the outside world, including religious ideas about the human spirit. According to one scholar, globalization is the "compression of the world and the intensification of consciousness of the world as a whole."[45]

Those in the United States tend to have a somewhat negative image of other people's religions, particularly Islam. But religious affiliation can help people in local communities adjust to globalization. Such people share a sense of community, basic moral and ethical values, self-discipline, humility, and willingness to accept rules established for the good of all. This combination can help overcome the alienation and insecurity associated with the collapse of traditional authority and rapid economic change. For example, in Egypt, Islamic movements have mushroomed to fill vacuums caused by the crisis in state legitimacy. These movements provide "a channel for informal political participation, a sense of identity and social justice, and the provision of basic needs and services for the underprivileged."[46] In Turkey and Kosovo, Islamic self-help groups have filled holes in the state's social safety net. Members of religious groups are also in a good position to report human rights abuses and other instances of injustice.

Much of the violence that occurs in the name of religion is a political backlash against dislocations associated with globalization. Fighting between Christians and Muslims in the Moluccas (formerly known as the Spice Islands and now part of Indonesia) stems in part from a sudden, destabilizing influx of migrants that upset the balance between the two groups. Hindu militancy is often political in nature, used to divert popular attention from problems or scandals. Politicians can invoke religious themes to foment separatism, anti-Americanism, or enthusiasm for war. They also use religion to whip up a martyr complex or justify a culture of victimhood, as in Serbia and Iran. Local elders can use religious language to perpetuate tribal customs (for example, genital cutting of girls) or to enforce tribal notions of honor (for example, keeping women and girls at home and "honor killings").

What is truly destabilizing and disintegrative is not the revival of genuine religious faith, but a total collapse of religion-based norms and ethics. This is what appears to be happening in some parts of sub-Saharan Africa (for example, Congo and Sierra Leone), as well as in many parts of the former Soviet Union. Even harsh justice meted out in the name of the Sharia (the Islamic code of justice) is better than a war of all against all.

Social, Demographic, and Environmental Effects of Globalization

Migration, Population, and the Role of Women. According to the International Labor Organization (ILO),[47] there are approximately 120 million migrants as of the year 2000—up from 75 million in 1965. While this surge is dramatic, it is not unprecedented. Between 1846 and 1939, some 59 million people emigrated from Europe. Prior to 1850, an estimated 15 million slaves were transported from Africa to the Americas. In the peak year of immigration, 1915, the United States accepted a level of immigration equivalent to 1.2 percent of its population, while in 1996 that figure was only 0.35 percent.

As the ILO makes clear,[48] what is new is the global nature of the migration. Between 1970 and 1990, the number of countries classified as major receivers of labor immigrants rose from 39 to 67, while the number of countries designated as major international labor suppliers rose from 29 to 55. The number of countries that are both suppliers and receivers rose from 4 to 15.

It is no longer true, if it ever was, that "capital migrates, but workers don't." A record number of people on the move are refugees from war. In the churning world of global trade and investment, those who are losing their livelihood often migrate as well.[49] Some migrate illegally; a new industry—trafficking in workers—generates an estimated $6 billion a year for smugglers and forgers, some of whom are members of international criminal networks.

The cross-border migration of workers has a number of benefits. It brings in people with the energy and courage to start a new life. It serves to fill low-wage jobs that a more affluent population no longer wants, such as street cleaning, janitorial services, and care of the aged. It provides new economic opportunities for both migrants and their host communities. It is another form of efficiency—the intersection of supply and demand.

Beyond a certain point, however, large-scale migration can be jarring and dehumanizing. The sudden influx of large clusters of immigrants strains local resources and often generates social tensions. Even in the United States, which is unusually receptive to immigrants, a racist backlash shut the door to Asians in the 1920s. After the Vietnam War, Vietnamese shrimp fishermen encountered violence in Texas. In Germany and Austria, where roughly 10 percent of the workforce is foreign-born, right-wing political parties that oppose further immigration have gained strength. In Spain, violence against North Africans escalated into several days of terror and destruction.

Migration to cities is a particularly urgent problem. Global agribusiness and other changes associated with globalization are driving or enticing many people from the land into overcrowded cities, creating massive social and health problems. In some countries, female infanticide distorts male-to-female ratios, compounding dissatisfaction with rural life. At the current rate, by 2010 the world will have at least a dozen more cities with populations of 8 million people or more. The supply of water, sewage systems, health facilities, schools, public transportation, roads, and practically everything else that people need to live decent lives will be in short supply. Even draconian measures to discourage such migrations, such as denial of work and residence permits in Chinese cities, do not seem to halt the flow.

Over time, migrants can build up resentment about their shabby treatment and low status. While parents may conclude that life in the city is still better than it was in the village, their unemployed sons may dismiss the comparison and take to the streets. Long-time residents can resent the intrusion of people whose customs and lifestyle are different. In the United States, the most recent comparable experience is probably the migration of African-Americans from the rural south to northern cities, a shift whose consequences are still felt decades later.

The movement of highly educated people to the United States and other developed countries—the so-called brain drain—is not new. What is new is that some of them are starting businesses in their country of origin even while maintaining their primary residence abroad (for example, Indian engineers living in Silicon Valley). This trend should send a pointed signal to governments whose policies do not permit this sort of entrepreneurship.

Population trends suggest that both the need for and the supply of migrant workers will continue for some time to come. Birth rates are stable or declining in most of the industrialized and industrializing world, as life choices diminish family size and better health care contributes to the "graying" of the population. As an Italian journalist puts it, "The fewer children we have, the more immigrants we need."[50] He might have added that in Africa and parts of the Middle East, the population is growing by as much as 5 to 6 percent, with the largest number of births occurring among the poor.

Many women take jobs outside the home because of economic desperation. Others do so because they want to take advantage of new opportunities swept in by globalization. Worldwide, women increased their participation in the labor force from 36 percent in 1970 to about 45 percent in 1994. This rate varies sharply by region. In Arab countries, for example, only one in four women are in the labor force, compared with 69 percent in East Asia.[51]

Other things being equal, the chance to earn money is likely to raise the status of women and improve the prospects for female literacy. In areas where women have long been allowed to earn money, such as southern Nigeria and the state of Kerala in India, the ratio of men to women is roughly normal because there is no economic reason to kill or starve female babies and girls. Over time, the empowerment of women could prove to be one of globalization's most positive contributions.

The Environment and Health. Globalization is clearly a catalyst for rapid growth, and untrammeled growth can take destructive forms. Many environmentalists associate globalization with the destruction of the rain forest, the disappearance of threatened plant and animal species, the depletion of marine resources, acid rain, chemical pollution, and a host of health concerns. The data tend to validate these concerns, at least in the near term.[52] For example, A.T. Kearney's survey found that rapid globalizers saw increases of 4 percent or more in their carbon dioxide emissions.[53] A major culprit in environmental deterioration is the uncontrolled use of resources backed by misguided and unbalanced development policies in developed and developing countries alike. Environmental destruction in the *un*globalized former communist empire, for example, was worse than most of what is observed today.

Over time, globalization tends to increase pressure for environmental protection, but the process is not automatic. Foreign investment often brings investors from the United States and Europe who are more sensitive to environmental values than local governments, if only because their shareholders are tracking their performance.[54] Foreign pressure to move toward free trade and investment can reduce wasteful subsidies that distort the use of resources. The drive for efficiency can introduce more rational pricing policies and the "polluter pays" principle. The spread of science and technology around the world can help to clean up the environment as well, but solutions are necessarily long-term in nature. In the meantime, the emphasis on growth must be linked with serious resource planning.

From a security perspective, the impact of globalization on the availability of natural resources is a key concern. The most urgent shortage of the first half of the 21st century will not be oil, which is still relatively abundant, but clean water. The demand for water is outstripping the supply. Control of water supplies has long been a strategic objective and is a tension-creating factor in many parts of the world.

The North China Plain is already in crisis. The water table around Beijing, for instance, has declined by 59 meters since the late 1960s. Plans to divert water from the South are controversial, environmentally destructive, and hugely expensive. Chinese intentions to build two dams across the Upper Mekong have sparked concerns about their impact on downstream agrarian communities in Indochina.[55] Other water-related concerns include the conflict between Syria and Israel over the Golan Heights,

Singapore's uneasy dependence on Malaysia, and the movement of Saharan Africans fleeing from the encroachment of the desert.

Another problem directly or indirectly associated with globalization is the spread of infectious disease. In particular, acquired immunodeficiency syndrome (AIDS) is a threat to U.S. security for several reasons. A globally mutating virus could return to threaten the United States and its allies, as well as strategically important countries such as Russia, Brazil, and India. There is already a conflict over access to life-saving drugs, and it could get worse. Finally, in some countries, there could be a breakdown of civil order as social, economic, and political systems crumble in the face of widespread disease and death from AIDS.

Besides AIDS, cholera, tuberculosis, and a variety of other diseases are rampant, and some are taking drug-resistant forms. The expansion of shipping has given a free ride to many germs and disease-bearing insects. In 1991, for example, a ship from China emptied ballast tanks containing the causative agent of cholera off the coast of Peru. Within weeks, outbreaks of cholera were reported in Peru when none had been found in the entire continent of Latin America for more than a century.[56]

Occupational illness has also been on the rise. Women, widely employed in electronics factories because of their manual dexterity, are regularly exposed to carcinogenic solvents, acids, and toxic fumes. Frequent use of microscopes has damaged their eyesight. Women who do fine sewing in the garment trade also report eye problems. Both women and men suffer from exposure to hazardous chemicals.

Public health is one area where the market alone cannot provide adequate solutions, but public funding for this and other transnational threats is skimpy compared to the need.[57]

Military Globalization

Military globalization parallels the history of conquest. It traces its ancestry to Cyrus of Persia, Alexander the Great, the Roman Empire, the Muslim conquerors, the Crusades, the Mongol invasions, and the age of colonialism, among others. But none of these people and events established a military-backed world system that was truly global. Even World War I was not a global war, and its post-war aims, a peaceful Germany and the League of Nations, both failed.

World War II was the first truly global war, and it gave rise to the structural elements of a global system. This system became operational in the economic arena to a greater degree than in most others, a fact that helps to explain why the global economic institutions and rules of today are far more highly developed than most noneconomic ones. The economic and social agencies of the United Nations, the World Bank, IMF, and the GATT (which later became the World Trade Organization) were pillars of a would-be global system consciously designed to knit together peace, growth, financial stability, trade, and investment. Mindful of the failed League of Nations, those who founded the United Nations skirted a true collective security system and subordinated security to the Security Council, where the five permanent members had a veto. When the Soviet Union emerged as a military threat, security arrangements took a regional form, of which NATO was the most prominent. The bipolar political lineup that froze into the Cold War determined who armed themselves against whom around the world, and with whose technology.

What is new about the structure of military globalization is that the end of the Cold War and the rash of global threats have thrown into question the rationale for an exclusively regional security system. The most important expression of regional security, NATO, has begun to expand both membership and mission, taking on a role that complements and may occasionally replace that of the UN Security Council. Members of NATO are searching for ways to match regional security resources and arrangements with threats arising outside the defined territory to be protected (so-called out-of-area threats). This search is hampered by inevitable tensions both within and among the various governments involved and by resistance to NATO hegemony on the part of Russia and China (and to some extent, France).

What is new about the content and characteristics of military globalization resembles what is new about globalization more generally—high-speed communications, the rise of criminal networks, piracy, the mobilization of local ethnic and religious groups, and all the other aspects of globalization previously described. Technology with potential military application glides around the world through commercial channels, as well as in the computers of criminals. Know-how on nuclear weapons and other weapons of mass destruction can be downloaded from the Internet. Shoulder-fired missiles easily find their way to terrorists.

With respect to industry, more rational patterns of production, prompted in part by global competition, have injected more efficiency into defense procurement. The defense industrial base is checkered with licensing deals and crisscrossed by strategic partnerships.[58,59] There has been a substantial consolidation of firms within both the U.S. and the European defense industry. While these firms often compete head-on for major arms contracts, considerable cross-investment has occurred, especially at the subcontractor level.

In some ways, the United States is superbly positioned to shape military globalization. Its technology is second to none. It is by far the world's largest and most competitive seller of arms. For decades, it has constructed an extensive web of military-to-military ties and trained numerous military personnel from abroad. Although Europe, Russia, and China rival the United States as global arms merchants, none enjoys close military relationships with other countries to the degree that the United States does.

Military resources alone, however, cannot cope with the combination of weapons proliferation and nuclear stockpiles, ethnic and religious violence, the explosion of crime, health and environmental disasters, massive migration, and the demand for humanitarian intervention to halt genocide. Arms sales and technology transfer can be destabilizing, and military-to-military ties serve U.S. interests only if the government in question is committed to the right goals. In the era of globalization, conflict prevention and institution building must be granted more priority space in the American toolbox. Just as gun control alone will not stop crime, the United States needs a comprehensive security strategy that transcends its military elements.

In sum, the benefits of globalization are substantial, but the risks are immediate and pressing. Globalization can facilitate solutions, but not overnight. In many parts of the world, globalization is linking together an emerging world community, while those left behind are angry and alienated. There are far too many small-scale conflicts, catastrophes, and threats, causing far too much human suffering and discontent. A global strategy must extend from dot-coms to demographics, from rockets to religion. Although security is an essential ingredient, the scope of such remedies extends way beyond the purview of the U.S. military and calls for a wide variety of expertise.

Globalization, Security, and the International System

Globalization in the current era is unprecedented, irreversible, highly uneven, and sometimes divisive in its effects. It has defining characteristics (for example, speed, networks, and flows) and a defining direction—toward integration. It is intertwined with economic development, politics, culture, religion, society, and the environment in ways that can produce both benefits and risks. Security policy is concerned with the risks. Shocks and disruptions associated with globalization have provoked outbursts of religious, cultural, political, and individual reaction, and sometimes crime, revolution, and war.[60] These eruptions can threaten U.S. security interests, expose the shortcomings of U.S. policy, and generate demands for intervention.

Globalization and Security Policy

Globalization has vastly expanded the scope of security policy. For individuals, communities, and nations alike, security has always meant freedom to pursue a freely chosen way of life without undue danger, interference, or uncertainty. Today, threats have proliferated in both number and in type. Globalization creates and exposes vulnerability to what had previously seemed remote or irrelevant.

External Threats. Traditionally, security has been an external, cross-border concept. City dwellers built walls and fought off invaders. Alternatively, their leaders went off and conquered their neighbors. The danger of a Soviet nuclear attack has disappeared, but the threat of conventional, territorial war has not (for example, the Korean Peninsula, the Taiwan Strait, the Spratly Islands, and Kashmir). Military forces are still organized geographically, and their most basic mission is to protect territorial integrity.

In the era of globalization, by contrast, external threats have increasingly assumed transnational forms. Information on making weapons of mass destruction can be gleaned from the Internet. Because of improvements in transportation and communications, globalization has multiplied the instances and destructiveness of covert criminal activities (for example, crime, drugs, terrorism, and trafficking in human beings) and given rise to new, invisible threats (for example, cyberterrorism and new forms of germ warfare).

Economic priorities figure prominently in the new security calculus. In the most recent national security strategy document issued by the White House, for example, the tasks of security are not only to protect territory and save lives but also "to promote the well-being and prosperity of the nation and its people."[61] The broad scope of this thinking brings U.S. security policy more into line with what leaders in ASEAN,

Japan, and elsewhere call *comprehensive security*. Security thinking in other parts of the world has been moving in this direction as well.[62]

Environmental and demographic changes also have cross-border effects. As national economies have become more integrated, hardship and crisis in one country can puncture livelihoods in the entire region. Environmental disasters—ranging from Chernobyl-type accidents and erosion-induced flooding to the polluting effects of slash-and-burn agriculture on a massive scale—can erode the health of people in neighboring countries. One example is the drifting of smoke and haze from burning fields in Indonesia to Malaysia and Singapore.

Internal Threats. In addition to coping with external, cross-border threats, security planners must now grapple with the internal dynamics that stoke those threats in the first place. A certain number of states are either too rigidly controlled or too weak at the center to cope with globalization, let alone take advantage of it. They are clustered in the geographical region extending from the former Soviet Union through the Middle East and down through much of sub-Saharan Africa. The so-called failed states—Somalia, Sudan, and possibly Sierra Leone and Pakistan—are in this region. Four states whose rulers are most at odds with emerging norms of the post-Cold War international order—Iraq, Iran, Libya, and Afghanistan—are also located there. (Two others are North Korea and Burma or Myanmar.) These states either deliberately isolate themselves from the international community or pursue policies known to invite isolation. In a slightly different category are a handful of states such as Colombia, whose governments contain or shelter criminals who are heavily engaged in the global drug trade.

The collapse of internal sovereignty can also become a regional security headache. What begins as a collapse of authority soon spawns rag-tag rebel armies, ethnic thugs, armed quasi-religious groups, drug traffickers, vigilantes, and shakedown artists.[63,64] Other countries can be drawn into internal problems if local violence spills across borders, if domestic insurgents and criminal elements receive funding and combat support from abroad, if insurgents take foreign hostages or launch a "holy war" against their neighbors, or if genocide occurs. Devising a global security policy now requires coming to grips with its internal aspect, which is individual and human, as well as its external aspect, which is collective and territorial.[65]

Sooner or later, the infusion of information technology and services into countries ruled by corrupt or repressive governments stimulates a drive for more political openness and predictability. It raises awareness of the outside world, encourages behavior that conforms to basic global norms and standards, fosters networking among NGOs, and brings abuses to global attention. But the near-term dangers are real and complex.

Both the external and internal dimensions of security call for a new definition of stability: peaceful adaptation to change. In the age of globalization, no government can isolate its people completely and forever or keep them from demanding political reform, religious freedom, more land, or whatever their need happens to be. Such demands frequently lead to abrupt change. The U.S. security community tends to see changes in the status quo as destabilizing, but they need not be threatening, even if they shake up regimes friendly to the United States. To paraphrase Rosenau, what matters is whether the change in question conforms to emerging global norms and whether it contributes to or detracts from the coherence of the system (that is, long-term sets of relationships and conditions).[66]

Strengthening National and International Security in the Era of Globalization: Goals, Strategies, and Process

Goals. The overarching objective of U.S. foreign and security policy in the era of globalization should be to shape the emerging world order in a way that protects U.S. interests and promotes U.S. and allied values. Protecting the territorial integrity of the United States and its treaty allies is obviously a vital interest,[67] but other interests and values are of relevance to the rest of the world as well. They include a stable peace; democratic governance based on inclusion, justice, and legitimacy; economic opportunity; basic respect for the individual; and social, cultural, and environmental health and well-being.

The goals required to carry out the overarching objective of shaping a benign world order include:

- Promotion of global norms through peaceful adaptation to change and integration, accompanied by the development of corresponding global rules and institutions. Steps include strengthening and expanding the multilateral trading and financial system, participating in various environmental and arms agreements for which there appears to be a global consensus, and devoting more resources to conflict prevention. The current governance gap between advanced rule making and dispute settlement in the trading system and weak or nonexistent guidelines and rules in other aspects of international life should be narrowed so that legitimate concerns are addressed and not targeted exclusively at economic institutions such as the WTO and the International Monetary Fund.
- Simultaneous nurturing of regional, national, local, group, and individual autonomy through active promotion of diversity and free choice, reflected in strong, accountable, and flexible domestic institutions. Steps include promoting democracy, supporting efforts to protect indigenous populations and cultures, and providing financial assistance for the poorest countries.
- Enhancement and expansion of institutions and instruments of cooperative security, founded on widely shared norms and respectful of autonomy and peaceful change, to contain or reduce existing threats and prevent the development of new ones. Steps should address the demand for weapons of mass destruction and advanced conventional armaments, as well as the supply—that is, the conditions that give rise to destabilizing arms buildups and violence in the first place. Actions should take account of how U.S. actions are perceived abroad, as well as the close link between traditional and nontraditional threats (for example, civil war and crime).

Of these three goals, promoting global norms is probably the most basic. World leaders are increasingly being challenged to subscribe to and put into practice an emerging set of global norms. The UN Millennium Declaration of September 2000 identified certain fundamental values as "essential to international relations in the twenty-first century." They are freedom, equality, solidarity (including equity and social justice), tolerance, respect for nature, and shared responsibility (for managing economic and social development, as well as threats to international peace and security).[68] This list downplays certain typical American themes (such as economic opportunity and basic human rights), but it is generally consistent with them.

Norms are usually at the heart of durable institutions.[69] Many of today's recognized workaday institutions started as shared basic norms, which the statesmen of the day then hammered into articles of agreement. A good example is the GATT and its successor organization, the WTO, whose complex rules on market access and elaborate system of dispute resolution evolved from and are rooted in the principle of nondiscrimination.

In the era of globalization, to use Rosenau's language, the evolution of shared norms is characteristic of the emerging global-domestic frontier and gives voice to the collective nature of shared challenges. It is not that a world society has consolidated its shared norms, leaving out a small minority, but that "enough evolution has occurred for traces of widely shared norms to be noticeable."[70] Even dictators often cloak their misdeeds in normative language. The phenomenon is not exactly new; La Rochefoucauld's 17th-century maxim that hypocrisy is the homage that vice pays to virtue probably applies to the entire sweep of political history. The difference today is that such language is global and so are its means of transmission.

The notion of emerging global norms is controversial. Who has the right to say what is "global"?[71] The debate about what is and is not "Western," as opposed to global or universal, has great bearing on the charge that globalization amounts to cultural imperialism, but almost every conflict that swims into global focus features recognizable demands for political participation, justice, and basic human rights (or some variation thereof).

Strategies. Achieving the three goals listed earlier—promoting global norms, nurturing autonomy, and creating new instruments for cooperative security—is a step-by-step process. Policymakers will have to continuously redefine and refine the substance and style of their daily work to correspond to the speed, intensity, opportunity, and potential for disaster associated with globalization. They will need a strategy based on cross-disciplinary analysis encompassing all aspects of globalization and all available tools and partnerships.

Cross-disciplinary analysis is necessary because of the interconnectedness of various aspects of global development. For instance, adequate security is a prerequisite for healthy economic growth. That growth in turn makes possible a reasonable level of defense spending and fosters a vibrant middle class. The growth of a middle class is associated with the demand for economic opportunity and, usually, more political freedom. And so on.[72]

Another crucial prerequisite is the ability to build consensus and to work as a genuine team with friends and allies, where necessary through compromise. Despite its hegemonic status, the United States cannot shape a world order adapted to emerging global norms, autonomy, and security all by itself. Building such a world order in the era of globalization requires help and cooperation from others—allies, friends, and governments that are not particularly friendly to the United States, but with which it has common interests. Moreover, globalization has increased the value of "soft" power, which depends on alliances and coalitions for maximum effect.[73]

There is still no meaningful strategic dialogue about coordinated policy responses to globalization between and among the United States and its allies. Building coalitions is a frequently stated objective, but proposed compromises to achieve those coalitions are often dismissed as "non-starters," meaning politically unacceptable. But giving in to this defeatist viewpoint is itself a non-starter. "Buy America" legislation, suspicion of foreign motives, and a residual instinct to go it alone still hamper the ability of the members of U.S.-led coalitions to cooperate internally[74]—to the detriment of U.S. security. In particular, the emphasis that the United States places on sanctions against would-be nuclear weapons states will have to be tailored and adapted to the security priorities and prescriptions of others if a more cooperative security strategy is to be feasible.

On some occasions, U.S. unilateral action may be appropriate, as in the initial response to the Iraq-Kuwait war of 1990–1991.[75] On other occasions, some missions will have to be carried out "the European way," "the Asian way," or whatever way is appropriate because others may be better equipped to do the job and/or the job is not a U.S. responsibility in the first place. In all cases, U.S. leaders should avoid sounding arrogant or sanctimonious.

Strategies designed to channel globalization toward a benign world order must transcend governments, making use of regional and international institutions as well as local public-private partnerships involving companies and/or nonprofit groups and organizations. Nongovernmental organizations are changing the face of politics all over the world. Aided by media attention, they have been regularly demanding a voice at international meetings and in the Congress. They are bound to be active in or around future combat or peacekeeping missions. The security community must come to grips with the new power and presence of nongovernmental organizations.

Global Systemic Strategies. Changes in the nature of security and stability have consequences for the structure and dynamics of the international system. As noted earlier, the global system that emerged after World War II tilted toward the economic arena, with security arrangements taking a regional form. Even a decade after the end of the Cold War, the global system remains asymmetrical.

For example, the development of international institutions is currently lopsided. Economic and financial institutions, notably the World Bank, IMF, and the WTO, are relatively well developed, with established procedures and rules and a proven record of accomplishment. So are certain technical organizations such as the World Health Organization and the International Telecommunications Union, both of which are specialized agencies of the United Nations. But there are many global problems for which no effective international institution exists or for which joint action is inadequate. The International Labor Organization provides an important forum for the relevant players (that is, government, labor, and employers), but it lacks "teeth." There is no functioning world environment organization, although one has been proposed.[76] The United Nations under Secretary General Kofi Annan is struggling to improve its performance in peacekeeping and humanitarian intervention. In all of these areas, global governance lags behind globalization.

Efforts to negotiate cooperative responses to the effects of globalization across the board are ongoing and must continue. It is important, for instance, to build and make operational a fair and accountable global economic system loosely linking trade, investment, finance, energy, and monetary affairs. Building a system does not call for a new bureaucracy, merely closer coordination of existing ones.

A linked economic system should coordinate national policy responses, stimulate cross-national policy thinking, and prompt communication across traditional lines (for example, between trade policy and international finance, monetary policy and development assistance, private investment and banking supervision). It should promote transparency, provide for emergency energy sharing, and stimulate the development and equitable diffusion of technology. Such a system must respond to the legitimate trade, investment, and debt-related needs of developing countries. It must provide for adequate resources to prevent extreme financial volatility and, if prevention fails, to deal swiftly with it. It must address legitimate labor and environmental concerns. It must provide a voice for those whose livelihoods are threatened by economic globalization, as well as for those who benefit from it. Launching another round of multilateral trade talks is a necessary step, but it addresses only one aspect of economic globalization.

Another priority is the enhancement and possible expansion of security institutions to prevent and contain conflicts. At the UN Millennium Summit, heads of state pledged to make the United Nations a more effective institution in the fight against violence, terror, and crime, and to intensify efforts to reform the UN Security Council. These promises raise a basic set of questions about roles and missions. What is NATO's mission, how does it mesh with the UN system, and how many security problems should the United States take on by itself? Specifically, is "humanitarian intervention" a legitimate and appropriate mission for U.S. and allied and/or UN forces? If so, what are its limits? According to the doctrine of "overwhelming and decisive force" (prevalent during the Reagan-Weinberger years), U.S. forces should be sent into battle only if political objectives are clear and measurable, overwhelming force can be applied quickly, and an exit strategy is in place. Armed intervention to halt "ethnic cleansing" or genocide is unlikely to meet those criteria.

A related question centers on the potential uses of military forces, besides fighting and preventing wars.[77] The challenge is to determine the boundaries of U.S. (and NATO) military deployment. A typical security mission of the future is likely to combine diverse operations in such varied fields as combat operations, peacekeeping, mine clearing, refugee protection and relocation, police training, law enforcement, antiterrorism, disaster relief, and reconstruction of transport and communication facilities. U.S. soldiers, sailors, airmen, and marines may be the best trained and equipped forces on the scene—but how many of these tasks should U.S. forces be expected to undertake?

No institution is politically prepared for this broad mixture of tasks either. NATO had a difficult time coping with the Balkan crisis. Elsewhere in the world, collective security organizations are either defunct (for example, the Southeast Asia Treaty Organization [SEATO]) or never existed at all. The UN Security Council is capable of functioning reasonably well in certain cases (for example, Iraq), and much if not all of what has been done in the Balkans bears the Council's seal of approval. Nevertheless, its structure is somewhat outdated, it is frequently incapable of action, and it does not adequately back up decisions with resources.

The European effort to develop a meaningful security and defense "identity" is a good idea, but it will be years before Europeans acquire sufficient hardware, skills, and transport capacity to translate their goals into action. (Helicopters for relief activities in Mozambique, for example, had to be ferried in aging transport planes from Ukraine.) Moreover, the further away a proposed out-of-area action, the less likely a European consensus or even majority approval for intervention.

The contrast between the wide range of global conflicts and the current inadequacy of institutions and resources is stimulating fresh thinking. For example, a new high-level report on the UN peacekeeping department recommends not only the provision of adequate support for peacekeeping but also an integrated task force for each mission that combines political analysis, military operations, civilian police, electoral assistance, aid to refugees and displaced people, public information, logistics, finance, and recruitment.[78] In the meantime, the United States can use its influence to bring existing allies together and encourage them to tackle security problems cooperatively.[79] The same approach can be tried in other parts of the world, beginning with bilateral dialogues. Successful security mechanisms developed in a bilateral context can and should gradually be extended to plurilateral relationships.

Global Issue-Specific Strategies. In parallel with systemic measures, globalization strategies can tackle specific problems that are worldwide in scope without waiting for institutions to catch up. The working group on money laundering set up within the Organization for Economic Cooperation and Development (OECD) is an example. Task forces on crime, cyberterrorism, piracy, and illegal resource depletion (for example, intensive fishing and trafficking in endangered species) are good candidates for a cooperative approach, and some work along these lines is under way. In the private sector, global organizations dedicated to fighting corruption (Transparency International) and providing health services to the world's poor (Doctors Without Frontiers) are pioneering examples.

Coordinated, effective, issue-specific responses to globalization require some degree of international consensus on the substantive issues to be negotiated. These responses should be drawn up and implemented in close partnership with relevant groups in the private sector. Peace, security, health, a clean environment, labor standards, and protection of important cultural landmarks are among the many examples of "global public goods," that is, public goods whose benefits are diffused among people in several countries.[80,81] Neither the marketplace nor governments on their own can relieve the shortage of such goods.

The United States, working closely with allies and friendly governments, needs to take more initiative to shape and strengthen the international system and to help solve specific global problems. Globalization calls for a comprehensive set of responses. Moreover, the governance gap that exists between economic institutions and most other forms of international decisionmaking should be narrowed.

In addressing these problems, the United States must be at the forefront with actions and resources, not soundbites and sermons. If the Nation profits from globalization, but does little or nothing to share its benefits and offset its risks, other countries are certain to shape the world of the future in ways that reflect neither U.S. interests nor U.S. and allied values.[82]

Regional and Subregional Strategies. For the most part, globalization works itself out in characteristic regional and subregional ways rather than on a uniform, worldwide basis. In an age of global media, U.S. policies toward various regions should not be inconsistent, although they need not be identical. Regional strategies permit policymakers not only to promote regional free trade and investment but also to address the social, political, and cultural concerns associated with globalization and linked to autonomy. These concerns include corruption, health and environmental issues, threats to cultural vitality, and a variety of other challenges.

A pillar of U.S. regional strategy continues to be the negotiation of regional free trade agreements. The major examples are the North American Free Trade Agreement (NAFTA), completed in 1993; the Free Trade Area of the Americas (FTAA), currently under negotiation with a deadline of 2005; and the APEC forum, which aims at open trade and investment by 2010 for developed countries and 2020 for developing ones. Imperfect as they may be from a labor or environmental perspective, these agreements and proposals have stimulated trade and investment, ratcheted up global standards, and advanced rules-based dispute settlement. They also have geopolitical significance. In addition, they have given a regional voice to global norms.[83]

The near-term future of FTAA and APEC negotiations is in doubt because the Clinton administration failed to secure the requisite political support and authority from the Congress (including so-called trade-promotion authority). This situation should be corrected as soon as possible. In addition, the United States has an interest in developing a strategic economic partnership with the European Union.[84] Provided that regional economic agreements are broadly consistent with the global system, U.S. negotiators should be empowered to pursue them as boldly and quickly as circumstances permit.

In many regions, coping with globalization will suggest open, flexible, ad hoc coalitions leading to informal security communities rather than to formal bipolar or multipolar commitments directed against particular governments. Conversely, regions in which governments fail to participate in such coalitions and groupings will miss out on the benefits of globalization and will suffer most from its ill effects. The mechanisms and processes established to promote regional economic cooperation, where they exist, can increasingly be used or built upon to address common security issues. For example, Russia and China already participate in the ASEAN Regional Forum, an extension of ASEAN that serves as an umbrella for discussions on regional political-security questions.

The United States is already actively promoting regional cooperation, but could do more. Tools of engagement and "soft" power projection include open trade and investment initiatives (backed by Congressional authorization and on terms beneficial both to developing and to industrialized countries), inclusion in regional and international decisionmaking bodies, and expanded educational and training opportunities, to name just a few. Aid resources, including officially guaranteed credits, should be championed as an integral component of U.S. national security strategy and bolstered accordingly. Joint exercises and other forms of noncombat military operations can also play an important role in strengthening systemic tendencies toward the peaceful resolution of disputes. A special effort should be devoted to building up a cadre of regional experts in law, arbitration, and conflict resolution.

The fate of certain swing or pivotal countries will influence the evolution of their regions or subregions. Russia and China, with their vast territory and ethnic diversity, are the two most important states whose future is still uncertain. Bringing them more fully into the various leadership "clubs" and elite consultative groups should be a high priority. In the developing world, one group of authors has identified "pivotal" states as Algeria, Brazil, Egypt, India, Indonesia, Mexico, Pakistan, South Africa, and Turkey.[85] The 12 "Big Emerging Markets" identified by the first Clinton administration on the basis of population, growth, and business opportunities were Argentina, Brazil, China, Hong Kong, India, Indonesia, Mexico, Poland, South Africa, South Korea, Taiwan, and Turkey. The countries on both lists are Brazil, India, Indonesia, Mexico, South Africa, and Turkey. (China was not ranked as a "developing" country but is obviously "pivotal," and Iran could emerge as a candidate.)

These countries are important and deserve more focused policy attention and inclusion than others. They have sufficient strength and presence to qualify them as regional powers. At the same time, their size, diversity, and residual poverty make them difficult to govern. Their readiness for globalization, their quality of governance, their security environment, and the nature of their cultures vary widely.

They should not be judged solely on the basis of whether they possess or are developing nuclear weapons (for example, India) or cooperating in the U.S. war on drugs (for example, Mexico). Public, annual, single-issue report cards on these countries should be abandoned, since they contribute little or nothing to what is already known and stir up anti-American resentment in the target country.

An inchoate strand of a regional strategy is giving priority attention to cities and coasts. Globalization permeates world-class cities and coastal communities faster than rural or landlocked ones, and its benefits and risks are correspondingly greater. Large cities constitute nodes in global networks of information and money. Coastal communities benefit disproportionately from trade and investment because of the transportation advantages afforded by access to large bodies of water. New jobs are more plentiful. Cultures in these areas are typically more cosmopolitan, less encumbered by caste and taboo. Educational standards are usually higher. Privacy and anonymity are more attainable for those who want them.

At the same time, globalization brings new threats to urban and coastal communities. Waves of migration from the impoverished countryside to already overcrowded cities severely strain resources; between 40 and 60 percent of urban growth is attributed to internal immigrants of this kind.[86] Inadequate sewage and air pollution compound health problems. Political discontent among those left behind can foster insurgencies or extremist movements. Global criminals and polluters take advantage of cities and coastlines to engage in drug trafficking, piracy, money laundering, illegal immigration, and the plundering of marine resources. Indonesia, a nation of islands and overcrowded cities, suffers from most, if not all, of these ills, but it is not alone.

A successful regional and subregional strategy would emphasize initiatives that build on shared norms while respecting local needs, cultures, and autonomy. It would include a security component. It would trim or drop programs that merely project onto other countries pet projects dreamed up in Washington. It would jettison outdated unilateral sanctions, if any. It would be carried out by well qualified ambassadors, not political hacks. A toolbox consisting of aid, credits, technical assistance, and simple presence on the ground would permit the United States to engage in activities tailored to the local scene. The mix might include, say, boosting job creation in the poorest rural areas (to dampen urban migration), strengthening and training local coast guard forces, training individuals to provide legal assistance, sponsoring exchanges of cultural and religious leaders, cooperating with environmental NGOs, and offering other components of a well thought out pattern.

Process. As every good bureaucrat knows, the daily work of the government consists largely of process rather than substance. Like most national governments, the U.S. Government is inadequately prepared and organized to deal with decisionmaking aspects of globalization. Pursuing the goals and strategies outlined earlier calls for setting up a process that conforms to the following guidelines.

First, devising a successful globalization strategy will require much closer coordination between the economic and security policymaking communities in Washington. There should be far more teamwork and dialogue between the two groups than there is now and a far higher level of coordination. The Office of Management and Budget (OMB) could take the lead. A revised personnel system should be established to reward, not punish, people who break down outdated bureaucratic barriers. Closer coordination will help to avoid costly mistakes, identify appropriate tools to cope with emerging problems, and lessen the likely need for a U.S. show of force or intervention.

Within the Executive Office of the President, the National Economic Council should be merged into the National Security Council to form a single policy council that integrates economic and security expertise, as well as other disciplines.[87] The State Department should consider similar measures to bridge the gap between its economic and political-military bureaus. U.S. policy should reflect a tightly coordinated blend of financial, commercial, and military resources and priorities.

Such coordination should begin at the top and become institutionalized by means of specific changes in each agency's personnel system. The President must set the tone. The Treasury Department, traditionally the most secretive and exclusive of all the major agencies (and in fairness, one of the most competent), must consult with and be consulted by the full range of players, including the Department of Defense, to a far greater degree than in the past. For their part, Congressional leaders should take corresponding steps to promote communication and cooperation among Congressional committees.

This new commingling could lead to small, but meaningful, changes in policy. For example, the United States may need to modulate its laissez-faire policy on international capital flows and place more emphasis on foreign bank supervision. It should also step up the pace of reducing its own barriers to exports from poor countries—for national security reasons as well as humanitarian ones.

Second, U.S. policymakers should unite in support of more funding for nonmilitary instruments of foreign policy to achieve a better balance with military ones. The ability to shape globalization rather than just react to it requires adequate resources and a better balance between "hard" and "soft" security.

Nonmilitary instruments of U.S. foreign policy, such as foreign aid, educational exchanges and scholarships, visitors' programs, public diplomacy, and contributions to humanitarian programs and multilateral organizations, are pitifully small in comparison with U.S. military power and global reach. Spending on these nonmilitary instruments has shrunk steadily over the last 20 years, from 4 percent of the Federal budget in the 1960s to 1 percent today.[88]

Although the number of U.S. troops overseas also declined in the 1990s, the American presence abroad is overwhelmingly dedicated to conflict-related missions—defense, law enforcement, and peacekeeping—rather than to conflict prevention, institution building, environmental cleanup, education, public diplomacy, and other peaceful missions. In the era of globalization, these latter missions are more important than ever. Neither U.S. companies nor U.S. troops should be expected to take primary responsibility for such missions, although they may make important contributions.

Generous education and training programs, development assistance, credit programs, conflict prevention, and old-fashioned diplomacy should receive higher priority. Officeholders in these fields should have adequate budgets and staff, as well as access to the White House. Their perspectives are essential to an integrated strategy.

Third, decisionmaking will have to become speedier, communications more direct, and organizations flatter and more streamlined. This will be difficult because of the greater variety of perspectives built into the strategy. But compartmentalized activities will no longer do. This is as true in the military services as it is in the rest of the foreign policy community. As outgoing Commander in Chief of the U.S. Central Command, General Anthony Zinni, put it, "Napoleon could reappear today and recognize my Central Command staff organization: J–1, administration stovepipe; J–2, intelligence stovepipe—you get the idea. . . . This must be fixed."[89]

Fourth, policymakers will have to learn more about historical, technological, cultural, religious, environmental, and other aspects of world affairs than they have to date. More people with expertise in these nonmainstream fields should be hired and utilized in mainstream positions. Where appropriate, representatives of religious groups should be recruited and assigned to diplomatic missions.[90] Nongovernment actors of all backgrounds should be consulted not occasionally and after the fact, but routinely and as far ahead of time as possible. Ambassadors should be appointed from the ranks of career diplomats or serious noncareer professionals capable of, and interested in, learning about the regions to which they are assigned.

Fifth, building and maintaining coalitions with friends and allies to channel globalization in constructive directions and mitigate its harshest aspects should receive higher priority. The United States cannot have everything its own way. Its officials cannot preach free trade, the rule of law, and other aspects of international order to others and make an exception for the United States. Relatively small commercial disputes should be settled promptly so that they do not sour prospects for cooperation on more important economic, political, or security issues. Laws and regulations that impinge on others' interests (for example, the economic sanctions legislation of the mid-1990s) should be avoided. The annual G–8 summit should revert to the pattern set by President Valery Giscard d'Estaing of France in 1975 (where the first such summit was held)—focused, intense, selective, informal discussions of pressing economic issues among leading heads of state.[91] (China should be added to the group.) No matter what the setting, the United States should take pains to avoid sounding sanctimonious, bullying, or arrogant.

Sixth, internal policy coordination should be such that domestic speeches and policies that have bearing on foreign and security policy could be modified, adapted, or at least reexamined in light of global public opinion. Globalization blurs the distinction between "domestic" and "foreign" policy. Foreigner bashing, bullying remarks and unilateral threats damage American interests abroad, even when uttered before domestic political audiences because the globalized media will flash them around the world. Policies may have a strong rationale at home, but their foreign policy and security costs may be too high. For instance, there is a strong security argument for reorienting the battle against drugs from suppression abroad and interdiction at the border to greatly expanded treatment and prevention of addiction at home. This shift would free major resources and remove a periodic irritant in U.S. relations with otherwise friendly countries.[92]

Finally, more effort must be made to gain domestic support for global engagement. Contrary to the perceived "isolationism" of the public, polls show that a majority of U.S. citizens are not opposed to engagement and intervention abroad, military or otherwise, but they will rightfully demand explanations for it from their elected leaders.[93] Instead of "grandstanding" and pandering to the politics of the moment, leaders should strive urgently to restore bipartisan support for vigorous U.S. engagement. Such support is needed not only from Congress but also from states, localities, and key nongovernment actors.

Conclusions and Recommendations

Globalization holds the promise of global pluralism—a state of society in which autonomous groups maintain and develop their culture, livelihoods, and interests within the confines of shared norms and a shared world order. This promise is broadly consistent with U.S. international security and foreign policy interests, as well as with the long-term needs of most of the world's people. Over time, globalization promotes openness, encourages political and economic reforms, strengthens the demand for the rule of law, and fosters norms-based integration.

From a security perspective, the worrisome phrase is "over time." In areas of the world where poverty is widespread and institutions are weak, economic globalization is outstripping the development of public and private means to help ordinary people cope with its effects. In the near term, globalization can sharpen class differences, feed rampant corruption, fortify dictators, and arm criminal elements and terrorists.

Sound environmental standards, access to clinics, and safety nets may exist only on paper, if at all. Shocks associated with rapid globalization, especially short-term financial flows, can shake up the body politic, throw more people into poverty, foment riots, and force a retreat from market-oriented reforms, whipping up anti-Americanism in the process.

The overarching objective of U.S. policy is to shape the emerging world order in a way that avoids these disasters and channels the wave of globalization in directions that ease adaptation to rapid change and peaceful integration. The United States should avoid policies that polarize the global community, concentrating instead on promoting global norms that are accompanied by global systems, institutions, and rules. At the same time, U.S. policymakers should place a premium on the protection of regional, national, local, group, and individual autonomy based on diversity and free choice; reflected in strong, accountable, and flexible domestic institutions; and sustained by the rule of law. Finally, the U.S. security community needs to work with others to enhance and expand institutions and instruments of cooperative security, founded on widely shared norms and respectful of autonomy, to contain, reduce, or prevent conflicts and other threats to a peaceful world order.

To pursue these goals, policymakers should be prepared to make necessary compromises with allies to gain their support as partners and forge new, flexible, ad hoc coalitions with friendly governments, NGOs, and private business. Most of these notions exist on paper, but are not considered relevant to national security. They are.

The strategy also requires a more balanced set of tools, namely, adequately funded *non*military instruments of foreign policy. Without a more well stocked and diversified toolbox, U.S. military forces will be under mounting pressure to solve problems for which military power is not well suited.

Finally, the strategic agenda should include a streamlined, flexible, and coordinated decisionmaking process adapted to the Internet Age and capable of responding quickly to fast-moving foreign crises. This process should be initiated by the White House and embedded in the goals and missions of the various departments and agencies. It should embody routine coordination between economic and security policies; draw in political, cultural, religious, environmental, demographic, and other perspectives; build support for active global engagement in Congress and the public; and seek common ground with those voicing legitimate concerns about globalization, both at home and abroad.

For their part, developing country governments can help to smooth adaptation to globalization by establishing the right policies and priorities. These include strengthening the rule of law, dismantling unnecessary regulatory restrictions, promoting education, punishing corruption, fostering inclusion, guaranteeing the peaceful transfer of power, emphasizing the adaptive elements of the prevailing political culture, and, where feasible, deepening trade and investment relationships with neighboring countries. These steps are far more important than geography and natural resources. Countries that are resource-poor, landlocked, or lacking in navigable rivers have to try harder, but if the policy climate is right, and if their neighbors are not waging war on them, they can often find a niche. Successful adaptation depends on the strength, flexibility, responsiveness, and openness of institutions; the cultures in which those institutions are embedded; and the ability of individual leaders to shape those institutions and cultures for a new era.

Those involved in setting U.S. priorities and allocating U.S. resources to deal with these challenges of globalization will have to work together far more closely, quickly, and flexibly than they have to date. They will need adequate tools and budgets. They need to avoid preaching and practice humility. They will have to develop a thorough understanding of globalization, shared criteria of success, a more considered ranking of the priorities at stake, and a more balanced application of resources, including but not limited to military forces—in short, a globalization agenda informed by strategic purpose.

Notes

The author is grateful to Frederick M. Montgomery for his extensive and insightful comments on earlier drafts of this chapter.

[1] Compare with "[Globalization] is morally neutral.... It can be good or bad, depending on the kind of content we give to it." Vaclav Havel, *The New York Times,* August 23, 2000, A8.

[2] The term *globality* is taken from Daniel Yergin and Joseph Stanislaw, *The Commanding Heights* (New York: Simon and Schuster, 1998), 14. Robert O. Keohane and Joseph S. Nye, Jr., prefer the word *globalism.* See their article in *Foreign Policy*, no. 118 (Spring 2000).

[3] Commission on Global Governance, *Our Global Neighborhood* (Oxford, England: Oxford University Press, 1995), 1.

[4] Thomas L. Friedman, *The Lexus and the Olive Tree: Understanding Globalization* (New York: Farrar, Straus and Giroux, 1999).

[5] Dani Rodrik, *Has Globalization Gone Too Far?* (Washington, DC: Institute for International Economics, 1997), 1.

[6] The White House, *A National Security Strategy for a New Century* (Washington, DC: Government Printing Office, December 1999), 1.

[7] Defense Science Board Task Force on Globalization and Security, *Globalization and Security*, i.

[8] David Held, Anthony McGrew, David Goldblatt, and Jonathan Perraton, *Global Transformations: Politics, Economics, and Culture* (Stanford, CA: Stanford University Press, 1999).

[9] Michael D. Bordo, Barry Eichengreen, and Douglas A. Irwin, "Is Globalization Today Really Different from Globalization a Hundred Years Ago?" *Brookings Trade Forum 1999* (Washington, DC: The Brookings Institution Press, 1999), 1–50.

[10] James N. Rosenau, *Along the Domestic-Foreign Frontier: Exploring Governance in a Turbulent World* (Cambridge, England: Cambridge University Press, 1997), especially chapters 4–6.

[11] National Defense University, Institute for National Strategic Studies, Project on Globalization and National Security, "Stability, Stasis, and Security: Reflections on Superpower Leadership," *Global Forum* 1, no. 1 (June 2000).

[12] Jessica T. Mathews, "Power Shift," *Foreign Affairs* 76, no. 1 (January/February 1997), 50–66.

[13] Rosenau, *Along the Domestic-Foreign Frontier.*

[14] Anne-Marie Slaughter, "The Real New World Order," *Foreign Affairs* 76, no. 5 (September/October 1997), 183–197.

[15] John Newhouse, "Europe's Rising Regionalism," *Foreign Affairs* 76, no. 1 (January/February 1997), 67–84.

[16] David C. Gompert, *Right Makes Might: Freedom and Power in the Information Age*, McNair Paper 59 (Washington, DC: National Defense University Press, May 1998).

[17] For a comprehensive discussion, see Wolfgang H. Reinecke, *Global Public Policy: Governing Without Governance?* (Washington, DC: The Brookings Institution Press, 1998).

[18] For a description of how Coca-Cola and McDonald's are coping with this trend, see "Fallen Icons," *The Financial Times*, February 1, 2000, 12.

[19] The Asian financial crisis demonstrated that the pace of financial liberalization exceeded institutional capacity to deal with credit booms and liquidity/currency "mismatches." See Morris Goldstein, *The Asian Financial Crisis: Causes, Cures, and Systemic Implications* (Washington, DC: Institute for International Economics, 1998).

[20] Anton Lukas, *WTO Report Card III: Globalization and Developing Countries*, Trade Briefing Paper No. 10 (The Cato Institute, June 20, 2000), 2.

[21] World Bank, *World Development Indicators 2000* (Washington, DC: The World Bank, 2000), 3.

[22] <http://www.turnpoint.org>. For similar perspectives and links, see also the Web site maintained by the International Forum on Globalization, <http://www.ifg.org> and <http://www.globalexchange.org>.

[23] See "Global Trade Watch" at Public Citizen's Web site, <http://www.citizen.org>.

[24] Lori Wallach and Michelle Sforza, *Whose Trade Organization?* (Washington, DC: Public Citizen, 1999).

[25] See the full-page newspaper advertisements criticizing globalization found at <www.turnpoint.org>.

[26] UN Development Program, *Human Development Report, 1999* (New York: Oxford University Press, 1999), 7.

[27] A new Asian monetary fund aimed at preventing or mitigating such crises, proposed by the Japanese, is now under discussion.

[28] Debraj Ray, *Development Economics* (Princeton, NJ: Princeton University Press, 1998), 29.

[29] For a clear-sighted analysis of the disappointing record of aid to Africa, see Carol Lancaster, *Aid to Africa: So Much to Do, So Little Done* (Chicago: Century Foundation and University of Chicago Press, 1999).

[30] For example, what Alan Greenspan calls *asset inflation*—the booming U.S. stock market—has created huge wealth, but that wealth has not been taken away from the poor. By contrast, the financial crisis in Asia in 1997–1998 temporarily crushed the livelihood of millions of people.

[31] World Economic Forum Task Force, *From the Global Digital Divide to the Global Digital Opportunity*, statement to the G–8 Kyushu-Okinawa Summit, July 21–23, 2000, www.weforum.org; Andrea Goldstein and David O'Connor, "Bridging the Digital Divide," *The Financial Times,* July 21, 2000, 15.

[32] A.T. Kearney, *Globalization Ledger*, April 2000, <www.atkearney.com>.

[33] The collapse of Hanbo Steel in Korea is one of many examples. See Kimberly Ann Elliott, "Corruption as an International Policy Problem: Overview and Recommendations," in *Corruption and the Global Economy*, ed. Elliott (Washington, DC: Institute for International Economics, 1997), 196.

[34] Patrick Glynn, Stephen J. Kobrin, and Moisés Naím, "The Globalization of Corruption," in *Corruption and the Global Economy*, ed. Elliott (Washington, DC: Institute for International Economics, 1997), 10.

[35] For a thoughtful survey of research on this topic, see Joan M. Nelson, *Poverty, Inequality, and Conflict in Developing Countries* (New York: Rockefeller Brothers Fund, 1998).

[36] Andrew Leonard, *Finland—The Open-Source Society*, 2000, <http://www.salon.com>.

[37] The author borrows this word from the late Benjamin I. Schwartz, who applied it to China to identify recurrent patterns in the face of change.

[38] See Lawrence E. Harrison and Samuel P. Huntington, eds., *Culture Matters* (New York: Basic Books, 2000); Samuel P. Huntington, *The Clash of Civilizations*, 2d ed. (New York: Touchstone Books, 1997); Kishore Mahbubani, *Can Asians Think?* (Singapore and Kuala Lumpur: Times Books International, 1998); J. Timmons Roberts and Amy Hite, eds., *From Modernization to Globalization: Perspectives on Development and Social Change* (Malden, MA: Blackwell Publishers, Inc., 2000); Robert Hefner, ed., *Market Cultures: Society and Values in the New Asian Capitalisms* (Singapore: Institute of Southeast Asian Studies, 1998); and World Bank, *The East Asian Miracle: Economic Growth and Public Policy* (New York: Oxford University Press, 1993).

[39] The index published by Freedom House ranks countries as *free*, *partly free*, or *not free*. See <www.freedomhouse.org>.

[40] A good example is Transparency International, which ranks countries according to the extent of corruption and has inspired unprecedented efforts to overcome it.

[41] Robert W. Hefner, "Introduction: Society and Morality in the New Asian Capitalisms," in *Market Culture: Society and Values in the New Asian Capitalisms*, ed. Robert Hefner (Boulder, CO, and Singapore: Westview Press and the Institute for Southeast Asian Studies, 1998), 3–5.

[42] McDonald's Corporation 1999 Annual Report, March 15, 2000, 1.

[43] Lee Hsien Loong, speech to the Williamsburg Conference, March 3, 2000 (press release).

[44] James Kurth argues that the "ideology of expressive individualism" can lead to "totalitarianism of the self," according to which human rights are nothing more than the rights of individuals, independent of community or traditions. See James Kurth, "Religion and Globalization," Foreign Policy Research Institute WIRE 7, no. 7 (May 1999). See also "Faith and Statecraft," a special issue of *Orbis* (Spring 1998).

[45] Roland Robertson, quoted in Meredith B. McGuire, *Religion: The Social Context* (Belmont, CA: Wadsworth Publishing Co., 1997), 373.

[46] Miranda Beshara, "Globalization and the Middle East: Growing Together or Apart?" Unpublished paper, Fall 1999, 9.

[47] International Labor Organization, *Workers without Frontiers: The Impact of Globalization on International Migration.*

[48] International Labor Organization, *Workers without Frontiers.*

[49] International Labor Organization, *World Migration Tops 120 Million, Says ILO*, Press Release (ILO/00/2), March 2, 2000.

[50] Giovanni Valentini, *La Repubblica* (Rome), July 14, 2000, translated in *World Press Review,* September 2000, 22.

[51] Joyce Akins, "Globalization and Women: Progress and Pain," unpublished paper, December 1999.

[52] For a comprehensive and readable summary of these concerns, see Hilary French, *Vanishing Borders: Protecting the Planet in the Age of Globalization* (New York and London: W.W. Norton, 2000).

[53] A.T. Kearney, *Globalization Ledger,* April 2000, 12, available at <www.atkearney.org>.

[54] The Aspen Institute, *The Convergence of U.S. National Security and the Global Environment*, Third Conference Report, November 12–16, 1998 (Washington, DC: The Aspen Institute, 1998), 6.

[55] James Kynge, "Yellow River Brings Further Sorrow to Chinese People," *The Financial Times,* January 4, 2000, 4.

[56] Nicholas Timmins, "World Health and Disease Is Now a Local Issue," *The Financial Times*, January 3, 2000, 13.

[57] Carol Lancaster, "Redesigning Foreign Aid," *Foreign Affairs* 79, no. 5 (September/October 2000), 74–76.

[58] For a more comprehensive treatment of military globalization, see David Held et al., eds., *Global Transformations*, chapter 2.

[59] William W. Keller, *Arm in Arm: The Political Economy of the Global Arms Trade* (New York: Basic Books, 1995).

[60] Samuel P. Huntington, *The Clash of Civilizations and the Remaking of World Order* (New York: Simon and Schuster, 1996), 36. Huntington sees these forces in cultural and "civilizational" terms.

[61] The White House, *A National Security Strategy for a New Century*.

[62] Paul B. Stares, ed., *The New Security Agenda: A Global Survey* (Tokyo and Washington: Japan Center for International Exchange and The Brookings Institution, 1998).

[63] Robert D. Kaplan, *The Ends of the Earth* (New York: Vintage Books, 1997).

[64] Robert D. Kaplan, *The Coming Anarchy* (New York: Random House, 2000).

[65] Reinecke, *Global Public Policy*, 224.

[66] Rosenau, "Stability, Stasis, and Security."

[67] For a discussion of U.S. interests and a grouping of those interests into priority categories, see The Commission on America's National Interests, *America's National Interests* (Washington, DC: Commission on America's National Interests, July 2000).

[68] UN Millennium Declaration, A/55/L.2, New York, September 6, 2000, 2, available at <www.un.org>.

[69] Webster's dictionary defines *norm* as a principle of right action binding upon the members of a group and serving to guide, control, or regulate proper and acceptable behavior.

[70] James N. Rosenau, *Along the Domestic-Foreign Frontier*, 180–181.

[71] Samuel P. Huntington warns us not to confuse "modern" norms and values with historically unique Western ones. According to him, the world is becoming "more modern and less Western." Huntington, *The Clash of Civilizations*, 78. Amartya Sen, by contrast, challenges the very notion that "Western" values such as liberty, justice, reason, and tolerance are uniquely Western. He points out, for example, that the great Indian ruler Akbar was codifying tolerance at a time when Giordano Bruno was burned at the stake for heresy. See Amartya Sen, "The Reach of Reason," *New York Review of Books* (July 20, 2000), 36. For an anthropological perspective, see Arjun Appadurai, *Modernity at Large: Cultural Dimensions of Globalization* (Minneapolis: University of Minnesota Press, 1996).

[72] To take a recent example, cracking down on intellectual property violations on the part of businesses run by China's People's Liberation Army should not be handled only as a trade issue, as it was in the mid-1990s. It should also be seen in the framework of the army's role in China's political and security evolution.

[73] The author is grateful to Sir Laurence Martin of the Center for Strategic and International Studies for this observation.

[74] US–CREST, *Coalition Military Operations: The Way Ahead Through Cooperability* (Arlington, VA: US–CREST, 2000), xv. *Cooperability* is defined as "the successful bridging between coalition partners of differences in doctrine, organization, concepts of operation, and culture."

[75] Peter W. Rodman has remarked that sometimes the charge of "unilateralism" leveled by U.S. allies against Washington is a code word for policy disagreements or "strategic escapism." See Peter W. Rodman, *Uneasy Giant: The Challenges to American Predominance* (Washington, DC: The Nixon Center, 2000), 51.

[76] Daniel C. Esty, *Greening the GATT: Trade, Environment, and the Future* (Washington, DC: Institute for International Economics, 1994).

[77] Lawrence J. Korb, "The Military: What Role in U.S. Foreign Policy?" in *Great Decisions* (Foreign Policy Association, 2000), 44.

[78] "UN Is Urged to Upgrade Peacekeeping Department," *The New York Times,* August 24, 2000, A10.

[79] Robert D. Blackwill, "An Action Agenda to Strengthen America's Alliances in the Asia-Pacific Region," in *America's Asian Alliances*, eds. Robert D. Blackwill and Paul Dibb (Cambridge, MA: MIT Press, 2000), 124–126.

[80] For a landmark study of this topic, see Inge Kaul et al., *Global Public Goods: International Cooperation in the 21st Century* (New York: Oxford University Press, published for the UN Development Program, 1999).

[81] Reinecke, *Global Public Policy*.

[82] Robert Kagan and William Kristol, "The Burden of Power Is Having to Wield It," *The Washington Post*, March 19, 2000, B3.

[83] In the late 1990s, when Paraguay appeared to be on the brink of a military coup, Brazil and Argentina indicated that membership in MERCOSUR would not be open to dictatorships. When Prime Minister Mahathir of Malaysia sacked and jailed his long-time deputy on what appeared to be trumped-up charges, the governments of Thailand and the Philippines expressed their dismay in the context of an APEC meeting.

[84] Ellen L. Frost, *Transatlantic Trade: A Strategic Agenda* (Washington, DC: Institute for International Economics, 1997). This study proposes the creation of a North Atlantic Economic Community, or NATEC.

[85] These observations, plus the list of "pivotal" states, are drawn from Philip Zelikow's review of Robert Chase, Emily Hill, and Paul Kennedy, eds., *The Pivotal States: A New Framework for U.S. Policy in the Developing World* (New York: W.W. Norton, 1998). The review appeared in *Foreign Affairs* 79, no. 3 (May/June 2000), 169. The major cross-cutting issues identified by the same editors are population growth, environment, ethnic conflict, human rights, and economics.

[86] National Research Council, *Our Common Journey: A Transition toward Sustainability* (Washington, DC: National Academy Press, 1999), 77.

[87] Doing so would require substantially augmenting economic expertise and giving more weight to environmental, cultural, social, and demographic concerns than exists at present.

[88] Richard Gardner, "The One Percent Solution: Shirking the Cost of World Leadership," *Foreign Affairs* 79, no. 2 (July/August 2000), 3.

[89] Anthony C. Zinni, farewell address, transcript of Robert McCormick Tribune Foundation—US Naval Institute Address, March 2000, 8.

[90] The author borrows this idea from Douglas Johnston, founder and president of the International Center for Religion and Diplomacy.

[91] Eric D.K. Melby, *Post-Okinawa—Re-Thinking the G–8 Process*, Issue Brief No. 00-05 (Washington, DC: The Forum for International Policy, August 7, 2000).

[92] Similarly, the execution of young and mentally retarded prisoners tarnishes America's image as a humane and tolerant society. Since the United States is a signatory (albeit with conditions) of the International Convention on Civil and Political Rights, such deaths also undermine U.S. credibility.

[93] John E. Rielly, ed., *American Public Opinion and U.S. Foreign Policy 1999* (Chicago: Chicago Council on Foreign Relations, 1999).

Chapter 3

Controlling Chaos: New Axial Strategic Principles

Richard L. Kugler

The dawn of a new century and millennium coincides with the arrival of a new era in world politics. The coming era likely will be one in which economics and security share center stage in determining how the world evolves. Rather than one dominating the other, the two will play equally powerful roles, and they will interact closely, exerting great influence over each other. In this setting, globalization is important partly because it is reshaping how the world economy operates and how people communicate with each other. But what makes it more significant is its potential impact—direct and indirect—on international politics and security affairs. This chapter does not definitively answer questions about the impact of globalization, for they are clouded by too many uncertainties for clear answers. Instead, this chapter provides a simple framework for thinking about these questions in illuminating ways. Based upon the previous chapter, its goal is to provide added tools for assessing globalization's impact in the strategic arena, where the great issues of war and peace will be decided. It assesses the implications for U.S. national security strategy, including the core endeavors and goals that are to drive its efforts in the coming years.

This chapter's thesis is simply stated: Globalization is not only creating opportunities but also dangers if worrisome trends are not handled wisely. *Whereas the great drama of the 20th century was democracy's struggle against totalitarianism, the defining issue of the early 21st century will be whether the democratic community can control chaotic strategic affairs in the vast, troubled regions outside its borders, which are not being made permanently peaceful by globalization.* Although the democratic community is making progress within its borders, it will face the challenge of fostering greater strategic stability at key places outside them, not only to protect its own interests and values but also to help progress take hold there. This challenge of suppressing new-era dangers while promoting healthy trends will especially fall on the United States. As superpower leader of the democratic community, it will need to blend its security and economic policies together and to use its military power wisely, as well as to mobilize help from its allies and partners. These tasks do not promise to be easy. Performing them effectively could play a major role in determining whether

---

Richard L. Kugler is a distinguished research professor in the Institute for National Strategic Studies at the National Defense University. He formerly was a research leader at RAND and a senior executive in the Department of Defense. Dr. Kugler is the author of many books and studies including Commitment to Purpose: How Alliance Partnership Won the Cold War.

the future produces growing tranquility, or instead goes up in smoke. The bottom line is that while globalization and other unfolding dynamics have the potential to elevate much of the world onto a higher plane of peace and prosperity, they also have the capacity to tear it apart in ways that produce a dark future. The challenge is to ensure that the former unfolds, not the latter.

The Need for a Simple but Powerful Framework

The strategic questions raised by globalization are critical. How will globalization affect foreign policy, diplomacy, and defense strategy around the world? Will it produce spreading tranquility and community-building, growing political conflict and strife, or some of both? What implications does it pose for U.S. policy and strategy abroad? Globalization necessitates that U.S. policy see the world as a whole, think globally, and act globally—while not losing sight of each region's unique features. What goals and priorities should the United States embrace in responding to globalization's opportunities, challenges, and dangers? In strategic terms, how should the United States act in a globalizing world? What should be its core strategic concepts, its aims, and its visions?

These questions require discriminating answers because our understanding of globalization's effects is maturing. A few years ago, a popular view held that globalization would make nearly the entire world peaceful by influencing countries everywhere to seek democracy, market economies, and cooperative relations with each other. This hope still prevails in important ways, but since then, a more complex reality has become apparent. Recent trends suggest that globalization may have a powerful impact in some regions, but not all regions, especially where traditional state interests, geopolitics, and aggressive instincts still abound. Even in places where globalization will shape the future, its impact will not always be positive. In some places, it likely will be an engine of progress. But in other places, it may have damaging effects, thereby exacerbating already serious problems. Globalization thus is likely to be uneven and hydra-headed. Its diverse strategic consequences need to be grasped if its weighty policy implications are to be understood.

Addressing these questions requires an intellectual framework for identifying the key factors at work. *For this framework to be potent, it must be simple.* Analysis will get nowhere if it portrays globalization in terms of 50 different activities affecting the world's 200 countries in separate ways. This approach will result in a picture of such hideous complexity that nobody, not even the authors, will be able to discern clear strategic messages. In virtually all disciplines, the best theories are those that reduce great complexity to a few simple ideas. Such theories lay a rock-solid foundation upon which increasingly elaborate formulas can be built. This is the case in analyzing globalization, where a blizzard of events can be understood only if the basics are brought into focus.

Accordingly, this chapter puts forth a set of six "axial strategic principles" for accomplishing the task. These principles deal with the fundamentals and essential elements from which everything else flows. They are propositions for organizing scholarly thought, not axioms for proclaiming irrefutable truths. They are not cast in concrete, but instead can evolve as knowledge of globalization matures. They aspire to simplicity because that is exactly where good analysis normally finds its strength: by bringing clarity and order to a picture of confusing complexity. Obviously, the world is more diverse than portrayed here. But the purpose of theory-building, however, is not to grasp every detail. Instead, theory-building works best when it offers a few ideas that have great explanatory power: covering not everything, but much of what is important.

The Phenomenon: Globalization in a Changing World

The first two strategic principles set the stage, first by distinguishing between structure and process in contemporary international affairs, and then by probing globalization's core features. By analyzing the dynamics of change and integration in some depth, they further highlight the extent to which the modern world of economics and security differs greatly from that of the Cold War, when change and integration seemed like foreign ideas.

> Principle 1: In analyzing world affairs, today's structure does matter, but change-producing processes that will shape the future are more important.

If globalization's strategic impact is to be understood, analysis must address *both* the current structure *and* the process of change in contemporary world affairs. There is a big difference between the two. As used here, "structure" refers to the physical characteristics of today's international system: the main actors, their relationships to each other, and their interactions. By contrast, "process" refers to the key dynamics by which the international system is changing in ways that alter today's system and create a different one tomorrow.[1]

During the Cold War, structure mattered most because the world was so frozen into rigid bipolarity that little change was occurring. *In today's setting, structure is still important, but analyzing the process of change is more critical to understanding the future.* The reason is that today's setting is fluid. Immense changes are at work, and many are neither linear nor evolutionary. They ensure that tomorrow's structure will be quite different from today's. Moreover, tomorrow's structure will not be frozen in concrete. The world is experiencing a period of great dynamism, spontaneous organization and reorganization, and perpetual novelty as it rapidly moves from one temporary structure to the next. The strategic situation is more akin to that of the first half of the 20th century, when the international system changed its core features four times in rapid succession, rather than to that of the last half of the century, when bipolarity formed early and hardly changed afterward.

This process of change may appear random, even chaotic. But at its fundamentals, it is being driven by forces that often have logic and purpose and that are capable of combining to produce orderly outcomes. As a result, things eventually may settle down and a new structure with enduring characteristics will emerge. This will not happen for a while—probably not for many years. In the interim, the United States and other countries will face the principal challenge of dealing with an ever-changing world, not a status quo world or even a world of features that last long enough to become familiar.

What lies ahead is to be seen, but it will be primarily determined by how nation-states act and interact. To a degree, the ability of national governments to control their destinies is being eroded by external constraints and internal pressures. Transnational actors now abound, and in some ways, the old Westphalian system is giving way to a post-Westphalian politics in which countries are no longer fully sovereign, much less supremely independent in everything they do. Within countries, moreover, pluralist politics is becoming the norm; interest groups in one country sometimes cooperate with those in other countries. Yet the nation-state will remain the most powerful actor on the world scene. Indeed, the number of countries has been increasing as old empires have collapsed. The growing importance of events abroad dictates that virtually all countries will have to pay more attention to foreign policy, including the three key components of politics, economics, and security. Because countries will be responding to their own interests and strategic situations, they will not behave in uniform ways. What unites them is that all will be dealing with a setting of major changes in the globalizing world.

> Principle 2: Globalization is a process producing a worldwide system and faster change.

Globalization involves the growing cross-border flows of trade, finance, capital, technology, information, ideas, and people that are driving countries and regions into an expanding web of ties. It is best seen as being mostly a process of change, not an already existing structure. Eventually, a fully globalized world structure may emerge, but it has not yet arrived. *What matters is the great transformation being brought about by globalization's dynamics.* Globalization's twin features—its impact on domestic affairs and on international affairs—merit discussion here.

The changes taking place in the domestic political and economic affairs of many countries, especially those within the democratic community, go back more than 20 years, long before globalization became a noticeable trend. One of these changes was democratization. Between 1978 and 1998, the number of democracies doubled: from only 43 countries to 88. As many as 53 other countries were partly free.[2] This trend was a result of political upheavals, demanding not only freedom but also better economic conditions in Latin America, Eastern Europe, and parts of Asia. A second big change was a major switch from state-owned and command economies to market economies in various guises. Prime Minister Margaret Thatcher's Britain was a pacesetter in its pursuit of denationalization and privatization, but its example was followed by many countries in Eastern Europe, the former Soviet Union, Latin America, South Asia, Asia, and Africa. A third change was the switch from protectionist economic strategies to export strategies, which was led by Asian countries but now is being followed by many others. In powerful ways, these three changes worked together to alter the world political and economic scene greatly. Whereas authoritarian governments, command economies, and protectionism often seemed the wave of the future in earlier decades, now they were in sharp retreat: not everywhere, but in many places. Replacing them in key regions, with varying degrees of fervor, were democratic governments, market economies, and a willingness to participate actively in the world economy.[3]

These three changes helped set the stage for today's globalizing dynamics. By drawing many countries into closer contact with international markets, globalization is putting added pressure on them to modernize their governments, societies, economies, and businesses to compete better. Not all are responding vigorously, but those trying to adapt are experiencing considerable change in their domestic arrangements. The transition is easiest for already modern countries, such as the United States, that possess democratic governments, capitalist economies, free-trade practices, skilled workforces, and information-era businesses capable of producing goods and services that sell profitably in international markets. It is more difficult for countries that are less well endowed with these assets. It is quite hard, sometimes impossible, for the many ill-prepared countries that lack virtually all of these assets. Around the world, as a result, some countries are responding effectively with alacrity, others are struggling, but making progress, and still others are falling behind the power curve, stagnating, or even regressing.

Those involved in efforts to forecast globalization's future impact on domestic affairs should remember that industrialization, modernization, technological growth, and communications have been at work for two centuries. Countries and cultures have responded in different ways (for example, Europe became democratic and capitalist, but until recently Russia remained authoritarian in its politics and economics). The result is a world of great diversity. This deeply entrenched diversity is not going to disappear overnight in response to globalization, which is, after all, only the latest in a long line of trends. Yet globalization is a powerful force. It likely will not propel the world toward a single model of domestic affairs, but because it brings about changes, it will help produce the multiple ways in which the future's diversity is manifested. Democracies likely will respond in one way, authoritarian countries in another way, and traditional countries in yet a third way. When the dust settles, these three types of countries may resemble each other in some features but still be significantly different in others. What unites them is that all will be significantly altered by globalization.

Equally important is globalization's impact on how modern international relations are being carried out in politics, economics, and security affairs. Here, too, a future of continuity and change seemingly lies in store. National foreign policies are influenced by geostrategic facts of nature that will not change. U.S. foreign policy, for example, is powerfully shaped by the country's sheer size, its location in the Western hemisphere, and its reliance on the Atlantic and Pacific Oceans for access to foreign markets. Comparably important but different geographical features help determine how Germany and Russia, or China and Japan, interact. The same applies in many other places. These geostrategic factors will remain constant, and all countries will bring their own values, perceptions, and attitudes to policymaking. Even so, globalization will be an influential factor, among many, bringing about important changes in how many countries view their premises and priorities in foreign policy.

The consequence will be a world of continuing great diversity in foreign policies, but, in one way or another, virtually all policies will be affected by globalization in two key ways. First, as outlined earlier, globalization, acting as a relentless but uneven dynamic, is fostering integration in the sense of bonding separate places and activities together in ways that make them increasingly connected and interactive. The consequence can be enhanced peace, but not necessarily so, for a variety of outcomes are possible, depending upon how these closer interactions play out. In the economic arena, for example, growing trade relations can draw countries closer together in political terms, even leading them to bury their hatchets over old conflicts. Conversely, history shows that economic changes can have the opposite effect, especially when they unfold unevenly. Some countries may take advantage of their growing wealth and power to bully vulnerable neighbors. Countries doing less well in economic markets might employ their military strength to gain resources and wealth through coercion or simply to lash out in frustration against more fortunate nations. In the geopolitical arena, globalization may prove to have similar hydra-headed effects. It may help to lessen some existing rivalries, but leave others untouched, while fanning still others and giving rise to entirely new ones.

The key point is that globalization is creating, for the first time in history, a true "international system": actors and actions in one place are starting to affect those in other places in important ways. In earlier eras, some regions were bonded internally to create a unified political and economic system: Europe before World War I is an example, one that ended unhappily. Worldwide, the globalization process has been under way since the mid-1800s, when the telegraph and modern naval vessels began drawing widely separated regions closer together. But never has the entire world been bonded together in the close ways emerging today. This trend is likely to intensify in the coming years.

A true system does not exist simply because key actors are located near each other. For a system to exist, these actors must interact like billiard balls—powerfully bouncing off each other as they roll across a pool table. Seen in formal terms, a fully developed system exists when a change in one component part, located somewhere on the system's outer periphery, causes a significant change in another part positioned on the opposite periphery. Chaos and complexity theorists call this the "butterfly effect" (for example, a political coup in Paraguay can cause policy tremors in Peking).[4] Simply stated, globalization's process of outward-spreading developments in multiple areas is making the world's actors more interconnected and interdependent.

As a consequence, separate regions are starting to affect each other more than in the past. The actions of a growing number of countries, not just the big superpowers, are starting to influence the policy calculations of other countries located far away. Also, separate functions and subsystems are now affecting each other more powerfully. Not only is a true "world economy" evolving, but its dynamics also are influencing security affairs in important ways. Conversely, globalizing security dynamics are starting to influence world economic trends in increasingly potent ways. The same is true in other functional areas. For example, global warming, struggles over natural resources, weapons of mass destruction (WMD) proliferation, and international organized crime are separate activities that are starting to influence each other significantly.

A good example of how regions may now influence each other is the recent Asian economic flu. It began in Southeast Asia, but quickly spread like a contagious disease around the world, damaging economies as far away as Russia and Latin America. Security affairs are still heavily regional and have not yet shown such contagious properties, but signs of growing cross-regional interactions are emerging. One reason is that the United States and other big powers are acting in multiple regions on behalf of global strategies. For example, China's diplomatic intervention in the Kosovo conflict shows how the influence of a powerful country now can be projected far beyond its immediate region. Many analysts believe that if WMD proliferation begins accelerating, it will have contagious properties and will engulf several regions. Even short of this, globalization means that future regional security affairs will not take place in isolation but will be increasingly influenced by the larger international setting.

The growing connection between economics and security affairs is already becoming manifest. For example, North Korea has been selling weapons abroad to earn hard currency, and its flirtation with long-range missiles may be intended to extract economic blackmail from the United States and other countries. Iraq continues menacing Kuwait and Saudi Arabia, not only for political reasons but also to gain control of Gulf oil and its profitable sale. A few years ago, China tried to intimidate Taiwan with missile tests apparently intended to deflate Taiwan's stock market and influence its elections. Elsewhere, key actors with more constructive goals in mind are showing an awareness of the connection between security and economics. In Europe, the Western democracies are trying to bring Eastern European countries into their fold by extending membership to them in both the North Atlantic Treaty Organization (NATO), their premier security body, and the European Union (EU), their premier economic body. Almost everywhere, countries face the task of harmonizing their foreign economic policies with their national security strategies. China and Russia both face this challenge, as do the countries of Europe and Japan. So does the United States.

These trends probably are a forerunner of bigger things to come. In today's world, a full-blown international system does not yet exist; however, because of globalization's tendency to accentuate interconnections, such a system is coming. In tomorrow's world, separate regions and functional subsystems will still exist, but they will no longer operate in a cocoon, driven solely by their internal structures and processes. Instead, they also will be influenced importantly by the larger international system as a whole.

Second, globalization is accelerating the rate at which changes occur on the world stage. Earlier, changes to the world structure tended to move slowly. No more. Owing to the Information Age, the emergence of new technologies, and other globalization dynamics, change is now taking place more rapidly, and its pace likely will continue accelerating in the coming years. Moreover, globalization by no means is the only change under way. In many places, countries are redefining their identities, goals, governments, and societies for reasons that go beyond globalization. As a result, the world is headed toward a future in which developments that once took decades to unfold will take only a few years, or even less. In this setting, swift and surprising reversals of direction will come with growing frequency. A good trend can quickly be replaced by a bad trend, and then reverse itself just as promptly. Something valued by the United States can suddenly disappear and be replaced by something dreadful, or the reverse. Also important, events will have contagious effects and cascade upon one another, creating rock slides and avalanches for good, or ill, or a combination of both. What exists today may not exist tomorrow—not only at sunset but also at sunrise.

This pace of globalization has major strategic consequences and implications for how the United States sees the world. As globalization gains momentum, it will acquire a growing capacity to alter the fundamentals of the world's structure, and it will do so far more rapidly than anything experienced in the past. This does not mean that globalization will rule the world or make it a homogeneous place. Its limits need to be recognized, for other powerful factors also will be shaping the future. Yet globalization will exert a substantial influence, bringing about changes of its own, some of which will help make the world more heterogeneous, not homogeneous.

As a result, the United States will need to think in properly responsive strategic terms. Rather than trying to manage an already existing and enduring world structure, it will need to focus primarily on channeling an ongoing process of change and bonding. It will need to grapple with a future whose destination is not only uncertain but also capable of moving in multiple directions, depending upon how key countries act and events play out. In this key sense, the future will always be "up for grabs," with the capacity to produce good or ill. The never-ending task will be one of continuously trying to grab the future, to shape it, and, sometimes, to hold on for dear life.

The Strategic Consequences of Globalization

Amid this setting, the strategic consequences can best be analyzed by first portraying the current international structure and then examining how globalization may alter it in the coming years. Axial principles 3 and 4 perform this task:

> Principle 3: Globalization is washing over an international structure that is mostly bimodal, composed of the democratic community and the outlying world.

In its fundamentals, the current international structure is bimodal because it is composed of two parts. This structure is not highly polarized; it is not organized into two competing camps in confrontation with each other. But in their politics and economics, these two parts of the world are about as different as different can be. This is the case not only in their physical characteristics but also in their current peacefulness and capacity for progress.

The bimodal nature of today's international structure can be seen by examining 10 key attributes of peace and progress in the various regions:

1. Democratic governments and rule of law
2. Market economics
3. Stable, modern societies
4. Wealthy economies
5. Constructive involvement in the world economy and the information era
6. Benign foreign policies and stable, nonconflictual security affairs

7. Benign economic policies that help promote political collaboration, not conflict
8. Major participation in multilateral institutions
9. Unthreatening defense policies and military preparedness
10. Support for democratization and community-building

For the most part, the democratic community scores quite high on all of these attributes. This especially is the case in North America, Europe, and democratic Asia. Latin America and some other democratic zones score lower, but this largely owes to their economic and social conditions, not to authoritarian governments or stressful security affairs. By contrast, many regions of the outlying world score low when all 10 attributes are taken into account. To be sure, there are pockets of peace and progress. Overall, however, these regions typically lack democratic governments, and their economic and social conditions are often troubled, their countries do not cooperate heavily in multilateral institutions, and their multipolar security affairs are often conflict-laden. Together, these conditions add up to a setting of potential strategic chaos far different from what prevails across the democratic community.

The democratic community includes those countries that not only have democratic governments but also participate in democracy's multilateral institutions in politics, economics, and security. For most of the 20th century, the democracies were besieged by deeply endangering totalitarian threats. Since the end of the Cold War and the Soviet-led bloc a decade ago, this troubled situation has been transformed into something far better. The democracies now find themselves not only free and prosperous but also possessing far greater strategic power, unity, and wider appeal than any rival. Moreover, their numbers have increased greatly, for their ability to combine liberal political values with successful economic performance through capitalist markets has proven attractive worldwide. The democracies, especially those with modern economies and high-technology industries prepared for the Information Age, are the countries best able to adapt successfully to globalization's pressures.[5]

With a recently enlarged membership of about 80 to 100 countries (depending upon how "democracy" and "membership" are defined), this community now includes about one-half of the world's nations, more than 70 percent of its wealth, and nearly one-third of its population (45 percent if India is counted). Its members vary greatly in their size, strength, culture, and unique features. What gives this community homogeneity is its agreement on common values. Inside their borders, its members regard political democracy and free-market economics as ideals, and, in varying degrees, most of them practice these values. Outside their borders, they pursue their legitimate interests, but they respect their neighbors and international law, and most readily participate in international organizations. Few show any sign of lingering ultranationalism or imperialism. This especially is the case among the older, well-established democracies that lead this community, which now are mostly secure from invasion and have the luxury of shaping their foreign policies with community-building, economic gain, and related priorities in mind.

What distinguishes the democratic community is the high degree of peace and tranquility within its boundaries. Its members often squabble over various issues: economic fissures were worrisome a decade ago and may be on the rise again. But on the whole, this large community contains few sharp interstate frictions and stressful geopolitical maneuvers in strongly polarized ways. Any lingering fear of war among them is fading into history. *Not only are they at peace with each other, but they also tend to cooperate in diplomacy and security even as they compete in the economic marketplace.* Their economic competition, moreover, tends to be mutually profitable. For most, Ricardo's model of comparative advantage is at work, and the rising tide is lifting all boats.[6] Globalization compels them to adjust their economies and sometimes to make painful changes, but provided they remain competitive, their long-range economic prospects are good. As a result, they tend to regard the increasingly integrated world economy as a good thing, and they mostly favor the idea of Western-leaning democracy enlarging further, thereby expanding their already large zone of peace and prosperity.

To be sure, this democratic community is not internally uniform or fully pristine. It has an "inner core" of about 30 powerful members, including the United States, Canada, the European Union, Japan, and a few other Asian democracies. These countries mostly have stable governments, liberal societies, and wealthy economies with an annual per capita gross domestic product (GDP) of $20,000 to $30,000, which is well above the worldwide average of only $7,000 (see table 1).[7] They are also united in collective security and defense alliances that cover most of them and in their foreign policies, they cooperate closely in a variety of bilateral and multilateral forums, such as the G–8 and NATO.

Table 1. Democratic Community

	Population (millions)	*Total GDP, 2000 ($ trillions)*	*GDP per Head, 2000 ($)*
North America	311	9.3	30,000
Europe	480	9.8	20,420
Asian Democracies	217	5.0	23,040
Latin America	492	3.0	6,100
Other	150	0.8	5,300

Note*:* Table 1 excludes India, which is a democracy but is counted in the outlying world because of its independent foreign policy and strategic circumstances.

The community's "outer core" includes about 50 countries in Latin America, plus parts of Asia, Africa, and other regions. These countries qualify as democracies in the sense of having elected governments, but for many, the commitment to liberal values and free-market economies tends to be weaker than in the inner core. The outer core countries are not nearly as wealthy as those of the inner core, nor do they cooperate closely in their diplomacy and security affairs. Lying beyond this outer core are about 35 countries struggling to adopt democracy and market economies, but making uncertain progress, facing tough struggles, and not cooperating in important ways.

Eastern Europe stands out as a region that has done a great deal to enlarge democracy's ranks. Little more than a decade ago, all of its countries had communist governments. Now, nearly all of them are democracies that are adopting market economies and beginning to join NATO and the European Union. Several Asian countries, including South Korea and Taiwan, have also recently joined the ranks. Latin America has added even more countries to the total. Over the past two decades, most of its 25 countries have abandoned traditional rule and corporatist economies to adopt democracy and capitalism. Many are now cooperating in various multilateral institutions, such as the North American Free Trade Agreement (NAFTA) and the *Mercado Común del Sur* (MERCOSUR)—the Common Market of the South. Latin America continues to face formidable problems. Most of the region is still poor, and several countries are afflicted with serious social tensions and shaky politics. Drug trafficking and organized crime in Colombia and some other countries add to the region's troubles. Yet Latin America, as well as Eastern Europe and parts of Asia, are steadily making progress and seem pointed toward becoming even fuller members of the democratic community in the coming years. Not coincidentally, many of these countries are benefiting from globalization more than being harmed by it.

Despite its internal diversity and blurred edges, this large democratic community is a readily identifiable strategic cluster on the world scene. In many ways, it is a well-developed "subsystem" in itself, with a widely perceived "sense of the whole" that marks it as distinctly separate from the rest of the world. Simply stated, its members have a great deal in common. They mostly view each other as friends and partners, and they behave accordingly. While this is especially true within the inner core, many countries in the outer core are trying to draw closer to the center, thereby further tightening the community's bonds and sharpening its already well-defined identity.

Beyond the borders of the democratic community, there lies the second part of the bimodal structure: the "outlying world," which is composed of multiple, diverse regions. This large cluster also totals about one-half of the world's countries, albeit a few have one foot, or at least a few toes, in the democratic community. It is primarily located in the huge geographical expanse of Eurasia, Asia, the Greater Middle East, and Africa. It is decidedly heterogeneous, not only in its physical structure but also in its values. Indeed, its lack of a common identity makes it highly amorphous and fragmented, lacking any sense of the whole. This outlying cluster contains many of the countries that are most ill-prepared to adapt to globalization, or at least to face the greatest transformations, because they lack the necessary foundations in government, society, and economics.

This strategic cluster includes such major powers as Russia, China, and India; a number of medium-sized, but locally potent, countries; and many small countries. Its members embrace a wide spectrum of political and economic ideologies that find expression in different internal policies. Democracy and market economics are sprouting up in key places, but in large part, this cluster is ruled by authoritarian or traditional regimes, and its national economies are often state-owned or otherwise corporatist. This cluster's societies, moreover, tend to be traditionalist, embracing values and structures not well suited for energetic participation in capitalism and the modern world economy.

The foreign policies of these numerous countries cover a wide spectrum. Perhaps the dominant stance is that most countries pursue their "national interests," defined in state-centric terms, rather than collectivist values or universalist visions. The majority of these countries are responsible in their intentions and peaceful in their conduct.

But not all act this way, and the presence of a few troublemakers can cause significant tensions in regions that lack the capacity for collective action. Even a setting of countries pursuing ostensibly legitimate interests can create difficulty when these interests are not fully compatible. In any event, the plethora of different foreign policy models, carried out by multiple countries of varying size, accounts for the various regions of the outlying world being so heterogeneous in their makeups and so significantly different from each other to boot. Eurasia, the Balkans, the greater Middle East, sub-Saharan Africa, South Asia, and nondemocratic Asia all have unique strategic contours that make them quite different from each other. What unites them is that all lack the democratic community's sense of unity and readily achievable progress in a globalizing world. Indeed, all are struggling to cope with the unique and multifaceted problems facing them.

In these multiple regions, several countries are trying to adopt democracy and market economies and to join the democratic community. Some actively cooperate with the United States and its close allies in security and economic affairs. Others admire or accept the democratic community, but choose to live quietly outside it, pursuing their independent values and interests in nonprovocative ways. Still others are mostly intent on preserving their traditional cultures and politics and thereby are preoccupied with warding off the intrusive effects of the democratic community and of globalization, not actively opposing them on the world stage.

Others, however, have different attitudes. *Russia, China, and India are large powers that can best be portrayed as "strategic challengers."* They bring dissimilar domestic arrangements to the strategic table, but they are similar in the sense of using their size to pursue traditional geostrategic interests in their foreign policies. All three seem eager to participate in the world economy to profit from it, but they are less enthused about accepting the security structure created by the United States and its democratic allies. Instead, they aspire to be influential strategic powers in their own right, at least in their own regions and perhaps beyond. Their strategic stance seems to be one of becoming wealthy on the world economy in order to gain the strength needed to put an imprint on the security structure, in ways that elbow aside the United States and its close allies to advance their interests and conceptions. If these three countries get their way, Russia will play an important role in Eurasia and Europe, China will dominate Asia, and India will hold sway in South Asia. The resulting global security system will differ considerably from that of today, and the world economy may change along with it.

Great powers have the capacity to contemplate such designs. As for lesser powers, some are angry and frustrated with the democratic community and their own lots but do not pursue aggressive foreign policies aimed at altering the status quo. Others, however, are so angry, frustrated, and ambitious that they are aggressively willing to challenge the status quo and to victimize their neighbors while menacing Western interests. The result can be nationalism, as witnessed in Serbia, or classic, raw-boned geopolitical behavior, as seen elsewhere. A few fall into the category of being genuine outlaw states and potential aggressors: North Korea and Iraq are examples. Elsewhere, several countries are troubled or failing in the sense that their governments are losing internal control and their societies are plunging into ethnic clashes, tribalism, and violence. Finally, a few are becoming a new breed of predator: criminal states that seek economic profit through terrorism, drugs, weapons profiteering, and other contraband.

Despite the heterogeneity of these diverse regions in the outlying world, core similarities unite many of them. They are not part of the democratic community, and owing to their preferences or conditions, most are unlikely to join it anytime soon. They are not wealthy: per capita GDPs hover at about $1,000 to $5,000 annually (table 2). While their economic fortunes vary, most of them are not prospering in the world economy in ways that point to great wealth in the future. For example, Russia has been victimized by a collapsing economy and a staggering loss of wealth in recent years. Although it has privatized much of its economy, only lately has it started to rebound. China has been strongly on the upswing, and some of its regions are modernizing rapidly; overall, however, it remains a poor country with a per capita GDP of about $4,000. With only a few exceptions, the countries of the greater Middle East and South Asia are poorer still, and Africa is mostly poverty-stricken. Apart from some pockets of progress, these countries mostly do not have Information Age economies. Many are still positioned in the Industrial Age or, in multiple cases, the Agrarian Age. To compound matters, many are saddled with dysfunctional governments and political systems, growing populations that cannot be housed, teeming masses living in decaying cities, weak medical systems, and poorly educated workforces. Such conditions leave many of these countries struggling to survive, not eagerly awaiting the beneficial effects of a globalizing world.

Table 2. Outlying World

	Population (millions)	*Total GDP, 2000 ($ trillions)*	*GDP per Head, 2000 ($)*
Russia and Eurasia	282	1.5	5,400
China and Asia	1,750	5.0	2,800
South Asia	1,316	1.7	1,300
Greater Middle East	315	1.8	5,700
Sub-Saharan Africa	560	0.6	1,100

This characterization of widespread troubles is not meant to imply that domestic conditions across the entire outlying world are uniformly glum and that future prospects are bleak everywhere. Although traditional or authoritarian regimes hold power in most countries, their behavior varies: some are cruel and exploitative of their societies, but others are more caring and enjoy popular support. Economic conditions also vary in ways resulting in a hierarchy within each region. In Asia, Malaysia's annual per person GDP of $11,000 is well above Indonesia's $4,500. In the greater Middle East, Saudi Arabia's per capita GDP of $10,000 is far higher than Jordan's $4,700. Even in relatively poor countries, there is often a wealthy upper class. This small elite presides over a large lower class whose income is very low. The missing element is a vibrant middle class. In these countries, the attitude of the lower classes varies: some are deeply frustrated by their poverty, but others seemingly are content because their values are not highly materialist. Thailand's countryside, for example, is poor but tranquil because many Thais are content with their lifestyles. Moreover, a number of countries are witnessing at least parts of their economies being energized by globalization in ways producing greater wealth, at least for some people. To a degree, truth in this arena is relative: it lies in the eyes of the beholder. Sometimes poor people are happy, as are people who lack liberty. Nonetheless, the basic point remains valid: most countries of the outlying world lack—by a wide margin—the health, wealth, freedoms, and safety enjoyed by the industrial democracies.

Across the outlying world, these struggles in domestic affairs recently have been accompanied by a worrisome surge of chaos, conflict, and violence in interstate affairs: not everywhere, but at sensitive spots in all key regions. In Europe, the Balkans have plunged into ethnic warfare in Bosnia and Kosovo in ways necessitating NATO intervention. In Eurasia, Russia, itself struggling in its politics and economics, has brutally invaded breakaway Chechnya, but with uncertain success. In the Persian Gulf, U.S. airplanes regularly bomb Iraq in enforcing no-fly zones even as Iraq and Iran both pursue WMD systems. In South Asia, India and Pakistan have detonated nuclear weapons and are building missiles even as they continue struggling over Kashmir. In Asia, China is threatening to invade democratic Taiwan if it proclaims independence. North Korea seems equally capable of collapsing of its own weight or of suddenly launching a powerful military attack on South Korea. In Southeast Asia, Indonesia recently experienced an internal upheaval, and the accompanying violence in East Timor was bad enough to necessitate intervention by international peacekeepers. In Africa, so many wars are being waged that the casual observer is hard-pressed to keep track of them. To be sure, these negative trends have been accompanied by positive signs—for example, the Israeli-Arab peace process and Iran's steps toward moderation. But the bottom line is clear. The idea that the outlying world is marked by strategic chaos is not a prediction of the future. Ample chaos, of a violent sort, already exists there. The only issue is whether that chaos will abate or grow as globalization gains steam and other changes take place.

While the future is uncertain, a key strategic reality is that nearly all countries in the outlying world are mostly left on their own in the international arena. Apart from a few alliances and partnerships of convenience, they seldom cooperate with one another, nor do they enjoy the benefits of powerful collective security mechanisms that underscore their safety. In the arena of security and defense affairs, they live in a setting of structural fragmentation and anarchy. They do not have the luxury of focusing their foreign policies on economic gain because they cannot take their physical safety for granted. Some are deeply endangered by their neighbors, and even those living in peace face the possibility that this situation could change overnight. Still others are deeply endangered by the political frictions, ethnic clashes, and tribal impulses that divide their own societies. In varying ways, and to greater or lesser degrees, all of these countries are being buffeted by the adverse chaotic trends that, along with positive trends, are now sweeping over the outlying world.

What are the strategic consequences of this bimodal structure? They are twofold and profound. Life for the democratic community is basically good: very good for the inner core, and reasonably good, or at least hopeful, for the outer core. Most of its members have the luxury of being able to focus on happiness and wealth. Their basic needs are being met. Their governments, economies, and societies are functioning effectively. With the Cold War gone and their strategic power no longer matched by menacing adversaries, they do not have to worry about their safety and survival being taken away by dangerous power politics outside their borders.

For much of the outlying world, by contrast, life is considerably worse and sometimes, wretched. Many of these countries are not being elevated by their internal health, by the globalizing world economy, or by a surrounding community of cooperating neighbors. In many places, the exact opposite applies, for many countries are struggling internally even as they face serious dangers externally, and globalization is pressuring them to make changes beyond their ken. Whereas the democratic community makes John Locke look like a prophet, the outlying world too often confirms Thomas Hobbes's worst instincts of life being nasty, brutish, and short. This basic difference between the good life for one-half of the world and a troubled life for much of the other half is what gives today's international system its distinctly bimodal structure, in ways that have immense practical consequences for people everywhere.

> Principle 4: Future directions point toward further progress for the democratic community and some other places, but chaos and turbulence for key parts of the outlying world.

Where is this bimodal structure headed? How will globalization affect it? Over the long term (50 to 100 years), it is possible, but far from certain, that democracy, markets, and cooperative communities will spread across the entire globe. The coming 5 to 20 years, however, are a different matter. During this shorter time, as matters now stand, these two components seemingly are headed toward different fates. For the democratic community, life in a globalizing world seems destined to become ever better: wealthier, more democratic, more peaceful, and more cooperative. For the outlying world, the future is uneven and not nearly so optimistic. While globalization is part of the solution there, it is only a partial solution of indeterminate power, and, in some respects, it is also part of the problem. For democracies and others situated to benefit from the positive effects while warding off the negative effects, globalization offers major opportunities to make further progress. But for many countries in the outlying world that are less favorably endowed to separate the good from the bad, globalization's hydra-headed effects not only offer opportunities but also spell trouble by adding new problems atop still existing old ones.

The democratic community is not only headed toward ever-growing prosperity and cooperation but also seems heavily on autopilot in key areas. That is, its progress has become so deeply embedded in underlying dynamics that it is sustainable almost on its own. True, governments must act to handle fissures and to ensure that temporary roadblocks and potholes on the road to progress are overcome. But they no longer have to labor at creating the road itself, for it has been largely built, and much of it is already paved. A good example is European unity. To be sure, the European Union faces many policy dilemmas and challenges in its efforts to broaden and to deepen. But the underlying impulse to create a unified and peaceful Europe is now so deeply entrenched and widely shared that the EU task is limited to creating an institutional architecture, not forging a basic political consensus on the wisdom of the fundamental enterprise.

The same judgment applies to the idea of sustaining the transatlantic and transpacific communities that bond the United States to its major European and Asian partners. In the coming years, many policy challenges will have to be faced in continuing to nourish and further develop these two communities as Europe unites and Asia's strength grows. But foundations have been laid already in common values, cooperative security, and mutually profitable economics. Provided future challenges are handled wisely, few sensible observers worry any longer that these communities will somehow fracture or drift apart in any fundamental way. The Americans, Europeans, and democratic Asians still quarrel about specifics, but these quarrels arise within a stable family. Barring some colossal strategic infidelity by one or more members, divorce is not in the cards.

Ten years ago, many observers feared for the future of the democratic core. Two concerns motivated them. One concern was that the Cold War's end would remove the need to keep alliances intact, and the alliance members consequently would drift slowly apart in security affairs. The other concern was that in this era of eroding security bonds, their mounting economic competition would drive core countries sharply apart, perhaps to the point of viewing each other as adversaries, not partners.[8] These concerns are still a preoccupation in some quarters. Yet the events of the past decade lead this study to judge that today's reality is more hopeful. Instead of dismantling their alliances, the democratic partners have been preserving and refurbishing them for new missions in a still dangerous world. With the world economy propelling all of them toward greater prosperity, the democratic partners have been using diplomacy to seek common approaches and have been more preoccupied with making their internal economies competitive rather than one-upping each other. None of this necessarily means that cooperation and progress will be the case in the future. Things could still fall apart if the partners do not cooperate adequately on new security missions, or if they allow normal economic competition to become strategic rivalry, or especially if both adverse trends unfold. The key point is that these countries already possess the well-oiled practices and common strategic perspectives not only to prevent disaster but also to build upon their successful legacy.

Within the democratic community, a key issue will be the extent to which the large outer core of about 55 countries will join the inner core of 30 countries. Heavily affected here are Latin America, Europe's peripheral countries, and parts of Asia and Africa. Progress probably will be made in this arena, and some countries that are only partly democratic and capitalist today likely will advance further in their transition. Southeast Asia is a region where economic gains and greater democratization may both occur, provided countries there can restart their sputtering economies. Nonetheless, an emerging reality is that the democratic community seems unlikely to grow in big ways in the coming years. *The rapid enlargement of the democratic community in recent years has been breathtaking, but it now seems to be slowing and approaching its limits.*

Democracy already has been adopted in most places likely to adopt it any time soon. Many parts of the outlying world are proving to be much harder nuts to crack. The core reason is that the conditions for creating democracy and market capitalism are not present in the necessary strength. Countries there typically lack the internal conditions for democracy to take hold: moderate pluralist politics, effective governments, cohesive societies with a strong middle class, and a hopeful economic future. They also lack the necessary external conditions, for democracy is hard-pressed to take hold when a country is deeply menaced by dangerous neighbors. This sobering reality has immense strategic consequences. *It means that democracy and capitalism cannot be relied upon to continue sweeping over the entire world, expanding on autopilot to bring stability and progress to the huge zones that continue to lack them.* Much of the outlying world will continue to face its current troubles, without democracy and capitalism to cure them.

This chaotic prospect does not necessarily mean that a catastrophe is looming everywhere in the outlying world, but it does mean that steady progress everywhere is not necessarily in the offing either. In important ways, a future of struggle, change, and turbulence apparently lies ahead. *Already today, an intensifying struggle is under way between two competing dynamics: progress leading to peaceful cooperation versus backsliding leading to fragmentation and conflict.* The outcome is uncertain and likely will vary from one region to the next. Depending on the specific place, things could get better, get worse, or at least mutate in ways that leave a welter of different but still imposing problems. The result will not only determine the fate of the outlying world but also will profoundly affect the safety and contentment of the democratic community.

Globalization enters the picture here. As said earlier, it likely will operate in most places as a dynamic that has an important, but not wholly transforming, impact. Its positive features will affect how many countries determine their future internal political and economic institutions. It also will influence how many countries pursue their relations with each other, and often to the good. But its overall impact likely will be moderate because it will be operating in a setting where the terrain often is not fertile to major progress and where other powerful dynamics, some of them not for the good, will also be at work. Globalization itself, moreover, seems likely to have hydra-headed effects, spawning a mixture of good and bad results. This reinforces the conclusion that it should be seen as a variable, not a constant, and that along with other factors, it will help propel the future in uneven ways and in multiple directions.

The good effects of globalization are well known. Globalization likely will combine with other dynamics to produce economic growth across major parts of the outlying world in the coming years. Annual growth rates of 2 to 4 percent will not make countries rich overnight, but will help improve conditions there. Opportunities for economic progress and access to information will help encourage adoption of democratic values. The bad effects are less well known but are real. For example, some countries doubtless will benefit in big ways from participating in the world economy's growing trade and financial patterns. But many others will benefit only modestly, some will remain largely unaffected, and a number seem likely to be damaged—in ways leaving them still poor, frustrated, and angry. What globalization likely will produce is not a homogeneous zone of prospering, happy capitalists, but instead a diverse pattern of winners, losers, and canoe paddlers—that is, countries struggling to stay afloat.[9]

Likewise, modern communications increase public awareness in more ways than one. One effect can be to spread enthusiasm for democracy and other liberal political values; another effect can be to fan anti-Western backlashes, nationalism, religious extremism, cultural antagonism, ethnicity, terrorism, and crime. Globalization can also erode the sovereignty of governments and weaken their ability to control their societies. To a degree, the recent revolutionary upheavals in East Timor, Chechnya, Africa, and the Balkans may be partly caused by the ability of modern communications to mobilize resentful social groups into action. Typically, nondemocratic governments presiding over societies with deep social cleavages find their stability threatened, not enhanced, by globalization. The collapse of such governments, and even of entire states, can unleash pent-up violence as ethnic groups and tribes are given license to attack each other.

Above all, the limits of globalization should be recognized. Globalization is washing over regions whose politics, economics, and security affairs are influenced by many other factors, some of them immensely powerful and capable of diluting globalization's positive impact. The notion that market economics and the information era will create a common political culture across the outlying world—complete with pro-Western attitudes—seems more facile by the day. The diverse political cultures in the outlying world are far too deeply entrenched for any such wholesale transformation, irrespective of how many multinational businesses, Hollywood movies, and McDonald's hamburger stands appear on the scene. The Russians will remain mostly as they are today and as history has made them: Slavic in their thinking. Likewise, the Chinese, the Asians, the Middle East Muslims, the Indians, the Pakistanis, and the sub-Saharan Africans will continue to see modern life through the lenses of their own experiences and values, and they will behave accordingly.

Amid this diverse cultural and economic setting, traditional geopolitics is not going to give way entirely to a new era of growing multilateral cooperation. Progress in some areas may be gained, but today's tensions probably will continue to exist in many places and even intensify in others. *The key reality is not solely that many countries in the outlying world dislike and distrust the democratic community. The more important reality is that they often dislike and distrust each other, including their immediate neighbors.* As a result, many of today's longstanding hot spots may continue to exist, and others may appear. Notwithstanding globalization, the Balkans, the Caucasus, the Middle East, South Asia, and sub-Saharan Africa are not likely to become zones of peace anytime soon.

Behind the scenes, a new era of geopolitics among the big powers may be emerging, partly spawned by globalization's diverse effects. Of special importance is that Russia is losing power while China is gaining it. Long a respected power, Russia seems likely to continue resenting its loss of status and to be left increasingly desperate to control deteriorating events around its borders and in its immediate Eurasian region. China will be feeling its oats as its power grows, and it increasingly will be prone to assert its strength and interests in Asia and elsewhere. Meanwhile, India, whose own power is growing, seems likely to assert itself in South Asia. All three of these countries will be pursuing traditional state interests, and none seems likely to have the United States in its gun sights. While they probably will not become close partners of the United States, neither will they be implacable enemies. But they may menace other countries around their borders that are closely tied to the United States, often in deeply binding security treaties. What the United States should fear is not direct rivalry with these big powers, but instead growing trouble in Russia's relations with Germany and the European Union, Russia's relations with China, China's relations with Japan and other Asian countries, and India's relations with China and Pakistan. If not managed carefully, these four key relationships have the potential to deteriorate into major geopolitical rivalries, in ways drawing in the United States because of its own interests and security ties with close friends and allies.

Looking at this complex geostrategic setting and knowing history, some experts forecast trouble ahead. Samuel Huntington foresees a cultural clash pitting the West against the rest of the world. Henry Kissinger and Zbigniew Brzezinski are worried about a world of restored geopolitical tensions. Hans Binnendijk frets about a new bipolar rivalry, pitting the U.S.-led Western alliance system against a new, interest-based bloc that unites Russia, China, and a large cast of regional rogues and troublemakers. While these forecasts are helpful, only time will tell how the outlying world evolves. What can be said is that today, this part of the world is littered with worrisome conditions. The list includes big powers pursuing traditional geopolitical interests, regional outlaws primed to commit aggression if the opportunity arises, and multiple interstate frictions. It also includes frustrated countries not making progress, failing states, criminal states, and transnational threats. Finally, there are a host of other countries that are well-meaning but that live isolated and vulnerable lives in fragmented zones utterly lacking in collective security. Globalization or not, this situation adds up to a future of turbulence and trouble in many places, not tranquility everywhere.[10]

The globalization trend especially to be feared is WMD proliferation, accompanied by changes in regional conventional military balances brought about by modern weapons and doctrines. Many regions in the outlying world are already pockmarked by dangerous military imbalances and security vacuums. In several cases, strong potential predators are located next door to weak and vulnerable neighbors whose security is important to the Western community. The oil-rich Persian Gulf is but one example. Especially because WMD proliferation will take place in an already unstable setting, it has the potential to transform, in highly damaging ways, strategic relationships along the entire southern belt stretching from Southeastern Europe, through the Middle East, to South Asia and Asia.

Russia and China already have nuclear weapons and long-range delivery systems. A growing danger is that WMD arsenals might be acquired by such countries as India, Pakistan, Iraq, Iran, and North Korea. An accompanying danger is that other countries might seek WMD systems in reaction. An especially serious danger is that aggressor countries might combine WMD arsenals with improved conventional forces capable of swift offensive strikes against their neighbors. These trends are already emerging and may be robustly on the scene within a decade or less. The exact consequences are hard to foresee, but they could be highly disruptive. Widespread WMD proliferation and other damaging military trends could alter already unstable security relationships in many places, making today's situation considerably worse in multiple regions.

As table 3 shows,[11] nearly 20 million active duty troops remain under arms worldwide—apart from the 1.4 million troops of the United States. What matters most in the strategic calculus is the unbalanced distribution of forces in key regions that already are unstable for political reasons. In Eurasia, Russia today fields only about 1.2 million troops and has a decaying military. It no longer has the offensive power to menace Europe, but it is far stronger than its immediate neighbors. In Asia, the Korean standoff is constantly tense, but the long-term concern is China's huge military force of nearly 3 million troops. China's military currently lacks the assets to project major power beyond its borders, but over time, modernization could provide this capability in ways that could menace its outnumbered Asian neighbors. In South Asia, India's military is twice the size of Pakistan's. In the Persian Gulf, Iraq and Iran both field forces that are considerably larger than those of Saudi Arabia and other Arab sheikdoms. Elsewhere, the sheer amount of well-armed military forces provides a major capability for violence if they are unleashed. The Balkans is an example.

Table 3. Military Forces in Key Regions

	Active Military Personnel (thousands)	*Defense Spending ($ billions)*
NATO and Europe	3,400	190
Russia and Eurasia	2,278	78
Greater Middle East	2,768	66
South Asia	2,009	30
Asia	6,815	202
Africa	1,005	25
Latin America	1,325	30
Total	19,600	621

These military imbalances might not be worrisome if they occurred in settings of stable political relations; however, many of them arise in settings that are highly unstable, even volatile. In particular, situations where potential aggressors enjoy a big military advantage over outnumbered victims are an open invitation to war. The lack of collective security mechanisms in most of these regions further exacerbates the problem because aggressors are not deterred from attacking and potential victims are not assured of their security. Often, the result is an atmosphere of chronic anxiety and, occasionally, war—as has occurred in the Persian Gulf and the Balkans in the past decade. As potential aggressors modernize their forces with weapons capable of offensive doctrines, this situation may worsen. WMD proliferation is deeply menacing because it promises to exacerbate these unstable situations further, thereby heightening anxieties and setting the stage for additional conflicts.

The troubled security conditions in key parts of the outlying world contribute importantly to their prospects for progress as globalization occurs. *The key issue is not whether globalization's positive features that are conducive to progress will be helpful in outlying regions, but whether these features alone can be relied upon to break the back of chaos at vital, unstable places where progress is hard to come by. An outcome this optimistic seems improbable.* Globalization alone probably will not stop savage ethnic war in the Balkans, prevent the Persian Gulf from remaining a permanent hot spot, cure Africa's poverty, prevent confrontation in South Asia, make Russia favorable to the European Union and NATO, or turn China into an ally of the United States. *Globalization will not solve these security problems, primarily because it operates in the sphere of economics and associated politics, which is outside the domain of security affairs.* If these problems are to be solved, it will be primarily through security politics and policies, not through globalization.

While the future is impossible to predict, hope for quick, sweeping progress in security affairs across nearly all of the outlying world seems misplaced. The idea that economic markets and natural political dynamics will empower such a wholesale transformation almost overnight is comforting. But it seriously underestimates the deeply rooted, intractable, and mounting security troubles facing the outlying world's diverse regions. Progress is not a forlorn aspiration, but a more plausible path is a slower, evolutionary progress, a checkered one that brings greater gains in some regions than in others. Over the long haul, an evolutionary progress that gradually chips away at problems—lessening some while preventing others from exploding—could have a strong cumulative effect. Even this gradual progress will not come, however, if economic markets and natural political forces are left to operate on their own devices. If this progress is to be achieved, it will have to come from the U.S. Government and other countries collaborating together in several key arenas: politics, security, diplomacy, and economics.

Looking at where the outlying world is headed, a future of major progress everywhere seems unlikely, but a steep descent almost everywhere seems equally improbable. If a steep descent begins, the Western democracies and other countries doubtless will act to halt it. Equally important, the emerging picture in the outlying world is far from entirely bleak. Although countries there will be pursuing their own interests in a setting of autarchy, most will remain inward-looking and will prefer peace to war. Globalization, moreover, will give many countries incentives to behave responsibly to preserve their access to the world economy and other benefits flowing from cordial relations with the democratic community. Only genuine outlaw states, such as Iraq and North Korea, will be permanent aggressors, but they will be few in number. Other states may be troublemakers from time to time, but mainly in fleeting ways.

Most likely, tomorrow's outlying world will show progress in some places, coupled with an overall level of shifting tension and danger in other areas that is about the same as, or modestly higher than, that of today. But this forecast assumes effective Western action. Moreover, tomorrow's dangers likely will be different from today's, and they will fluctuate over time. Some of today's dangers (for example, a new Korean war) may abate, but others may rise to take their place (such as a nuclear war in the Middle East), only to be replaced by others eventually. The United States may find itself temporarily struggling to find common ground with Russia in one period and facing trouble with China in the next. It may have to confront a Balkan aggressor one year and intervene forcefully in a collapsing Middle Eastern or African state the following year. A future of shifting dangers is considerably less menacing than is a worldwide thunderstorm of permanent crises and wars, but it is hardly innocuous. *It will require the United States to show a great deal more flexibility and adaptivity than was needed during the Cold War or even over the last decade.*

This middle-range forecast, however, is not the only plausible outcome. A worse future could transpire if events take a bad course, control of them is lost, and the democratic community does not respond in time. Rampant WMD proliferation is one dynamic that could bring about a steep descent, especially if it unfolds in a setting of stressful regional tensions, growing transnational threats, big power assertiveness, and Western bungling. If a global thunderstorm occurs, it likely will not stem from the appearance of a new superpower or peer competitor to challenge the Western community worldwide. *Instead, it likely will come, at least initially, from the outlying world's sheer fragmentation, multipolarity, chaotic turbulence, multiple dangerous trends, and interactive dynamics.* If so, this outcome will be of small comfort to the democratic community, for a chaotically dangerous world could prove to be quite hard to handle for reasons of its own. After all, the prospect of having to put out multiple forest fires, caused by lightning strikes in many separate places, is hardly a prescription for a tranquil existence.

Implications for U.S. Policy and Strategy

Globalization thus is combining with other dynamics to make the democratic community increasingly peaceful and prosperous, but the outlying world is still chaotically turbulent, perhaps more so in some places. This strategic trend has important policy and strategy implications in two key areas, both of which will impose significant demands on American resourcefulness and superpower leadership: mobilizing the democratic community to act in the outlying world and setting strategic goals there.

For the United States, the need to craft a strategic policy for the outlying world is not a prescription for being heavily involved everywhere. Because U.S. resources are limited, a clear sense of interests will be needed in determining where to become involved and where to stand back. Recent trends suggest that U.S. interests are enlarging outward into new regions. But not all interests are the same in weight. In theory, U.S. interests are vital, important, or peripheral. Vital interests are so critical that they always mandate large efforts, sacrifices, and risks to protect them. Important interests can be critical, too, but they fall into a lower category and therefore mandate a keen sense of feasibility and cost-effectiveness in deciding whether and how to protect them. Peripheral interests have intrinsic value but normally do not justify expenditure of major resources. This threefold distinction can be hard to apply, especially when gray area important interests are at stake. For example, some important interests can be derivative of vital interests: strongly defending them may be necessary to prevent major threats to vital interests from arising later. Yet the costs and risks of protecting important interests sometimes can prove to be higher than originally thought—sometimes too high. Each situation must be judged on its own merits; in general, U.S. involvement should be selective, focused on matters of truly strategic importance in which the consequences of acting, or not acting, are widespread, not purely local.[12]

The same judgment applies to the role of values in U.S. foreign policy. Especially because the United States is a global power with a major leadership role, the days are long gone when it could anchor its foreign policy in a Palmerstonian concept of pragmatic interests defined in narrow geostrategic terms. U.S. foreign policy necessarily must favor and promote the spread of democracy, humanitarianism, peaceful conduct, respect for law and rules, and international cooperation in zones beyond its old Cold War perimeters. Indeed, the widespread adoption of these values is a powerful way, over the long haul, to promote American and common interests. But recognizing the important role of values does not translate into the conclusion that overly weighty burdens, unnecessary risks, and impossible dreams should drive U.S. policy. Here, too, a prudent sense of selectivity and restraint is needed.

The bottom line is that U.S. interests and values are a powerful prescription for a foreign policy of activism, not passivity, toward both the democratic community and the outlying world. An activist policy must be well construed and guided by a clear sense of strategy; it must embody a coherent relationship between ends and means and apply its scarce resources wisely, through sound plans and programs. In particular, it must be as effective as possible. In the coming years, the hallmark of a sound U.S. foreign policy will be its ability actually to achieve its goals rather than to watch in confusion or frustrated angst as the future unfolds.

Owing to globalization and other dynamics, U.S. foreign policy will need to think globally; it will need to see the world as a whole because it is becoming a single place of tightening geography and shortening time. U.S. policy also will need to focus intently on the future. Nobody can pretend to know what today's changes will produce tomorrow. To a degree, the early 21st century reflects what Charles Dickens said about Europe in the late 19th century: that because it was the "best of times and the worst of times," the world seemed headed both toward heaven and in the opposite direction. If this is the case today, it says something profound about the coming agenda. The United States should not view the future as predestined to unfold along a single, linear path. Instead, it should view the future as a variable, as capable of producing a wide variety of outcomes, ranging from good to ill, depending upon how events play out and key countries act. Above all, the United States should not adapt a passive stance by assuming that great progress is ensured by the natural forces of economics, politics, and human evolution. Some observers have said that the current era resurrects the Enlightenment's long-buried faith in progress. Perhaps so, but if progress is to come, it will have to be created out of a setting that is equally capable of producing the opposite.

The idea that governments can play a positive role in helping shape the strategic future has gone out of fashion in recent years. Whether this is true in economics can be debated, but it is decidedly untrue in security affairs. There, wise government action will be the key to determining whether the future produces progress or descent. An activist U.S. foreign policy seems best advised to focus on three strategic imperatives. First, U.S. policy should endeavor to handle wisely today's opportunities and challenges while adjusting its actions as the strategic situation unfolds. Second, it should try to encourage further progress at places where this is possible. Third, it should work with other countries to set up strong roadblocks against any major descent in global security affairs. If U.S. policy can accomplish these three key strategic tasks, it will enhance its chances to produce a safe and healthy future in which progress is possible because potentially crippling dangers have been surmounted.

> Principle 5: U.S. policy toward the democratic community will need to focus on getting it to project organized engagement and power into the outlying world.

During the Cold War, U.S. policy was compelled to focus intently on the challenge of keeping the besieged Western world united and protected, while staying prepared for a global war. That challenge has been replaced by the vastly improved situation of today. The danger of global war is gone, as is rivalry with a determined, powerful opponent. By a wide margin, the democratic community is now the strongest and most unified actor on the world scene, possessing both immense strategic assets and appealing values. In contrast to the course that it took throughout most of the 20th century, Europe is now headed toward unifying peace under democracy, and large parts of Asia and Latin America are pointed there as well. *This development makes the strategic task facing the United States far easier, for it no longer has to worry about the entire world going up in flames.*

Clearly, U.S. policy should continue carefully nurturing the democratic community's health and progress, which cannot be taken for granted. Keeping the United States closely bonded to unifying Europe and key Asia allies will be critical to preserving a stable world as well as to promoting progress. Nonetheless, this central strategic task is far easier than in the past, for the democratic community's further internal development is now heavily on autopilot. Many challenges lie ahead in ensuring that democracy takes hold in new converts and in promoting fair economic competition and burden-sharing, but these are policy particulars. *The unifying strategic essence and upward direction of the democratic community is already established as a core foundation of modern life in a globalizing world.* Barring something truly disruptive, this community will continue becoming more democratic, unifying internally and prospering almost on its own.

Yet this community faces a demanding strategic challenge. It cannot expect to remain secure and prosperous if it walls itself off from the outlying world. If this still-troubled portion of the world goes up in flames, the democratic community eventually will be consumed as well. Strategic isolationism is impossible precisely because globalization is making the world ever more connected and interdependent. The need for a selective interpretation of involvements does not alter the fact that for good reasons, U.S. and Western interests and values are marching outward into previously peripheral areas—as was evidenced by NATO intervention in Kosovo and the Balkans. In the coming years, some interests will be truly vital—for example, retaining access to Persian Gulf oil. Other interests will be powerfully derivative—not vital in themselves, but closely tied to vital interests. An example is halting WMD proliferation in South Asia so that it does not spread to the Middle East. Still other interests will be less critical, but often important enough to merit protection and advancement. On occasion, purely humanitarian interests and values will justify intervention, as will the need to enforce international codes of conduct. The presence of serious dangers to such compelling interests and values outside the democratic community's borders is what makes strategic isolationism implausible.

As a consequence, the democratic community needs a proactive policy of engagement, strategic shaping, and responding to dangerous events in the outlying world. Indeed, the United States and its democratic partners need to define their interests carefully and act selectively; a new global crusade would be unnecessary and unwise. The larger strategic reality is that the democratic community will need not only to act effectively in the outlying world but also to act together as a whole insofar as possible. Combined action is needed because even though the United States is a superpower, its assets are spread thin by its global involvements, and it cannot be present everywhere at once. It needs help from allies and partners. When the democratic powers act separately, their effectiveness is diluted. But when they join together, their effectiveness is greatly magnified.

Unfortunately, the democratic community does not have a unified policy and strategy in this arena. It is good at defending its own borders, nourishing its internal values, and promoting its own prosperity. When it comes to working together to project its interests, values, and power outward, however, it is disunited, weak, and ineffective because it has no combined strategy and comprehensive program. As a consequence, the United States is left carrying too many burdens in the security and defense arena. It singly plays the role of projecting major military power in peace, crisis, and war because its European and Asian allies remain largely focused on defending old Cold War borders against fading threats. Even in the few arenas of security and economics where the allies are active, they heavily pursue incompatible goals and uncoordinated policies—not only in relation to U.S. policies but also in relation to each other.

Absent is the sense of democratic commitment and strength that won the Cold War. What exists instead is a potpourri of disconnected policies, many of them lacking adequate resources and combined strategy. *The specifics of these policies can be debated endlessly, but the bottom line is clear: today's worrisome situation is a recipe for strategic drift and maybe failure.* Something better is needed by the inner core and, to the extent possible, by the entire democratic community. Fortunately, there are signs of progress—witness NATO's new Defense Capabilities Initiative in Europe and Japan's willingness to accept some new military missions in Asia. But much more needs to be done. The United States will need to continue encouraging its allies to respond strongly and to work closely with them in creating combined approaches in economics and security. The allies will need to rise to the occasion with greater willpower and resource commitments. Precisely how this change is to be brought about and how subsequent activities are to take shape are complex issues requiring considerable analysis and political dialogue. But as these problems are addressed, it is critical not to lose sight of the strategic basics. *Mobilizing the power and purpose of the democratic community to act effectively in the outlying world is a main challenge in a globalizing era.*

Action by the democratic community is needed because any attempt by the United States to act unilaterally would both overstretch its resources and brand it as an unwelcome hegemonic superpower. In addition, nearly all of today's existing multilateral institutions—from NATO to the Asia-Pacific Economic Cooperation (APEC) forum and the International Monetary Fund—seem overloaded and hard-pressed both to reform themselves and to cope with the complex challenges of a globalizing world. They can be brought to greater life and refocused only if their key members join together on behalf of common enterprises. While a global strategic response is needed, multilateral efforts at specific places clearly cannot be mounted by the democratic community as a whole. What will be needed are several smaller coalitions of the committed and able, composed of countries with bedrock interests at stake in key regions and possessing the assets and inclinations to work together. Thus, different coalitions will be needed to carry out strategic activities in Europe and its environs, Eurasia, the Greater Middle East and Persian Gulf, Africa, South Asia, and Asia.

Building such coalitions has already begun in Europe, but the effort is only beginning to make headway elsewhere. The core issue is not the worthiness of the enterprise, but instead its feasibility in the face of today's powerful political constraints. Strong leadership by the United States in all key regions can provide considerable energy and thereby elevate the chances for success. Potential allies and partners will have strong motives to act because their own interests increasingly are at stake, and cooperation with the United States and other countries can greatly magnify their ability to protect these interests. The strategic advantage of multilateralism is that it can allow many countries to commit only modest resources and still aim for ambitious goals. It thus may have more appeal than often is realized, provided countries awaken to the challenges facing them.

Prospects are best in Europe, where the commitment to multilateralism and positive experience with it are strongest, owing to NATO and the European Union. Europeans are accustomed to focusing their security policies on their own region, but their global economic interests and involvements are giving them a growing incentive to think more broadly, if not globally, about security. Experience at multilateralism is less deeply planted in the greater Middle East, but the Persian Gulf War shows that strong coalitions can be assembled during times of great danger. The looming challenge is one of applying this lesson to build greater peacetime cooperation. Progress may be stimulated if the Israeli-Arab peace process gains momentum and WMD proliferation creates growing incentives for countries to bond together in security affairs to protect themselves.

Asia is a region where multilateralism has little anchoring in history and where countries are separated not only by their wary attitudes toward each other but also by their sheer distances from one another. Yet globalization is drawing Asia together in economics and security affairs, impelling greater security cooperation if steady economic progress is to be made by the key countries. Asia already has nascent multilateral institutions: APEC and the Association of Southeast Asian Nations are examples. The issue is whether they will take hold and grow in ways that affect not only politics and economics but also security affairs. Much will depend upon whether U.S. leadership can convince such key countries as Japan, South Korea, Australia, the Philippines, Indonesia, Singapore, and others to begin blending their security policies and defense planning. Prospects seem best in the arenas of peacekeeping, humanitarian aid, and maritime operations, where collaborative efforts can be aimed at protecting key sea-lanes while not signaling hostile intent to the sovereignty and security of any Asian country. Progress at first may be slow, but in the long run, perhaps momentum can be built.

For the United States, the attractions of success make the effort worthwhile. Cooperating with allies and partners is never easy, but history shows that when a coalition acts, it does so with great power in politics, security, and economics. Simply stated, coalitions can accomplish a great deal in enduring ways—far more than can be achieved by countries acting separately. This is the case because coalitions often are synergetic instruments: their whole is greater than the sum of their parts. Clearly, the United States cannot hope to replicate the NATO experience in regions where such intense multilateral cooperation lies decades away. However, efforts to create less formal coalitions in security affairs and economics may offer viable prospects in the sense of being both potentially successful and effective enough to get the strategic job done.

If this agenda of multilateral coalition-building is pursued more intently than now, it doubtless will be complex, demanding, and often frustrating: progress will be measured in small degrees and experienced over a period of years and decades, not months.

If the United States does not achieve progress in this arena, it will increasingly find itself carrying overloading strategic burdens around the world almost alone. If the democratic countries and other friendly powers of key regions do not cooperate and work with the United States, their own regions could go up in smoke, and their interests and safety along with it. To an important degree, globalization leaves all participants no other alternative but to act together: not to achieve strategic miracles, but to strengthen their capacity to handle the challenges ahead.

> Principle 6: In dealing with the outlying world, promoting strategic stability is rapidly becoming not only a key goal in itself but also a precondition for attaining progress.

Several years ago, a prevailing hope was that the outlying world would benefit powerfully from the positive trends now sweeping over the democratic community. A common expectation was that owing to irresistible forces of democracy, free markets, and multilateral cooperation, the outlying world would itself go on autopilot, destined for a future of steady integrating progress. Whether because of globalization or in spite of it, this comforting vision recently has been going up in smoke. From Russia to the Middle East and Asia, recent downward trends show clearly that the countervailing dynamics of chaotic fragmentation and deterioration are too powerful for the autopilot mechanism to work on its own. In today's outlying world, there is too much growing political conflict, economic strife, social dislocation, geopolitical maneuvering, military competition, and WMD proliferation to suggest otherwise.

The key policy questions facing the democratic community are: Exactly what is to be done? How should an effective common policy and strategy take shape? *The growing turbulence in the outlying world is ample reason for a basic judgment: before steady progress can be made there, strategic stability must be achieved.* The term *strategic stability* does not mean stasis or a great slowdown in change; in today's world, neither is possible, and in many places, they are not desirable. What strategic stability means is a marked lessening of the damaging conditions and dynamics that create great friction in interstate relations and domestic affairs and that thereby set the stage for widespread deterioration, conflict, and war. An unstable situation is prone to a big explosion any time a match is lighted. By contrast, a truly stable situation is characterized by strategic affairs that are healthy, enduring, and peace-pursuing.

If U.S. strategy is to be anchored in sensible goals, it should first be a strategy of stability, and only then a strategy of progress. The reasons are apparent. Chaos at key places in the outlying world not only endangers U.S. and allied interests but also poses a menace to peace worldwide. If allowed to fester and grow, it could propel major parts of the world, including the big powers, back toward the kind of geopolitical maneuvers and endemic conflicts that set the stage for the 20th century's long-lasting troubles. Because the democratic community's common resources are finite, it must set priorities. Indeed, the democratic community will not be able to aim for strategic stability everywhere; instead, it must focus on the conditions and dynamics that matter most—those that affect not only local places but also multiple regions.

Equally important, a foundation of strategic stability is a precondition for enduring progress. Globalization's good features and other positive trends cannot take hold if they are planted in quicksand. The same holds true for the inspiring values of democracy and free markets, which will not take hold if the preconditions for their success are lacking. The paramount need to foster strategic stability is not a recipe for diluted values and lowered horizons; it merely means that the horse must come before the cart if the cargo is to arrive at its destination. Strategic stability in the outlying world will be difficult to achieve. If stability is attained, however, it will help accelerate the rate at which progress unfolds.

A proactive strategy of promoting stability must be anchored in a clear sense of how the three goals of seeking economic prosperity, healthy security affairs, and democracy-building are to work together. Clearly, all three goals are interactive: success at one helps achieve the other two. Equally clear, U.S. policy in endangered zones cannot aim for economic growth and democratization in the misplaced confidence that peaceful security relationships will flow in the aftermath. To an important degree, the need to create stable security affairs should be seen as a precondition for economic gains and democracy to take hold. This is how the democratic community was built during the Cold War. The same formula of cause and effect likely will apply to taming key parts of the outlying world in the coming era.

In promoting strategic stability as a foundation for progress, should the United States and its democratic partners pursue a truly global strategy or separate regional strategies? The answer seemingly is a sensible combination of both approaches, carried out in ways that harmonize economic and security policies. In the economic arena, as Robert Gilpin has said, global strategies are needed to promote common rules, policies, expectations, and coordinated actions. Regional economic strategies can contribute, but only if they serve as stepping stones, not stumbling blocks, to handling truly global issues.[13] The same applies in security affairs. Global strategies are needed in such critical areas as arms control, diplomacy, and international law. Regional strategies are needed to mobilize the common military and security assets that will be available for use in dealing with regional problems. Whereas global strategies can lack the focused power to handle regional affairs on a case-by-case basis, regional strategies can lead to fragmentation and localism. Separately, neither approach offers a solution. But together, they can work effectively if they are properly blended in ways that make them mutually supportive.

Globalization's unifying effects create compelling reasons for the democratic community to see the world as a whole, rather than as disconnected regions. A sense of the whole will assist the critical tasks of setting priorities among regions and of coordinating efforts to handle each of them on behalf of a common strategic enterprise. Once this task is performed, policies can then be forged that respond to the unique features of individual regions. Most likely, U.S. strategy will seek to consolidate Europe's unification, preserve stable relations with Russia and China, defuse poisonous nationalism and ethnic hatreds in the Balkans and Caucasus, keep the lid on the explosive Middle East and Persian Gulf while dampening the effects of WMD proliferation, prevent South Asia's troubles from infecting other regions, and prevent Asia from sliding into geopolitical competition as China's power grows.

In each region, U.S.-allied strategy will need to be anchored in the proper combination of goals aimed at shaping the strategic terrain, including reforming alliances, promoting broader multilateral combination, reaching out to new partners, reassuring vulnerable countries, stabilizing competitive dynamics, and deterring improper conduct. As success is achieved in preventing negative trends, emphasis can shift toward pursuing positive developments. In this way, the troubled security affairs of dangerously chaotic regions perhaps can gradually give way to an atmosphere of growing tranquility and cooperation. This improving strategic stability can help set the stage for further progress in building democracy, market economies, greater wealth, and political communities. Progress in these areas, in turn, can help reinforce the trend toward strategic stability in security affairs.

The vision of strategic stability and progress put forth here does not imply that concepts of security order crafted by the United States and its close allies should be, or can be, artificially imposed on key regions. Nor does it mean that the political and economic values of countries in these regions necessarily must mimic those of the democratic community. If stability and progress are to be achieved, they will need to be attained in organic ways that reflect the history, values, and evolving practices of the regions themselves. Ultimately, they will need to be achieved by the countries of each region, not sustained by outsiders in ways not welcomed by insiders. The proper process for defining how the future should be built is multilateral consensus-building among insiders and outsiders. All participants must be guided by legitimate interests and responsible conduct. This is the case for outsiders, but it also is the case for insiders, including those possessing the physical strength and willpower to impose their own unhealthy conceptions on their neighbors. In the final analysis, the world will and should remain a diverse place; however, if stability and progress are to be achieved, some common themes will apply to all regions. The legal rights and legitimate interests of all countries will need to be respected, human rights will need to be honored, and security and economics will need to work together.

Although policies will vary among these regions, similar guidelines will apply. The United States and its partners will need to forge their multiple policy instruments together. Their diplomacy, political activities, economic policies, security efforts, and defense plans will need to work on behalf of a coherent strategy, rather than operate in separate domains or even at cross-purposes. These policy efforts must be backed by adequate resources and be carried out by economizing plans and programs that gain the maximum mileage from the resources expended. By acting wisely in these ways, the democratic community will enhance its prospects for success in dealing with a turbulent setting where success will not come easy.

One of the biggest challenges faced by U.S. strategy will be that of crafting coordinated, complementary economic policies and security policies. If these two policy components can be forged together on behalf of common purposes, they will greatly magnify the effectiveness of U.S. strategy. If they do not work together, or even compete with each other, their impact will be greatly diminished. The specific challenges to be faced will vary from region to region. In the transatlantic relationship, collective defense already exists, but building a more harmonious economic relationship as the European Union enlarges and deepens promises to be both important and difficult. In Asia, the opposite situation prevails. Prospects for cooperative economics appear good, but the region lacks collective security: its architecture is held together by bilateral ties between the United States and multiple allies. Building upon these bilateral ties to create a greater sense of multilateral cooperation likely will be a key endeavor, for its success not only will affect Asia's stability but also will have an important impact on economic progress. The same judgment applies to the Middle East and the Persian Gulf, where economic progress and democracy-building are badly needed but will remain problematic unless today's crippling security problems can be lessened.

Likewise, coordinated policies will be needed in dealing with key strategic challengers: Russia, China, and India. Ushering these three big powers into the world economy makes sense as part of a strategy for market-building and global economic growth, but this step will be advisable only if there are credible assurances that these countries will use their economic opportunities to play constructive, not destructive, roles in security affairs. An even sterner judgment applies to outlaws and potential aggressors. Until they alter their demeanor, they will continue to need deterrence through political-military pressure and economic sanctions. Offering them economic inducements can be a viable way to influence their behavior only if it ensures that they will act responsibly. Owing to different but equally thorny dynamics, dealing with troubled and failing states in Africa and elsewhere will also require coordinated economic and security policies. For most of these poverty-stricken countries, economic progress is vital, but it will not come easily, and it cannot take hold unless effective governments and security conditions are first created. The United States will not be able to help all of them, but it will be compelled to help some of them. To do so, it will need to blend its economic and security efforts wisely.

Doubtless, debates will continue raging about how to coordinate economic and security policies in specific cases. But participants in them should be able to agree on one core judgment: these two key policy instruments must be blended to support a common strategy. The same applies to using other instruments of national power. If this coordination can be achieved, a comprehensive, well-conceived strategy, led by the United States and backed by key allies, will stand a good chance to succeed—perhaps not everywhere, but at enough places to make a big difference. In this event, dealing with the outlying world's chaos will prove to be less difficult and dangerous than otherwise could be the case. If islands of strategic stability can be built there and gradually expanded outward, the chances for economic progress and democracy-building will increase commensurately. To the extent this effort succeeds, the democratic community will find itself looking outward and seeing opportunities, not dangers.

Diplomacy, politics, economic activities, security efforts, and arms control can make a major contribution to this strategy, but in the final analysis, sensible Western military commitments and actions will be critical. The reason is that in the turbulent outlying world, security and defense conditions will have an important bearing on whether the future produces growing stability or mounting chaos. For the United States and its allies, this reality means that they will need to remain skillful at using military power—not only during crises and wars but also in peacetime.

American military forces will need to remain well armed, capable of winning wars and able to handle the crisis interventions and other operations ahead, including peacekeeping. This will remain a top priority, regardless of how the future unfolds. At the same time, these forces seem destined to play an enduringly important role in U.S. efforts to shape the strategic environment in peacetime, especially in turbulent geographical zones where critical interests and security goals are at stake. Shaping the environment will take many forms, ranging from building coalitions to reassuring vulnerable countries to warning potential aggressors. These disparate activities likely will be guided by a common strategic mission: laying a foundation of stability not only to safeguard U.S. and allied interests but also to help encourage the progress coming from globalization's positive features.

The idea of using U.S. military power to help shape the strategic environment is nothing new, for it was done continuously throughout the Cold War. Back then, however, the task was different: it was to uphold the bipolar order by defending key alliances through such precepts as containment, deterrence, forward defense, and flexible response. Now, the task of creating strategic stability is different because the world is no longer bipolar, but is considerably more complex. Today's world is vulnerable to being torn apart not by the actions of a single large enemy, but by many dynamics capable of conspiring together to create a bubbling stew of interacting troubles. Helping calm these diverse troubles before they reach the boiling point likely will be a core strategic purpose of U.S. military power.

The manner in which U.S. military forces are used also seems destined to be different from that of the Cold War. Then, U.S. ground and air forces, carrying out continental strategies, were the main instruments of peacetime strategic shaping: naval forces normally played important but supplementary roles. In the coming era, the new geostrategic setting of the outlying world is elevating the role played by naval forces and operations in U.S. strategy for peacetime shaping. Clearly naval forces will remain embedded in joint operations: experience shows that "jointness" is the best approach to using U.S. military power effectively. All the same, U.S. strategy faces a new intellectual challenge. It is one of figuring out how to use naval power and joint maritime operations for peacetime political impact in a highly complex, fluid setting where the relationship between cause and effect is anything but clear.

Mastering this challenge does not promise to be easy, but in this era of globalization, few things are easy.

Conclusion

Globalization is washing over the entire world, increasingly bonding its separate parts together and intensifying the pace of change. The strategic consequence is not preordained. It can be progress, descent, or a mixture of both. Much depends upon how countries everywhere act, for in the final analysis, globalization will become what they decide to make of it. How the future will unfold is impossible to know. What can be said is that there is a major difference between the democratic community and the diverse regions of the outlying world. Whereas the democratic community seems headed toward growing progress, the direction of the outlying world is less clear. It has the potential for progress, but major parts of it also have the potential to slide into chaos in ways that might not only consume them but also damage the democratic community. Controlling this potential chaos is a main strategic challenge: not only to protect the interests and values of the democratic community but also to give the outlying regions a better chance to take part in the undeniably positive benefits of globalization. The future hangs in the balance—for people everywhere.

Notes

[1] For an overview of current global security affairs, see the Institute for National Strategic Studies, *Strategic Assessment 1999: Priorities for a Turbulent World* (Washington, DC: National Defense University, 1999). For a journalistic account of globalization, see Thomas L. Friedman, *The Lexus and the Olive Tree: Understanding Globalization* (New York: Farrar, Straus and Giroux, 1999). See also John Micklethwait and Adrian Wooldridge, *A Future Perfect: The Challenge and Hidden Promise of Globalization* (New York: Crown Business, 2000). A scholarly appraisal is presented in Robert Gilpin, *The Challenge of Global Capitalism: The World Economy in the 21st Century* (Princeton, NJ: Princeton University Press, 2000).

[2] For an appraisal of trends in recent decades, see Samuel P. Huntington, *The Third Wave: Democratization in the Late Twentieth Century* (Norman and London: University of Oklahoma Press, 1991). For a more recent overview, see "The Democratic Core: How Large, How Effective?" in *Strategic Assessment 1999: Priorities for a Turbulent World* (Washington, DC: National Defense University, 1999), 189–204.

[3] For more analysis, see Daniel Yergin and Joseph Stanislaw, *The Commanding Heights: The Battle between Government and the Marketplace That Is Remaking the Modern World* (New York: Touchstone, 1998).

[4] Mitchell M. Waldrop, *Complexity: The Emerging Science at the Edge of Order and Chaos* (New York: Simon and Schuster, 1992).

[5] For analysis, see David C. Gompert, *Right Makes Might,* McNair Paper 59 (Washington, DC: National Defense University Press, 1997).

[6] For a technical description of the Ricardo model and other models, see Paul R. Krugman and Maurice Obstfeld, *International Economics: Theory and Policy* (New York: Addison-Wesley, 1997).

[7] For more economic data, see David Held, Anthony McGrew, David Goldblatt, and Jonathan Perraton, *Global Transformations: Politics, Economics, and Culture* (Stanford, CA: Stanford University Press, 1999).

[8] Lester Thurow, *Head to Head: The Coming Economic Battle among Japan, Europe, and America* (New York: William Morrow and Company, 1992).

[9] For additional analysis, see Robert Gilpin, *The Challenge of Global Capitalism*; for a pessimistic portrayal of where future global economic trends could head, see Paul R. Krugman, "The Return of Depression Economics," *Foreign Affairs* (January/February 1999).

[10] See Samuel P. Huntington, *The Clash of Civilizations and the Remaking of World Order* (New York: Simon and Schuster, 1996); Henry A. Kissinger, *Diplomacy* (New York: Simon and Schuster, 1994); Zbigniew Brzezinski, *The Grand Chessboard: American Primacy and Its Geostrategic Imperatives* (New York: Basic Books, 1997); Hans Binnendijk, "Back to Bipolarity," *Washington Quarterly* 22 (1999), 4.

[11] For more detail, see "Global Military Balance: Stable or Unstable?" in *Strategic Assessment 1999: Priorities for a Turbulent World* (Washington, DC: National Defense University, 1999), 55–68.

[12] For more analysis of U.S. interests, see Joseph S. Nye, Jr., "Redefining the National Interest," *Foreign Affairs* (July/August 1999).

[13] Gilpin, *The Challenge of Global Capitalism*, 329–357.

Chapter 4

Global Economics and Unsteady Regional Geopolitics

Robert E. Hunter

During recent years, increasing attention has been paid to a phenomenon—or, rather, phenomena—that is generically termed *globalization*. Defining it precisely, however, has proved elusive. There is a widespread, instinctive sense that much is in the process of changing, and changing rapidly, in a wide variety of fields and activities, especially because of advances in a number of technical areas—notably, transportation, communications, digitization, sensors, and computation. Yet no common definition of globalization has yet emerged, no basic standard of reference. That is part of the phenomenon itself: that so much of what is happening is uncertain, both in its current scope and in its future direction. Predicting what advances in technology will be most consequential has proved to be difficult enough (anecdotal evidence is legion about current developments that were not forecast only a few years ago); even more difficult is predicting what economic, political, social, and other consequences will flow from the technologies of globalization and their applications.

Thus, any effort to predict the impact of globalization suffers at the outset from the lack of a commonly accepted framework for analysis. For purposes of this analysis, globalization is viewed primarily in what could prove to be an overly restrictive way, namely, in terms of those developments that are increasing the pace and extent of interaction among nations, societies, and peoples, and of the speed with which information can be transmitted and processed. (Also critical are some ancillary developments, especially in high-technology military capabilities.) This definition reveals one conclusion: that, at least on one level, what we call globalization is not historically unique in terms of causing change. Because international interaction has been intensifying for many centuries, it may be appropriate to call it the "Gutenberg and Marco Polo effects." Perhaps the rate of change is accelerating, but the fact and direction of it, as well as its causal role in shaping the international environment, are not. At another level, however, quantity can become quality—that is, the way in which relations among peoples are developing, as well as the ways in which they are viewed (the political effects)—can establish new ways and create new patterns of behavior precisely because the pace of change is so great and the degree of penetra-

---

Robert E. Hunter is a senior advisor at RAND and vice chairman of the Atlantic Treaty Association. He is a member of the Defense Policy Board and associate of the Belfer Center at Harvard University. He served as both U.S. Ambassador to NATO and U.S. Representative to the Western European Union and has been a member of the National Security Council Staff.

tion into domestic affairs is so high. Consider the instantaneous engagement in transnational communication of far more people than was ever before possible, including to a high degree in nonlinear broadcast terms: leaping technical, interactive, and even conceptual barriers. Judging these political effects is most difficult of all; perhaps it is impossible. For the policymaker, this puts a premium both on process and on contingency—doing those things that, as far as can be told, are most likely to take account of a wide range of possible developments and potential changes that could have the greatest consequences in terms of their impact on a hierarchy of interests and values.

Globalization and the Post-Cold War Era

Globalization cannot be separated from other developments in international society; indeed, it cannot be understood outside the broader context. In regard to the strategic environment, the most important change has been the impact of the end of the Cold War—which itself is in part the product of an earlier stage of globalization as the term is being used here. The hollowing out of the Soviet Union (along with the rest of the Soviet empire) was certainly hastened by radical advances in telecommunications and computation, which accelerated the spread of ideas throughout the empire and permitted millions of people who previously had been institutionally excluded from that process—the essence of totalitarianism—to participate in the development of society and its evolution. Ironically, it was Mikhail Gorbachev's effort to modernize the Soviet economy in order to reform and thus to "save" both communism and the Soviet Union—enshrined in his policies of *glasnost* ("opening") and *perestroika* ("restructuring")—that helped to legitimize and to give impetus to the underlying forces that spelled the downfall of the totalitarian system and its appendages. This also provides a first lesson about the impact of globalization, in the sense that it is a phenomenon that marries technology to the spread of ideas, resulting in great difficulty in predicting the ultimate impact of globalization on societies, both domestic and international.

The End of Paradigms

The end of the Cold War brought what is sometimes called a return to normal international politics (that is, a more fluid system of relations among states and other entities) such as existed before the beginning of the great Ice Age of global politics that was the Cold War. In particular, the post-Cold War era has not been marked by the emergence of any small set of paradigms, as viewed by the most consequential leaderships, to govern large sections of the international system or the behavior of individual states within that system. For the United States, for example, Cold War policy could be reduced to its essence as three propositions: to contain the Soviet Union, its allies, and acolytes; to constrain and confound communism; and to lead a growing global economy. Obviously, this is an exaggeration: much that happened in the world during the Cold War fell outside the parameters of these three paradigms. Nevertheless, whenever there was tension between these paradigms and other possibilities or choices for national action, the requirements of managing the Cold War—in particular the central strategic relationship with the Soviet Union—tended to take precedence.

Since the Cold War's end, the first two of these three paradigms—at least as they apply to the world beyond Cuba, China, North Korea, and parts of Indochina—are no longer relevant. The third paradigm—to lead a growing global economy—remains a critical goal of U.S. policy but has changed significantly in terms of its motivations and qualities. Of course, the idea of normal international politics also begs many questions. International society is different from what it was prior to the Cold War, in part because of progressive developments now lumped together as globalization. In some aspects, however, international society is similar to that of the past. (Also, even during the Cold War, what happened in various parts of the world was not just a function of the Cold War framework: regional developments, with their own dynamics, coexisted with the demands of Cold War management.) This similarity can be seen particularly in the continued use, in various places, of some classic tools of statecraft, such as the balance of power, the pursuit of regional hegemony, and deterrence. The term *normal*, therefore, is used here to indicate international and regional politics that are not distorted by some overarching global framework.

Also important as a method of foreign policy analysis and action, there is today what could be termed a paradigm gap: namely, it is unlikely that there will emerge a relatively small set of propositions that can describe, much less govern, the international system overall, certainly not to the degree that the Cold War paradigms "governed" the world of that era. Nor is it likely, for the foreseeable future, that the United States and its Western partners will see the emergence of a country seeking global hegemony (even an assertive China would be unlikely to have the worldwide ambitions of the old Soviet Union) or, with even stronger reason, a new ideology with the Earth-spanning pretensions of communism.

Limits on Mobilizing Power?

Globalization, in terms of communications and the spread of ideas, can be viewed as helping to reinforce this lack of a new anti-Western ideology, certainly one applying to the assertiveness of states and to the development of a single stance with widespread appeal in different regions of the world. In the former case is the argument—not systematically proved, but often asserted to have at least intuitive value—that "democracies do not make war on other democracies." At least part of this idea can be stated in another way: the spread of information, radically promoted by advances in telecommunications, can inhibit central governments in their efforts to mobilize national power for aggressive purposes, unless there is some compelling national ethos that can withstand the test of relentless exposure. At times, nationalism and ethnicity have had such a quality; witness the capacity of Slobodan Milosevic to mobilize power to destructive ends in today's Serbia. It still has not been proved, however, that such moods of national assertiveness can be sustained over time in a communications-rich environment in the absence of palpable threats that can rally domestic opinion decisively. The possibility of sustaining such a mood is likely to be particularly questionable in societies whose politics place a significant value on human life and whose governments cannot obscure losses from conflict (losses measured in blood, if not treasure) or stifle popular access to attacks on their propaganda.

An Ideological Response to Globalization?

At one level, the more rapid transmission of information, with greater penetration within and among societies, could acquaint large numbers of people with the same ideas and help to build broad transnational coalitions. At another level, however, the same technological capabilities can rob a proselytizing ideology of exclusiveness in terms of access to individuals, such as has been a hallmark of ideologies that have been exploited by totalitarian regimes. One important qualification should be noted: a new ideology (or a use of an old ideology for contemporary political purposes) might prove to be so compelling, as a response to stresses within a society, as to drown out competing information. There is precedent, though not in this age of telecommunications—namely, the emergence of the three principal European-origin ideologies that developed, over a century and a half, in response to the Industrial Revolution: liberal capitalism, communism (and its cousin, socialism), and fascism. It is conceivable that the age of globalization will produce economic and social disparities and dislocations of such a magnitude as to spawn one or more ideologies in reaction, but even if they do, it is quite another thing for such ideologies to have a global reach. A religion with global reach is possible, but none of today's major religions is a candidate. Fears of some commentators that a sort of political Islam would fill this role already have been confounded.

At a more modest level, reactions to globalization have already set in. The angry protests at the Seattle meeting of the World Trade Organization in 1999 should not be extrapolated as conclusive evidence of a new era in attitudes toward economics, society, and relations among nations, peoples, institutions, and private sector entities. Nonetheless, it is clear that there is "push back" against some of globalization's trends and that this reaction is coming from a diverse set of sources and perspectives that reflect, in part, differential rates of adaptation to the disruptions caused by globalization. There is also a generalized reaction to the identity-reducing quality of some aspects of globalization, relating even to developments such as the formation of the European Union (EU), which has witnessed increased regionalization within Western Europe. In part, this regionalization has been a search for meaning in an era when, in Europe, the nation-state has become less relevant than it once was. Nevertheless, these trends cannot be seen, at least not yet, as the emergence of some globe-spanning response to globalization that will evolve into a new paradigm of analysis and, possibly, of action.

The basic lesson, therefore, is that in the era since the end of the Cold War, owing to the new fluidity in world politics and the onset of a new and intense phase of technology-driven globalization, a few simple paradigms for describing the international system, much less governing it, are unlikely to emerge. Indeed, there could be even more fragmentation, especially in regard to the role that perception plays in determining the nature of the international system. ("There is nothing either good or bad, but thinking makes it so.") By the same token, it is difficult, if not impossible, to ascribe to globalization specific effects in regard to the international political and economic system that occur without reference to other developments. In short, the world as we know it and see it evolving must be taken all of a piece, with an effort, however imperfect, to ascribe to globalization at least some causes of change.

Globalization as a Marriage of Technology and Ideas

There is a basic distinction to be made between instruments and effects. In terms of developments in the international system, instruments of globalization are most prominent in technology, as reflected particularly in transportation, communications, and the making sense (computation) of the information that is thus transmitted or acquired. The most important technological developments of globalization (that is, those that are relevant to international relations in the broadest sense of the term) are likely to continue to be increased speed and volume of transport in all of its aspects, information technology, sensors, and computational capacity—the getting of people, things, and information from place to place and the manipulating of the information that is involved. Understanding the significance and impact of these technological developments also requires dealing with their effects—what do the technologies, as they are applied, actually do within political, economic, and social contexts? Of course, the very complexity, interrelationships, rapid development, and unpredictable evolution of technologies (instruments) combine with vagaries regarding their effects to create a great deal of uncertainty. Nevertheless, for policymakers, that statement is no answer, and further efforts at analysis—making distinctions and searching for predictability regarding causes and effects—need to be made.

Trends

During the next decade or so, the evolution of the international political and economic system is likely to be deeply affected by a variety of trends. A major challenge for governments, including the U.S. Government, will be to understand how these trends interact, how they affect one another politically, economically, militarily, socially, and culturally, and how to make relevant decisions about foreign policy in such an environment. Two trends help to illustrate the broader phenomenon of globalization and the differential development of aspects of international life that stem at least in part from globalization and its effects.

Trend One: Global Financial Marketplace

There will certainly be increased globalization in finance, as a result of the capacity to move the denominators of wealth (capital) from place to place at speeds that were inconceivable only a few years ago. It may not be an exaggeration to say that, within a limited time, there will be, in the absence of controls imposed by governments or international institutions, a single global financial market, for that is the direction in which the organization of capital markets is moving. This phenomenon is made possible by the technical capacities of moving capital in "real time," if not also of making decisions at a comparable pace. In all systems, friction is a fact, but the concept of a truly efficient global capital market is no longer just a pipe dream of theoretical economists.

The implications of this form of globalization, even if significantly inhibited in terms of timing, scope, or limitations deliberately placed upon it, are profound. For several years, certain trends have been accelerating, driven by technology and the organization and systems development that it facilitates, with uneven application in different countries and regions, but moving toward significant uniformity in open market situations. These trends include a decreasing capacity of governments to control capital markets within their frontiers; a rising risk associated with uncertainties; lessening efficacy of traditional economy-regulating methods available to governments and internal markets (for example, interest rates, exchange rates, money supply); increasing costs of competition to retain financial assets ("beggar-thy-neighbor" policies as a structured response to globalization); and decreasing confidence in any form of planning that assumes some predictable supply of financial assets at a cost within a relatively narrow range. A distinction can still be made between financial assets that are highly, even instantaneously, mobile on a global basis and other economic instruments (such as invested capital and labor) that are relatively fixed. Nevertheless, the impact of the former can still have a major distorting effect on the latter—especially in reducing the capacity for self-management of governments and even of whole economies. This analysis, moreover, does not account for the differential impact that a new global financial marketplace can have within individual economies, among different sectors, and within classes of society. This provides a dual meaning for the concept of "digital divide"—not just as between countries, but also as between individuals within a society (who is "digital," and who is not?).

The phenomenon of an emerging global financial marketplace can have diverse effects. Some of these could be characterized as good. They would include increasing the efficiency of markets, stimulating economic growth and trade, and helping to provide a basis for long-term increases in productivity and standards of living. Other effects could be characterized as bad. They include increased disparities among groups within domestic economies, social dislocations and increased stresses, the stimulus to populist and xenophobic politics, potentially increased differences in economic performance between "advanced" and "retarded" economies (coupled with increased alienation between "rich" and "poor" countries), and, perhaps, a greater reluctance on the part of some countries to cooperate with other countries or with international institutions. At the same time, it is not clear what impacts on broader global politics will stem from changes in financial markets or other economic developments that will be deeply affected by globalization.

Trend Two: Strategic Regionalization

In partial tension with the increased globalization of the financial marketplace and—with somewhat less force and effect—with broader international economic relationships (involving less mobile factors), the trend toward strategic regionalization is found in the realm of geopolitics (the intersection of forces and effects that deals primarily with strategic, military, and political matters). As a function of the end of the

Cold War and the loss of two of that era's three central paradigms, at least as viewed by the United States and much of the West, geostrategic coherence has also dwindled.

By the same token, there has been a reassertion of the importance of regional developments. This has been true in two senses: first, in terms of the inherent significance of regional developments (for example, less competition for attention from the requirements of an overarching global geostrategic framework) and, second, in terms of a lack of relationships among regions, and of developments within a region, of a nature that was enforced by that overarching framework. This is most clearly seen in the end of concerns that developments in one region or another could escalate—politically or militarily—to engagement of another region, with the implication, finally, that there could be some form of global conflict. There still do exist interrelationships among regions and even situations of potential escalation, however modest: thus, the Kosovo conflict entailed a requirement for NATO to extend temporary protection to Macedonia and Albania. Similarly, a military attack by the People's Republic of China on Taiwan would be unlikely to be contained within the immediate region. There are several circumstances in which the use, or threat of use, of weapons of mass destruction (WMD) would have effects across regions.

Nevertheless, in general, the end of the Cold War means that events within individual regions, including events of major significance to the world's great powers, are more likely than before to play out within the region itself, or at least primarily within its neighborhood. As early as 1991, during the Persian Gulf War—sometimes called the first major post-Cold War conflict—the theater of political as well as of military combat was more constrained geographically than would have been true only a few years earlier. There was little risk of an East-West conflict—centering on the United States and the Soviet Union—emanating from regional events that, in the Cold War, could have been cause for a major crisis and very likely superpower collusion to keep the crisis under control. It is not even clear that an event so regionally cataclysmic as an India-Pakistan war that introduced nuclear weapons would have critical, direct effects outside that region, beyond the precedent that such use of nuclear weapons would obviously set.

The CNN Effect

It is often argued that one major aspect of globalization—namely, widespread access to immediate information about what is happening in distant regions—will cause attention to be paid to physically distant events and actions to be taken, at least by morally sensitive countries, even where there is little or no connection to the classic interests of outside observers. This is sometimes called the *CNN effect*. The evidence for such an effect, however, is not conclusive or at least is not universally applicable. To be sure, it is now possible to bring events into the "global living room" from just about any point on the globe—media "point and shoot"—but it is not clear that this translates into mobilization for action. That is, it is not clear that simple media exposure creates a connection or an interest where none might otherwise have existed.

This point can be illustrated by several recent events. For example, the United States and other states in the West eventually responded to visual evidence of horrific suffering in Bosnia and later Kosovo, but they were less sensitive to, and less motivated to action by, events in East Timor; moreover, they were virtually unresponsive to events in Afghanistan and Rwanda. Some commentators might attribute these different reactions to an accumulating anesthetic quality of suffering portrayed by the media; however, the differences might also be ascribed to the relevance of the regions where the viewed events were taking place to the interests of the countries that were doing the viewing. The status of East Timor does relate to the broader question of Indonesia's future, which, in turn, relates to long-term issues of development and stability in Southeast Asia, and events in both Bosnia and Kosovo were taking place in Europe (demonstrating the importance of moral relativity in the CNN effect). At the same time, the very existence of these conflicts struck at the basis of political support for NATO and the European Union to pursue what were seen to be other, more important objectives. The events in Afghanistan, Rwanda, Kashmir, Sri Lanka, the Congo, Angola, and elsewhere were widely viewed—and were important—in human terms, but they were not judged as particularly important by the United States and other Western states in terms of geopolitics.

The point also can be illustrated by viewing the CNN effect from the reverse angle. Efforts by Saddam Hussein's Iraq to develop weapons of mass destruction and otherwise to avoid meeting the requirements of the 1991 cease-fire in the Persian Gulf War are of consequence to the West. During several crises in recent years, widespread media attention has been paid to developments in Iraq, and the U.S. administration has thus been put under intense political pressure to take action. Notably, however, within days—if not hours—of the "resolution" of each of these crises, media attention rapidly shifted elsewhere. The "crisis" has had no lasting impact in terms of media coverage and, concomitantly, there has not been an insistent public outcry for U.S. officials to deal with the issue on a continuing basis.

Regional Contexts

This geostrategic situation is not to deny that there will be significant connections among regions in the post-Cold War era, or that factors of globalization, overall, will be important. For example, the spread of military technologies can enable states not only to employ force beyond their immediate region with greater facility than previously (for example, ballistic missiles and, should warhead technologies spread, especially nuclear weapons), but also to act militarily in ways that are out of proportion to their national power as measured by classic means. (This has always been one fear of nuclear proliferation; it is coupled with assessments made by some observers about whether particular countries can be dissuaded through the use of the classic instruments of deterrence from using WMD.) Of course, the spread of weaponry is as old as history, and it cannot be ascribed to globalization as such. However, the reach of some modern military technologies, as well as their effectiveness—factors that owe in major part to the same range of technologies that are at the core of globalization—does lead some weaponry to outstrip geography. That is, weapons become more effective at longer ranges, but the world itself is not expanding. Thus, weapon X can enable relatively small country Y to apply military power well beyond its earlier, natural limits.

Some geopolitical connections among regions may actually increase in the post-Cold War era, in part because they are not part of the former era's larger perspective, with the risks of escalation and prospects for discipline imposed by the superpowers. These connections among regions may be abetted by globalization, but that is only a matter of intensity or pace, not primary cause. The increase in the number of state actors, especially in regions that are judged by the great powers of the Northern Hemisphere to have some sort of inherent importance, is also producing classic problems and gambits of geopolitics, in some cases extending to relationships among regions. This is particularly true of countries bordering the former Soviet Union. Thus, Western states concerned with stability in Europe focus once again on imponderables in Central Europe, extending all the way to the Balkans—which, among other things, has gained importance as the back door to other Western concerns in the Aegean and Middle East. Hence, both NATO and the European Union are trying to create a permanent stability by engaging the Central European countries, in one form or another, within their compass of security; hence, as well, NATO evinces a special concern about the future of Ukraine.

Western interests, whether direct (for example, energy) or indirect (for example, stability), also extend to other unstable or not-yet-predictable areas of the Russian periphery. For example:

- There is increasing Western concern about the Caucasus (North and South), in part as a function of calculations about the future of Russia, its integrity, and the West's role in promoting its evolution into a stable, democratic society, and in part as a matter of helping the Transcaucasian states to ratify their independence and to secure their capacity to produce energy (Azerbaijan) or provide transit for it (Georgia).
- The West has similar concerns (including about energy) about the Central Asian states.
- To varying degrees, in all eight of the states along the southern border of Russia, a rudimentary "great game" has begun. The players in this game are not completely clear or consistent, but they include regional states (such as Uzbekistan), Russia, Turkey, Iran, the United States and—to the east—China.
- A new geostrategic context is evolving that has Russo-Chinese relations at its core (while also extending to Central Asia and parts of the Middle East).

At the same time, the end of the Cold War has seen the emergence of new areas of real or incipient contention. For example, relations among states in the Persian Gulf, partly frozen during the past decade and left in a strategic limbo by the U.S. dual containment of Iraq and Iran, are becoming more complex. During the next several years, they are likely to develop into an elaborate system of balancing elements. India, Pakistan, Kashmir, Afghanistan, and Iran are emerging as a particular regional subsystem that overlaps with others. China's status in East Asia will clearly be a major focus of both regional and international developments for the foreseeable future; it will also involve Japan, Korea, Southeast Asia, India, Pakistan, Russia, and the United States. Recent diplomatic moves on the Korean Peninsula have provided particular evidence of the potential for a large impact on the broader East Asian system. The development of a regional system embracing these countries will have some mixture of politics, economics, military power, and strategic interests and concerns. Meanwhile, Arab-Israeli relations will continue to be important, even though one major impetus for U.S. concern—the risk that regional conflict could escalate to conflict with the Soviet Union—no longer applies.

All of these developments, and others in different regions, will be affected by globalization, in various ways and to a greater or lesser degree. They do not spring from globalization, however, nor is their course—and valid responses to them—likely to depend fundamentally upon globalization and its effects, as opposed to more classic aspects and instruments of geopolitics.

Bridging Geoeconomics and Geopolitics

To be sure, issues of trade and resource flows will continue to provide a bridge between the worlds of geoeconomics and geopolitics—and between the regional and global contexts, as witnessed by the growth of regional trading and related agreements, such as *Mercado Común del Sur* (MERCOSUR)—the Common Market of the South, the Association of Southeast Asian Nations, and the European Union. It should not be surprising that oil—its discovery, control, production, transport, refining, and marketing—retains its formative character for many issues in the globalization era, as it did under the "old economy." This is true because fueling economies remains critically important, whether the balance within Western economies tilts toward goods or services, tangibles or intangibles, the "real" or the "virtual." Indeed, the impact of oil on geopolitics is still significant, even with a low likelihood of future efforts to embargo exports as a function of Arab-Israeli conflict, not just because the Organization of Petroleum Exporting Countries retains considerable ability to set oil prices, but because there are new concerns about the production and export of oil from the Transcaucasus and Central Asia. The matter of the pipeline routes to the West has taken on major economic and political significance, with widespread effects on regional developments and on the relationship between public and private sectors in setting foreign policy.

Terrorism also is often cited in discussions of the impact of increasing globalization on international politics. At one level, the greater ease of transportation theoretically increases the capacity of terrorists to act in different places, even those remote from their home locations. Information about the methods of terrorism, including instructions for creating powerful weapons, is carried on the Internet. At another level, images of terrorist acts can be broadcast worldwide. Of course, this is not new. Indeed, much of the Middle East-based terrorism of the 1970s to 1990s relied for its effects on the potential for getting peoples remote from the events to identify with the victims of those terrorist acts—an identification essential to classifying such acts as terrorism, with its goal of seeking to provoke compliant political action.

Here, as in the case of weapons of mass destruction, modern technology can be seen to increase vulnerability in target states, including the United States. Whether these technological advances can be categorized as globalization, they help to provide a potential for what is termed *asymmetrical warfare*—the ability of a relatively small power (or a nonstate actor) to cause destruction and hence to have a political impact even where the overall balance of forces overwhelmingly favors the opponent. This can be particularly true in circumstances where the tolerance of the more militarily advanced society to sustain casualties is relatively low, as was evident in the U.S. engagement in Somalia in 1993 and for all of the NATO allies in Kosovo in 1999. In the future, leaders of relatively small military powers around the world will likely make their own calculations about this factor.

Implications for Policy

In the era embracing the parallel developments of the post-Cold War paradigm gap and intensified globalization, some features will have a particular impact on the way in which the United States will need to look at the outside world, its role in it, and decisions to be made about that role. These features include the following:

Role of Nonstate Actors

Decisions in areas of the greatest globalization will increasingly be taken by nonstate actors—especially in the private sector. It is in these areas and with these actors that some of the more significant cultural and political challenges to globalization will be found. This will be especially true where its impact exacerbates differences among and within societies in terms of information, wealth, and social structure. Many of these nonstate actors will be labeled—accurately or not—as "made in America," a phenomenon that parallels the widespread tendency to conflate the terms *modernization*, *globalization*, and *Americanization*. As a result, the United States is likely to be saddled, for good or ill, with responsibility for much of what American nonstate actors do.

Indeed, it is increasingly obvious that U.S. foreign policy, as it affects both the corpus of U.S. interests in the world and the perceptions by others of what the United States does, is not limited to government action. Other countries will not care very much whether U.S.-origin actions are manifested by formal government agencies, by U.S. nongovernmental organizations (NGOs), or by U.S. private sector entities. This creates added difficulties for the U.S. Government in managing—much less controlling—the Nation's role abroad, promoting some sense of broad, shared interest, and relating different instruments of foreign policy to one another. For example, a U.S.-based private financial institution may be able to move capital to a country that the U.S. Government wishes to contain, and Washington may have little ability to impose controls. Likewise, an offshore firm, with major U.S. ownership, could transfer defense goods to a third country with little control by Washington, except to the extent that it could identify "U.S. content" subject to licensing restrictions and possible sanctions.

Continuation of the Nation-State

At the same time, it is certainly premature to write off the nation-state as a major actor on the global scene. In terms of mobilizing military power, nation-states do not have a complete monopoly. Except for what is still comparatively limited nonstate-sponsored terrorism, however, countries muster the overwhelming bulk of military power and decisions on its use. By the same token, most actions within the broad framework of geopolitics reflect decisions taken by sovereign governments. Certainly, in terms of developing policy toward the congeries of regional foreign policy challenges, what the U.S. Government does will have far and away a greater impact than what is done by nonstate entities, whether NGOs or the private sector. This point is sometimes overlooked in analysis of the impact that globalization is having in the economic realm, as well as in the spread of information directly to populations, which reduces the relative dominance of governments over what has classically been called "intelligence collection."

Even within institutions in which diminution of sovereignty is a key goal—as is certainly true in the European Union, for example—the role of individual states in the conduct of what can be called foreign policy is still dominant. In this case, the European Commission has responsibility for trade negotiations for all 15 member states in the European Union. Even so, the EU Common Foreign and Security Policy and European Security and Defense Policy are still firmly in the bailiwick of the European Council, which represents the sovereign states, and critical decisions in these areas are still taken by consensus.

Nor is it likely that the nation-state will lose significance in the conduct of foreign policy, at least for the foreseeable future. This does not deny that globalization will have its effects or that the authority of governments is in some measure being challenged. It is rather to caution against expectations that the age of globalization is rapidly bringing both the emergence of effective supranational bodies and the paralysis of national governments to act in this realm.

U.S. Military Power

Also in this era, a handful of countries (especially the United States) are finding that the capacity to project military power abroad is increasing dramatically. For the foreseeable future, the United States will almost surely remain the world's dominant military power; however, its role may be challenged militarily in niche areas (for example, because of geographical features, nonconventional weaponry, or attrition tactics by adversaries trying to exceed U.S. political tolerance for casualties). Or the United States could be challenged politically and economically where military superiority is not particularly relevant. For example, asymmetrical warfare need not be just about military capabilities and their application, but rather can be found in other areas that affect U.S. interests. Thus, there is rising concern about so-called cyberwarfare, which would employ technological weapons—targeted at hardware, at software, or simply at processes—that in many cases should properly be seen as economic in character. For example, the disrupting of commercial and financial information flows can have a crippling effect on a nation's capacity to function, an effect that is analogous to military destruction. How serious such threats may become is open to debate, however, along with the potential for counteraction, protection, redundancy, and reassurance, provided in part by the sheer size and proliferation of information flows.

At the same time, it is not clear in what circumstances the United States will be prepared to use military force in pursuit of its interests—or how precisely, especially in advance, to define those interests. In the post-Cold War era, there has emerged a sort of "paradox of military supremacy," whereby the United States has the capacity to apply power almost anywhere and, in some cases, with little or no risk to itself. But in the 1990s, the United States has also adopted, informally, a number of self-limiting ordinances. These can be seen both in recent actions regarding Iraq and, especially, in the conduct of the Kosovo conflict. In major part, this reflects an implicit calculation, in popular American imagination, that relates the value of interests to the willingness to sustain casualties. There is a spectrum, extending from interests for whose protection it is clearly worth running severe risks (for example, repelling Iraq's 1990 invasion of Kuwait and the further threat to oil throughout the Persian Gulf) to those that are not worth risking more than minimal casualties (such as the Kosovo conflict, which was waged without any allied combat fatalities). The crossover point is not clear, and this lack of clarity may be exploited by leaders who seek to broaden the limits of what they can do by effectively deterring the United States, especially through posing credible risks of U.S. combat casualties out of proportion to the perceived U.S. interests at stake.

In part because of this phenomenon, the United States has already moved significantly toward resolving, in practice, the domestic political issue of its preparation to use military power unilaterally or primarily when it can act within a coalition. Since the end of the Cold War, certainly the U.S. predilection—from the Persian Gulf War to Kosovo—has been to seek coalitions. Among other things, this raises important questions relating directly to military developments that draw on the same technologies that are most evident in promoting globalization. Within the Atlantic Alliance, for example, there is a serious risk of a "hollowing out" of NATO, provoked by the differential rates of force modernization, especially in taking full advantage of developments in high technology. Indeed, tomorrow's U.S. forces may be unable to fight in collaboration with allied forces that remain stuck essentially at today's technological levels. Trying to remedy this situation, even before considering whether NATO as a whole would be involved militarily beyond the confines of Europe, is a key premise of the NATO Defense Capabilities Initiative that was agreed upon at the 1999 Washington Summit.

Economic Sanctions

At the same time, the use of one principal nonmilitary instrument, economic sanctions, is increasingly suspect as an effective means of promoting U.S. interests. There are the classic problems posed by sanctions, including the difficulties of impacting on the right targets in terms of goods embargoed and populations affected (that is, leadership elites versus the poor); gaining the support from other countries that is needed to prevent circumvention or "leakage"; and limiting the possibilities for import substitution, which sometimes even leads countries facing sanctions to become stronger economically and more autarchic militarily than they would be if free of embargoes. Now there is a reduced incentive for allies to accept the disciplines of imposing sanctions, in the absence of Cold War requirements and in the face of the decreasing national character of large segments of the private sector, especially large entities with global reach, in both finance and other economic activity. Furthermore, governments have less control over elements of the private sector, especially finance, which inhibits their effectiveness in applying sanctions even if they were inclined to do so. In general, therefore, economic sanctions have dwindling value in a globalized world.

Strategic Analysis and Policy

Because of all the factors that have been discussed, notably the intersection of post-Cold War developments and globalization, the U.S. Government's promotion and defense of U.S. interests abroad will require a significantly different overall approach to policy. The conduct of international relations will include a challenge to manage the interplay between the differential rates and impact of trends and countertrends to a degree never before required. This will be especially important where major aspects of a globalized world will be dominated by private sector activity, while governments will have primary responsibility for more regional matters of geopolitics.

At one level, there must be a resurrection of the qualities of strategic analysis that marked the two decades after the end of World War II, when the United States had to devise the first long-term grand strategy in its history, along with coherent substrategies for prosecuting the Cold War—qualities of analysis that have tended to fall into disuse.

At the same time, there must be a radically increased capacity in the United States to identify, develop, and integrate different elements and instruments of policy—such as political, diplomatic, economic, and military—and to make choices, in terms both of investments in instruments and of geographical and functional concentration. This point should be obvious, but in all too many areas, it is not, in part as a product of habits developed during the Cold War, in which the classic triad of foreign policy instruments—political, economic, and military—came to be seen in terms of a hierarchy, with military instruments (and especially those instruments required for deterrence of war with the Soviet Union) in the ascendant. In the post-Cold War era, by contrast, the other elements of the classic triad have again come into their own, as a more normal, or at least less skewed, functioning of international politics. This is especially so where military instruments of policy may be far less relevant to meeting national interest requirements than at least appeared to be true during the Cold War.

This integration of policy instruments must also take adequate account of the possibilities—and especially of the limitations—of the role played by nongovernment entities, especially financial and commercial, in determining what the United States can do abroad. The institutional and political structure of U.S. administrations is not well suited to make these connections, to do the relevant strategic and policy analysis, and to translate conclusions into decision and implementation. Nor is the relationship between administrations and Congress structured in a way (nor is Congress itself so structured) to facilitate decisions, choices, tradeoffs, planning, and organization to create and to carry out comprehensive and integrated policies in the post-Cold War, globalizing world. The dwindling ratio of "signal to noise" in policy, in part as an effect of communications technologies and the consequent explosion of information and its dispersion, make developing strategies and applying them that much more difficult, as well as that much more necessary. This is the policy universe in which the United States and its leaders must now increasingly operate, with the same requirements as before of taking care to protect the interests of the Nation, to the extent that this concept can be defined coherently and consistently.

Basic Requirements for Policy

In the absence of any major unifying focus in security challenges (such as a hostile China), in order to advance U.S. interests overall, the U.S. Government must be able to develop new skills, techniques, and practices. In addition to those highlighted earlier, others include the need to:

1. Design and employ military forces in significantly different ways from those of the past. Some of the implications of this statement are already being seen, for example, in the increased role for high technology in the evolving structure of the Armed Forces, all of which are becoming more capital-intensive; in the capacity for integrating military activities across different environments, as well as among the services; in higher expectations in regard to the performance of weaponry ("if you can detect a target through sensors, you can destroy it with your weapons"); and in power projection rapidly across great distances, with implications for issues such as basing requirements and force structure and employment. In addition, there is an increased premium on integrating military and political-military functions, as seen in some key active uses of U.S. military forces in the last decade in Europe, including peacekeeping in Bosnia and Kosovo, peace observation in Macedonia, and training of other countries' militaries through the Partnership for Peace (PFP).

2. Interact effectively with NGOs (for example, financial institutions, private sector organizations). This will include a need, even within traditional areas of foreign policy and national security, to develop public-private partnerships in which the interests and activities of nongovernment entities can be brought into some degree of concert with government efforts, in terms of incentives and common interests (as between government and private sector goals), rather than through coercion.

3. Deal with the "paradox of information," defined in the following way: The more access there is to information, the greater challenge there is to the ability of free society governments to decide on national interests and to mobilize action, especially action requiring sustained effort or imposing high costs, in terms of blood or treasure. The relative lessening of the primacy of governments in gaining access to information about events and developments in other countries is having an impact on the crafting and implementing of policy, as well as on the building of support for it with Congress and the American people. This is a different form of the CNN effect that makes it more difficult for government officials to claim superior "expertise."

4. Revise, as necessary and appropriate, methods of making and carrying out U.S. foreign policy within the administration, and between it and the Congress, to deal with post-Cold War requirements and possibilities. This revision is especially important in regard to integrating various approaches and instruments of policy. This also means inculcating within U.S. Government councils a much greater emphasis on strategic analysis, cross-disciplinary interaction (including realms of technology that give life to globalization), long-term planning, and political leadership prepared to make choices, commit resources, and build political support for courses of action that are not demanded immediately, but that can be critical in terms of shaping an environment that will be congenial to the United States.

5. Reconcile the competing demands of domestic special interests toward the outside world with some sort of shared national interest that can be broadly sustained in U.S. domestic politics. This has become more of a problem in the post-Cold War era as the requirements of prosecuting that conflict within some broader, national framework of interest have disappeared and as popular attention to foreign policy, on a national basis, has declined, while a wide variety of special interests pursue their own agendas.

6. Build international institutions, practices, processes, and relationships that can be sustained over time and that will engage a broad range of other countries in collaboration with the United States.

This last point may prove to be the most significant, in terms of the long-term U.S. response both to developments in the post-Cold War era and to the growth of globalization. It is key to turning power into influence in a world where the United States has more incipient power—military, economic, and to a considerable extent, political and cultural—than does any other country, perhaps since the collapse of the Roman Empire, but where the United States and its people do not have the aspiration, temperament, tradition, or organization to exploit this potential for purposes of national aggrandizement. This is very different from the attitudes and behavior of other countries in the past, some of which have sought to translate relative superiority in the instruments of power into hegemony or empire. A building process that seeks to promote long-term U.S. interests by promoting those of other countries and peoples as well is not only likely to have more staying power than does a policy that focuses on the short-term pursuit of unilateral advantage, but is also more likely to help the United States deal with the onset, at some point in the future, of a relative diminution of the relative advantages in power that it now possesses. At the same time, this kind of building process can help the United States deal with responses by other countries that are tempted to see in the current U.S. position a need to seek ways of confounding U.S. advantages. Indeed, this movement toward finding ways of offsetting U.S. power and influence is already being seen, not just in countries such as Russia and China, but also among some friends and allies of the United States.

The virtues of seeking, with others, to build international institutions, practices, processes, and relationships that can endure have already been shown in the effort during the 1990s to recreate and adapt NATO to the challenges and opportunities of the 21st century. Within the Alliance, this has included an effort to engage a wide range of countries in Europe and the former Soviet Union in pursuit of an overarching security structure that can provide benefits for each country—at least those that see advantages in this cooperation. Thus, NATO has pursued five key goals: (1) to keep the United States permanently engaged on the Continent as a European power; (2) to preserve the best of its past, including the integrated military command structure; (3) to engage Central European states fully in the West; (4) to draw Russia productively out of a self-imposed isolation that has lasted more than 70 years; and (5) to stop actual and incipient conflict within Europe. To achieve these goals, the Allies have adopted a series of interlocking initiatives. In addition to its military activities in the Balkans, NATO has begun taking in new members while keeping the door open to others, launched the successful PFP program and accompanying Euro-Atlantic Partnership Council, negotiated a NATO-Russia Founding Act and NATO-Ukraine Charter, redesigned the Alliance command structure and strategy, and made room for the European allies to assume greater responsibilities for security, in terms of both structure and force contributions, through the EU European Security and Defense Policy. All of these efforts are bent upon testing whether it is possible to create a "Europe whole and free"—the first time in history when such an experiment could even be attempted.

As part of the broader purposes of building an institution that will command the support of as many Euro-Atlantic countries as possible, it has been critical that the redesigning of NATO, while carried out with a strong measure of U.S. leadership and essential engagement, has the support of all the NATO allies. Indeed, all can claim a share of the credit for creating this promising security structure and practice. At the same time, the way in which the Alliance is defining security extends far beyond the concept's military aspects and encompasses economic developments in parallel areas (under the leadership of the EU), a role for the EU Common Foreign and Security Policy and European Security and Defense Policy, the Council of Europe, the Organization for Security and Cooperation in Europe (OSCE), and the engagement of the private sector. While still a "work in progress" and subject to the requirements of political will and provision of adequate resources, this recasting of European security for the 21st century has prepared a framework that makes sense and that holds significant promise for dealing effectively not just with the interests and values of the several nations involved, but also with changes that are taking place within the rubric of globalization.

Of course, the possibilities in Europe for building international institutions, practices, processes, and relationships are not to be found in many other places around the world. Common interests and common values are not so similar in form and substance as to promote a duplication of the NATO experience elsewhere. Nevertheless, what has been learned in Europe during this past decade does validate propositions about integrating different instruments of power, planning for the long term, engaging different countries in looking for common interests, and applying the full range of techniques of strategic analysis. This, ultimately, is the way to balance the new requirements of a globalizing world with the classic dictates of power, purpose, and position in shaping the future.

Chapter 5

Stability, Stasis, and Change: A *Fragmegrating* World

James N. Rosenau

Can an unparalleled superpower committed to building a democratic world shake off a tendency to equate stability with stasis rather than with change? That is a central challenge facing the United States today. To meet the challenge, an elaborate and incisive conception of stability is required, one that joins the value and analytical dimensions of stability in such a way as to make it clear that *change is to stability and democracy as stasis is to disarray and authoritarian rule*. Only through change can democracies prosper, and only through stasis can the antidemocratic forces in the world sustain themselves and the disarray on which they thrive.[1]

It remains to be seen whether the United States has the wisdom and discipline to perceive, promote, and accept the necessary forms of stable change and to avoid seeking or preserving situations marked by stasis. Admittedly, in a rapidly changing world there is much that even an unparalleled superpower cannot accomplish; at the same time, there is little it can do if it lacks the conceptual equipment necessary to comprehend the transformations that are altering the course of events.

Setting the Stage

Although the nature of democracy is often articulated in crude and simplistic terms, its essential core is well understood and serves as the basis of a widespread consensus in American thought. This cannot be said about the degrees of understanding that surround notions of stability. Everyone favors it, but few pause to explicate how they know stable situations when they see them. What is the relationship between stability and change, between stability and order, between stability and stasis? Can there be stable change or unstable order? When are stable conditions acceptable, and when are they unacceptable?

Two reasons for the lack of attention to such questions stand out. One is that globalization is vastly increasing the number of variables that conduce to a stable, orderly, and desirable world. The other concerns the nature of global leadership. With

---

James N. Rosenau is university professor of international affairs at The George Washington University. He is the author of Turbulence in World Politics: A Theory of Change and Continuity *and* Along the Domestic-Foreign Frontier: Exploring Governance in a Turbulent World, *as well as the co-author of* Thinking Theory Thoroughly: Coherent Approaches to an Incoherent World.

its policymakers and publics conceiving of the United States as the world's only superpower, as responsible for and capable of controlling the course of events, this country is likely to be increasingly wedded to preserving stable situations and to presuming that any basic alteration in the structure of countries or situations abroad may lead to instability. Such an orientation is built into being a superpower, given that only through maintaining the prevailing global arrangements can its leadership endure. Under these circumstances, it is all too easy to take the concept of stability for granted and not be preoccupied with the need for a clear-cut conception of its constitutive elements under varying conditions.

Put differently, Americans are inclined to view threats to stability as likely anywhere, to equate global leadership with the maintenance of a stable world scene, and to be unsettled by rapid and profound change, even to see it as a threat to the country's well-being. To be sure, the United States is not unwaveringly committed to the status quo. As illustrated by recent policies toward the Middle East, Northern Ireland, and the former Yugoslavia, the United States is not averse to trying to change the arrangements prevailing in some countries or situations, but its rare efforts to alter the status quo are also cast as the obligations of superpower leadership, as actions designed to infuse an acceptable order into situations susceptible to collapsing into ever greater disarray. Such efforts are seen as promoting a more secure form of stability in place of one that violates basic democratic values or is marked by an absence of societal harmony. In other words, whether it promotes or prevents change in the name of stability, the United States tends to act without paying much, if any, conceptual attention to the dynamics that differentiate degrees and types of stability or to the long-term processes and conditions within and among societies that are likely to lessen or foster varying degrees and forms of stable change.

Viewed in this way, for example, it is not surprising that the United States failed to support the Shi'ites and Kurds toward the end of the Persian Gulf War on the grounds that a splintered Iraq would destabilize that region of the world. Likewise, the United States opposed independence for Kosovo on the grounds that stability in the Balkans would be that much harder to establish. Whatever their empirical accuracy, such presumptions are worrisome because they normally do not derive from an explicit conception of the underpinnings of stable situations, and they unknowingly tend to equate stability with order, even with stasis, thereby according it a higher status than any other values. But stability need not be the equivalent of either order or stasis. It is, rather, only one form of order, a dynamic form, and it surely is not stasis if by stasis is meant a standing still and the absence of change.

Given the potential for misreadings of policy situations based on an underdeveloped and complex concept, it is plainly time to return to the conceptual drawing board and unpack the concepts of stability, change, and order in the process of tracing the impact of globalization and the probable directions in which world affairs are headed. The task is not easy. One could fall back on equilibrium theory and extrapolate likely future trends, but such an approach seems too simple in the current milieu. There are just too many ambiguities and contradictions in the emergent epoch to proceed in the usual ways, especially as the contradictions and uncertainties are multiplying as the pace of change accelerates exponentially. If this is so, and if it is also the case that in many ways the course of events is out of control and possibly headed toward dire outcomes, then it is all the more important that a nuanced return to the drawing board be undertaken and that temptations to simplify the dynamics of stability and change be resisted. In short, it is necessary to ponder the links between stability and stasis, between change and continuity, between dynamics and inertia, between macro collectivities and micro individuals, and between globalizing and localizing forces.

Fragmegration

The most all-encompassing of these polarities involves the links between the globalizing and localizing dynamics that are propelling the course of events everywhere. My label for these interactions is *fragmegration*[2]—a contrived word designed to capture in a single phrase the fragmentation-integration, localization-globalization, and decentralization-centralization tensions so pervasive throughout the world that it can fairly be said the present age is not one of globalization, but one of fragmegration.[3] Just as it is fruitless to assess whether the chicken or the egg came first, it matters little whether globalizing forces have been the driving forces of history and localizing forces merely reactions to them, or vice versa. The point is that today, the two are inextricably linked.

More specifically, such a perspective treats the world as short on clear-cut boundaries that differentiate domestic and foreign affairs, with the result that local problems often become transnational in scope even as global challenges have repercussions for small communities.[4] Indeed, the multiplicity of opposites, of contradictions that promote tension, are so pervasive that one can discern fragmegrative dynamics in virtually any situation at every level, from the individual to the local community to the national state to the global system. Among the more conspicuous of these dynamics are the tensions between core and periphery, between national and transnational systems, between communitarianism and cosmopolitanism, between cultures and subcultures, between states and markets, between territory and cyberspace, between decentralization and centralization, between universalism and particularism, between flow and closure, between pace and space, between self and other, and between the distant and the proximate. Each of these tensions is marked by numerous variants; they take different forms in different parts of the world, in different countries, in different markets, in different communities, in different professions, and in different cyberspaces, with the result that there is enormous diversity in the way people experience the tensions that beset their lives.

In our heavily wired world, the integrating and fragmenting events usually occur simultaneously. Moreover, they often are causally related, with the causal links tending to cumulate and to generate a momentum such that integrative increments tend to give rise to disintegrative increments, and vice versa. This momentum highlights the pervasiveness of the interactive foundations of the diverse tensions. The simultaneity of the good and the bad, the integrative and the disintegrative, and the coherent and the incoherent lies at the heart of global affairs today. As one analyst puts it, ". . . the distinction between the global and the local is becoming very complex and problematic."[5]

Nor have the contradictions of the emergent epoch escaped the attention of publics. With the fragmenting forces of localization and the integrating dynamics of globalization so interwoven as to be products of each other, people have become increasingly aware of how fragmegration has intensified old identities and fostered new ones. However they may articulate their understanding, individuals everywhere have come to expect that the advance of globalization poses threats to longstanding local and national ties, that some groups will contest, even violently fight, the intrusion of global norms even as others will seek to obtain goods, larger market shares, or generalized support beyond their communities.

The forces of fragmentation are rooted in the psychic comfort people derive from the familiar, close-at-hand values and practices of their neighborhoods, just as the forces of integration stem from people's aspirations to benefit from the distant products of the global economy, to realize the efficiencies of regional unity, to counter environmental degradation, to achieve coherent communities through policies of inclusion that expand their democratic institutions, and to acknowledge the meaning of the pictures taken in outer space that depict the Earth as a solitary entity in a huge universe. In the succinct words of one astute observer, "There is a constant struggle between the collectivist and individualist elements within each human."[6]

Like stability, the concepts of integration and fragmentation are not as self-evident as may seem to be the case at first glance. Most notably, a distinction needs to be drawn that allows for the many situations in which actions foster both the integration of a system and the fragmentation of its subsystems, and vice versa. When integration occurs at both levels, it can be regarded as "progress-enhancing integration," whereas "strife-enhancing integration" marks those situations when integration occurs at only one of the levels while the other undergoes fragmentation. The former is illustrated by the European Union and its subsidiary principle that facilitates Union-wide integration while at the same time enabling individual countries to maintain their own practices and authority when necessary. On the other hand, strife-enhancing integration was evident in the recent Austrian elections, which resulted in divisiveness for the country even as it solidified the victorious parties. Similarly, the Cold War was integrative for each of the two warring coalitions even as it intensified the antagonisms between them. Lastly, in "strife-enhancing fragmentation," both a system and its subsystems undergo fragmentation.[7] A good example is the prolonged and intense conflict in Northern Ireland, which fostered fragmentation as well as dissension within its Catholic and Protestant factions.

Stability

Given pervasive contradictions, tensions, and ambiguities at every level of community, the need to sort through and rethink the concept of stability as it pertains to world affairs is compelling. The puzzles are numerous: How is stability distinguishable from order? What conditions obtain when individuals, communities, organizations, states, regions, and the global system are judged to be stable or unstable? Does instability set in as some of the authority of nation-states undergoes disaggregation upward to transnational entities, sideward to social movements and nongovernmental organizations (NGOs), and downward to subnational entities? Can the concepts of stability and instability be framed in such a way that they can be applied to individuals as well as to collectivities, and, if so, is stability at the micro level of individuals a prerequisite for stability at the macro level of collectivities, and vice versa?

It is important to recognize, first, that most of the time both individuals and collectivities undergo change. The pace at which change occurs—such as the degree of aging and the extent of movement toward or away from goals—can vary considerably, from infinitesimal to incremental to abrupt. Second, it follows that stability is a form of change and that what counts is whether the change is acceptable or unacceptable and whether it contributes to or detracts from the system's coherence and capacity to endure.

It follows that it is possible to distinguish between two dimensions of stability. One is its value dimension, which involves the degree to which the prevailing stability or instability is judged to be acceptable. The other is its analytical dimension, by which is meant the extent to which the prevailing stability or instability is assessed to be marked by systemic coherence, by being able to persist through time more or less intact (that is, to be sufficiently coherent to overcome internal conflicts such that goals can be framed, decisions made, and policies implemented). The distinction between the two dimensions is not easily sustained, however. Perhaps as often as not, the two dimensions are at odds, thus making it all too easy to confound—to shift unknowingly back and forth between—them when assessing situations from a liberal democratic perspective. Not infrequently, for example, a coherent system lacking in basic democratic practices has been treated as acceptable, just as a democratic system on the brink of collapse has been regarded as unacceptable, with the former then being assessed as a desirable order and the latter as a noxious disorder. The readiness of the United States to support authoritarian systems during the Cold War is illustrative of how undemocratic systems can be viewed as acceptable, and the current U.S. concern about the potential for civil war in Colombia exemplifies how a certain type of democratic system can be seen as a noxious and unacceptable disorder.

In other words, sustaining the analytical-value distinction is difficult because order and stability overlap and because they are both value-laden and analytical concepts. Order refers to the conditions and structural arrangements that prevail in any situation at a given time, and these conditions can be either stable or unstable, depending on the values of those who assess them. One observer's stable order may be another's unstable disorder in the sense that what may be judged to be a disorderly system is nonetheless founded on a set of underlying structural arrangements that shape how its people and collectivities interact with each other, even if impulse and violence mark their interactions. Treating disorder as a form of order in this way serves to limit the overlap by holding constant the value problem associated with the concept of order.[8] It facilitates conceiving of stability and instability as subcategories of order, thereby reducing the value problem to the distinction between degrees of acceptable stability and unacceptable instability.

This remaining value problem, however, is no small challenge. Although detached analytical criteria for delineating between stable and unstable systems can be developed in terms of their capacity to remain coherent and durable, the criteria are bound to derive from values that shape what is viewed as acceptable or unacceptable in any situation. Here the value foundations are conceived to consist of two clusters that may or may not be mutually reinforcing. As indicated earlier, one cluster is composed of the various values associated with the premises and processes of liberal democracies, while the other is comprised of the values linked to system coherence that allow for movement toward goals. In what follows, "acceptable stability" is viewed as characterizing coherent systems that protect or promote democratic procedures, while "unacceptable stability" or "instability" is judged to prevail when a system does not promote democratic practices and is unable to sustain its coherence without relying on high degrees of coercion.

There are two difficulties here, however. One, the question of whose judgment of acceptability is involved, is the easier to resolve. The other, by contrast, is endlessly perplexing and probably not subject to a satisfactory resolution. This is the problem of how to assess acceptability when analyzing situations either where systemic coherence and undemocratic procedures are judged to prevail or where democratic processes are judged to be operative in deteriorating systems that are increasingly short on coherence. Other things being equal, the resolution of these dilemmas may be to treat democratic practices as more acceptable than systemic coherence when a choice between the two cannot be avoided.

The 1999 situations in Pakistan and East Timor are illustrative in this regard. In the former case, a corrupt and deteriorating democratic system was overthrown by a military coup that initially appeared to have substantially reduced disarray and restored a goodly measure of systemic coherence acceptable to many Pakistanis. But was this an acceptable or unacceptable stability? My answer reflects the inapplicability of a hard-and-fast rule: in the very short term, the coup appeared to have laid the foundation for a return to a more effective democracy, but in the long term, or even the medium term, stability in Pakistan requires the reestablishment of democratic procedures. The longer military rule prevails in the country, in other words, the more are the prevailing arrangements judged to be an unacceptable form of stability, a conclusion that is consistent with the positions voiced by U.S. foreign policy officials at the time and shared soon thereafter by the people of Pakistan.[9] In the case of East Timor, on the other hand, not even a brief period of systemic coherence followed the electoral coup. Coherence had been maintained by Indonesia, and East Timor collapsed into sheer disarray when its public successfully demanded independence. From a liberal democratic perspective, both the pre- and the post-independence arrangements in East Timor were unacceptable, which is why members of the United Nations (UN) Security Council felt compelled to authorize UN forces to take over the duties of governance in the situation.

These examples highlight the question of whose criteria are employed when judgments of acceptability are applied to systems or situations. It is misleading to infer from the U.S. and UN assessments in the Pakistan and East Timor cases that the only criteria of acceptability that count are those employed by the actors making such judgments, be they officials in the public domain, observers in the private world, or the top echelons of the U.S. military. For in both the U.S. and UN policy establishments—not to mention those elsewhere in the world and among military officers as well—there are officials and observers who rely on different sets of priorities and arrive at different syntheses.

How, then, to answer the acceptable-to-whom question in using the concept of acceptability as a measure of stability? Given the absence of a consensus in particular circumstances, the answer lies with the individuals making the stability assessments or, in the case of collective agencies such as governments, in the official policies pursued or advocated by the interested parties. A situation may provoke divided assessments within an agency, and these divisions can be duly noted; however, what counts is whose criteria ultimately prevail in judging its acceptability.

In sum, my guidelines for differentiating between stable and unstable situations in world affairs involve both an analytical and a value dimension, with the former focusing on degrees of systemic coherence and the latter focusing on degrees of acceptability. Figure 1 presents a 2×2 matrix that highlights this distinction between these two dimensions. The entries in the cells are examples drawn from my own values and analytical judgments about contemporary systems or situations. Assuming the distinctions between high and low system coherence and between acceptable and unacceptable situations are adequately operationalized (a task not undertaken here), any policies of governments or assessments of observers can be readily classified in one of the cells, thus providing a first cut at locating what are considered to be the stable and unstable features of the world scene. Second and third cuts are suggested below by identifying four structures of stability and four paces at which situations may or may not change.

Figure 1. Stability along Two Dimensions

		VALUE DIMENSION	
		Acceptable	**Unacceptable**
ANALYTICAL DIMENSION	**High System Coherence**	–Chinese reforms –European Union	–Burma –North Korea
	Low System Coherence	–Indonesia –Russia	–Kosovo –Apartheid in South Africa

The four structures of stability are conceived to consist of those that develop at the level of individuals (micro stability), those that prevail within collectivities (macro stability), those that persist among both individuals and collectivities (micro-macro stability), and those that operate among collectivities (macro-macro stability). All four structures have a common quality. All are based on the premise that stability consists of acceptable change, with change being conceived as alterations between two points in time and with acceptable change being viewed as any alterations that are not characterized by low system coherence and do not generate widespread efforts to resist, prevent, or undo them.

It is here where complexity and nuance become central: distinctions have to be drawn between the priorities that are attached to the analytical and value dimensions of change by each stability structure. Most notably, different consequences can follow when change is differentially accepted at the micro level on the one hand and the other three levels on the other hand. More often than not, the perception of unacceptable change at the micro level will not be matched by a similar perception among ruling elites and governments at the macro and macro-macro levels because the latter tend to accord higher priority to systemic coherence than to the value dimension of stability. Only when micro-macro structures become operative and sizable publics press their values on governments—as was the case with apartheid in South Africa or with Elián González, the Cuban 6-year-old rescued at sea—does a prevailing situation become defined as both a threat to systemic coherence and an unacceptable situation in terms of values. In most situations, publics are uninterested in or oblivious to the acceptability of distant situations and thus do not become preoccupied with change and stability elsewhere in the world. But at least some elites and government agencies are charged with being sensitive to low-system coherence abroad and thus may be quick to perceive unacceptable stability. From the superpower perspective of U.S. officials, for example, the world is pervaded with numerous situations that appear susceptible to undermining national security and call for efforts to resist, prevent, or undo them.

It follows that whatever may be the pace of change, global stability prevails as long as the change is widely acceptable at the micro level of individuals, the macro level of collectivities and their leaders, and the macro-macro level of other collectivities. It is here where complexity and nuance again become pivotal. Global stability is rare because only infrequently are any of the rates of change acceptable to most actors at every level. The advent of global television exemplifies an abrupt change that did not undermine global stability because it was widely accepted by people and collectivities everywhere. On the other hand, the abrupt changes that accompany successful revolutions or invasions are likely to be widely accepted at the micro level of the revolutionaries and invaders and the macro level of their collectivities, but at the same time such changes will foster macro-macro instability if other countries view the revolution or invasion as a threat to systemic coherence and undertake to reverse it. Likewise, infinitesimal or incremental economic growth will be acceptable to those with vested interests in the growth at micro and macro levels, but such change is likely to be unacceptable to the poor (and their spokespersons), who do not participate in the processes of growth. In addition, the more infinitesimal change borders on the absence of change (as may be the case in highly authoritarian regimes that prevent change), and stasis can be said to prevail—although in all likelihood it will not prevail for long because in the emergent epoch, stasis runs against the grain of individuals, who will become restless and aspire to at least a modicum of change the more the stasis persists and the less responsive are their society's institutions.

Although no effort is made here to operationalize clear-cut measures for differentiating infinitesimal, incremental, and abrupt change, the distinctions are hardly trivial. *Infinitesimal* change is just barely noticeable. It is rooted in the tendencies of collectivities toward inertia and of individuals toward habit, with the result that a high degree of certainty will prevail wherever and whenever infinitesimal change is occurring. Infinitesimal change is also likely to be accompanied by a resistance to the acceleration of change and thus amounts to a form of stability that is marked by inequalities, exploitation, and the absence of meaningful progress. *Incremental* change, on the other hand, involves steady and discernible movement toward the goals of individuals and collectivities. The more incremental the change, the less will be the uncertainty and the greater will be the stability of people and collectivities. *Abrupt* change is sharp, extensive, and subject to volatile shifts in direction. Consequently, the more abrupt and explosive the changes, the more will people and collectivities experience uncertainty over the likelihood of high systemic coherence and thus the less acceptable will be such changes. In short, it is possible to conceive of a stability-instability continuum on which the location of individuals and collectivities is defined by the degree to which acceptable or unacceptable change is fostered in their daily routines.

Given this linking of stability to change, it is clear that stability exists when most individuals accept, either by explicitly welcoming or implicitly acknowledging, that progress and movement toward goals are occurring without also fostering low system coherence. On the contrary, instability exists when any changes unfold in the opposite direction, when most persons resist or reject the goals being sought and perceive a decline of high system coherence. The locales in a collectivity, a region, or the world that are stable and those that are unstable are determined by applying the same criteria. Variability along these lines, of course, is the norm in world affairs.

Table 1 permits an elaboration on the value and analytical dimensions of stability. Employing the value and system coherence criteria to assess acceptable or unacceptable systems or situations on the current world scene, table 1 makes clear that, irrespective of the pace of change or the structure of stability, some situations are acceptable and some are not, depending on the value and analytical perspectives that different observers bring to bear. Change is considered noxious when it is perceived as undermining the well-being of people and/or the coherence of their collectivities by perpetuating poverty, racial prejudice, and a host of other injustices at the individual level or by jeopardizing systemic coherence at the collective level. In this sense, the processes that sustain some stable macro structures ought to be rendered unstable from a value perspective. (South Africa under apartheid comes quickly to mind.) Likewise, if change involves movement in noxious directions (for example, the advent of authoritarian regimes or the collapse of economies), there is reason for concern.

On the other hand, change is beneficial and acceptable when it enlarges the well-being and competence of individuals and communities, thereby leading to the improvement of the human condition and to higher system coherence. Viewed in this way, neither unstable nor uncertain situations need be feared by policymakers if they involve steady movement toward goals marked by fluctuations within an acceptable range. In short, as indicated earlier, change can be a dynamic form of stability or instability, one that allows for progress on the part of communities and their members or for a deterioration of their circumstances. Table 1 suggests that under certain conditions even stasis may be acceptable, although it can also serve as a bulwark against change that might lead to even more satisfying conditions.

Table 1. Stability and Instability in World Affairs: Examples from the 1990s

Pace of Change		*Stability Structure*			
		Micro	*Macro*	*Macro–Macro*	*Micro–Macro*
Stasis	U	Vigilantes	North Korea	Arms trade	Burma
Infinitesimal change	A	Patriotism	Japanese culture	U.S.–British relations	Post-war Bosnia
	U	Drug consumption	Colombia	Middle East decline of populations	Northern Ireland
	A	Decline of AIDS	Iran		Human rights
Incremental change	U	Rich–poor gap	Russia	UN financing	Afghanistan
	A	Emergence of Chinese middle class	Spread of democracy	International election monitoring	European Union
Abrupt change	U	Flight of refugees	East Timor	Nuclear proliferation	Asian financial crisis
	A	Fall of the Berlin Wall	Collapse of the Soviet Union	End of Cold War	End of Apartheid in South Africa

Key: A, acceptable; U, unacceptable.

On the other hand, change is beneficial and acceptable when it enlarges the well-being and competence of individuals and communities, thereby leading to the improvement of the human condition and to higher system coherence. Viewed in this way, neither unstable nor uncertain situations need be feared by policymakers if they involve steady movement toward goals marked by fluctuations within an acceptable range. In short, as indicated earlier, change can be a dynamic form of stability or instability, one that allows for progress on the part of communities and their members or for a deterioration of their circumstances. Table 1 suggests that under certain conditions even stasis may be acceptable, although it can also serve as a bulwark against change that might lead to even more satisfying conditions.

Also implied in the foregoing discussion is the large degree to which stability and change are part and parcel of the close links between collectivities at the macro level and individuals at the micro level. Exceptions aside, these links are often symmetrical in the sense that changes at one level can generate comparable changes at other levels. Cases of abrupt change are most conspicuous in this regard: the instability that accompanies unacceptable abrupt change at one level is likely to precipitate parallel changes at other levels. Iraq's abrupt invasion of Kuwait in 1990, for example, disrupted the prevailing macro-macro stability and generated abrupt macro change on the part of the countries that joined to form the 32-nation coalition to reverse the situation. Similarly, incremental and progressive change at one level is likely to be matched by acceptable change at other levels, as is illustrated by, say, those situations in which close links are established between domestic publics and governmental policies over environmental regulations. In general, therefore, it is reasonable to presume that comparable and symmetrical degrees of change and stability among collectivities and people go hand in hand, each reinforcing the other.

There are, however, important exceptions to this rule. As previously noted, the most conspicuous asymmetry occurs when individuals at the micro level are oblivious to or unconcerned about distant situations even as their governments may nevertheless perceive some of them as threatening a diminution of system coherence and act to prevent further deterioration. Similarly, incremental micro changes can, on occasion, foster abrupt macro changes. For instance, one analyst who studied the micro level in the United States over three decades "finally" found that

> . . . societies learn and react differently than individuals. Surprisingly, social learning is often far more abrupt than individual learning. It is more extreme. It is less incremental . . . [A] typical pattern of social change starts with a sharp lurch in the opposite direction which is then followed by a complex series of modifications based on trial and error learning. . . . We have found that two factors usually precipitate such lurches: a change in circumstances and a lack of responsiveness to the change on the part of institutions.[10]

Fragmegrative Sources of Stability and Change

One way to portray the sources and consequences of fragmegration succinctly is to note four flows of influence that shape the underpinnings of fragmegrative changes and tensions: (1) a technological revolution has facilitated the rapid flow of ideas, information, pictures, and money across continents; (2) a transportation revolution has hastened the boundary-spanning flow of elites, ordinary folk, and whole populations; (3) an organizational revolution has shifted the flow of authority, influence, and power beyond traditional boundaries; and (4) an economic revolution has redirected the flow of goods, services, capital, and ownership among countries. Taken together, these flows have fostered a cumulative process that is both the source and consequence of eroding boundaries, integrating regions, proliferating networks, diminishing territorial attachments, coalescing social movements, weakening states, contracting sovereignty, dispersing authority, demanding publics, and expanding citizen skills—all of which also serve to generate counterreactions intended to contest, contain, or reverse the multiple flows and thereby preserve communities and reduce inequities. While each of these sources is powerful, none of them can be listed as primary. They are all interactive, and each reinforces the others. None is sufficient, but all are necessary to sustain the age of fragmegration.

Among the substantial number and variety of sources that sustain fragmegrative processes and flows, eight are especially noteworthy inasmuch as they serve to illustrate the ways in which the structures of stability are shaped by the dynamics of fragmegration (table 2). One of these sources consists of "the skill revolution," wherein people everywhere are increasingly able to construct scenarios that trace the course of distant events back into their homes and pocketbooks.[11] A second source involves the large degree to which collectivities around the world are undergoing authority crises, by which is meant the paralysis and stalemates that prevent them from framing and moving toward their goals.[12] A third focuses on the bifurcation of global structures whereby the long-standing state-centric world now has a rival in an emergent multicentric world of diverse actors such as ethnic minorities, NGOs, professional societies, transnational corporations, and the many other types of private collectivities that now crowd the global stage.[13] A fourth is the "organizational explosion" that has witnessed a huge proliferation of associations and networks at every level of community.[14] A fifth is the "mobility upheaval," by which is meant the vast and ever-growing movement of people around the world, a movement that includes everyone from the tourist to the terrorist and from the jet-setter to the immigrant.[15] A sixth consists of the many microelectronic and transportation technologies that have collapsed time and space.[16] A seventh involves the complex processes through which territoriality, states, and sovereignty have weakened to the point where it can be reasonably asserted that landscapes have been supplemented—and in some cases replaced—by mediascapes, financescapes, technoscapes, ethnoscapes, and ideoscapes.[17] An eighth concerns the large degree to which national economies have been globalized.[18]

Unstable Responses to Fragmegrative Tensions

The enormous analytical challenge posed by how these eight major dynamics (and the many others that could be identified) interactively generate and sustain fragmegration is suggested in table 2. The rows of the table list the eight dynamics, and the entries in the cells indicate the diverse ways in which the sources of fragmegration can significantly shape the four structures of stability listed in table 1. In some instances, their impact fosters further integration; in other instances, they add to the processes of fragmentation. Indeed, although not easily depicted in the table, each of the dynamics is likely to have both integrating and fragmenting consequences. For present purposes, however, table 2 serves to make clear that the obstacles to stable change are considerable and that each of the structures of stability is vulnerable to a variety of undermining influences. Stated differently, unstable situations around the world that portend low system coherence or are otherwise unacceptable are in large part a consequence of the dynamics whereby ordinary folk, elites, collectivities, and global structures respond to and sustain the conflicting pressures in global and local directions. More than that, in often subtle and circuitous ways, the stability at each level of aggregation is affected by the ways in which actors at the other levels cope with fragmegrative tensions.

Micro Actors: Ordinary Folk

Table 2 also makes clear that people at the micro level—citizens and aliens, consumers and investors, migrants and workers, rural peasants and computer technicians, the poor and the wealthy—are under assault by fragmegrative dynamics. For some, the assault is destabilizing in the sense that longstanding habits and affiliations are challenged; for others, it has beneficial consequences in the sense that their enhanced skills enable them to form and to join organizations, to shoulder new responsibilities, and to aspire to new accomplishments. In other words, many subtleties accompany the impact of fragmegrative dynamics at the micro level. None of them has singularly stabilizing or destabilizing consequences, but all of them can serve both to promote and to undermine the stability of the lives and routines of ordinary people. For our purposes, then, it is useful to identify the ways in which the dynamics of the emergent epoch may foster abrupt or incremental changes at the micro level that are sufficiently widespread to feed into the behavior of collectivities at the macro and macro-macro levels. Every individual everywhere probably experiences one or more consequences of the clash between globalizing and localizing forces, but these consequences become meaningful only in terms of micro instabilities that cumulate and result in collective unease or action to which policymakers must attend.

Perhaps the most destabilizing consequences of fragmegration at the micro level that can cumulate into a powerful collective force are the insecurities that stem from the many rapid and bewildering transformations engendered by fragmegrative dynamics. With their worlds turned upside-down by the multiple flows of ideas, goods, people, crime, drugs, and pollution that are part and parcel of the emergent epoch, numerous people experience an uprooting of their daily routines. They feel lost and threatened by the changes that accompany a global economy and a collapse of time and space. Often, they cope with this sense of loss by seeking comfort through religion, by joining labor unions, by supporting protest organizations, by clinging ever more fervently to local mores and norms, and by a host of other means of valuing the local and rejecting the global. When such reactions and fears are aggregated into collective action through the mobilizing efforts of elites, they result in abrupt changes that can roil societies and become salient pockets of instability on the world stage. The Iranian revolution of 1979 is an example of this potential for instability, as are secession movements in the former Soviet Union, Indonesia, and elsewhere. In such cases, support at the micro level of mass publics can be abruptly generated by leaders who, for various reasons and by means of diverse techniques, are able to tap into people's need for a sense of belonging. Given an epoch marked by a skill revolution, an organizational explosion, and weakened states, it is hardly surprising that micro-macro dynamics underlie a rapid proliferation of secessionist movements that, from a U.S. perspective, loom as serious pockets of instability.

Table 2. Stability and Instability in World Affairs: Examples from the 1990s

Consequences of Fragmegration	*Stability Structures*			
	Micro	*Macro*	*Macro-Macro*	*Micro-Macro*
Skill Revolution	Expands people's horizons on a global scale; sensitizes them to new meanings of security; facilitates a reversion to local concerns.	Enlarges the capacity of government agencies to think "out of the box" and analyze security challenges.	Multiplies quantity and enhances quality of links among states; solidifies their alliances and enmities.	Constrains security policies through increased capacity of individuals to know when, where, and how to engage in collective action.
Authority Crises	Redirect loyalties; encourage individuals to replace traditional criteria of legitimacy with performance criteria.	Weaken ability of governments and other organizations to frame and implement policies.	Enlarge the competence of some International Government Organizations and NGOs; stall diplomatic negotiations.	Facilitate the capacity of publics to press and/or paralyze their governments, the World Trade Organization, and other organizations.
Bifurcation of Global Structures	Adds to role conflicts, divides loyalties, and foments tensions among individuals; encourages local preoccupations.	Facilitates formation and consolidation of collectivities in the multicentric world.	Generates institutional arrangements for cooperation on major global issues such as trade and the environment.	Provides opportunities for special interests to pursue influence through diverse channels.
Organizational Explosion	Facilitates multiple identities, subgroupism, and affiliation with transnational advocacy networks.	Enables opposition groups to form and press for altered policies; divides publics from their elites.	Renders the global stage ever more transnational and dense with nongovernment actors.	Contributes to the pluralism of authority; heightens the probability of authority crises.

Table 2. Stability and Instability in World Affairs: Examples from the 1990s (continued)

Consequences of Fragmegration	*Stability Structures*			
	Micro	*Macro*	*Macro-Macro*	*Micro-Macro*
Mobility Upheaval	Provides people with more extensive contacts with foreign cultures; contributes to both hate of and fondness for the United States.	Enlarges the size and relevance of subcultures and ethnic conflicts as people seek new opportunities abroad.	Heightens need for international cooperation to control the flow of drugs, money, and terrorists.	Increases movement across borders that lessens capacity of governments to control national boundaries.
Microelectronic Technologies	Enable like-minded people anywhere in the world to be in touch with each other.	Empower governments to mobilize support; render their secrets vulnerable to spying.	Accelerate diplomatic processes; facilitate electronic surveillance and intelligence work.	Constrain governments by enabling opposition groups to mobilize more effectively.
Weakening of Territoriality, States, and Sovereignty	Undermines national loyalties and increases distrust of governments and other institutions.	Adds to the porosity of national boundaries and the difficulty of formulating national policies.	Increases need for interstate cooperation on global issues; lessens control over cascading events.	Lessens confidence in governments; renders a nationwide consensus difficult to achieve and maintain.
339	Swells ranks of consumers; promotes uniform tastes; heightens anxiety about jobs.	Complicates tasks of state governments vis-à-vis markets; promotes business alliances.	Intensifies trade and investment conflicts; generates incentives for building global financial institutions.	Increases efforts to protect local cultures and industries; facilitates vigor of protest movements.

Abrupt changes at the micro level are not always the result of gifted leaders or demagogues. Sometimes circumstances evolve in such a way that multitudes of individuals react abruptly in the same way without prior provocation by their leaders and, in so doing, create as much instability at the macro level as is the case when publics are mobilized. The sudden flight of refugees responding to a shared fear of pending aggression is a frequent instance of unstable situations that evolve swiftly out of uncoordinated micro actions. A sharp collapse of a currency or stock market is another case in point. As investors and traders interpret new economic data as portending problems ahead, so will their separate acts of withdrawing investments, selling stock, or trading currencies conduce to macro instabilities.

The aggregation of individuals in the absence of mobilization by leaders does not always result in abrupt change. Often the aggregation occurs incrementally, as more and more people are induced to move in the same direction with the passage of time. When fearful reactions spread widely through incremental change that eventually cumulates to the point where large numbers of people are in distress and thus potentially prepared for mobilization, they may well evoke responses from their government at the macro level that, in turn, create an unstable situation. The Falun Gong movement in China is a recent instance of incremental and spontaneous micro aggregation in response to a perceived need for spiritual guidance to cope with the complexities of globalization that gave rise to an unstable situation. As Chinese leaders came to view the movement as a threat to their party's rule and their country's stability, they clamped down on it and fulfilled their own prophecy of instability. Much the same can be said about the massacre at Tiananmen Square in 1989. It, too, was precipitated by uncoordinated individual actions that ultimately cumulated in a mass movement that macro leaders felt obliged to suppress.

In sum, there are many routes through which developments can be unacceptable at the micro level of individuals and thus generate unstable macro or macro-macro circumstances. Indeed, it can reasonably be anticipated that in the present era, the unease fostered by globalizing dynamics, combined with the skill revolution and the organizational explosion, will increase the prospects for collective action and generate an ever greater number of diverse situations marked by instability. This conclusion renders ever more difficult the task of policymakers charged with being sensitive to patterns that can get out of hand and foster low system coherence elsewhere in the world. It means that their analytical antennae must be as geared to the grassroots as to the more easily comprehended threats that may evolve at the macro level of governments and societies.

Micro Actors: Elites

Although elites—politicians, business executives, labor leaders, NGO heads, journalists, intellectuals, entertainers, sports stars, and those in many other fields of endeavor—could be considered macro actors inasmuch as they normally speak and act on behalf of the concerns of macro collectivities, they are best regarded as individuals with aspirations, fears, and commitments that are responsive to fragmegrative dynamics. As elites, cosmopolitans, or symbolic analysts (as they are sometimes called), they are the individuals who form and sustain the micro-macro links and thus need to be separately assessed. It is they who sustain and often initiate the processes whereby authority undergoes disaggregation and change, who worry about the stability of situations, who calculate whether events are tending toward low system maintenance, and who seek to guide or to mobilize ordinary folk in directions derived from their values and leadership roles. Their worries, calculations, and leadership may be sound or inaccurate, appropriate or inappropriate, constructive or counterproductive, sufficient or inadequate, but in any event, their actions substantially shape the course of world affairs.

Surprisingly, very little systematic knowledge is available about the activities, orientations, affiliations, and loyalties of the elites on the cutting edge of globalization and fragmegration. As indicated by the quotations listed later, it is easy to gather numerous seemingly astute observations about what is transpiring in elite circles, but all such commentaries are essentially impressionistic.[19] Investigators have yet to undertake the extensive systematic surveys of cosmopolitans who straddle the globalizing-localizing divide comparable to those of national elites that were compiled in earlier eras. It would be helpful, for example, if systematic studies of those who attend the annual World Economic Forum in Davos, Switzerland, or of the 25,986 persons from 37 countries who flew at least 100,000 miles on United Airlines in 1995 were conducted,[20] but efforts to raise funds for such studies have been unsuccessful, and thus one has to fall back on undocumented, varied, and contradictory (but often not implausible) impressions.[21]

One recurring theme in these impressionistic commentaries stands out as highly relevant to fragmegrative dynamics if it turns out to be supported by systematic data. It is that many elites supportive of globalizing processes may be increasingly cut off from the larger societies in which they live and work. Their global networks and responsibilities appear to be weakening their ties to their home communities and their countries, leading them to reside in gated enclaves when they return to their families, to give resources to transnational organizations rather than local charities, and to see themselves as jet-setters whose field of play is global rather than national or local in scope. Consequently, they see themselves either as citizens of the world or, perhaps more frequently, as lacking any meaningful citizenship. Some observers contend that in particular subsets of leaders, an insulated subculture may be evolving that is new, consequential, and—most important—apart from any extant cultures. An example of speculation along these lines is plainly evident in this interpretation of a particular subculture that may be developing among leaders who attend the annual meetings of the World Economic Forum:

> Participants in this culture know how to deal with computers, cellular phones, airline schedules, currency exchange, and the like. But they also dress alike, exhibit the same amicable informality, relieve tensions by similar attempts at humor, and of course most of them interact in English. Since most of these cultural traits are of Western (and mostly American) provenance, individuals coming from different backgrounds must go through a process of socialization that will allow them to engage in this behavior with seemingly effortless spontaneity. . . . But it would be a mistake to think that the "Davos culture" operates only in the offices, boardrooms, and hotel

> suites in which international business is transacted. It carries over into the lifestyles and presumably also the values of those who participate in it. Thus, for example, the frenetic pace of contemporary business is carried over into the leisure activities and the family life of business people. There is a yuppie style in the corporation, but also in the body-building studio and in the bedroom. And notions of costs, benefits, and maximization spill over from work into private life. The "Davos culture" is a culture of the elite and . . . of those aspiring to join the elite. Its principal social location is in the business world, but since elites intermingle, it also affects at least the political elites. There is, as it were, a yuppie internationale.[22]

Assuming there is more than a little truth in the notion of global elite subcultures, what might be the consequences insofar as the stability of the situations that mark the world scene at any moment in time? One obvious answer is that such subcultures might serve to disrupt, distort, attenuate, or otherwise intrude upon micro-macro interactions, thus adding to the instability of situations where unease is widespread among ordinary folk. Some analysts are deeply troubled by this possibility, even though they do not cast it as a source of potential instability:

> Without national attachments . . . people have little inclination to make sacrifices or to accept responsibility for their actions. . . . The new elites are at home only in transit, en route to a high-level conference, to the grand opening of a new franchise, to an international film festival, or to an undiscovered resort. Theirs is essentially a tourist's view of the world—not a perspective likely to encourage a passionate devotion to democracy. . . . To an alarming extent the privileged classes . . . have made themselves independent not only of crumbling industrial cities but [also] of public services in general. . . . In effect, they have removed themselves from the common life. . . . Many of them have ceased to think of themselves as Americans in any important sense, implicated in America's destiny for better or worse. Their ties to an international culture of work and leisure . . . make many of them deeply indifferent to the prospect of American national decline.[23]

> But will the cosmopolitan with a global perspective choose to act fairly and compassionately? Will our current and future symbolic analysts—lacking any special sense of responsibility toward a particular nation and its citizens—share their wealth with the less fortunate of the world and devote their resources and energies to improving the chances that others may contribute to the world's wealth? Here we find the darker side of cosmopolitanism. For without strong attachments and loyalties extending beyond family and friends, symbolic analysts may never develop the habits and attitudes of social responsibility. They will be world citizens, but without accepting or even acknowledging any of the obligations that citizenship in a polity normally implies.[24]

> . . . a new breed of men and women for whom religion, culture, and ethnic nationality are marginal elements in a working identity . . . the word foreign has no meaning to the ambitious global businessperson. . . . How can the physical distinction between domestic and foreign have any resonance in a

> virtual world defined by electronic communications and intrinsically unbounded markets?[25]

If such commentaries are accurate, large segments of the world's leadership may not be sufficiently involved in the processes of globalization to be sensitive to all the potential ways in which unstable situations can evolve. On the other hand, there is also a segment of elites that is aware of the negative consequences of a globalizing world and thus inclined to champion localizing dynamics. The latter may not be as numerous or powerful as the former, but as indicated by the protests in Seattle during the World Trade Organization (WTO) meeting in December 1999, their ranks are large enough to prevent a worldwide consensus on the virtues of globalization. Presumably, fragmegrative dynamics are just as operative in elite circles as they are at every other level of aggregation.

The Maintenance and Coherence of Collectivities

The prime task of those who analyze such matters as system coherence is one of trying to comprehend the factors that enable systems to get from one day, week, month, and year to the next. This task can be restated as one of understanding how and why so many of the stable situations in the world persist. Such a perspective inhibits analysts from focusing exclusively on instabilities and thus does not provide a baseline for assessing when situations might deteriorate. It facilitates grasping when and where instability is likely to set in by compelling analysts to be sensitive to factors that can undermine high-maintenance systems. It suggests that analysts should be just as attentive to the stable as to the unstable circumstances that sustain the course of events.

The previous enumeration of the sources of fragmegration indicates where analytical antennae should be focused in the vast complexity that constitutes the global scene. Clearly, the skill revolution, the organizational explosion, and the mobility upheaval have heightened the probabilities of micro-macro processes moving systems closer to the edge of collapse. That is, the enhanced skills of people and the proliferation of organizations through which they can channel their enlarged talents, along with the deterritorialization that has accompanied their wide movement around the world, are likely to generate and intensify ever greater numbers of authority crises. Whatever the nature of the dynamics that sustain ethnic sensitivities, religious fervor, and independence movements, or that otherwise lead to the spread of multicultural societies, and quite apart from the virtues of multicultural arrangements, it is reasonable to speculate that more and more communities will be wracked by divisiveness and efforts to decentralize authority. As many extant situations today demonstrate, the intensification of subgroupism and the relocation of authority tend to weaken states and their capacity to maintain high levels of systemic coherence.

Our analytical antennae also need to be attentive to those fragmegrative dynamics that serve to reinforce and deepen the coherence of other situations. Against the factors that may eat away at the maintenance of collectivities are the adaptive ways in which authority is being transferred upward, downward, and sideward out of the state-centric world and relocated in new spheres of authority (SOAs) throughout the multicentric world. In effect, the SOAs serve as mechanisms for constructively absorbing the dynamics of fragmegration. The dialectical process embedded in fragmegration may in the long run give rise to new forms of political authority—that the syntheses emanating from globalizing forces as theses and localizing forces as antitheses may well be new social contracts that govern the SOAs to which decentralizing and disaggregating processes are giving rise and within which localizing dynamics and the needs of individuals can be accommodated.[26] To enumerate just a few of the possible SOAs, they might consist of issue regimes, professional organizations, neighborhoods, credit-rating agencies, local networks of the like-minded, truth commissions, codes of conduct for business (for example, the Sullivan principles), social movements, provincial governments, diaspora, regional unions, loose confederations of NGOs, transnational advocacy groups, and so on across all the diverse collectivities that have become major sources of decisional authority in the ever more complex multicentric world.

There is another, well-documented way in which adaptive processes counter the undermining impact of globalization. The possibility of individuals and communities losing their identity in the face of homogenizing global dynamics can be readily exaggerated. Not only is there a variety of local resistances to the lures of global commodities and media but also, perhaps even more widespread, there are individuals and communities that absorb global norms, practices, and products by transforming them in such a way as to render them consistent with their own local cultures. Cricket in India, for example, is no longer British cricket; it is Indian cricket, a feature of Indian culture.[27] Strong and powerful as fragmegrative tensions may be, so are the means that have been developed to work around and avoid these tensions. A compelling generalization of this conclusion is offered by an astute anthropologist:

> The new global cultural system *promotes difference* instead of suppressing it, but difference of a particular kind. Its hegemony is not of content, but of form. Global structures organize diversity, rather than replicating uniformity. . . . In other words, we are not all becoming the same, but we are portraying, dramatising and communicating our differences to each other in ways that are more widely intelligible. The globalizing hegemony is to be found in *structures of common difference*, which celebrate particular kinds of diversity while submerging, deflating or suppressing others. The global system is a common code, but its purpose is not common identification; it is the expression of distinctions, boundaries and disjunctures. The 'local,' 'ethnic' and the 'national' cannot therefore be seen as opposed to or resisting global culture, but instead, insofar as they can be domesticated and categorised, they are essential *parts* of global culture.[28]

In sum, analysts seeking to differentiate situations that are likely to remain stable from those that have the potential of deteriorating and becoming increasingly unstable have no easy task. Some situations and countries are moving toward ever more acceptable levels of systemic coherence, while others are prone to decline into prolonged instability. The surface clues as to which direction a country or situation may be headed, such as the robustness of economies and the nature and support of the prevailing political leadership and the forces opposed to it, should be supplemented with assessments of trickier variables, such as the orientations and commitments of ordinary folk, their receptivity to new forms and loci of authority, and their readiness to engage in the organizational life of their communities or countries.

Lessons for U.S. National Security

Although the conceptual underpinnings of stability have been taken for granted by policymakers and academics alike, the same cannot be said of the concept of security. Keenly aware that the end of the Cold War meant that U.S. security was no longer centrally dependent on military preparedness and advanced weapons technologies, that rather the country was subject to challenges from a wide variety of new and unfamiliar sources, many observers returned to their conceptual drawing boards in the hope of clarifying what national security involves in a world free of a superpower rivalry. In so doing, it became clear that, as difficult and precarious as the circumstances of the Cold War were, they were at least founded on certainties as to who the enemy was and what the threats were. The age of fragmegration, however, is pervaded with such a vast array of uncertainties that analysts were impelled to broaden the concept of national security to allow for a world in which protecting territory was less salient and compelling than was advancing the well-being of individuals and their societies. One inquiry, for example, focused on "human security," which was conceived to include physical, psychological, gender, social, economic, political, cultural, and environmental security, as well as military security.[29]

Even though progress in developing this broader conception has yet to result in a widely shared and clearly specified operational meaning of national security, its outlines are consistent with the formulation of stability developed here. More accurately, it seems clear that none of the various forms of national security can be achieved or maintained unless it is founded on a dynamic conception of stability that allows for change and avoids stasis. Even more precisely, the more a situation or system is marked by high and acceptable systemic coherence, the more can the values that attach to national security, however defined, be realized.

Locating U.S. national security concerns in the context of the foregoing elaboration of the concept of stability leads to several insights. First and foremost, perhaps, policymakers need to appreciate that micro-macro interactions are crucial to many of the situations around the world of concern to the United States and that their ability to exercise control over such situations is severely limited. In Kosovo, Serbia, East Timor, Russia, Colombia, and a host of other places, public moods, evolving identities, and long-standing aspirations are predominant variables that cannot be readily controlled by native politicians, much less by distant foreign offices. Indeed, the necessity of being sensitive to micro-macro phenomena throughout the world places a huge burden on the intelligence agencies of governments. Anticipating how and when people will act collectively—what stimuli will move them and under what conditions they will remain quiescent—is perhaps the most difficult task confronting those who analyze developments elsewhere in the world.

In addition, as evidenced by hackers who break into Internet sites and files with a fair amount of ease, the pace at which micro actions get converted into macro actions is accelerating, and the range of individuals who can have macro consequences is broadening. In effect, the skill revolution has become a threat as well as an asset insofar as the security of communities at every level of aggregation is concerned. The very technological training that societies need to provide their citizens and military personnel can also be used against them by those in their ranks who become alienated and employ their skills to roam around cyberspace, creating havoc for their societies.

Second, the predominance of micro-macro processes suggests that heads of state, prime ministers, and cabinets often hold office under precarious circumstances and that therefore commitments to them ought not be unqualified. To attempt to shore up a favored prime minister through foreign policy statements and gestures is to run the danger of ending up on the wrong side, in the event abrupt changes move a situation toward the edge of collapse.

Third, and no less important, policymakers need to avoid excessive confidence that favorable situations abroad marked by infinitesimal or no change are likely to continue to be benign. They need to frequently remind themselves that the acceleration of micro-macro dynamics renders all situations susceptible to sudden and rapid deterioration. More than that, as the skill revolution gathers momentum, and more and more people begin to sense the contribution they can make to collective actions, the greater is the likelihood that internal conflicts will be increasingly shrill, intense, and confrontational.

Fourth, it seems clear that stability and instability come in various forms. Stable foundations may lie at the root of situations that convey a surface appearance of crisis, and unstable conditions may underlie situations seemingly free of crisis. The possibility of being misled in these regards highlights the need of policymakers to be clear in their own minds as to the criteria of systemic coherence they employ when they assess the long-term prospects of countries and the short-term likelihood that situations of concern will spin further out of control. No less important, they need to be keenly sensitive to the ways in which degrees of stability and instability vary from country to country and region to region. Clearly, for example, just as China's stability is different from Israel's, so are the dynamics of change in Europe different from those in Asia—truisms, to be sure, but easily overlooked if policymakers try to impose a singular conception of stability on the diverse situations comprising the global agenda.

Fifth, strategic discourse needs to recognize that a powerful form of the mobility upheaval—millions upon millions of refugees—can be a central feature of the new wars that mark the fragmegrative epoch. Not to anticipate that a major consequence of military campaigns today may be an unmanageable flow of displaced persons whose plight needs immediate and energetic attention is to risk losing control over the reasons for which such actions were undertaken. Not only might control be lost on the ground where the combat ensued, but losses might also be incurred in the struggle to stay on a high moral ground where human rights norms are valued. The organizational explosion and the bifurcation of global structures make it difficult to wage military campaigns in which the world remains oblivious to their unintended consequences.

Sixth, the deepening and broadening of fragmegrative dynamics has led to such great complexity within and among communities that the aforementioned applicability of the concept of security to so many aspects of community life poses the risk of confounding the variability of its meanings. If the security of all institutions, groups, and practices is endangered, as indeed can be the case under fragmegrative conditions, then discourse needs to be specific about what kinds of threats to what kinds of situations reference is made. Moreover, if the scope of security is now all-encompassing, there is a danger that the ambiguities thus involved will be avoided by recourse to excessively narrow conceptions of where the main threats to security may be located. There can be little doubt, for example, that new technologies have intensified terrorism as a threat to the security dilemmas of societies, but it would be a grave mistake to become so preoccupied with such threats as to overlook, or even to define away, the numerous threats that are less to physical well-being and more to economic, political, or social institutions.

Seventh, perhaps the key to coping with a fast-changing, complex world in which nonlinearity prevails is adaptability, that is, being able to adjust to the unexpected in creative and appropriate ways, rather than being surprised and perforce falling back on established strategy that failed to anticipate the unexpected. One organization has managed to build such a perspective into its operating procedures: the Marine Corps. Because they must confront new and unexpected challenges, Marine platoons have become adept at adjusting to the unforeseen,[30] and there is no reason why their success in this regard cannot be emulated across an entire policymaking organization. To do so is to be ready to ignore, work around, modify, or otherwise bypass established bureaucratic procedures and the inertia they sustain. It is hoped that the nature of fragmegrative challenges will encourage, even compel, the U.S. policymaking organizations to overcome inertia and become more adaptable.

Eighth, if adaptability is the key to effective security policies in the future, then it is crucial that policymaking organizations beware of excessive single-mindedness toward any perceived threat. To think out of the box is not to move to a small enclosure with room for only one new idea. To be sure, a vast and creative literature on the potentials of information warfare, the nature of new weaponry, and other new forms of military operations is now available, and it is pervaded with valuable insights and recommendations.[31] Nevertheless, all too often a new problem tends to get exaggerated into *the* problem and is then placed so high on the list of priorities that all other problems get downgraded and, in effect, slighted or ignored. The fear of new kinds of terrorism and germ warfare sometimes exhibits this characteristic, especially after these problems were elevated to the fastest growing category of military defense spending in the United States. As one observer puts it, the perception of such threats "has begun to outpace the facts. . . . [The government should be] acting and spending smart and not spending and talking big."[32] Even more specifically, anthrax came to be viewed by the Department of Defense as a vehicle for germ warfare that constituted such a huge threat as to necessitate an order that all members of the Armed Forces have an anthrax vaccination, a policy that not only became a central preoccupation at the highest levels of government but also proved to be ill-founded because the vaccine was subsequently judged to be of questionable value. As one analyst puts it, "Obsessing over operational and tactical details—like anthrax—as a pretext for permitting leaders to dodge fundamental strategic issues has become unacceptable."[33]

Ninth, there may be lessons to be learned from the world's recent experience with the perceived dangers of Y2K. The community of experts on the subject has gone through, and is still going through, much soul-searching on why their dire expectations fell so far short of reality. It appears that the lessons can be clustered under three headings: strategic, informational, and managerial. Since the transition from December 31, 1999, to January 1, 2000, was a successful (and extremely rare) case of worldwide cooperation rooted in and sustained by micro-macro interactions, its lessons may have relevance for the framing of approaches to coping with challenges to security in a fragmegrative world. Given the prevalence of conflict among people and countries, that is, there may be something to be learned from those moments when the tensions yielded to cooperation. Six *strategic* lessons stand out: (1) a common menace and cross-border interdependencies were keys to success; (2) networking and information work; (3) leapfrogging (that is, learning from those who started early) is good; (4) infrastructures are both connected and resilient; (5) public-private partnerships can work; and (6) technology can be managed. Likewise, six *informational* lessons seem salient: (1) facts build confidence; (2) self-reporting should be valued; (3) those close to a situation understand it best (for example, the United States had doubts about Russian natural gas going to Europe, but the Finns, who depend on Russian natural gas, had studied the pipelines in Russia and were very confident); (4) details count; (5) the information lag should not be overlooked (reporting on repairs completed lagged behind making the repairs); and (6) information cartels have marginal value (that is, organizations that charged for information did not have better information than what was publicly available). In addition, five *managerial* lessons loom large: (1) explain the program in "plain English"; (2) realize that information and communications technology are mission-critical; (3) know the systems, suppliers, and business processes; (4) manage risks proactively; and (5) prioritize requirements for results.[34] Taken together, these 17 lessons highlight the large extent to which the maintenance of stability involves innovative, thorough, and perhaps even aggressive approaches to a challenging world.

Finally, and by way of summary, these observations highlight the central themes of the preceding discussion:

> We must develop an ideology of perpetual renewal. The reality of globality—the time compression and the pressures of complexity or, in other words, the death of distance, the death of sequentiality and the death of traditional structures—require from each society, from each organization, and each individual an integrated and internalized capacity for renewal. . . . Particularly, a society can only flourish if it is based on change and stability. A fast-changing society requires societal glue provided by the preservation of cultural traditions and shared values.[35]

Conclusion

With the advent of a bifurcation of global structures and a vigorous multicentric world of diverse collectivities that is adding substantially to the density of actors on the global stage, it might seem as if the world is headed for increasing unrest and instability. The ever-widening interdependence of publics, economies, societies, and polities generated by a microelectronic revolution that has collapsed time and space would also seem to have rendered instabilities in one part of the world vulnerable to spreading quickly to other parts. Terrorists emulate each other; currency collapses cascade quickly across national boundaries; secessionist movements are contagious; environmental, human rights, and labor groups join protests against the policies of the International Monetary Fund (IMF), World Bank, and the WTO—developments that cumulatively suggest ever-widening pockets of instability on a global scale.

Yet, for all the world's problems and the insecurities they generate, it is possible to conclude on an upbeat note. While policymakers need to monitor the innumerable present and potential situations at work in the world for signs of further breakdown, they can also take comfort in the sheer numbers of organizations active on the global stage. These organizations can serve as a bulwark against instability or at least against a continual and worldwide spread of deteriorating conditions. The processes are hardly democratic, but the evolving bifurcation at the global level is making it increasingly difficult for a few collectivities or situations to dominate the others. Localization is no less a powerful force than globalization, and the tendencies toward decentralization undergirding localism may offer as many saving graces as there are in the centralization that accompanies globalism.

Notes

The author is grateful to Ellen L. Frost, Richard L. Kugler, and Hongying Wang for their reactions to earlier drafts of this chapter.

[1] Indeed, in the case of the current regime in Vietnam, caught between a communist system and capitalist world, the overall policy orientation appears to be one of "frenetic stasis." Seth Mydans, "Vietnam Hesitates on Globalization," *International Herald Tribune*, April 14, 2000, 2.

[2] Other terms suggestive of the contradictory tensions that pull systems toward both coherence and collapse are *chaord*, a label that juxtaposes the dynamics of chaos and order; *glocalization*, which points to the simultaneity of globalizing and localizing dynamics; and *regcal*, a term designed to focus attention on the links between regional and local phenomena. The chaord designation is proposed in Dee Hock, *Birth of the Chaordic Age* (San Francisco: Berrett-Koehler Publishers, 1999); the glocalization concept is elaborately developed in Roland Robertson, "Globalization: Time-Space and Homogeneity-Heterogeneity," in *Global Modernities*, eds. Mike Featherstone, Scott Lash, and Roland Robertson (Thousand Oaks, CA: Sage Publications, 1995), 25–44; and the regcal formulation can be found in Susan H.C. Tai and Y.H. Wong, "Advertising Decisionmaking in Asia: 'Glocal' versus 'Regcal' Approach," *Journal of Managerial Issues* 10 (Fall 1998), 318–339. Here the term *fragmegration* is preferred because it does not imply a territorial scale and broadens the focus to include tensions at work in organizations as well as those that pervade communities.

[3] This concept was first developed in James N. Rosenau, "'Fragmegrative' Challenges to National Security," in *Understanding U.S. Strategy: A Reader*, ed. Terry L. Heyns (Washington, DC: National Defense University Press, 1983), 65–82. For subsequent and more elaborate formulations, see James N. Rosenau, "New Dimensions of Security: The Interaction of Globalizing and Localizing Dynamics," *Security Dialogue* 25 (September 1994), 255–282.

[4] For an extended inquiry into the dynamics that have obscured the boundaries between national and international affairs, see James N. Rosenau, *Along the Domestic-Foreign Frontier: Exploring Governance in a Turbulent World* (Cambridge, Great Britain: Cambridge University Press, 1997).

[5] Roland Robertson, "Mapping the Global Condition: Globalization as the Central Concept," in *Global Culture: Nationalism, Globalization, and Modernity*, ed. Mike Featherstone (London: Sage Publications, 1990), 19.

[6] Harry C. Triandis, *Individualism and Collectivism* (Boulder, CO: Westview Press, 1995), xiv.

[7] The author is indebted to Richard L. Kugler for calling my attention to these distinctions.

[8] For an elaboration of a formulation that treats disorder as a form of order, see James N. Rosenau, *Turbulence in World Politics: A Theory of Change and Continuity* (Princeton, NJ: Princeton University Press, 1990).

[9] Some 5 months after the coup, it was reported that the Pakistani public began to find it unacceptable. See Celia W. Dugger, "In Pakistan, Disillusionment with New Rulers Is Widespread," *International Herald Tribune*, March 7, 2000, 1.

[10] Daniel Yankelovich, "How American Individualism Is Evolving," *The Public Perspective* 9, no. 2 (February/March 1998), 4.

[11] For a full discussion of the skill revolution, see Rosenau, *Turbulence in World Politics*; James N. Rosenau and W. Michael Fagen, "Increasingly Skillful Citizens: A New Dynamism in World Politics?" *International Studies Quarterly* 41, no. 4 (December 1997), 655–686; and Ulric Neisser, *The Rising Curve: Long-Term Gains in IQ and Related Measures* (Washington, DC: American Psychological Association, 1998).

[12] For an effort to explain the pervasiveness of authority crises, see Rosenau, *Turbulence in World Politics*, 186–191.

[13] The bifurcation of global structures is elaborated at length in Rosenau, *Turbulence in World Politics*, chapter 10.

[14] Lester M. Salamon, "The Global Associational Revolution: The Rise of the Third Sector on the World Scene," *Foreign Affairs* (July/August 1994), 109–122. For a cogent assessment of the proliferation and significance of networks, see John Arquilla and David Ronfeldt, "A New Epoch—and Spectrum—of Conflict," in *In Athena's Camp: Preparing for Conflict in the Information Age*, eds. J. Arquilla and D. Ronfeldt (Santa Monica, CA: RAND, 1997), 5.

[15] The consequences of the mobility upheaval are creatively explored in Arjun Appadurai, *Modernity at Large: Cultural Dimensions of Globalization* (Minneapolis: University of Minnesota Press, 1996).

[16] Rosenau, *Beyond Globalization*, chapter 8.

[17] Rosenau, *Along the Domestic-Foreign Frontier,* chapters 7, 11, and 18. The various "scapes" are discussed in Appadurai, *Modernity at Large*, 33–37.

[18] For a cogent, data-based analysis of the dynamics involved in the emergence of a global economy, see Geoffrey Garrett, "The Causes of Globalization," a paper presented at the Conference on Development and the Nation-State in the Crosscurrents of Globalization and Decentralization, Washington University, St. Louis, April 8, 2000.

[19] For a more extensive collection of such commentaries, see James N. Rosenau, "Emergent Spaces, New Places, and Old Faces: Proliferating Identities in a Globalizing World," a paper presented at the Conference on Globalization and Cultural Security: Migration and Negotiations of Identity, sponsored by the House of World Cultures Berlin and the Toda Institute, Berlin, October 14–17, 1999, 17–21.

[20] Stephanie Burnham, personal communication, May 23, 1996.

[21] With extremely limited resources (less than $5,000), my office recently sent a mail questionnaire to a sample of some 3,000 leaders listed in *Who's Who in America*—hardly an adequate solution to the problem, but at least a beginning in the sense that the survey sought to identify persons on the cutting

edge of globalization by including a number of items designed to uncover the global responsibilities, orientations, and affiliations of the respondents. As of January 10, 2000, approximately 850 questionnaires had been returned.

[22] Peter L. Berger, "Four Faces of Global Culture," *The National Interest* 49 (Fall 1997), 24.

[23] Christopher Lasch, *The Revolt of the Elites and the Betrayal of Democracy* (New York: W.W. Norton, 1995), 6, 45, 47.

[24] Robert Reich, *The Work of Nations: Preparing Ourselves for 21st Century Capitalism* (New York: Alfred A. Knopf, 1991), 309.

[25] Benjamin R. Barber, *Jihad vs. McWorld* (New York: Times Books, 1995), 17, 29.

[26] James N. Rosenau, "In Search of Institutional Contexts," a paper presented at the Conference on International Institutions: Global Processes-Domestic Consequences, Duke University, April 9–11, 1999.

[27] Appadurai, *Modernity at Large*, chapter 5.

[28] Richard Wilk, "Learning to Be Local in Belize: Global Systems of Common Difference," in *Worlds Apart: Modernity through the Prism of the Local*, ed. Daniel Miller (London: Routledge, 1996), 118.

[29] Laura Reed, "Rethinking Security from the Ground Up," *Breakthroughs* IX (Spring 2000), 21–27.

[30] This adeptness has been supplemented by the development of the platoon as what was earlier described as an "all channel network, in which every node can communicate with every other node." See Joel Garreau, "Point Men for a Revolution: Can the Marines Survive a Shift from Hierarchies to Networks?" *The Washington Post* (March 6, 1999), 1.

[31] See, for example, Arquilla and Ronfeldt, "A New Epoch—and Spectrum—of Conflict," and Martin C. Libicki, *What Is Information Warfare?* (Washington, DC: National Defense University Press, 1996).

[32] Paul Richter, "Doubt on 'New Terrorism,'" *International Herald Tribune* (February 9, 2000), 3.

[33] Andrew J. Bacevich, "Anthrax Vaccination and the Deeper Problems of Leadership," distributed by email by the Foreign Policy Research Institute, Philadelphia, March 11, 2000, 4.

[34] International Y2K Coordination Center, *Y2K: Starting the Century Right*, <http://www.iy2kcc.org/February2000Report.htm>. The listing is from the executive summary at <http://www.iy2kcc.org/ExecutiveSummary.htm>.

[35] Klaus Schwab, *Opening Remarks* (Davos, Switzerland: World Economic Forum, February 2000).

Chapter 6

Military Power and Maritime Forces

Seymour J. Deitchman

The United States is the dominant power in the global economy and its Armed Forces are the premier in today's globalizing world. It might be thought, therefore, that our national security would be assured in this world. But much of our economic power involves links with the rest of the world, and the nature of those links affects both the underlying strength of our unprecedented military power and how we can use it to protect and further our global interests. Some related, important perceptions on the part of the American public also affect such use. Together, these constraints shape the directions in which our military forces, and especially our naval forces, can and must evolve to serve the Nation in the future. The sources and the nature of the constraints and future strategic needs must be examined before we can specify the naval force characteristics to be sought.

Globalization, the End of the Cold War, and National Security

As has been amply described elsewhere in this volume, *globalization* is the term used to describe the spread of commercial and financial enterprise around the world, with all of its concomitants. The enterprises and their derivatives cross national borders; they are centered in "Anyland," with the centers of control and the flow of the assets distributed internationally. Control and ownership are concentrated in the advanced industrialized nations: the United States; the European Union and its outliers in places like Australia; Japan and the Republic of Korea in the Far East; and a few financial centers such as Hong Kong and Singapore. The United States has a role as "first among equals" in this array, simply through the sheer size of its economy and its military power. This global economy is supported by, and depends on, flows of resources from undeveloped or less developed nations—clustered conceptually in what was called the Third World during the Cold War—to centers of production and to the centers of advanced economic power.

Seymour J. Deitchman is a consultant on national security. He previously served as vice president for programs at the Institute for Defense Analyses. He has also held various positions both in government and on advisory panels and is the author of six books, including On Being a Superpower: And Not Knowing What to Do about It, Beyond the Thaw: A New National Strategy, *and* After the Cold War: U.S. Security for the Future.

Global enterprises are characterized by centralized policymaking with decentralized execution of policies. This pattern is enabled by the ubiquity of information across an enterprise at multiple levels of command, made available through the technologies (for example, computing, communication, transportation) that have driven the modern globalization phenomena. Those technologies, although their greatest recent advances originated in national security concerns and endeavors, are now the mainstay of the commercial world. That world dominates the markets for, and the further development of, the technologies. It therefore also affects the shape and capabilities of the armed forces.

While the spread of global enterprise as such is not a brand-new phenomenon, having begun centuries ago with the onset of the European colonial period, its current manifestation, with its distributed management, rapid flow of people and resources, and instant financial transfers, is unique, both because of the technologies and because of the organizational patterns and resource dependencies that they have induced. Now, less industrialized nations—for example, Russia, China, India, Brazil, other countries on the Pacific Rim—are joining the global industrial and commercial community. And globalization has come to characterize criminal enterprises as well—mafias, drug traders, smugglers of people and goods.

This internationalization of wealth-creating enterprises has been accompanied by the spread of culture and ideological concepts, strongly and consciously U.S.-driven: democratic government, human rights, ethical business practices, and particular freedoms for the media. From this background, the United States views globalization as providing strong support for the national security of the participating countries, including the United States. History shows that democratic governments rarely, if ever, go to war with each other. On the whole, therefore, and allowing for internal dissension about hardships attending its evolution, we tend to view globalization as leading to a more orderly world, at least for the countries benefiting from it.

There are, however, downsides to globalization for the United States. It engenders jealousies and resentments in many nations and groups who aspire to join the globalized economy, but are not yet a part of it, among those furnishing its raw resources, and among members of any groups who are feeling hurt by it in the short run. It induces rivalries over competition for resources and markets among the industrialized nations, affecting how they try to face the "outsiders" and weakening their mutual cohesion. All this is added to the residues of international tensions among the advanced nations (note, for example, the tentative pace at which the United Kingdom is becoming fully committed to the European Union), and to the effects of ethnic hatreds and strife within and among the less developed ones.

Also, there is a tendency among U.S. policymakers and the general public to think that since the rest of the world seems to be absorbing American and Western culture, it also thinks as we do and has similar values—such as respect for human life and notions of fair play. We tend, in our policy advocacy and policymaking, to ignore others' values and cultures, which do not change very fast and are not the same as ours, in much of the world with which we must interact—parts of Europe, Russia, the Middle East, Africa, India, and the Far East. This leads to misunderstandings between us and other nations, and perceptions of American arrogance on their part. It exacerbates the resentments attending globalization, and, worst of all for the United States, it colors and confuses our own ability to obtain accurate intelligence estimates and interpretations regarding potential trouble areas.

Overall, globalization bespeaks a world in transition, to a future that is far from understood. Like all states of transition, there is much progress, but it is proceeding unevenly, with many instabilities and conflicts—economic, political, outright military, and quasi-military. The last—the quasi-military conflicts—are the worst kind for the United States because of their ambiguity about whether and how they may affect us, whether and how we should get involved, who the players are and what they stand for, who in our government is responsible for what, and the difficulty of cross-agency coordination on policies where the overall problem definition and therefore policy guidance is unclear and there are differences with our allies about how to respond.

The biggest current U.S. advantage in this world, beyond our domination of information technology, is our ability to capitalize on that technology to synthesize large-scale systems. That is, our "secret weapon" in mastery of globalization is in technique and organization, as much as or more than in technology per se (although military technology is an important piece of the technology spectrum, and there are some militarily relevant technology areas in which we still excel—sensors, stealth, precision missile guidance, submarine design, and large-scale combat systems, for example). U.S. superiority in the globalization transition is supported by our vast people resources and ownership of, or ready access to, natural resources. This superiority could be transitory, as our industrialized companion countries are gaining on, and sometimes exceeding, our technical capability in many areas relevant to the global economy (for example, the United Kingdom, France, and Germany together in Europe; Japan in the Far East). Indeed, as fallout from the inequalities of military capability, which became apparent in Kosovo, we want these allies to learn to do what we are able to do as well as we can do it. But others, whom we may not be so eager to teach, learn as well (partly through our own help, which comes to them via the global economy, whether we intend it or not). And they may use what they learn against us.

The end of the Cold War interacts with the effects of globalization to affect the U.S. strategic position in the world and therefore the requirements for, and modes of, use of military power. The Cold War exerted a kind of perverse discipline because most U.S. actions overseas had a counter-Soviet imperialism focus, and most Soviet actions had the objective of spreading communism and countering the resistance of the United States and the North Atlantic Treaty Organization (NATO) to that. Therefore, although all the kinds of Third World involvements and conflicts we see today were extant then, we became engaged in them then as part of the strategy to prevent the spread of the hostile communist ideology and the concurrent growth of Soviet imperial power. Hence, for example, we fought major regional wars in Korea and Vietnam; we intervened to affect the directions of government changes in Central and South America; in Iran, we aided in the resistance to the Soviet invasion of Afghanistan; and we provided security assistance to many other nations to keep them from falling within the Soviet sphere.

The Cold War focus, including nuclear deterrence and thinking about national missile defense, was, along with everything else, a matter of national survival. The contest with communism was a contest for political and economic control of the world and its resources. The end of the Cold War meant that national survival concerns in U.S. international relations subsided for the foreseeable future. Even current threats to our homeland—terrorist, cyberwar, or the possible use of weapons of mass destruction (WMDs) by "rogue" states—while capable of inflicting severe damage, do not threaten our immediate national survival. Thus, our foreign policy focus now is on trade, the impact of globalization on our economy, the availability of resources, cultural exchanges, advancement of the human condition, and promotion of a world of international relationships that are conducive to those things or, conversely, conflict with national or transnational forces that threaten them. That is, international affairs for the United States have changed from matters of survival to furthering and protecting "interests" in all these areas. Attacks on those interests can threaten our national survival in the long run, but the threats do not appear imminent, as, for example, was the threat of nuclear destruction during the Cold War.

As a result, our Nation's strategic threat structure is now different from what it was during the Cold War. Our vital interests still include threats of attack that can inflict serious damage on our homeland, our economy, and our closest allies. We must now, however, be concerned that such attacks can come from widely dispersed nations, small as well as large, and from transnational groups that threaten us in many ways and our allies along the way. Ambiguity has entered threat considerations. For example, is drug traffic to the United States and the European Community from the Caribbean, which debilitates a significant part of our populations, a threat to our vital interests? Is the risk of control over a large fraction of Europe's and Japan's oil supply by a dictator hostile to the United States a threat to our vital interests? Less than vital, but nonetheless important, threats to our own interests and to our obligations to support and help protect our allies (who are in great measure the other industrialized nations involved in the global economy and democratic fellowship), also appear in more dispersed parts of the globe. The threat to NATO cohesion by genocide on Western Europe's doorstep in the Balkans, together with the attending humanitarian considerations, surely falls in this category. An attempt by China to occupy Taiwan by force, could, if unresisted, challenge our reliability as an ally and a proponent of democracy in the Far East, and consequently our long-term viability as a power on the Pacific Rim.

Because of this diffusion of threat, the character of our military deployments, pre-positioning, and operations has been reoriented. Instead of focusing on continental Eurasia, with a large permanent presence of the land-based ground and air forces in Europe and preservation of seagoing access to Europe by the Navy, we are now focused on the southern and eastern regions of the Eurasian land mass, North Africa and the Middle East, and Southeast Asia/Oceania, with major distractions in Africa south of the Sahara and Latin America as well. The Armed Forces' orientation has shifted toward expeditionary warfare, and we have had to pre-position equipment and supplies on ships in the Indian Ocean, at Diego Garcia, in addition to supplies and equipment still stored in Europe.

For strategic planning, there has to be more than a random character to this structure. Since it is generally accepted that "he who defends everywhere defends nowhere," the Nation must work out a hierarchy of interests that helps establish priorities for defense. Although little publicized, such a hierarchy was proposed in 1996 by the Commission on America's National Interests.[1] The Commission, sponsored by a consortium including the Harvard Center for Science and International Affairs, the Nixon Center for Peace and Freedom, the RAND Corporation, and the Hauser Foundation, and chaired by Robert Ellsworth, Andrew Goodpaster, and Rita Hauser, divided the national interests of the United States into four major categories: *Vital, Extremely Important, Just Important,* and *Less Important* or *Secondary.* The following kinds of security threats or overseas events are included in each category (this is not a complete list, and it is paraphrased):

- *Vital interests* require attention to eventualities that would threaten the United States directly: minimizing the risk of attacks on the United States by nuclear, chemical, or biological weapons; preventing the emergence of a hostile "hegemon"—a dominant power—in Europe or Asia, or the emergence of a hostile major power on U.S. borders; preventing the catastrophic collapse of major global systems for managing trade, finance, energy, and environmental matters; and ensuring the survival of our allies (since they help ensure our own survival).
- *Extremely Important interests* are less important only in that they deal with matters outside the United States that can have serious impacts on our security, rather than those that would affect our country directly. Examples of such matters include preventing WMD proliferation or use anywhere; preventing the emergence of a hostile regional "hegemon" in areas important for our national well-being or that of our allies, such as the Persian Gulf; protecting our allies from significant external aggression; suppressing, containing, and combating terrorism, transnational crime, and drugs; and preventing genocide.
- *Just Important interests* cover a host of activities that make up the substance of the day-to-day dealings of the United States with other nations. They include such things as discouraging massive human rights violations in other countries; promoting freedom, democracy, and stability in strategically important states; preventing nationalization of U.S. assets abroad and protecting U.S. citizens from terrorist attacks or kidnappings; promoting beneficial international environmental policies; and maximizing American economic growth from international trade and investment.
- Finally, the *Less Important or Secondary interests* cover many more items and activities perpetually in the news, such as balancing bilateral trade deficits, enlarging democracy elsewhere for its own sake (in places like Congo, Haiti, or Cuba), and helping other states who are not allies preserve their territorial integrity.

This kind of strategic definition of U.S. interests is helpful in determining where the Armed Forces may have to be used. Careful scrutiny of the array, however, reinforces the dispersed and ubiquitous nature of the threats that the Nation and the Armed Forces must be ready to meet. Those that are lower in the hierarchy can move higher quickly, as the examples of Korea in 1950, Kuwait in 1990, and Kosovo in 1999 indicate. An action by a rogue or a normally hostile government (if we can tell the difference) can change a stable, but uncertain, situation to a threatening one overnight. This is not new—it happened, for example, when the Soviet Union invaded Afghanistan in 1979. These complexities are made even more intense by the domestic political tensions that can be generated by actions at the lower levels of the hierarchy (in Panama, Somalia, and Haiti, for example), and by the uncertainties about whether any development has, indeed, moved up the ladder (in the Balkans, for example). All this simply affirms that the Armed Forces must be versatile and adaptable, and capable of action at many levels on a world scale, even more than was required during the Cold War.

Significance for U.S. Military and Naval Forces and Their Use

The design of our Armed Forces is following that of the commercial enterprise, both driven and enabled by the technology of that enterprise: substitution of capital for labor—exemplified by the use of instrumentation and automation to reduce crew size in ships of comparable size and capability (as in the reduction in our guided missile destroyers from about 300 in the existing DDG–51 to 95 in the coming DD–21); changed cost structure; use of information, communication, and transportation technology to shape organizations and their modus operandi; and centralized decision-making with decentralized execution. In the fast-moving actions that are anticipated, forces in the field are more likely to be given mission-type orders after campaigns are planned by the regional CINC headquarters, with more responsibility to be delegated to lower commanders. That this pattern will depend totally on the quality of information available at all levels of command was illustrated by several instances during the Persian Gulf War when General Norman Schwarzkopf slowed the movement of some elements of his forces because of uncertainty about their exact positions and fear that they might engage each other.[2]

There also exists the concern that the National Command Authorities, also having that information at their disposal, might be tempted to intervene and would thereby adversely affect prosecution of a military action, as the Armed Forces felt happened too often in the Vietnam War. The problem is that when a central authority perceives an imminent action or a risk attending one that, it is feared, could jeopardize wider political and economic goals, it is very difficult to sustain a "hands off, wait and see how it turns out" attitude. For example, much of President Lyndon Johnson's personal intervention in Vietnam was generated by concern about whether China might be provoked to enter the war, and other kinds of concerns beyond the immediate operations attended the decision to end the Persian Gulf War short of total destruction of the retreating Iraqi forces. (It should be noted that problems of analogous vital importance face global commercial enterprises as well.)

One way to avoid such dilemmas is to complete a military mission fast enough to minimize the chance that the concerns will arise. Our Armed Forces are being designed for rapid military success, for the standard reasons that Armed Forces always have for quick success, but also for the obvious policy reasons attending globalization and the end of the Cold War. More detailed insight into the direction of evolution of the Armed Forces and their operational characteristics can be obtained from the Joint Chiefs of Staff *Joint Vision 2010* and the emerging update, *Joint Vision 2020*.[3] The terminology describing the operational concepts of the future forces captures their orientation: "dominant maneuver; precision engagement; focused logistics; full-dimensional protection"—with information superiority, in joint operations, with allied and coalition partners.

For military-to-military engagements, this orientation enables fast-response forces, basing their operations on broad knowledge of the forces and equipment that the opponent fields and what the opponent can and does do with them. It enables precision disabling attacks against the heart of the opponent's capabilities.[4] It allows fast movement to dominate the battlefield and defeat opposing forces.

These capabilities can be, and have been, extended to the quasi-military domain—for example, the Panama invasion in 1989, the Somalia landing in 1992, and the 1998 attack on Osama bin Laden's camps in Afghanistan. But in this area, the use of military forces is far more subject to all the kinds of ambiguities noted earlier, given the interests at stake. In consequence of the latter, our fast-response, highly effective military capability is subject to the delays attending political decisionmaking, which can obviate some, much, and sometimes all of the advantage conferred by the forces' technical capability. This means that our forces rarely have strategic surprise on their side, although they can achieve operational and tactical surprise by how they operate. A positive example of the latter is the way the Persian Gulf War coalition was able to use a flanking attack to drive Iraqi forces out of Kuwait; an example of the negative strategic effect of publicly argued delay in alliance decisionmaking is the way that Serb forces moved inside NATO's timeline to destroy the civilian community in Kosovo.

The spread of military technology to the rest of the world; the dominance of commercial technology in the critical information and communication areas of military endeavor; ready access to space systems, including commercial space surveillance capability and the Global Positioning System (GPS) for navigation and weapon guidance; and the possibility that our opponents will jam the GPS to deny us its use for these purposes all create serious vulnerabilities for U.S. forces. This makes the U.S. forces' hold on their current supreme position vis-à-vis the rest of world's forces more precarious than is commonly realized.

The risks to our forces operate on three levels: *conventional military, quasi-military/terrorist,* and the *potential for WMD use*. At the *conventional military* level, there are many opposing capabilities, some of which we are not yet able to counter: ballistic missiles (it will be only a matter of time until such missiles have guided or homing warheads for deployment against ships of the fleet and ground targets); stealthy and/or fast antiship cruise missiles; advanced conventional submarines, which are especially hard to counter in littoral waters; mine warfare; advanced versions of antiaircraft missile systems spread by former Soviet countries to any who can afford to buy them; and shoulder-fired surface-to-air missiles (SAMs) against our forces' air mobility. In addition, commercially available space surveillance equipment and space surveillance capabilities of hostile governments can make achieving surprise with maneuvers such as the flanking attack used by coalition forces in the Persian Gulf War much more difficult.

These threats are in direct opposition to the developing directions of our Armed Forces' maneuver and combat techniques: rapid maneuvers in unexpected directions against enemy areas of weakness and command locations; heavy dependence on tactical attack aviation and air mobility in combat zones; strategic- and operational-level air and sea movement for major force operations; dependence on the use of ports and airfields of sometimes wavering coalition partners; a consequent tendency to concentrate supplies at a few points or in a few ships converging on the area of action; and heavy dependence on worldwide commercial communication networks for information transfer and command and control of the forces. These threats will not put our forces out of action, but they will require extensive (and expensive) attention to the conventional as well as the new, unconventional types of attack that the forces will face.

At both the *conventional military* and *quasi-military/terrorist* levels, our forces are vulnerable to manipulation and breaking of the heavily space-based information/communication and navigation/guidance links—by jamming, deception, cyberwar, and antisatellite attacks (which can use high-powered lasers and microwave weapons from the ground rather than antisatellite weapons launched into space). Anyone, from a hostile nation to one of the increasingly sophisticated terrorist or criminal groups, can attack against these vulnerabilities at some level. And they must be expected to try, as we become increasingly and obviously dependent on those links for the evolving style of operation in the mode of *Joint Vision 2010*. Our overseas bases, ports, and military personnel are also vulnerable to terrorist strikes, as are our civilians, embassies, and commercial infrastructure. We will never have perfect security in any dimension. Therefore, intelligence is crucial to our force protection as well as civilian protection. And in geographical areas with which we are not familiar, help from our allies is also crucial. But in the perverse manner that is characteristic of the "globalized" world, such help is also a vulnerability because it is an additional source of leakage of information and technology to hostile quarters. There is not anything to be done about that, since recent experience in the globalized economy has demonstrated that we cannot either retreat into a shell or coerce our allies into holding the technology close; it simply makes the task of maintaining force superiority more difficult.

Another problem facing the military forces derives from the merging of the conventional military with the quasi-military kinds of opposing capability. Recent data show that on average about two-thirds of the world's population is concentrated within about 250 miles of an ocean shoreline. Also, most of the world's population growth is in urban areas, in growing megacities that tend to be concentrated within those zones along the littoral. This makes the objective areas for decisive military action more accessible to expeditionary forces, but it also means that the decisive action will have to take place in urban terrain—built-up areas where combat to achieve rapid results is very difficult. It also makes available to defenders, who may well have fewer scruples about human life and chivalric concepts of civilian protection than we do, the opportunity to use civilian populations as shields for military operations and to stimulate civilian mobs to interfere with military movements against strategic locations. Thus, as the Russians found in Grozny, plans for rapid success in an urbanized environment might easily be foiled.

Also at both these levels, the slow *WMD diffusion* constitutes a danger not only to civilians who may be terrorist targets but also to our Armed Forces when they operate in hostile environments. Nuclear weapons are in a class by themselves in ability to deliver sudden and widespread devastation. Nuclear proliferation may be slow, but we can expect it to proceed, as it has been. In addition to the five original nuclear powers, Israel is presumed to have weapons holdings, and India and Pakistan have recently demonstrated their nuclear capabilities. Iraq and North Korea are known to be pursuing them, with what actual success we do not know. We lean on Russia not to pass to Iran nuclear technology that can be turned into weapons, but with only partial success. China and North Korea have been sources of leakage of missile technology, and this could extend to nuclear weapons technology if strategic rivalry between them and the United States should heat up. While this kind of creeping proliferation suggests that nuclear weapons may be a phenomenon of nations and will not become a terrorist weapon soon, that is only a matter of degree. Even if terrorists per se have more difficulty making the much feared "nuclear weapon in a basement" than is usually supposed, nuclear-armed hostile countries that may fear or be unable to attack the United States or its forces directly with nuclear-armed missiles can easily use terrorist groups and techniques to deliver such weapons.

In addition to possible nuclear weapons use, there is some concern about chemical and biological weapons as weapons of choice for poor nations who wish us or our forces ill. It is apparent that any of these weapons, which are usually lumped with other WMDs but have distinctive scope-of-action and time constants, can threaten our forces and, if used against them by surprise can essentially destroy—certainly defeat—a major military operation.

Quasi-military/terrorist actions and *WMD use* are now being lumped under the rubric "asymmetrical warfare." This is simply another manifestation of the historical strivings of people to find ways to attack strength from weakness. In our own recent history, during the Cold War, the Soviet and Chinese support for Wars of National Liberation against countries to whom we had extended our protection, which led us into the debilitating conflict in Vietnam, was a major example of an asymmetrical warfare strategy. The implication of such a strategy, of course, is that the Armed Forces have to be able to engage seriously in both the conventional military and quasi-military arenas. This is an important understanding to achieve—there has been a tendency in discussions of design of the Armed Forces, recently, to view "asymmetrical warfare" as something that "displaces" the conventional warfare for which our Armed Forces have been designed and must be kept ready.[5] The fact that it is an addition to their already full plate makes their design all the more complex, difficult, and expensive.

Then there are the military operations other than war (MOOTW). Generally, they involve keeping the peace in some area, or conveying humanitarian assistance after a natural or man-made disaster. Why must military rather than civilian resources be used for such operations? The reasons lie in their structure and training: they are well organized and disciplined, they know how to marshal resources rapidly and have the wherewithal to do so, and they can fight if needed. These qualities figured in Panama, Somalia, and the Balkans. And Congress has called on the military to undertake such activities—for example, to participate in drug interdiction in the Caribbean. Why was the U.S. military committed in places like Somalia, where we have no obvious need to intervene except the humanitarian one, or in Bosnia, which is much more accessible to our European allies? Mainly, it appears, because we are the only ones whose armed forces have worldwide reach; because we do not have the residual political inhibitions that still act after centuries of historical rivalry among the nations that are now united in alliance with the United States; and because as the leader of those alliances, we are expected to lead by example.

Theoretically, civilian administrations are supposed to take over from the military in areas where the military initiated the action, but the civilian agencies have not yet proved equal to the task. The United States has provided no civilian agency for exercising civilian administrative control overseas, and our ethos dictates that we not run some other country's government. At best, we want to help the local people do it, but in the absence of local training and a tradition of effective civilian administration, that is a very long-term proposition—at a time and place where fast action is needed. We tend to rely on the United Nations to establish civilian administration where the alternative is chaos. It takes a long time to muster the resources, however, and even then there is no real authority or functioning organization to impose its will and discipline locally. Thus, a brilliantly executed military mission to set up some situation for effective civilian government often seems to have failed, or else it requires a continued military presence; the latter is often also viewed as a failure. Such purported failures have often been cited as reasons not to undertake the next such operation—in Europe as well as in the United States.

The U.S. military has become aware of, and has tried to deal with, this strategic need earlier than our civilian government—especially the Congress, which is put off by the financial and human cost of it. Transition to life in a globalized economic world in the absence of a Cold War requires that the government and the military come to terms with the new mission needs. In particular, the non-Department of Defense (non-DOD) agencies must see how the government can be better organized to deal with the spectrum of conflict more efficiently than it can at present, and the policies permitting such activity by those agencies must be put in place by Congress and the administration.

Many civilian agencies outside DOD and the national intelligence agencies must become involved in the broad spectrum of activity short of formal warfare that derives from the hierarchy of interests defined by the Commission on America's National Interests. Those agencies include the State Department and its bureaus, for economic assistance, information, intelligence, and technology transfer (in addition to the Diplomatic Corps); Justice, including the Federal Bureau of Investigation and the Drug Enforcement Agency; Transportation, for the Coast Guard and for the investigation of disasters that may have been instigated by terrorists; Treasury, for the Bureau of Alcohol, Tobacco, and Firearms; Energy, on matters involving nuclear weapons or a threat against our nuclear power plants and other nuclear installations;

Health and Human Services, for the Centers for Disease Control; and others, for specific assistance as needed.

Currently, these activities are controlled by Presidential directives specifying agency responsibilities and establishing coordination from the White House. These directives deal mainly with the possibility of terrorist attacks on the United States, and they fall short of dealing with all of them—for example, a cyberattack on our banking, power grid, or air traffic system, which could also involve other parts of the Treasury Department, the Commerce Department, the Federal Communications Commission, and the Federal Aviation Administration. A comparable structure must be established to deal with the aftermath of an overseas military operation involving peacekeeping or humanitarian assistance in a chaotic, combat-prone situation such as the one that characterized Somalia or Haiti at the time of our entry, or that followed the entry of NATO military forces into Kosovo. In particular, the relative roles of the military and the civilian agencies and the relationships between the parts of such actions devolving to the United States, its allies, and the United Nations must be clarified in both American and international law.

The significance of, and need for, working with other nations is often neglected in U.S. public discourse about events that may invite military action. Interlocking economies mean interdependence with other nations, and this enhances the importance of alliances even though the Cold War is over. It also means that the United States cannot undertake military action in isolation from others' involvement, and that for such action to be as effective as possible we must share technology and know-how with them. This is simply another force creating both the advantage of leadership and the risk of losing it; in being leaders we can at least influence policy in favor of our interests, but, as noted earlier, in sharing the capabilities that confer leadership, we indirectly impart those capabilities to others who would challenge us.

Also, worldwide engagement means worldwide military presence and force projection capability. That, in turn, implies the need for a mix of pre-positioned overseas assets (for rapid deployment to conflict areas) and overseas military bases (currently at about half the number that were available during the Cold War). All this suggests the need for coalition actions in all cases except direct defense of our homeland (and even that is often tied up in alliances and treaties, such as those with Canada involved in the North American Aerospace Defense Command). Dependence on overseas bases means that the allies or other nations want to have a say in the purpose and nature of military operations that are undertaken from the bases on their territory—for example, Germany asked us not to use NATO airbases in Germany to fly supplies to Israel during the 1973 war; Turkey has passed on whether and when we could use airbases on Turkish territory to attack Iraq; and Italy proposed to restrict some aircraft operations out of Aviano during the Kosovo air campaign.

Thus, as noted at the outset of this chapter, a main characteristic of U.S. inextricable involvement in (indeed, leadership of) the globalized economy is that we have global interests to protect, but cannot operate as free agents in doing so. Our very dominant global position leads to constraints on our ability to use military power as we alone would wish to, and makes deterrence just as important now as it was during the Cold War, although by different mechanisms. It also enhances the importance of naval forces, since those forces can operate for extended periods in forward positions without challenging any nation's sovereignty, and they can exercise forward, friendly engagement through port visits, all with but a few forward support bases in especially secure areas.

Even within the above structure, the Armed Forces cannot be clear about whom, where, or when they will have to fight. They must be ready for actions in any area of instability where our interests may be challenged, in any of the ways described, but within the coalition constraints sketched earlier. This diffuse "threat" makes it especially difficult to provide a planning base for structuring the Armed Forces. Therefore, we have chosen the two major theater war strategy, the ability to fight two major regional wars of roughly Persian Gulf War size nearly simultaneously, which we may not be able to sustain in terms of budget. For example, it is the pressure of keeping the available forces ready to fight two major regional conflicts that at least in part raises the level of tension in Congress about whether the Armed Forces should be used for peacekeeping and humanitarian missions. For this reason, it may well prove necessary to change our military planning strategy to one of being ready to fight one major regional conflict while being ready to deter another—that is, use our remaining aerospace and sea power to stand off an attack on our interests in another region until we can deal with it effectively. This could free up resources and forces to engage in the military operations other than war that bid fair to be a continuing part of our post-Cold War geopolitical landscape, while keeping the bulk of the forces ready for the more conventional and demanding war fighting.

The nature of the potential opposition and the wide geographical separation of our forces' possible operating areas show the deployment capability, military systems, and preparation to operate in the exotic environments that our forces need. With respect to where and who, the forces will have to be adaptable, and train to be so. There will also be a premium on intelligence, including surveillance operations and derivative strategic interpretations of "signs"—for example, trends in attitudes, propaganda, subtle preparations for subversion or war—to allow as much time as possible to prepare for and execute deployments to specific locations against specific forces when the need arises. A change in attention to intelligence will be of crucial importance. We decreased expenditures and the scope of intelligence activities after the end of the Cold War. However, they should have been, and must in the future be, increased because there are more areas of concern to cover, and a greater need to learn about potentially hostile societies and their activities beyond what can be learned through national technical means alone, and more analysis of data that must be gathered from all sources.

The changes in strategic outlook also affect our views of overseas military engagement. We are not as willing to risk treasure and military casualties in support of "interests" as we were when survival was at stake. The question—Is this worth one American life?—arises, and the case has to be made—as it was in the Persian Gulf, and in Bosnia and Kosovo—about why any particular engagement is worth risking our servicemen's and servicewomen's lives and the expenditure of national budget that could be used to meet internal civilian needs.[6] This attitude extends to our allies in the sense that the longer a military conflict goes on, the more questions arise as to the purpose and value of it (we saw this tendency operate in the Persian Gulf War and the Kosovo bombing campaigns), and the more likely it becomes that the coalition will weaken or fall apart. The latter problem is exacerbated by any visible U.S reluctance to incur casualties—a natural concomitant of asking the question above—and by the inferred tendency of the United States to want to lead by saying, "Do this," rather than by saying, "Follow me."

Moreover, human rights considerations have broadened to the point that a large body of U.S. and allied opinion runs against inflicting heavy damage on opposing forces, and in particular heavy civilian casualties—this in contradistinction to the tendency to condemn and punish their nefarious leaders. Arguments about sanctions and the bombing campaign against Iraq, as well as arguments within NATO about the severity of the air campaign against Serbia over Kosovo, attest to this change of attitude. In consequence, deterrence of conflict has become much more important at the conventional, tactical, and operational levels than it was before. These deterrence considerations bear little relation to the strategic deterrence of the counter-Soviet era, and the distinctions have had a marked effect on our military planning.

Let us consider the military planning first. Since drawn-out wars in support of "mere interests" are not likely to garner public support in the United States or abroad,[7] we are planning (as described in *Joint Vision 2010*'s "dominant maneuver, precision engagement") for fast, decisive actions that will be over rapidly and involve few casualties. Actually, even our industrial plant that supports the Armed Forces is no longer designed for support of a prolonged conflict that uses up extensive materiel. It is spread very thin, has little expansion capability, and depends on the rest of the world for much material support, such as electronic components and oil for fuel and petrochemicals. Accordingly, a determined opponent, for whom war would not be for "interests," but for survival and position in a competitive world, could seek to defeat our strategy by turning our attempt to achieve a rapid, decisive military victory into a protracted war—for example, by sustaining a guerrilla war against us, our allies, or a friendly nation. Twentieth century military history is replete with miscalculations that a war can be kept short: World War I, World War II, Korea, Vietnam, Chechnya. We must take these lessons into our military planning, by being careful never to underestimate our opponents—another reason for an enhanced intelligence effort.

This suggests that we need to know more about the cultures and values of friends and potential foes, what *they* deem important enough for a fight to the death, and how they would organize for one. Think, for example, about potential directions and outcomes of a conflict with China over a Chinese military campaign to dominate Taiwan. As pointed out in a recent study of post-Cold War deterrence commissioned by the Navy and performed by the Naval Studies Board of the National Research Council,[8] even the so-called rogue governments have rationales for challenging us, and they have different culture-specific values that cause them to fight wars in ways that we would not anticipate and that we must come to understand. That study put forth the idea of embedding a group of "strategic worriers" in DOD planning structure, with the mission of knowing other cultures and their leaders' value systems, and then anticipating their strategic moves on the world scene. The knowledge gained by this group would be used to inform war games and training exercises for engagements in various parts of the world, as well as to inform intelligence estimates for contingency planning and crisis response.

Such knowledge would greatly enhance our ability to deter actions against our own and our allied interests. As in all the other areas of military concern, the new deterrence needs are built on the old ones. Strategic deterrence in the Cold War sense is still with us. We still need forces that can counter the large remaining numbers of Russian nuclear weapons holdings, in case that country should gradually turn hostile again and reconstitute its strategic nuclear forces. In addition, our own strategic nuclear forces are now viewed as necessary to deter the use of nuclear weapons—and in some circumstances, chemical and biological weapons—by rogue or hostile states or transnational forces against U.S. forces, our homeland, or our allies. There is no need to remind the reader that the Navy, with its strategic ballistic missile submarines, is a key component of the strategic nuclear deterrent force.

In addition, to deter conventional attacks against our forces and interests overseas, we need credible conventional forces and related capabilities. To be credible, these capabilities must be demonstrated, in conflict if necessary, but by other means wherever possible. And, especially, there must be demonstration of the will to use them wisely, in furtherance of our interests, and not to squander them to no obvious gain.

As part of that demonstration, steps must be taken in advance of crises to create an environment in which challenges to our interests are less likely to arise. This must be done at many levels: political, diplomatic, economic. Then, the military forces become part of the total effort, through "forward engagement" and continuous contact with nations that are neutral or friendly, and even with some that may later turn hostile. This includes visits, military schools, personnel exchanges, and joint training and maneuvers. Such contact has multiple benefits: it helps others come to know our military; it demonstrates our capabilities in a benign, friendly environment; it helps our own soldiers, sailors, marines, and airmen to become acquainted with and understand potential partners and opponents; and it represents the beginning of coalition building that will come to the fore in times of crisis. (We should note that these methods, and even demonstrated military action, may not deter terrorists, who are driven by ideology and who think they have a strategy that can defeat our strengths. This includes the few nations that would make war on us using terrorist tactics in "peacetime." Such transgressors may, however, be deterred for an uncertain time by severe military punishment. How long does it take for the lessons of a Persian Gulf War, or a Kosovo campaign, or a strike against a Muammar Gaddafi or an Osama bin Laden to wear off?)

Naval forces are ideally situated and constituted for forward engagement. This has been recognized in the Navy's "Forward . . . from the Sea" concept. They can be in an area for extended periods while not wearing out their welcome in any particular spot. Carriers and other warships are highly visible signs of military power. The movement of such forces in time of crisis sends strong diplomatic as well as military signals; it is easier than moving land-based forces because entry of land-based forces may be especially sensitive just at the time of crisis and therefore not wanted by a recipient country, even one that typically avails itself of our military protection. If a crisis calls for military force, naval forces can land from the sea, with or without ports, and if the latter, they can establish and hold a base area until land-based forces arrive. This capability, too, in modernized form, is described in the Marines' developing "operational maneuver from the sea" (OMFTS) concept.

The naval forces are positioning themselves to meet the new conditions of warfare and the new strategic needs. Under the "network-centric warfare" concept,[9] together with the OMFTS concept, they will be positioned to have the information superiority and to carry out the "dominant maneuver" of *Joint Vision 2010*. They are also acquiring advanced tactical aircraft—the current-generation F/A–18 E/F and, together with the Air Force, the Joint Strike Fighter—for the next generation of Navy and Marine aircraft. The Navy has the capability to launch "precision engagements" using current aircraft and surface-fired weapons, and that capability will increase in the future.[10] And both the Navy and the Marine Corps are developing the operational concepts and doctrines that will enable them to undertake the full spectrum of missions from friendly engagement to intense combat.

Specific Current and Future Naval Force Design Needs

It can be assumed that the basic naval force structure of carrier battle groups, amphibious ready groups, and strategic ballistic missile submarines, including all their new-generation ships, aircraft, weapons systems, and the concepts of operation that go with them, will continue into the indefinite future. This structure has been evolving steadily since World War II to meet changing world conditions, and, as the preceding discussion has shown, the forces within the structure will come to be even more appropriate to the Nation's needs in the future. The evolution of the force structure and its modes of operation will not cease, of course, and it will take some directions that derive from the current state of the world's technology, economy, and geopolitics.

The key conditioner of the modern use of naval power is that the days of independent naval force operation are long gone. Although in the current organizational trend they have much autonomy in tactical operations and even at the operational level once an action is committed, naval forces must not only keep in close touch with regional CINCs and the National Command Authorities for policy reasons, but also they are heavily dependent on external technical support for successful operations. They are particularly embedded in the information web, as attested to by the growth of the network-centric warfare concept. And for this, while they have many of their own assets at the tactical level, naval forces depend heavily both on the Air Force and on national space assets for surveillance, reconnaissance, communication, and navigation attending military action. Further, although the Marines are designed to take territory from the sea and set up protected operating bases on land, they are not fundamentally constituted or oriented to hold territory indefinitely as a ground force (although they have had to do so, and have done it very effectively, in Korea, Vietnam, and the Persian Gulf).

This is not simply a one-way dependency. The ground forces and land-based air forces depend on the sea for heavy lift, and therefore on Navy protection of the sea-lanes. They depend on the Navy for surveillance, reconnaissance, and electronic warfare support in open ocean areas that they may have to transit or in or near littoral areas from which they may have to operate. And as just noted, they may depend on the Navy/Marine Corps team and sea-based Special Operations Forces to take and secure operating bases where safe entry and close support are needed, but not available.

Also, there is a natural partnership between naval aviation and the intercontinental bomber force. The latter cannot hold position in a theater of operations for extended periods, nor can it necessarily feel secure about safe passage through antiaircraft defenses that may prepare for their arrival during the period preceding the arrival of a sortie in a target area. It was possible to anticipate B–52 raids from Guam through surveillance of the base area during the Vietnam War, and surveillance techniques have become considerably more sophisticated since then. On the other side of the equation, naval forces can only penetrate inland to the range of carrier-based aviation and, at the longer distances, the deliverable payload of attack aircraft becomes limited. However, the Navy can maintain sustained contact and clear the way for the heavy, deep-strike forces based off-shore or in the continental United States, in addition to conducting strike warfare along the littoral and 100 to 200 miles inland. Further, the coming era of tactical and theater-level defense against ballistic and cruise missiles will clearly require the fielding of complementary systems by all the services to ensure multilayer protection of areas at risk of nuclear or even conventional missile strike—including defense of Air Force and Army concentrations on land, allied cities and forces, and naval forces at sea.

The bottom line is that, in the post-Cold War, globalized world, military forces will have to operate jointly, both because of the geographical separation among possible areas of action and the fact that in the new (*Joint Vision 2010*/*Joint Vision 2020*) modes of operation, the critical assets for rapid decisionmaking are distributed among the forces; none of the forces can be as self-sufficient as they once were, or as they may have thought they once were. This development is coming to be accepted by the services, in recognition of the authority that the Goldwater-Nichols Department of Defense Reorganization Act of 1986 granted to CINCs for establishing the military requirements as well as commanding the military operations in their areas of responsibility. The formal command structure below the level of CINC still largely follows the lines established during the Cold War, in that service component commanders report to the CINCs and are responsible for the operations of their force elements: fleets, carrier battle groups, air forces, and so forth. However, mutual support among these force elements is ensured by direction from the CINC and by CINC approval of battle plans.

The arrangement of areas of responsibility and authority of the regional CINCs already covers much of the world's areas where military action may have to take place: the Atlantic and the Mediterranean; the Middle East and the Indian Ocean; the Pacific, including the Far East; and Latin America. The key area where shortening of command lines is taking place is at the lower operational and tactical levels, where it has come to be recognized that combat forces "at the point" cannot wait for engagement orders—for example, strike sorties, battalion maneuvers—to percolate through several command levels before action is authorized after the combat information network yields data on enemy maneuvers and shifting targets.

It has become clear from the lessons of the Persian Gulf War and operations in the Balkans that the traditional military operational command structure is evolving under operational pressures, just as the commercial command structure for global operations has been evolving. It is expected that in future military operations, especially those under the developing Marine OMFTS concept, forward units will often fight dispersed and in apparent isolation, making them hard for opposing forces to find and giving them a great deal of autonomy as they exercise their power—and mission—to call in heavy surface and air firepower from the fleet. However, they will have to be tied to the joint combat information and command network to do that and to operate as a coherent total force. Forward ground force units of any service will depend on air defense and aviation units of their own and other services for air defense and for offensive tactical air, mobility, and logistics support. The tactical air forces will rely on the forward ground units for accurate targeting information. Thus, even though the battlefield structure may appear to be one involving small, widely dispersed units that are apparently operating on their own, they will in fact be closely coupled in a joint operational structure. That is, indeed, the strength of the new tactical expression of network-centric operations. It is too early to say what the final structure will look like; it will be conditioned by future operations, and will have to be adaptable to remain responsive to the needs of the occasion.

The first requirement for naval forces in this environment is to make certain that they are fully connected, along with all the other services and the regional CINCs, into the worldwide command, control, communications, computers, intelligence, surveillance, and reconnaissance (C^4ISR) network, and that they appropriately furnish their important parts of that network. Information comes from many and diverse service and national sources, ranging from troops and aircraft in contact with the enemy to systems in space. Naval forces need compatible terminals to receive the information aboard ships, and at the headquarters of Marine units at various command levels on land. They also need communications that are interoperable among the services. The needs extend further, to include intelligence, ranging from opponents' intentions and capabilities to their actual tactical movements and actions, on land and at sea, in preparation for military engagement. Naval forces also need rapid intelligence on the effects of their actions. Such intelligence is commonly thought of as "bomb damage assessment," but it amounts to much more than that. The forces need to know the broader and longer term effects of any action—whether strike or maneuver—on their opponents' activity and plans early enough to anticipate and counter enemy moves before they can have any effect. Only through building toward such an information advantage can the forces make the rapid decisions needed in the current and future strategic environment.

In the naval forces operational environment, mines and submarines can be showstoppers. Mines conditioned the activity of the fleet and the Marines off Kuwait during the Persian Gulf War. Loss of a ship—for example, a major warship or a prepositioning ship steaming toward the scene of an action—to a submarine torpedo could effect a marked change in the outlook of the American public on an engagement in defense of a "mere interest," thereby either triggering an undesirable expansion of a modest military action or prompting an embarrassing stand-down. A significant part of the British naval effort during the Falklands war was devoted to guarding against Argentine diesel submarines that were feared to be in the theater of operations.

From the naval force point of view, the needed intelligence includes knowledge of opponents' mine warfare capability, moves to deploy mines, and the locations and extent of minefields. Knowledge of opposing fleet and air activity must also include submarine activity. Although the Navy and Marines have begun to give concerted attention to the risks and problems of mine warfare, which can be carried out by irregulars as well as by organized military forces (swimmers attaching limpet mines to ships in harbors, for example, or small boats loaded with explosives going off next to a warship), serious attention to antisubmarine warfare (ASW) essentially stopped with the end of the Cold War.

Antisubmarine warfare has been largely ignored in the competition for resources characteristic of our post-Cold War military planning. We have largely stood down from the heavy ASW emphasis of the Cold War era, both in research and development (R&D) and in actual operations at sea.[11] Yet, many potentially hostile nations and others who might want to interfere with U.S. and allied fleet and logistics operations are acquiring modern, quiet submarine capability. Such nations include China, North Korea, Iran, Pakistan, and India—not to mention the remaining and very substantial Russian submarine capability, which although reduced in recent years can be reactivated if they perceive the Navy as a hostile force. At the same time, our naval forces are focusing on the littoral area, in shallow waters where the underwater physics is much more difficult than in the deep, open oceans where we had concentrated our ASW attention during the Cold War. We have not yet solved the problems of finding and defeating hostile submarines in the relatively shallow waters of the continental shelves.

Mine and submarine warfare pose two serious vulnerabilities that must be remedied to permit the most effective use of our naval forces in defense of our interests. Failure in that effort would pose a serious threat to our developing military strategy of achieving fast decision with minimal casualties—a strategy that we have seen is needed in this era in which "interests" rather than survival dominate our global orientation.

The Marine Corps must be organized and prepared to deal with the prospect of having to achieve rapid success in urban environments that have, in addition to hostile populations, military or quasi-military defenders who know how to use buildings and rubble for cover, concealment, and offensive resistance. And they may have to achieve this under the watchful eyes of the news media's cameras, which will assuredly be focused on the most intense areas of death and destruction. The Marines are well aware of this need and have been preparing for what they call military operations in urban terrain (MOUT), or what has elsewhere been called military operations in built-up areas. This preparation has involved a series of exercises by the Commandant's Battle Lab whose purpose is to develop appropriate tactics and training, and through R&D to develop matching sensors and weapons, all with a view to capturing built-up areas rapidly, without destroying them—as we saw happen in Chechnya. Part of this preparation includes experimentation with nonlethal means of securing sections of streets and controlling the movements of mobs, both to avoid casualties to the civilian population and to prevent the civilians from being caught up in, and interfering with, combat operations.

The preparation must also build understanding of local cultures, customs, and values and include education training to impart this knowledge to our forces and their leadership. Such understanding and training could help forces anticipate the defense techniques of urban resistance groups and, if successfully integrated with the combat techniques being developed for MOUT, could eventually change the character—extended combat, heavy destruction, heavy casualties—of fighting in built-up areas. The need for such understanding and training emphasizes the need for, and value of, coalition operations, particularly operations with military forces and civilian administrators in or near the area of prospective combat. They will have much relevant information to provide, and our forces should be trained to seek out and heed it.

Summary of Areas for Naval Force Concentration

It is now possible to compile, from the preceding discussion, a compact summary of the particular needs of the naval forces in the globalizing, post-Cold War world of globalization that go beyond continual fleet, aviation, and weapons system modernization:

- All-source intelligence, surveillance, and reconnaissance input is crucial to naval force operations. Navy and Marine systems contribute to such input, but they also depend heavily on other services and national agencies for it. In this environment they must make their needs known and ensure that they are met, or their operations will be severely hampered.
- The naval forces' combat information systems must be a fully interoperable part of the theater- and worldwide intelligence and combat information network. Accomplishing this will entail developing ideas for network-centric operations that have been emerging from the Naval War College and several Navy-sponsored studies. These concepts include the idea of a balance between centralized policymaking and decentralized execution within the information and command network. The naval forces will have to work to extend that network physically and conceptually, working in conjunction with related efforts of the other services and the regional unified commands.
- The naval forces will need a precision land strike capability, which can operate autonomously as necessary or jointly with either the intercontinental bomber force or theater land-based air and ground forces. Capability in this area, already substantial, is being continually augmented, and that augmentation will continue so that the naval forces can take full advantage of joint targeting assets such as the high-altitude, long-endurance, unpiloted aircraft *Global Hawk* and the Joint Surveillance and Target Attack Radar System.
- The naval forces will have to give close, sustained attention to antimine and antisubmarine capability in the littoral environment. Mines and modern, quiet, non-nuclear submarines represent "poor-man's weapons" against a major naval power. They are easily purchased, they are appearing in increasing numbers

around the world, and they constitute a major U.S. vulnerability. The naval forces must be prepared to counter them.

- The Navy and Marines will need surface combat capability against stealthy antiship cruise missiles (or hostile ships) such as is being pursued in the current Cooperative Engagement Capability program and its extension to joint experiments with land-based air defense systems. These experiments will have to be continued until we are capable of providing cruise missile protection of an entire combined-arms combat force extending from far out at sea to far inland.
- The Navy must partner with other theater forces in theater ballistic missile defense, and it must be able to float such defense into place at appropriate locations at sea to undertake the defense alone in some circumstances (for example, defending Taiwan or Japan ad hoc from the sea, when political considerations may have precluded assistance "on the ground" before eruption of a crisis).
- Naval ships and the Marines must be defended against WMD effects. Ship protection would include positive pressure in ventilation systems, rapid washdown and decontamination capability, and immunization or treatment for chemical or biological attacks. The Marines must learn and practice how to operate in an environment where nuclear weapons have been or may be used, and how to operate in a chemical environment while wearing protective gear. And they must work with the Army and U.S. allies to acquire better, less debilitating protection. Also, for all the forces, continued research is needed on the detection of biological agents and on immunization or field application of antidotes for them.
- The naval forces need the ability to land marines rapidly, overcome resistance rapidly (including sustaining civil order by nonlethal means, since much of the action will be in urban or built-up areas), and secure ports and areas where follow-on land and expeditionary air forces can enter and undertake sustained operations; that is, they must continue to develop OMFTS and the techniques and equipment for military operations in urban terrain or built-up areas.
- The Navy will have to be able to protect logistics support fleets from any threats—air, surface, or subsurface—as they transit to a theater of operations.
- The naval forces will need counterterrorism capability for ships and their crews in ports and for marines ashore. This must include intelligence conducive to the anticipation and interdiction of terrorist attacks.
- To engage in the operations with coalitions that can be foreseen, to forestall terrorism, and to make it easier to subdue hostile urban areas when necessary, the naval forces will need the ability to work well with allies and other potential coalition partners. The knowledge and capabilities will have to be adaptable to many areas of the world. This will require the training of officers and commanders to enhance knowledge of diverse cultures and value systems, and of crews to adapt to those cultures and value systems (not to adopt them, but to be able to work in harmony with them). National policy must provide for the exchange of technical capabilities with allies. Such education, training, and knowledge will be needed at all levels, from small combat units or ships' crews to commanders in chief. The naval forces must not only train their own people in these areas, but also they must work with the other services in their related efforts. Whether, when, and

how to tailor capabilities to specific geographical areas, the provision of resident experts for consultation with the CINCs, and the nature of, and readiness for, ad hoc training for unexpected contingencies—all are matters yet to be taken up. The naval forces should promote their resolution at the policy levels of DOD and the Department of the Navy, and then diffusion of the results through the fleet and the Marines.

- Continuous training for both conventional military and quasi-military operations, including military operations other than war, is needed. The naval forces must work out ways to build and sustain proficiency in both areas—for example, by having different parts of forces in training and deployment for different aspects at different times; one part can at one time be preparing for, and deployed in, MOOTW and defense against asymmetrical warfare, while the other part is involved in training and preparation for conventional network-centric war fighting. The fractions of the forces to be assigned to each kind of activity at various times, rotation policies between them, the nature of the education and training, and other relevant matters—these too remain to be worked out. This is a major policy issue that must be worked out if the Nation and its naval and other military forces are to adapt effectively to a post-Cold War world having a global economy and posing major challenges to U.S. interests and security.

Notes

[1] Commission on America's National Interests, *America's National Interests* (Santa Monica, CA: The RAND Corporation, July 1996).

[2] Michael R. Gordon and Bernard E. Trainor, *The Generals' War* (Boston: Little, Brown and Company, 1995).

[3] John M. Shalikashvili, *Joint Vision 2010*, Joint Chiefs of Staff (Washington, DC: The Pentagon, 1997).

[4] Of course there can be mistakes, fratricide, and so forth; military operations are rarely perfect. But we can compare the World War II air raids against Dresden, which caused hundreds of thousands of civilian casualties, with the air war against Belgrade in 1999, which the Serbs claimed caused some dozens of civilian casualties, for similar operational effects.

[5] National Defense Panel, *Transforming Defense: National Security in the 21st Century* (Washington, DC: Government Printing Office, 1997).

[6] It should be noted that since our Civil War, at least, the United States has always been interested in minimizing combat casualties. We have eschewed such tactics as the Russian practice of committing division after division to be chewed up in combat to achieve a breakthrough, or the likes of Chinese "human wave" tactics, which spend personnel freely "now" in the expectation that that will hasten victory downstream. But the notion that troops should lay down their lives in what is viewed by much of the public as a sort of geopolitical game, rather than for the Nation's freedom and survival, adds further to the desire to avoid casualties in military action.

[7] A test we should not want to undertake, for example, would be to find out whether military conflict with China over Taiwan, as a war of principle, if it became protracted, would also fail for lack of support.

[8] Naval Studies Board, National Research Council, *Post-Cold War Conflict Deterrence* (Washington, DC: National Academy Press, 1997).

[9] The concept and its modus operandi are described in detail in the report of a study sponsored by the Chief of Naval Operations: Naval Studies Board, National Research Council, *Network-Centric Naval Forces: A Transition Strategy For Enhancing Operational Capabilities* (Washington, DC: National Academy Press, 2000).

[10] The current inventory includes the joint direct attack munition guided bomb and laser-guided bombs. Under development for the services' future inventory are the joint standoff weapon and the joint air-to-surface standoff missile. There are also surface-fired, precision-guided weapons such as the current *Tomahawk* and extended-range standoff land attack missile and, in the future, the gun-fired extended-range guided munition (ERGM) and a land attack version of the standard missile with extended range. This missile, as well as the *Tomahawk*, the ERGM, and the joint air-launched missiles will have the ability to attack targets with unitary warheads or submunitions, including the brilliant antitank submunition.

[11] Naval Studies Board, National Research Council, "Overview," vol. 1 of *Technology for the United States Navy and Marine Corps, 2000–2035* (Washington, DC: National Academy Press, 1997).

PART II.
U.S. NATIONAL SECURITY POLICY: EMERGING PRIORITIES

Chapter 7

A Global Agenda for Foreign and Defense Policy

Jonathan T. Howe

This paper explores in broad terms how continued globalization is likely to affect U.S. foreign policy and diplomacy over this new decade and beyond. It then examines some of the implications of this newly configured foreign policy for national defense and the requirements for maritime forces.

Foreign Policy

Three striking changes launched the period of fundamental alteration in the context for U.S. foreign policy that began in the 1990s. The Soviet empire collapsed, ending the Cold War; the United States emerged as the only superpower, with an unprecedented opportunity to influence the world; and America became more connected internationally as the process of globalization was fueled by technology. In addressing the impact that globalization is likely to have on U.S. foreign policy in this decade, it must first be acknowledged that there are many other trends, factors, and complexities that will shape the arena and global framework for which foreign policy is designed and implemented. Globalization is just one among many trends; and as others have observed, a "trend" is not necessarily a "destiny."[1] Nonetheless, the "rapid, ongoing, and uneven expansion of cross-border flows of goods, services, money, technology, ideas, information, culture and people" is likely to have a profound influence on future U.S. foreign policy and national security requirements.[2]

The United States no longer has the option of avoiding entangling foreign relationships. Forces beyond the control of any one nation are shaping a world that will be increasingly linked and enmeshed. Whether an open democracy or an insular dictatorship, no nation will be able to shield its citizens entirely from the impact of globalization. George Washington's hope "in extending" American "commercial relations" to have "as little political connection as possible" with "foreign nations" spoke to a profoundly different era of U.S. foreign policy.[3] Whatever foreign policy choices we make today in pursuing goals that enhance our interests, we must envisage that we will be dealing with a more tightly connected and interdependent world.

Admiral Jonathan T. Howe, USN (Ret.), served as national security advisor to the President and Vice President and has been a member of the National Security Council staff, the Office of the Secretary of Defense, and the Joint Staff. He commanded Allied Forces Southern Europe and U.S. Naval Forces Europe, and directed UN operations in Somalia.

Global interdependence is not a new phenomenon. Policymakers have been talking about it with increasing intensity over the last 30 years. For example, President Richard Nixon's report to the Congress on *U.S. Foreign Policy for the 1970s* observed, "Increasingly we see new issues that transcend geographic and ideological borders and confront the world community of nations. Many flow from the nature of modern technology. They reflect a shrinking globe and expanding interdependence."[4] During the preceding three decades, movement toward closer integration has been steady and substantial. In the 1990s, the pace became unrelenting and unprecedented.

Globalization alone is not likely to create new foreign policy demands. Rather, the acceleration of existing trends will have consequences both for policy and for the way Americans respond to future challenges. Globalization is providing both obstacles and opportunities. It is, for example, shrinking the time frame in which we must act. To be effective, foreign policy will have to deal with more problems at an earlier stage.

Impacts of Globalization on Foreign Policy

Among the many components of globalization, a few stand out as having a significant effect on foreign policy requirements. These include finance and trade, information, education, porosity of borders, and shared dependence.

Finance and Trade. The growing linkage of world economies will clearly influence future foreign policy. In spite of the November 1999 protests against the World Trade Organization (WTO) in Seattle and against the World Bank and International Monetary Fund (IMF) in Washington, DC, in April 2000, there does not appear to be any insurmountable barrier to the further integration of global financial markets and world trade. The pace, however, may be halting at times, with an uneven development of market economies and a growing gap between "have" and "have-not" nations.[5] Ability of governments to control the flow of money internationally has diminished as an estimated $1 trillion exchanges hands daily. Free financial flow adds to volatility. Even the strongest and largest economy in the world is not isolated from fluctuations in other markets, as demonstrated in recent years by the effects of disruptions in Mexico, Latin America, and East Asia on the American market.

The exchange of goods and services is also accelerating as American companies become more invested in markets overseas and as more foreign companies become an integral part of the American economy. The United States is the world's largest importer and exporter, and by 2010 will be dependent on trade for an estimated one-third of its gross domestic product (GDP). McDonald's, Coca-Cola, Goodyear, Johnson & Johnson, Exxon-Mobil, Gillette, Xerox, Intel, and Citicorp have joined the growing list of American companies that depend on overseas markets for more than half their earnings. Many foreign companies, such as the Japanese carmakers, have built plants in the United States or own American companies. Whether in the entertainment, beverage, insurance, banking, communications, or a range of other industries, the links forged among global businesses are multiplying at unprecedented rates. The merger of Chrysler/Daimler and Ford/Volvo are recent examples of the globalization of companies along product lines and new transnational alliances that help penetrate markets. We are confronted daily with reports of global mergers and acquisitions. Random House is now a German firm; a Denver company is buying a German cable television network. A British-Dutch conglomerate has acquired Ben & Jerry's Homemade Ice Cream, and a British company has bought New England Electric. An American group has purchased a major Japanese bank. A Spanish company is trying to buy Lycos.

E-commerce has introduced still another force that is promoting linkages. Although we will be increasingly connected electronically, the spread of an American presence in nations all over the world is also likely to accelerate. U.S. citizens will participate in all phases of economic life throughout the world. As a General Electric official has said, "Geographical and functional barriers must evaporate entirely. People must be as comfortable in New Delhi and Seoul as in Louisville or Schenectady."[6] A down side of this activity will be more U.S. citizens who are exposed and vulnerable to the vicissitudes of unstable countries and groups. Overseas businesses have always been targets, but there are more of them today and likely to be even larger numbers tomorrow. For instance, even if run by local entrepreneurs, McDonald's restaurants have become popular symbols of American enterprise targeted by protesters overseas.

What does this closer economic linkage mean for U.S. foreign policy? Clearly, we have an interest in the stability of an increasing number of countries and segments of countries for economic as well as political and mutual security reasons. No longer can we sustain the growth of our economy through the internal trade of goods and services. Our economic expansion is increasingly dependent on markets abroad. Therefore, a shared prosperity and an equitable trading system will be even more in our interest in the future than it is today. This economic dimension also has political ramifications. Growing competition for global markets may generate political tensions. Economic interdependence may also facilitate the building of better relations. For example, China's free market and desire to trade with the rest of the world could eventually lead to greater internal political freedom. Iran may be moderating internally as it seeks to restore trading relations with the United States.

As economic globalization continues, the map of foreign policy interests and national security requirements is likely to change. Economic components of foreign policy may have heavier weight. New economic alliances, partnerships, and friendships may have greater influence in defining national security priorities.

Information. Even in the early stages of the Information Revolution, the implications for foreign policy are profound. We have only begun to exploit the potential of the Internet, email, satellite telephones, and global television networks. In the early 1980s, a keen observer of the Soviet Union told me that what the Kremlin feared most was the spread of computing networks. Soon it would no longer be possible to suppress the flow of information or control the spread of ideas within or from outside Soviet society. The Internet was only in its infancy at the time. Certainly, there are still areas of the world where populations are isolated and where efforts continue to censor and distort the flow of information. The Internet and other pervasive media sources alone will not produce complete transparency. Propaganda and manipulation are not yet endangered. Nevertheless, the degree of control that any government exerts on the flow of information or powerful ideas to its citizens is likely to diminish over time. The opposition Malaysian political party Harakar's recent turn to the Internet is one example.

This free flow of information and ideas has many other implications. As the economic gap between the so-called developing and developed nations widens, it may exacerbate the discontent of the "have-nots," who begin to perceive that the conditions in which they live are not foreordained and that they need not be tolerated stoically. The flow of populations creates looming problems in certain countries as restive global nomads are drawn across borders in search of political freedom and respite from the ravages of ethnic cleansing or out of desperate need for economic opportunity or simply enough food and water. Such movements can lead to tensions, as the forceful return of Albanians by the Italians or the unrelenting struggle with illegal aliens on the southwestern U.S. border demonstrates. The majority of persons on the move across the world's borders are economic refugees. As the media connect more citizens with disturbing images, it becomes difficult in the "have" world to ignore the plight of peoples dying of starvation as a result of a natural disaster or an ethnic conflict. Pictures of the exodus of ethnic Albanians driven from Kosovo provided the evidence that ensured international support for North Atlantic Treaty Organization (NATO) bombing. This CNN effect can be powerful. Thus, information can both stimulate population flows and influence responses to them.

During a recent meeting in Jacksonville, Florida, with a small group from Punjab, India, calling cards and email addresses were exchanged. New connections had been established. Similar informal linkages occur daily and multiply exponentially. Over time, there will be millions of linkages among individual citizens and nongovernmental organizations (NGOs). These individual connections may link people with common global interests or causes (for example, preserving the environment or preventing the spread of the human immunodeficiency virus [HIV]) and either reduce government influence or convince governments to change policies. The 1997 Nobel Peace Prize, which recognized the grass-roots efforts of Jody Williams and associates to ban and clear antipersonnel land mines, is one example of this potential.

These new networks of formal and informal linkages also create vulnerabilities. Hackers are intruding into supposedly secure computers with regularity. Whether stealing identities or credit card numbers, breaking into confidential government networks or simply testing skills, cybercriminals present a continuing challenge. The arrest of young Israelis who broke into the Department of Defense (DOD) network is one recent example; another is the Scandinavian hacker who managed to tie up the 911 systems in Florida. The shutdown of global email by the "I Love You" virus is one in a series of incidents that illustrate the pervasiveness of these worldwide linkages and their vulnerability. As we become more dependent upon the Internet, our vulnerability to and the threat of cyberterrorism will grow.

What does this sharing of information and connectedness across global boundaries mean for U.S. foreign policy? A few implications are:

- Governments will have greater difficulty controlling commerce, movement of peoples, and the flow of information and ideas.

- The awareness of the plight of distant peoples will be much higher, and there will be pressures to use capabilities to assist where feasible.
- Tensions may rise as individuals become more aware of and discontented with the uneven distribution of wealth and move across state boundaries in search of a better life.
- Resentments may build as American culture proliferates around the globe.

We are only beginning to understand the likely influence on foreign affairs of this profound Information Revolution.

Education. Closely linked to information is the increasing globalization of higher education. The internationalization of education is illustrative of what is happening in practically every other profession. For example, it is routine in college libraries to search collections abroad for materials. The librarian of Davidson College recounts the story of a frantic email message from a student in Scandinavia who had become electronically locked in the North Carolina library and was pleading for a way to get out. The sharing of documents and information means that with the click of a mouse, under-resourced institutions can multiply the access that their students have to global sources of information.

Education is an essential underpinning of the preparation necessary to deal with the effects of globalization. Nonetheless, we are only at the beginning of the monumental effort needed to prepare U.S. citizens to operate effectively in this new world. As the new head of Claremont McKenna College observed, if we do not become more seriously engaged in the study and analysis of global issues, "America will gradually lose its relative economic, military, political weight in the world, while it also becomes more economically integrated and exposed to external environmental factors that will be increasingly more difficult to control."[7] In the United States, higher education is just starting to take innovative steps to respond to this future. Larger percentages of graduates have spent a semester abroad,[8] courses are reflecting a broader approach to the world across curricula, and language requirements are making a comeback. Distance learning provides new ways of connecting classrooms, and there are growing examples of students in different countries jointly taking the same courses or earning degrees online in another nation.

Although there are encouraging initiatives to get more American college students overseas during their undergraduate years, many foreign countries are far ahead of the United States in this regard. There is an alarming trade imbalance in higher education. This is one area in which the United States has a four-to-one exchange surplus: it educates far more students from foreign countries than it sends abroad. As American institutions strive for more geographically diverse student bodies, foreign students gain a deeper understanding of the United States. The experience of American students also is broadened; however, rubbing elbows with foreign students who are spending time in the United States is no substitute for going overseas to study. Interestingly, eight of the top ten providers of students to the United States are Asian nations, but the majority of American students (64 percent) who go abroad to study still choose Europe.[9]

There is also a growing international partnership among educational institutions. The joint venture between Massachusetts Institute of Technology (MIT) and the University of Cambridge that formed the $135 million Cambridge-MIT Institute is a recent example.[10] Foreign scholars are also joining American academic associations in significant numbers. For example, more than one-third of the membership of the American Mathematical Society is foreign.[11]

In order for its foreign policy to be more effective, the United States will need not only informed diplomats, international economists, intelligence specialists, and military officers, but also citizens in every profession who speak foreign languages, understand foreign cultures, and know how to operate in the world. If the United States is going to sustain a leadership role in the decades to come, it must begin now to develop greater numbers of citizens with deeper understanding of the multiplicity of global cultures that approach life in starkly different ways.

Porosity of Borders. As the financial, information, and education flows demonstrate, national borders are eroding as barriers to international interaction. Growing connections across permeable borders have both positive and negative implications for nation-states. On the down side, it has eased access for global crime syndicates and drug cartels, exposed nations to terrorism, and contributed to the proliferation of arms around the world. The spread of weapons of mass destruction (that is, chemical, biological, and nuclear arms and their delivery systems) is facilitated by ease of access and global connections. At the same time, globalization offers tools for combating these menaces to civil societies. It is clear that nations must cooperate much more closely if they are going to combat such criminal activities. The rapid expansion of legitimate international connections provides a mechanism for doing so. However, this essential coordination among nations also contributes to the erosion of their individual sovereignty.

The internal breakdown of nation-states that occurs as a result of ethnic struggles—struggles that global media bring to our living rooms—has raised a major new foreign policy question: At what point is it appropriate for the world community to act within the sovereign boundaries of a country? Somalia, Haiti, Kosovo, and the Congo are recent examples of this dilemma.

Shared Dependence. International cooperation is also essential to ensure that resources meet the needs of a growing world population and to find solutions to the common challenges of a shared environment. It has long been recognized that the oceans, environment, energy, food supply, air, and weather affect the world—not just individual states—and that preservation of ecological systems requires global solutions. World water demands are "expected to double in the next 30 years,"[12] and global food requirements are estimated to double in the next 25 years. According to the Archer Daniels Midland Company, "Food security has become the single most important issue in international trade negotiation," and the world's food economy has become "truly global this past decade."[13] The world's need for energy and delays in developing economically viable alternative sources underline the importance of ensuring that oil supplies and other important natural resources remain in the hands of nations friendly to the outside world. From mad cow disease to acquired immunodeficiency syndrome (AIDS), world health standards are also important to long-term survival. Cooperation among nations is essential, since microbes carry no passports. Similarly, from fishing to forests, the impact of excesses and the failure to preserve biodiversity are mortgaging the health and quality of life of future generations.

Whether dealing with acid rain, biodiversity, or oil spills, there also is a deeper understanding that it is in the mutual interests of nations to find shared solutions to common environmental problems. Nations share the consequences of environmental degradation. In the future, we will live even more closely together. We have seen that the fallout from a Chernobyl can endanger agriculture thousands of miles away. Nations have conflicting interests, and finding practical and equitable solutions is seldom easy. A major task of foreign policy is to achieve international cooperation in addressing these common problems.

In examining the potential negative consequences of globalization in the future, the White House has reiterated that U.S. citizens "have a direct and increasing stake in the prosperity and stability of other nations, in their support for international norms and human rights, in their ability to combat international crime, in their open markets, and in their efforts to protect the environment."[14]

Foreign Policy Objectives

Over the past decade, there has been little change in how American presidents have defined core national security objectives. The broad goals described by the White House in late 1999 in *A National Security for a New Century* are similar to those outlined by President George Bush at the beginning of the last decade. Essentially, these core goals have been to enhance security, to bolster economic prosperity, and to promote democracy abroad.[15] It can be argued that we have worked successfully in the last decade to "advance the welfare of our people by contributing to an international environment of peace, freedom and progress within which our democracy—and other free nations—can flourish."[16]

How we succeed in the new century in accomplishing these historic and enduring elements of national strategy will depend increasingly on how we deal with the challenges presented by a more closely linked and globalized world. The three core objectives are intertwined. Economic prosperity will increasingly be a shared global experience. The promotion of peace, prosperity, and representative government are complementary endeavors. The freer flow of ideas, stimulated by globalization, should facilitate the growth of democracy. A free economy provides incentives for peace and representative government.

Former National Security Advisor to the President Sandy Berger said, "The central phenomenon of our time, globalization, plays to America's greatest strengths—to our creative and entrepreneurial spirit—and spreads our most cherished ideals of openness and freedom."[17] The somewhat simplistic notion that democracies seldom fight or jeopardize intertwined economies, often referred to as the "McDonald's rule,"[18,19] has become a modern axiom. However, some scholars have cautioned that in the "short run, democratic transitions often promote war and undermine economic reform."[20] During the United Nations (UN) intervention in Somalia in 1993, it appeared to be the fear that more representative government would mean the loss of power for warlord General Mohamed Farah Aidid that motivated him to oppose the United Nations so violently.

The core goals of security, prosperity, and democracy are more likely to be advanced in an atmosphere of relative global stability than in an atmosphere that is unstable. Promoting stability and peace in this increasingly networked and changing world will be central to future foreign policy and is likely to create new defense challenges and priorities.

To a considerable extent, the U.S. approach to this challenging world will be influenced by the strategy adopted by the administration elected in November 2000. Roughly, there are three variations in the way a new administration might approach its foreign policy and national security responsibilities while professing the same core agenda of past administrations. In broad terms, these approaches, and in a sense attitudes, can be described as protective, reactive, and proactive. Each approach will influence the strategies employed:

- *Protective.* A protective strategy would be characterized by minimizing exposure abroad, limiting participation and support of international organizations, adopting more protectionist measures with regard to the impact of trade on American workers, reducing treaty alliances and limiting new commitments, and very narrowly defining U.S. interests in terms of when U.S. forces should be committed.
- *Reactive.* A reactive strategy would involve allowing situations to evolve and responding to critical requirements as they presented themselves. With this ad hoc approach, we would develop and select in each instance the best possible option.
- *Proactive.* A proactive strategy would involve providing leadership in world organizations, developing long-term strategies, and moving aggressively and preemptively to solve problems. The United States would be a leader in working with other nations to try to anticipate and to resolve world problems.

What are the consequences of these strategies for U.S. national security policy in a globalizing world? A protective approach would put priority on such issues as the preservation of American jobs. The North American Free Trade Agreement (NAFTA), the WTO, the World Bank, the United Nations, and other global organizations and arrangements would be seen as threats to our sovereignty. An effort would be made to limit the "damage" of these manifestations of globalization. Such an approach would run counter to the strong and relentless current of inevitable change. What might appear to be "progress" in the short term would probably leave the United States farther behind in the long run. Resort to protection would amount to the world's most powerful nation trying to duck an unwanted leadership position.

An ad hoc approach would take a more measured middle road between the other two strategies and might mitigate rancor generated by a perception of overweening U.S. activism. It would sacrifice, however, the concerted strategy that is probably necessary to influence the world in directions favorable to the United States. It would slowly abandon the opportunity for leadership provided by our economic, political, and military position in the world.

A proactive approach would require developing and conducting a well thought-out strategy. It would give the United States the largest role in shaping global outcomes. However, such a strategy would probably mean more U.S. involvement in controversial activities such as peacekeeping and in schemes designed to contain conflicts and bound problems without actually solving them. A proactive approach would raise resentments in some areas of the world and could be seen as threatening in others. Nonetheless, it appears to be the approach most consistent with operating successfully in a globalized world.

In implementing a proactive policy, the cross-cutting issues of globalization that sometimes have been relegated to the back burner would need to have greater priority. Terrorism, crime, drugs, pollution, and the proliferation of weapons of mass destruction and their means of delivery can no longer be seen as problems of an individual country or even of a region. These problems are global in nature and require global solutions. It will take our most innovative and determined individuals to fashion solutions. It will not be enough that goals are reflected in high-sounding rhetoric; meeting these challenges must be the day-to-day passion of an administration.

Diplomacy

Even if the United States chooses a very protective foreign policy, the age of globalization is likely to call for a different approach to implementing it. We will need a much more dynamic diplomacy to help meet the prolific demands of a new age, and it will need to be backed by military power.

As linkages become tighter and news travels faster, we enter a world in which there is an increasing magnification and resonance of events. Ramifications ripple farther and faster, and responses need to be more rapid and effective. This calls for a new kind of diplomacy that has some of these features:

- More connection to governments and to other power centers in a given country.
- Rapid consultation, cooperation, and coordination with allies and friends.
- A better informed country team in the field, and an ability to react more quickly in Washington with informed decisionmaking.
- A tightly coordinated national security team that fully integrates political, military, and economic factors. This may call for reorganization, as international businesses are doing, along functional rather than regional lines. More power may need to be shifted to the functional bureaus of the Department of State, for example, from the traditionally dominant regional bureaus.
- A military that is better positioned and has the means to react quickly in both the prevention and crisis phases of potential conflicts.

Although the practice of diplomacy will need to change in response to a faster moving age, one historical axiom remains valid. To be effective, diplomacy designed to promote peace and defuse crises must be backed by military strength. This relationship is one of the enduring reasons for maintaining a responsive and respected military capability in a period such as the one ahead.

A central task for diplomacy and DOD will be building cooperative relations with friends and allies. In promoting stability around the world, a network of allies and friends will be essential. The very nature of globalization means that partnerships will need to be an important component of resolving critical concerns and problems. Worldwide crime organizations, for example, must be confronted by resolute global partners. In the same way, it will take nations working cooperatively to meet the vast needs of economic and political security and stability. Just as the purposeful investment in alliance building and containment was relevant to the Cold War, a strong network of partnerships for stability will be essential to this new world.

Defense

As the world becomes more interdependent, the need for the skillful exercise of a blend of diplomacy and power and the need for partnerships with other nations will not diminish. As discussed earlier, maintaining stability in various critical regions of the world will continue to be one of the dominant objectives of U.S. foreign policy. It is also likely that the list of geographical locations in which the United States has interests will be much longer and contain unfamiliar names. The forces of globalization may also lead to new functional priorities and changing alliance structures. Although some locations will have greater priority than others, as American goods, services, culture, and people spread to remote areas of the globe, U.S. citizens may become more tightly linked with new societies.

The continuing march of globalization is likely to generate a more diverse and less predictable set of requirements over a wider area of the world. As the scope of economic interests spreads farther and penetrates deeper, driven by new multilateral companies and the pervasive network of entrepreneurial dot-coms that know no boundaries or barriers, the United States will require a more active and better informed foreign and commercial policy backed by a more flexible and agile defense organization.

Decisionmaking. The forces of globalization are helping create a national security environment that calls for rapid and sound decisionmaking. The pressures alone to be "out front" of globalized media call for faster and more flexible responses. The combination of unpredictable situations and far-flung interests requires Washington to overcome its historical inability to concentrate on more than one foreign crisis at a time and to be able to manage multiple crises simultaneously across the globe. This imperative of timeliness, however, does not offer an excuse for poorly thought-out policies, knee-jerk reactions, and avoidance of the "And then what?" question. Rather, it calls for rising to a new level of performance.

A number of elements will be required to retool the national security machinery to meet the responsibilities of this changing world. They include a much deeper and wider intelligence base from which to inform decisionmaking, a well thought-out and well formulated policy framework from which to make crisis decisions, and tighter coordination based on a strong and responsive National Security Council (NSC) system. This will require closer policy integration across concerned departments—both horizontally and vertically—and a team of talented, selfless individuals who are genuinely devoted to putting the national interest before bureaucratic self-interest.

Partnership between State and Defense starts with a close relationship between the secretaries of these departments. Other players will need to be integrated. For example, given the global economy, the Secretary of the Treasury must be more involved in national security decisionmaking.

There also will be no substitute for the personal involvement and leadership of the President. It is the one area in our system of checks and balances in which a President has clear-cut leadership and Constitutional responsibilities. Failure to prepare for and skillfully handle national security challenges could be the downfall of this Nation. On key issues, the President must be engaged in national security policy formulation from its inception. A framework of goals and objectives must be established in the quiet prevention phases of impending crises, long before they move to the media glare of the near-conflict stage. The national security advisor should be instrumental in seeing that this is the case. Focusing on the economy should not provide an excuse for turning inward; instead, in a global economy, it should underline the need to turn outward.

Requirements. The demands of defense in an age of complex globalization are imposing. What appears to be needed is a streamlining comparable to that which major companies have undertaken in order to remain competitive and to take commanding leadership in the global marketplace. With the commitment of the President and adequate resources, this is a task well within the competence of our entrepreneurial Armed Forces. As we contemplate the future impact of globalization, it is helpful to consider the changing imperatives of prevention, deterrence, commitment, crisis response, and success in conflict.

Prevention. In the future, it will not suffice for the armed services simply to provide a "911 force" for rescuing failed policies. Instead, DOD must be a full partner with State, the Central Intelligence Agency (CIA), and other members of an expanded national security organization in making a long-term investment in the knowledge, global relationships, and confidence building that will reduce the number of emergency calls. In a globalizing world, successful prevention will require a comprehensive strategy and a concerted effort across the entire cabinet—not just the traditional national security community. An effective strategy will also require working more closely with the private sector. Conflict prevention is one of the most difficult challenges ahead, but greater attention must be focused on the early phase of meeting selected global responsibilities. We will need to devote more assets to shaping the environment in which we must operate. Just as medicine has begun to learn that investment in prevention pays, the national security establishment will need to become involved earlier in trying to head off difficulties in the era ahead.

Historically, DOD has played an important role in prevention, but it will have to operate with greater anticipation and skill than in the past, when decisions on where to invest preventive attention could be made in the context of a more clearly defined Cold War framework. Overseas bases, for example, are still important to a responsive global defense structure, but new locations may be needed and others should be abandoned. Sites will have to be selected with the sensitivities of potential host nations in mind. The Marine Corps barracks bombing in Lebanon in 1983 and the terrorist bombing of the Air Force Khobar Tower barracks in Saudi Arabia in 1996 are reminders of the challenges of placing forces statically in tense areas.

Prevention also requires a better understanding of the swirling cultural differences in this new world and a keener grasp of potential nation-state and nontraditional adversaries as well as friends. This job is not limited to intelligence agencies. It requires the pooling of relevant governmental, private, and public resources, especially in overseas missions. With Internet newspapers, global radio and television, and knowledgeable businesspersons operating all over the world, there are numerous sources of information, often untapped, that must be integrated into the equation. Pervasive globalization presents complex challenges to defense, but it also offers tools for becoming better informed and thus better prepared.

Deterrence. An important question related to prevention in this new period is, What constitutes effective deterrence? Closely linked to this question is the importance of *credibility*. The time-honored ingredients of credible deterrence may be harder to achieve, but appear to be just as relevant in a more globalized world as they were in former times. If challenges are to be kept to the minimum, the warnings of diplomats or peacemakers must be backed by a force that adversaries anticipate will be used with relative impunity and that will have an impact on the things they value most.

With this requirement in mind, there must be a closer partnership between diplomats and military commanders. Diplomacy must be undergirded by ready forces whose power and capability are unquestioned. There must also be a belief in the commitments made by the President of the United States. This requires a willingness to act boldly when it is in U.S. interests to do so. Such commitments must also be based on a determination to persevere when the going gets rough and on the readiness to provide sufficient means for the military to accomplish assigned missions.

American credibility has ebbed and flowed in recent years. The United States did not start to close the global credibility gap caused by its handling of the Vietnam War and by the failed Iran rescue attempt in 1980 until 1983, when the quick victory in Grenada demonstrated that the United States could and would still act decisively. The collapse of the Soviet empire and the *Desert Storm* response to the invasion of Kuwait raised U.S. military credibility in the early 1990s to an all-time high. Some of this capital was squandered when the United States decided in 1993 to pull its forces out of Somalia and shortly afterward appeared to be intimidated from acting in Haiti. One of the major reasons given for the recent intervention in Kosovo was the future credibility and survival of the NATO alliance. Whatever the legitimate criticisms of the Kosovo process, it has given new life to NATO and was an impressive demonstration of standoff power.

These latter crises had more to do with where we draw the boundary lines of national interests requiring sacrifice than with the capabilities of our forces. They bring home, however, the importance of careful consideration of which commitments are sufficiently in our interests to include a willingness to sacrifice lives to defend those interests. American military power will need to command respect from a vast range of potential adversaries—from individual terrorists such as Osama bin Laden to future peer competitors.

Commitment. In an era of globalization, the U.S. definition of national interests is likely to expand. In recent years, the President has committed to defending national interests and values. Values are even more wide open to interpretation than are traditional national security interests. There are many instruments besides military forces for defending interests and values. However, it is likely that future armed services, in addition to preparing for current priority contingencies in Asia and the Middle East and for the unanticipated crisis and hedging against a peer competitor, will be contributing to peacekeeping, peace enforcement, humanitarian recovery, and a broad agenda of other global challenges. These may include ethnic cleansing, terrorism, the war on drugs, nonproliferation, and defending against asymmetrical warfare. While it might be ideal to concentrate on fewer, better defined missions, the realistic expectation is that the spectrum of mission requirements is likely to expand, rather than narrow, in this uncertain period.

Whether a major or a minor conflict, the consequences of the commitment of U.S. forces should be thought through before it is undertaken or before participation is expanded. However, the underlying need for perseverance and follow-through, once a commitment is made, will not change, nor will the global consequences to credibility from pulling out.

Related to participating in complex emergencies is the unrealistic expectation that American casualties will be minimal and that we can be successful without paying a cost in lives. While we must always strive to minimize casualties, the much lower than predicted losses in the Persian Gulf War and the surgical approach to Kosovo have fed misleading notions that U.S. power can be effective with little risk to our forces. The United States should strive aggressively for a technical edge that raises probabilities of rapidly achieving goals, but in deciding to commit forces, we must weigh the costs carefully in advance and accept that there are always consequences (sometimes unintended), dangers, and risks to using military force. Appropriate preparation of U.S. citizens for these eventualities is essential.

Crisis Response. Even with optimum intelligence and an active program of conflict prevention, globalization is unlikely to change the fact that there will be instances when national security surprises require rapid crisis response. In cases in which we enter with our eyes wide open because a laborious process of diplomacy and prevention has preceded intervention, we will undoubtedly be prepared to respond with the full measure of diplomatic and military capabilities. However, we are not likely again to have the luxury of the 6-month buildup period of *Desert Shield.* Our future will surely have its share of surprises and "come-as-you-are" emergencies requiring immediate action. Delaying, hedging, or postponing tough decisions should never be the only feasible option. The defense establishment must be rapid in its response, agile in its employment of appropriate instruments of power, and fully capable of bringing pressure to bear effectively. This will require having the right instruments and being able to use them in a timely manner. We also must have developed the peacetime diplomatic and military relationships that help convince allies and friends to provide their political and practical support in times of potential conflict.

Success in Conflict. As history demonstrates, the combination of skillful execution of diplomacy backed by available force is not always enough to deter conflict.

There will undoubtedly be a wide range of circumstances requiring a variety of responses such as coercive diplomacy, retaliation, or restoration of a pre-existing situation (as in *Desert Storm*). Forces will also still need the capability to respond to major theater contingencies. Whatever the shape of the conflict, forces must be able to persuade an adversary to capitulate quickly. They must be able to bend the will of an adversary and demonstrate convincingly that there is more to lose with each passing day of conflict. This requires forces that are clearly superior and able to target accurately, and with relative impunity, things of value to an adversary.[21,22] We must be able not only to conclude military actions successfully but also to deal with post-conflict activities that ultimately may determine the long-term success or failure of a military operation.

Design of Forces. Designing forces to operate effectively in a globalizing world is a daunting task. Building a "force for all missions" would be challenging, even in an ideal world unencumbered by an outdated procurement system and the historical American inclination not to invest in future security when there is no overriding threat. Clearly, greater flexibility, versatility, responsiveness, speed, reach, and accuracy are dictated by likely responsibilities and contingencies in a globalizing world. The Army and Air Force are moving toward greater flexibility with air expeditionary forces and more rapidly deployable Army brigades that complement the traditional expeditionary capabilities offered by the Navy and Marine Corps; however, a much higher level of joint integration in warfare is needed. Innovative concepts such as "Rapid Dominance" that exploit the potential of advances in rapidity, information, control, and brilliance[23] need to compete with more conventional approaches to preparing for the future. We should take advantage of American entrepreneurial capacity to adapt to this new age. "Dot-com" ingenuity, boldness, and determination reflect some of the new spirit and energy needed.

The Maritime Mission. It is also clear that in the period immediately ahead, it will be necessary to orchestrate more skillfully the unique capabilities that each service brings to the battle. The seamless optimizing of joint forces is essential in a period in which diffuse and unanticipated requirements may be the norm and the size of the armed services has been cut significantly. All of the services, including the Coast Guard, will need to continue to contribute to traditional maritime missions; however, the Navy and Marine Corps will likely retain a primary role, especially in the prevention and crisis response roles that will be an important part of day-to-day maritime operations.

As the United States extends its economic and political reach into unfamiliar corners of the globe, naval and marine forces afloat provide a visible reminder that Americans on the ground are backed by a full coverage insurance policy. The peacetime missions of the 6th and 7th Fleets, and now the 5th Fleet in the Persian Gulf, and regular cruises to other regions (for example, South America, West Africa, and the South Pacific) have been traditional solidifiers of good will, confidence, and stability. As some nations become more secure and independent, one can legitimately ask whether a reassuring presence is still relevant. Is this an anachronistic vestige of the Cold War struggle for the Third World or a return to "gunboat diplomacy" of the 19th century? In the less defined world ahead, there will be changing relationships and needs. Some nations may become more secure; others will experience increased insecurity and possibly internal fragmentation. In this volatile period, the overseas presence mission, although difficult to sustain, will still be relevant.

The relationships established while exercising with friendly armed forces have long-term benefits. As a preventive tool, they demonstrate readiness to act together to defend mutual interests. They help pave the way for access to territorial waters and straits or hurried air transit or tanker overflight clearances in times of crisis. The groundwork is prepared for more effective coalition warfare in conflict. The foundation for long-standing relationships needs to be built in periods of peace, just as access to U.S. military schools and exchanges of people promote lasting friendships and provide the basis for better understanding complex societies. These traditional tools of prevention are just as relevant in an uncertain period of globalization as they were in the Cold War.

In crisis, there is still no substitute for a warship or carrier aircraft appearing offshore or beginning training with local forces during times of tension and impending crisis. Such symbols of capability, backed by the credibility of a government that means what it says, can translate into powerfully persuasive messages of peace and restraint. The numbers of crises that need to be defused in their early stages by the visible expression of commitment are not likely to diminish in this new restless decade.

The Navy and Marine Corps have traditionally been effective symbols of U.S. interests in areas in which the United States does not have a usable base structure for land-based assets. Depending upon the circumstances, they can sustain a presence or withdraw over the horizon. Even in well established relationships, there have been recent reminders that potential host nations are not always prepared to offer access to their facilities. Saudi reluctance to authorize use of bases for Operation *Desert Fox* is a vivid reminder that the United States needs to have a full array of flexible sea-borne weapons platforms. When crises erupt, the Navy and Marine Corps provide a valuable means for responding in remote areas and for teaming with other joint forces in bringing weapons to bear on an adversary.

Historical maritime requirements to protect the open ocean sea-lanes and ensure access through strategic chokepoints (such as the Suez Canal, the Strait of Hormuz, or the Strait of Malacca) are not likely to disappear. Most of the logistical flow to support ground-based forces continues to go by sea, and the industrial West, including Japan, still depends on the free flow of energy and other materials.

The Navy and Marine Corps also will need to provide their full range of warfighting capabilities to strike from the sea and influence events ashore in support of joint efforts to respond to regional contingencies and to hedge against the emergence of a peer competitor. For example, the Navy cannot assume that no submarine force will ever rise to challenge its free access of the open ocean as the Soviet Union once did.

How does the increase in globalization affect these historical missions? Will they be different in the future? Are new tools necessary, and are old ones anachronistic? Clearly, maritime forces will have to continue to change with the times. Better weapons should be developed as technology advances, and other services may become stronger contributors to the maritime mission.

Because of globalization and a variety of other influences, such as the collapse of the Soviet empire and the breakup of nation-states, in the next two decades the United States is likely to confront tough national security choices in a more complex and unstable world. As long as stability is a major foreign policy mission, maritime forces will be critical instruments for maintaining it.

Globalization, therefore, has two immediate effects on the national security requirements for maritime forces. First, the scope of coverage needed and the responsiveness required to protect U.S. interests are likely to increase. Second, the short-term effect of globalization may contribute to increasing instabilities in some areas while tightening the bonds between like-minded societies in others.

Conclusions

The period of accelerating globalization ahead will introduce forces for stability and instability. It will offer both opportunities and challenges for achieving foreign policy goals. The long-term influence of globalization may be to help create a more peaceful and stable world in which closely linked and interdependent global citizens have a growing stake in a shared prosperity and political freedom. However, over the next several decades, globalization will also be one of the factors that stimulate reverberating tensions and unleash forces of change.

In meeting the demands of national security during this uncharted period of transition, tension, and turbulence, the United States will need highly effective, mobile, and responsive forces capable of meeting a wide range of complex and challenging contingencies in both new and familiar trouble spots. It must also make a concerted investment in conflict prevention. In such an unsettled time, maritime forces can provide a number of answers. The Navy's "anytime, anywhere" approach to preparing for this period appears to be on target. It would be appropriate to add to that assertion, "We deliver."

Notes

[1] Jaime Lerner, quoted in the *1997 Annual Report* of The Geraldine R. Dodge Foundation, 13.

[2] This is the definition used throughout this book. The White House describes globalization as "the process of accelerating economic, technological, cultural and political integration." The White House, *A National Security Strategy for a New Century* (Washington, DC: Government Printing Office, December 1999), 4.

[3] George Washington, farewell address, *The Record of American Diplomacy* (New York: Alfred A. Knopf, 1964), 87.

[4] Richard M. Nixon, The White House, *U.S. Foreign Policy for the 1970s, Building for Peace* (Washington, DC: Government Printing Office, February 25, 1971), 5.

[5] The share of global income possessed by the 85 percent of the world's population living in emerging nations is estimated to be only slightly above 20 percent. *The Babson Staff Letter,* Cambridge, MA, March 3, 2000.

[6] Dennis D. Dammerman, "Educating People for the 21st Century," remarks to a conference of Jesuit Advancement Administrators, *Fairfield Now* (Spring 1997), 2.

[7] Pamela Brooks Gann, inaugural address, Claremont McKenna College, October 23, 1999.

[8] Only about 9 percent of U.S. college students currently study abroad, and fewer than one-third of these spend at least a semester in a foreign country. A. Lee Fritschler, as quoted in an article by Stephen Burd, *The Chronicle of Higher Education* 46, no. 35 (May 5, 2000).

[9] Paul Desruisseaux, "15% Rise in American Students Abroad Shows Popularity of Non-European Destinations," *The Chronicle of Higher Education* 46, no. 16 (December 16, 1999), A60.

[10] Alina Tugend, "MIT and U. Cambridge Announce $135-Million Joint Venture," *The Chronicle of Higher Education* 46, no. 13 (November 19, 1999), A71.

[11] Beth McMurtie, "America's Scholarly Societies Raise Their Flags Abroad," *The Chronicle of Higher Education* 46, no. 21 (January 28, 2000), A53.

[12] The Nature Conservancy, *The Nature Conservancy's Freshwater Initiative*, Arlington, VA, 1999, 10.

[13] G. Allen Andreas, *ADM this Quarter*, November 29, 1999, 2–3.

[14] The White House, *A National Security Strategy*, 4.

[15] The White House, *1999 National Security Strategy Report*, press release, January 4, 2000. The actual report adds "and human rights" to the third objective.

[16] The White House, *National Security of the United States* (Washington, DC: Government Printing Office, March 1990), 1.

[17] Samuel R. Berger, *American Leadership in the 21st Century*, remarks to the National Press Club, Washington, DC, January 6, 2000.

[18] See, for example, J. Brady Anderson, "Waging Democracy—The McDonald's Rule," *Rhodes College* 7, no. 1 (Winter 2000).

[19] Richard Saul Warren, *Understanding*, 1999 report of The Markle Foundation.

[20] Edward D. Mansfield, "And Now the Bad News," *Hoover Digest*, no. 4 (1999), 77.

[21] For more on the Rapid Dominance concept, see Harlan K. Ullman and James P. Wade, *Shock and Awe: Achieving Rapid Dominance* (Washington, DC: National Defense University/Government Printing Office, 1996).

[22] Harlan K. Ullman and James P. Wade, *Rapid Dominance—A Force for All Seasons* (London: RUSI Whitehall Paper Series, 1998).

[23] Ullman and Wade, *Rapid Dominance—A Force for All Seasons.*

Chapter 8

Beyond Global-Regional Thinking

Alan K. Henrikson

The globalization of American foreign policy, including national security policy, is not mainly a product of having a single "global" *idea*—a unifying "world" view, a "large" economic outlook, a "grand" military strategy. It is not, essentially, *ideo*logical, whatever its scale. It is, rather, *logical*—a continuing rational process of seeing and, consequently, making connections between and among the diverse situations overseas in which the United States, through different periods, has been involved, is currently involved, and might soon become involved. In a word, policy globalization is a dynamic of linkage—not only outward linkage across space (geographical linkage) but also backward and forward linkage over time (historical linkage). It is the *text*, or reasoned articulation, of the defense of American interests and the promotion of American values in a progressively more international *context*, an ever-bigger, indeed ultimately globewide setting for the making and the carrying out of American policy.

Globalization, it thus here will be emphasized, is not only an "external" historical process of changing technological, economic, social, and political conditions, but it is also an "internal" process of constant policy transformation—a development of the policy world itself. It proceeds when issues that "come up" in one issue area, functional as well as geographical, are connected, or linked, with issues arising in other areas; and thereby, progressively, the space of policy discourse is extended. Eventually, this sphere of policy ratiocination becomes worldwide in scope and comprehensive in content—"global" in both the spatial and the substantive senses of the word.

This is not to suggest, however, that "links" are completely arbitrary. Nor are they just imaginary. "One of the principal tasks of statesmanship," Henry Kissinger has written, "is to understand which subjects are truly related and can be used to reinforce each other. For the most part, the policymaker has little choice in the matter; ultimately, it is reality, not policy, that links events. The statesman's role is to recognize the relationship when it does exist—in other words, to create a network of incentives and penalties to produce the most favorable outcome."[1] Indeed, the most effective foreign policy "linkage" normally is that which is based on real-world relationships, on cause-and-effect patterns that, when understood, show how the world "truly" works. Ideally, diplomatic "linkage" is self-enforcing, for the operation of the

---

Alan K. Henrikson is associate professor of diplomatic history in the Fletcher School of Law and Diplomacy at Tufts University. He has served as director of the Fletcher Roundtable on a New World Order and has been a visiting professor at the Foreign Affairs College (UN Development Program) and the Department of State.

world-system itself will provide the incentives and impose the penalties. Issues are thus connected subjectively because they also may be related objectively, in a deeper historical causality.

The enlargement of the geographical scope and the functional span of American national policy—ultimately, its globalization—is historically, and very powerfully, connected with the expansion of the world-system, including the technological, economic, social, and political factors that continue to produce international interaction. That is to say, external or *objective* globalization drives internal or *subjective* globalization. To a lesser, but increasing extent, there is a reverse influence as well. The reciprocal effects—those of American policy and policy action on world processes—have become more and more pronounced, although it is very difficult, analytically, to distinguish the effects of deliberate state action, or U.S. policy moves, from those of America's emanations abroad in general.[2]

At the very beginning of the 20th century, when the United States first began to be spoken of as a "world power,"[3] there was much international speculation, both hopeful and fearful, about the possible "Americanization" of the world.[4] America's influence was clearly felt. Globalization is sometimes treated, though too freely, as virtually the same as the Americanization that long has been remarked on.

Globalization is, first and foremost, a process of the development of the world-system, not the actions of a single country. This is the context within which American policy has been conducted, if sometimes in ways that interact with and modify the global system. It has been argued that what we today call globalization means not merely the expansion of the world-system, but its *closure*. This argument, first advanced in a policy-relevant way by the British political geographer Halford Mackinder, produced a profound new complication for policymakers, one whose implications still are not well understood. Thenceforth, action taken in, or with regard to, one part of the world reverberated in others, and around "the globe" at large, and created a new, unprecedented need for statesmen to take into account these globe-wide effects, including the policy reactions of other governments. Merely local or even regional policy, in a geographical sense, became impossible thereafter. Policy, even if focused on localities, had to be global.

The intricacy of the American "global" concept reflects the actual history through which it has emerged. The story proceeds, logicohistorically, from what will be termed the intercontinental phase through the multiregional phase to the present global-regional phase to a coming global-local phase to a conceivable global-global phase, which though not likely, provides a conceptual capstone and a measure for all the rest. The historical stages described, though successive, naturally overlap somewhat. Moreover, and very important to note, the earlier stages are not forgotten. They remain influential as residues and recollections of policy—traditions, precedents, and also ambitions and aversions—that, over time, become an intellectual and emotional composite rather than a single, simple thing.

Origins of the "Post-Columbian" World System

From the discovery of the New World to roughly the turn of the 20th century, as Mackinder observed in a 1904 lecture before the Royal Geographical Society, "the outline of the map of the world has been completed with approximate accuracy, and even in the polar regions the voyages of Nansen and Scott have very narrowly reduced the last possibility of dramatic discoveries." The preceding 400 years, foreshortened, might come to be seen, Mackinder suggested, as "the Columbian epoch." The essential characteristic of that almost half-millennium, he argued, was "the expansion of Europe against almost negligible resistances."[5] To Europeans, and by extension Euro-Americans, the world was fundamentally an open place, and its horizons had seemed, and for most practical purposes were, unlimited.

What are the factors that generated this dynamic expansionary process, centered mainly in Europe but not focused there exclusively, which worked to complete, and to end, the "Columbian" world-system? Among the most important factors are, surely, the advances of science and technology. These made physically possible the overspreading of the world in terms of time and space. The steam engine, applied both to shipping and to rail transport, made distant seas and remote lands not merely more accessible, but more accessible on a regular, even commercially scheduled basis. Nonetheless, in the latter half of the 19th century when many of these developments occurred, transport and travel were not easy. They were, by present-day standards, slow. Communication between countries did speed up. The electromagnetic telegraph, especially when submarine cables were laid across the Atlantic and through the Mediterranean and Indian Oceans into Asia and part way across the Pacific Ocean, began to facilitate almost real-time communication, but only for a limited number of people in the right places. The radio, though its messages were widely broadcast, did not have anything like comparable range.

Despite their restrictions and incomplete coverage, these particular applications of new forms of energy did make possible, indeed necessary, some of the earliest forms of international organization. Some business magnates, notably the American financier Edward H. Harriman, had synergistic dreams of "girdling the earth" with a unified railroad-steamship system that would connect the Americas and Eurasia via the Bering Strait.[6] But while they were the main planners and participants, shipping and railroad companies like White Star Line and the Union Pacific and communications operators like Cable and Wireless were not the only ones that profited from and promoted the technological innovations.

Governments, too, were involved in earth-girdling, even though this was an era of laissez faire. The International Telegraph Union (forerunner of the present International Telecommunication Union) was formed by an international convention signed in Paris in 1865. In order to standardize time, which became an issue especially in those countries (for example, the United States) having a vast east-west geographical extent and a number of railroad firms that each kept time according its own individual clock, the U.S. Congress authorized an International Meridian Conference. This was held in Washington, DC, in 1884. An international gathering of some 25 countries, the Washington Conference adopted a "universal day" to begin at midnight at the meridian running through the Observatory of Greenwich in the United Kingdom. Thus, with somewhat competing reference centers, the earth was divided into 24 world time zones of 15 degrees each.[7,8]

The naval and military implications of not merely the new technology, but also the national and international standardization efforts that accompanied it, made possible strategic planning and coordinated tactical operations on a larger scale. Many examples are provided by history. The French adoption of steam-powered ships of war able to cross the Channel in almost any weather created invasion scares in Britain. The skillful use of railroads by the Northern side in the American Civil War enabled General Ulysses S. Grant to overcome the Southern geographical advantage of interior lines of communication. Signaling, too, became easier. The telegraph, as the historian William McNeill has pointed out, "allowed an advancing army to keep contact with a distant headquarters simply by playing out wire as it advanced." During Prussia's war against France, for instance, King Wilhelm and his Chief of General Staff, Helmut von Moltke, thereby "could maintain accurate check on large-scale military movements."[9] On April 25, 1898, when the United States declared war against Spain, Commodore George Dewey, whose Asiatic Squadron lay in Hong Kong's harbor, received (via Europe) a cabled message to "proceed at once to the Philippine Islands." After destroying the Spanish fleet in the bay at Manila, which was linked to Hong Kong by cable, Dewey asked the Spanish Governor General of the Philippines to allow him to communicate with Washington. "When the Spaniard refused," as Robert Love relates the story, "Dewey cut the cable, and thus was on his own."[10] The importance of the geopolitics of control over telegraphy quickly became evident to all nations. A subcommittee of the British Committee for Imperial Defence, quoting from A. Roper's *Die Unterseekabel,* published in Leipzig in 1910, recognized with Roper that "the course and result of a naval war may depend on the opportune arrival of commands and information by submarine cable." The British report also quoted an essay by Captain George Owen Squier of the United States asserting that in time of war submarine cables would be "more important than battleships or cruisers."[11]

The sheer industrialization, especially of the Western world, during the 19th century and the concomitant increase of trade with markets overseas profoundly altered the international security field. It repeatedly tipped power balances. David Landes in *The Unbound Prometheus* points out that "when the Prussian coalition defeated France in 1870, numerous Britons, including the Queen, rejoiced to see the traditional Gallic enemy and disturber of the peace humbled by the honest, sober Teuton." This was an outmoded perspective. Very soon, Germany's industrial and other growth had raised it "to Continental hegemony and left France far behind." Landes adds, "This was one of the longest 'double-takes' in history: the British had been fighting the Corsican ogre, dead fifty years and more, while Bismarck went his way."[12]

The "New Empire" of the United States after the Civil War, argues Walter LaFeber, also was basically a product of the Industrial Revolution, reinforced by a political power shift from the planters of the South to more progressive Northern industrialists and financiers. The distinctive manifestation of the "New" as opposed to the "Old" kind of Empire was not the conquest of more territory abroad but the search for foreign markets—that is, commercial rather than territorial "expansion."[13] Government leaders in Washington, like the political authorities of other industrializing nations with insufficient domestic markets, were expected in one way or another to provide outlets for the surplus product. The writings of the American naval strategist Alfred Thayer Mahan are eloquent testimony to the power of this industrial-commercial motive and resulting expansionism. His concept of "sea power" appropriately included a civilian merchant marine as well as naval forces proper, which were considerably enhanced by the Navy's shipbuilding program that his advocacy helped to inspire.[14]

Social processes, including demographic growth and overseas migration, also fundamentally changed the international field of force in the 19th century. "To many of the migrations in ancient and modern times the adjective, 'great,' has been applied," reflected the historian of the subject Marcus Lee Hansen. "It *aptly* describes that westward movement of Europeans which began with the discovery of the New World and has continued until our era."[15] Toward the end of the 19th century, the sources of transatlantic migration shifted somewhat, from western and northern to eastern and southern Europe. This fact caused anxieties in the United States, fearful about its identity as well as its economy. Yet this population influx proved to be another source of strength for the United States vis-à-vis the Old World. In an era such as that one, when ideas about race supported claims about national superiority and inferiority, and worries about the "mongrelization" of America or submergence in a social "melting pot" were frequently expressed, immigration in fact produced many benefits—in the context of international competition as well as internally. Not the least of these was a constant downward pressure on wage rates, which, paradoxically (as it seemed to some theorists), increased employment—and production—levels. "Everywhere immigrants have enriched and strengthened the fabric of American life," as President John F. Kennedy years later affirmed. He quoted with approval the lines of Walt Whitman appropriate to a more international age: "The States are the amplest poem,/Here is not merely a nation but/a teeming Nation of nations."[16] The United States, like Canada, Australia, Brazil, and rather few other immigrant-absorbing countries, brought "the world" into itself. It is therefore, despite isolationist tendencies in its policy, "global."

The Darwinian Age of the late 19th and early 20th centuries has too often been interpreted only in terms of a "power struggle," narrowly defined in terms of armies and battleships. "*Weltpolitik*," "imperialism," and, in the American lexicon, "world power"[17] included much more. These catch-all notions were a summation of the many forces at work in the world. Yet geopolitics and geo-economics arguably were at the core. Historian William L. Langer has epitomized the complexity and sequences of such forces in terms of Europe's alliances and alignments and the diplomacy of imperialist rivalry during the 1890s. The story of European international relations in that decade, he posits, "is the story of the assault of Russia and France upon the territorial position of Britain in Asia and Africa, and the story of the great economic duel between England and her all-too-efficient German rival."[18] The United States enters the world picture mainly via Latin America and the Far East. America's arrival was announced by the victory over Spain in the Spanish-American

War and President Theodore Roosevelt's dispatch of his "Great White Fleet" around the world—from Hampton Roads around Cape Horn to the West Coast and then across the Pacific to New Zealand, Australia, the Philippines, Japan, and China, and from there across the Indian Ocean to Suez and on through the Mediterranean to Gibraltar and back to Hampton Roads (December 16, 1907–February 22, 1909).[19]

The "world powers"—that is, the European Great Powers with overseas interests, the United States, and Imperial Japan—competed in what they increasingly felt was a "contracting" world. Mackinder, concluding in his 1904 Royal Geographical Society lecture that it was no longer possible for Europe, as it had done during the Columbian age, to expand "against almost negligible resistances," then proclaimed, "From the present time forth, in the post-Columbian age, we shall again have to deal with a closed political system, and none the less that it will be one of world-wide scope."[20] For the first time, world history was, in a new and literally true sense, global. International activity had reached its ultimate geographical limit—the opposite end, approached from all directions, of the round Earth. There was nothing—no horizon—anywhere beyond it, thus no place farther to go. (Of course, Mackinder could not then realistically imagine the possibility of space exploration, though his imagination soared.)

It was the "closure" of the new global situation of mankind, not just the widened scope of it, that seemed to Mackinder the most profoundly significant—and potentially disruptive—fact. From that point on, the outward energies of the Western civilized powers would be turned back, and their forces would be directed against each other—and across everything in between. For Earth had become, not only physically, a vast echo chamber: "Every explosion of social forces, instead of being dissipated in a surrounding circuit of unknown space and barbaric chaos, will be sharply re-echoed from the far side of the globe," warned Mackinder, "and weak elements in the political and economic organism of the world will be shattered in consequence."

"There is a vast difference of effect," this early British globalist added to make his point more immediately geographical, "in the fall of a shell into an earthwork and its fall amid the closed spaces and rigid structures of a great building or ship." Probably some "half-consciousness" of this, he speculated, had begun to divert the attention of statesmen around the world from "territorial expansion" to the "struggle for relative efficiency."[21] (We would today say "competitiveness.") Although formulated in metaphorical language, and not readily subject to scientific analysis or careful measurement, Mackinder's deep insight, made at the beginning of what may be called the Global Age, merits contemplation today. It is historically wrong to think that globalization is just now beginning.

From the beginning of the 20th century, the basic sphere of human affairs, within which everything would of necessity thereafter have to be apportioned, was the "globe." For scientific purposes, this meant, as Mackinder further suggested, that "we are for the first time in a position to attempt, with some degree of completeness, a correlation between the larger geographical and the larger historical generalizations." That is to say, with events taking place "on the stage of the whole world," we may "seek a formula which shall express certain aspects, at any rate, of geographical causation in universal history."[22]

While this may seem excessive, it is the historical-geographical dimension of the *globalization* phenomenon that should be emphasized. It is the bedrock of all else. Within this new context, the "westward march of empire,"[23] of which the movement of the western frontier of the United States was but one small part,[24] was destined also to come to an end. The U.S. conquest of the Philippines, which was the high-water mark of American physical imperialism, seemed to confirm this perception. The weight of this American policy move, though somewhat "accidental" in the sense of being a by-product of a conflict over Cuba, had an impact on the overall global equilibrium. Mackinder himself remarked, "The United States has recently become an eastern power, affecting the European balance not directly, but through Russia, and she will construct the Panama canal to make her Mississippi and Atlantic resources available in the Pacific. From this point of view the real divide between east and west is to be found in the Atlantic Ocean."[25] From the perspective of Europe, and America, too, it seemed as if the frame of the world-system had shifted somewhat.

The Historical-Geographic Dialectic of U.S. Foreign Policy

When did the United States of America acquire a foreign "policy," in the sense of a body of guidelines for taking future action in defense of American interests in a consistent and coordinated way? Although it is generally assumed that the U.S. Government has had foreign policies from almost its beginning, notably Washington's Farewell Address (1796) with its counsel against permanent alliances and the Monroe Doctrine (1823) with its assertion of American hemispheric separateness, there is good reason to place the beginning of U.S. foreign policy proper, especially that of an incipiently "global" shape, in a much later period. Not until approximately the year 1890 did American political leaders and government officials begin to make decisions regarding U.S. relations with the world that were required, not just by the many and varied circumstances that Americans happened to encounter abroad, but also by the imperative, which is here emphasized, of policy consistency, or greater coherence, among those decisions.

The historian Robert Beisner, using this stricter definition of the term *policy*, writes in *From the Old Diplomacy to the New, 1865–1900*, that around 1890:

> the old reactive and unsystematic conduct of U.S. foreign relations was replaced by the formulation of a real "policy" in international affairs and its more-or-less systematic execution. Thus hypothetically speaking, while a Secretary of State in 1880 would probably have reacted separately and disjointedly to events in, say, Mexico, Canada, and China, his successor in 1900 would have anticipated the need for decision before events overtook him, perhaps pondered both events and decision in a framework calculated to advance a general foreign policy, and then acted accordingly.[26]

It is thus perhaps no accident that Secretary of State John Hay's "Open Door" notes in 1899 and 1900, calling for nondiscrimination by other powers against American interests in the China market (and by implication markets elsewhere in the world), quickly became known as the Open Door *Policy*.

There is a dialectic—a weighing and reconciling of juxtaposed facts and arguments about them—in the development of policy. The consideration of one case leads, logically and progressively, to the consideration of others, actual and hypothetical; and a constant refitting of formulations to ever-wider and more complicated reality results. Thus, American foreign policy—national security policy as well as economic and other kinds of policy—became "globalized." This process has occurred by stages. So far, three historical phases of policy expansion, in this sense, have been experienced. We may now be entering a fourth phase. These stages are chronological, though they do overlap to some extent.

The first stage in the globalization of American foreign policy extends from the late 19th century to World War I. This was a period dominated by intercontinental reasoning. In this interval, and for some time afterward, American leaders and officials, basing their thinking on the geographical premise of the American "continent" (a concept often used to cover the whole Western Hemisphere), argumentatively juxtaposed their policy ideas regarding the Americas (viz. the Monroe Doctrine) with prospective thoughts about involvement on other continents. These tentatively held visions, because of the Monroe Doctrine, were considered, by some policymakers and certainly many commentators, as quite illicit. The Monroe Doctrine—"America for the Americans"—obviously implied "Europe for the Europeans" and, more remotely, "Asia for the Asians." How, then, could it happen that the United States, though by the turn of the century it had become the predominant power in the New World, legitimately became engaged in the affairs of any part of the world, particularly the Old World? Something, it seemed, had to "give" logically—either American geographical self-restriction or the Monroe Doctrine itself. Underlying this issue was a comparison of continents, and of the appropriateness of American involvement in the affairs of different continents—the comparative "base" always being "this hemisphere."[27,28]

The issue was posed in a prominent way by the unprecedented U.S. participation in 1884 in the Berlin Conference concerning the Congo. In the opinion of some critics at home, this involvement was a clear violation of the Monroe Doctrine. Worse, assuming that there is an in-built reciprocity in the Monroe Doctrine (though this logic is not spelled out in Monroe's text), the critics warned that American official participation at Berlin, especially if it resulted in the acceptance by the United States of political obligations regarding the Congo, could release the European powers from any obligation to respect the political independence of the American republics (excepting their own remaining colonies in the Western Hemisphere). They had, of course, never acknowledged the validity of the Monroe Doctrine in the first place. The thought of Europeans proposing "a conference to settle American affairs, especially the problem of an isthmian canal" caused the U.S. Government to shy away from further involvement.[29]

The Harvard professor Archibald Cary Coolidge, writing some 20 years later about the U.S. participation in the Berlin Conference (and also American participation in the 1906 Algeciras conference concerning Morocco, as well as Secretary Hay's protests against Romania's oppression of Jews in Romania and the Kishinev massacre in Russia), asked, rhetorically but compellingly, "[I]f the United States is going to abandon that portion of the Monroe Doctrine which forbids interference in

European affairs, how can it insist that Europe shall not meddle in those of America?" Giving his own response, he suggested how a doctrine of "paramountcy" might be used to preserve the core of the Monroe Doctrine (that is, its prohibition on European meddling in American affairs) while asserting, on the general theory of the "national welfare," the right of the United States to address situations outside the Western Hemisphere to which its "interests" may have spread. The actual growth of American power and interest, he was in effect arguing, gave the United States "legitimate" reason to protest against abuses of freedom elsewhere. He explained:

> Logically, perhaps, it can not; but, on the broad ground of national welfare, it might maintain that its interests were "paramount" in one region without necessarily being nonexistent elsewhere. An attitude of this sort would, however, be somewhat weak morally, and would give the European powers a legitimate cause of complaint against the restrictions now imposed upon them. This is one reason why the Americans are anxious to keep out of purely European questions. Whether they will be able to do so is another matter.[30]

Continentalism was already in conflict with globalism. The received notion of the political separateness of "hemispheres" was at odds with the growing, and spreading, economic and even security interests of the United States. The Monroe Doctrine did not preclude formal American annexation of the Hawaiian Islands in 1898. Nor, although some influential people argued that it should, did it stop the United States from establishing a protectorate in the Philippines. Senator George F. Hoar of Massachusetts warned that American intervention in Asia would invalidate the Monroe Doctrine, encourage "every European nation, every European alliance" to "acquire dominion in this hemisphere," and, moreover, change America into "a cheapjack country, raking after the cart for the leavings of European tyranny."[31] His reasoning did not prevail, for American control of the Philippines was a fait accompli. "Asia," at least island Asia, was henceforth not beyond American bounds. The U.S. involvement in World War I showed that the "American" and "European" spheres were not completely separable either, though the U.S. Senate's rejection of membership in the League of Nations restored a semblance of the traditional separation of the Old World and the New World. This image lingers today, though it is usually drawn rhetorically, and in official policy terms, in the language of "regionalism."

The second major stage in the progressive globalization of American foreign policy, encompassing World War II and most of the Cold War, is that of multiregional reasoning. During this period, U.S. policymakers began to think in narrower and somewhat better defined terms of "regions," rather than whole "continents" (or more abstract "hemispheres"). This conceptual approach was more generic; it could embrace a larger number of situations in a comparative, juxtaposing way. Rather than comparing possible American relations with other parts of the world only with the "base" pattern of the Western Hemisphere, including the continental United States, they began to see possible connections and to draw analogies between distant regions themselves, without, necessarily, any reference to the U.S. continental or hemispheric base. Their focus had shifted outward.

For example, during the late 1930s, Secretary of State Cordell Hull was opposed to concluding a revised commercial treaty with Italy (even though doing so might help detach Mussolini from Hitler) because signing such a document would entail treating with the King of Italy—who was formally also the Emperor of Ethiopia, Italian forces having displaced Emperor Haile Selassie—and thus would imply that the U.S. Government might also accept Japan's military takeover of Manchuria. Hull's concern, though he was formerly a judge, was not only law-like but also realistic. In a globalizing world, what was happening in one region or was being decided with regard to one region would quickly become known in other regions. In a more interdependent world-diplomatic system, to sign a new U.S.-Italian treaty seemingly at the expense of Ethiopia could be considered tantamount to recognizing the Japanese puppet regime of *Manchukuo* and condemning thousands of Chinese to permanent servitude. Journalists and others in Japan might even have interpreted a new U.S.-Italian commercial treaty as an American green light for military aggression against other territory in Asia. Thus, concluding a new treaty could even have been dangerous. At one point during the Ethiopian crisis, the Italian ambassador to the United States, Augusto Rosso, asked Hull, according to the Secretary's account in his *Memoirs*, "if we had taken up with Japan the situation in North China. I immediately jumped him and said that the Italo-Ethiopian conflict was the most serious single factor in precipitating the Japanese-Chinese crisis!"[32]

What this shows is the new power, in a more communicative and closely organized world, of the logic of inter-regional comparison in the making of foreign policy. A new treaty of amity and commerce with Italy, seemingly at the expense of Ethiopia, which implicated politically the Mediterranean and Horn of Africa regions, could have spilled over into Northeast Asia and beyond. Hull's inhibition—though based theoretically on the universalist Kellogg-Briand Pact (1928), the Washington Nine Power Treaty (1922), and the Stimson Nonrecognition Doctrine (1932), pertaining specifically to the Far East—was also a pragmatic response to the stricter requirement of cross-regional policy consistency in a more globalized, and thus more complicated and perilous, geopolitical setting. The United States could not and would not condone an action in one region if it were afraid of the consequences of doing so in another region, even on the opposite side of the globe. Whether this fear was well founded in the international political realities of the time, Hull and many other State Department officials, in their own minds, could not be sure. But most of them felt they could not take the risk. Thus they further "globalized" America's recognition policy.

Somewhat similarly, following the war in June 1950, President Harry Truman decided, despite a Joint Chiefs of Staff determination that the Korean Peninsula was only of secondary strategic importance, that he could not afford to allow North Korea to succeed in its aggressive move against South Korea because that could suggest weakness vis-à-vis the Soviet Union in Europe as well as in Asia and risk the onset of World War III. Making a global geopolitical analogy, he even said, pointing to Korea on a globe, "This is the Greece of the Far East. If we are tough enough now there won't be any next step [anywhere]."[33] He had already, in the so-called Truman Doctrine of March 1947, declared it to be "the policy of the United States to support free peoples who are resisting attempted subjugation by armed minorities or by outside pressures."[34] In a way, that seemed to some officials, like George Kennan, to be too multiregional. Truman did not really generalize his earlier doctrine, in practical or theoretical terms, until the Soviet-backed North Korean military drive across the 38th parallel made him see the need for consistency of action in support of a coherent policy worldwide. Region-to-region reasoning thus "globalized" American policy further.

The Eisenhower administration, too, was mindful of the interplay of region-centered issues and of the need to respond to threats in different regions in a weighing and reconciling fashion. One expression of this was the replication of "regional" alliances, on the model of the North Atlantic Treaty (1949) and the earlier Inter-American Treaty of Reciprocal Assistance (1947). Secretary of State John Foster Dulles hopped the globe to build new regional security arrangements comparable and complementary to the North Atlantic Treaty Organization (NATO). He even sought to form these assorted regional pacts, including the very different Organization of American States (OAS), the newer Southeast Asia Treaty Organization (SEATO), and the British-sponsored Baghdad Pact, later transformed into the Central Treaty Organization, into a loose multiregional arrangement. Reminding his fellow NATO allies at a North Atlantic Council meeting in Paris in December 1957 of the collective security roles of the OAS, SEATO, and the Baghdad Pact, Secretary Dulles suggested that the Secretary General of NATO, Paul-Henri Spaak, "explore closer ties between the various organizations."[35] Nothing, however, came of his multiregional design.

During the next decade, Dean Rusk, Secretary of State in the Kennedy and Johnson administrations, also emphasized the inter-regional linkages of issues, particularly the possible ramifications, globewide, of the Vietnam conflict. Secretary Rusk, with youthful experience in Europe and military experience in Asia, had a strong sense of the political, moral, and legal interconnections of Cold War challenges in different regions, even those remote from the United States. If the United States did not meet these, its credibility would be at stake. Partly under Rusk's influence, President Lyndon Johnson stated in his first speech to the Nation, "This nation will keep its commitments from South Vietnam to West Berlin."[36] Secretary Rusk often relied on regional organizations, notably the OAS over Cuba and SEATO over Vietnam, for policy legitimization. Although this was done in part because the central world political body, the United Nations (UN), was handicapped by the near certainty of a Soviet veto, it also reflected a genuine sense of regional organizations as major building blocks of world order.

The third stage in the globalization of American policy, covering the post-Cold War era into the present, may be characterized as that of global-regional thinking. To some degree, this style of reasoning originated in the previous period, when the U.S.-Soviet strategic nuclear rivalry overshadowed everything. American policymakers, notably Henry Kissinger, stated quite bluntly that the United States had "global" interests and responsibilities. The major European countries, though America's close NATO allies, had merely "regional" ones.[37,38] The American nuclear umbrella overarched the globe.

With the end of the Cold War and the political collapse of the Soviet Union, the United States emerged as the "sole surviving superpower," with seemingly unlimited sway over world affairs. Its new global role has made possible, and perhaps even has required, the withdrawal of U.S. military assets from certain particularly heavy regional tasks it had long been performing—notably, the maintenance of large standing forces in Western Europe, now unlikely to be invaded. The 1990–1991 Persian Gulf War accelerated this process of relocation, but by shifting assets temporarily to another region, one that was threatened internally. Following the success of Operation *Desert Storm*, many American troops were returned home, rather than to Europe, in part so as to be better placed for possible "global" action—anywhere. The focus had shifted back to the center.

The Gulf operation, a U.S.-led "coalition-of-the-willing" effort, was authorized, unprecedentedly, by a UN Security Council resolution supported by a Russian "yes" and enabled by China's abstention. Collective security seemed to be working for the first time since the United Nations was founded. A strong presumption was created, from the very beginning of the 1990s, that, henceforth, any international military action including intervention in intrastate conflicts, in order to be considered legitimate, would have to receive approval of the UN Security Council—at least after the fact. The dialectic of international policymaking, including that of the U.S. Government, was working in that direction.

To some degree, regional organizations, notably NATO (though not formally a "regional" organization in the sense of chapter VIII of the UN Charter), became "subcontractors." Some global idealists, and even reality-minded multilateralists, tended to favor the new dependence of military alliances on that world body for authority and direction. Others, opposing the hierarchical subordination to NATO, believed that alliances ought to be autonomous, as their members, alone or together, still enjoyed "the inherent right of individual or collective self-defence" recognized in the UN Charter.

Both philosophically and procedurally, a kind of global-regional "partnership" was beginning to develop.[39] The United Nations, because its membership is universal (or nearly so), can express the will of "the international community." NATO, however, plainly has more physical power to uphold international order than the global body, the United Nations, does. The United Nations has so far proved incapable of forming a rapid-reaction force, or even gathering sufficient resources to support small-scale peacekeeping operations in a logistically sustained way. NATO has neither the internal or the external support to become a "global NATO"—this despite some (mainly American) enthusiasm expressed for the idea around the time of the alliance's 50th anniversary summit in Washington, DC, in 1999. To be sure, as Secretary of State Madeleine Albright said before that meeting, her predecessor Dean Acheson had pointed out 50 years before that "while the Washington Treaty involves commitments to collective defense, it also allows us to come together to meet common threats that might emanate from beyond the North Atlantic."[40] Yet the North Atlantic alliance clearly has no mandate to act (though its members can indeed strategically consult) globally.[41,42] Objectively, the two organizations, the United Nations and NATO, need each other.

Subsequent experience has, however, revealed the difficulties of coordinating global and regional organizational action. The balance between the two levels is very difficult to maintain. The pattern of cooperation is also uneven. In some parts of the world—for example, Northeast Asia—there are no regional organizations even to strike a balance. The present global-regional "system" thus lacks substance as well as uniformity. The logic of it—deriving from the policymaker's demand for symmetry—makes a powerful case, however. It points not only toward a strengthening of the United Nations but also to the sponsorship of new regional bodies. Even so, to some degree, the historical-geographical "opportunity" for further globalization-regionalization in the security sphere may have passed.

The next, the coming fourth stage in the globalization of American policy, which could become clarified by around the year 2010, may be a period of global-local reasoning. Rather than relying largely on regional security arrangements such as NATO to keep the peace, the United States may find itself, even for the purpose of maintaining security broadly conceived, also working with global economic institutions, some of them affiliated with the United Nations. In many instances, the management crises that emerge all around the world will be geographically localized. These can be addressed only in an essentially ad hoc fashion. Action typically will be taken after the fact, when an outbreak of some kind occurs. The treatment of "hot spots" can in theory be preventive as well, however. Partly for that reason, the International Monetary Fund, the World Bank, the World Trade Organization, and even the informal Group of Seven/Eight may become the first recourse, in the sense that their timely general relief measures might preclude the incidence of violence or other disturbances. With this surely in mind, the leaders of the major industrialized nations, including Russia, at their July 2000 summit meeting in Okinawa, committed themselves to helping poor countries reduce their debt burden as well as to helping them develop by improving their access to education, health care, and information technology.[43]

The problems that arise in the future may not fall neatly within the parameters of regional organization. The crisis in East Timor, for example, "fell between the cracks" regionally and finally was handled, fairly decisively, by the Secretary General and the Security Council of the United Nations, local security action being led by relatively nearby Australia, outside any formal regional-organizational context. "Policy" in the future may have to be customized to fit very particular situations. Some of these, like the East Timor case, may be on a very small scale, though their urgency may be intense. Regionalization, which requires known and knowable geographical parameters, may thus be challenged by hard reality and, as regards the policy dialectic, by localization as well as globalization.

Many international and intranational crises today have more dimensions than do existing regional bodies. NATO, however, is more and more taking on broad peace stabilization functions, particularly in the Balkans. The European Union, in its origin (though perhaps not basic motivation) an economic organization, is now proceeding to develop a genuine European Security and Defence Identity (ESDI). These regionally based organizations, like others elsewhere, face a changed world, even within their own locales. "NATO's new security vocation," as Canadian Foreign Minister Lloyd Axworthy terms it, is to respond to new conflicts that are "accompanied by large-scale atrocities, violent crime, and terrorism." The solutions to these "human security" problems, like the problems themselves, are complex. They must "rely on a variety of instruments—political, civilian and military." Axworthy may be right in saying, "Only through a wider and deeper recognition of the importance of human security to peace and stability will NATO retain its relevance and effectiveness in facing the diverse challenges of the coming century."[44]

A recurrent feature of these global-local predicaments, centered increasingly on small states and even on breakaway sections of larger states, is most likely to be extreme economic exigency, threatening social collapse. This is not insecurity that can be addressed only in politico-military terms. Therefore, American and international responses will, as suggested, have to become more multifaceted than ever before. The handling of "complex emergencies," and of course their prevention, requires competencies of all kinds, from police training to electoral advice to legal assistance to public health provision—a task akin to "nation building," or in many of the actual cases today, "nation *re*building."

Any consistency, let alone philosophical coherence, in this historically accumulating pattern of emergencies and international responses to them may be hard to find. Yet the "rationalizing" pressures of budgetary shortfalls and other stresses felt by national governments such as that of the United States and by international institutions such as the United Nations and NATO, and the "lessons learned" from repeated, hard experience may bring about more cogent policies and principles.

Toward a Full Globalization of American Policy?

An ultimate global-global model of reasoning—a full merging of the objective (real-world) and subjective (policy-world) processes of globalization, so to speak—is conceivable. Such a final dialectical synthesis of fact and fancy may be unlikely, but the logical development of American foreign policy over time suggests it nonetheless. The very notion of policy is to face the future, which cannot be certainly known. All trends in the development of political reasoning, including strategic thought and diplomatic craft, are "futuristic." The concept of a global-global matching of the sphere of action with the scope of policy has, at the very least, a heuristic value.

This notion—a global-global culmination—would imply that all major problems abroad would be deemed to be global in character and to admit of, even require, global solutions. Those that did not rise to this level could, under a pure globalist doctrine, be safely ignored, for they would not have universal significance or systemic importance. Far from meaning that all problems everywhere would have to be dealt with, it means that some problems simply would not rise to a level warranting policy consideration. Indeed, this raises the specter of a "new isolationism," which has always been "the other side" of a perfectionist global vision. The essential point here is that a distinction between "global" and "nonglobal" can be made and that such a distinction permits some freedom of choice as to whether to be involved or not to be involved.

As Secretary of State Albright, speaking before the Senate Appropriations Committee on Foreign Operations, observed, "To protect the security and prosperity of our citizens, we are engaged in every region on every continent"—quite a change from the historical beginning of American policy. "Many of our initiatives and concerns are directed," as she noted, "at particular countries or parts of the world"—suggesting a localizing trend—"[while] others are more encompassing and can best be considered in global terms." In both cases, some selection—priority "targeting"—is in order. But it is hard to know exactly how to choose, for, as she affirmed from her historical perspective, "We must heed the central lesson of this century, which is that problems abroad, if left unattended, will all too often come home to America."[45]

The basic answer to the question of selecting—or prioritizing—surely must be to know globalization, and to address those situations and act on those issues that, through the known and predictable processes of globalization, really will "come home to America." The difference between "then" and "now"—between the period a century ago when the United States was still on a periphery of world affairs and the present when it is at their center—is that its own actions can shape the world environment, affecting the very processes of globalization that can entangle and entrap it. Its "policy," therefore, is at once national and global, though not to the same degree.

The lessons of the foregoing analysis, historical and geographical, with an emphasis on the logic of policy development in response to occurrences in places abroad, are not simple. They are rich in detail, more than can be presented in the necessarily brief account given. Nonetheless, certain points do stand out. One is that "global" policy does not develop in the abstract, but rather in concrete response to actual cases, juxtaposed for the policymaker's weighing and reconcilement—in the American case, in a pluralistic governmental setting. A second is that a categorization of issues simply as "military," "political," or "economic" can be erroneous and can lead to inadequate or even counterproductive responses. A third is that projection into the future is needed, from the known and knowable into the unknown, lest policymakers constantly be "catching up" with the current events or, worse, "getting blindsided" by historical trends.

Finally, there is the most difficult historical lesson of all. The story told in the foregoing pages suggests an alarming conclusion: Because of globalization, herein described, it has become almost impossible to make policy decisions pertinent to a particular case solely on the merits of that case, for the spatially outward and temporally backward and forward linkages of every policy decision act and "reverberate" globally—that is, in the echo chamber that Halford Mackinder described. Thus, in a sense, the only kind of comprehensive policy that is possible today is global policy.

Notes

[1] Henry A. Kissinger, *Diplomacy* (New York: Simon and Schuster, 1994), 717.

[2] Alan K. Henrikson, "The Emanation of Power," *International Security* 6, no. 1 (Summer 1981), 152–164.

[3] Thomas A. Bailey, "America's Emergence as a World Power: The Myth and the Verity," *Pacific Historical Review* 30, no. 1 (February 1961), 1–16.

[4] W.T. Stead, *The Americanization of the World: or, The Trend of the Twentieth Century* (London: H. Marckley, 1901).

[5] Halford J. Mackinder, *Democratic Ideals and Reality*, ed. Anthony J. Pearce (New York: W. W. Norton, 1962), 241–242.

[6] John Curtis Perry, *Facing West: Americans and the Opening of the Pacific* (Westport, CT: Praeger, 1994), 156–165.

[7] Lloyd A. Brown, *The Story of Maps* (New York: Dover Publications, Inc.), 296–298.

[8] Alan K. Henrikson, "America's Changing Place in the World: From 'Periphery' to 'Centre'?" in *Centre and Periphery: Spatial Variation in Politics*, ed. Jean Gottmann (Beverly Hills: Sage Publications, 1980), 73–100.

[9] William H. McNeill, *The Pursuit of Power: Technology, Armed Forces, and Society Since A.D. 1000* (Chicago: University of Chicago Press, 1982), 248.

[10] Robert W. Love, Jr., *History of the Navy, 1775–1941* (Harrisburg, PA: Stackpole Books, 1992), 390–391.

[11] Peter J. Hughill, *Global Communications Since 1844: Geopolitics and Technology* (Baltimore: The Johns Hopkins University Press, 1999), 43.

[12] David S. Landes, *The Unbound Prometheus: Technological Change and Industrial Development in Western Europe from 1750 to the Present* (Cambridge, England: Cambridge University Press, 1969), 327.

[13] Walter LaFeber, *The New Empire: An Interpretation of American Expansionism, 1860–1898* (Ithaca, NY: Cornell University Press, 1963), 1–7.

[14] Robert Seager II, *Alfred Thayer Mahan* (Annapolis, MD: Naval Institute Press, 1975).

[15] Marcus Lee Hansen, *The Atlantic Migration, 1607–1860: A History of the Continuing Settlement of the United States* (Cambridge, MA: Harvard University Press, 1941), 280, emphasis added.

[16] John F. Kennedy, *A Nation of Immigrants,* rev. and enl. (New York: Harper and Row, 1986), 3.

[17] Archibald Cary Coolidge, *The United States as a World Power* (New York: The Macmillan Company, 1908).

[18] William L. Langer, *The Diplomacy of Imperialism, 1890–1902*, 2d ed. (New York: Alfred A. Knopf, 1960), 415.

[19] Robert A. Hart, *The Great White Fleet: Its Voyage Around the World, 1907–1909* (Boston: Little, Brown and Company, 1965).

[20] Mackinder, *Democratic Ideals and Reality*, 242.

[21] Ibid.

[22] Ibid.

[23] Ibid.

[24] Walter Prescott Webb, *The Great Frontier* (Boston: Houghton Mifflin Company, 1952).

[25] Mackinder, *Democratic Ideals and Reality*, 262.

[26] Robert L. Beisner, *From the Old Diplomacy to the New, 1865–1900* (New York: Thomas Y. Crowell Company, 1975), 35.

[27] S.W. Boggs, "This Hemisphere," *U.S. Department of State Bulletin* 12, no. 306 (July 1940), 845–850.

[28] Arthur P. Whitaker, *The Western Hemisphere Idea: Its Rise and Decline* (Ithaca, NY: Cornell University Press, 1954).

[29] Edward Younger, *John A. Kasson: Politics and Diplomacy from Lincoln to McKinley* (Iowa City, IA: State Historical Society of Iowa, 1955), 336–337.

[30] Coolidge, *The United States as a World Power*, 119–120.

[31] Robert L. Beisner, *Twelve Against Empire: The Anti-Imperialists, 1898–1900* (New York: McGraw-Hill Book Company, 1968), 155.

[32] Cordell Hull, *The Memoirs of Cordell Hull*, 2 vols. (New York: The Macmillan Company, 1948), II 440.

[33] Ernest R. May, *"Lessons" of the Past: The Use and Misuse of History in American Foreign Policy* (New York: Oxford University Press, 1973), 71.

[34] Harry S. Truman, "Message to Congress," May 12, 1947, *The New York Times*, March 13, 1947.

[35] Alan K. Henrikson, "East-West Rivalry in Latin America: 'Between the Eagle and the Bear,'" in *East-West Rivalry in the Third World: Security Issues and Regional Perspectives*, ed. Robert W. Clawson (Wilmington, DE: Scholarly Resources, Inc., 1986), 283.

[36] Thomas J. Schoenbaum, *Waging Peace and War: Dean Rusk in the Truman, Kennedy, and Johnson Years* (New York: Simon and Schuster, 1988), 409.

[37] Henry A. Kissinger, "The Year of Europe," address to the Associated Press Annual Luncheon, New York, April 23, 1973.

[38] Henry A. Kissinger, *American Foreign Policy*, 3d ed. (New York: W. W. Norton, 1997), 105.

[39] Alan K. Henrikson, "The Growth of Regional Organizations and the Role of the United Nations," in *Regionalism in World Politics: Regional Organizations and the International Order*, eds. Louise Fawcett and Andrew Hurrell (Oxford, England: Oxford University Press, 1995), 122–168.

[40] Madeleine K. Albright, "The NATO Summit: Defining Purpose and Direction for the 21st Century," *United States Department of State Dispatch* 9, no. 5 (June 1998), 8.

[41] Alan K. Henrikson, "The Creation of the North Atlantic Alliance," *American Defense Policy*, 5th ed., eds. John F. Reichart and Steven R. Sturm (Baltimore: The Johns Hopkins University Press, 1982), 296–320.

[42] Alan K. Henrikson, "The North Atlantic Alliance as a Form of World Order," in *Negotiating World Order: The Artisanship and Architecture of Global Diplomacy*, ed. Alan K. Henrikson (Wilmington, DE: Scholarly Resources, Inc., 1986), 111–135.

[43] Calvin Sims, "Group of 8 Pledges to Help Poor Countries," *The New York Times*, July 24, 2000, A6.

[44] Lloyd Axworthy, "NATO's New Security Vocation," *NATO Review* 47, no. 4 (Winter 1999), 8–11.

[45] Madeleine K. Albright, "U.S. Foreign Operations Budget," *U.S. Department of State Dispatch* 10, no. 5 (June 1999), 8, 12.

Chapter 9

Foreign Policy in the Information Age

David J. Rothkopf

To hear the debate within Washington, it would be easy to conclude that little has changed in foreign policy circles since the days when every bright young man was speaking of throw weights and the Fulda Gap. Some of the names have changed, of course. The bright young men are now the venerable, gray-haired regulars of the think tank panel discussion circuit. The Cold War is over, so now some people worry a little more about China and a little less about Russia than they used to. Some argue that economic concerns are now more important than before. The names of the treaties being debated change, and the amounts of money that Senators balk at spending also ebb and flow. But inside the Beltway, the casual observer might conclude that U.S. international policy, U.S. power, and global relations are similar if not identical in character and conduct to what they have always been.

It is a little akin to Europe in the years immediately after Columbus landed in the Americas. Europe still felt like Europe. Dynastic kings still ruled from their ancient thrones. America was new, but it was there to fit into their old views of the world, to be made to serve Europe. Maybe the earth was flat, maybe it was not. That hardly mattered so long as European flags flew over these new lands. The character of the world had not changed, just some of the names and numbers on the map.

Of course, the fallacies rife in these views would soon be revealed. In a world that moved much more slowly than our own, discovery of the Americas would soon mean not a world of more Europe, more European ways, and more Europeans, but something entirely different. To be sure, there was a period of time when it looked liked the Eurocentric view might prevail. The Incas, Mayas, Aztecs, as well as the Sioux, Algonquins, and Seminoles—all were crushed. But European seeds planted in American soil grew into something entirely new, something that changed not just this hemisphere, but Europe and the world.

So it is today. A revolution in world affairs is afoot that possesses all the import, sweep, and potential impact of the discovery of the "new world" in the Americas or the onset of the Industrial Revolution or the Cold War itself. The very character of

---

David J. Rothkopf is chairman and CEO of Intellibridge Corporation. Previously, he was managing director of Kissinger Associates and served as Acting Under Secretary of Commerce for International Trade Policy. He is also adjunct professor of international affairs at Columbia University and the author of The Price of Peace: Emergency Economic Intervention and U.S. Foreign Policy.

international affairs is changing—of power, of its application, of its roots, and of the challenges that we as a Nation will face.

This watershed in international relations has not yet been fully accepted in foreign policy circles, but the debates are starting. It has not produced new security theories, but the seeds have been planted. It has not produced new visions for leadership, but the void is becoming more apparent and the need to fill it ever more urgent.

The watershed has been triggered by a technological revolution unlike any other in history, one that is changing even the most fundamental assumptions about societies, governments, businesses, individuals, and their roles, as well as the nature of change, of risk, of opportunity, and of the future.

Just outside Washington, one of the world's great technological hubs is rising. Inside Washington, the Information Revolution is still seen as an incremental force, a minor adjustment to be made in old formulations.

A different view is called for. A new approach to U.S. foreign policy is urgently needed—one based on an in-depth reassessment of American interests and our ability to advance them. Call it the Global Era or call it the Information Age, it is time to set aside Flat Earth strategies and to try to understand the properties of this other new world, ironically, one of which may be that we are moving to an Earth that in some ways has become flatter after all.

This chapter will seek to lay a foundation for that new view by exploring the specific changes in the character of international relations that have resulted and will result from the continuing Information Revolution. In addition, it will illustrate those changes in character with a special look at how they have resulted and will result in a new and rapidly changing set of threats to the national interests of the United States.

Proving the Obvious: The Case for the New Era

To make the case that a new era has begun presents many challenges. Many, of course, have announced this change and attempted to plumb its subsequent challenges. How many articles and volumes and speeches have there been on the end of the Cold War or the onset of the Information Age? There have been books on the *End of History,* the imminent *Clash of Civilizations,* and on a *Jihad vs. McWorld.* In his book *The Lexus and the Olive Tree*, *The New York Times* foreign policy columnist Thomas L. Friedman asserts:

> Sustainable globalization requires a stable power structure and no country is more essential than the United States. All the Internet and other technologies that Silicon Valley has designed to carry digital voices, videos and data around the world, all the trade and financial integration it is promoting through its innovations and all the wealth this is generating are happening in a world stabilized by a benign superpower, with its capital in Washington, DC . . . ideas and technology don't just spread on their own.

In other words, ideas and technology need to be backed by a credible currency, such as the weight of American, European, or Asian innovation. The implications of this change are not yet felt by many policymakers. Daniel Yergin and Joseph Stanislaw reiterate this point in their book *The Commanding Heights*:

> A new reality is emerging. This is not a process but a condition—a globality, a world economy in which the traditional and familiar boundaries are being surmounted or made irrelevant. The end of the Soviet Union and communism has redrawn the map of world politics and subdued ideology as a dominating factor in international affairs. The growth of capital markets and the continued lowering of barriers to trade and investment are further tying markets together—and promoting a freer flow of ideas. The advent of emerging markets brings dynamism and opportunity on a massive scale to the international economy. . . . Paralleling and facilitating much of this is a technological revolution of momentous but uncertain consequences.

But can such a sea change be proven? At what point does the critical mass of smaller changes in communications infrastructures, information-processing tools, and related technological developments in areas such as transportation, health care, and other industries produce a larger scale phenomenon? At what point did the Middle Ages end and the Renaissance begin? How many factories had to be in place before the Industrial Revolution had officially started? Obviously, such dividing lines are not easily drawn, and inevitably they are drawn by historians secure in the perspective offered by hindsight.

The problem for policymakers is that they cannot wait for such thresholds to be limned. They must constantly reassess the world around them and determine whether their old metrics and systems still apply, or whether it is time to go back to the drawing board in a broader way.

It is also just as clear that, at such times, there will be plenty of those who note all that is the same and use this line of reasoning to trivialize the major change that has taken place. We hear such arguments today in the context of discussions of globalization. Contrarians are fond of pointing out that global trade as a percentage of world output is the same today as it was at the turn of the last century and that thus we are no more globalized now than we were then. What they neglect to assess is whether the character of international interaction has changed in such a substantial way that theirs is too narrow a measure.

One hundred years ago, while plenty of trade was taking place, it was mostly within and between a handful of empires and a few companies. It took place slowly via the seas. The vast majority of international interaction was limited to the courier and telegraphic links between nations, states, or cities. Nations in conflict could only very slowly mount attacks, moving overland at the speed of horses and across the seas at the speeds of comparatively early steamships. To say this international interaction is the same as today's is like saying that because the first printing press enabled books to go to more of the elites and to a comparatively small set of libraries worldwide, thus upping access to the written word by thousands of percent within a century, it is of the same consequence as the Internet connecting over 300 million people to virtually limitless information in less than a decade. While there are some similarities, they are hardly the same. And if one were a consumer or manufacturer of information, it would hardly make sense to use Gutenberg-era strategies, or even the communications strategies of the immediate pre-Internet era, to operate in the new environment.

In the same vein, it makes little sense to assert that because we had nations and armies and an international economy before this new age that the new age is nothing really different. Instead, what we must do is examine whether and how and to what degree the character of the drivers of international relations have changed. We must use all the tools at our disposal to do this. Statistical tools. Assessment of meaningful anecdotal observations. The evaluations of experienced observers. We need to collect evidence and then to weigh it. And once we have done so, we need to assess the consequences of that evidence.

Hype or Revolution?

How do we measure the degree of a revolution, especially one that is only in a nascent stage? We can note that 5 years ago there were 16 million people with Internet access and that in the past 5 years that number has grown by 1,902 percent to 304.36 million. Six months ago, the number of people online was 201.05 million, or 4.18 percent of the world's population. We can note that today, 1 in 3 Americans has Internet access, while 1 in 4 Koreans has it, and 1 in 20 Brazilians. And Internet penetration grows daily. We can note that Internet use is expected to grow 40 percent in the next 5 years, that the number of individuals with a computer worldwide will grow from 250 million to 350 million. We can note that e-commerce in the United States alone is expected to rise from $51 billion in sales in 1998 to $1.439 trillion in 5 years. We can emphasize the fact that despite the many people in the world who are untouched by this, every country is touched by it, every government, and every major corporation. Every credible member of his or her nation's elite is dealing with the new realities caused by this revolution.

As an alternative approach, consider for a moment the following anecdotes while asking yourself whether the scope of this change is indeed revolutionary. These are isolated examples, some very distant from the world of geopolitics and threat assessments that strategic thinkers are most comfortable with. But taken together, they suggest as evocatively as do the numbers cited earlier the breadth and depth and scope of the changes now afoot thanks to the technological revolution that is defining our era.

In the days of the Tiananmen uprising in China, foreign media sources were censored by the Chinese government, but protestors videotaped satellite feeds and faxed news briefs and circulated news nationwide without the cooperation of their leaders. From Chiapas to Tibet to Sarajevo to Seattle, the Internet has been used as a powerful tool for subversion, resistance and organization. Many feel that the fall of the Soviet empire was in large part due to the fact that closed societies could no longer compete in the Information Age, blind as they were to all the forces that drove the marketplace.

On Wall Street, the Internet and high-technology boom transformed the markets, drove them to new records, and forced a complete change in the rules of corporate valuation. But these changes also transformed Wall Street itself. From e-trading to the coming disenfranchisement of the intermediaries from brokers to traders to the creation of complex new algorithm-driven swaps and programmed trading techniques to the instant, global scope of increasingly volatile 24/7 markets, the Information Age has forced the financial industry to reinvent itself from the ground up. Even stodgy old "white shoe" firms have gone to casual attire every day in a desperate attempt to attract those best and brightest who are now being drawn to the dot-com world.

The transformations in the financial markets have extended further. Not only have markets seen remarkable share volumes and indices seen remarkable point swings, but the interconnection of markets thanks to global information systems has also produced new phenomena like market contagion. In the past, of course, events in one market would touch others. But never so quickly or so profoundly as in modern markets. When in the emerging markets' financial crisis of the late 1990s, speculators in the Russian market were caught off-guard by Russia's decision to devalue the ruble, their margin calls forced them to withdraw money immediately from other markets. The one that felt this impact most acutely was Brazil, a country that until then had been viewed as having followed many of the financial prescriptions of the market and its advocates. Similarly, it was a crisis that spread across the markets of Asia that ultimately triggered the weakness in Russia. There are not independent markets any more, regardless of regulatory regimes. There is one global pool of capital that ebbs and flows from risk to reward globally.

This global flow of capital has, of course, had many other profound effects. In the wake of the end of the Cold War, as public sector capital flows from the United States and Russia to emerging markets shrank, as did the flows from the institutions they had controlled to serve directly or indirectly their Cold War objectives, these markets became more dependent on flows from capital markets. Thanks to the "wired markets" phenomenon described earlier, many of these flows were from the portfolios of institutions seeking near-term gain, so-called hot money that would come and go overnight. These funds, controlled by perhaps 30,000 equity, debt, and other securities traders worldwide, became a critical source of hard currency and capital on which these markets depended for growth. Consequently, how these 30,000 traders viewed public policies became as important to leaders wanting to implement change as were the views of local voters. These leaders now had two constituencies. One was at home where it had always been, Main Street—poorer, less cosmopolitan, less interested in global issues. The other was on "Wall Street" (in financial communities)—rich, globalist, concerned with maintaining liquidity and financial stability above all social concerns. This created a "dual-constituency conundrum" in which virtually all world leaders became servants to two sets of masters. To illustrate the importance of this factor, it is important to note that a decade ago, only 20 percent of the capital flowing into emerging markets came from the private sector; today it is 80 percent.

Of that 80 percent, the portion that does not come from market portfolios comes from global corporations. Their world too, has been profoundly changed by the technology revolution. Global multinational corporations face the challenges and seek to seize the opportunities created by global markets. This has forced consolidation on an unprecedented scale (for example, DaimlerChrysler, Vodafone-Mannesman-Airtouch, the dozens of once independent financial organizations that now make up Citigroup or Deutsche Bank, the airline alliances). This scale has grown so great that it challenges many of the basic underpinnings of traditional antitrust law—laws written in the age when a single company's domination of a national market was a threat, but before the age when the national scale was only a fraction of that required to compete internationally. Global companies have goals and interests that therefore extend far beyond national borders. Where once companies were part of a country, today they are increasingly apart from any one country, producing, selling, hiring, and raising money in all corners of the world.

The global information system required to support these companies has led in large part to the growth of the Internet and international telecom and transportation infrastructures that are the backbone of the technology revolution. But the existence of these global connections has also produced the first signs of new threats in the form of mischief and crime and sabotage, in which individual actors and nations have used the Web to disrupt business worldwide in an instant, as in the case of the "Melissa" and "I Love You" viruses; to steal billions; to alter national information resources for propaganda purposes; to shut down critical systems; and to consider new and more powerful ways to do all these things. The rise of cyberterrorism and hacking threats is therefore also a visible and important new development we can observe in this newly wired environment. It comes at a time when, increasingly, the financial and information flows of the world—personal and corporate and national resources that once sat isolated and safe in vaults—are now accessible via the open doors of the e-infrastructure.

These new technologies have had the effect of opening up the world to anyone with a computer. An individual can now sit at a desk and touch millions around the world, shop anywhere, find any information, sell to anyone, buy from anyone, and do it all in an instant. This effect is empowering and democratizing. It is also destabilizing, as it reshuffles power up to the global corporations cited earlier even as it gives individual actors unprecedented power and options—from tiny companies that can plug into global capital markets and grow more rapidly than ever before (witness the explosion of Internet companies) to hackers and cyberterrorists. These actors work in cyberspace, or the "infosphere," a region in which national borders are unclear and where it is harder to define jurisdiction, tax transactions, manage developments, or intervene.

This revolution has at the same time produced significant increases in productivity. The unprecedented economic expansion of the United States is now considered by some leading economists to be significantly (15 to 30 percent) due to the productivity increases resulting from the use of technology to save costs in production, employment, and marketing; eliminate middlemen; increase speed to market; refine supply chain management; and increase procurement efficiencies At the same time, many feel that central bankers have failed to adapt their formulas for assessing whether the pace of growth is consistent with the new reality. Technology sector leaders like John Chambers of Cisco and Bill Gates of Microsoft and new economy economists have wondered aloud whether the efforts of the Federal Reserve Bank of the United States to tighten money supply in the face of increasing growth rates are based on antiquated ideas of what is possible. But because there is no consensus on this, the policymakers act to tighten and possibly undermine the potential for greater and faster growth in the near to medium term.

The current revolution is one that has emerged in the private sector and has developed so quickly that public sector policymakers have been unable to keep up with it. Regulations and responses from the government therefore have become lagging indicators of this change. Unfortunately, as in any market-driven phenomenon, there is a tendency to focus efforts, resources, and change on those places where returns can be greatest rather than those where social equity is the principal driver. This produces another paradox. The factors that can create superpowered economic growth and integration are the same factors that can create a global digital divide in which information haves benefit and information have-nots fall rapidly behind. The fear of this phenomenon has led to a highly publicized backlash against the forces of globalization (seen as a manifestation of the technology revolution). This backlash was manifested in the streets of Seattle during the World Trade Organization (WTO) ministerial meeting in late 1999, in the streets of Washington and Prague during the recent meetings of the International Monetary Fund (IMF) and the World Bank, in the discussions that dominated the World Economic Forum meetings in Davos, and in countless other media and localized—and Web—forums.

Such anecdotal *tours d'horizon* are not always illuminating or meaningful. But the sweep of what is happening as a consequence of the technology revolution is so great and so manifest in so many respects that it conveys much more effectively than do sterile statistics the breadth, depth, and character of such changes.

But because we have had the opportunity to see how the information and related technological revolutions have affected sectors like business and finance, how they have transformed markets and the roles of nations and individuals, and how they have transformed the nature of interactions and conflicts, we also have another opportunity. We can use our experience to date to explore whether these transformations are of a similar character in any way, and whether they share common traits that can offer insights into coming changes or a better understanding of how this revolution will affect international relations or should affect international strategic considerations.

The Character of Change in the Information Age

On the basis of an analysis of how the technological developments of the past decade have changed industries from finance to manufacturing, changed nations and marketplaces, changed warfare and the media, it is possible to identify 9 and perhaps 10 separate characteristics of change that are linked to the Information Age. These characteristics are all factors that differentiate in some substantial way this new era from that which preceded it, either in degree or in terms of a deeper transformation. To understand them is the first step to understanding not only how this new age is unlike those that came before but also how to rise to its challenges and seize its opportunities—whether in terms of foreign policy, military affairs, or business itself.

Perhaps the first and most obvious change is *acceleration*. Thanks to new technologies in information and in transportation, things move much faster in the current era than at any time before. Transactions are conducted in a fraction of a second. Manufacturing processes are accelerated thanks to automation, refined supply chain management, enhanced delivery capabilities, and greater efficiencies at every stop of every process. Communications are accelerated thanks to the profusion of new communications technologies, enhanced competition, greater bandwidth, and more robust alternative switching and dissemination mechanisms. Political reactions to events thus become more rapid because more people can see what is happening anywhere in the world sooner and share their reactions more quickly. Disruptions can also happen much more quickly as moods are changed and groups react with stunning swiftness. This is as true in markets as it is with uprisings. Consider the market contagion noted earlier, or the speed with which demonstrations erupted across China in the wake of the U.S. bombing of the Chinese Embassy in Belgrade.

The next fundamental change in character is *amplification.* The roots of the technology revolution go back to the transistor. This device was transforming because it enabled the amplification of weak electrical signals. Now virtually all the offspring of this device do the same in broader social, economic, political, military, and other ways. A single actor at a computer can start a computer virus that can touch a majority of the businesses on the planet Earth within hours. A single voice can be heard by millions. A single market actor can attract the attention of all capital providers. A single incident can thus have much greater consequences than before, and produce a greater reaction. Take the accelerating nature of most businesses and combine it with the ability to impact large numbers of people—touch many quickly—and the consequences of actions amplify.

The combination of acceleration and amplification yields the third characteristic of this changed world: *volatility.* No one who has lived through the market upheavals of the past few years needs to have them explained. Moves that once would have taken months take days. Volumes of trades have increased by magnitudes of 10 over a decade ago. Greater volumes in less time and a greater ability to absorb and synthesize information produce faster travel through cycles of reaction to an event. Consequently, market cycles are condensed. The same characteristic can be seen impacting elections and public opinion. Witness the huge outpouring of sympathy around the death of Princess Diana: huge populations spread around the entire world responded and were transfixed for several days. Witness the swiftness with which political fortunes can change. Yesterday's bull market very quickly becomes today's bear market; yesterday's hero, today's villain; yesterday's peace, today's conflict.

Another consequence of combining acceleration and amplification is that fewer people can have a bigger impact than ever before—call it *asymmetry.* This phenomenon is very familiar to military strategists, who have been contemplating asymmetrical warfare as a new and growing class of threat for several years now. Essentially, it comes down to the fact that new technologies allow either individuals or small groups to have much greater power than ever before possible, power that once was available only to the largest companies or governments. Once only a government had the ability to shut down the infrastructure of an enemy or to destroy a city. Now, cyberattacks or attacks with weapons of mass destruction (WMDs), managed and carried out by a few people, can do the same. Once it would be unthinkable that a tiny company could compete globally with a giant, but today small companies are plugged into every market, can process vast amounts of information, and can be visible everywhere—all via the Web. In the past, the capital-intensive business of building global infrastructure and delivery mechanisms was a barrier that protected the power of the large. Today, the infrastructure is in place for global communications and delivery, and, thanks to miniaturization, small devices with great power (or, thanks to advances in biotechnology, new classes of microbial threat) can be sent anywhere, anytime, easily. This phenomenon comes at a time when the balance of the bipolar Cold War world is gone, and threats exist essentially along those fault lines where U.S. national interests appear gray or distant and smaller actors are the dominant threats to peace. But small does not mean what it once did; ask the Russians who faced a few thousand Chechens with cell phones and computers and the ability to move around with ease. Indeed, the reality is that one no longer requires the resources of a state to attack another state or society. Nonstate actors are a growing source of asymmetrical threats. This fact is complicated, of course, by the fact that U.S. power has been crafted to handle global challenges at the highest level. We are very good at thermonuclear war, less good at more limited conflicts. So, the little guy is not only empowered but also is striking a comparatively vulnerable area (worse still if he is attacking a country or region without our protection). This produces what could be called the David syndrome, in which the small—who are so numerous—become an increasingly important threat to the large. This is an increasingly important phenomenon in the world of cyberpolitik, in which balance of power calculations and tactics need to take into consideration more than just great powers.

This problem can itself be exacerbated by yet another factor of the new environment, *interconnectivity*. This is the nature of the Net, of course, a world in which the infrastructure is already in place to link everyone to everyone else. These linkages create new systems, new relationships, and new bonds that defy old structures. Geography is less important, and thanks to acceleration and amplification, new systems can be created overnight. This creates the possibility for virtual alliances that combine and recombine to meet different threats or serve different objectives. It takes parts of the world that seem remote from one another and it links them—so that Boris Yeltsin can "go to bed drunk, and Brazil can wake up with a hangover." Or so that a threat in Pakistan has implications in the Straits of Taiwan. Or so that companies can engage easily in "co-opetition," the process by which they cooperate with a company in the morning, then compete with it in the afternoon. Or so that alliances of nongovernmental organizations (NGOs) can form quickly. And so on. To make the United States a great Nation, first came the railroads, then the highways that linked us together. The infrastructure—for example, satellites, fiber optics, wireless links, traditional copper cables, air transport networks—to link the world is already in place, a public asset, more or less, to be used by anyone to link with anyone else. Consequently interconnectivity produces one of the most challenging consequences of this age: contagion—be it economic, political, social, or security-related.

The reality of a permanently connected, networked world has a number of other implications. One of the most important is *decentralization*, the redistribution of power thanks to the Web. Asymmetry is an element of it. But it is also linked to the fact that most power became "centralized" within a place or an institution because it had to be to maximize efficiency. Power was centralized around Wall Street because traders had to meet to exchange securities. Capital was linked to productive assets; consequently, in a more capital-intensive world than that of the knowledge economy, economies of scale were only available when there was a concentration of productive capacity and power. In the new environment, individual actors have tools, powers, and options once available only to central authorities. In parallel with the rise of the information economy, moreover, central actors have begun to lose some of their strength for other reasons. Governments in particular have increasingly ceded power to markets, which apportion it among those who have the means to seize it. Also, as knowledge itself is distributed more broadly, the prerogatives associated with having a close hold on special knowledge dissipate. There is, however, a flip side to this argument. The creation of enterprises of sufficient scale to operate globally has produced new actors with even greater concentrations of some kinds of power than before. Decentralization does not simply eliminate the center, it moves it around; it creates a kind of "virtual" center that changes with each new combination of actors involved in any particular interaction—within a company, between companies, between countries, and among and between actors of all sorts.

Associated with decentralization in many of these interactions is what happened when people no longer had to deal with centralized authorities as in the past: they ceased requiring the services of those who had access to the center. They could deal more directly with the center or those at the top. Everyone is an email away. People do not need a broker or a trader to intervene in the marketplace when they can do it themselves. They do not need a middle manager to channel their views to top management when they can contact him or her themselves, and he or she has new means by which to filter more and more incoming information. People do not need a broadcast network or a newspaper to deliver their message to a large audience when the Internet connects them to the desks of hundreds of millions. This related phenomenon is *disintermediation.* Why do countries need ambassadors to relay messages when they can deal more directly via telecommunications media, transport media, or the Internet itself? They do not. One of the ironic realities of the Information Revolution is that it is producing a world that is not only smaller but one that is flatter. The flat earth is a world in which layer upon layer is proving unnecessary, and direct communication is proving easier. The effects on institutions, social structures, interpretation of information, clarity of communication, and many other elements of international relations are significant and growing with each passing day.

Just as profound is the shift away from a land-based world order. For most of human history, land was the fundamental source of wealth and the fundamental measure of power. This is because it is on land that we lived and because it was off the land that we survived. Gradually, as we moved toward more industrial societies, power shifted slightly to nations with access to nonagricultural resources required for industrial production. Now, in the post-Industrial Age, much of wealth exists as information, knowledge assets are more important, and exchanges take place not at a location on land, but in the infosphere. The result is what could be called *dislocation.* It is not that territory is no longer important. It is just that we live in a time in which territorial demarcations are becoming increasingly anachronistic. Data flows across borders are undetectable, uncontrollable. Huge flows of capital and of goods, once measurable and taxable and controllable, take place beyond the purview or ken of governments. Borders are increasingly meaningless. Economic units are increasingly differing in size from political units. This is both a result of trade liberalization and a result of the changing nature of trade in ideas as well as in intellectual property and services. Dislocation also manifests itself in the idea that ad hoc or permanent groups of nonaffiliated individuals acting together within the infosphere can take actions that once only nations could take; they can pose threats and do so under the umbrella of state sovereignty. One thing governments are very bad at is dealing with this meta-world of virtual communities that have interests conflicting with those of nation-states. How do they communicate with them? How do they enforce their views without upsetting the order among nations? How do they tax those who seek to keep transactions above and beyond borders? How do they account for the flows of wealth that never adhere too long to a particular parcel of land? Indeed, how will they deal with the reality that there are now increasingly global communities in many countries that, thanks to new technologies, have much more in common with distant like-groups than they do with their own countrymen?

Related to dislocation and to volatility (impermanence), acceleration, and disintermediation is the ability of groups to recombine at will. This has created the growth of outsourcing and ephemeral communities such as those cited earlier. This then becomes the ninth characteristic of changes associated with this new world: *virtualness*. Virtual alliances, virtual enemies, and virtual nations such as those cited above are just some of the consequences of this characteristic that are worthy of consideration in the context of planning for this new environment.

Finally, the tenth factor that may be worthy of consideration is one that has been raised several times already. That is that virtually every driver of change in the Information Age is a double-edged sword. Each has the capacity to help and to harm, to build and to destroy. Interactions accelerate, and in so doing they present everyone with countless more choices, information sources, communications, and counterparties. Speed creates glut; the ability to process more creates more to process. Amplification can enhance the power of individual actors and of great players already on the stage. It can also offset power by creating more powerful defenses. Volatility creates wild swings in markets and the public mood, but as we see, people grow accustomed to these oscillations, time frames for assessing swings change, and tools for coping with volatility render it less meaningful. We have already discussed the fact that asymmetry is in fact a product of a paradox, the rise of great nations to be so powerful that they can hardly deal with the small without overkilling, overreaching, and losing their advantage. Decentralization creates new centers, even if they may be short-lived (volatility). Disintermediation creates new opportunities for intermediation through new networks or among members of virtual networks. Dislocation and virtualness are among the factors that have contributed to a backlash to globalization born of the sense that old land-based identities are at risk, and consequently to a new nationalism. So it goes in any period of revolution and great change; the issue is upheaval and coping with transition as much as it is trying to determine where in the long run we shall be. In the case of each of the changes in the character associated with the Information Revolution that have been cited, the trick is understanding the change and the consequences of, or reaction to, the change.

The changing character of international affairs in the Information Age has called into serious question many of the old models used to predict or manage international behavior. Most affected are economic and political models—for example, models of market performance, state revenue collection, international conflict, power distribution worldwide, the creation or management of political opinion or will. We have seen an era begin with a continuous decline in the relative power of the state, and we have seen the incipient rise of nonstate actors. We have seen the decline in the relevance of political borders and a growing disconnect between political and economic entities, structures, and systems. (Despite the rise of a global economy and regional economies, weakening nation-states remain the norm.) We note that the government and multilateral entities do not include the new players who are of rising importance in this new mix. Perhaps most important, we have seen that the speed of the changes in question is severely challenging the ability of institutions (government, military, and business) to keep up even as the stakes rise rapidly for remaining in step with these changes.

Fifty Challenges: U.S. Foreign Policy in the Information Age

There is no reason to limit to 50 the number of major challenges that U.S. foreign policymakers will face in this new era. But it is a large enough number to suggest that the changes in place are so sweeping that much greater urgency is required in considering and responding to them. That number is sufficient to illustrate the situation we are up against and why it is significantly more profound than much of the action within the government and the policy community to date would suggest. The impact of the technological revolution of the past 10 years and the next 10 years on U.S. foreign policy may well prove to be as defining in scope and character as was the onset of the Cold War.

International Economic Policies

It is worth beginning with international economic policies for two reasons. One, the changes in question are more widely accepted there. Technological change has been embraced more enthusiastically by markets than almost anywhere else, and the consequences of that change have been better understood. Furthermore, economic tensions, economic interpretations of national interests, and other economic drivers often underlie broader foreign policy concerns, even ones draped in the rhetoric of higher motives.

1. New development models are required for the new global economy. Most of the models still in place focus on the lessons and approaches of the "old economy." They address industrial development. The new economy is different. To attract capital, new regulatory and infrastructure standards must be met, labor forces must be trained accordingly, and entrepreneurship must be cultivated. Private equity rather than debt capital must be more widely available. The leading role of the private sector in these changes must be accepted. The ability of e-commerce to eliminate middlemen, assist global marketing efforts, and bridge oceans and cultural divides must be harnessed. The list goes on. The drivers of wealth creation are changing.

2. New regulatory and institutional frameworks are required for a global economy. Transactions cross borders by the thousands each second. Throughout history such transactions have been regulated to protect consumers, to ensure justice, to reduce crime, to enhance the public health. But national and international institutions are inadequate to even assess what has changed, much less regulate it. The institutional gap is accompanied by a jurisdictional gap. An overarching policy review is needed to address these gaps.

3. Global capital markets require transnational oversight and regulation. The point raised in item 2 must begin with recognition that global capital market flows can be destabilizing to smaller nations, that power is concentrated within these markets, that new technologies make the consequences of volatility and abuse greater than ever, and that just as these markets have been regulated nationally, they must be regulated internationally. More important is that they must be overseen by disinterested panels that anticipate problems and correct them before they happen. This will require not only new entities and laws, but it will also require changes in political and financial attitudes.

4. Global e-commerce requires transnational oversight and regulation. There has been an effort afoot in the technology community to treat e-commerce as a separate class of economic interchange. The flaws in this approach will soon be realized, as other sectors are already beginning to protest this lack of regulation as a "subsidy." Such "subsidies" also create a false sense of the economics of e-commerce businesses, which translate into valuation misunderstandings in the markets. Furthermore, beyond the need to address issues of market-to-market equity, the overall public goods cited earlier must be regulated in this new area—and mechanisms must be created that adapt to the rapid development of new models, business approaches, and business abuses within the e-commerce arena.

5. The role of IMF must be reevaluated to ensure its ability to cope with the changing nature of financial crises in the global information economy. This process began in the wake of the financial crises of the emerging markets in the late 1990s. The reality, though, is that the debate over the future of the International Monetary Fund has not taken fully into consideration the diminishing capacity of governments to influence the market activities with which the International Monetary Fund is concerned. Furthermore, many of the orthodox approaches used by the International Monetary Fund in prescribing fixes for emerging economies are not adjusted for the new realities in question. Finally, the swiftness with which changes happen in the marketplace requires not only that institutional structures be more fluid, but also that all the players involved—private and public sector alike—be at the table when crises are dealt with. This is currently not the case. Lack of transparency between the International Monetary Fund and countries will not be tolerated by the markets in the new environment, either. In short, an overhaul is called for.

6. The role of multilateral development banks must be reevaluated in the context of the new dynamics of the global information economy. This is just as true at the International Bank for Reconstruction and Development, the Inter-American Development

Bank, the European Bank for Reconstruction and Development, the Asian Development Bank, and the African Development Bank. United Nations (UN) Development Program, the UN Industrial Development Organization, and other such groups also must be reevaluated in the new context. The roles of these institutions will likely shift to addressing the growing divide between information haves and have-nots (see below), gaps that exist not just between countries, but within them. Furthermore, they will focus more on those national economies that are effectively disconnected from any viable economic base, the poorest of the poor. Since most capital will come from the private sector, their role will atrophy. And those that remain will have to implement the new policy prescriptions identified in point 1 above.

7. The monetary policy implications of new global foreign exchange realities must be weighed, in particular those of dollarization. Already there is a dollar on one side or another of virtually every foreign exchange transaction in the world. The same is true for commodity transactions. The reality is that old ideas of currencies are being overtaken by electronic realities. Money is just an algorithm in a computer, a formula for converting from one ostensible unit of value to another. Most national currencies are already a figment of local imaginations, and increasingly useless as borders are crossed. International trade efficiencies will require fewer currencies of which the dollar will be dominant. What does this mean for the United States? Should we advocate it? How far should we let it go? Can we control the outcome?

8. The implications of the consolidation of global stock markets must be taken into consideration. The merger of the Frankfurt and London stock exchanges is just the latest in a trend that will continue over the next few years. The old idea of a stock exchange as a place people meet to swap securities is dead. These transactions all take place 24 hours a day in virtual space. National pride will result in retaining a few such operations, but they will primarily exist for regulatory and clearing purposes, home to servers rather than traders. What are the implications of the massive regional markets that will replace the local markets? How do we manage the process?

9. We must assess and understand the capital market implications of the growing, Web-enabled retailization of markets, including the volatility and thus enhanced risk. The character of markets has changed, too. Where once the majority of stock trading in the American markets was institutional, today most trades are in retail-size 1,000-share units. Whereas in 1929, 8 percent of the populace owned stocks, today almost 80 percent do. Market movements are therefore not an issue of concern only to the rich. Furthermore, market decisions are being made by a class of less well-informed investors who are able to absorb less punishment or do not manage risk as well as large institutions. What does this mean for the future of markets and their relationship with consumer confidence and other macro-economic drivers?

10. We must understand and manage the growth of global unregulated markets in hedge funds and other such vehicles. Some financial vehicles, such as hedge funds, will grow in use thanks to these new technologies and the desire to manage risk in new ways. These funds, however, have their own inherent risks as we have seen in the past several years, and they are not regulated even nationally as other similar investment alternatives are. This sort of gap will also have to be addressed.

11. The implications of dislocations of transactions from national tax bases must be assessed and dealt with. There is already a body of work focusing on how the dislocation of transactions from national borders and the ease of creating complex chains of transactions globally will impact national tax revenues. Means of tracking, measuring, and taxing such transactions will be an imperative in this new environment.

12. Antitrust laws must be redrawn to account for growing global consolidation of industry and requirements for global scale. As noted earlier, American and other national antitrust laws date to times when monopoly domination of national markets was the fear. Today many companies that are monopolies in national markets lack the scale to compete globally. Furthermore, new alliances across industries are required to adapt to the changing realities of knowledge economies. (America Online-Time Warner is an example.) All these raise questions about the value of old laws and the need for new ones and new transnational enforcement and monitoring mechanisms.

13. New growth models are required to account for the enhanced productivity of the current and coming eras, and old models must be adjusted or set aside. Many business leaders today feel that the U.S. Federal Reserve is being too cautious regarding growth rates. They feel that the board at the Federal Reserve is focusing on old metrics to determine when an economy becomes overheated without fully taking into account the heightened productivity made possible by new technologies and the new explosion in wealth drivers resulting from the creation of that economy. These assertions need to be evaluated, and, if deemed necessary, new metrics and related growth management policies will have to be devised.

14. Tensions caused by the development of new global labor disequilibria must be addressed. As the new global information economy develops, 1 billion new workers will enter the labor force, most of them in developing economies. If these workers are disconnected from the real wealth drivers in the global economy, capital will not flow to their countries, and they will live in poverty and be doing hard labor to support the richer, knowledge economies that will be exporting "bad" jobs to these markets. This will inevitably cause great tensions. At the same time, globalization will enable countries with large, low-cost labor forces to harness information technologies to better compete and actually create better jobs, leading to the perception in the developed world that those jobs were "stolen" from the developing countries. Witness the labor reaction to globalization in the United States. This tension is likely to be an increasingly important driver in U.S. international affairs in a world in which labor, capital, and corporate mobility, as well as the ability to rapidly manage change over great distances within short times, will all conspire to reshape global labor market dynamics.

One change touches all areas of U.S. international policy and poses a challenge that should be at the forefront of those we consider actively and attentively:

15. We must contain the growing digital divide and the related, growing disparity in the wealth between the information haves and have-nots in the world. In 1946, the average per capita income in the world's richest nation was 3 times that in the poorest nation. It is now 77 times higher. While the Internet revolution has transformed American and developed societies with now one in three people in the United States online, the majority of people in the world have never heard a telephone dial tone. Three billion people live on $2.00 a day or less. The Information Revolution can accelerate the growth and prosperity of those who harness it—and leave them farther and farther apart from those who do not have the chance to plug in. This will cause growing tensions, not just between nations, but within them. In fact, elites in the emerging world do have access to these technologies and capital resources, and they are integrating into the "global" economy even as their countrymen are not. The gaps between rich and poor, haves and have-nots, have driven most of the conflicts known to man. But today, new technologies also make it possible for the poorest to have hitherto unimaginable power—thanks to the availability of cheap WMD technologies. Discontent over the growing gaps could thus produce highly costly conflicts. If there is comfort to be had, it is in the fact that new technologies also give us the ability to knit these societies back together, educate more people faster, improve health care across distances, and reduce social inequities. There is a choice involved. It may be the single greatest choice human society currently confronts.

International Security Policy

Given the destabilizing nature of several of these challenges, should they not be addressed, it is natural to turn our focus to security concerns prompted specifically by the nature of the new era.

16. We must assess and address growing asymmetrical threats. Asymmetrical threats have already occupied the attention of many strategic thinkers. That said, new threats are emerging all the time, and there has certainly not been a shift to addressing these threats that is commensurate to the proportion of our attention that they will demand. Further complicating this is the fact that asymmetrical threats may emanate from within sovereign territory not directly linked to the threat. We have had some limited experience in this regard, but it is certainly not something that our diplomacy or the international system is well equipped to deal with. We must be able to exploit national means to deal with non-national actors, be they individuals, terrorist cells, political groups, NGOs, businesses, or others who now act as nations once did, but do so in a way that is either invisible to our current systems or so ill-suited to them that we are ineffective in containing threats until they have manifested themselves as crises.

17. We must assess and address the implications of global systemic shock in this new environment. Acceleration and amplification produce volatility on a scale not foreseen by past policy models. A financial breakdown in one region causes a global panic. Similarly, political upheaval on one side of the world can spread rapidly to like-minded individuals anywhere in the world. A virus can shut down computer systems worldwide in hours. The disadvantage of living within a connected system is that all parts can be made to feel pain quickly. We are better prepared to deal with simple regional crises than complex chains of economic, political, social, and security challenges that spread across the globe, mutating according to local circumstances. But this character change—related to what the financial markets call contagion—may have massive foreign policy implications in certain future crises.

18. We must assess and address the regional corollaries of global systemic shock in the new environment. If global systemic shock is possible, regional systemic shock is even more likely. Just as markets view negative developments in Thailand as having serious consequences for the Association of Southeast Asian Nations (ASEAN) or Asia in its entirety, so too will future crises of a noneconomic nature be more likely to become regional in their significance. Colombia is not a localized problem. It is an international commercial problem that has burgeoned for the same reasons as globalization has let other businesses burgeon, enhanced by the same technical tools. It now touches the entire Andean region, Brazil, Panama, Mexico, and the United States. Drug organizations and regional insurgents alike draw on international trade in illicit weapons and technologies from groups as far away as the Russian Mafia to support their efforts. When pressure is placed on a group, it is easier to move when so many financial and information assets exist in the infosphere. This is an example of how new technologies are changing the character of old problems and converting national concerns into regional and international ones.

19. We need to consider the underlying consequences of greater market shocks, security shocks, environmental shocks, and others. Another corollary to the notion of shocks within the system is that the consequences of market upheavals, environmental upheavals, and political upheavals are more easily spread. They can therefore grow in scale and become more likely to produce security challenges. Thailand's real estate markets melt down, ASEAN is hit, Indonesia's economic house of cards collapses, Suharto falls, and Timor and Aceh become security problems. These changes took place rapidly. Future changes will do so as well, but the threats of each will differ in magnitude, location, and nature.

20. A new definition of rapid response to over-the-horizon and multiple-theater challenges will have to be developed for a world of proliferating serious threats. We once trained our military to fight a Cold War. Following that, we looked at low-intensity conflicts and developed strategies to deal with two large regional conflicts. Today, however, we face a world in which scores of threats can arise at any moment, such threats can impact one another overnight, and virtual alliances can be formed among our enemies rapidly—all of which poses the risk of a rapidly changing constellation of threats that will demand much more fluid responses from us.

21. Cybernetic, biological, and other enhanced technical threats must be dealt with. It goes without saying that one of the results of the technology revolution is the development of new technologies of war fighting. Cyberwarfare and biowarfare and other such new sources of threats will grow, and our ability to contain them, track them, and respond to them and the proliferation of WMDs in the new environment will be critical.

22. We must continue the work being done to identify and protect national information assets. What are our most important sources of information—that is, commercial information resources, software developers, computer security specialists? Which commercial resources now exceed our Federal resources? Which academic resources do? How do we identify them? Who identifies them? How do we protect them? This is a new class of assets, a changing class, and one that is increasingly important.

23. We must also identify and protect critical national infrastructures. More progress has been made in this area. The Y2K exercise and the National Critical Infrastructure Initiative have produced excellent public-private models for protecting information assets as well as infrastructures. But new threats will emerge, new infrastructures will be created, and the process needs to evolve to meet those challenges.

24. We must enhance our ability to fight and win cyberwars. Electronic warfare battalions have been introduced, and we have begun to make inroads in exploring the strategies required for winning cyberwars. But the doctrine is not fully developed, and new resources will be required to translate what we have learned for offensive use.

25. We must enhance our ability to contain cyberterrorism. The potential power of cyberterrorist attacks has been illustrated by hacking attacks on commercial information systems. Governments have also employed cyberterrorism or cyberattack techniques in peacetime assaults on the information apparatuses of their enemies (for example, across the Straits of Taiwan). New units are required to address this threat—even as we must acknowledge that the skills and resources of the people we have fighting these threats may never be commensurate with those of the people initiating them.

26. We must prepare to fight technology-empowered enemies in an era in which U.S. information hegemony is resented and fought by our allies. The Information Revolution will lead to the spread of destructive technologies, even as it fuels our ability to maintain our technology leadership. We must expect to fight increasingly technologically enabled foes while at the same time confronting growing resentment from allies and others who see our technological strength as a lever of power in all manner of negotiations. We have already seen within certain alliances that the dependence on U.S. information warfare dominance has produced tensions and a desire to develop alternative systems and resources outside the United States.

27. We must assess and address the realities of coping with the "electronic democracy" (e-democracy) speed of shifts in American public opinion. As noted below, American public opinion is a small vessel afloat on an ocean of information. It will be easily swept in one direction or another—turned, righted, and turned again. Internet and satellite feeds suddenly make one misfired weapon or one ill-considered target a decisive factor in the war to maintain public support for international action. Given this potential for error magnification, militaries will have to move increasingly to a zero-tolerance-for-error model. Owing mainly to the unpredictability of battle, such a model has eluded militaries since the dawn of time. The result: an environment in which the political information war around the military information war will gain increasingly in importance—even beyond the importance it has already achieved.

Just as we identify new threats and new enemies directly related to emergent technologies, we must strive to understand the drivers underlying threats and how best to manage them. Consequently, we must also consider international politics.

International Politics

A number of policy challenges arise in this area:

28. We must understand the sources and drivers of power in this new era as we did those of the past era. During World War II, we produced steel, ships, and aircraft because we saw these as the sources of our power. During the nuclear age, we did the same. Now, we must reassess where power comes from in the Information Age. Surely, we will need ships, and we will still require strategic weapons. But there are other sources of power in this age...new systems, new constellations of satellites, new human resources, new education resources, new concerns with private sector proliferation of technological capabilities, that must be studied as a new calculus of power is developed.

29. Understanding how our national interests are altered in the new era is essential. As the interests of our citizens and companies globalize, and as our interests in the roots of Information Age power as a source of security and prosperity evolve, so too will our assessment of our national interests. Driving that assessment, of course, will be the immutable desire for peace and prosperity. But as the determinants of peace, prosperity, and related factors change, so too must our sense of national interests. Where are the stakes highest? Where are the threats greatest? What threats do we take most seriously? Which do we wish to contain? Which allies are likely to be most loyal or most important? This is the foundation of all foreign policy, and we need to examine it.

30. Efforts must be made to develop an understanding of the global fault lines of the Information Age. Are the fault lines in fact between information haves and information have-nots? Are they between the rich and the poor of the world? Are they between those Internet-linked nations whose cultures converge and those disconnected nations who see the Internet as a threat to culture? Does the Internet enable new alliances among those with common languages, cultures, and experiences? Where do our national interests suggest we are willing to intervene? Regardless of the answers, we can rest assured that as long as we are so dominant, the fault lines will lie just beyond the borders defining places we will certainly intervene—that is, in those gray areas in which the ambitious will feel that they can seek gain without paying too high a price.

31. We must develop more fluid institutional structures for a more fluid era. The North Atlantic Treaty Organization (NATO) has proved too slow to act, even against a comparatively weak enemy—for example, the Serbs. Can alliances that are consensus-driven function in an environment of information-empowered warfare? The simple answer is that they cannot, and thus new decisionmaking apparatuses have to be developed—or new alliances.

32. Mechanisms must be developed to deal with nonstate actors. The U.S. Department of State has no bureau to deal with foreign companies or foreign individuals that pose threats. It deals only state-to-state. As we have repeatedly noted, a new set of challenges has arisen, and new mechanisms will have to be developed—and perhaps old ones scrapped.

33. Strategic innovation will be required to manage foreign policy in the era of virtual alliances and co-opetition. Governments should take their cue from companies that have dispensed with old models to enable the virtual strategic alliances and co-opetition crucial to success in the Information Age. Perhaps the first such virtual alliance was that formed by the Bush administration during the Persian Gulf War. Disparate groups came together for a purpose, then disbanded. We have since seen that one of the problems of such alliances is the difficulty of maintaining them to address future contingencies. But we are not good at groupings in which our leverage differs from group to group. Our bureaucrats like pre-existing structures so that they can have pre-existing plans. This makes less sense in this new era. We might benefit from considering whether companies that operated like our State Department or intelligence agencies would successfully compete or lose in the current global environment. The answer is painfully clear.

34. We will have to be more effective in managing transnational problems—from environment to drugs to terrorism. We see a growth of transnational problems in the global environment, but we do not have effective multilateral institutions to deal with them. Those we do have are ineffective and constantly weakened by our inability to invest real political and economic capital in them. Without new institutions, we will continue to struggle to deal with these growing problems—and, in a global environment, that could prove to be a very serious flaw in our foreign policy apparatus.

35. The information leadership of the United States should be maintained. We are the leader now in most information technologies. We are the leader in software and in most hardware. We are the home to the system of higher education that is producing the most important and valuable technologists. Our language has become the language of these new industries. Our intellectual property is the backbone of much of this technology growth. Our companies are dominant in many sectors of the information and other technology industries. Do we leave this leadership to the marketplace? It is, after all, what produced the leadership. Are there ways of protecting the lead that do not, like many trade protection measures, for example, do more harm than good?

36. Strategies must be developed to continue the information dominance of the United States. How far are we willing to go? Are we willing to actively work to promote English as the language of business, and our standards as the standards of the Information Age? Are we willing to do what we can to fund new developments, to encourage companies to spend more money on research and development, to encourage foreign students to stay in the United States, to make our regulatory environment more attractive than any other, and to protect our intellectual property rights more vigorously? Do we want to increase our lead? Do we want to counteract threats? Is this even a matter for a nation to consider? It is not politically correct, but the path of enlightened self-interest in such matters has always been worth serious consideration.

37. We must address the technical empowerment of criminals. Just as cyberterrorism is growing, so are international criminal cartels, six or eight of which may represent the most serious near-term threat to our national interests of any entities on the planet. These are the entities that are killing tens of thousands of Americans a year thanks to illegal drugs, and stealing hundreds of millions of dollars a year in cyber-crimes that have barely stirred public awareness to date. These are international entities representing domestic and foreign policy concerns of the first order. Stopping them will require new plans and initiatives, international cooperation, and sophisticated and costly information resources.

38. The power of the Internet and related information technologies should be exploited to change, subvert, and politically motivate societies (overtly and covertly). Just as the Internet can be used to move public opinion by independent actors, so can the United States and other governments use it. We need to study the example of NGOs and insurgencies that have done so and consider where and when we would employ similar tactics. We need to take advantage of the ability to do so covertly, and we need to recognize the ability of others to do the same to us.

39. It is important to develop new intelligence models for the open source-rich information era. Through the use of open sources and modern technologies, it may be possible to produce a better intelligence product than the vast majority of the output of the U.S. intelligence community. It is certainly possible to create an information and knowledge management system within the U.S. Government that would allow intelligence users to better interact with intelligence gatherers and analysts, to manipulate information better, to seek it better, to receive it in a more useful form, and probably to do it all in a more secure fashion, notwithstanding fears about agency-to-agency information sharing. Indeed, given the realities of the Information Age, the information-gathering arm of the U.S. Government is probably the arm of government most amenable to a complete overhaul.

40. Immigration policy must reflect the realities of a mobile world in which a premium is placed on technically knowledgeable workers. Attracting and keeping knowledgeable workers, retaining the output of our system of higher education, finding workers to perform tasks more educated workers will not do, and doing this in the context of uncertainty about the implications of globalization for labor forces—all this will require a reassessment of our immigration policies and procedures.

41. Foreign policy controls are required in an era in which the role of the Executive Branch is shrinking, the role of government is shrinking, and U.S. special interests are being realigned globally. Foreign policy prerogatives are being seized by the Congress, by the states, and by companies. It is becoming increasingly difficult to define who and what the U.S. Government's constituents are. Voters? Voters who work for foreign companies? American companies with most of their operations overseas? Government is less important than before. Interest groups are converging on the Internet despite borders. The result is a world in which the very core understanding of who does what for whom in U.S. foreign policy is being altered.

Domestic Policy Concerns with International Implications

Naturally, to implement and address many of these issues, domestic policy changes must be considered and implemented. They include the following:

42. The U.S. Government must be restructured to better reflect these new realities (making it flatter, more fluid, better able to deal with nongovernment entities). Reinventing government is a nice slogan. However, until we get rid of outmoded agencies, permit government restructurers to fire employees, give government workers the tools that they need to communicate with each other and compete with their counterparts in other governments and nonstate actors around the world, it will remain a slogan. Government really has to be reinvented.

43. Definitive steps should be taken to improve understanding and management of e-democracy (opportunities, threats, and the pace of change). One threat to—and hope of—the reinvented government will be that the very nature of electronic democracy will change. The threat is that it will do so in an unplanned way that produces not leaders but individuals who respond to a never-ending series of polls and referenda. This could produce the kind of deficiencies decried by political theorists from Plato to Alexander Hamilton, James Madison, and John Jay. It also could paralyze real action. It may seem a distant threat, but consider the degree to which electronic media and polls drive decisionmaking today. The reality is that the foundations of politics are now firmly planted (is this possible?) in the infosphere. On the other hand, enabling greater involvement of the people and greater dialogue among government and nongovernment actors with common interests can only conduce to the enhancement of democracy in this new era. What dominates and defines the character of the change remains to be seen; to a large degree, however, it is up to us.

44. Efforts should be made to improve understanding and management of e-government (opportunities, threats, and the pace of change). The ability to deliver government services via the Internet is on the rise. How rapidly will this happen? What does it mean to register voters, to recruit soldiers and sailors, to manage Social Security accounts, to distribute passports and other government documentation—all online? What does it mean to put in place extremely transparent government procurement systems, or to make information about public officials and programs more accessible to the public? Government here and abroad will change profoundly in how it operates, how it interacts with people, and how it is perceived. What does this mean for the future of democracy?

45. Education policy (distance education, cross-border education) will have to be adapted to the Information Age. Education is of paramount importance in a knowledge economy. The Information Age promises many changes in this regard. Children everywhere will have access to schools and libraries everywhere via the Internet. The best teachers will be available online—but only to those who will pay their higher prices. Will they be available through universities or via their own Web sites?

Knowledge resources—including education resources—will cross borders more easily. Should we build universities in Africa or simply erect satellite links to schools in the United States or Europe? Should we educate a world of scholars or use information technologies to take undereducated workers and walk them through the steps of jobs that once required more training? Do we educate or do we just enable? How will the basic theories of education policy be changed as the media via which we educate change? What are the implications of career-long education for those who can get it—and for those who cannot?

46. We will have to confront intelligently the health care and Social Security policy implications of biotechnology, which may dwarf the political implications of the Information Revolution. Like distance learning, distance medicine has already attracted considerable attention for its ability to attract the attentions of top doctors to rural and other formerly inaccessible regions and patients. But behind the question of how the Information Revolution changes health care is the bigger and substantially more profound question of how the biotechnology revolution will change global societies. In the next two decades, advances in biotechnology will produce dramatically longer life expectancies—for those who can afford the innovations. It is therefore reasonable to anticipate an aging, developed world that requires the exertions of the more youthful, underpaid labor forces of the developing world to pay for their extended retirements. This is likely to negate all pre-existing assumptions about Social Security and health care systems and how they are funded, and it could prove to be a source of serious societal tension. It will also, inevitably, give rise to new biowarfare threats and options. It is a revolution made possible by the increased computing power that is the hallmark of the Information Revolution, and thus it can be reasonably argued that the two should be considered together.

47. Structural models for policy should be based on the Internet model rather than the obsolete hierarchical model. Our old structural models were the product of societies and organizations run by councils that gathered in a single room at the hub of centralized infrastructures that they managed. Hierarchies dominated. The new environment's decentralization, dislocation, and virtualness argue for structures that are more like the Internet (that is, more matrix-like), wherein information flows differ depending on the recipients and the purpose of the interaction. The various levels of international actors—supranational, regional, national, transnational (for example, corporate), and individual—will have to have mechanisms for dealing with one another within and across borders as circumstances dictate. Structures will be flatter and more fluid. They will also be virtual, with resources held in virtual spaces for timely deployment in support of meetings and interactions.

48. Strategies must be developed to overcome the difficulty in attracting quality individuals to government. Recruitment power has shifted to the private sector; the old days when the State Department attracted the best and the brightest individuals with international interests are long gone. Government is finding it increasingly difficult to compete with private industry in attracting talented employees, and this will only get worse as government's influence shrinks and private sector opportunities proliferate. It will also be increasingly difficult to attract senior officials in a world in which active e-empowered media can penetrate to the most intimate level of personal lives and thus make service a considerable risk. The Information Age will not obviate the requirement for talented leaders, but increasingly those leaders are likely to have to be borrowed (briefly) or hired from the private sector.

49. It will be necessary to cope with growing pressure to cede to supranational entities the authority to address growing global and regional problems. The domestic implications of this are illustrated best by the reactions to the WTO manifested in the streets of Seattle and those to IMF and World Bank in Washington, DC. The reality is that such institutions are needed, and yet we have not found an effective way to sell them to the public. In the absence of support for them, they will falter and thereby weaken, correspondingly weakening the trading, financial, and other systems that they are intended to support.

50. We must combat the backlash against globalization and the associated rising tide of nationalism. The current backlash against globalization is linked to resentment of American domination of the Information Age and to emerging challenges to our leadership in related affairs. Nationalism, the predominant countervailing force, is observable in the politics of all kinds of national leaders, from Mahathir bin Mohammed in Malaysia to Joerg Haider in Austria, from Pat Buchanan in the United States to Hugo Chavez in Venezuela, and from Vladimir Zhirinovsky in Russia to the old hard-liners in Beijing and Tehran. When sweeping changes occur, it is natural for the forces of reaction to be brought into line. Our interests lie not in appeasing them, but rather in containing the threat they pose. Consequently, we must find a way to advance our views in ways that persuade or weaken them.

Conclusion: Broader Implications and Beyond

There are many significant implications of this new era for U.S. national policies. And there are a host of related questions that we will be forced to answer. How do we feel about our role as the current undisputed Information Hegemon? Do we feel the same about our role as the undisputed Technology Hegemon? Is it in our best interests to protect and preserve these roles, regardless of the economic impacts on our allies and less fortunate nations, or the consequences in terms of the world's view of us? Should technology dissemination accelerate thanks to the ubiquity of information in the Information Age? Who will be the new threats? India? China? Brazil? Our European allies? Do we wish to promote growth and thus stability by giving up some of the information assets that would ensure our continued dominance? Recognizing that the digital divide is also a capital divide—capital and information travel together—is there an alternative to promoting global participation in this revolution that does not promote such economic tensions as to engender protracted global conflict? As information has flowed more freely, we have seen a weakening U.S. resolve to put our men and material at risk globally. Is this trend likely to continue? In the absence of the U.S. police officer, what will become of world order? In the absence of Cold War pressures that once kept nations unified—threat of civil conflict produced alignment with either the U.S. or Soviet side and raised the stakes for division—will we see atomization of the planet as new technologies give smaller and smaller states the ability to operate effectively internationally? Does this mean a growing disconnect between political and economic units? Do political units become more ethnically driven? Are we, in fact, entering a new era of polarization of the planet between haves and have-nots, between those for whom stability is the predominant interest (those with assets and market interests) and those who require upheaval to advance? Where are the fault lines in this new global tug-of-war?

The world is being transformed by the Information Revolution. The result is globalization, and with it new wealth and productivity. On the model of the industrial era, a by-product of which may have been the ability to feed and clothe every human being, the by-product of this era may be the ability to educate every human being. New international cohesiveness is possible, born of a new sense of shared interests.

Or we may falter. We may be whipsawed by the transition and stumble. New conflicts and divisions may arise and be exacerbated. The stakes of technologically empowered conflict will certainly grow. And the future may see greater and costlier conflicts rather than fewer if we do not rise to the challenges of the new era.

The first step is recognizing that something new and profound is afoot. The next is recognizing the character of change in the new era. Then we can begin to develop and implement enlightened policies to address that change.

We have not begun to take these steps; we have just begun to consider them. As a consequence, this moment is likely to be seen as a watershed in our history—and we shall be judged by history on the basis of our ability to recognize and rise to its challenges.

Chapter 10

Economics and National Security: The Dangers of Overcommitment

David P.H. Denoon

As the global economy races ahead, more and more demands for U.S. security services are surfacing throughout the world. With this rapidly evolving scenario comes a pressing need for the United States to study the situation carefully and develop a comprehensive strategy in this arena. How best to proceed, from an economist's point of view, is explored in this chapter.

The crux of the problem is the growing connection between the global economy and security policy, including defense plans. The fact that such a connection exists should come as no surprise, for national policy saw these entities as connected during the Cold War. During that conflict, containment strategy sought to bottle up the Soviet bloc and employed a strong defense effort to support it. In tandem, U.S. policy also sought sustained economic growth across the entire Western alliance system, both to achieve prosperity and to build strategic strength for containment. In the current era of globalization, policies for security and economics must still be blended, but in ways different from those of the past. The United States has an interest in fostering worldwide economic growth as one way to help promote peace. It also needs an active security policy to address the turmoil and dangers that have bubbled up in the wake of the Cold War. A strong U.S. defense posture will be needed. It should be guided by economic thinking not only in using scarce resources wisely but also in being selective about military involvement and in prodding allies to contribute more to common defense burdens.

The focus of U.S. defense economics has shifted dramatically in the past 5 decades. In the 1950s, the shortages of World War II were still paramount in the thinking of most analysts. The United States was still essentially an industrial economy, and the Paley Commission report to President Harry Truman did an impressive job of projecting materials requirements and identifying countries and regions that were the source for vital American inputs.[1] The concentration on minerals and access to oil were also key factors in the way that strategists ranked defense priorities.

By the 1960s, the United States was at full employment, and the principal defense economics issue was how to get greater efficiency out of defense spending while still maintaining nuclear deterrence and a 2½ war conventional force strategy.

David P.H. Denoon is professor of politics and economics at New York University. He has served as a program economist for the U.S. Agency for International Development in Indonesia and vice president of the U.S. Export-Import Bank.

These circumstances and the soaring costs of the Vietnam War strengthened the position of Secretary of Defense Robert McNamara and his systems analysts. Defense economics thus shifted predominantly to a focus on budgeting and micro issues.[2]

As the Vietnam War wound down, however, it became clear that the United States faced a continuing global competition with the Soviet Union, and there was renewed interest in the relationship between economics and global strategy.[3] As the Reagan defense buildup proceeded in the 1980s, there was intense controversy over the macroeconomic effects of defense spending[4] and increased interest in ways to encourage Allies to pay a larger share of defense burdens.[5]

It was not until the 1990s and the end of the Cold War, however, that economists started linking structural changes in the global economy to more fundamental questions about strategy. For example, if production and assembly of "American products" were going to be done on a truly global basis, where should the lines be drawn between vital and merely important interests? Also, if the defense industry was going to be downsized, to what extent could the Department of Defense rely on foreign suppliers for vital parts and cooperation during a war?[6]

Neither the Bush nor Clinton administrations made much progress on developing a grand strategy to replace containment as an overarching set of guidelines for U.S. security policy.[7] The Bush administration recognized that, after 1989, the probability of a global military conflict had declined significantly and thus turned its attention to regional flashpoints that could potentially escalate to major wars. The East Asian strategy initiative was designed to reassure states in the Pacific Basin that the United States was not withdrawing its defense guarantees, and the Persian Gulf War of 1990–1991 promptly illustrated that U.S. power would still be used to protect access to vital fuel supplies.

On balance, however, this still left the United States without a clear set of international security priorities. The Clinton administration never faced a decision about a major war and used the military primarily to defend the no-fly zone in Iraq and to participate in a series of humanitarian interventions in Somalia, Haiti, Bosnia, and Kosovo. These latter interventions alerted observers to the virtually unlimited supply of ethnic and religious animosities around the globe that could flare into violence and lead to calls for troops to restore order.

Demand for troops is rising because the United States currently dominates the international stage in a truly unprecedented manner. It is the world's leading trading state, has the world's largest capital markets, and is the principal source of technical innovation in the globe's fastest growing business sectors (that is, telecommunications, computers, Internet-related business, and biotechnology).[8] In addition, American culture is widely accepted around the globe, especially by the young who will shape trends in future decades; the U.S. political system, particularly open democracy, is broadly respected; and American civil society, with its large number of nongovernmental organizations, has had a profound influence on the press and the nature of international public discourse.[9] Academics have long debated how to define hegemony, but there is little doubt that a state dominant economically, politically, and militarily is able to shape the world agenda.

The Perspective of Defense Economics

Within the broader patterns of economic change discussed earlier, two major developments in the 1990s fundamentally altered the way a defense economist would see the security calculus.

Clearly, the most critical change was the disintegration of the Soviet Union. Although Russia still possesses a vast arsenal of nuclear weapons, it no longer has the economic strength to project conventional power beyond its borders. This means that defense choices can be made without an ever-present worry about a threatening response from Moscow.[10] American defense economics is thus freed from the constraint of bipolarity and can concentrate on choosing an optimal force size with long-term structural objectives in mind.

The second development is the liberalization and rapid growth of the world economy. As barriers to trade have fallen and the global transfer of capital and technology has soared, there is no question that the very nature of the world economy has been transformed. As recently as three decades ago, it was reasonable for economists to assume that countries had relatively fixed endowments of land, labor, and technology and that these "givens" could change only gradually through specialization in trade or from new investments.[11] Today there is dramatic evidence of how improvements in finance, communications infrastructure, and the process of transferring technology have made it possible for formerly agricultural states to be producing high-technology products.

The scale of the transformation is stunning. World trade in goods and services grew at an annual average of 4.7 percent in the 1980s and accelerated to a yearly growth rate of 6.1 percent in the 1990s. Even accounting for the volatility of the past few years, real gross domestic product (GDP) annual growth rates in the developing countries increased from an average of 4.2 percent in the 1980s to 5.4 percent in the 1990s.[12]

The driving force behind this transformation, and the destination for many of the world's exports, has been the United States. The openness of the American economy, the breadth and versatility of its capital markets, and the extraordinary rate of technical innovation have led most countries to plan their economic expansion on access to American markets. The current account deficit (goods and services plus net transfers) has skyrocketed from $4.1 billion in 1991 to an estimated $300+ billion in 2000. This pattern, where the United States is the sponge for the world's goods, is not sustainable in the long run. Yet, shutting U.S. borders would throw the world into recession and raise prices for consumers. Consequently, adjustments need to be gradual and carefully thought out.

The Pros and Cons of Being the World's Dominant Economy

The United States has two enormous advantages at this moment in time, as the world's economy is being globalized. First, our domestic currency is the world's primary medium of exchange. This means that the United States can run trade deficits and many foreign individuals, corporations, and governments are willing to accept U.S. dollars in payment. This currently allows the United States to consume more than it produces. At some point, the rest of the world's appetite for dollars will drop. Until that time, most Americans have an artificially higher standard of living than they would otherwise.

Second, being the dominant economy allows American firms to set the standards in fast-growing industries like software, microprocessors, and biotechnology. Even where foreign suppliers may have superior technology, American firms have a significant edge because the scale and openness of the economy means that few producers will risk going against standards set in the United States. Moreover, since there are supernormal profits to be gained by being the first in many knowledge-based industries (because the incremental cost of producing is much lower than the cost of the first unit), American firms are likely to reap above-average returns until there is a true technological challenger. This permits high rates of research and development spending, which helps maintain economic dominance. Most residents in the United States do not fully appreciate these advantages but benefit from them nonetheless.

There are two distinct disadvantages in the current position, however. The most immediate concern is the soaring current account deficit. In the 1980s, many economists took the position that the trade deficit was not overly worrisome because the United States was the world's leading exporter of services, from architectural design to financial management. It was widely claimed that the deficit in traded goods was being overemphasized and that surpluses on services would counterbalance deficits on trade. Surging imports in the 1990s and growing payments to foreign lenders and investors discredited the naïve optimism of the 1980s, and the United States now runs massive trade and current account deficits. This matters because American profligacy is piling up hundreds of billions of dollars held by foreigners. These dollars are essentially IOUs. As long as overseas holders of American dollars prefer the dollar to other currencies, the United States can continue to print little green pieces of paper and take other countries' goods in return. At some point, this officially sanctioned approach will be fully understood, and many holders of U.S. dollars will sell them. Then, the dollar will drop in value; imports will go up in price, causing inflation; and the average U.S. citizen will experience a drop in his or her living standard.

The second major disadvantage of the current U.S. global dominance is that most Americans think this is a normal situation. It is not, and it will not last.

The danger in thinking that preeminence is normal and will continue indefinitely is that it leads to overcommitments of resources and resentment by less powerful states. Overcommitment of resources can be self-correcting; however, once coalitions of resentful nations are formed, they could last for long periods and persistently pursue measures to inhibit U.S. actions and values.

The following discussion will distill these introductory remarks into seven propositions and then attempt to relate the broader trends experienced in globalization to specific implications for U.S. security policy.

Seven Propositions

Before laying out the propositions, it is necessary to define some terms. *Globalization* will be used to mean the creation of truly worldwide markets on the input side for labor, capital, and technology and on the output side for final products and services. Although it may be true that trade accounted for a higher percentage of world GDP during several decades of the 19th century than is the case today, that is not central to the issues before us now. It is the change in the character and the extent of international interaction that make globalization today more intrusive and more important than the forms it took in the Victorian period.[13]

Specifically, there are two aspects of globalization today that make it different from past periods of open trade: the pervasiveness of outside political and cultural influences makes it extremely difficult for non-Western cultures to preserve their autonomy,[14] and the speed with which orders for trade, capital, and technology are carried out makes it much harder for governments to respond when a crisis develops.[15] Since open capital markets often put unsustainable stress on the banking, insurance, and regulatory sectors of developing countries, it is not surprising that countries like China, India, and Malaysia have chosen various forms of capital controls and resistance to aspects of economic globalization.

The term *industrial democracies* is self-defining and will be used as synonymous with the members of the Organization for Economic Cooperation and Development. All of the industrial democracies are intricately linked to the global economy. The term *transition states* will be used, in its economic sense, for countries that are partially integrated within the global economy.[16] Transition states are typically ones that have a vibrant modern sector of high per capita incomes and modern technology coexisting with a traditional sector of agriculture and extractive industries. Governments of the transition states, which include a mixture of authoritarian and democratic states, are often deeply ambivalent about how closely they want to be linked to the global economy and frequently attempt to limit the influence of outside economic, political, or cultural influences.[17] *Traditional states* will be defined as those in Asia, Africa, the Middle East, Latin America, and parts of the former Soviet Union that often have low incomes, low levels of technical skills, and only rudimentary links to the world economy.

The seven propositions that form the core argument of this chapter are the following:

1. In the next decade, fundamental security challenges (those that threaten large parts of the American population) are likely to come only from the large transition states that have the economic strength and technical prowess to inflict widespread physical damage or massive economic disorder.

2. Smaller transition and traditional states, as well as assorted terrorist groups, might be able to damage selected areas of the United States but are unlikely to be able to threaten the basic integrity of American society.

3. Overall globalization is an accelerating trend with such a large number of complex interactions that it is impossible to adequately model or accurately predict the full range of its social, political, and military implications.

4. However, the economic aspects of globalization have been under way for a sufficiently long time that the United States can probably make acceptable estimates of the likely direction and impact that world economic integration is having and ways in which the character of the world economy will evolve in the next decade.

5. Current levels of U.S. defense spending do not significantly detract from the long-term growth potential of the economy; given the plausible challenges of the next decade, the United States is fully capable of defending itself against direct threats to its population and national integrity.

6. Nevertheless, because the United States is so dominant economically and militarily, its allies and many other nations expect it to provide stability and security protection in large parts of the globe where vital national interests are not involved. Much of the future debate about linkage between economics and security will thus be focused on the extent to which American taxpayers should provide systems maintenance for the world.

7. If the current trend of increasing U.S. involvement in police actions and maintenance of order in the Third World continues, military readiness will be affected; also, it will be harder to maintain military superiority and research and development levels necessary for military dominance. Hence, it will be essential to develop criteria for deciding when to participate in police actions and limiting the tendency of allies and independent states to free-ride on the provision of global security protection.

To put the current problems associated with globalization in perspective, it is useful to review briefly how the United States developed policies to smooth the effects of business cycles and limit instability in the financial sector. It took the United States almost 140 years to develop resilient financial institutions and several generations (between the 1890s and the 1960s) to develop a consensus on the appropriate role for the United States in the international economic arena. This is critical for policymakers and security analysts in Washington to understand because Americans are often impatient with developing countries that resist opening their traded-goods and capital markets.

In most cases, the Department of Defense (DOD) does not need to formally intervene in Government deliberations on macroeconomic policy toward the Third World. However, the economics profession has been chastened by the havoc wrought by capital market liberalization in East Asia in the early 1990s, when few countries were adequately prepared for it. Thus, it is helpful to understand the problems that the United States had in developing sound financial institutions and a consistent direction for its international economic policy.

U.S. Economic Policy in Historical Perspective

It is hard for present-day Americans to understand how vulnerable the American economy was to external shocks and financial panics before the establishment of a competent central bank and a Federal commitment to full employment. Countries in the Third World must develop sufficiently resilient institutions so that they, too, can weather the vicissitudes of inevitable shocks from fluctuations in financial flows and assorted business collapses.

Although it is well known that in the 19th century there were long-standing differences between the American states of the North and of the South regarding tariffs,[18] the most bitter economic policy debate at the time was over whether to establish a central bank. Secretary of the Treasury Alexander Hamilton and the Federalists favored a Bank of the United States, while Thomas Jefferson and James Madison opposed it.[19] The Bank was established, but subsequently its charter was revoked. For much of the 19th century, individual banks issued their own currencies, and there were frequent bank panics. Banking regulation was intermittent until 1913, when the Federal Reserve System was established. Moreover, it was not until the end of World War II that the principle of Federal Reserve independence was fully accepted.

Trade policy in the United States has gone through similar swings in sentiment, at times favoring free trade but also having long periods of protectionism. By the 1890s, American manufacturing was booming, the United States began to run a trade surplus, and many businessmen favored a mercantilist strategy. As a Congressman, William McKinley pushed through a highly protective tariff, and protectionist sentiment dominated even through the Progressive Era up to the enactment of the Smoot-Hawley Tariff of 1929.[20]

The panic of 1896 made the public aware that a completely unregulated economy was prone to dangerous cycles, but the free silver movement and deep skepticism about concentrating power in Washington still prevented the creation of an American central bank for another two decades. Thus, it should come as no surprise today if developing countries have difficulty in deciding how to regulate their financial sectors.

Interestingly, however, it was in the 1890s when the United States developed its first modern conception of the links between economic and security policy. Alfred Thayer Mahan was a prominent advocate of using sea power to project American values and influence,[21] and there was growing acceptance of the need to develop sophisticated capital markets and gain access in foreign countries for American exports.[22] This approach clearly influenced Congressional and executive branch thinking at the time of the Spanish-American War and during the advocacy of the open door policy toward China.

The mercantilist worldview dominated until the downward spiral of the Depression in the 1930s. It was only with the intellectual ferment over how to deal with the devastation of the Depression and how to restructure international trade and finance after World War II that the current liberal synthesis was developed. United States economists and financiers took the lead in 1945 in creating a sharply different conception of how the United States should interact with the world economy.

The post-World War II conception was based on three elements: (1) careful bank regulation and an active monetary policy guided by the Federal Reserve System, (2) countercyclical fiscal policy and a commitment to full employment, and (3) open markets and efforts to stimulate world economic growth, using the World Bank and International Monetary Fund.[23]

There was a consensus among economists that the Federal Reserve had been too contractionary in the 1929–1935 period, so it needed to see growth and inflation as tradeoffs and aim for an appropriate balance. The Full Employment Act of 1947 was a key commitment to lower income workers, demonstrating that their interests would be considered if they would go along with a less protectionist, open economy.[24] The international financial institutions (World Bank and IMF) were to help moderate the type of mercantilist behavior that had deepened the Depression.[25]

In summary, it took the United States almost 60 years from its rise as an industrial power, until 1945, to settle on a consistent conception of how it should deal with the world economy. Since then, there have been various efforts at shifting U.S. policy in a more protectionist direction, but there has been a broad consensus that U.S. interests are best promoted in an open-trading and financial system. Clearly, countries that have less competitive industry and fragile capital markets will be threatened by an open, globalized economy. Unless they can develop adequate domestic employment growth and sufficiently resilient banks, they will continue to prefer mercantilism for themselves and a free trade stance by the United States.

Formal Links between U.S. Economic and Security Policy

Many texts on defense economics concentrate first on microeconomic issues and then present the connection between defense topics and the broader economy.[26] In the following discussion that process will be reversed, as American trade, capital, and technology have a far greater effect on the world economy than do specific choices about U.S. defense spending.

The U.S. Global Presence

Concerning U.S. security policy, it is absolutely essential that the U.S. role in the world economy be appreciated as a key asset for leverage. To put it bluntly, most of our allies and many of our antagonists need us far more than we need them.

Although there is no question that the United States benefits from an open world economy, those countries that trade with the United States benefit even more. China, for example, sends over 40 percent of its exports to the United States alone and currently has a $60 billion annual trade surplus with the United States. American exporters would be hurt if trade were cut off with China, especially in the aircraft, machinery, and power equipment sectors. However, China's entire economic development strategy would be crushed if it were denied access to the American market.[27] Unfortunately, in the process of pursuing open global markets (which is definitely in the long-term interest of the United States), U.S. policymakers often neglect the specific bilateral influence that the United States has.[28]

The size and openness of American markets is an enormous inducement for other countries to cooperate with the United States. Similarly, American influence in the World Bank and IMF provides an indirect but substantial form of additional inducements. Recent protests in Seattle against the World Trade Organization and in Washington against the World Bank and IMF may appear to undercut the legitimacy of these international organizations but in fact are a true sign of their power, as it is pointless to protest against an entity that has no influence.

The United States also has three forms of bilateral assistance that can be used to strengthen its security position: aid, investment guarantees, and export financing. The U.S. Agency for International Development, the Overseas Private Investment Corporation, and the U.S. Export-Import Bank can all provide key resources to vital countries.

Thus, in addition to its political, military, and cultural influence, the United States has a truly unmatched range of economic options for dealing with cooperative or antagonistic states. In the future, security planners need to look more closely at the tradeoffs between using military or economic options. Both have costs and both can generate adverse reactions, but they should increasingly be seen as complements, not supplements.

The Defense Industrial Base

True globalization of trade, capital, and technology flows provides both opportunities and difficulties for maintaining the American industrial base. On balance, it makes the process of getting standardized parts far easier because they are available from a greater variety of vendors. It also improves interoperability with allies, as globalized markets reward interchangeable parts and compatibility in software.[29]

By the same token, however, globalization makes it easier for antagonists of the United States to get American technology, to train with it, and—presumably—to learn how to foil it. This places a premium on keeping a U.S. lead in essential defense technologies and having the wherewithal to tell even close allies that certain items simply cannot be shared.

Jacques Gansler provides sensible advice in noting that adapting to the post-Cold War environment requires major adjustments on the part of both government and business, by allowing contractors more flexibility in sourcing; continuing to emphasize technological leadership; and upgrading the quality of the U.S. workforce at all levels.[30] The implications of these trends are explored below. It is clear that the military services will need to develop a greater capacity for working directly with a broader range of private contractors (domestic and foreign) in peacetime and wartime.

Natural Resource Planning

As the United States has shifted from an industrial to a service economy, the livelihood of its citizens depends less on imported raw materials than it did at the time of the Paley Commission. The United States is less worried about chrome from East Africa or copper from Chile than it once was. Also, as materials science has become more sophisticated, it has yielded a host of synthetic products that can directly substitute for natural ones or prior manufactured ones.[31]

The principal exception to this pattern is oil. In the highly suburbanized society that the United States has become, there is still no substitute for gasoline. Natural gas could, eventually, heat most homes. Also, at some point there may be cars with combination battery-powered and internal combustion engines. Yet, unless there are some unforeseen major technological breakthroughs, the United States will remain highly dependent upon imported oil and the world will be increasingly dependent upon Persian Gulf oil.

States in the Persian Gulf area that are members of OPEC are expected to increase their daily exports of oil from 25 million barrels per day (mbd) in the year 2000 to 45 mbd in 2020.[32] Even with secondary and tertiary recovery techniques being employed, most other areas of the world will see only modest changes in levels of production. This means that the Persian Gulf will remain an absolutely vital region of U.S. security concern and, by some measures, could become even more important in our calculus than it is today.

So, although materials in general will be less important in shaping security priorities in the future than now, maintaining stability in the Persian Gulf and an adequate strategic petroleum reserve (SPR) will warrant even greater attention. Since our principal allies (Europe, Japan, and South Korea) are far more dependent on Persian Gulf oil than we are, this natural resource vulnerability will require extensive future discussions on burden-sharing.

Implications of Economic Globalization for Security Interests

Economic globalization has three principal implications for U.S. security interests: the distinction between the defense sector and the economy at large is diminishing and will require DOD to adopt more efficient techniques for gaining the benefits of links to the global economy; more preparations need to be made for dealing with the effects of market disruption; and there are various unresolved policy dilemmas that will affect the way the United States deals with economic issues in developing countries. Although the military services will not have the lead in shaping these initiatives, DOD needs to be attentive to them.

Adapting to the New Economy

United States private sector firms are now spending hundreds of billions of dollars to upgrade their computer and information handling systems. This, in turn, is fundamentally reshaping the way "just in time" production, warehousing, and distribution is done.[33] If DOD does not stay current with these changes, it will not be able to gain the full advantages of lower cost supplies and wider availability of parts.[34] Business-to-business Web sites now offer thousands of standardized and customized products in such diverse areas as steel plate and dynamic random access memories.

Not only will DOD need to use these sources for its own purchasing, but also it will need to develop adequate intelligence methods for ensuring that its products are not contaminated, while at the same time figuring out the weaknesses of its antagonists' supplies. Adjusting to these changes is already under way, but it will remain a costly and ever-present feature of DOD operations because the training involved and the assorted downtimes associated with systems failure are likely to be more costly than the equipment itself.

The U.S. Government as a whole must also become more realistic about sanctions. When parts can be bought anonymously or with fake identifications, it will be increasingly difficult to impose effective boycotts. This, combined with the greater speed of technology transfer through the Internet, could mean ironically that the

United States may need to overwhelm certain antagonists with quantity because quality differentials in weapons have been reduced.

Preparations for Market Disruptions

The oil shocks of 1973–1974 and 1978–1979 led to the creation of the International Energy Agency and various strategic petroleum reserves in the major industrial countries. This has had a calming effect in the intervening two decades as businesses and consumers were reassured that basic needs could be met in new crisis periods.[35] Obviously, the United States needs to keep its SPR at adequate levels, given anticipated future demand.

The more difficult issue is how to deal with financial contagion. Former Secretary of the Treasury Robert Rubin is now publicly acknowledging how close the world came to a financial sector implosion in 1997–1998 as the East Asian crisis spread to Russia and Brazil and as highly leveraged hedge funds such as Long-Term Capital Management collapsed. Dealing with these issues will always be primarily a Treasury function, but DOD needs to have staff who understands the issues and can analyze the implications of such crises for U.S. security commitments. There also may be instances where DOD short-term interests are hurt by efforts to achieve longer term stability of the financial system. For example, it may be more important to build up crisis stabilization funds at Treasury and IMF than it is to write off specific country debt under DOD loan programs.[36]

Unresolved Policy Dilemmas

The globalization trend has spawned at least three policy questions that provoke fundamental disagreement among specialists: Should lower income countries try to maximize their economic growth rates? How far should countries go in opening their capital markets? Will greater integration with the global economy reduce or accentuate inequality within traditional and transition states?

For the last half of the 20th century, most economists assumed that countries should try to maximize, or at least increase, their GDP growth rates. Although there have been sharp differences over how to achieve greater equity in income distribution, the general presumption was that more growth and a larger GDP were better.[37] Moreover, by the middle 1990s, there was broad agreement among Western development economists that a common set of policies was likely to achieve promising results. According to this view, the emphasis should be on balanced budgets, low inflation, high savings and investment rates, and the use of open markets as a means to force efficiency in the economy. Because the World Bank, IMF, and the U.S. Government supported this view, it became known as the Washington Consensus.

The World Bank was so confident of this approach that in 1993 it published a primer on how the East Asian states had used this model to achieve their rapid growth rates.[38] However, the slowdown of the Japanese economy in the 1990s and the East Asian crash of 1997 brought more scrutiny to the debate. The linchpin of growth for the East Asian states had been their strategies to emphasize exports (and particularly access to the American market) as a way to generate foreign exchange to pay for imports that modernized their economies. Today, a sizable group of economists is skeptical of the wrenching changes that the East Asian states went through to achieve their export-oriented growth, and there is now interest in strategies that focus more on internal changes and accept lower GDP growth.[39]

The debate over how open an economy should be is a longstanding one. French mercantilists favored protection in the 1700s, the United States was protectionist for long periods, and most developing countries have pursued a mix of some protection and export promotion. In the 1950s, Ragnar Nurkse stressed the problem that raw material exporters faced with the high volatility and low-income elasticity of demand for their products.[40] The East Asian states became even more vulnerable because they tied their growth prospects to foreign markets, foreign technology, and foreign capital. Paul Krugman sees the weaknesses of the East Asian development pattern as relying too much on high savings and investment rates and not placing sufficient focus on selecting efficient investments and improving productivity.[41] Jeffrey Sachs, on the other hand, sharply criticizes IMF and the Washington Consensus for advocating a risky strategy to begin with and then imposing an overly contractionary policy once the 1997 crisis was under way.[42]

A key element in the growth debate is intense controversy over the desirability of linking the small capital markets of traditional and transition states with the large and highly liquid markets found in Tokyo, London, and New York.[43] The Washington Consensus stressed the opening of capital markets as a way to move money to its most efficient use, but many countries have found volatile flows in and out too difficult to handle.[44] Hence, after the East Asian crisis and the turmoil in Brazil and Russia, there is a heightened caution about capital market openness.[45]

These challenges to the Washington Consensus have led to an even broader critique of economic development strategies. Amartya Sen, for example, has argued that democracy is a desirable goal on its own and that enfranchised citizens will press for more equitable growth policies; these, in turn, will ultimately prove a more stable basis for development because citizens will then have both choice and growth.[46]

The growth, market integration, and equity debates are clearly unresolved, but they do bring into question the desirability of U.S. pressure on countries to open their capital markets, unless new kinds of protective buffers can be found for those with fragile economies. It would also be prudent for DOD to anticipate increasing challenges to the argument that globalization is good for all. Growing democratization might also be expected to lead to protectionism and nationalism, rather than to the acceptance of common world standards for economic and social policy as advocated so frequently by some in Washington.[47]

Conclusions

The foregoing analysis of the links between economic globalization and U.S. national security leads to four basic conclusions.

The Military Services and OSD Need Better Economic Analysis

The military services and the Office of the Secretary of Defense (OSD) have long had a small group of systems analysts who are skilled and effective at using quantitative techniques on budgeting questions. As it is clear that global economic issues will be increasingly affecting military choices, DOD should consider two initiatives to improve its capability to deal with economic topics: contracting for economic information tailored to military needs at all levels of the officer corps and civilian leadership and supporting a larger number of officers to obtain training in economics at the M.A. and Ph.D. level so that DOD will have a broader range of trained staff to deal with future economic topics.

DOD Should Acknowledge the Value of Steady, Sustainable Growth in Developing Countries

There is no perfect correlation between economic growth and political stability. In fact, the recent East Asian economic crisis illustrates that rapid growth can be destabilizing. However, in the long run, stability depends upon creating jobs and opportunity for young people entering the job market and a rising living standard for those already working. This requires economic growth.

Steady sustainable growth is important because high variability in growth rates leads to speculative behavior during booms and deep pessimism and resentment during downturns. Hence, DOD and the military services need to recognize that their interests and the interests of vulnerable economies are often intertwined. This may well mean that DOD personnel will need to pay more attention to economic behavior in traditional and transition states, by being more attentive to levels of defense spending, corruption, demography, and ways to dovetail defense programs with broader development objectives.

The United States Should Resist Overcommitment

In the Cold War period, many administrations were prone to overcommitment because they saw global jockeying for power as a zero-sum game with the Soviet Union. The Sino-Soviet split provided an opportunity for more complex brokerage and enabled President Richard Nixon to proceed with the opening to China and the Guam doctrine simultaneously.[48]

The United States has even more maneuverability today. It has no direct military challenge. Unfortunately, however, since 1989 DOD has been asked to take on a growing list of police actions that are not linked to U.S. vital interests. Maintaining the no-fly zone in Iraq is questionable policy, but it is clearly in a vital country. The interventions in Somalia, Haiti, Bosnia, and Kosovo illustrate the fact that crises lead to calls for action and, unless the United States is willing to be strict with its commitments, there will be virtually infinite demand for its police services. In the future, the American economy may not be so vibrant, and the United States will regret its presidents' essentially unlimited commitments of U.S. peacekeepers.

In Somalia, Haiti, and Bosnia, the United States has used essentially main force troops for police functions. Many of the troops were not trained for these tasks. Most importantly, the world was left with the impression that U.S. forces would be available for global police duty. If a conflict is occurring in a country or region of vital interest to the United States, using U.S. troops to enforce peace is legitimate. Policing or peace maintenance should be done by international organizations, however. Otherwise, the United States will get involved in a vast array of inconsequential disputes that no great power can afford. Hence, the United States should see value in supporting competent international peacekeeping forces under United Nations or regional organization command.

The United States Should Minimize Free-Riding

During the 1950s and 1960s, U.S. allies had an incentive to underinvest in conventional defense because they were confident about the U.S. nuclear guarantee or were unsure if a war was worth winning if it was fought on their soil. Only with great effort did the United States ultimately convince its allies that increased spending on conventional forces increased their military options.

Unfortunately, in the post-Cold War period, the United States has lost its leverage with its allies because, with the exception of China, there is no major state that is sharply increasing defense expenditures or seems likely to coerce its neighbors. In this environment, only the states on China's periphery and those in the Middle East have enough concern about being attacked that they will join with the United States to agree on maintaining prespecified defense capabilities.

Consequently, most U.S. allies (except those that feel truly vulnerable) have an incentive to free-ride on U.S. security protection. In fact, even countries that are neutral or hostile to the United States free-ride, enjoying U.S. defense of the sea-lanes and U.S. intervention to calm quarrelsome neighbors. Most Dominicans were privately glad that U.S. troops occupied Haiti; many Ethiopians were pleased when U.S. forces intervened in Somalia; and many Croats and Slovenes appreciated outside troops' restoring order in Bosnia. Yet, none of these countries has the slightest sense of obligation to help defray U.S. expenses. That pattern will not change unless the United States is more sparing in its commitments. Therefore, the United States must make the distinction between vital and peripheral interests. Otherwise, the rest of the world will have an incentive to exhaust American goodwill and resources.

Summary

In sum, it is possible to identify the broad directions that economic globalization is taking. There are strong incentives for producers and consumers to take advantage of the global marketplace. This will make it difficult for countries to cut off the access that their firms and citizens have to outside suppliers of capital, goods, technology, and information.

Nevertheless, if the turmoil caused by massive capital flows is great, if competition against local producers is daunting, and if outside information threatens regimes, efforts will certainly be made to limit the impact of global markets. Thus, it is substantially harder to predict the political, cultural, and security implications of globalization.

Because the current level of DOD spending does not adversely affect the American economy, the United States does not face the kind of built-in limits to defense spending that it did during the Cold War. Hence, it is important for U.S. decisionmakers to set limits to U.S. commitments. Otherwise, U.S. resources will be spread around the globe on low-priority problems, and inadequate investments will be made to maintain readiness and military superiority.

Notes

[1] William S. Paley, *The Report of the President's Materials Policy Commission* (Washington, DC: Government Printing Office, June 1952).

[2] Alain C. Enthoven and K. Wayne Smith, *How Much Is Enough? Shaping the Defense Program, 1961–1969* (New York: Harper and Row, 1971).

[3] Charles J. Hitch and Roland N. McKean, *The Economics of Defense in the Nuclear Age* (New York: Atheneum, 1975).

[4] Lester Thurow, "How to Wreck the Economy," *New York Review of Books* (May 14, 1981), 3–8.

[5] David B.H. Denoon, ed., *Constraints on Strategy: The Economics of Western Security* (Washington, DC: Pergamon-Brassey's, 1986).

[6] Jacques Gansler, *Defense Conversion* (Cambridge, MA: MIT Press, 1995), 85–102.

[7] For a discussion of how different nations have developed national strategies, see Paul Kennedy, ed., *Grand Strategies in War and Peace* (New Haven, CT: Yale University Press, 1991).

[8] Council of Economic Advisors, *Annual Report of the Council of Economic Advisors* (Washington, DC: Government Printing Office, January 2000), 7–128.

[9] Robert Keohane and Joseph S. Nye, Jr., "Globalization: What's New? What's Not? (And So What?)" *Foreign Policy* 118 (Spring 2000), 104–118. For example, the number of international nongovernmental organizations has grown from about 6,000 in 1990 to over 26,000 in 2000.

[10] President Vladimir Putin's decision to visit Pyongyang in July 2000 (announced 5 days after his June 2000 summit with President Clinton) is an indication that the Russians intend to pursue an independent foreign policy, which, to the extent possible, maintains Moscow's influence in Asia.

[11] Charles Kindleberger, *International Trade* (Homewood, IL: Irwin, 1963), chapter 7.

[12] These growth rates for trade and services in the 1990s even overcame the effects of the Mexican and Asian financial crises. See International Monetary Fund, *The World Economic Outlook—1999* (Washington, DC: International Monetary Fund, May 1999), 145, 167.

[13] For a debate on these points, see Sylvia Ostry and Richard Nelson, *Techno-Nationalism and Techno-Globalism* (Washington, DC: The Brookings Institution, 1995), especially chapter 1, "The Decline of American Hegemony," 1–27.

[14] D. Nettle and S. Romaine, *Vanishing Views: The Extinction of the World's Languages* (New York: Oxford University Press, 2000).

[15] S. Arndt, "Globalization and the Open Economy," *North American Journal of Economics and Finance* 8, no. 3 (1997), 71–79.

[16] This is a different use of the term *transition* than in the literature dealing with the change from authoritarian to democratic states.

[17] There are some similarities between my term *transitional states* and Paul Kennedy's term *pivotal states*, but they are not identical because, clearly, not all transitional states are pivotal. See R. Chase,

Emily Hill, and P. Kennedy, "Pivotal States and U.S. Strategy," *Foreign Affairs* 75, no. 1 (January/February 1996), 33–51.

[18] The North with a budding industrial sector favored protection, while the South was primarily agricultural and favored free trade (so it could get manufactured imports at the lowest possible prices).

[19] John Garraty and Peter Gay, eds., *The Columbia History of the World* (New York: Harper and Row, 1981), 793.

[20] Thomas Paterson, ed., *Major Problems in American Foreign Policy—Volume I: to 1914* (Lexington, MA: DC Heath, 1989), 353.

[21] Alfred Thayer Mahan, *The Influence of Sea Power on History 1660–1805*, repr. (Englewood Cliffs, NJ: Prentice Hall, 1980).

[22] Robert Beisner, *From the Old Diplomacy to the New* (New York: Harlan Davidson, Inc., 1986), 32–34.

[23] The designers of the World Bank and IMF had hoped to create the International Trade Organization as well, but the U.S. Congress balked at ceding this much power to an international trade body. So, the weaker General Agreement on Tariffs and Trade was formed instead.

[24] President Truman proposed a mixture of pro-labor and pro-business legislation in the early post-World War II years. See Michael Barone, *Our Country—The Shaping of America from Roosevelt to Reagan* (New York: Free Press, 1990), 185.

[25] For an overview of how these institutions were created, see Robert Solomon, *The International Monetary System* (New York: Harper and Row, 1977).

[26] See, for example, Lee R. Olvey, James D. Golden, and Robert Kelly, *The Economics of National Security: Weighing the Costs of Defense* (Wayne, NJ: Avery, 1984).

[27] For discussion of the pros and cons of different types of sanctions, see David Baldwin, "The Sanctions Debate and Logic of Choice," *International Security* 24, no. 3 (Winter 1999/2000), 80–107.

[28] The U.S. decision to enter the World Trade Organization limits the circumstances under which Washington could impose bilateral sanctions, but they are not forbidden if the imperative of national security is invoked.

[29] This may make it less necessary for the United States to subsidize its allies through coproduction and codevelopment programs. For an overview of those programs from the 1950s to 1980s, see D.H. Denoon, *Arms Collaboration, Co-production and Industrial Participation Agreements* (Washington, DC: U.S. Department of Defense, August 1983).

[30] Gansler, *Defense Conversion*, 147.

[31] Carbon-carbon fibers replacing steel and aluminum is one notable example of the growing use of substitutes.

[32] Energy Information Administration, *International Energy Outlook* (Washington, DC: Energy Information Administration, 1999), Appendix D.

[33] For an overview of how high-technology companies are competing and the way in which their services are changing, see David Bunnell, *Making the Cisco Connection* (New York: Wiley, 2000).

[34] As an example of this pattern, it is now known that the Defense Advanced Research Projects Agency was able to get a new "friend vs. foe" identifying system bought and in the field within 16 days during the Persian Gulf War. If the contracting had been done under normal DOD procedures, it would doubtless have taken years.

[35] The oil price increases of 1973–1974 and 1978–1979 led to a widespread set of adjustments: power companies demonstrated that they could switch to cheaper fuels, firms reduced the energy content of their products, and consumers rewarded auto and appliance makers who produced fuel-efficient goods. This served notice to OPEC member-states that it was counterproductive to raise the price of oil to the level where it seriously affected demand.

[36] For a summary of policy options regarding the destabilizing effects of financial flows, see Carmen and Vincent Reinhart, "Some Lessons for Policy Makers Who Deal with the Mixed Blessing of Capital Flows," in *Capital Flows and Financial Crises*, ed. Miles Kahler (Ithaca, NY: Cornell University Press, 1998), 93–127.

[37] For an overview of this debate, see Gerald Meier, ed., *Leading Issues in Economic Development* (Oxford: Oxford University Press, 1995), 3–66.

[38] World Bank, *The East Asian Miracle* (Oxford: Oxford University Press, 1993).

[39] Dani Rodrik, *Has Globalization Gone Too Far?* (Washington, DC: Institute of International Economics, 1998).

[40] Ragnar Nurkse, *Problems of Capital Formation in Underdeveloped Countries* (New York: Oxford University Press, 1953).

[41] Paul Krugman, "The Myth of Asia's Miracle," *Foreign Affairs* 73, no. 6 (November/December 1994), 62–78.

[42] Jeffrey Sachs, "International Economics: Unlocking the Mysteries of Globalization," *Foreign Policy* 110 (Spring 1998), 97–111.

[43] In 1996–1997, the International Monetary Fund designated capital market liberalization as one of its highest priorities.

[44] For an overview of the magnitudes involved and the difficulties that capital flows pose, see Barry Eichengreen and Albert Fishlow, "Contending with Capital Flows: What Is Different About the 1990s," in *Capital Flows and Financial Crises*, ed. Miles Kahler (Ithaca, NY: Cornell University Press, 1998), 23–68.

[45] For an argument that countries do not need open capital markets to get the benefits of trade competitiveness, see J. Bhagwati, "The Capital Myth," *Foreign Affairs* 77, no. 3 (May/June 1998), 7–12.

[46] Amartya Sen, *Development as Freedom* (New York: Knopf, 1998).

[47] See, for example, The White House, *A National Security Strategy for a New Century* (Washington, DC: Government Printing Office, December 1999), 3–4.

[48] In the Guam Doctrine, enunciated in July 1969, President Nixon urged U.S. allies to share a large part of the global defense burden. Nixon promised more military assistance but said the United States would make fewer direct military commitments overseas.

Chapter 11

Toward Alliance Reform

Ronald D. Asmus

Globalization is forcing everyone to rethink—not least of all the strategic studies and policymaking community. As is true in other areas, our community is still coming to grips with what globalization is, what it means for foreign and defense policy, and how strategic studies and policymakers need to reorient their traditional ways of thinking and working in an increasingly globalized world.

Many of the excellent contributions in this volume are conceptual, historical, or highly empirical. They help illuminate the critical and often detailed issues that are at the center of the globalization debate and that we must grapple and come to terms with if we as a community are to build a consensus on U.S. foreign and defense policy in an increasingly globalized era. My goal in this chapter is somewhat different. It is to step back and be speculative by asking the following questions: What kind of policies would we ideally want to have for the United States in a globalized world? How do they compare to where we are today? Is it possible to close the gap?

My perspective is that of someone who has spent his career in both the think-tank world working on policy initiatives and in the government trying to implement them. Most of that experience has been in the U.S.-European relationship. Our relationship with Europe is particularly interesting, for Europe is a part of the world that is coming together after the end of the Cold War while also going global in a number of areas.

For the United States, Europe remains strategically important but for new and different reasons. It is no longer just a place we are committed to defend, but also a potential global partner at a time when there is a growing imperative in U.S. foreign policy to find partners to manage a global agenda. Europe is an ally that, unlike other parts of the world, has officially embraced the goal of pursuing common goals and interests with the United States on a global scale. It is the part of the world with which we have the most mature alliance relationships and with which we currently have at least the beginnings of a more global dialogue and agenda. It is a natural ally in trying to manage the strategic challenges of globalization.

This is why the Clinton administration made Europe and the creation of a new post-Cold War U.S.-European partnership one of its top foreign policy priorities. Secretary of State Madeleine Albright often said that one of the basic rules of politics is to protect your base, and that, in foreign policy terms, Europe is our base. American support for North Atlantic Treaty Organization (NATO) and European Union

---

Ronald D. Asmus is a senior fellow at the Council on Foreign Relations. He also has served as Deputy Assistant Secretary of State for Europe and a senior analyst at both RAND and Radio Free Europe.

(EU) enlargement, as well as U.S. proposals to restructure and expand the scope of the U.S.–EU relationship, was driven by several factors. But one of the most important motivations was the desire to move this relationship away from its original Cold War rationale and to create a modern partnership to work together in an increasingly globalized world.

Today our relationship with Europe and the U.S.-European partnership are still largely dominated by the need to finish what one might call the "in-Europe agenda"—the creation of a Europe whole and free in alliance with the United States. As we move forward with this project, we must also continue to lay the foundation for what might be called the "beyond-Europe" agenda—the issue of whether and how a unified Europe and the United States can cooperate on global strategic issues.

Globalization: Is It Good or Bad for the United States?

Strategists and policymakers are trying to understand and cope with two dramatic shifts that have occurred in the last decade. The first was the collapse of communism in the Soviet Union and Eastern Europe, the end of the Cold War, and the passing of the bipolar system that shaped so much of our strategic agenda for half of a century. The second is the accelerating trend toward globalization. The two are, of course, related. Globalization helped accelerate the collapse of communism as it widened the gap in the economic performance of the West and the Soviet Union. The spread of information fueled the development of civil society and undercut communist rule. At the same time, the collapse of communism unleashed a set of new forces that has helped contribute to globalization's acceleration in the 1990s.

As someone who approaches the issue as an amateur, I do not pretend to be conversant in the nuances and quasi-theological arguments over how to define, measure, or quantify globalization. In my mind, the key characteristics of this trend are pretty straightforward: the growing surge of economic, cultural, and political cross-border flows; the growing integration and interdependency of markets; and the growing formation of multinational corporations and other institutions in response to these trends. Many of the characteristics of globalization strike me as the same trends that we see and have seen in terms of regional integration, albeit on a global scale and at a new, more accelerated and less controlled pace. This is a trend that, in a macro-sense, is mostly a positive one both for the United States and for the world.

That is an important point to make because integration is almost universally accepted as a positive trend. True, globalization is seen by some critics as being much more ambiguous, if not threatening, but I do not share that skepticism. I think that globalization has had several positive strategic consequences:

- Strengthening and consolidating the core of democratic, market-based countries around the world, especially in North America, the European Union, and Northeast Asia.
- Improving the prospects for the successful transition to democracy and market-based economics in other areas (Eastern Europe, Latin America, and Southeast Asia) as well as key swing states such as Russia, China, India, and Indonesia.

- Creating huge pressure for the opening up of closed societies and for reform in those countries whose leaders are still trying to resist change.

In short, globalization has thus far led to a big improvement in the prospect for a more democratic, peaceful, and prosperous world. If one were to plot a chart of the world, one axis measuring how open or closed societies are and the other how autonomous or integrated a country is, it would show a huge shift toward a more open and integrated world since 1989. If globalization were a product of a consciously pursued Grand Strategy, we would declare it a success. To a degree, this success has been a product of our policy and strategy, but it also has been produced by natural forces of change. In the future, globalization will continue being influenced by natural forces, but conscious and strong government policies will be needed to channel it in the right directions.

For the United States, globalization has been a special bonus. It is not a coincidence that this last decade has simultaneously witnessed the acceleration of globalization and one of the greatest increases in American economic growth, technological innovation, self-confidence, and power. Economically, we are well positioned to prosper from this trend. Politically, our society has shown itself to be more flexible and able to absorb the domestic shocks and backlash of globalization than most other countries, including other Western industrial democracies. Culturally, globalization is an American and English-language phenomenon. Strategically, globalization has reinforced the fact that we are the sole remaining military superpower with a global reach and capability.

At the same time, globalization has produced not only winners in a political, economic, or cultural sense but has also been a double-edged sword; that is, there have been both winners and losers within states and in the international arena. While countries may be doing better in a macro-sense, various sectors or segments of society have clearly suffered. All of our countries have experienced a political backlash against some of the effects of globalization. Even the United States has not been immune to these trends, as was evident in the protests against the World Trade Organization summit in Seattle.

Internationally, the dramatic opening of societies and states in the international system has also been a double-edged sword. While we generally accept the growing interdependence of the world as a net plus, this has also been accompanied by the emergence of new threats, risks, and vulnerabilities. These include, but are by no means limited to, the following: the diffusion of potentially dangerous technologies, especially in the area of weapons of mass destruction (WMD); the weakening or failure of states, along with the rise of troublesome nonstate actors; the lack of accountability or democratic control over many of the new transnational global actors; the vulnerabilities to attack that arise from an integrated global infrastructure; and a much more likely contagion or knock-on effect from one part of the world to another.

Proliferation is the most obvious and oft-discussed example of globalism. But it also remains unclear which way important transition states such as Russia or China will go. The inability to adapt to, or cope with, the pressures of globalization can also create instability and produce failed regimes and failed states. While we all pledge our faith to the market and growing interdependence as a peaceful antidote to nationalism and geopolitics, and cross our fingers that Frank Fukuyama was right in his thesis on the end of history, we are still not 100 percent sure and harbor concerns that maybe he was wrong and that there still may be modern-day dictators who harness nationalism and modern-day capitalism for evil purposes. As one of the greatest beneficiaries of globalization, the United States is also the focal point of much of the envy, frustration, and hatred it has engendered. For that reason, we may be a more vulnerable target for that frustration.

There are also some caveats when it comes to the United States. There is little doubt that the United States has benefited tremendously from globalization. But it also has placed new pressures on the United States to become more involved in issues and in regions where it has not been engaged before. The fact that there is no agreed-upon international framework to manage this process has left a void and created additional pressures for the United States to somehow help fill this void. What some countries see as an enormous benefit to the United States and a chance for the country to maximize its influence by becoming a kind of global policeman, however, is viewed by many U.S. citizens as a significant and almost frightening version of mission creep, which is capable of overtaxing our resources and overextending our military forces.

Applying Einstein's *Gedankenexperiment* to Foreign Policy

One of the great pitfalls when one is in government or even when one works in the broader think-tank community that tries to affect policy decisions is the tendency to work from, and at times become intellectually captive or hostage to, the conceptual agenda set by existing government thinking and policy. There is an almost inevitable tendency when in government to use the status quo as the point of departure. Such an approach often makes sense. But at other times, it can be constraining, even counterproductive. Anyone who has served in government has probably witnessed or been involved in a policy review where such an approach was bureaucratically comfortable but led to an intellectual dead end. This is particularly true when governments or branches of government are forced to confront significant changes in their external environment or paradigm shifts of one or the other form.

Does globalization present that kind of change or paradigm shift for U.S. foreign policy and strategy? Are we adapting or adjusting our policies in the right way to meet this challenge? One way to test the adequacy of our current policies is to conduct a rather simple intellectual exercise. The goal here is to step back, set aside the status quo and its constraints as much as possible, and instead try to sketch out the ideal state of affairs—that is, what the goal of our strategy should be. One can then compare that ideal state to the status quo to see how we are doing. If the two are the same, then we are in pretty good shape. If they are not, then we can identify the gap, the reasons for it, and start thinking about whether and how it is possible to move from Point A to Point B. To employ a phrase that Albert Einstein used for scientific theories, we could conduct a *Gedankenexperiment* (thought experiment) to help us discover something that might or should exist but that we are not aware of at the moment.[1]

If asked to try to design from scratch a strategy for the United States in a globalized world, what might it look like? I would suggest that our options should be guided by the following principles. First, we should recognize and accept the fact that globalization is happening whether we like it or not. It cannot be stopped. It has many beneficial aspects, in particular for a country the size of the United States, which has such a dominant position in the international arena. This position, however, imposes a unique responsibility on us to help create and sustain an international system that is equitable, and one that must be seen as equitable if it is to be accepted by the vast majority of other participating states. The point of departure for our strategy should therefore be how we can best shape this system in a fashion that is conducive to our interests as well as those of the world community.

Second, at a time when the United States is more integrated into an increasingly interdependent world, the importance of allies and partners and international institutions should be going up, not down. Globalization is indeed global. The logical goal of globalization in the realms of foreign and defense policy is greater integration. In short, we should seek alliances to help manage the strategic consequences of this trend. The United States cannot and should not aspire to "go it alone" and carry the full responsibility of managing this emerging global system. An imperative of globalization is therefore that we need partners—as much if not more than in the past. This leaves us with a certain paradox. Even though the Cold War is over and we do not face any imminent existential threats (and find ourselves with fewer resources for the conduct of both foreign and defense policy), our strategy should be oriented to building and sustaining alliances and partnerships, not neglecting them. A globalizing world demands them in order to ensure that it produces progress, not troubles and disasters.

A top strategic priority should be to organize the core group of democratic or like-minded countries who benefit from, and are willing and able to shoulder the international responsibilities of creating and managing, a framework in which the challenges of globalization are addressed. There will be, and should be, a great deal of cogitation and debate over how one does this—by strengthening truly global institutions or by transforming existing regional relationships and organizations. But the strategic thrust of our policy is nonetheless clear. In an increasingly interdependent world where the United States is more integrated and exposed to external influences, alliances and partnerships with key players are an asset, not a liability.

Third, there must be an answer to the immediate question: allies and partners to do what? What should these alliances be focused on in terms of mission? Who should be included and who should not? At least part of the answer to this question is that we need alliances whose mission is to provide the international or regional framework for globalization and to address the new risks and vulnerabilities that result from it. Because the nations of the world are so interdependent, the main goal of our strategy should be to keep that world safe by guarding against the risks that do exist. At a time of growing interdependence, when the consequences of crises spread faster, cross more borders, and can affect more people in disparate countries, we need alliances not only to deter or fight wars but also to help shape that interdependent system in peacetime. A higher premium should be placed on what many strategists like to call "environment shaping"; that is, in the absence of an immediate threat, but in a world where integration and globalization are accelerating, the importance of environment shaping should increase relative to crisis management and war fighting.

Such alliances would, of course, not just be military, but also political, economic, and security organizations. Their goal would not be limited to only creating regional military balances of power or defending countries against an acute military threat. Such thinking is increasingly anachronistic in a globalized world. Instead, they would, ideally, integrate all of our policy tools from money to military power in order to maximize our ability to shape both regional theaters as well as this new global environment. They would bring together "soft" and "hard" power, to use Joseph Nye's terminology, as part of a grander strategy for shaping a new international system.[2]

A point that often gets lost in much of the current literature on globalization is the important link between economics and security and the role that security and alliance have played and can continue to play in fostering integration at different levels. To paraphrase a well-known political slogan from the 1992 American presidential campaign, It is not just the economy, stupid! Security matters, and it is often the precondition for successful economic integration and reconciliation. It is a lot easier for a country to trade and integrate across borders if it is not worried about being invaded, securing its sovereignty, or competing militarily with its neighbors.

If we look at the European experience, historically and today, security alliances have played and continue to play a crucial role in fostering regional integration and reconciliation. For example, Franco-German reconciliation as well as the start of European integration would have been impossible without NATO and the security umbrella that the Atlantic Alliance provided. NATO enlargement to East-Central Europe has made EU enlargement eastward easier. It has also eased German-Polish reconciliation and is likely, in my view, to be a precondition for the eventual reconciliation between Russia and its Eastern European neighbors. Poland today is far more confident and willing to trade with Russia and to work for Russia's inclusion in broader Euro-Atlantic structures, now that its own security is protected by NATO. The same concepts and principles can be applied to different regions as well as on a broader, even international, scale.

Fourth, our strategy should, of course, not be limited to the task of environment shaping. It would have to cover the full spectrum, including both crisis management and war fighting. Globalization is likely to increase the pressures on us for early crisis intervention and management of conflicts in order to stop or contain them and to prevent such instability from spreading or escalating into major conflicts. Therefore, we would ideally want to have political support at home, civilian and military capabilities nationally, and coalitions for effective crisis management.

Fifth, we obviously should have the right kinds of military forces, properly trained and equipped, to confront and defeat our adversaries in a globalized world when required to do so. Globalization will not make war obsolete, but it may change the nature of warfare. For example, adversaries may seek to gain advantage over us by exploiting whatever new vulnerabilities we face in a globalized world through asymmetrical warfare.

In short, our strategy should be global in scope, focused first and foremost on shaping the international environment through a better integration of soft and hard power; more reliant on political, economic, and security alliances with allies and partners, as well as international institutions; outfitted with both the civilian and military capabilities for early and effective crisis management; and, last but not least, equipped with the military forces necessary to deter and fight the kinds of new wars most likely in this new era.

Performance of U.S. Foreign Policy Today

If this list provides a useful approximation of the kind of strategy the United States would want to pursue in an era of globalization, then clearly we have some work to do in order to meet that standard. Neither the policymaking world nor the strategic community that tries to support the policymakers is currently doing a very good job on many of these fronts.

The problem starts with the fact that the strategic issues associated with globalization are not yet well understood, let alone integrated into our work. They have not become part of the mainstream work of diplomats, soldiers, or even think-tankers in the strategic community. They are rarely on the agenda for summits or even regular consultations with key allies. In an era in which governments and bureaucracies are all too often compartmentalized, global issues are all too often handled in newly created bureaus or divisions that are not at the center of, or influential in, the foreign policymaking process. They are still considered trendy, somewhat exotic issues that are to be addressed, yet often only as an afterthought or after the heavy lifting on more traditional issues has been accomplished.

For example, let us take the experience of U.S.-European relations over the last decade. Both the United States and our key European allies have, in various forms, embraced the principle that we should become closer partners in managing global issues. But I suspect that the strategic challenges of globalization would not be high on the list of issues that our leaders have spent their time discussing. We still have to move beyond rhetoric and define the kind of workable agenda that will turn that principle into reality.

Moreover, while we all nod our heads in agreement when someone talks about the need for better environment shaping and crisis management strategies, the reality is that implementing these strategies is easier said than done. For example, there is a growing recognition that we need to better integrate our economic and security policies in order to be more effective in creating or shaping an environment where instability and new threats might arise. But the gap between economic and political or military policymakers in the United States and in Europe remains as wide as ever. The U.S. Government has taken some steps—for example, creation of the National Economic Council—to raise the profile of and integrate economic issues and factors in the national security decisionmaking process. But my sense is that we still have a long way to go in this regard. If one looks at the resources we make available for economic policy tools, one finds that the record is hardly an encouraging one. In view of the very mixed record on sanctions, it is not clear that they are a success story in terms of the interplay between economics and security either.

I would argue that NATO enlargement was one of the great acts of soft strategic environment shaping of the last decade. We enlarged NATO in order to foster European integration and unification at a time of peace and in the absence of any immediate military threat. We all probably would agree that a coordinated enlargement of NATO and the European Union would have been ideal. In theory, it would certainly have made strategic sense to have an open dialogue, if not coordination, between these two institutions. But that was simply not doable because of institutional sensitivities and competition. Since then, we have progressed to the point where we allow NATO Secretary General Lord Robertson and EU Special Representative Javier Solana to meet for coffee, and we may soon agree to low-level informal working groups. But we clearly still have a long way to go to have an effective impact.

Similarly, it seems obvious that a better integration of soft and hard security instruments as part of a broader, common U.S.-European approach would also necessitate an overhaul of the U.S.–EU relationship. The European Union is a major provider of soft security on a global scale. The United States should want to transform that relationship into one in which it coordinates its approaches on soft security and then backs them up with hard security through NATO and ad hoc military coalitions of the willing. But the U.S.–EU relationship today remains largely nonstrategic and dominated by the management of U.S.-European trade disputes.

When it comes to crisis management, we have obviously learned a lot in the last decade from our experiences in peacekeeping and peacemaking in various parts of the world—Haiti, the Balkans, Africa, or East Timor. But part of what we have learned is that we need to be able to do a much better job at it. Let me highlight two issues that I think are illustrative of the kinds of issues that will become more important, but maybe also contentious, as we move into a globalized world. One is the question of the international legitimacy of different forms of early intervention. Intellectually and strategically, we understand that at times it can be more effective and cheaper to intervene early in a conflict, before it escalates, and thereby nip a crisis in the bud.

But that is often difficult politically, in part because we cannot get the international mandate for intervention, a situation that has prompted increasing debate among international legal experts. The Kosovo conflict highlighted just how important different interpretations of international law can be to flexibility in a crisis. There is also another political reality: it often is not possible for governments to secure a political consensus on early involvement or intervention precisely because the stakes and risks are not immediately apparent to all.

Another challenge is the need for a more robust and effective civilian component to crisis management missions. This is the most conspicuous lesson of our peacekeeping experience in Europe over the last decade. We see, again and again, the clear asymmetry between the military and civilian resources that can be brought to bear in a conflict. While the analytical and policymaking community recognizes this need, again fixing this problem is often difficult.

For example, in 1998, the U.S. Government proposed to create under the auspices of the Organization for Security and Cooperation in Europe something called Rapid Expert Advisory and Cooperation Teams, or REACT. We recognized the need to have a more robust capability to rapidly deploy civilian resources to crises just like the U.S. military does. The basic idea was to have a team of civilian experts that either could be deployed rapidly to other countries to help defuse crises in their early stages or could be partnered as a separate unit with military forces in peacekeeping or peace enforcement missions. While the program was eventually launched on a very modest basis, trying to build a political constituency for this idea and convincing governments to invest any resources at all in it were painstakingly difficult.

In addition, we do not have much of a strategic dialogue on globalization with our key allies and partners around the world. We have only begun to try to recast Cold War alliances for a post-Cold War globalized world. Again, let us start with our own strategic community and Europe. Considering the fact that annually we have dozens, if not hundreds, of conferences with our European colleagues in the strategic community on a huge number of issues, it is striking how infrequently we see a conference whose agenda is focused on the strategic consequences of globalization for the United States and Europe.

If we look at the official level, our leaders get together and spend great amounts of time going over detailed issues on the Balkans' other hot spots, but rarely do they step back and talk about how we together can shape a strategy to pursue our common interests in an increasingly globalized world. The part of our government that is responsible for tending to our relations with Europe is staffed by Europeanists who are often the wrong interlocutors for a global strategic dialogue. Although policy and planning staffs could and should be thinking about issues that cut across regional portfolios, they find it difficult to perform that function as well. Paradoxically, globalization and the acceleration of information have accelerated the pace of diplomacy, with the result that planners have all too often been pulled into the day-to-day management of foreign affairs.

The problem is not necessarily convincing leaders or senior officials that in principle there is a need to make the necessary changes. The vast majority of senior U.S. and European leaders and officials would probably embrace the basic hypothesis that the United States and Europe are natural allies or partners in a globalized world, that we have common interests, and that we need to find ways to pursue those interests. They would also probably agree in principle that the United States and Europe should have some kind of common strategy toward Europe's periphery as broadly defined—Russia, the great Middle East, the Persian Gulf, and the Mediterranean; that we need a better common strategy on key functional issues such as WMD; and that we should also be trying to work together on regional issues such as China and Taiwan.

But turning that into reality is not easy on either side of the Atlantic. Europe today is a global actor commercially but only a regional actor strategically. Europe today is more insular in its strategic thinking than it was a century ago—the result of two World Wars and the Cold War. Our basic venue for discussing economic and global issues is the U.S.–EU relationship. But neither this relationship nor this dialogue is a strategic one. It is unfortunately dominated by the management of trade disputes rather than the coordination of strategies for putting hard and soft power to use in a common purpose.

Our basic venue for discussing military strategy with the Europeans is NATO. On paper, we have succeeded in transforming it from an alliance that defended the western half of Europe against a Soviet threat to a post-Cold War alliance between the United States and a Europe that is embracing new democracies from the Baltic to the Black Sea. In addition to defending alliance members' territory, the alliance has now pledged itself to defend common transatlantic interests beyond its immediate borders as well. In the Washington Declaration issued at the NATO 50th anniversary summit in April 1999, alliance leaders underscored a simple but profound principle for the future: it must be as effective in dealing with new threats as it was in meeting the Soviet threat during the Cold War.

The issue of just how far NATO common interests might stretch in the future is clearly a sensitive one. In the negotiations over the new strategic concept, the real issue was whether it would limit itself to language implying that it would go no further than "in and around Europe" or would talk about the security of Europe—thereby leaving the door open to future involvement in regions such as the Persian Gulf. As often is the case, we reached a carefully worded compromise with our allies. But the political and strategic reality is that we have succeeded in stretching the center of gravity in alliance thinking from the Fulda Gap to the periphery of Europe—an important accomplishment in its own right—but not any further. We must still make that vision a reality and then build on it if we are to create this global strategic agenda.

The area in which the United States is probably doing the best in terms of preparing for the future of globalization is in ensuring that we have the military forces needed for this new world. Other contributions in this volume address the specific issues involved for the U.S. military. I would make only two brief observations.

We are in better shape in this regard than in other areas because the U.S. military is working at this issue in its usual professional manner, has a better resource base to prepare for this kind of a future, and, more than most other foreign policy agencies, has the capability and tradition of having to think long term. To be sure, there are many problems, unresolved issues, and fights over the kind of forces and force packages that we need and can afford. Yet progress is being made in the military arena.

But the challenge and problem for the U.S. military is also that it can only function as part of the overall foreign and defense policy team, and that, ideally, we should be able to operate in a coalition of countries with similar capabilities. Many of the challenges and problems laid out here, as well as the changes that would be required, go well beyond the U.S. military or the Department of Defense. They affect the way in which we think, conduct, and manage foreign policy. In many ways, this may be the area in which we are weakest and need to rethink the most.

The reality is that we often turn to U.S. military forces to compensate for our weaknesses in other areas. We turn to them to compensate for our inability to develop or field the appropriate civilian expertise in crises. We expect the glue of our military alliances to help hold together political and economic relationships with key allies. Having denuded ourselves of meaningful policy tools for economic aid and assistance, tools that are likely to be in greater demand as a result of globalization, we often rely on our military-to-military contacts to sustain relationships with developing countries. Other countries often turn to us and the U.S. military because they themselves have not created the capabilities that might allow them to perform a mission without us or at least to assume a larger share of the burden. This is an unhealthy imbalance that cries out for improvement.

The purpose of this brief survey has not been to criticize. It is always easier to analyze what is wrong or missing in current policy than to come up with the answer. But by drawing the contrast between the kind of strategy we would want for an era of globalization and comparing it with the status quo, we can break out of the existing bureaucratic mindset that all too often limits or inhibits our thinking and illuminate the path we need to take.

Performing Better: A National Agenda

Can we do better? The answer to this question is that we must. How? We are clearly in the midst of a kind of paradigm shift, the implications of which we are still in the process of sorting out. Against this backdrop and without any claim to definitiveness, here is nevertheless a short list of steps we can take to help produce better policies in the future.

First, we must obviously expand and accelerate the intellectual and strategic dialogue on globalization and what it means. The issues involved in globalization must move from the periphery to the center of the strategic and policymaking debate. The globalization debate has heretofore been largely nonstrategic. It should become part of our mainstream work and debate in the foreign policy and strategic studies community, not an add-on often done as an afterthought to check a box. For a whole host of reasons, governments are going to find it hard to do this alone. They are not set up to do it; indeed, the way they are organized often inhibits it. Nor is it always their strength to look beyond the horizon or to integrate issues that cut across bureaucratic fiefdoms.

The necessary change can only happen in the context of an intellectual and analytical partnership between the government and the strategic community. That partnership must include not only the Department of Defense but also other parts of the government. As we have seen as a result of this cursory exploration, one of the key challenges we face is whether and how we not only can better integrate foreign and defense policy in a globalized world but also do a better job of bringing economic and security together as well.

Second, we need a more systemic exploration and understanding of a set of key issues that this chapter has unearthed. One special need is better identification of the new vulnerabilities—political, economic, and military—that the United States faces as a result of globalization to provide a basis for better thinking about strategies needed to counter them. Another is better policy tools and better integration of the tremendous nonmilitary resources of the United States in order to pursue a more conscious and effective environment-shaping strategy. Equally important, we need to think about how we can contribute to and help create the kind of international institutions and systems that are needed in a globalized world. In this context, we also need to tackle the question of how we can continue or start to transform existing alliance systems whose origins are rooted in the Cold War and adapt them to the challenges of globalization. We have made a solid start on that in the case of Europe; we have not really started that discussion when it comes to Asia.

Third, we must be aware that this debate is not an abstract or a merely intellectual one. It is also about resources, organization, and turf. In many cases, we have a reasonably good idea, at least in principle, of some of what is needed, be it in the area of civilian crisis management or how to apply the lessons of the revolution in military affairs to a globalized world. But it is still a long way from developing a good concept on the drawing board to creating the kinds of capabilities that are deployable on the ground. One has to build constituencies in order to forge the consensus necessary to acquire the resources. My view is that we, for a variety of reasons, are in much worse shape when it comes to the civilian component than the military one.

Fourth, while our priority must be getting our own strategic house in order, we must also realize that it is in our own interests to start the dialogue on all of these issues with our allies and partners. There is no escaping the fact that in a globalized and increasingly interdependent world, the United States will have to rely more, not less, on coalitions to pursue our goals. Cooperation with allies and partners will become more important, our own strength notwithstanding. And our alliances will have to change, in some cases radically. There will and should be lots of legitimate debate over how best to do this, but in an age in which new global alliances and partnerships are being established every day in the area of politics, commerce, and culture, why should we think that our field will be any different? A primary challenge for the United States will be to come up with creative incentives to get our allies to work with us to continue to transform Cold War relationships into post-Cold War alliances.

Fifth and finally, let me state the obvious. While we need a broader and more integrated portfolio of foreign and defense policy tools, we also need to ensure that we have the right kind of military wherewithal at the end of the day to protect our territory and interests, and that our allies and partners have sufficient forces so that we do not have to bear this burden alone.

This is an ambitious but exciting agenda. Some will look at it and say it cannot be done. Others will look at it and say we have no choice. The best answer is to get started and see how far we get and how good a job we can do. In the final analysis, we have no alternative.

Notes

[1] The point is that Einstein, as a theoretical physicist and mathematician, was skilled at creating conceptual systems in the absence of major empirical data portraying their operations or even their existence. See Nigel Calder, *Einstein's Universe* (New York: Viking Press, 1979).

[2] Joseph S. Nye, Jr., "Redefining the National Interest," *Foreign Affairs* 78, no. 4 (July/August 1999), 22–35.

Chapter 12

The Globalization of Energy Markets

Martha Caldwell Harris

Energy market globalization is deepening and broadening, not only through international trade but also through cross-investments, deregulation of domestic markets, and industrial restructuring that links the older energy industries to the new global political economy. This transformation of energy industries and markets is apparent around the world, and it offers great promise in terms of economic efficiency, technology development, and consumer choice.

The process of energy globalization is uneven, however, and some of its impacts will present new challenges for strategic planners. What new relationships are developing between producers and consumers, and between buyers and sellers? Who are the winners and losers? In a context of opening energy markets, why is there renewed concern about energy security around the world today? What types of security challenges will energy globalization present during the next two decades?

There are varying approaches to energy security in a context of market globalization. The United States supports market-oriented energy policies at home and abroad that open traditionally closed markets to new forms of competition and restructuring. Asia, a region where the United States has vast security stakes and where the most rapid increases in oil and gas imports are projected in the next two decades, deserves special attention. Policymakers in Asia and other countries worry that the market alone will not ensure energy security. The United States has generally pursued energy security on a different track, making Persian Gulf security a high priority.

To promote the cooperation and mutual interdependence that open energy markets require, it will be necessary to explore different approaches to energy security, analyze some of the unintended security risks that globalization of energy markets entails, and draw conclusions about the implications for U.S. security. Although the United States has already made large investments in Asian security, new multilateral approaches will be needed to pre-empt and mitigate the energy-related disruptions that may lie ahead. Defending the sea-lanes, to take an example, will be more important than ever in the future, but ensuring freedom of transit will require new multilateral efforts that cannot be simply subsumed under traditional alliances. Although the

---

Martha Caldwell Harris is a senior fellow at the Atlantic Council of the United States. She has served as Deputy Assistant Secretary of State in the Bureau of Political Military Affairs. Dr. Harris has also held positions at the Asia Foundation, National Research Council, and Office of Technology Assessment.

United States will have adequate access to energy supplies, it may be drawn into energy-related disputes, as weak states fragment, and producers and others seek to exert political leverage via energy supplies and infrastructure. Despite the uncertainties and difficulties of multilateral initiatives, it will be necessary to use them to address myriad energy-related security problems that are likely to arise as unintended consequences of energy market globalization. Failure to move proactively will result in requirements for more costly and demanding responses further down the road.

Asymmetrical Interdependence

Globalization of energy markets is not a new phenomenon. The major oil producers have for years been quintessential "multinational corporations," and fossil fuels have been internationally traded for centuries. Today, however, energy market globalization is unprecedented in its pace, range, and depth.

Networks of interconnection in energy development, supply, and use among actors in different countries on different continents render obsolete the traditional energy policy approaches directed toward national autonomy and control. National markets are increasingly integrated with global markets through more open access to resources, international agreements such as the Energy Charter, electronic international exchanges, corporate linkages and industry restructuring, cross-border pipelines, and electric power grids. Global energy trade grew much faster than did energy consumption between 1990 and 1997. Deregulation of electric power, one of the bastions of regulated monopoly operated for "public good" purposes, is a global trend. Consumers around the world are buying electricity from non-national firms operating in expanding regional markets.

The unevenness of the globalization process and the asymmetrical nature of relationships among key actors present new challenges for energy policymakers and security planners. In the developing world, there are 700 million more people today who do not have access to electricity than there were 25 years ago. Although 1.3 billion people have been added to central power grids, the population has grown by 2 billion.[1] The traditional model of centralized grids and state control has left many literally in the dark. Fuel subsidies have favored larger users, while lower income populations and smaller businesses have been squeezed when fossil fuel prices soared, in some cases as an industrial restructuring precondition for access to international capital. Developing nations, moreover, have suffered disproportionately from high oil prices in the past year.

In the midst of energy market globalization, regions are faring differently. Whether one argues that the outlook is for an oil glut or for continuing high prices and constrained supplies, differences among regions will be clear in the next 20 years. Forecasters agree that Asia will become much more dependent on Middle East oil in the two decades ahead,[2] as demand surges and local production levels off. Although oil trading has certainly become more transparent and global, Asian nations are at a critical juncture in deciding how much to rely on market forces. They have traditionally paid more for oil than have buyers in Europe and the West, and they continue to rely on long-term contracts and special relationships. One nation's choices will affect the calculus of neighbors. As China courted Saudi Arabia with promises of assured imports in recent months, Japan was rocked with the loss of the Arabian oil concession. Whether Asian nations will rely on global energy markets or old-style resource diplomacy is an open question. Growing dependence on Middle East oil imports will distinguish the Asian region for decades to come and create new imperatives to strengthen relationships with suppliers.

International cross-investment, another indicator of globalization in energy markets,[3] has grown rapidly in recent years. Decisions to privatize energy industries stimulated global transactions valued at more than $65 billion in the period 1991–1997 alone.[4] Foreign-based firms have taken advantage of these opportunities in the United Kingdom, Latin America, Northern Europe, and around the world—including the United States. (It's not your father's electric company any more.) Privatization and deregulation have brought significant benefits in electricity price decreases, but large industrial users have benefited more than have residential consumers. Furthermore, industry consolidation involves wrenching changes for workers as well as for managers. Deregulation has opened energy markets to new players who are selling new services and developing joint ventures that leverage resources of energy companies in new areas such as telecommunications and the Internet. Corporate linkages among firms based on different continents have in some cases streamlined operations and produced new resources for innovation. Market liberalization, nevertheless, is progressing at different rates around the world, and new problems are emerging that require new forms of government action, such as setting rules of the road that enhance market competition in electricity transmission.

Many argue that technological change provides the solution to global energy problems by lowering the costs of exploration and development and by promoting more efficient production and use of energy. New technologies can also help address environmental problems likely to grow even more serious as the world population increases to 9 billion people in the next 50 years. Fossil-fuel use is the major cause of environmental problems, particularly in developing nations where local and regional pollution is growing. Despite the promise of hybrid cars and distributed energy generation (for example, small turbines and decentralized power generation), market signals have been inadequate to support early commercialization. Political will (rather than government noninvolvement) is necessary to promote sustainable solutions that require joint governance. The uneven application of new technologies to address global energy and environmental problems is another dimension of the asymmetrical impacts of globalization of markets.

Renewed Concerns about Energy Security

Although energy security has been dismissed as old-think in a world of integrated energy markets, public concern heightened in the United States as gasoline prices rose in the past year. In Europe and Japan, where energy security never disappeared as an issue, perceptions of the problem nevertheless differ. A recent survey found that 60 percent of Japan's energy policy experts have big concerns about energy security—a percentage that only slightly exceeds similar concerns of all others surveyed.[5]

The biggest danger was growing demand for energy in Asia, followed by concerns about possible conflict in the Middle East and constraints in nuclear power. Japanese energy experts see global warming as a major threat, and they believe that as the phenomenon becomes more apparent, there will be negative impacts on energy security. Japanese perceptions of energy security today reflect a broader definition of risk—and a greater focus on the Asian region—than did the preoccupation with security of oil supplies in the 1970s' "oil shock" period.

In Europe, there is renewed concern about energy security today. A recent forecast projects that the overall import dependence of the European Union (EU) will rise to almost 70 percent for natural gas, 80 percent for coal, and 90 percent for oil by 2020. Imports of Russian gas could reach 45 percent of the union's total.[6] As demand for energy in the developing world rises to surpass the demand of the Organization for Economic Cooperation and Development during this time frame, the EU share of global energy demand will shrink to slightly more than 10 percent. The European Union has begun an effort to sort out the strategic implications by the end of 2000 and, in the meantime, to work on a transit protocol to implement the Energy Charter, an international agreement that includes EU nations as well as others. As Europe grapples with rising dependence on imported energy, the European Union places strong emphasis on environmental concerns and (more so than Asia) on continuing market liberalization. While the European Union stresses the benefits of competitive markets in terms of flexibility and avoidance of market control, however, it is clear that different countries have different perspectives. In 1999, the union brought legal action against France, for example, for missing the deadline on the introduction of national legislation to implement the electricity market-opening directive.

In the United States, rising gasoline prices in mid-2000 brought energy security back to the center of public attention. Over the past decade, a consensus around market-oriented policies has developed. In this context, public debate about energy security has focused on negative impacts of price hikes—increases that seem minuscule compared with those in other nations where taxes are high—on consumers. With a large U.S. strategic petroleum reserve and the increasing interconnection of North American energy markets, politicians worry about the uneven impacts of oil price increases—for example, on heating oil consumers in the Northeast compared with truckers—and about the reliability of the electricity transmission in a deregulated market. With inventories tight, planners were surprised by the jump in prices, and American officials turned their attention back to jawboning with the Organization of Petroleum Exporting Countries. Although the quest for Caspian oil has been a major pursuit of U.S. energy diplomacy, the tangible results have been limited. Meanwhile, the international coalition that supported military action against Iraq in the Persian Gulf crisis has lost its traction as major European countries push for loosening of sanctions.

In Asia, Europe, and the United States, these different approaches to energy security reflect different resource endowments, traditions, and institutions. Asian countries, understandably concerned about oil supply disruptions, are moving toward new forms of regional cooperation as pollution and environmental problems increase. European approaches resemble those of Asian countries, but with an important distinction. The European Union has made market competition a high priority and has the legal and institutional resources to push laggards forward. The United States has also in the past decade placed great priority on energy market liberalization, but the 50 states are moving at different paces and experimenting with different approaches. In addition, investments in Persian Gulf security, freedom of the sea-lanes, and maintenance of the strategic petroleum reserve provide a security underpinning. In the United States, however, the security and market opening dimensions are pursued on parallel (some would say unintegrated) tracks by different agencies.

Energy Market Globalization in Asia: Challenges Ahead

Does it matter that globalization is unfolding unevenly and that policy priorities for enhancing energy security are defined differently in the United States, Europe, and Asia? Traditionally, analysts have focused on the potential for military conflict over energy resources as the primary threat. Extrapolating 20 years ahead, based on consensus supply-and-demand projections that show sharp increases in Asia's energy requirements, a number of energy-related issues are likely to generate new types of problems and unintended consequences associated with deepening globalization. To the extent that globalized energy markets more deeply integrate economies in the region, of course, investment resources, entrepreneurial skills, and experience in governance will be available to mitigate the downsides. At the same time, U.S. officials responsible for security as well as for economic policy need to anticipate problems—many of them unintended consequences of globalization—that they may be required to address. Focusing on Asia, where there is no overarching, institutionalized security framework and where energy market globalization offers perhaps the biggest uncertainties as well as great promise, brings potential problems into sharper view.

Among the countries of the Asia-Pacific Economic Cooperation (APEC) group, electricity demand is projected to increase 60 percent by 2010, with China's electricity demand likely increasing by almost 6.4 percent annually.[7] In India, the International Energy Agency (IEA) forecasts that electricity consumption will more than double between 1995 and 2010. These forecasts (revised after the Asian economic downturn) imply major additions to generating capacity and to grids. Coal will likely continue to play the major role in electric power generation, but substantial increases in gas-fired generation are expected. Asia now has only limited intercountry electricity trade and pipeline systems. A number of countries, China in particular, have substantial energy resources located far from industrial and population centers.

Most of developing Asia is part of the global energy system, but because of inadequate investment in infrastructure as well as weak political leadership, the connections are in some cases tenuous. Rapid population growth and pressures for economic restructuring and deregulation have already produced some wrenching changes. Twenty thousand miners rioted in Northeast China in early 2000 after an announcement that a large mine had gone bankrupt, and workers were offered a one-time severance package equal to $68 per working year. The army was brought in to restore order, but the incident was not reported in the press for weeks.[8] Industrial unrest is rising in China's resources sector, where inefficient plants must be closed in line with government restructuring plans and ambitions to enter the World Trade Organization.

Russia exemplifies another type of political complication associated with market integration. In Russia, the country with the world's largest natural gas reserves, a good portion of which are located in the Far East, there are frequent blackouts. Gazprom cut gas supplies to RAO Unified Energy Systems (UES) recently in response to nonpayment. Gazprom is not investing enough to keep its gas flowing, and UES has warned that its old network of power stations and lines needs $75 billion in investment if Russia is to avoid blackouts.[9] Europeans and Asians hoping to import more Russian gas are rightly concerned about supply security in light of Russia's status as a nonsignatory of the energy charter, which includes transit provisions.

These examples illustrate the potential political fallout when energy market globalization occurs in developing and transitional economies that lack experience with market competition. As markets and infrastructure are connected across national borders, fuel substitution and economic benefits accrue. At the same time, new vulnerabilities are created. Energy infrastructure such as power grids can be the target of terrorists and opposition groups.[10] These concerns are not unique to developing countries, of course. The President's Critical Infrastructure Commission has outlined serious threats to the U.S. energy system from a number of sources—including hostile governments, terrorist groups, and disgruntled employees—as well as accidents.

For some groups in developing economies, the sharp changes in fortune that accompany restructuring and global energy market integration can create a political backlash that threatens the security of neighbors who buy energy from them or import it through their territories. Intense discussions are now under way in Northeast Asia about cooperation in pipelines and high-voltage transmission lines extending from Russia into China. According to some estimates, Eastern Russia could supply half of Northeast Asia's natural gas needs by 2020. These projects offer great promise in meeting energy demand and in hands-on cooperation among countries that have been historical competitors and enemies. The United States and countries in the region need to discuss the security implications of growing and asymmetrical interdependence, however, at an early stage. Joint planning and scenario analysis involving government as well as private sector organizations will be needed to anticipate and mitigate risks. The United States could lend support for discussions involving public officials and private sector representatives from Japan and South Korea, but Russia and China also need to be involved. In addition to high-level discussions on rules of the road for cooperative energy development, there is a need for joint efforts among environmental experts to assess potential effects, among regulatory authorities to discuss harmonization of equipment and industrial standards, and among legal experts to clarify issues such as transit rights and reciprocal tax treatment.

In developing Asia, where energy market integration is uneven, energy demand will grow sharply; because the infrastructure is inadequate and vulnerable, security-related problems are likely to grow. Attacks on energy infrastructure in friendly nations could lead to requests for U.S. assistance—both official and private. U.S. cooperation in the APEC and other regional initiatives to promote common standards and shared infrastructure are, in this light, a good investment. Although U.S. support for APEC energy market liberalization initiatives has been strong, energy security concerns have been treated with less urgency. U.S. industry and government could make this a higher priority and share expertise for assessing and mitigating risks.

A second dimension of uneven globalization—Asia's growing dependence on Middle East oil—also will present new challenges. The United States has made great investments in Persian Gulf security and has gone to war to ensure the stability of the region and its oil production. In the future, the narrow, shallow Straits of Malacca and the sea-lanes between the Middle East and Asia will be more congested with tankers and other ships carrying fuel and commodities. Today, 90 percent of Japan's oil imports and most of South Korea's and Taiwan's oil imports flow through these waters. More than 200 vessels pass through the Malacca, Sundra, and Lombok Straits and the South China Sea daily. In 1994, more than $1 trillion in international trade passed through these waters, which have seen an increase in serious accidents since the early 1990s. Piracy, kidnapping, and other acts of violence by nonstate actors, such as left-wing rebels in the Philippines, are also on the rise. China has fortified small islets in the South China Sea with fort-like structures, and the number of incidents involving fishing and naval vessels from Southeast Asian countries has increased.

Although some argue that territorial chokepoints such as these narrow water passageways are no longer security concerns in an age of globally integrated electronic markets that permit rerouting of cargo and fuel switching, securing freedom of the sea-lanes may well be more of a security challenge in the future. Competing claims among six claimants to the Spratly Islands, differing interpretations of the United Nations Law of the Sea, and the inability of the International Maritime Organization to establish safety and environmental standards of sufficiently high quality all contribute to a sort of maritime anarchy.[11] At the urging of the Philippines and other Southeast Asian states, the Association of Southeast Asian Nations (ASEAN) Regional Forum has agreed to take up the question of a code of conduct for the South China Sea; however, China opposes legally binding agreements and prefers to deal separately with each country. Other countries favor demilitarization and joint development, with the geographically closest claimant country taking stewardship over disputed areas. In this context, the potential for military conflict remains significant. By supporting efforts of regional states to address these issues, the United States can add momentum and expertise.

In the future, accidents and acts of terrorism and piracy will be even more likely throughout the region. Some have called for a change in the transit passage law enshrined by the Law of the Sea separating commercial and military traffic.[12] The objective would be increased regulation of commercial vessels in the Straits of Malacca to ensure navigation safety without affecting military or government vessels. Such a regime would involve not only the key states but also shipping concerns and user states such as Japan, China, and the United States. Another approach has been led by a working group on maritime security cooperation of the Council for Security Cooperation in the Asia Pacific, a nonofficial organization that provides input to the ASEAN Regional Forum. The working group has developed guidelines for maritime cooperation and plans to examine the Law of the Sea to identify areas that need clarification in order to ensure maritime security in South Asia.[13] These efforts suggest that addressing maritime security problems in Asia will be a challenging task, but arguably a good investment in preventive diplomacy. Cleaning up after a major oil spill and relief efforts to deal with terrorism or piracy could be much more costly after the fact.

Another way to address vulnerabilities in energy transportation through the sealanes is to develop regional emergency response mechanisms. Japan, Australia, and New Zealand are the only Asian members of the IEA, although South Korea is following IEA activities closely, and programs for nonmember states such as China have recently expanded. Asia lacks a viable regionwide program of emergency response or oil stockpiles. Although the impulse is strong for many of the Asian countries to pursue old-style resource diplomacy to secure supplies of Middle East oil, a more effective approach would be to build cooperative emergency response measures.

Market-oriented approaches can also contribute to solutions. Asian countries could permit cross-investment in downstream facilities so that refinery operations could be streamlined and efficiencies improved, encouraging Middle East countries to consider establishing storage facilities in the region. In addition, government involvement in emergency response and stockpile development is needed. American political support, technical expertise, and approvals to use international development assistance funding would help significantly in addressing energy security concerns in Asia and in bolstering the confidence and mutual trust required to sustain energy market liberalization policies over the long haul.

International corporate linkages in Asian energy markets are most extensive in the upstream resource exploration and development areas. Japanese firms have for years been mining coal in Australia, developing natural gas resources in Indonesia, and purchasing oil from China. With greater openness come new possibilities. Tokyo Electric Power has stakes in new power-generating ventures in Malaysia and Vietnam. Enron has teamed up with ORIX Leasing to compete in Japan's energy services and electric power markets. Marubeni, a Japanese trading company, and Sithe Energies, an independent U.S. power producer, plan to buy power plants and market electricity in Japan. Gas and electric power are the focus of networks of growing international joint ventures that include firms from many Asian countries, as well as from the United States.

These corporate linkages today extend further and deeper into the domestic economies and, in some cases, can stimulate market-oriented corporate restructuring and advanced technology development. They can also lead to new security challenges. In 1996, Japan imported almost one-fifth of its natural gas from Indonesia, a country where violent independence movements have threatened central authority in some regions. Electric power, gas, and steel companies have long-term contracts for liquefied natural gas (LNG) imports from Indonesia that stretch more than a decade ahead in some cases. Two-fifths of Indonesia's LNG exports come from Aceh, at the western end of Sumatra. Aceh is overwhelmingly Islamic; its rural people resent the wealth of the Javanese who run the industrial enclave. Disputes and violence have erupted. The potential fragmentation of energy- and resource-rich regions poses problems not only for central government but also for the importers whose investments become vulnerabilities.[14] The United States, Japan, and others have an interest in developing multilateral approaches toward assistance that leverage the resources of the international community and address the basic grievances that have led to strife and tension.

Advanced technology is diffusing through energy development, presenting another double-edged sword from a security perspective. Japan, South Korea, Russia, China, Taiwan, India, and Pakistan have commercial nuclear power programs, and four of these states have tested and/or developed nuclear weapons. For Japan, nuclear power has been the central pillar of its energy policy—seen as Japan's only hope for gaining a degree of autonomous control (through technology indigenization) and for meeting environmental commitments. However, the serious criticality accident that took place recently at a fuel fabrication plant shook Japan's energy policy leadership enough for the government to announce a comprehensive review. Japan's ambitious plan to develop the complete fuel cycle has proved to be expensive and technically difficult. Such problems aside, Asia has become the new center of gravity for the global nuclear industry, as additions to capacity in this region are projected to make up three-quarters or more of the world's total over the next two decades.

For safety, environmental, and nonproliferation reasons, advanced technology cooperation in energy among Asian nations is essential. Working with other nations around the world, the industrial operators and research institutions of Asia need to develop a stronger safety culture. In addition, governments will need to work to strengthen nonproliferation norms (a very difficult task in South Asia) and to build cooperation in material protection, accounting, and export controls. Weapons of mass destruction proliferation is clearly a major threat to the stability of a region where the security framework is weak. Two of the benefits of addressing the North Korea problem have been an expansion of security cooperation between Japan and South Korea and a broadening of dialogue involving China.

Other forms of cooperation are also needed to make the most of new technologies that are coming on stream. They include microturbines and fuel-efficient vehicles that offer promise not only for industrialized countries but also for many developing nations. Regulatory barriers, as well as established business practices, may present obstacles to the application of new equipment and systems. Government leadership in eliminating regulatory obstacles and in supporting international partnerships could speed up penetration and assimilation of technologies—with environmental gains for all concerned.

As energy market globalization proceeds in Asia, the likelihood that the United States will be forced to deal with threats that stem from unintended consequences will increase. Multiple actors will be involved, and solutions will in most cases need to be constructed—at least in the near term—in the absence of established frameworks and institutions.

Conclusion

Energy market globalization brings significant benefits for producers and consumers, if the political will can be mustered to implement thoroughgoing, market-oriented reforms. In many countries, this process is still in its early stages and remains vulnerable to reversals. The United States has much to gain from more open energy markets, and deeper cooperation and sustained leadership are needed.

The potential security risks stem in large part from the unintended consequences of uneven globalization in a context of partial market liberalization. In the current transitional phase, critical choices are being made about financial investments, partnerships, technology development, and fuels that will affect evolving and multidimensional interdependent relations among actors. Addressing energy security concerns, rather than dismissing them, is a requirement for promoting market-oriented policies.

In this fluid context, the United States should take pre-emptive action, investing resources in preventive diplomacy and building security communities on specific issues in order to avoid the need for military force deployment down the road. Despite the uncertainties and inadequacies of multilateral approaches, there is really no alternative. The investments will be costly (not so much in terms of hardware, but in terms of time) and will challenge the skills of strategists trained to deal with more traditional security threats. Security specialists will need to work more closely with economic policymakers and the private sector, bridging the traditional separation between security and economic policy domains.

Asia offers the most striking example of both the potential risks of neglecting these issues and the tremendous gains that can come from devising new ways to address the concrete problem of energy security. China and India, the emerging new energy giants, will need assistance in meeting energy requirements and addressing concerns about energy security—if they are to contribute to, rather than detract from, Asian security. The United States will need to work proactively with them and with other countries in the region, forming new communities to deal with specific energy security concerns. In many cases, doing so will require focused dialogue not only with close allies and friends but also with other countries. Issues that require attention include disputes over energy-rich areas such as the South China Sea, the absence of an emergency response program in Asia to deal with oil supply interruptions, and the need for cooperation in resource development and efficient and environmentally sound energy use in the Russian Far East and China, as well as the potential for expanded energy cooperation involving South and North Korea, if progress continues in building trust and reducing threats on the Korean Peninsula.

Efforts to address specific problems such as piracy as a threat to shipping in South and Southeast Asia provide a platform for building lines of communication, experience with working together, and synergies with energy-related challenges, such as ensuring free and safe transit for energy resources. Cooperation with the Regional Piracy Center in Kuala Lumpur, a minimally manned but potentially important effort, is a case in point. There are signs that countries in Asia are beginning to take positive steps to deal with the piracy problem. China reportedly has improved the capabilities of the People's Armed Police for dealing with piracy and has shown new commitment to prosecute criminals. In addition, the Philippine Navy has expanded its coastal patrol effort, and merchant vessels have applied new technology, such as automatic tracking systems that make it possible to locate hijacked vessels quickly and allow ship owners to track vessels by using the Internet.[15] Meanwhile, Japan's Defense

Agency has talked with Vietnamese counterparts about cooperation in search-and-rescue operations for civilian ships and has reached agreement for use of Singapore bases in the event of a peacekeeping operation. Japan also has been talking to India about cooperation in antipiracy efforts. These and other efforts illustrate the potential benefits, as well as limitations, of myriad approaches.

The challenge for U.S. policymakers, security specialists, and economic affairs officials, as well as private sector leaders, is to determine how and when to work with existing organizations, where new approaches are necessary, and how to work most effectively with a diverse range of stakeholders. In some cases, U.S. leadership may be necessary; in others, thoughtful U.S. "followership" and support may best serve to build security coalitions on specific issues. Economic organizations may provide the needed framework for cooperation in some instances, but military cooperation and leadership will be essential in others. Determining the appropriate approach, finding needed resources (funding, expertise, and technology), and ensuring implementation and follow-up will require new modes of cooperation among U.S. Government agencies. Building multilateral security communities on energy security issues will not be easy, but the globalization of energy markets makes it a necessity.

Notes

[1] James Bond, Director and Chair of World Bank Sector Board of Energy, Mining and Telecommunications Department of the World Bank, "Global Energy Policies Must Be Updated for the 21st Century," *European Affairs* 1, no. 1 (Winter 2000), 74.

[2] The Department of Energy forecasts that by 2010, developing countries in Asia will consume 24.3 million barrels a day of oil, about the same amount as the United States at that time. See *International Energy Outlook*, 1999.

[3] Daniel Yergen has pointed to cross-investments as the key indicator of "globality" in energy markets, a term that he uses to stress that in the future traditional boundaries will be increasingly irrelevant.

[4] See Enron Energy Outlook 1999–2020, 9.

[5] *Shakai Keizai Seisansei Honbu* [Japan Productivity Center], *Enerugi Sekurite no Kakuritsu to 21 Seiki no Enerugi Seisaku no Arikata* [Approaches to Ensuring Energy Security and 21st Century Energy Policy], (March 2000).

[6] European Commission, Directorate-General for Energy, *Energy in Europe: Economic Foundations for Energy Policy*, Special Issue (December 1999).

[7] Asia Pacific Energy Research Center, *APEC Energy Demand and Supply Outlook* (Tokyo: Updated September 1998).

[8] James Kynge, "Chinese Miners Riot over Severance Pay," *Financial Times,* London, April 3, 2000.

[9] Jeanne Whalen, "Russian Energy Dispute Reflects Threat to Country's Gas, Electricity Supplies," *The Wall Street Journal*, April 12, 2000.

[10] Leftwing guerrillas bombed hundreds of electricity pylons in Colombia, causing severe problems for the government, which is attempting to privatize the industry. The grid has been split in two. See James Wilson, "Security Fears Dog Colombia's Privatization Plans," *Financial Times, London*, April 5, 2000.

[11] Mark J. Valencia, "Maritime Management in the Malacca/Singapore Straits: Lessons Learned," report for the GEF/UNDP/IMO Regional Programme, draft (August 1999).

[12] Mark J. Valencia, "Time for a New Regime in the Straits of Malacca?" *The Business Times*, April 25, 1998.

[13] The Pacific Forum Center for Strategic and International Studies has also conducted workshops on maritime security issues. See Ralph A. Cossa, *Security Implications of Conflict in the South China Sea: Exploring Potential Triggers of Conflict* (Honolulu: Pacific Forum, March 1998).

[14] A cease-fire agreement was signed on May 12, 2000, but unrest continues. See Jay Solomon, "Mobil Sees Gas Plant Become Rallying Point for Indonesian Rebels," *The Wall Street Journal*, September 7, 2000.

[15] "Repelling the Pirates," *Jane's Security*, June 14, 2000; homepage <www.janes.com>.

Chapter 13

Dealing with Rogue States

Kori N. Schake and Justin P. Bernier

It is yet unclear whether globalization has effected an increase in the number of so-called rogue states; however, their ability to threaten U.S. interests is increasing. The spread of information, access to communications technology, mobility of people and assets, emergence of markets in scientific expertise and weapons materials, maturation of dual-use technologies, and commercial pressure for market access—all characteristics of globalization—facilitate the work of rogue states and organizations.

The effect of rogues is compounded because globalization also seems to be impeding states' abilities to sustain their traditional realms of national power. Globalization is reducing the ability of states to maintain monopolies of information and the use of force, regulate the permeability of borders, and amass treasuries beyond the magnitude of nonstate actors. Thus, globalization seems to be increasing the prospects of rogues while diminishing U.S. capabilities to counter them.

Current U.S. policies intended to manage rogue states emphasize three elements: economic and political isolation; international regimes[1] to prevent the spread of technology and weapons; and punitive military actions. The first two of these elements are particularly vulnerable to diminished effectiveness as a result of globalization. The limits of U.S. knowledge about states newly able to threaten U.S. interests will complicate efforts to use military force for limited political purposes. A new strategy is needed to protect and advance U.S. interests as globalization reshapes the international environment.

The United States needs to develop new strategies that capitalize on globalization's effects, rather than seeking to forestall them. Some strategies with particular promise are ending states' political and economic isolation, increasing reliance on narrow sanctions, and making greater use of media and financial interventions. As a prudent hedging strategy, the United States should also improve its national defenses. This approach would increase the vulnerability of rogue and other potentially dangerous states to the most powerful U.S. assets—globalization's economic benefits and the attractiveness of the American way of life—while increasing U.S. protection against attacks and intimidation.

Kori N. Schake is a senior research professor in the Institute for National Strategic Studies at the National Defense University. Previously, she served on the Joint Staff and in the Office of the Secretary of Defense. Dr. Schake has taught at the University of California at San Diego and the School of Public Affairs at the University of Maryland. Justin P. Bernier was a member of the Quadrennial Defense Review 2001 Working Group in the Institute for National Strategic Studies at the National Defense University.

Will Globalization Produce More Rogues?

For at least the last 6 years, U.S. foreign policy has operated on the assumption that there exists a particular category of states that neither accept the norms of international behavior nor respond to usual means of suasion. In 1994, National Security Advisor Anthony Lake noted that U.S. foreign policy "must face the reality of recalcitrant and outlaw states that not only choose to remain outside the family but also to assault its basic values," and for which the United States has "a special responsibility for developing a strategy to *neutralize*, *contain*, and, through selective pressure, perhaps eventually *transform* these backlash states into constructive members of the international community."[2] These states—namely, Cuba, Iraq, Libya, North Korea, and Iran—eventually became commonly known as "rogues." Although officially known as "states of concern" today, U.S. policy toward these states remained largely unchanged.[3]

What makes a state a rogue? The U.S. Government definition has had neither satisfactory explanatory power in categorizing the constituent states about which the United States is concerned nor sufficient persuasiveness to sustain international consensus. Nonetheless, the states categorized as rogues have several common features: they are all authoritarian regimes that govern without the consent of their populations; they tend to define their interests in hostile opposition to the United States; they are all on the U.S. State Department list of state sponsors of terrorism; and, finally, as Ellen Laipson has argued, they are characterized by their isolation from international political norms and trends.[4]

The sum of these shared attributes has tended to make the United States particularly wary of the so-called rogue states. There is greater uncertainty about the behavior of rogues because their respective societies are less transparent and less familiar, and they have leaders who are less restrained by institutions and public opinion. That rogue states support terrorism as a means of foreign policy engagement furthers suspicion that they will not engage politically or militarily in expected or predictable ways.

Rogues, however, also have many important differences that make a uniform approach to them a less than optimal U.S. policy. Some, like North Korea and Cuba, seem to have chosen international isolation to strengthen the hold of the regime. Others, such as Iraq and Sudan, would welcome engagement by the international community but are isolated against their will by multilateral concerns and effective U.S. action. So-called rogues also differ in their degree of hostility to U.S. interests and their means of contesting U.S. policies and international norms. North Korea, whose weapons of mass destruction (WMD) and conventional capabilities could severely damage U.S. interests, is a much greater security concern than Cuba, whose military power pales in comparison. Some rogue regimes rule forcibly, while others may be accurate reflections of society. Such differences suggest that a uniform approach may be ill conceived.

The number of rogue states has remained surprisingly stable. None of them has been consistently isolated, let alone reformed, by U.S. policies. Cuba enjoys political and economic relations with the rest of the world, including the closest U.S. allies, while President Fidel Castro restricts basic political freedoms. Muammar Gaddafi remains in power and continues to make diplomatic progress with the West even though Libya continues to seek ballistic missiles capable of reaching Europe and beyond.[5] With Washington's blessing, its European allies and South Korea are cultivating their relationships with North Korea despite the regime's threatening posture toward the United States and its Asian allies.[6,7] Even the United States has begun normalizing relations with some of the rogues: Washington has encouraged state-to-state relations with Iran following President Mohammad Khatami's 1996 election and recently completed an exchange of high-level officials with North Korea for the first time ever.

Isolation has succeeded best against Iraq. Sanctions initiated in 1991 and subsequent bombing raids have seemingly curbed its programs to develop weapons of mass destruction. However, Saddam Hussein remains in power and implacably hostile to U.S. interests, and the policy imposes substantial material and political costs on the United States and its Persian Gulf partners. Moreover, this quarantine is eroding, as France teams up with Russia at the United Nations (UN) in efforts to lift the sanctions against Iraq and humanitarian organizations become increasingly concerned about the disastrous effects of broad sanctions on the Iraqi people.

The concept of rogue states has never been fully accepted outside the United States, in part because the Clinton administration never developed a standard that could be neutrally applied to replicate their results—rogues seem to be any state hostile to the United States. Even the list of state sponsors of terrorism[8] is politicized: Washington has considered removing North Korea from the list to facilitate talks with Pyongyang; Syria was a candidate for removal in order to advance the Middle East peace process, even though it supports Hezbollah; and Pakistan is not included in the face of its support of terrorists in Kashmir.[9,10]

Even if it were possible to clearly delineate rogue states in ways that would build international support, such a categorization is not beneficial in dealing effectively with those states and may ultimately be counterproductive. Stigmatizing states—even those hostile to U.S. interests such as Cuba, Libya, North Korea, and Iraq—reduces Washington's ability to engage them when it is conducive to U.S. interests to do so and undercuts international support for U.S. efforts to confront these states.

This is especially the case since other states in the family have begun to assault its basic values. In 1998, India and Pakistan crossed the nuclear threshold and engaged in a rising spiral of threats over Kashmir. Both Russia and China continue serial proliferation of their WMD arsenals and expertise, as the former conducts a brutal military campaign in Chechnya, allegedly in response to apartment bombings in Moscow during the fall of 1999. U.S. and European attempts to influence Russia's policy both during and after the Chechnya conflict have proven futile. To intimidate Taiwanese voters in advance of the 2000 elections, China has increased its ballistic missile holdings adjacent to Taiwan and threatened to attack the island if it moves toward independence, although it has been virtually independent for nearly 50 years. All of these behaviors assault basic U.S. values, yet it would hardly be productive for the United States to term any of these states rogues. With a doubtful factual basis for judging certain states as rogues, the capacity to isolate them decreasing internationally, and Washington engaging in normal foreign policy tradeoffs with so-called rogues, the United States should revisit its scarlet letter policy and delineate behaviors that threaten U.S. interests.

States that are hostile to the United States *and* either possess WMD programs or engage in international terrorism are likely to pose the greatest danger and be least amenable to more engagement: Afghanistan, Iran, Iraq, Libya, North Korea, and Sudan (table 1). States that are not hostile to the United States but that possess WMD programs or engage in international terrorism are not necessarily a threat to the United States, but they nonetheless have the means to negatively affect U.S. interests.

The number of states and organizations hostile to U.S. interests may grow in the short run as globalization exacerbates the gap between rich and poor, and states unable to cope with globalization lash out at the United States as its dominant symbol. As Director for Central Intelligence George Tenet has stated, "That we are arguably the world's most powerful nation . . . may make us a larger target for those who don't share our interests, values, or beliefs."[11] The world's authoritarian regimes are busier than ever fighting the tide of Western ideas, values, practices, and products. Hermit states such as North Korea, Afghanistan, and Sudan will likely continue to use opposition to the United States to justify their hostile actions because they cannot find ways to balance their values with the press of globalization.

According to Ellen Laipson, rogue states are unable to take advantage of globalization's benefits because their "centers" are too controlling (North Korea, Cuba) or too collapsed (Sudan). In either case, the benefits of globalization are passing these states by because they are unable to establish helpful national policies or effectively bargain with their underdeveloped or corrupt private sectors. Even so, controlling states will find it impossible to shut out globalization's effects indefinitely, as unregulated media challenge their monopoly on information and trade. Eventually, states that try to take advantage of some globalization benefits—for example, freer flows of capital—will find it exceedingly difficult to suppress other aspects—such as an even freer exchange of ideas.

In the longer run, the centripetal effects of globalization are likely to reduce the number of states that either can or want to prevent the effects of globalization. In the shorter run, the United States cannot prevent the emergence of hostile states or coalitions among disaffected states reeling from the effects of globalization. There is much the United States can do to minimize their negative impact in the interim, however.

Harnessing Globalization to Effect Positive Change?

As noted earlier, U.S. policy relies on three main elements: economic and political isolation; international regimes to prevent the spread of technology and weapons; and punitive military actions. Globalization is affecting all three.

Table 1. The Strategic Consequences of WMD Proliferation

State	Hostile	WMD Programs	Terrorism Sponsor
Countries posing national security threat to the United States			
Afghanistan	Yes	No	Yes
Iran	Yes	Yes	Yes
Iraq	Yes	Yes	Yes
Libya	Yes	Yes	Yes
North Korea	Yes	Yes	Yes
Sudan	Yes	Yes	Yes
Countries for which security threat to the United States is unclear			
Algeria	No	Yes	Yes
China	?	Yes	No
Cuba	Yes	No[1]	No[2]
Russia	?	Yes	No
Serbia	?	Yes	No
Syria	No	Yes	Yes
Countries posing no national security threat to the United States			
Egypt	No	Yes	No
India	No	Yes	No
Israel	No	Yes	No
Pakistan	No	Yes	Yes
Saudi Arabia	No	Yes	No
South Korea	No	Yes	No

[1]In June 1999, the Department of State said it had no evidence that Cuba is stockpiling or has mass-produced any biological warfare agents.

[2]The State Department explains Cuba's presence on its list of state sponsors of international terrorism with the following assertion: "Cuba continued to provide safe haven to several terrorists and U.S. fugitives in 1999. A number of Basque ETA [Euskadi Ta Askatasuna, "Basque Homeland and Liberty," separatist group in Spain] terrorists who gained sanctuary in Cuba some years ago continued to live on the island, as did several U.S. terrorist fugitives. Havana also maintained ties to other state sponsors of terrorism and Latin American insurgents. Colombia's two largest terrorist organizations, the Revolutionary Armed Forces of Colombia and the National Liberation Army (ELN) [Ejercito de Liberacion Nacional], both maintained a permanent presence on the island. In late 1999, Cuba hosted a series of meetings between Colombian government officials and ELN leaders." While this explanation may technically justify its presence on the list, the authors do not judge it adequate.

Economic and Political Isolation

Clearly, the ability of the United States to maintain international sanctions against rogue regimes is eroding. The State Department estimates that 100,000 barrels of oil are smuggled out of Iraq each day, much of it going to Turkey with tacit U.S. approval.[12] With government encouragement, the French oil firm Total is engaged in Iranian oil exploration. The political isolation of Iran and Libya is ending as the European Union's "critical dialogue" makes sporadic, but undeniable, inroads. U.S. allies reject the legitimacy of extraterritorial acts, like the Iran-Libya Sanctions Act and the Helms-Burton Act, that sanction foreign firms whose investments undermine U.S. policy.

Whatever the fate of individual efforts, the trend is away from effective international sanctions because other states are decreasingly likely to comply. Sanctions remain a popular tool in the United States because they create a public symbol of U.S. disapproval and the American body politic tends to support principled international actions.[13] However, the United States cannot sustain broad sanctions alone.

Even if broad sanctions could be sustained, it is not clear that their effect is wholly positive. Morally, it is unpalatable to harm societies in authoritarian states for the choices of their leaders. It punishes the already punished without—in most cases—affecting the lives of ruling elites.[14] Practically, it reinforces the leaders' control (as the distributors of scarce resources) and gives them the ability to externalize responsibility for societal suffering (by virtue of their control of information). Also, broad sanctions provide others the economic advantage of not having to compete with American companies in sanctioned markets. In this vein, the U.S. decision to lift its 50-year trade embargo against North Korea, while leaving in place trade rules barring any export of American technology or equipment that could have military applications, is a step in the right direction. The Congressional decision to grant permanent normalized trade relations to China—although not widely considered a rogue—is also encouraging.

Narrow sanctions punishing individuals and companies involved in criminal or reprehensible activities fare much better and are on the rise in U.S. policy, as Senator Jesse Helms (R–NC) has persuasively argued.[15] Recently, Congress passed legislation sanctioning a Russian firm known to have aided Iranian nuclear programs and prohibited the Clinton administration from spending $500 million for cooperative work on the space station because of a suspected diversion of funds.[16] This approach would end the economic isolation of rogue states, opening them up to the pressures of globalization, while continuing to target individuals and firms involved in activities that increase danger to U.S. interests.

Nonproliferation Regimes

According to the White House's 1999 National Security Strategy, "weapons of mass destruction pose the greatest potential threat to global stability and security."[17] The United States has constructed and relied upon nonproliferation regimes to slow the spread of weapons and technologies most threatening to U.S. interests. However, globalization is also eroding these regimes by facilitating a transnational market in

WMD, cloaking the participants, and facilitating the clandestine movement of people and resources across borders.

International monitoring and control regimes have not worked to the degree expected (table 2).[18] China continues to sell missile technology to Iran and Pakistan, despite a promise to adhere to Missile Technology Control Regime (MTCR) restrictions.[19] Russia (or at least Russian firms) continue to sell WMD technology and expertise to Iran and other states.[20] Tehran has biological and chemical weapons programs and may already have nuclear weapons, despite membership in the Nonproliferation Treaty (NPT), Chemical Weapons Convention (CWC), and Biological and Toxic Weapons Convention (BTWC).[21] The extent of Iraqi nuclear, chemical, and biological programs discovered after the 1991 Persian Gulf War shattered confidence that the regime of international treaties and monitoring can be effective.

Unfortunately, official, documented arms control violations only begin to capture the magnitude of the WMD proliferation problem. Many states' proliferation activities are not widely known, or are not publicized, because of secrecy, indifference within the international community, or the limited membership of particular treaties. For example, although the International Atomic Energy Association holds that Iran is NPT-compliant, the Central Intelligence Agency has testified that "Iran is actively pursuing the acquisition of fissile material and the expertise and technology necessary to form the material into nuclear weapons."[22] These efforts may place Tehran in violation of the NPT, which does not permit non-nuclear members to "seek or receive any assistance in the manufacture of nuclear weapons or other nuclear explosive devices."[23] This trend is not limited to international institutions and rogue states: for years the United States refused to acknowledge the fact that India and Pakistan were de facto nuclear weapons states, as it continues to ignore Israel's nuclear weapons status in order to avoid challenging the legitimacy of the NPT and other nonproliferation efforts.

Moreover, the international norm condemning possession of weapons of mass destruction that nonproliferation regimes were intended to create no longer dominates state calculations, as Indian and Pakistani nuclear tests demonstrate. Possession of weapons of mass destruction may even be a more powerful status symbol and a potential equalizer to weak states than to states of greater political, economic, and military power. The norm against WMD possession will likely be further eroded by tepid international reaction to the Indian and Pakistani tests. The lesson for potential proliferators is that the strongest states in the system may even accord greater status to new nuclear states. President Clinton's visit to India and Pakistan in the spring of 2000 sends an unfortunate signal in this regard.

Table 2. Arms Control Treaty Violations

State	*Non-proliferation Treaty*	*Biological and Toxic Weapons Convention*	*Chemical Weapons Convention*	*Missile Technology Control Regime*	*Other*[1]
Afghanistan					
Algeria	In violation		In violation		
Argentina		In violation	?		
Brazil		In violation	?		
China	In violation	In violation	In violation	In violation[2]	In violation[3]
Cuba					
Egypt		In violation			
Ethiopia			In violation		
India		?	In violation		
Iran	In violation	In violation	In violation		
Iraq	In violation	In violation			In violation[4]
Israel			In violation[5]		
Libya	In violation	In violation			
North Korea	In violation				In violation[6]
Pakistan		In violation	In violation		
Russia	?	In violation	In violation	In violation	In violation[7]
Saudi Arabia			In violation		
Serbia	?				
South Korea					?
South Africa				?	?
Sudan					
Syria	In violation	In violation[5]			
Taiwan					

[1]Includes formal and informal arms control agreements related to weapons of mass destruction.

[2]On October 4, 1994, the United States and China issued a joint statement on China's adherence to the MTCR. In exchange, the United States promised to waive sanctions imposed on August 23, 1993, allowing the export of high technology satellites to China.

[3]On May 11, 1996, Beijing agreed not to provide assistance to unsafeguarded nuclear facilities after the U.S. State Department announced sanctions would not be levied against China for violating the NPT by supplying 5,000 ring magnets (used exclusively for uranium enrichment) to an unsafeguarded Pakistani nuclear facility.

[4]UN Security Council Resolution 687, which Baghdad formally agreed to after the Gulf War, requires Iraq to abandon its nuclear, biological, and chemical programs and all programs and capabilities related to ballistic missiles with a range greater than 150 km.

[5]State is signatory of treaty.

[6]Under the 1994 Agreed Framework, North Korea agreed to freeze the construction and operation of its existing nuclear reactors and related facilities, to eventually dismantle this equipment, and to comply with the NPT. In exchange, the United States pledged to help North Korea acquire two light-water nuclear reactors and to arrange for deliveries of 500,000 metric tons of heavy fuel oil annually until the first reactor was completed. The reactors and fuel are to be used for electricity generation and heating only.

[7]In 1995, President Boris Yeltsin agreed to order Russia's Ministry of Atomic Energy to drop plans to provide equipment and advice to Iran's effort to mine uranium ore and process it to use as reactor fuel.

States hostile to the United States that have significant WMD programs include North Korea, Iran, Iraq, Libya, and Sudan. North Korea is the closest to developing ballistic missiles capable of threatening the United States, having tested the Taepo Dong-1 and demonstrated work on an even longer range Taepo Dong-2.[24] Pyongyang, which has advanced biological and chemical weapons programs, is thought to have enough plutonium for at least one, possibly two, nuclear weapons.[25] Although North Korea formally agreed to halt its nuclear weapons programs in a 1994 deal, the United States is unable to certify its compliance with that agreement or subsequent commitments to freeze its long-range ballistic missile program while talks with the United States continue.[26]

Iran has achieved the capability to deploy the Shahab-3, a 1,300-kilometer range missile that can reach targets in Europe, and is believed to have two even longer range missiles under development.[27] Tehran has used chemical weapons in the past and is thought to have advanced biological and nuclear programs as well; in December 1999, the Central Intelligence Agency warned President Clinton that it could not rule out the possibility that Iran already has nuclear weapons.[28] The regime also engages in the planning and execution of terrorist acts, including assassinations outside Iran.[29]

With UN inspections no longer in place and economic sanctions in question, Iraq could be well along the road to reconstituting its WMD programs despite a formal post-Persian Gulf War agreement to eliminate them. Targeted bombing by the United States and United Kingdom has failed to destroy most of the facilities where Iraq is storing its nuclear equipment, and there is evidence to suggest that it has stepped up efforts to produce the weapons-grade plutonium and uranium necessary for an atomic bomb.[30] Iraq, which loaded biological and chemical weapons into ballistic missiles before the Persian Gulf War, maintains the skills and industrial capabilities needed to reconstitute its long-range ballistic missile program.[31] Intelligence reports say that Iraq could test an intercontinental ballistic missile capable of hitting the United States with a nuclear, biological, or chemical (NBC) weapon by 2015—sooner with foreign assistance.[32]

Libya continues to obtain foreign assistance for its WMD program. In September 2000, shortly after UN sanctions were lifted against Libya, Gaddafi took delivery of a consignment of North Korean No Dong ballistic missiles capable of reaching not only Israel but also several NATO states in southern Europe with either conventional or NBC warheads.[33] Gaddafi commands chemical weapons—which Libya has used against Chadian troops—and maintains a biological weapons program despite membership in the BTWC. Even though Libya finally cooperated with the United Kingdom on the 1988 Lockerbie bombing case and has not been implicated in any similar act for several years, it continues to support international terrorism publicly and privately.[34]

Sudan, the least technologically advanced of the five hostile states, is a member of the CWC but is developing the capability to produce chemical weapons with help from Iraq.[35] In 1999, the United States conducted military strikes against a pharmaceutical plant in Khartoum it suspected of manufacturing chemical weapons and associating with terrorists. Sudan is a major sponsor of international terrorism, acting as a meeting place, safe haven, and training hub for international terrorist groups, among them, Osama bin Laden's al-Qaida network, which is probably targeting the United States.[36]

Preventing proliferation of nuclear expertise and materials has been a U.S. priority since the advent of the Nuclear Age. While the effort has succeeded in many instances, international controls and international norms are insufficient to prevent a determined proliferator such as Iraq or North Korea from acquiring weapons of mass destruction and long-range delivery means, even when these states are successfully isolated, politically and economically.

Military Responses

The third element of U.S. policy toward rogues has been the threat of military action. In an effort to deter the use of weapons of mass destruction against the United States or its allies, the United States does not rule out the use of any means in responding to WMD attacks. Recent military actions suggest a trend away from general punishments of societies; instead, the United States has targeted individual terrorists and military facilities within states in response to attacks on the United States. U.S. cruise missile strikes against Osama bin Laden and purported WMD facilities in Sudan in 1998, while widely criticized, demonstrate the personalization of foreign policy as organizations and individuals begin to possess the means of damaging U.S. interests.

As states such as North Korea, Iraq, Serbia, and Sudan challenge U.S. interests, the United States will need a world-class intelligence community to understand the leaders and social mores of these rogue states. Otherwise, military action may increase a leader's standing or fail to inflict expected harm. If the United States lacks understanding of the political calculus of states and organizations, then careful calibration of military force for political purposes (as currently practiced in Serbia, Bosnia, Iraq, North Korea, and Sudan) and against terrorist groups may not suffice to defend U.S. interests.

The audit of U.S. intelligence capabilities conducted by retired Admiral David Jeremiah to determine why the United States failed to predict India's and Pakistan's nuclear tests concluded that the United States is far from having that sophisticated understanding. The report placed special emphasis on the intelligence community's "mindset" problem—the challenge of viewing other states through Western interpretation.[37] In classified testimony to Congress, Jeremiah is reported to have described an intelligence community plagued by ineffective central management, overstretched analytical resources, limited human intelligence capabilities, and "poorly suited" satellite collection techniques that are "vulnerable to simple detection."[38] To date, it is yet to be seen what, if any, measures the U.S. intelligence community has taken to improve this state of affairs.

The spread of NBC weapons and missile technology could drastically alter U.S. foreign policy and overall strategy. A number of potential adversaries, reluctant to engage the U.S. military on its terms, have turned to asymmetrical warfighting strategies, one of which involves the deployment of long-range ballistic missiles with NBC warheads. By deploying even a modest WMD arsenal, a conventionally inferior state might believe it could threaten U.S. territory and overseas forces in a crisis, thereby narrowing Washington's range of options to an unpalatable few or deterring it from taking any action altogether. Such weapons could also be used in terrorist attacks on the U.S. homeland aimed at sapping political support for its overseas commitments.

This argues for a substantial increase in U.S. defenses. The United States will not have the luxury of relying solely on efforts to prevent proliferation or likely have sufficient confidence in the U.S. intelligence community's ability to accurately interpret the intentions and actions of hostile states.

Crafting More Effective Policies to Counter Enemies?

Policies intended to isolate states and prevent the spread of weapons of mass destruction are built on foundations that are being eroded by globalization. Given that the current course is one of diminishing effectiveness, the United States needs to decide whether to redouble efforts to shore up the current approach, resign itself to a world of more and better armed rogues, or try to find ways to achieve the objective of a world with fewer states hostile to, and able to threaten, the United States and its fundamental interests.

Strengthening the current approach would entail committing greater resources to the tasks of isolating rogues and strengthening nonproliferation regimes. Isolating rogues would require constructing a much stronger international consensus on both the threat that these states pose to the international community (as opposed to just the United States) and on isolation as the appropriate tactic to contain the threat. The United States is unlikely to achieve consensus by persuasion. Other states—not least Washington's closest allies—simply do not believe that their interests are served by shunning regimes hostile to the United States. Creating an international regime aimed at containing rogues would require enormous political attention; in fact, it would likely displace all other issues on the foreign and defense policy agendas. It would probably require resurrection of a system such as that associated with the Coordinating Committee on Export Controls and more legislation with extraterritorial reach and stronger enforcement against violators of current legislation, an unpleasant prospect given the determined resistance, both foreign and domestic, to the Helms-Burton and Iran-Libya Sanctions Acts. It would also probably require denial of American markets to violators and political acquiescence to popular arms control treaties (which may not be in American best interest) in order to entice international cooperation.

This approach would likely result in European allies reciprocating with extraterritorial legislation, companies choosing not to do business in the United States to avoid the prospect of sanctions, and opposition from nongovernmental organizations and human rights organizations concerned about the effects of broad sanctions on publics in rogue states. In short, it would cement the stereotype of the United States as a bully that must be constrained by the rest of the international community. Even if the United States could muster sufficient political and economic resources to make the current approach successful in the long run, this approach would be self-defeating. The price that the United States would have to pay in order to make rogues the defining issue on the international security agenda and pull the international community into a common approach would be prohibitively high.

A second possible course of action would be to forego trying to hold back the tide of globalization that is eroding current policies and accept the fact that the world is becoming a more uncertain and dangerous place for U.S. interests. This strategy would seek to continue current policies even as their effectiveness declines but would not risk alienating allies or require heroic measures to create international regimes to isolate hostile states. It would seek to lower the political and economic costs of current policies and would introduce new approaches intended to better protect the United States from hostile states armed with weapons of mass destruction. These new approaches would include a strengthened national missile defense, theater missile defenses, and cruise missile defenses; more active intelligence collection within and outside the United States; more active border controls; and NBC response teams operating in the United States and training civilian populations in urban areas.

This approach would gradually open rogue societies to the positive economic effects of globalization as current practices become less effective. However, the withering of current policies could embolden hostile states to believe that the United States would no longer uphold its commitments, creating challenges to U.S. interests. This course would require shifts in resources to dramatically improve border controls and might even include military policing of American borders. It would be likely to raise public concern in the United States about the protection of civil liberties and increase isolationism to the extent that U.S. engagements overseas are seen as "creating" the threat of WMD attack. This pessimistic and resigned approach appears unsuited to American political culture.

The third and most promising alternative strategy would end economic isolation while increasing U.S. defenses and targeting the interests of hostile individuals or groups. It would entail ending broad economic sanctions against Cuba, Iraq, North Korea, and Iran. It could retain targeted sanctions intended to undermine hostile individuals and regimes without affecting the general public, including travel restrictions, international criminal indictments, cyberoperations to erase bank holdings and identity markers, and prohibitions on regime-owned companies doing business in the United States and allied markets. Since the effects of globalization differ from state to state, a proper mix of such measures should be developed to maximize their impact on the regime in question.[39] It might be especially beneficial to introduce the prospective policy changes as part of a deal with U.S. allies to end broad sanctions in return for commitments to create and enforce a regime of targeted sanctions, intelligence sharing, and revitalized export restrictions on key technologies. This approach would also include improving U.S. defenses as a hedge against globalization producing more states and organizations that are both hostile and dangerous to the United States. While not going as far as the previous option, this strategy would still necessitate a strong national missile defense, theater ballistic missile defenses, and cruise missile defenses, plus some additional domestic preparation for responding to WMD attacks.

This approach would capitalize on the effects of globalization to create opportunities for change in rogue societies. The attractive power of the American way of life and the prosperity inherent in globalization constitute the best hope for reducing the risk of states hostile to the United States and its interests. These attributes should be used to the advantage of U.S. policies. Ending economic isolation would open rogue societies—particularly their emergent middle classes—to the benefits of economic advancement and weave their regimes into the international system, where other states could assist the United States in shaping their behavior. This approach would better protect the United States from the damaging effects of WMD attacks without requiring major adjustments in the openness of American society. It would end restrictions that disadvantage American businesses in the international marketplace. It would emphasize the separation between rogue regimes and the people unfortunate enough to be living under their control. It could perhaps build a broader coalition of support for action against rogue individuals and regimes by the international community. Finally, it would reduce friction between the United States and its allies.

The main drawback to this approach is the political difficulty and ethical dissatisfaction of ending sanctions. Whatever their effectiveness, sanctions send a signal of American disapproval that is important to Congress and valuable in building the public basis for other action against these states. Unquestionably, it would be politically costly for any U.S. administration to convince Congress to repeal sanctions legislation. However, globalization is driving up the costs to the United States and diminishing the benefits of the current U.S. strategy. The question is not whether to sustain the current approach or move to a different strategy. The current approach will not be sustainable because of globalization effects beyond U.S. control. A comprehensive package of initiatives to end broad sanctions, increase sanctions targeted at individuals or regimes, improve U.S. defenses, and rebuild international support for a narrow set of export controls and monitoring would best defend and advance U.S. interests as globalization progresses. Moreover, instead of working against globalization, as the current U.S. policy does, this course would harness the driving forces of globalization to propel a more successful policy.

Notes

[1] As used here, *regime* refers to a set of treaties, laws, codes of conduct, members, and enforcement mechanisms for regulating some aspect of international behavior.

[2] Anthony Lake, "Confronting Backlash States," *Foreign Affairs* 2 (1994), 45–46.

[3] Steven Mufson, "What's in a Name? U.S. Drops Term 'Rogue State,'" *The Washington Post*, June 20, 2000, A16.

[4] The authors thank Ellen Laipson for her insights on the key phenomena of globalization and rogues.

[5] Peter Ford, "EU's Outreach to 'Pariah' States," *The Christian Science Monitor*, January 12, 2000, 6.

[6] "Britain, Germany to Recognize N. Korea," *The Washington Post*, October 20, 2000, A34.

[7] Office of the Secretary of Defense, 2000 Report to Congress: Military Situation on the Korean Peninsula, September 12, 2000.

[8] Cuba, Iran, Iraq, Libya, North Korea, Sudan, and Syria are the seven governments that the U.S. Secretary of State has designated as state sponsors of international terrorism in *Patterns of Global Terrorism, 1999*.

[9] James P. Rubin, U.S. Department of State, Daily Press Briefing, February 10, 2000.

[10] Philip Shenon, "U.S. Warns Pakistan It May be Branded a Sponsor of Terrorism," *The New York Times*, January 28, 2000, A8.

[11] George Tenet, quoted in Justin Brown, "More Furtive Enemies Threaten US in New Century," *The Christian Science Monitor*, February 4, 2000, USA 2.

[12] Robin Wright, "Iran Opens Key Isle to Iraqi Oil Smugglers, U.S. Says," *The Los Angeles Times*, July 3, 2000, 1.; Robert Suro and John Lancaster, "Navy Detains Russian Oil Tanker," *The Washington*

Post, February 4, 2000, A25; James Risen, "Iraq Is Smuggling Oil to the Turks under Gaze of U.S.," *The New York Times*, June 19, 1998, A1.

[13] Stephen Kull and I..M. Destler, *Misreading the Public: The Myth of a New Isolationism* (Washington, DC: The Brookings Institution Press, 1999).

[14] Richard N. Haass, ed., *Economic Sanctions and American Diplomacy* (New York: Council on Foreign Relations, 1998).

[15] Jesse Helms, "What Sanctions Epidemic?" *Foreign Affairs* 1 (1999), 3.

[16] Audrey Hudson, "Unanimous House Backs Sanctions on Russia Due to Arms Deal with Iran," *The Washington Times*, March 2, 2000.

[17] The White House, *A National Security Strategy for a New Century* (Washington, DC: Government Printing Office, December 1999), 2.

[18] Office of the Director of Central Intelligence, Unclassified Report to Congress on the Acquisition of Technology Relating to Weapons of Mass Destruction and Advanced Conventional Munitions, July 1–December 31, 1999 (Washington, DC: Government Printing Office, August); Office of the Secretary of Defense, Proliferation: Threat and Response, November 1997; U.S. State Department, Adherence to and Compliance with Arms Control Agreements, 1998.

[19] Office of the Director of Central Intelligence, Unclassified Report to Congress, 9.

[20] Ibid., 10.

[21] James Risen and Judith Miller, "C.I.A. Tells Clinton an Iranian A-Bomb Can't Be Ruled Out," *The New York Times*, January 17, 2000, A1.

[22] U.S. Senate, Statement by Deputy Director, DCI Nonproliferation Center A. Norman Schindler on Iran's Weapons of Mass Destruction Programs to the International Security, Proliferation and Federal Services Subcommittee of the Senate Governmental Affairs Committee, September 21, 2000.

[23] Treaty on the Non-Proliferation of Nuclear Weapons, Article II.

[24] U.S. National Intelligence Council, *Foreign Missile Developments and the Ballistic Missile Threat to the United States Through 2015* (Washington, DC: Government Printing Office, September 1999), 9.

[25] Office of the Director of Central Intelligence, Unclassified Report to Congress on the Acquisition of Technology Relating to Weapons of Mass Destruction and Advanced Conventional Munitions, January 1–June 30, 1999 (Washington, DC: Government Printing Office, February 2, 2000), 4.

[26] "North Korea Continues To Develop Missiles," *The Washington Times*, October 28, 1999.

[27] Steve Rodan, "Iran Now Able to Deploy Shahab-3," *Jane's Defence Weekly*, March 22, 2000.

[28] Risen and Miller, "C.I.A. Tells Clinton an Iranian A-Bomb Can't Be Ruled Out."

[29] U.S. Department of State, *Overview of State-Sponsored Terrorism*, available at <www.state.gov/www/global/terrorism/1998Report/sponsor.html>.

[30] Kenneth R. Timmerman, "Saddam May Soon Have the Bomb," *The Wall Street Journal*, March 18, 1999, A22.

[31] R. Jeffrey Smith, "U.N. Says Iraqis Prepared Germ Weapons in Gulf War; Baghdad Balked, Fearing U.S. Nuclear Retaliation," *The Washington Post*, August 26, 1995, A1; U.S. Congress, Report of the Commission to Assess the Ballistic Missile Threat to the United States (Washington, DC: Government Printing Office, July 15, 1998), 14.

[32] U.S. National Intelligence Council, *Foreign Missile Developments and the Ballistic Missile Threat*, 10.

[33] Con Coughlin, "Missiles Deal Puts Israel in Gaddafi Sights," *London Sunday Telegraph*, September 24, 2000, 27.

[34] U.S. Department of State, Overview of State-Sponsored Terrorism.

[35] Office of the Director of Central Intelligence, Unclassified Report to Congress, 5.

[36] U.S. Department of State, Overview of State-Sponsored Terrorism.

[37] Office of the Director of Central Intelligence, CIA Press Release: Jeremiah News Conference, June 2, 1998.

[38] Walter Pincus, "Spy Agencies Faulted for Missing Indian Tests; Wide Range of Failures Cited by Review Panel, But No Firings Recommended," *The Washington Post*, June 3, 1998, A18.

Chapter 14

Deterrence, Intervention, and Weapons of Mass Destruction

William Miller

Although globalization may enhance stability in certain key ways, the proliferation of weapons of mass destruction (WMDs) threatens to damage it. The United States will need new strategy precepts because the old nuclear doctrines of the Cold War—for example, deterrence, mutual assured destruction, flexible response, and controlled escalation—may no longer apply. Today's aggressors may not be as restrained as the Soviet Union was during the Cold War, but they will not be as powerful. A world of nuclear plenty does not mean that the United States will be stripped of its capacity to deter aggression or to intervene forcefully in crises where its interests are at stake. It does mean, however, that the United States will need to develop new military doctrines aimed at employing forces wisely in reaction to the political situations at hand in peace, crisis, and war.

Emerging Trends toward WMD Proliferation

The Nonproliferation Treaty and other arms control accords provide important bulwarks against WMD proliferation. Yet recent trends suggest that proliferation is now gaining momentum. The governments of India, Pakistan, Iraq, Iran, North Korea, and other countries are trying to create nuclear arsenals and effective delivery systems. What does this trend mean in strategic terms? Will it be greatly destabilizing or not? How will U.S. strategy be affected?

Answering these questions requires understanding how globalization helps create today's setting for WMD proliferation. In the 1970s, the United States and its key allies took steps to allow flexible currency exchange rates and to promote increased flows of capital, trade, and investment across national boundaries. At the same time, information technology took giant steps forward. This combination was the underpinning of economic globalization. The important implication is that globalization began in the very midst of the Cold War. Although a large part of the world was not participating in this process, Western countries were opening their economies to one another, strengthening the nucleus of today's political and economic community of democracies.

William Miller is a consultant with Booz-Allen and Hamilton. He previously worked in the Institute for National Strategic Studies at the National Defense University and also at the Riverside Research Institute.

This experience might suggest that peace is not a necessary condition for the progress associated with globalization. Stability and security, however, are essential. Despite the severe tensions of the Cold War, the international environment was characterized by stability in the sense that it was mostly peaceful and did not constantly threaten the outbreak of war. It was in this environment that democracy and capitalism could succeed, relatively unmolested, within those countries that constituted the "West" (including Japan). The Western democracies first created strong security ties to protect themselves from communist aggression. Only by doing so were they able to start growing together politically and economically.

Cold War era stability stemmed from two factors in addition to the Western alliance system: the bipolar international system, which allowed the two superpowers to manage their political conflict peacefully, and nuclear weapons, which provided them with a strong incentive to do so. Within this context, the United States and the Soviet Union shared a common interest in preventing the proliferation of nuclear weapons to other parties. Because most countries fell within one of the two competing blocs, superpower military aid and implied direct involvement in crises dampened the pursuit of indigenous nuclear postures on the part of client states. Extended deterrence enabled both the United States and the Soviet Union to stabilize the superpower conflict and thereby lessen the likelihood of war through miscalculation. Limited wars occurred, but they were conventional, not nuclear, and the involvement of the superpowers was carefully orchestrated.

Some nuclear proliferation, nonetheless, did occur during the Cold War. To a degree, the entry of additional states into the nuclear club adversely affected the stability of the bipolar conflict, but not in catastrophic ways. In 1960, France developed its own nuclear capability and a few years later opted out of the North Atlantic Treaty Organization (NATO) Integrated Military Command. In the mid-1960s, China detonated first an atomic bomb and then a hydrogen bomb. By the end of that decade, the Sino-Soviet bloc had split asunder. Both instances of nuclear proliferation thus reshuffled the strategic deck between the superpowers, providing them with opportunities and hazards.

For the United States, the effects were complex. French possession of nuclear weapons increased the likelihood that a military conflict between NATO and the Warsaw Pact would escalate. On the other hand, by extending diplomatic recognition to China, the United States opened a new front against the Soviet Union. This step obligated the Soviets to divert both conventional and strategic forces to face this new threat, lessening their ability to launch a concerted attack against Western Europe. In neither the French nor the Chinese case did the acquisition of nuclear weapons originate the tensions that developed between these countries and their respective superpower patrons. Instead, nuclear weapons allowed both France and China to wriggle out from underneath the dominance of the superpowers. Nuclear weapons served as enablers, allowing these two previously junior partners to strike out in pursuit of their own strategic interests. However, this limited proliferation did not fundamentally transform international politics.

In today's setting, WMD proliferation is likely to have similarly complicated effects. The scope of globalization continues to expand, but this is an ongoing, uneven, and erratic process. Governments representing a large part of the world's population have slowly turned away from autarky and protectionism to engage in the global economy as economic partners of the West. Their national priorities have shifted, with economic well-being now ranking along with physical security as the primary national concern. Other countries are actively resisting the norms embraced by the nations of the more globalized West. Some are seeking WMD systems in order to buttress their strategic fortunes rather than relying on globalization to do so.

The evolution of national autonomy is similarly uneven. While the Western democracies may be undergoing a process of "denationalization,"[1] in which countries are trading their sovereignty for collective endeavors, within other regions the state symbolizes hard-won independence from colonial powers. Now that the state has finally evolved into a cohesive unit, with distinct interests and ambitions, its leaders are not about to trade in that independence for subjugation to rules devised by wealthy Western countries.

For the industrialized democracies, the shift in priorities to commercial gain has resulted in the easing of export controls, including those over high-technology products. The Cold War restrictions associated with the Coordinating Committee on Multilateral Export Controls, in which one country could veto the export of certain goods and technologies, have been replaced by the much looser Wassenaar Arrangement, which merely suggests guidelines. Accordingly, world markets are becoming buyer's markets, where countries are often eager to export materials, equipment, services, and technology that can be employed to develop nuclear weapons. No longer do countries that seek to acquire nuclear weapons have to rely solely on national industries and scientific establishments, or the aid of friendly nuclear powers, to provide the necessary technology. Lowering economic barriers and accelerating transactions allow information and expertise to flow more freely across national borders. Moreover, highly technical information is available on the Web. This more open environment enables countries to develop nuclear weaponry that would have been impossible for them to create indigenously.

Iraq's near-development of nuclear weapons demonstrates the ability of resourceful countries to tap into Western technology to aid in the development of their nuclear weapons programs. Material and equipment purchased from companies based in Austria, Finland, Germany, Britain, and Switzerland were instrumental in allowing Iraq to create its nuclear weapons infrastructure. Perhaps some deals went through in which the Western exporters knew full well the ultimate purpose of these items. In other instances, however, Iraq went through the effort of setting up numerous front companies to deflect suspicion and to facilitate technology imports. Iraqi deception was at least partially successful because the majority of technology and equipment purchased fell within the category of legitimate dual-use goods and technologies (those with the potential for both a civilian and a military application). If not sold by one company, they could be bought from another. The Iraqi experience suggests that as these technologies diffuse and as the competition for contracts increases in the global economy, export controls are likely to be harder to enforce and easier to contravene.

Within the West, economic incentive is a primary accomplice in permitting the spread of dual-use technologies. For other countries, the motives are more mixed.

Revenue remains a definite factor. In addition, countries may spread this technology in order to receive services in kind or for reasons of geopolitics (for example, to send political signals of dissatisfaction or merely to play the role of spoiler). Whereas the Iraqi nuclear program depended largely on technology and equipment bought from the West, the Iranian program draws from this second category of countries. Iran's WMD program began when it received short-range Scud missile systems from Syria and Libya. It extended the range of its missile forces with technology purchased from North Korea. Purchase of missile technology from Russia extended the range of Iranian systems even further, and Russia continues to provide technical assistance in the construction of the Bushehr nuclear plant. In a sense, the Iran example helps illustrate how proliferation is becoming a classic case of the free rider problem. Largely unconcerned with the ramifications of nuclear weapons outside their regions, some states will have less incentive to cooperate in nonproliferation efforts when, through providing technology and hardware, they may gain an edge in the global marketplace or further their own parochial interests.

Globalization exacerbates WMD proliferation and its consequences in other ways as well. With nuclear technologies becoming increasingly available, the effect of a single country's acquisition of nuclear weapons is likely to reverberate throughout the international system. The increase in range of North Korean ballistic missiles has served as a primary motivator for the United States to develop a national missile defense (NMD) system. As deployment nears, this prospect has created antagonism between the United States and Russia because the planned NMD system could violate the 1972 Antiballistic Missile (ABM) Treaty. Significantly, the country that has been most vocal in its opposition to the U.S. NMD system is China, which fears that its smaller nuclear arsenal may be counteracted and that it will thereby lose its deterrent capability against the United States. Similar systemic effects of accelerating nuclear proliferation are in evidence among China, India, and Pakistan, as well as Israel, Iraq, and Iran. In the Cold War bipolar system, the escalation and de-escalation of tensions often was the result of conscious actions made for reasons of state policy. Because the number of variables is increasing in today's setting, the international equation is becoming more complex and difficult to understand and influence. Indeed, actions taken to address one set of circumstances are having unforeseen and unpredictable ramifications in other settings.

Globalization is also stimulating proliferation as nuclear powers try to enlarge and upgrade their existing arsenals. As technology becomes increasingly available, countries with rudimentary nuclear arsenals will seek to increase the capabilities of their nuclear weapons and delivery systems. Encouraging Chinese involvement within the global economy is often viewed as a means of exposing China to democratic norms of behavior and bolstering democratic forces within that country. At the same time, Chinese business arrangements with Western companies may have improved Chinese military capability, including its long-range missile systems. Meanwhile, China's impressive economic growth and burgeoning technological development—both the result of involvement within the global economy—are broadening the scope of its regional political ambition and influence.

China has recently enhanced its nuclear capabilities by deploying the DF–31 intercontinental missile and by developing MIRVed warheads. One probable motivation for these actions is to deter the United States from involvement within China's expanded sphere of influence in Asia. In response, Taiwan, concerned about the weakening of implied U.S. security guarantees, is feeling a greater need for its own deterrent capability. As in the case of China, Taiwan's involvement in the world economy provides it with access to the technology needed to obtain this deterrent if it chooses to do so. Japan and other non-nuclear Asian countries are similarly situated to join the nuclear club, if they choose to do so.

If nuclear weapons were a key stabilizing element in the Cold War, why should nuclear proliferation be destabilizing now? A small but respected group of academics argues that the spread of nuclear weapons may be, on the whole, a positive phenomenon. This "more may be better" school holds that because the costs of total war between nuclear powers will exceed any possible gains, states will have no motivation for waging war. Because all states allegedly will be mutually deterred, Kenneth Waltz says, "the probability of major war among states having nuclear weapons approaches zero."[2]

Three points will suffice to rebut this thesis. First, the "more may be better" argument relies on a logic of nuclear deterrence in which the costs of actually using nuclear weapons are intuitively understood and commonly appreciated. During the Cold War, the United States and the Soviet Union shared this perspective. Whether the leaders of other countries will see things in similar terms is not clear. They do not have to be insane or emotional to bring a different calculus to decisions. Iraq has employed chemical weapons against Iran, and other countries might be inclined to use such weapons as well. Second, the nuclear balance of terror during the Cold War was stable because both the United States and the Soviet Union had invulnerable second-strike postures. A future of multiple countries with vulnerable first-strike postures could be a recipe for great instability. Third, even if nuclear deterrence does impose stability on the international environment, the nature of that stability may be opposed to U.S. national interests. Any stability achieved through the proliferation of nuclear weapons would not be one that results from mutual trust and interdependence, but instead from suspicion. Such an environment will not be conducive to prospects for future peace and community-building.

Such a world promises increased difficulties for the United States in carrying out its superpower roles in security affairs and economics. The current global economy has largely been constructed under U.S. auspices. A large measure of the innovation, capital, and leadership that promotes increased world interconnectedness is American in origin. The development and enforcement of international norms of behavior, as well as standard trading practices, reflects American (and European) initiative. The United States is not only the primary country supporting globalization but also its ultimate guarantor. Unrivaled in its ability to project power, the sophistication of its military forces, and the depth of its financial resources, the United States has been acting to ensure that the process of globalization continues unimpeded. The risk is that the U.S. capacity to continue performing this role will erode if WMD proliferation accelerates, especially if it produces countries willing to employ these weapons, either directly or indirectly, as instruments of statecraft.

The ability of the United States to act forcefully is partly a product of today's favorable strategic conditions. In the last decade, the United States has intervened in at least three crises that could have stunted globalization. In 1991, the United States expelled Iraq from Kuwait, thereby ensuring the free flow of oil that powers the global economy. In 1999, the United States led NATO in an air campaign against Serbia in order to preserve stability in the Balkans and Europe. Along with both of these events, but often overlooked, was the U.S. intervention in the Taiwan Straits in 1995. Although not a full-fledged crisis, the event was serious enough. China launched missiles that landed in the vicinity of Taiwan in an attempt to intimidate the Taiwanese electorate away from pro-independence candidates. In response, the United States moved 7th Fleet forces toward the Straits. Had the United States not intervened, China likely would not have invaded, but nonaction would have encouraged China to continue pressuring the Taiwanese overtly.

During this period of tension with China, the United States demonstrated resolve, but it did not employ force. Had China launched missiles against Taiwan, U.S. policymakers would have been faced with two unpalatable options: respond with force against the People's Republic of China and accept the possibility of Chinese retaliation against U.S. territory, or stand idly by. The proliferation of nuclear weapons will likely make such political conundrums more commonplace. The question among many countries will be whether the United States will be willing in such situations to intervene and to enforce international norms of behavior.

Other things being equal, if the United States does not continue performing this role, aggressive states could be encouraged to establish spheres of influence, as did the Soviet Union during the Cold War. The existence of two or three such spheres would damage the freedom of trade and ideas because suspicious regional powers likely would persuade or coerce weaker neighbors from cooperating with the democratic community. Bandwagoning behavior on the part of weak states could result in the formation of hostile, WMD-armed regional blocs. Suspicion, not cooperation and peaceful competition, would become the main characteristic of state-to-state relations. Globalization would be replaced by unstable regionalization.

Globalization has yet to reveal its full consequences. Likewise, WMD proliferation has yet to show its full colors. But there is already plenty to worry about even if WMD proliferation does not result in such a damaging outcome. The irony is that WMD proliferation is being stimulated by globalization's negative effects in ways that could undermine its positive effects.

Strategic Consequences for the United States

If WMD proliferation accelerates, the emerging challenge for the United States will be to remain involved and to shape international events in the tense setting of a world of nuclear plenty. Most likely, the United States will soon face an increasing number of nuclear powers of varying capability and with differing strategic intentions. It will need to devise an appropriate response. Current U.S. nuclear strategy remains grounded in concepts stemming from the Cold War. During this period, the focus of U.S. nuclear strategy was on a single power. The Soviet Union, although hostile, was conservative in its actions and politically stable. In addition, its nuclear capability was comparable to that of the United States. The strategic environment was characterized by duality, stability, and equality. The future portends a radically different environment in which these characteristics are replaced by their opposites. The consequence will be to increase pressures on the United States to change its nuclear doctrines in appropriate ways.

Multiplicity, Instability, and Inequality

Proliferation likely will result in many non-nuclear friends and allies seeking protective shelter in the form of U.S. security guarantees aimed at warding off the threat or use of weapons of mass destruction against them. Indeed, this trend is already emerging in Asia and the Middle East. In both regions, the United States is discussing future goals and priorities with key partners. In Asia, discussions about theater missile defense and other options are under way with such key countries as Japan and South Korea. In the Middle East, the United States is pursuing a Cooperative Defense Initiative with the Gulf Cooperation Council countries, Jordan, and Egypt. What these efforts ultimately will produce remains to be seen. What can be said is that the act of providing extended deterrence coverage over NATO and Europe in the Cold War was one thing; creating it in new places, especially in zones where the peacetime stationing of large numbers of U.S. forces is not a politically feasible option, may be a different thing entirely. Whereas providing such coverage will further entangle the United States in the security affairs of turbulent regions, failure to do so could leave friends and allies exposed to new dangers and create incentives for them to develop their own nuclear arsenal or make political accommodations with adversaries. Dealing with these tradeoffs and making appropriate decisions will be among the most important challenges facing U.S. defense strategy in the coming years.

Dealing with nuclear-armed powers will be equally challenging. The relationship with a nuclear ally that has posed the least difficulty and most benefit for the United States has been its relationship with Great Britain. During the Cold War, U.S. and British nuclear policies were closely linked. Both countries shared the same risk perceptions, and the hierarchy of the partnership was fully understood: the United States led, Britain followed. The U.S.-British alliance therefore strengthened deterrence without heightening risk as a result of autonomous British actions. In the future, however, the U.S.-British relationship is likely to be the exception. The U.S. experience with France is more likely to be the norm. In such an often stressful relationship, there exist both benefits and risks. By acquiring nuclear weapons, U.S. allies will become more capable of shouldering their own security burdens. Yet these same weapons may embolden them to take autonomous action adverse to U.S. interests, thus increasing the likelihood that the United States will become involved in a nuclear crisis not of its own making.

Israel's alleged possession of nuclear weapons has lessened the likelihood of its being attacked by its Arab neighbors and thereby has helped stabilize Arab-Israeli conflict. The same beneficial side effects could be predicted for Taiwan or South Korea, with regard to China and North Korea, respectively. Yet in these cases, were a nuclear-armed ally to become involved in conflict with another nuclear power, the United States would become linked to a conflict over which it might have little direct control. Whereas the proliferation of nuclear weapons on the part of an ally could provide short-term and localized benefits, the potential consequences posed to U.S. interests could be damaging in broad ways over the long haul.

Nuclear-armed states that have neutral relations with the United States and, by implication, do not threaten its allies pose the least immediate menace. India and Pakistan are two examples; U.S. involvement in the India-Pakistan conflict is limited, and the United States may even serve as a neutral arbitrator between them. India and China are a second pair where the United States is unlikely to suffer directly from a conflict. Yet the interaction of such countries can have ripple effects elsewhere, often engaging U.S. interests more directly.

Last are those countries that will possess nuclear weapons and that are openly hostile to the United States. The candidates at the top of the list include Iraq, Iran, and North Korea. These states either threaten U.S. allies or are in direct opposition to U.S. interests. Yet hostility toward Washington is not necessarily their sole or even main motive. A number of such countries have security concerns only tangentially related to the United States. Their situations also are transitory. Iran's potential nuclear capability will remain a concern but will not be regarded as a direct threat if Tehran achieves reconciliation with its neighbors, particularly Iraq, Saudi Arabia, and the United States. Similarly, North Korea may not survive as a state beyond this decade. If North Korea is peaceably incorporated with South Korea, the threat of war on the Korean Peninsula will disappear. Yet the United States and its friends and allies in Asia will still face strategic dilemmas because a unified Korea might well possess nuclear weapons.

The nature of the nuclear postures acquired by countries gaining nuclear capabilities will help determine the strategic consequences. States that possess both stable political situations and secure second-strike capabilities may be expected to act according to the logic of mutual deterrence. By contrast, states with a small number of relatively vulnerable systems are more likely to fear a preemptive strike. During periods of conflict, they may be tempted to employ their weapons on a first-use basis rather than risk their being destroyed—especially if they can hope to disarm their opponents before they themselves are disarmed. Any country in confrontation with such a nuclear power would have to exercise extreme caution when employing military force. In addition, states with only a rudimentary nuclear capability are unlikely to have either adequate command and control capabilities or nuclear safeguards built into their nuclear infrastructure. Coupled with political instability, this situation increases the likelihood of both accidental launch and autonomous actions, such as renegade military units or terrorist organizations gaining possession of these weapons and using them.

In today's environment, actions taken by one state may have unintended consequences that reverberate across the international system. A great risk is that WMD proliferation will be contagious, producing an action-reaction cycle that motivates other countries to acquire these weapons and delivery systems. The calculus of deterrence will be less dependable because not all of these states will be politically stable. The smallest and least sophisticated may well be the most dangerous. This prospect calls for new thinking about how nuclear weapons are to be used in peace and war.

Nuclear Principles in the Globalization Era: Old and New

U.S. strategy and doctrine will need to remain flexible and adaptive because the strategic situation probably will vary considerably from one region to another. Most likely no single doctrinal formula will apply equally everywhere. Yet some common themes stand out in ways that will help create a similar framework for forging strategy and doctrine in each place.

While a number of countries will possess the WMD assets to inflict huge damage on their neighbors and elsewhere, the very act of owning these assets will make them natural lightning rods for countervailing actions, including devastating U.S. nuclear strikes if necessary. As a result, deterrence may not work in the straightforward psychological ways of the Cold War, although in new and cruder ways, it may still work all the same. The key point is not that the logic of deterrence will no longer apply, but that new and different ways may need to be found to make it work again in a manner that responds to the local politics and strategic affairs of each region.

Another dampening factor is that, in many cases, the proliferation of nuclear weapons will impose tighter upward limits on the intensity and ultimate objectives of conventional warfare. In a conventional conflict between two nuclear-armed states, military forces will be constrained from intensively targeting either civilian areas or nuclear infrastructures of the opponent. Fear of nuclear retaliation may also prohibit a country whose military forces are victorious on the battlefield from forcibly changing the regime of a vanquished nuclear-armed state. Removing a hostile regime from power by force of arms, as was done by the United States with Nazi Germany and Imperial Japan, could become a thing of the past in dealing with nuclear-armed states. A foretaste of these new restrictions has already been experienced during the aftermath of the Persian Gulf War. Clearly, one of the considerations involved in not occupying Baghdad and ousting Saddam Hussein was fear that chemical weapons would be launched against Israel, Saudi Arabia, or U.S. forces in the region. This upward ceiling on warfare may mean that many conflicts between states likely will not be resolved but will instead have to be managed. In political ways, such management will assuredly include violence, albeit strictly controlled. So, while nuclear proliferation could trigger escalation in some cases, its main effect might be to help limit wars in other cases.

Even so, the proliferation of WMD systems may give rise to a growing number of acts of aggression by countries possessing these weapons—not necessarily nuclear attacks, but a wide spectrum of actions ranging from peacetime bullying to conventional aggression. As was true in the Cold War, the ceiling imposed on conflict by nuclear weapons may tempt countries to run the risk of trying to pursue limited objectives, reassured by the logic that the United States will view small incursions as not worth the danger of unleashing nuclear devastation. Such logic allowed the Soviet Union to mount the Berlin blockade in 1948, China to enter the Korean War in 1950, and Egypt and Syria to attack Israel in 1973. The same phenomenon characterized the intensification of the Pakistani-Indian conflict over Kashmir in 1999. The dilemma for U.S. policymakers is that aggressive countries may use small, aggressive actions in order to acquire, over time, their strategic objectives. If so, no single action will cross the threshold in ways justifying a nuclear response, but taken as a whole, or even singly, all such actions could be detrimental to U.S. interests. Unable to invade and occupy the entire peninsula, for example, North Korea may be tempted to capture Seoul. Even so, the nuclear threshold—the point at which nuclear weapons actually are detonated—will likely remain high. If so, the ultimate result could be more small wars, but few, if any, nuclear attacks.

On balance, nuclear weapons will most likely remain primarily political symbols of power in peacetime and only secondarily military instruments of force in wartime. If so, nuclear strategy will retain its anchor in the nonuse of these weapons. One reason is that actually using these weapons in war will invite devastating retaliation. Moreover, most countries will probably lack the reliable delivery systems, command and control systems, and accuracy to employ these weapons for anything other than the crude targeting of cities. Using them on the battlefield will remain a difficult act. This too argues against their use, except in extremis.

In theory, mutual deterrence will extend to tomorrow's nuclear-armed countries with smaller arsenals because they will have substantial destructive power; the marginal difference between tens and hundreds of nuclear weapons is insignificant. Like the French *Force de Frappe* and China's posture, these limited nuclear arsenals assuredly will help deter outright aggression. In each case, however, such weapons must be highly reliable and attain a high level of confidence that they can be delivered to their targets. A country that possesses nuclear weapons but lacks such capability may find that its arsenal is a plausible deterrent but not a convincing instrument of coercion.

The current environment offers several examples. Scientists monitoring the 1995 Pakistani nuclear test dispute that country's claim of detonating an 18-kiloton nuclear device, instead stating that the yield may have been one-third of this level. If so, the test was a partial failure. Similarly, during a test, Iran's Shahab missile was destroyed in flight prior to impact, which suggests that the missile test was not a complete success. These weapons are still in the development phase. But the limited resources of these countries, international pressure, and bans on testing significantly reduce their ability to put these weapons and delivery systems through a rigorous series of tests to attain and demonstrate reliability. A state with such a dubious nuclear capability may still employ this capability to threaten, but if confronted, it would be wise to demur and seek compromise, lest its capability fail at a critical moment.

As for defensive systems, these may have greater utility than during the Cold War. The logic behind the ABM Treaty is firmly rooted in the Cold War standoff in which both countries shared mutual vulnerability. Any attempt to pursue defensive measures could result in offsetting offensive countermeasures or simply increase the number of weapons delivered. The result would be a continued arms race of no benefit to either side. This logic applied then, but whether it still applies today, especially in universal ways, is another matter.

With or without the deployment of an NMD system, the mutual vulnerability that existed between the United States and the Soviet Union will continue to exist in the U.S.-Russian relationship into the foreseeable future. At a certain level, it is inconsequential whether hundreds or thousands of nuclear missiles can reach their targets. The U.S.-Russian relationship may not be the norm, however. As with credibility, there is a point at which the potential damage that a country can inflict no longer has the same deterrent effect. Most future nuclear powers will be unable to rectify this situation because the cost of development and production will not allow them to produce enough weapons to ensure their ability to both overwhelm defensive systems and to inflict sufficient damage on the other state. Simply stated, a number of countries may acquire nuclear weapons and delivery systems, but these postures will remain small enough to contemplate defense against them. In such a world of nuclear power, ballistic missile defense may make sense.

Policy and Strategy Implications

During the Cold War, U.S. military doctrine for theater warfare against nuclear-armed opponents was animated by the concepts of deterrence, forward defense, and flexible response. These concepts arose largely in reaction to the NATO-Warsaw Pact standoff in Central Europe. Essentially, the United States and NATO tried to deter aggression by maintaining adequate nuclear and conventional force postures. In the event of aggression, their plan called for an initial forward defense of West Germany's exposed borders. If this did not hold, and the NATO conventional force buckled, the next step would involve crossing the nuclear threshold and gradually escalating in an effort to persuade the Soviet Union to desist rather than face total destruction. They retained the option for massive retaliation, but only as a last resort in the event that conventional defense and limited nuclear responses both failed.

In all probability, these old concepts will not be directly applicable to the regional crises of the future because the relevant political-military conditions will differ dramatically from those in Central Europe during the Cold War. Unyielding forward defense may not be as important as during the Cold War, thus lessening pressures in the United States to escalate prematurely. Instead, the United States might find itself rushing to deploy forces to distant areas in order to prevent an aggressor from consolidating gains through a surprise attack. The main task will be one of halting the aggression, building up strong U.S. and allied forces while degrading the enemy, and then launching a strong counterattack.

Efforts to create a new doctrine for a nuclear weapon-proliferating world will need to address the challenge of how to deal with such new situations, not those of the Cold War. These situations will be difficult and dangerous for reasons of their own, but perhaps not as troublesome as facing down a threat of 90 Warsaw Pact divisions armed with 5,000 nuclear weapons, and not yielding an inch of German territory. If U.S. strategy could find a sensible way to blend nuclear and conventional operations then, it likely will be able to do so again. The coming task is one of crafting a new doctrine that will allow U.S. forces to achieve their political-military goals while not triggering a nuclear exchange, or the use of chemical and biological weapons, in the process.

U.S. military forces have already begun the process of acquiring new capabilities to meet the counterproliferation challenges ahead. Under the mantle of *Joint Vision 2010*, U.S. forces are developing a better capacity to conduct precision strikes against enemy WMD targets with cruise missiles and other smart weapons. They also are developing theater air and missile defense (TAMD) systems and other means to help protect U.S. and allied forces through dispersal, protective gear, and the like. As these measures mature, they will enhance the physical capabilities of U.S. forces. But if U.S. forces are to become fully effective, they will also need appropriate doctrines for skillfully employing their assets in crises and wars. To what degree will the existing doctrines of deploying swiftly and operating decisively, with ambitious battlefield objectives in mind, still apply? Will the goal still be to inflict total battlefield defeat on enemy forces, or will different goals, of a political nature, rise to the fore? The answers are not apparent, but the questions will need to be addressed.

The nature and variety of threats are so large that seeking to deter all of them through the threat of nuclear weapons would be unrealistic. In this world of multiple nuclear powers, moreover, the United States will not be seeking so much to deter nuclear aggression as to retain its ability to intervene once conventional aggression occurs. Often, it should be able to succeed in doing so. Whereas aggressive states may seek to change the status quo through incremental actions that remain below the U.S. nuclear threshold, the United States may resist these same actions by means that themselves remain below the nuclear threshold of the aggressor states.

Within this realm of limited conflict, the United States will possess distinct advantages. Washington will often be able to employ its leadership status as well as political and economic leverage to convince others to act according to international norms. In the event of military conflict, the United States will retain superiority in conventional forces that may be used to punish, deny, and compel states that seek to change the status quo. By maintaining superiority in this realm, the United States can reinforce deterrence, for if states understand that the United States retains both the willingness and the ability to intervene militarily in world affairs, they are less likely to engage in aggressive action, even if they possess nuclear weapons. Simply put, the United States will enjoy much more leverage than will its opponents.

Being able to react promptly to aggression is critical to its prevention. By taking sudden action, a country may seek to bypass the standard protocols of deterrence by which the United States presents the aggressor state with first a verbal warning and then a demonstration of resolve. If possible, aggressor states may seek to present the United States and the world with a fait accompli.

One key to avoiding such situations is timely and accurate intelligence. Because other countries do not have the capability to move large numbers of forces quickly, the United States, through its intelligence capabilities, must be able to anticipate and discern aggressive action. Potential aggressors can then be put on warning that their action will not be tolerated. If its warning is ignored, the United States can engage in an appropriate military response. Even if warned, the aggressor country may hope that the sustained buildup of U.S. forces will leave an open opportunity to grab and keep significant gains. In this regard, the United States must have the ability to respond, if it so chooses, before and as the situation unfolds. The level of required response, of course, is variable, and could include anything from the positioning of aircraft carriers in the area of interest to standoff strikes against advancing forces.

To be able to strike the forces and infrastructure of a hostile state through the use of standoff weaponry is of undoubted utility in protecting the lives of U.S. military personnel. Often overlooked, however, is the role that standoff weaponry can play in deterrence. If a state realizes that the United States can oppose its aggressive actions at little direct cost to itself, the aggressor country can no longer calculate that the United States will hesitate before interposing U.S. forces between a hostile military force and its goals. The ability to engage a hostile state from a distance at low cost takes away an important disincentive to U.S. action.

On the battlefield, at every level of conventional escalation, a hostile power will be confronted by the superior capabilities of the U.S. military. Countries with lesser capabilities will likely be able to apply force only along a few and widely spaced rungs on the escalation ladder. An aggressor's inability to use force in carefully graduated amounts may create pressure to overshoot the objective of its escalatory response, something that it would be loathe to undertake. Therefore, as the United States maintains a high level of conventional superiority, "a sufficient asymmetry of capabilities at lower levels would ensure that an intolerable burden would be put on the side forced to raise the stakes."[3] In crises, most often it will be an enemy, not the United States, facing the choice between escalation and capitulation.

While nuclear weapons clearly make enemies stronger, deployed U.S. forces would probably be less vulnerable to them than surface appearances suggest. For example, an Army division is normally spread out along a 50-mile front and in equal depth; it would take multiple accurate nuclear strikes—not just one—to cripple the division's maneuver battalions and other formations. U.S. naval forces are also hard to destroy because their ships are moving and widely dispersed. When in flight, tactical air forces are even harder to damage. Because airbases, seaports, and supply dumps are stationary and concentrated, they seem more vulnerable. But because these entities are typically located long distances behind front lines, enemy aircraft and missiles must penetrate thick air defenses to reach these targets and also require accurate data on their locations to strike effectively. As a result, an enemy must possess a fairly large nuclear inventory, effective delivery systems, and good intelligence in order to carry out a battlefield campaign against U.S. forces. Even then, their prospects would not be good. During the Cold War, many studies of nuclear war in Europe produced a key conclusion. Theater nuclear war is not a good way for an outgunned force to compete against a more powerful force that also has nuclear weapons. It merely accelerates the ability of the stronger force to win quickly and decisively. The same conclusion likely would apply to any future adversary unfortunate enough to become locked in combat with high-technology U.S. forces.

The United States will retain freedom of action in conventional operations, so long as the intensity and objectives of U.S. military action remain below an aggressor state's nuclear threshold. Crossing such a threshold and triggering a nuclear response is not in the U.S. interest and is clearly to be avoided. For this reason, it is important for the United States to match its methods and targets with its understanding of the other country's level of tolerance. Full-fledged invasions by hostile states will remain relatively rare, and often U.S. policy objectives will be to punish a country for a specific action or compel it to desist from some form of behavior. In such a case, the utility of immediacy and distance remains in effect. The intensity of the response will, of course, be commensurate to the aggressive action and therefore will likely remain below the aggressor state's retaliatory threshold.

In the case of major conflicts, where the possibility of nuclear retaliation must be taken into consideration, the intensity and targets of U.S. action will have to be chosen with great discrimination, for inappropriate escalation may result in a retaliatory response. This situation in no way implies that the U.S. response should be dictated by the aggressor state, but that the United States must comprehend what actions are most likely to trigger retaliation. A few common sense guidelines may be useful to remember. Attack by remote platforms (aircraft, cruise missiles, artillery), although destructive, will leave the regime of the aggressor state in possession of what remains. The regime is weakened, but its ultimate objective, retention of power, is not threatened. Advancing armies, however, are far more menacing, for they imply the destruction of the regime. A regime with a foreign army approaching the capital will have little to lose if confronted with ouster, death at the hands of its citizens, or a war crimes tribunal. It is at this juncture that the nuclear threshold might be crossed. The employment of land forces in a conventional military role, therefore, should be cautious and their objectives remain limited.

The retaliatory capabilities of a state are the ultimate guarantors of the regime's survival. In the event of a conflict with North Korea, for example, the United States would have to think carefully about destroying vulnerable long-range North Korean systems. If attacked, and not destroyed, the North Korean regime might take this step as evidence that its destruction is the object of U.S. action. Prior to the commencement of air strikes against Iraq on January 8, 1991, Saddam Hussein had dispersed his arsenal of missiles. Consequently, attacks upon missile storage sites had the effect of closing the barn door after the proverbial horse was gone. Consider, however, if the United States had been successful in destroying the majority of these systems. How would Saddam Hussein have responded if he had in his control a handful of missiles, and the United States Army was approaching the city limits of Baghdad? The answer suggests that allowing a hostile and aggressive state to retain its retaliatory capability may reinforce and strengthen the nuclear threshold. In effect, the United States could approach the upper limit of that threshold more closely, thereby enabling U.S. forces to degrade a country's war-making capabilities.

There is no mutually understood agreement as to which actions remain below the nuclear threshold and which surpass it. The United States must therefore be cognizant of signals sent by aggressor states as to when this threshold is being approached, yet willing to call a state's bluff if the United States feels that further action is required to achieve its military and political objectives. Undoubtedly, there is a danger that the United States may cross this threshold prematurely, but the ultimate guarantor of deterrence—retaliation—must not be put into effect unnecessarily or unwisely. Nuclear retaliatory weapons are tools of strategy, and their use must take the form in which a state can apply them successfully.

The same judgment of relating means to ends applies to U.S. efforts to develop a TAMD and an NMD system. Both are tools that can aid in enabling the United States to intervene in the case of aggressor states' taking hostile action against their neighbors. A TAMD system allows the United States to protect its troops and limit the ability of hostile states to intimidate their neighbors into denying the United States forward basing. Both NMD and TAMD systems provide the last opportunity to protect the United States or its allies from significant harm. If a WMD-tipped missile is successfully intercepted, the United States retains options. It may return to a level of hostility that falls below the nuclear threshold, undertake some form of intensified yet limited retaliation, or attempt to remove the offending regime. These considerations argue for deploying such defense systems.

However, deploying missile defenses, especially NMD, could have significant negative ramifications if applied incorrectly. As an NMD system becomes more sophisticated, the risk exists of creating an arms race between the United States and the more advanced nuclear powers, Russia and China. To alleviate this problem, first and foremost an NMD system must remain limited. Only by U.S. limitation of interceptors will these countries feel that they will still possess sufficient nuclear weaponry to ensure a credible retaliatory capability. The difficulty is finding the correct balance in which advanced nuclear powers remain relatively unconcerned with U.S. NMD, while providing sufficient protection against possible nuclear use by less powerful states.

Conclusion

The strategic bottom line is that the prospect of accelerating WMD proliferation not only poses a major threat to global stability but also raises major implications for how U.S. military doctrine views the use of force in regional crises and wars. The United States will face the task of deterring WMD-armed hostile states from launching nuclear attacks against vulnerable allies and friends. Accomplishing this task may be easier than deterring and defending against states that employ their nuclear postures as an umbrella to carry out purely conventional aggression for limited political purposes.

The proper U.S. response will be neither to shrink from this challenge nor to apply the old doctrinal precepts inherited from the Cold War, but rather to craft new doctrinal precepts that apply to the fresh situations at hand. The time for thinking seriously about this subject is now at hand.

Notes

[1] David Held et al., *Global Transformations* (Stanford, CA: Stanford University Press, 1999), 3.

[2] Kenneth N. Waltz, "Nuclear Myths and Political Realities," *American Political Science Review* 84, no. 3 (September 1990), 740.

[3] Lawrence Freedman, "The First Two Generations of Nuclear Strategists," in Peter Paret, ed., *Makers of Modern Strategy: From Machiavelli to the Nuclear Age* (Princeton, NJ: Princeton University Press, 1986), 764.

Chapter 15

Peace Operations: Political-Military Coordination

Michael J. Dziedzic

Peace operations are linked to globalization because this paradoxical process generates both winners and losers. The great promise is that it can bring democracy, prosperity, and peace to regions previously lacking these qualities. Although this positive dynamic is occurring in many places, the losers in the globalization sweepstakes are the "failed states" that have become a leading source of instability in the contemporary era.

Globalization and the Failed State Phenomenon

As globalization has accelerated, peace operations aimed at dealing with troubled and dysfunctional states have correspondingly increased in frequency, difficulty, and duration. The effect has been to involve the United States and other participating countries in a host of areas that would have been dismissed as peripheral only a decade ago. Owing to this association with the enduring phenomenon of globalization, the demand for peace operations is likely to persist. Accordingly, the United States and its allies must become proficient at the demanding art of peace operations. This requires the ability to harmonize and integrate the actions of military forces with those of their civilian counterparts.

Under the influence of globalization, economic survival has become increasingly dependent on a vibrant trading relationship. This can place immense strains on authoritarian regimes that refuse to open their economies to outside competition or on aspiring democracies that mismanage the transition to market economics.

Globalization will likely contribute to the failure of autocratic rulers who reject free trade because they will find their capacity to meet the needs of their citizens inexorably declining. To retain power, rulers in such regimes typically opt to suppress making demands, which translates into heavy reliance on state security forces (military, paramilitary, intelligence, and police). One alternative source of revenue to sustain such repressive regimes in the short run may be the raw material resources of the state (for example, oil, diamonds, gold). This option has been prevalent in Africa,

---

Colonel Michael J. Dziedzic, USAF, is a senior military fellow in the Institute for National Strategic Studies at the National Defense University. He recently has served as the strategic planner for the UN Mission in Kosovo. Colonel Dziedzic has taught at both the National War College and the U.S. Air Force Academy.

reducing politics to rapacious rivalry between competing warlords (such as in Liberia, Sierra Leone, and Angola). An alternative source of funds to prop up such noncompetitive political economies is smuggling and other forms of transnational criminal activity (for example, the Balkans, North Korea). In either case, a downward spiral is often set in motion that ultimately concludes with the masses being driven by economic privation to a bare subsistence level or by internal conflict into camps where they become wards of the international community. External actors may unintentionally abet this process by imposing economic sanctions aimed at pressuring repressive regimes to reform. As in Haiti, victims of this process will flee to neighboring states if they have the means to do so. If they do not, mass starvation may occur, as in North Korea, unless the regime collapses or is overthrown.

A governability crisis can also be generated when erstwhile dictatorships attempt to open their markets to global competition. Former communist states and other nascent democracies have been particularly vulnerable when they confront the challenges of simultaneously privatizing their economies and pluralizing their political systems. Without the institutional safeguards and rule of law to manage the turbulent forces that are inevitably unleashed, the result has sometimes been perverse. If the privatization process is unduly influenced by political rather than economic desiderata, the outcome can be a bonanza for shady, underworld elements that insinuate themselves into emerging corporate and political power structures (for example, Russia and the remnants of Yugoslavia). This is another path by which globalization can contribute to the collapse of the state.

Globalization also renders it more difficult for statesmen to ignore the consequences of state failure. This process draws the world together in an ever-tightening web of instant awareness and interdependence. During this decade, Europe has discovered that it cannot treat the Balkans as an isolated backwater because events there have profound consequences for its own process of peaceful unification. Europe now finds itself entangled there, seeking to create stability by integrating that restive region into a protective cocoon of political, economic, and security structures. If recent events are an indicator, prosperous countries of Asia are reaching a similar conclusion about poor and unstable neighbors in Southeast Asia. Although Africa has not reached a comparable level of strategic importance, it cannot be neglected either, and not only for humanitarian reasons. If major parts of the continent slide into chaotic violence, the economic and political interests of certain big powers will be harmed, and the inevitable effects will unsettle the regional order. For these reasons, the plight of troubled and failing states has become a matter of growing concern for the democratic community and the entire international system.

International Trends

Weak States Have Become a Chronic Source of Global Instability

Troubled and potentially anarchic states are distinguished by their chronic incapacity to meet the basic needs of their people and, beyond this, often by the savage repression of major segments of societies. In such situations, government institutions are apt to be tested to the fullest, regardless of whether they are being used to respond to the demands of the populace or to suppress them.[1] In either case, grave doubt will be cast on the legitimacy of the governments. Recent examples include total collapse of the state (Somalia), economic bankruptcy coupled with brutal repression (Haiti), and genocidal assault by the state on an element of its own citizenry (Rwanda, Bosnia, Kosovo).

As the process of state disintegration unfolds, humanitarian catastrophes inevitably ensue, disrupting the internal social or political balance of surrounding states (for example, Haiti, Rwanda, Bosnia, Kosovo). The failure of institutions of law and order, moreover, can convert the failed state into an incubator of transnational threats, such as organized crime, terrorism, arms trafficking, and even proliferation of weapons of mass destruction. Troubled states are strategically significant, therefore, because they lie at the core of many contemporary security challenges. In an era of permeable borders, free trade, and an omnipresent media, a state in chaos anywhere is apt to send reverberations across the globe.

Transnational security threats are a major factor in the institutional deterioration that produces dysfunctional states. The relationship cuts the other way as well because the failure of a state creates an institutional void that may be exploited by transnational actors of various sorts. Osama bin Laden's terrorist network, for example, has exploited turbulent conditions in Afghanistan to establish a base of operations there. The absence of law enforcement in Albania, moreover, was used to project his operation throughout Western Europe and to support operations against American embassies in Kenya and Tanzania. Drug traffickers have also exploited anarchy in the Balkans, expanding their smuggling networks across Europe to Scandinavia. In point of fact, half of the heroin traffickers presently in Swedish jails and 80 percent in Norwegian jails originated in Kosovo and Albania.[2] In an era in which continued prosperity depends on the international exchange of products, money, and information, sealing American borders against these threats is not a realistic option. Although globalization is a boon for consumers, its corollary will be domestic insecurity unless transnational threats emanating from troubled states can be contained.

Demands Posed by Anarchic States Exceed the Capacity to Respond

Peacekeeping, a United Nations (UN) innovation during the Cold War, was intended to help keep interstate conflict from spiraling out of control and sparking a superpower conflagration. During its first four decades, the United Nations was called on to conduct 18 peacekeeping missions (an average of one new mission every other year), almost all of which resulted from conflict between states.[3] Between 1990 and 1999, the United Nations conducted 31 peace operations, or an average of 3 per year. Almost all have responded to "internal" conflicts in troubled states. However, the United Nations has been unable to deal adequately with this surge of new missions. Factors contributing to this failure include the high cost in terms of financial assessments to member states, an inability to recruit sufficient numbers of qualified peacekeeping troops and police, a lack of perceived national interests, a limited understanding of how to rehabilitate a failed state, and political embarrassment in Somalia and Bosnia. One consequence is that some failing states have been neglected, with dire consequences. Rwanda and Zaire are examples.

Another serious limiting factor is the incapacity of the United Nations to conduct the type of large-scale military operations that have often been required.[4] The United Nations is well suited for particular peacekeeping activities, such as monitoring and verification, which are premised on strategic consent among the disputants about the role of the intervening force. These conditions characterized the traditional peacekeeping of inter-state disputes during the Cold War. When consent was lost, UN forces withdrew, as occurred prior to the 1967 Arab-Israeli War.

Troubled states have been the focus of post-Cold War peace operations, and consent has been more conditional and fragile. In successful cases such as El Salvador and Mozambique, the conflict had been stimulated in part by superpower rivalry. Once this rivalry ceased to be a factor, local consent became obtainable. The United Nations has foundered when consent has been marginal and the need to wield force credibly has been high. The United Nations lacks a standing military capability, a viable command-and-control system, and consensus among UN Security Council members regarding use of coercive force in internal conflicts. As a result, it cannot manage the robust enforcement operations often required, at least initially, to deal with troubled and failing states.

These serious deficiencies are unlikely to be remedied any time soon. Many countries, including the United States, oppose an autonomous military capability for the United Nations. Even administrative initiatives, such as a rapidly deployable mission headquarters, have been resisted. Measures to enhance the capabilities of the UN Department of Peace-Keeping Operations (DPKO) may have reached their high-water mark. The establishment of a 24-hour command post was an essential improvement, as was the development of a mechanism for mobilizing standby military forces from member states. Another crucial practice, the use of "gratis" military officers from willing member states, has been abolished within the DPKO, however, at the behest of developing nations who insist that all positions be filled by paid UN personnel. Thus, the DPKO capacity to conduct even its current missions has been diminishing.

The United Nations has recognized its limitations in dealing with troubled states since the setbacks in Somalia and Bosnia. The Security Council has been willing to approve peace enforcement operations conducted by "coalitions of the willing" (such as the Multinational Force in Haiti, the Australian-led force in East Timor) rather than the United Nations, and by competent regional security organizations (for example, the North Atlantic Treaty Organization [NATO] in Bosnia and Kosovo). As a practical matter, this practice has meant that only troubled states of high importance to the members of the Security Council can be managed. There has been little enthusiasm for large, expensive operations in regions of marginal strategic consequence, such as sub-Saharan Africa. United States arrears from previous peacekeeping activities and a tendency to use the United Nations as a scapegoat for failed peacekeeping activities have served as further disincentives to undertake new operations, though this situation has improved somewhat.[5] Even when the United States is willing to support new missions financially, other countries may be reluctant to participate unless the United States also takes the lead militarily.[6]

Moreover, even when a troubled state affects U.S. strategic interests, other Security Council members may be reluctant to provide an unambiguous mandate for intervention. This is especially true where a brutal despot is suppressing his people (for example, Slobodan Milosevic and the Kosovars) because some Security Council members find it vital to respect sovereign prerogatives in this regard. Thus, there are regions, such as sub-Saharan Africa, in which the Security Council has been unwilling to act. There are also circumstances, such as ethnic barbarism, where the Security Council may be paralyzed. The greatest constraint, however, stems from the incapacity of the United Nations to manage the use of force credibly. Hence, future UN-led peace missions will be inclined to rather benign circumstances where the consent of the disputants is reasonably assured and international will is reasonably strong.

Despite these limitations, the United Nations performs several essential functions in managing troubled states. No other international body possesses the same degree of legitimacy to issue a mandate for intervening in a sovereign, but dysfunctional, state. Various UN representatives, such as the High Commissioner for Refugees and the High Commissioner for Human Rights, make vital contributions to mitigating the consequences of state failure, especially in the early stages. The United Nations has also developed extensive expertise in election monitoring and civilian policing, and it has an established mechanism to fund peacekeeping activities through assessments on member states. Owing to these competencies, the United Nations is well suited for the later phases of a peace operation, when the emphasis is on long-term institution building (as in Haiti).[7] The United Nations also has the potential to prevent the regionalization of internal conflicts by mounting preventive deployments in areas bordering a troubled state (such as the UN Preventive Deployment [UNPREDEP] Force in Macedonia).

The greatest deficiency, therefore, arises during the initial phases of an intervention, when a credible coercive capability may be essential for peacemaking or peace enforcement. The United Nations cannot be relied upon for this mission. Thus, this is a key area where demand exceeds capacity, at least until other mechanisms are adapted for this purpose. During the later stages, the United Nations can be more effective, but only if it can sustain the large numbers of skilled military personnel that often must remain deployed for long periods.

Intervention Is Occurring Before There Is a Peace to Keep

The international community continues to search for the proper set of tools to manage troubled and anarchic states, but the task has simultaneously become more demanding because the threshold for intervention has been lowered. Until recently, there was a sense that a peace mission should occur only after a dispute had become "ripe" for resolution. That is, the parties should have first exhausted themselves, moderated their war aims, and demonstrated a willingness to adhere to a peace accord. By following this prescription, the international community can avoid prolonged entanglements in violent conflicts; however, it also means that instances of genocide would be allowed to unfold, and surrounding regions might be destabilized before effective action is taken. By the time such situations become ripe for intervention on the ground, the cost in terms of lives and resources can burgeon. Having learned the price of delay in Bosnia and Rwanda, the United States and its European allies sought to avoid a repetition in Kosovo. Consequently, the Organization for Security and Cooperation in Europe (OSCE) fielded the unarmed Kosovo Verification Mission in late 1998 with merely the promise of a final agreement between the government of Yugoslavia and representatives of the Kosovar community. When this effort failed, NATO became enmeshed in a war with Serbia to stanch its assault on the ethnic Albanian population.

Two factors contribute to this trend toward early intervention. First, the vast majority of wars are now internal to the state, and it is these conflicts that have increasingly become the focus of international interventions. Second, many of these internal conflicts involve wanton use of force by armed elements against civilian masses. As in Iraq, Somalia, Bosnia, Rwanda, and Kosovo, humanitarian catastrophes are a likely result. Indicative of this trend, civilians today suffer the preponderance of casualties from armed conflict, whereas a century ago most casualties were military combatants.[8]

When a humanitarian calamity looms, immense pressure often is brought to bear from the media and concerned interest groups to "do something." Aware of this, secessionist forces such as the Kosovo Liberation Army are more likely to pursue a media "war of attention" than they are to conduct a guerrilla war of attrition. Because norms of international conduct are evolving, sovereignty no longer confers an absolute right on autocratic rulers to wield unbridled violence against their own people. By the action that has been taken on behalf of the Kurds in Iraq and ethnic Albanians in Kosovo, the international community has begun to establish a tenuous, countervailing legal right to intervene to prevent wholesale slaughter and displacement of civilian populations. By thus lowering the threshold for intervention, it has become easier to get involved but more difficult to get out and riskier to remain. The policy dilemmas associated with managing this aspect of the troubled state will not simply disappear. Indeed, the NATO intervention in Kosovo may be a watershed event. The uncertainty of engaging in similar actions in the future will be heavily influenced by the degree of success ultimately obtained there.

Strategic Implications for Force Operations

The strategic implications of these trends, in the United States and other countries participating in peace operations, are manifold.

The Impact on Military Readiness

In earlier years, peace operations often required only modest forces. For example, a neutral zone between two armies could be patrolled by a few hundred peacekeepers. Modern peace operations aimed at saving failed states are far more demanding. In the early stages, forcible intervention can require thousands of heavily armed troops of division or even corps size (60,000 troops or more). Later stages can also require large forces, for although combat missions are no longer necessary, other missions must be performed, and they can demand large troop deployments. For example, a peace support force composed of a few combat battalions, military police, intelligence and communications units, construction engineers, medical units, maintenance units, civil affairs units, training and educational units, other logistics support, and other special skills can require 20,000 to 60,000 troops. Moreover, these peacekeeping units might have to remain on station for years. Deployed troops must be rotated home after a tour of duty, and replacements trained in advance. This process requires a large replacement pool that can be two to three times larger than the actual deployment.

The post-Cold War "peace dividend" has now been collected, and the U.S. defense establishment is scarcely two-thirds the size it was at the end of the 1980s. Operational deployments, however, have tripled. Not all this increase is attributable to the exigencies of troubled states: natural disasters and more conventional security challenges, such as Iraq and North Korea, account for much of this trend. Nevertheless, there are legitimate concerns as to whether the Armed Forces can retain their fighting edge while engaged in continuous operations aimed at managing troubled states.

Peace support operations, considered in isolation, do not necessarily result in a degradation of military readiness. The experiences of the 25th Infantry Division in Haiti (as part of the Multinational Force) and the 1st Armored Division in Bosnia (as part of the Implementation Force [IFOR]) provide invaluable insights. In both cases, a minor but temporary degradation of some perishable combat skills (for example, gunnery) occurred. However, these skills were quickly restored and within a couple of months were at predeployment levels. The impact on leadership skills and organizational proficiency in complex warfighting tasks, in contrast, was significant and enduring. Daily patrolling in the challenging and unpredictable environments of Haiti and Bosnia placed a premium on decentralized decisionmaking and small-unit leadership. Such maturation could not have been achieved in artificial training environments. These are capabilities that will be central, moreover, to the decentralized and digitized battlefields envisioned for the future. By virtue of this refreshing of perishable skill sets, therefore, both units were deemed to be more combat-capable after the peace operation than before.

To achieve this outcome, certain essential steps had to be taken. Unit integrity was maintained,[9] and commanders conducted an active training program throughout the deployment. Finally, they went in with overwhelming force so as to be prepared for a worst-case scenario. Under the more benign circumstances actually encountered, it was possible to satisfy requirements of both the peace mission and an active training program.[10]

Thus, while the direct impact of peace missions on readiness is not necessarily negative, the cumulative impact, along with numerous other smaller scale contingencies and continuing exercise commitments, has produced an unacceptably high tempo of operations and an adverse impact on quality of life and personnel retention. This tempo cannot be sustained with the present force posture, for it is having a major impact on specialized career fields such as military police and civil affairs, which have uniquely valuable skills for managing troubled states. Beyond this, the United States today has only 10 active Army and 3 active Marine divisions. All are needed to meet combat needs in the event of major regional wars. The same applies to Air Force and Navy units. When forces are deployed for peace missions, they are not readily convertible for war fighting. Small deployments might not be highly damaging, but big deployments could have this effect.

The allegedly deleterious impact on the readiness of U.S. forces for combat operations is often decried. An equally potent example is the trend now taking place in Europe. The European Union is now setting out to create a full corps that can be employed for peace support missions. This corps is designed to include 60,000 full-time, active-duty troops. Beyond this, the Europeans are deciding to earmark fully 140,000 troops to provide this corps with individual replacements and staying power for deployments of many months. A strategic case can be made that the Europeans require a robust peace support force of this size. But there is a serious risk that these troops will come at the expense of manning the existing NATO Rapid Reaction Corps, which is tailored to heavy combat missions, as well as NATO efforts to create additional heavy corps for this purpose. The key point is that participating in peace operations may be a strategic necessity, but it is not a free lunch, and it can impose opportunity costs on other forms of preparedness for both U.S. and allied forces.

Civil-Military Interdependence

Peace operations bear little resemblance to the high-intensity battlefields that our forces are so well prepared to dominate. This use of the military differs from traditional combat operations because mission accomplishment is as dependent on the skill of civilians and effective civil-military integration as it is on military prowess. Deficiencies in this civil-military dimension impede the emergence of a durable peace and increase the burdens and risks borne by military units. Owing to the interdependence between civilian and military participants in complex contingencies, unity of effort is a key determinant of success. Whereas the Goldwater-Nichols Act successfully institutionalized "jointness" among the military services, the need today is for similar structural adaptation "beyond jointness" in civil-military collaboration.

The military contingent typically receives a mandate to establish a safe and secure environment. A stable peace can be put in place, however, only by working in concert with civilian counterparts, who have the expertise to help repair a broken state and mend a fractured society. Unity of effort is vital, therefore, because it enables the burdens to be shared more broadly, the tasks to be divided more competently, and the transition to a durable peace to be accomplished more expeditiously. Among the major activities requiring an effective civil-military partnership are:

- *Humanitarian relief.* In anarchic situations, humanitarian relief workers may be unable to provide life-sustaining assistance without protection from an international military force. While such forces have substantial capabilities that can be converted to humanitarian purposes, they are not specialized in the delivery of relief services. Thus, the military must nurture a symbiotic relationship with organizations established for this purpose.
- *Ending of hostilities and demobilizing of former warring factions.* Obtaining agreement to terminate a conflict often requires the international community to exercise a combination of force and diplomacy. Implementing the accord, more-

over, requires the presence of international human rights observers to monitor and investigate politically motivated violence. This effort often must be supported by a military contingent to monitor and verify compliance with activities such as a separation of forces, the cantonment of combatants and weapons, disarmament, and the demobilization of ex-combatants.

- *Public security and administration of justice.* At the inception of a peace mission, there tends to be a void in public security that the military contingent must fill, by default, until an international civilian police (CIVPOL) force can be deployed. As the CIVPOL element becomes operational, responsibility for maintaining public order will normally be transferred to it in a phased manner. Until police and judicial assistance programs can develop an indigenous public security establishment that serves the community rather than preying on it, the departure of military peacekeepers can be destabilizing.
- *War crimes and human rights.* An international tribunal may have a mandate to gather evidence about war crimes. The military contingent may be called upon to provide security for investigation of atrocity sites and to assist in the apprehension of indicted war criminals. The broader human rights community will also require a secure context for the development of local human rights organizations, independent media, and public attitudes that will serve as safeguards against government abuse of power once the peace operation ends.
- *Governance.* The incapacity of the state to respond to the elementary needs of its citizens is almost always an immediate concern of any peace operation. There is invariably a lag between the arrival of the military peace force and the period when international assistance begins to have an impact on the delivery of government services. United States Army civil affairs specialists in public administration, education, and health often perform a vital role, therefore, during the early phases of an operation. If a durable peace is to be constructed, ballots rather than bullets must determine who should govern. Civilian specialists play a central role by promoting grass-roots political development and by organizing electoral systems. The military contingent must provide a secure context for the conduct of campaigning and voting.

> *It is beyond tinkering and turning the screw even at the tactical level. It is more of a problem than just tuning up the CMOC, or making sure that the military and the NGOs just hold hands and sing 'Kumbya' at the end of the hour. . . . I would say that you are talking about a Goldwater-Nichols Act for the whole interagency process. Not just for the military. If we want to go 'beyond jointness,' we need to restructure radically. Maybe we need to look at the way we are internally structured and change.*
> — Anthony C. Zinni

- *Economic reconstruction.* Military combat engineers and civil affairs personnel will typically provide a capability to repair portions of the infrastructure that are vital for execution of the military mission. Examples are water, electricity, sewage, telecommunications, roads, railways, and bridges. Civilian reconstruction programs must not only restore basic services, but they also must stimulate the local economy and generate jobs, in particular for ex-combatants, if peace is to be self-sustaining.

Recommendations

Peace operations are inherently political, highly complex, and not susceptible to ready military solutions. Military force normally plays a key role, but it must be employed with specific political ends in mind and in concert with nonmilitary instruments. There is no substitute for wise strategic decisionmaking about when, where, and how they should be embarked upon. In general, they should be approached with restraint and resolve—restraint about mounting them at all, and resolve in carrying them out when mounted. Even when wise decisions are made to pursue them, the manner in which they are implemented matters a great deal in determining their ultimate success or failure.

The following practical measures could improve the efficiency of peace operations, perhaps in significant ways. They emphasize steps to better integrate the use of military forces with civilian assets in difficult settings where both must be employed adroitly in the service of common goals and policies. Just as the Goldwater-Nichols reforms institutionalized jointness in U.S. forces for combat operations, these measures could help bring greater coherence to peace operations that extend "beyond jointness." In future peace support operations, prospects for success will hinge on the effective blending of military and civilian endeavors. This task will never be easy, especially when U.S. assets must work with those of other nations. But it could become easier, and more effective, if the following measures are pursued.

Improve Instruments for Managing Anarchic States

Although the United States cannot be the world's policeman, this proposition provides little insight into who else should deal with the instability generated by troubled states. No amount of reform at the United Nations is likely to address this source of global instability fully. Two alternatives remain: regional security organizations and ad hoc coalitions of the willing.

Regional security organizations have made limited contributions to managing troubled states in Africa and Latin America. The most significant operations in Africa have been carried out under the aegis of the Economic Organization of West African States (ECOWAS). Dominated by Nigeria, which has supplied the bulk of the troops and material support, ECOWAS has been involved in bringing an end to the civil war in Liberia and is presently a protagonist in the civil war in Sierra Leone. The Organization of American States has also contributed to resolving regional security concerns in Nicaragua and Haiti.

In general, however, few regional security organizations have much potential to address the more demanding tasks of peacemaking and peace enforcement. Since they operate on consensus, they will often be paralyzed when faced with situations that might require using coercive force. Unlike the United Nations, where only five states wield a veto, any member can thwart action. Even if a mandate is forthcoming, member states are likely to have competing national interests in the troubled state that will militate against a coherent and constructive response. Thus, most regional organizations suffer from the same defects as the United Nations in dealing with the use of force. In more benign situations where the disputants provide their consent for an external intervention, the United Nations would normally be the preferred option, on the basis of its greater legitimacy, extensive experience, and established procedures for cost sharing.

NATO is qualitatively different—in large part because of U.S. leadership and the alliance's demonstrated capacity to conduct multilateral operations. NATO allies also share a set of values and interests that can be put at risk by a troubled state on their periphery, such as the former Yugoslavia. Indeed, a non-Article 5 mission provoked the alliance's first operational use in Bosnia and first use of force in Kosovo. Dealing with such challenges is also a major component of the alliance's new strategic concept. In addition, NATO continues to incorporate partner states into its operations in the Balkans and to develop civil affairs capabilities in many allied military establishments to facilitate collaboration with international and nongovernmental organizations.

Despite NATO's considerable advantages, its freedom to act will continue to be constrained by concerns about a mandate. In spite of the precedent set by bombing Kosovo without an explicit mandate from the UN Security Council, many allies will be reluctant to undertake an intervention in the absence of a specific UN mandate. It remains possible for a regional body, such as OSCE, to provide an alternative mechanism for legitimizing collective action. But as of today, this option is a theoretical hope, not a practical reality.

Another potential response would be for European states to develop the capacity to act alone when the United States opts to remain on the sidelines. Although the experience of the UN Protection Force in Bosnia was unfavorable, the inefficacy of that mission had much to do with the unworkable dual-key command-and-control arrangement with the United Nations. One way to develop an all-European capability is the European Security and Defense Policy, which essentially would involve European and NATO capabilities without active U.S. participation.

As a regional organization, NATO cannot address troubled states everywhere. Nevertheless, it has given itself a measure of flexibility because it has refrained from defining its out-of-area interests in narrow geographical terms. This flexibility would theoretically allow the alliance to mount operations anywhere, were there a consensus that its security interests were sufficiently threatened. Realistically, however, such operations are likely to be confined to Europe's periphery. The long-term consequences of intervention in Kosovo are likely to leave the alliance without surplus capacity or appetite for similar ventures for a considerable period. NATO is also limited in its ability to address the nonmilitary aspects of rehabilitating a dysfunctional state. Although the United Nations remains the leading potential partner for this effort, OSCE was called upon to conduct the Kosovo Verification Mission, and it is a major participant in Kosovo, performing such activities as organizing elections and building institutions.

To cope with troubled states beyond the NATO security umbrella, "coalitions of the willing" may be the only other alternative. For situations with a potential for high-intensity combat, or at least forcible entry, the United States will undoubtedly be indispensable, as it was for the Multinational Force in Haiti. If the scenario is more permissive, such as the lawless conditions encountered after a nationwide financial scam in Albania, an operation might be built around another lead nation, as Italy demonstrated in that case. Use of ad hoc coalitions will be contingent on the availability of capable coalition partners and a mandate from the United Nations or an appropriate regional security organization.

Because Africa has the greatest concentration of fragile states, the United States (via the African Crisis Response Initiative), France, and the United Kingdom have all undertaken programs to train and equip chosen African military forces to enhance their peacekeeping capabilities. The operational use of this capability, however, can be risky unless confined to considerable benign peacekeeping activities, as events in Sierra Leone have demonstrated.

Asia is the other major region with a potential for serious instability from future troubled states. Until the mission in East Timor, the only other post-Cold War peace operation in Asia had been in Cambodia. Asian nations had been involved primarily as troop contributors for missions in other regions. Future developments in Indonesia or the deterioration of such fragile regimes as those in North Korea or Malaysia could provide an incentive to develop a collective regional capacity to respond to failing states in Asia.

Expand Nonlethal Capabilities

Normally, an international mandate directs a peace mission to establish a safe and secure internal environment. During the initial phase of an intervention, the military contingent will often be the only source of order. It is apt to be tested by civil disturbances, violent clashes between antagonistic local factions, and theft of its own resources. The military can be a blunt instrument, however, and if even a single incident is mishandled through the use of excessive force, the entire mission can suffer because local consent may be squandered. Inaction, on the other hand, can risk the loss of credibility (for example, the disorders that accompanied transfer of the Sarajevo suburbs under the IFOR). The media spotlight will be unavoidable, and the consequences for success of the peace mission can be enduring.

To limit loss of life and destruction of property in the anarchic circumstances often encountered at the outset of a peace mission, nonlethal capabilities should be included in the initial force. Constabulary or armed police organizations with training and expertise in crowd control, nonlethal force options, and general policing could be deployed simultaneously with the military contingent. Until a CIVPOL contingent became operational, the constabulary could also begin organizing an interim local security cadre and monitoring their performance.[11] In this manner, a constabulary presence could help accelerate the process of reconstituting the local police force.

In addition to reestablishing order, a multilateral peace operation must also shape the political context in a manner favorable to the peace process. Unless this step is done successfully and peace becomes self-sustaining, other reconstruction and peacebuilding activities will be stillborn.[12] Because disgruntled political elites or "spoilers" may attempt to disrupt the peace process, military peacekeepers may be required to respond to various forms of violent resistance, including civil disturbances.

Military forces are reluctant to engage in confrontations with civilians because they are generally not trained in the measured use of force, riot control, negotiating techniques, or de-escalation of conflict. Neither are unarmed CIVPOL personnel capable of handling such violent challenges. Constabulary forces can counter this vulnerability to stage-managed civil unrest, as demonstrated by the deployment of the Multinational Specialized Unit (MSU) as a part of the Stabilization Force (SFOR) in Bosnia in mid-1998.[13] Composed initially of Italian carabinieri and Argentine gendarmes, the MSU has given SFOR the information-gathering capability to detect incipient unrest and to deter it by concentrating MSU patrols in restive areas. The MSU also has successfully defused potentially violent confrontations through negotiation. Only very rarely has the MSU actually had to use force, suggesting that by eliminating this gap in SFOR capabilities, the likelihood that the peace force will be challenged in this manner has been greatly diminished.[14]

Build a Capacity for Long-Term Management

For peace to be sustainable, core institutions of government such as the courts, prisons, and police require more than training and restructuring. Their fundamental mode of operation must be transformed. Indigenous institutions must be coaxed into functioning in rough accordance with internationally acceptable standards. This effort will usually entail a radical transformation of the culture of law enforcement. The local public security apparatus will often have operated as an instrument of state repression. It must begin to serve the public interest and function in a manner that respects the political and human rights of members of all groups, regardless of whether their members wield political power. Success requires time and patient effort.

Training a new police force and building the capacity of the judiciary and corrections systems are a multiyear project. Subsequently, the conduct of police, judges, and jailers must be effectively monitored and supervised. Without such oversight, the training and assistance that the international community provides could merely result in making these forces more competent at repressing their own people. Reconciliation will never occur under such conditions.

Innovative approaches to this challenge have been attempted in Bosnia by the International Police Task Force (IPTF). The concept developed there, termed "collocation," entails placing seasoned IPTF police officers alongside local police chiefs and senior Interior Ministry officials. In Kosovo, international judges and prosecutors have been introduced into district and supreme courts to assist their local colleagues in resisting the extrajudicial influences that abound there. Similar programs would also be warranted for penal systems. One of the primary constraints on implementing such a transitional phase is the lack of adequate international mechanisms to mobilize and field such highly qualified personnel.

Integrate Civil and Military Contributions

Troubled and anarchic states are distinguished by their failure to perform such essential functions as sustaining life, resolving political conflict, maintaining public order, and generating employment.[15] Mounting an effective response to such abysmal political, social, and economic conditions requires the integration of a wide array of military and civilian specialties.[16] The key lies in recognizing the interdependent relationship of military and civil components of contemporary peace missions and constructing effective regimes for their collaboration.

Integration of international efforts will always be imperfect because, inevitably, the states, organizations, and NGOs involved will all have their own interests in any given situation. American leadership is often essential to mount an international response. This leadership can be used to ensure the establishment of mechanisms that produce an integrated effort. Among these mechanisms would be steps to designate a single political manager (for example, a Special Representative of the Secretary General for a UN-led operation) to oversee implementation of the peace process and a common operations center for key international agencies involved. Fully exploiting the integrative potential of information technology (such as geographical information systems) could greatly facilitate information sharing, which is the first step toward task sharing and coordinated planning. Additionally, civil affairs personnel (known as Civil-Military Cooperation in NATO) perform an invaluable integrative function during interventions of this sort, and proper account needs to be made for this function in designing the force. Improvement is also needed in the capacity to mobilize CIVPOL personnel, to address the judicial reform issue, and to disperse funds for reconstruction activities in the early stages of an intervention.

Military commanders have historically been ill prepared to deal with the ambiguities of civil-military operations or to integrate their efforts effectively with the diverse array of multinational and civilian partners involved. Most military officers are unfamiliar with the capabilities and operational culture of the array of civilian actors—humanitarian relief workers, human rights monitors, election supervisors, police trainers, public administrators, and politicians—with whom they must collaborate. Most of the learning has been on the job. Even though these deficiencies have been repeatedly identified as "lessons to be learned" in after-action reviews over the past decade, the same shortcomings repeat themselves with monotonous regularity. These shortcomings will need to be overcome if future operations are to be successful.

Civil-military unity of effort is as vital to mission accomplishment as jointness is for combat operations. Yet this goal is even more difficult to attain because of the lack of formal authority to foster collaboration. The record of IFOR in Bosnia demonstrates the futility of seeking to divorce military and civilian implementation from each other. Absorption of this fundamental lesson—that an acceptable military end-state is unattainable without parallel progress in the civilian dimension—is crucial to unity of effort, as is mutual awareness of capabilities, responsibilities, and motivations. Success also depends on effective mechanisms for coordination and cooperation, the C–2 of civil-military operations (as opposed to command and control, the C–2 of military operations).

Civilian policy guidance or a strategic political-military plan is the starting point for effective civil-military collaboration. If the U.S. Government has not clarified what role its own civil and military agencies ought to play and what its expectations are for their international counterparts, the tendency will be to produce fragmented, uncoordinated, wasteful, and ultimately unsatisfactory operations. The second challenge is to link this planning effort with those individuals who must execute operations in the field. There are two dimensions to this challenge. The challenge for the

United States is to assemble the required experts—in civil and military affairs—in order to oversee the process of implementation. In the field, further complications arise because the primary responsibility for execution will commonly not lie with U.S. agencies but rather with various international groups and nongovernmental organizations. Effective remedies, therefore, will require structural adaptation at the strategic and operational levels.

The capacity of interagency officials to conduct strategic planning, as described in Presidential Decision Directive 56, needs to be enhanced. This will require institutionalizing a cadre of specialists with the expertise necessary to conduct training in the art of political-military planning and to provide a surge capability for developing such plans in crisis situations. This cadre of political-military planners should be drawn from across the cabinet agencies involved. The recently established Contingency Planning Interagency Working Group, if adequately supported and permanently institutionalized, could address the essential issues.

Interagency training activities should be conducted in concert with the regional commanders in chief (CINCs), addressing likely complex contingencies. The focus should be global and regional and should respond to the areas of responsibility of the commanders in chief. In this fashion, participants would not only gain general proficiency in developing political-military plans but would also help produce such plans.[17] Simulations should incorporate participation by those NGOs and international organizations most likely to be involved as de facto partners in peace operations. During an actual peace operation or humanitarian crisis, the members of the CINC political-military team could assist the Joint Task Force Commander or senior U.S. diplomatic representative in operational-level planning, deployment in theater, and execution of the political-military plan.

Education and Training

The U.S. military services have enhanced their capacity to function jointly by having their personnel learn about the unique capabilities and cultures of the other services, study together in advanced schools, train and conduct exercises together, and plan together. The same approach would be warranted for peace operations, humanitarian assistance, and civil-military operations. However, military schools have not adequately kept pace with what has been happening in the field, leaving the bulk of the learning to on-the-job experimentation.

After-action reports and lessons-learned reviews conducted with veterans of these operations indicate that military task forces often arrive uncertain about how to coordinate and integrate their efforts with NGOs and international organizations already on the scene. This initial response period, when confusion is greatest, is frequently critical to determining the outcome of an operation. The community of NGOs and international organizations also needs to learn more about military thought processes, *modus operandi*, capabilities, and limitations, as well as how to work effectively together. Prior education for both communities could significantly reduce this period of confusion and perhaps even lead to advanced planning, integrated execution, and ultimately enhanced mission accomplishment.

To institutionalize learning about operations that require integrated efforts, the dedicated, strategic-level cadre suggested earlier should also:

- Identify areas in which civilian and military professionals lack understanding of these operations, and develop educational resources to address them.
- Develop short courses for senior civil and military officials designed to foster expertise in managing complex contingencies.
- Assist in developing relevant scenarios for military training exercises and in obtaining experienced civilian practitioners to serve as role players.

Resources

Regional CINCs require specialized personnel to plan and execute complex peace operations successfully. Civil affairs and psychological operations personnel are among the primary resources for addressing the civil-military complexities of these operations and thus have been in particular demand. Owing to the nature of these contingencies, personnel may need to be mobilized rapidly, and substantial numbers may need to be sustained in the field for a period of years. Almost all civil affairs assets are in the Reserve component, however, where the basic commitment is to serve 1 weekend a month and 2 weeks in the summer, except in national emergencies. Even with a seldom-used Presidential Selective Reserve Call-up, the availability of civil affairs personnel is seriously constrained in numbers and in the frequency and length of deployment. Thus, the Reserve force is being called upon to address a national security challenge for which it was not designed and is not suitably configured. This contributes to retention problems and chronic personnel shortages because there are increasing difficulties in finding sufficient volunteers to satisfy all requirements for demanding missions like those in Haiti, Bosnia, and now Kosovo. To have fully capable civil affairs elements available for duty on short notice requires an investment in highly trained and deployable civil affairs units well in advance of operational requirements.

The regional CINCs need to have adequate expertise in political-military planning and implementation at their disposal.[18] At a minimum, there should be at least one senior, experienced civil-military affairs advisor in each regional CINC headquarters working closely with, or for, the political advisor, aided by the J–5 and senior civil affairs officer. Other desirable structural adaptations include:

- Expediting the increase of the civil affairs structure by 1,100 Reservists.
- Considering the formation of a second active-duty civil affairs brigade.
- Reviewing promotions and career incentives for civil affairs personnel.
- Determining which functional specialties have been in greatest demand.
- Filling shortages with civilian specialists on contract, including retired civil affairs personnel.
- Cataloging other potential sources of relevant civilian expertise in government agencies, the private sector, international organizations, and NGOs for rapid contact during the planning phase of operations.

Avert the Collapse of Troubled States

The fundamental challenge associated with averting the demands for future peace support operations to rescue troubled states is not early warning. It is a matter of early response in cases where preventive action can make a difference and where the United States has an interest to try. Potential cases would include either democratic regimes under extreme duress (for example, Colombia) or countries aspiring to a democratic transition that falter, in part, because of external or transnational sources of instability (such as Macedonia or Indonesia).

Preventive action normally begins with a traditional package of diplomatic, military, and economic assistance programs. If one source of instability is the spillover of conflict from a neighboring state, then the international community could mount a preventive peace operation similar to UNPREDEP in Macedonia. If these efforts fail and a general climate of lawlessness develops, there will not be time to await the results of typical training and assistance programs. Reversing this downward spiral requires prompt reinforcement of the performance and legitimacy of state institutions, especially those dedicated to providing law, order, and justice.

The option of using an unarmed international CIVPOL organization would probably be inappropriate in such circumstances because it would be incapable of self-defense. An international constabulary or armed police organization, however, could be mobilized to monitor, train, and operationally assist local police and judicial authorities. The guiding principle would be to inculcate in the local public security establishment principles of democratic policing and equality before the law. In extreme cases, a constabulary force might also require reinforcement by an international military contingent. Mounting an effective border patrol could also be extremely important in such situations. Over the long term, public security assistance offered by international organizations, individual governments, and NGOs would play a valuable role in the evolution of stable governance.

Mitigate the Humanitarian Consequences of State Anarchy

Relief workers have traditionally depended on an unarmed, nonthreatening posture and neutrality as their primary means of defense. These principles lose their protective value, however, when the relief community is seeking to assist a population that has itself become a primary target in the domestic conflict (for example, the ethnic cleansing of Albanians in Kosovo). The risks will be compounded if refugee camps become safe havens for rebel forces. Under such circumstances, humanitarian workers may be targeted for kidnapping or assassination. The International Committee of the Red Cross, for example, has suffered deadly consequences in recent years in Rwanda and the Chechen Republic. Rival armed groups may commandeer relief supplies, and order at warehouses and distribution centers may also be precarious owing to food riots and the activities of armed gangs. Unless security can be provided, relief activities may need to be suspended, or they may even be too perilous to mount in the first place.

Protecting the delivery of humanitarian assistance could entail a range of tasks, including:

- Security for convoys, warehouses, and quarters of humanitarian workers.
- Protection of refugees and safe areas.
- Demilitarization and disarmament of combatants.
- Public security within refugee camps.

Each of these tasks may require a different combination of capabilities, since none of the protection options is without significant liabilities.

Standard military combat units are not well suited for the task of protecting humanitarian assistance. Lacking nonlethal force options, the danger of excessive use of force can be high, as befell the elite Canadian airborne brigade during the Unified Interim Task Force in Somalia. Military forces can perform a crucial function, however, by ensuring that legitimate law enforcement agencies are able to establish their writ over throngs of refugees.

One way to address the security void in refugee camps might be to deploy units of constabulary or armed police to work with the international relief community. Operating in concert with local security forces to the maximum extent possible, they could keep armed elements (gangs or guerrillas) away from refugee camps and help to maintain order at food distribution points. The mere presence of a capable international security force of this sort would tend to encourage local civilian and military security forces to perform their duties more responsibly. A constabulary force might help local authorities curtail the activities of armed gangs inside refugee camps by using investigative techniques, expertise at community policing, and, when confronted, nonlethal control measures. This would improve the security climate within the camps and increase the likelihood that humanitarian assistance would reach the hands of the neediest rather than the most heavily armed.

Civilian police units typically comprise individual volunteers from various countries. Thus, they do not have an organized capability to conduct operations, such as demilitarizing refugee camps. Moreover, they traditionally are unarmed. Once a secure environment has been established, however, they can remove abusive personnel from existing police forces, recruit trainees, establish training programs, and monitor the performance of the entire public security apparatus. Bilateral assistance programs, coordinated with or managed by CIVPOL, provide the bulk of financial and technical support for retraining of domestic police forces.

One common alternative, especially for humanitarian organizations dealing with internally displaced persons, has been to hire local security guards. This can be risky, however, since these personnel may be aligned with one of the warring factions, which could invite retaliation from their rivals. Private international security firms are another alternative. They may be cheaper than an intervention force, but quality control and adherence to human rights could end up being compromised.

Governments hosting refugees have the greatest obligation to provide for their security. In reality, however, they often lack the capability to do so. One attractive option, therefore, is to provide international assistance, through CIVPOL and bilateral assistance programs, to local security forces so they can perform this mission more competently. Local governments will be more likely to cooperate with the relief effort, moreover, if they receive something in the bargain. Monitoring would also be required to prevent further victimization of refugees by a police force alien to them.

Another promising option would be to train cadres from the refugee community itself to maintain law and order inside the camps. Known as "encadrement," this would provide employment for military-age males who might otherwise cause problems and also create a security force familiar with the refugees' distinctive legal traditions. This option would require international training assistance and monitoring and would normally work best if implemented in concert with local police, judicial, and penal systems.

In general, humanitarian protection missions that are the least reliant on military resources are the most likely to receive an international mandate. Nevertheless, there remains a need to develop concepts and coordination mechanisms for integrating military quick reaction forces effectively with constabulary units, international civilian police monitors, and local authorities. One way to promote this sort of collaborative effort would be to establish a protection coordinator for every situation requiring protection of humanitarian relief.

Conclusion

The national security of the United States is most effectively buttressed by the consolidation of democratic regimes and by expansion of the realm of prosperous market economies. United States policy seeks, therefore, to encourage the democratization of autocratic regimes and to strengthen emerging democracies. The forces of globalization will bring increasing pressure to open up closed political and economic systems. Despots, however, sensing that power is slipping from their grasp, will be far more likely to go down with a bang than with a whimper. As Slobodan Milosevic has demonstrated in Kosovo, the internal humanitarian consequences of these ruthless attempts to cling to power can be abhorrent, and the destabilizing impact on surrounding states can directly imperil prominent U.S. interests. Democratic regimes, moreover, are at their weakest in their infancy, and it will be during the transition to democracy that many regimes will be prone to failure.

One effective antidote is the international peace operation. Civil-military collaboration will be essential to reinforcing the capacity of the international community to mount these operations in a timely manner and to conclude them successfully. This may be the most troublesome challenge for soldiers and statesmen in the future. Rather than the divide between East and West or North and South, it may be the gulf between governments that function and those that do not that concerns us most.

Notes

[1] These manifestations of a seriously challenged state have in common the failure of institutions to resolve disputes in a peaceful manner, maintain public order, generate employment or income, and allocate the scarce resources of society in a way that avoids massive suffering and mortality. Thus, the conflicts that arise are internal to the state and driven by the failure of political or economic institutions, as opposed to natural disasters. Until such elemental activities have been regenerated, the affected state and society will be unlikely to sustain peace autonomously. Consequently, the surrounding region will be at continued risk of destabilization.

[2] Swedish Foreign Minister Jan Eliasson pointed this out in a conversation with Ambassador Robert B. Oakley and the author on March 6, 1998, in Stockholm.

[3] The Congo operation was the major exception.

[4] John Hillen, *The Blue Helmets: The Strategy of UN Military Operations* (Washington, DC: Brassey's, 1998).

[5] The United States is presently responsible for funding 30.7 percent of each peace operation, and the costs associated with intervening in an internal conflict vastly exceed those involved in a simple monitoring mission between two rival states.

[6] For example, none of the 19 states that had designated standby forces was willing to make them available to the UN when a mission was proposed for Rwanda.

[7] The Haiti mission transitioned from a coalition of the willing, the Multinational Force, to the UN Mission in Haiti.

[8] Dan Smith, *The State of War and Peace Atlas* (Oslo: International Peace Research Institute, 1997), 14.

[9] If units had been formed from individuals drawn from across the Army, the impact on readiness would have been decidedly negative.

[10] The First Armored Division in Bosnia had an advantage in this regard because ranges were available in theater for periodic use by their units.

[11] The rules of engagement would be identical to those for the military force, most likely authorizing use of force to prevent loss of life or serious injury to members of the international community and, if indigenous authorities are unresponsive, innocent local civilians.

[12] If the peace process falters, refugees will be extremely reluctant to return to their homes; private investors assuredly will calculate that the risk to their venture capital outweighs any potential gain; the outcome of future elections could easily be determined more by bullets than by ballots; and resources spent on relief and reconstruction could merely result in a prolongation of the conflict. Transnational criminal organizations, moreover, are prone to seize upon such openings to intimidate or suborn even senior officials and insinuate themselves into positions of influence.

[13] This does not negate the overarching objective of placing the burden of policing on local authorities. Until the dominant sources of political resistance have been quashed, however, it would be unwise to rely totally on a politically motivated police establishment to maintain order.

[14] The controversial decision regarding the status of Brcko was announced in March 1999, and in spite of Serb verbal protests about the outcome, there was no orchestrated campaign of public disturbances.

[15] *Essential functions* are defined as clusters of related activities (political, social, or economic) that must be performed at least at some minimal level to preclude a return to conditions that originally provoked the international intervention.

[16] Where a peace operation is undertaken, the extent to which these essential functions are regenerated will vary. Some may not be addressed at all (with likely implications for achieving a stable outcome). However, all peace operations will address at least some of the areas.

[17] This is consistent with current efforts to develop Annex V of the Standard Operations Plan.

[18] Several have already taken steps to answer this need—for example, the PACOM Center for Excellence and the SOUTHCOM Center for Disaster Management and Humanitarian Assistance.

Chapter 16

Export Controls: A Clash of Imperatives

Charles B. Shotwell

This chapter examines the difficult challenge facing the U.S. Government in a globalizing world: forging sound export control policies for selling or releasing advanced technologies abroad.[1] The purpose of this assessment is not advocacy, but education. It seeks to illuminate the complex issues and trade-offs at stake and to portray the governmental processes by which export control policies are being made. The chapter begins by examining the emergence of the issue in recent years. It then appraises its impact on international security affairs and its implications for U.S. interests and policy. Finally, the chapter offers some observations on how the Federal Government might be able to strengthen its ability to handle the welter of tough export control decisions that doubtless lies ahead as globalization accelerates.

The thesis of this chapter is that in this policy arena, the United States faces a clash of imperatives. The prospect of a dangerous world creates powerful incentives to control the spread of destabilizing technologies that could fall into the hands of rogues or promote damaging weapons proliferation. At the same time, there are compelling reasons for helping allies remain militarily prepared and for using high-technology exports to help promote American economic prosperity and competitiveness in world markets. The United States always acts unilaterally: working closely with other countries often is critically important, and these countries have views of their own. Striking an appropriate policy balance among these sometimes competing concerns is not easy, and it is made harder by a properly democratic process that employs complex bureaucratic and political machinery to make decisions.

This chapter judges that there are no magic formulas for handling the export control challenge: there are neither simple strategic formulas nor equally simple procedural steps for getting the job done far better than it is done now. The tough decisions ahead will have to continue to be handled on a case-by-case basis by the executive branch and the Congress. Improvements can be made, however, in several key areas to bring better strategic guidance, analysis, coherence, and consistency to the export control review process. The bottom line is that this challenge can be handled effectively. If the U.S. Government consistently uses the instruments at its disposal clearly

---

Lieutenant Colonel Charles B. Shotwell, USAF (Ret.), served as a senior military fellow in the Institute for National Strategic Studies at the National Defense University. He was assigned to the Joint Staff and the U.S. Air Force Academy and also held a fellowship at the Fletcher School of Law and Diplomacy at Tufts University.

and acts wisely, it will stand a good chance of both protecting its security and advancing its economic prosperity in the coming years.

Setting the Stage

Globalization challenges the current regime of export controls in many respects. As borders have become more porous, economies more international, and technology/information more transportable, the underlying assumptions of programs to stem the flow of dual-use technologies and commodities come under question. The task facing the United States is to design export control policies that respond to the current era and the years ahead.

Export controls themselves are hardly new. U.S. export controls date back to a 1775 act of the Continental Congress outlawing the export of goods to Great Britain. Subsequent legislation imposing export controls included the Embargo Act, the Trading with the Enemy Act, and the Neutrality Act. The Export Control Act of 1949 gave the Department of Commerce (DOC) primary responsibility to administer and enforce export controls on dual-use commodities and, for the first time, defined three reasons for the imposition of these controls: to preserve national security, to advance foreign policy goals, and to prevent short supply.

During the Nixon-Kissinger era of détente, export controls were relaxed but later were reinvigorated when East-West tensions mounted with the Soviet invasion of Afghanistan. The end of the Cold War shifted focus to economic concerns over national security concerns and to the targeting of so-called rogue states. More recently, the continuing trend toward globalization (together with the post-Cold War defense drawdown) has meant that key industries in the technology sector are more dependent upon international trade for investment capital and overall economic viability. In turn, the military has grown more reliant on technologies from the private sector. These developments have created the framework for shaping export control policies.

Key Phenomena, Dynamics, and Trends

During the Cold War, the Soviet Union and the People's Republic of China and their client states were the focal points of U.S. export control policy. The Coordinating Committee on Multilateral Export Controls (COCOM) was designed to prevent certain commodities and technologies from acquisition and use by the Soviet Union. As a reflection of the Cold War's demise, COCOM was disbanded in 1994. The Wassenaar Arrangement on Export Controls for Conventional Arms and Dual-Use Goods and Technologies was created as a successor regime in 1996, but with Russia and many former Warsaw Pact states as parties rather than adversaries.[2] By its own terms, the arrangement

> has been established in order to contribute to regional and international security and stability, by promoting transparency and greater responsibility in transfers of conventional arms and dual-use goods and technologies, thus preventing destabilizing accumulations. Participating nations will seek, through their national policies, to ensure that transfers of these items do not

> contribute to the development or enhancement of military capabilities which undermine these goals, and are not diverted to support such capabilities.[3]

This is a broad-based multilateral arrangement, focusing on exports of arms and sensitive dual-use equipment and technologies. There are key differences between COCOM and the Wassenaar Arrangement. The latter's policy development is based on the consensus of all 33 members to bar exports as opposed to COCOM, where a single country (often the United States) could veto exports.

In terms of enforcement, however, the Wassenaar Arrangement is weaker than its predecessor was. COCOM had mandated export controls, but Wassenaar relies upon national discretion to implement controls. The Wassenaar Arrangement provides guidance, but it is not binding per se. Despite the arrangement's statement that measures "will not be directed against any state or group of states" and although the targets of the regime are not publicly stated, it is understood that the arrangement aims to control exports to four states: Iran, Iraq, Libya, and North Korea.

Essentially, the Wassenaar Arrangement provides for export controls for items not covered by regimes for weapons of mass destruction (WMD) and missile technology. In addition to controlling exports to four pariah states, it provides guidance regarding the export of arms to Africa and provides a mechanism for the review of export control lists in light of rapid technology developments. Most recently, the arrangement has served as an effective forum for American concerns about exports of high-performance computers and data encryption. Even so, some have argued that the Wassenaar Arrangement would be more effective if it had the discipline of COCOM and had legally binding authority over export controls.

The Wassenaar Arrangement operates in a new international setting vastly different from that of the Cold War. The end of the Cold War brought about a new emphasis on market economies and the promotion of global free trade, as evidenced by the objectives of organizations such as the North American Free Trade Agreement (NAFTA), the European Union (EU), and the World Trade Organization (WTO). The fall of communism also meant a precipitous decrease in the U.S. defense budget, defense industry consolidation, and a frenzied scramble for new markets, including foreign ones, for defense industry products.

The procurement budget of the Department of Defense (DOD) has shrunk to about one-half of what it was in 1990.[4] Following up on efforts begun by the Bush administration, the Clinton administration made efforts to reduce or remove controls as impediments to free trade, reducing the value of restricted goods from $6.1 billion per quarter in 1993 to $2.7 billion per quarter in 1995.[5] Export controls were liberalized for chemicals, software, computers, and telecommunications products.[6] As a result of export liberalization, the number of license cases dropped from a high of 120,000 per year under the Reagan administration to 9,000 in 1996.[7] Nevertheless, a dynamic tension continued between the imperative of enhancing American competitiveness and the imperative of denying certain technologies to potential adversaries. The DOC Bureau of Export Administration (BXA) has made a deliberate effort to publicize its objective to "enhance international competitiveness of American industry by making our export control system more efficient and effective."[8]

Ironically, many defense manufacturers initially opposed the liberalization of exports. The changing nature and consolidation of the defense industry have resulted in a shift in attitude. In 1992, General Dynamics, Martin Marietta, McDonnell Douglas, and Rockwell International all resisted easing government restrictions toward Russia and China, particularly for satellite launchers.[9] Hughes, Loral, and General Electric Aerospace favored easing access to low-cost foreign launchers. By 1995, Lockheed, GE Aerospace, and Martin had merged and developed a joint venture (International Launch Services) to sell launches on Russian boosters.[10] McDonnell Douglas and Rockwell were acquired by Boeing, which had an arrangement to use Ukrainian Zenit boosters for its Sea Launch Venture. Industry attitudes toward the foreign defense industry's access to American technology are also shifting as the shrinking defense market and other globalization trends compel defense firms to look at international partners and mergers. DaimlerChrysler Aerospace (DASA) and the speculated Lockheed Martin-GEC-Marconi merger demonstrate that the internationalization of defense is a key consideration and complication for national technology controls.

At the same time, manufacturers increasingly depend on access to the global economy, and profit margins are often driven by exports. This is particularly true of the aerospace industry.[11] It is also true of semiconductor and machine tool manufacturers.[12] Government contracts no longer drive the industry.

Impact of International Politics and Security Affairs

Studies of export controls show that the experiences for different technologies and commodities vary greatly. A key variant is the *fungibility* of the technology.[13] As time passes, the relative currency of the technology, its relative availability, and, hence, the need to keep it secure (in theory) decrease. Technologies that are considered state of the art one year are not necessarily the most advanced technologies a year later. Fungibility is important not only because a technology can quickly go from state of the art to antique, but also because new technologies are being invented and brought to market very quickly—possibly before a judgment about national security implications can be made. As Holman Jenkins has said, "What was yesterday's supercomputer is today's mass-produced cheapo PC."[14] On the other hand, even old technology may be very useful militarily to potential opponents. Exactly what technology should be controlled often depends upon a case-by-case determination, based upon a careful assessment of what enhanced capabilities will mean for an opponent and whether the opponent is likely to acquire that technology in spite of export controls.

Computers: Processing Speed. In 1994, the United States raised the control level for desktop personal computers from 12.5 million to 500 million theoretical operations per second (MTOPS), freeing about $30 billion in computer exports.[15] Under heavy industry pressure (in 1993, President Clinton had made a pledge to computer executives to liberalize controls), the control level was raised to 710 MTOPS in 1996. The administration, in effect, made the exporter responsible for deciding whether a license was required. The decision was based upon, inter alia, a Stanford University study (commissioned by DOC and DOD) that found these high-performance computers to be already available around the world. A 1998 General Accounting Office (GAO) report (prepared at the behest of the Senate Subcommittee on International Security, Proliferation, and Federal Services) criticized the study as empirically flawed and lacking any national security threat analysis, particularly with regard to military implications for Russia and China.[16] A major concern was that these "supercomputers" can assist in the design of ballistic missiles.[17] The National Defense Authorization Act for Fiscal Year 1998 requires exporters to notify BXA when they intend to export or re-export high-performance computers from 2,000 to 7,000 MTOPS to end users in Tier 3 countries (for example, China, India, or Pakistan).[18]

In January 1999, leading computer industry chief executive officers (CEOs) strongly urged Secretary of Commerce William Daley to loosen controls on computer exports and pressed him to resist Cox Commission recommendations to tighten controls.[19] In July 1999, on the basis of a survey of advances in technology and widespread availability of existing technology, President Clinton raised the export limit to 6,500 MTOPS without an individual license for military end users and up to 12,300 MTOPS for civilian end users.[20] In February 2000, those limits were raised to 12,500 MTOPS for military end users and 20,000 MTOPS for civilian end users.[21] American companies plan to sell chips capable of 5,000 MTOPS by late 2000. Under the Enhanced Proliferation Control Initiative, the administration retains the power to block export of computers at any level where particular end uses or end users pose concerns or risks of nefarious proliferation.

Computers: Data Scrambling/Encryption. Originally, the Wassenaar Arrangement control list covered all encryption, despite the objections of many countries. In November 1998, a new consensus was achieved. At the request of the United States, the Wassenaar group agreed to restrict the export of mass-market encryption software with numerical keys above 64 bits, Data Encryption Standard, in length. The United States has long disallowed the export of "strong encryption" software (currently defined as greater than 56 bits) but was concerned about the lack of controls for foreign exporters.[22] Groups such as the Economic Strategy Institute claim that these export controls will cost the American industry $96 billion over the next 5 years.[23] The United States uses 128-bit encryption to protect financial transactions. The new Wassenaar Arrangement is intended to reduce criticism from the American high-technology industry about the competitive disadvantage placed upon it by unilateral export controls. Nations such as Germany and Finland have opposed any restrictions on the export of encryption software. Nevertheless, even the House National Security Committee (after persuasive classified briefings by the National Security Agency and the Federal Bureau of Investigation) voted 45 to 1 to strengthen, rather than ease, export restrictions on export technology in September 1997.[24]

Computers: Hardware/Components. During the Cold War, almost all semiconductor manufacturing gear and materials were subject to export controls under COCOM. With the end of the Cold War, controls have been loosened and the industry has grown at a phenomenal rate. The so-called Moore's Law (named after Intel Corporation co-founder Gordon Moore) holds that the quantity of information storable on a computer chip doubles every 18 months, while the costs of manufacturing the chip are cut in half. The United States holds about 50 percent of the world market share of semiconductor equipment. Current controls date back to the 1990 COCOM "Core List."

China is emerging as one of the most lucrative markets. One trade association predicts that the market for semiconductors in China will grow to $2 billion by the year 2000.[25] China envies South Korea's and Taiwan's burgeoning chip-manufacturing industries and has targeted this area as a vital industry for its own investment. Export limitations, along with uncertainties and delays in the American export license process, may have played a role in China's selection of Japan's NEC, rather than an American manufacturer, to build a $1-billion semiconductor plant in a joint venture, according to industry sources.[26] The China-NEC agreement will implement a .35-micron line width processing capability. Industry advocates claim that American and Japanese manufacturing capability has proceeded well beyond the .35-micron level.[27] The industry is displeased with the control of the export of cluster tools essential for enhanced manufacture of semiconductors. Its advocates believe that controls on computers have not changed enough from the old COCOM "Core List" days. Flat panel display equipment is another American industry that is having a hard time competing with foreign exporters. IBM recently paid fines for violating export controls for computers. IBM was the top PC vendor in China in 1996, with $382 million in sales.[28] Intel ran into problems with its $198-million flash memory packaging plant in Shanghai because test equipment was limited to not more than 60 megahertz.[29]

Missile Technology. Much U.S. effort has focused on reining in the flow of missile technology from Russia and China to Iran and Iraq. Even so, there has been a lack of consistent will on the part of the United States and other governments to take action against Russia and China for their support of Iranian missile development. In June 1998, Congress passed (but President Clinton vetoed) the Iran Missile Sanctions Act, which would have imposed tough economic sanctions on the Russian government if it did not stop technology transfers to Iran.[30] China claims that its sales to Iran are legal because NP–110 (170-km range) ballistic missile technology is not prohibited under the Missile Technology Control Regime (MTCR).[31] Although technically correct, this stance provides effective cover for transfer of prohibited technology. On July 21, 1998, Iran tested the Shahab-3 missile, which has a range of 800 to 930 miles. Among the accusations investigated by the Cox Commission is that U.S. aerospace firms and satellite makers allowed China to "dramatically shorten the timetable" for developing the DF–31 intercontinental ballistic missile, which will have a range in excess of 4,500 miles (capable of hitting the American Midwest).[32]

Satellites. The Bush administration began and the Clinton administration implemented efforts to transfer authority for export control decisions over commercial satellites from the State Department Munitions Control List to the DOC Control List, shifting not only the departmental authority but also allegedly the balance, in favor of exports.[33] President Clinton overruled Secretary of State Warren Christopher in 1996 when the administration opened up billions of dollars of satellite sales to Chinese companies.[34] The attraction to the private sector was the availability of relatively inexpensive Chinese launch vehicles. Congressional disenchantment with the decision in 1996 can be seen in the October 1998 reversal of administration policy by the return of satellite export control to the State Department. Fears of technology leaks have dampened joint ventures such as the Boeing Sea Launch program (commercial satellite launches) with Russia and Ukraine, where a Russian-born translator (granted asylum in the United States) was caught with computer disks with codes to access the National Aeronautic and Space Administration's highly classified Tracking Data and Relay Satellite System. Both Hughes Electronics and Loral have been investigated for transfers of prohibited satellite technology in connection with the Sea Launch program.[35] On July 27, 1998, the State Department suspended Boeing's technical assistance agreement and most work on the Sea Launch program.[36] In the wake of the Congressional investigation, the administration canceled plans to eliminate U.S. launch quotas for Russian and Chinese boosters.[37]

The Office of the U.S. Trade Representative is responsible for reviewing interagency launch quotas. A current agreement with China allows up to 20 geosynchronous launches through 2001. Industry executives point out that other sources, particularly Europe, where export regulations are less stringent, are available for satellite technology.[38] Hughes Space and Communications Company emphasized that its security personnel always accompany the satellites while in China, in response to criticism that Office of the Secretary of Defense monitors were absent during the launch of Hughes satellites on Chinese Long March boosters in 1994, 1995, and 1996.[39] The 1996 crash of a rocket carrying a Loral satellite allegedly led to Chinese possession of an encrypted circuit board, though some believe the encryption technology was old and widely available anyway.[40] In June 2000, Lockheed Martin Corporation agreed to pay a $13-million fine for selling satellite technology to China in 1994, though the company did not admit guilt.[41]

Recent discussions have focused on making synthetic aperture radar and hyperspectral imaging technology (both used on satellites) available commercially. Although the technology has been used for military purposes, civilian demands for the technology and products thereof have been burgeoning. These types of demands put further pressure on the U.S. bureaucracy to open up exports.

Export controls can have consequences for manufacturers in the face of market demands. The Aerospace Industries Association claims that the shift of commercial satellite licensing from DOC to the State Department cut American export orders by 40 percent over the last year, though total sales exceeded $32.6 billion in 1999.[42]

Other Technology/Commodities. As the private sector has leaped ahead in the development of civilian applications for military technology, commercial demand often contributes to making certain technologies widely available. Night vision goggles were covered by the Munitions List yet were available through L.L. Bean. Global positioning system (GPS) technology is also commercially available, with more than 250,000 GPS receivers being sold each month.[43] Localized satellite imagery is available over the Internet. In the area of manufacturing, the export of machine tools is of much concern, particularly those that assist in perfecting the manufacture of nuclear weapons casings and advanced artillery. Other current areas of concern are wafers (for computer chips) and jet engine hot technology.

According to DOD, only about 0.5 percent of all American exports require an export license, and those items lie mainly in the high-technology sector. Most exports go to friendly, industrial nations. Only 2 to 3 percent of license requests are denied.

The recipient nations of concern, although not stated in official communications, are Iran, Iraq, Libya, and North Korea. The Cox Commission report turned the focus toward China and Russia. This tried to reverse a trend begun with the Bush administration to "decontrol" sensitive military technology, particularly for China. The Clinton administration continued and greatly expanded the effort in this area.

Implications for U.S. Interests, Strategies, Policies, and Goals

The onset of a new era in international affairs, influenced by globalization's dynamics, means that the task of designing sound export control policies is becoming more complicated and thornier by the day. It also has become both political and administrative in nature, in a setting where difficult tradeoffs must be balanced in a large number of controversial cases. President Clinton personally promised to sell Boeing Apache attack helicopters to Singapore in 1999; however, when Singaporean officials attempted to consummate the sale, American officials repeatedly denied export requests until there was high-level executive intervention.[44] Clearly, the unrestricted export of certain commodities and technologies is contrary to U.S. national security interests when it provides enhanced military capabilities for potential adversaries.[45] It now appears, however, that certain export policies hurt relations (and interoperability) with friends and allies. Furthermore, the long-term effect of inappropriate export controls in competitive industries (such as semiconductors) may actually hurt U.S national security more than the target state.[46]

During the Cold War, export controls were used to maintain a qualitative advantage for the United States and its allies against the Warsaw Pact and the People's Republic of China.[47] Historically, other objectives for export controls have included support for mercantilist policies, "starvation" of adversaries, and prevention of domestic scarcity.[48] In addition to the prevention of adversarial access to enhanced military capabilities generally, current controls are maintained for purposes of nuclear nonproliferation under the Nuclear Nonproliferation Act of 1978, which implements provisions of the Nuclear Nonproliferation Treaty. But the globalization of national economies has changed the dynamics by making key industries dependent upon exports for their economic vitality.

Current Export Controls Framework

The primary authorizing legislation for many years was the Export Administration Act of 1979, as amended by subsequent acts, and currently implemented by authority of Executive Order (EO) 12924 in 1994. Congress allowed the act to lapse in 1994, and President Clinton continued administration of the export control system by EO 12924 under the International Emergency Economic Powers Act. In addition, the United States is party to a number of international export control regimes, including the Wassenaar Arrangement, the MTCR, the Australia Group, and the Nuclear Suppliers Group. The United States also is party to the Nuclear Nonproliferation Treaty, the Biological and Toxicological Weapons Convention, and the Chemical Weapons Convention, which contain limitations on export of certain commodities and technologies.

Current agreements and regimes restrict the export of certain items and technology through the required use of export licenses. Commodity jurisdiction is divided between DOC and State Department. These two agencies administer critical lists. The BXA (under DOC) controls dual-use commodities and technical data exported from the United States and its territories and possessions or re-exported to foreign countries. The Commerce Control List (CCL) identifies commodities and technologies that were created (or were designed and developed) for civilian purposes but can have military applicability. Maintaining the CCL creates an institutional challenge for the BXA, since DOC is charged with the promotion of commerce and may be viewed as unofficially representing the interests of industry. DOC interfaces with international institutions, too, such as the Wassenaar Arrangement. The Wassenaar Arrangement Dual-Use List is incorporated into the CCL.

The State Department's Political-Military Affairs Bureau administers the U.S. Munitions List, which ostensibly identifies technology designed primarily for military purposes (unless exclusively controlled by other agencies). In reality, some dual-use items (communications satellites and encryption software) have appeared on the Munitions List.[49] The Munitions List identifies registered munitions manufacturers and provides generalized descriptions of controlled items. Certain commodities have been moved from the Munitions List to the CCL.

In 1996, as a result of high-level executive branch intervention, satellites and certain encryption items were transferred from the Munitions List to the CCL. Congress intervened in October 1998 to move satellites back to the Munitions List as a result of the Cox Commission investigation into divulgence of advanced technical data to China.[50] New regulations provide DOC with a voice, but not a vote, in the process.[51] In addition to DOC, the Departments of Energy and Transportation, along with the U.S. Trade Representative, have an advisory role in the process. A new goal was set for the State Department to complete the review process for satellite export applications within 90 days of submission.[52]

In addition to the State Department Munitions List, DOD maintains the Military Critical Technologies List (MCTL), which originated in 1981. The list was previously maintained by the Office of the Secretary of Defense, Office of Acquisition and Technology (Defense Technical Security Administration [DTSA]), but was assumed by the newly formed Defense Threat Reduction Agency (DTRA) in October 1998. DTSA, along with the On-Site Inspection Agency and the Defense Special Weapons Agency, now reports to DTRA. The MCTL is intended for U.S. Government guidance but is not binding in any form and does not automatically subject items to export controls. Current areas of concern from the DOD perspective are communication satellites, machine tools, and high-performance computers. Most machine tools are not controlled. Other machine tools are listed on the CCL. Machine tools are critically advantageous as they guide the cutting and shaping of metal and produce complex, geometric shapes and components. This technology is critical in the production of aircraft with Stealth attributes and the manufacture of nuclear weapons.

The Interagency Process: Help or Hindrance?

The interagency process has become the epicenter for contentious cases. DOC has the charter to administer and enforce export controls on all CCL dual-use technology, while the State Department oversees munitions and defense trade exports. The lead agencies participating in the review process are the State Department; the Arms Control and Disarmament Agency (ACDA), which was incorporated into the State Department effective March 1999; DOC; DOD; and the Department of Energy (DOE). The principal agencies for the licensing referral process are DOD for national security items, DOE for nuclear nonproliferation-controlled items, and the State Department for chemical, biological, and missile-related nonproliferation-controlled items. The Nuclear Regulatory Commission oversees reactor materials, whereas DOE focuses on technologies. Based on EO 12981, issued in 1995, the scope of the interagency review has been broadened. The State Department, ACDA, DOE, and DOD are notified of pending export licenses and have the authority to review any license application submitted to DOC and must justify applications they will not review (for example, because of not having pertinent expertise and not being related to designated mission). Other government agencies, including intelligence agencies, may also be requested to participate in the review process.

The National Security Council (NSC) has a coordinating role in the interagency export controls policy process, particularly regarding appeals. The Interagency Working Group for Nonproliferation originally encompassed export controls, but now export control policy is headed by the State Department. The NSC also works with the President's Export Council and leads a working group composed primarily of engineers from private industry.

In contrast to dual-use items on the CCL, exports of defense articles on the Munitions List are more tightly controlled by the State Department and the Department of Defense.[53] Because of their predominantly military nature, many of these items are sold under Foreign Military Sales programs or as authorized Direct Commercial Sales and are subject to close scrutiny by regulatory agencies such as the Defense Security Assistance Agency. More often than not, foreign militaries are the recipient of these items pursuant to bilateral agreements with the foreign government. In Munitions List cases, agencies other than the State Department or DOD play merely advisory roles and do not have a vote in the process.

There is a rough balance of views in the interagency process. In some ways, the contentious nature of the process is a good thing because it allows a full debate of views at the upper levels. The dynamic balance of the interagency process, however, can be skewed when the White House or Congress intervenes for its respective purposes. Congress has intervened on satellite sales and technology transfers to China. The White House, in turn, has criticized legislation like the Helms-Burton Act and the "new propensity for the Congress to take a direct hand in the direction and conduct of foreign policy vis-à-vis unacceptable behaviors of Third-World countries by utilizing unilateral economic sanctions in a much more prescriptive manner."[54] The reality is that the process for reviewing export controls has become bureaucratized and politicized. The challenge is to manage this complex process so that it produces wise decisions.

Cooperation with Allies

Allies have openly complained that American export controls have impeded defense cooperation and contributed to the so-called technology/capabilities gap between the United States and its allies. Something as simple as obtaining an export license to sell a tank clutch to the United Kingdom took an average of 89 days last year.[55] If a U.S.-supplied part broke, it required another set of licenses to return the part to the United States and to re-export the repaired part back. Export controls were a significant factor in the UK decision to buy a European-built missile to arm the Eurofighter.[56]

On December 16, 1999, Dutch Ambassador Joris Vos wrote a letter to Secretary Albright (signed by senior diplomats from 16 other states) criticizing U.S. export controls as "a serious impediment to defense cooperation."[57] This came on the heels of a request from Manfred Bischoff, president and CEO of Germany's DASA, to Secretary Albright to streamline export procedures and his company's decision to look for alternate sources for American-made components. The particular problem for DASA was satellite components. During the March–June 1999 intervention in Kosovo, U.S. export controls prevented allies from having sufficient numbers of precision-guided munitions. Ironically, in April 1999, at the 50th-anniversary NATO summit in Washington, the United States announced the Defense Capabilities Initiative to bridge the gap between U.S. and allied technology and capabilities. As Bischoff pointed out, transatlantic defense cooperation is difficult when technical assistance agreements require months (100 days on average) to process.

More recently, the administration has taken steps to loosen export controls for NATO members and close allies such as Australia and Japan.[58] This Defense Trade Security Initiative (DTSI) was officially announced at the May 24, 2000, NATO Ministerial in Florence, Italy. The measures include 17 improvements to the export controls system, including speeding up the processing of license applications (to about 10 days for allies), extending program licensing from 4 to 8 years, streamlining authorizations for technology transfer, revising the U.S. Munitions List, and permitting American firms to export certain technical data in support of DOD bid proposals without a license.[59] Also proposed is a $30 million computer link between the Departments of Defense, State, and Commerce, an action that will require the approval of and funding from Congress.

Cooperative development and production programs have suffered because of restrictive American export policies and unilateralist tendencies. In recent decades, the NATO Sea Sparrow and Rolling Airframe Missile programs have been among the few successes in cooperative efforts. Often joint and international programs, such as the Medium Extended Air Defense System with Italy and Germany, suffer because of service and Congressional support for single-service programs or U.S.-only programs. The U.S.-UK Joint Strike Fighter and Tracer Scout Vehicle programs are becoming victims to similar interests in the Pentagon and on Capitol Hill.[60] Though support of these programs is as much a question of funding as of export controls, the resistance to cooperation with allies is sired by the same unilateralist orientation. Nevertheless, DTSI has moved in the right direction by paving the way for a pending joint venture between Raytheon and France's Thomson CSF.[61] DTSI provides for blanket license approvals for major collaborative projects.

Are Current Regimes Effective?

Multilateral regimes can be more effective than unilateral regimes for obvious reasons. The number of participants, however, is not the sole critical factor. Effectiveness of regimes is dependent on careful selection of commodities appropriate for restrictions, participation of key producer nations, and adherence to agreed-upon restrictions by participating nations. The participants need only be a select group if they are the sole and leading producers of a particular commodity, whereas a more common technology requires a far greater partnership. In the latter case, it is necessary to encompass a greater range of technical knowledge and production and to uniformly enforce an agreed-upon common set of export controls. In some cases, bilateral regimes may be appropriate. Bilateral regimes may effectively supplement multilateral regimes with enforceable standards, such as agreements made with Hong Kong under the Wassenaar Arrangement. Bilateral agreements may better assist newly formed nations such as Kazakhstan in developing their export control policies.

Unilateral export controls and sanctions are contentious and usually ineffective.[62] They can be effective only if the nation that applies them is the sole producer and owner of the commodity or technology or otherwise substantially controls its availability. The United States has historically applied unilateral sanctions more than have other nations.[63] As was the case with the U.S. embargo of wheat to the Soviet Union in 1979, unilateral sanctions often result in the target nation seeking supplies elsewhere, resulting in long-term loss of markets for American producers. The Aerospace Industries Association recommends that unilateral U.S. export controls be limited to those technologies that are exclusively available from the United States.[64] Oftentimes, in spite of the futility of such measures, unilateral controls are used by policymakers to emphasize national and political "resolve." Despite the purported symbolic value, unilateral actions have historically had little impact, especially on nations whose economy or national security is hardly linked to the United States. More effective measures have resulted from the exercise of American leadership to forge multilateral sanctions targeting the most dangerous behaviors.[65] Ultimately, export controls cannot forever hinder nations from developing alternative technologies if other exporters are willing to provide them.

In addition to the question of effectiveness of unilateral controls is the issue of the impact of these controls on American exporters. As was the case with the wheat embargo of the Soviet Union, foreign competitors benefit from new markets. Investment capital, in turn, can lead to increased competitive strength, particularly for high-technology industries. That loss of investment capital can have serious implications for industries with long lead times and high infrastructure costs, such as the aerospace industry.[66] The interdependence of national security policy, foreign policy, and economic interests in a global context underscores the importance of multilateral agreements, particularly in light of the diminishing role of the United States as a sole provider for many technologies and commodities.

Security Implications

A 1984 Reagan administration study recommended loosening controls against China to balance the Soviet threat. More recently, at least one participant in the study, Paul Wolfowitz (Under Secretary for Defense Policy in the Bush administration) recommended tightening controls against China because of its export of missile technology to Iran and Pakistan, as well as its emergence as a "strategic competitor and potential threat to the U.S. and its allies in the first half of the next century."[67] By 1995, approximately $1.9 billion in sales to China had been removed from Federal regulation. This removed the requirement for export licenses for many categories of sales and resulted in the absence of any record of sales for many dual-use items.

In October 1998, Congress created a senior Pentagon position for technology security after concluding that the DOD role in controlling exports had been "significantly and improperly reduced over the years."[68] In July 1998, the Rumsfeld Commission reported that looser controls and lax enforcement increased the possibility that rogue states such as Iran or North Korea would build missiles that could hit the United States as a result of exports from China. In the words of the report:

> Trends in the commercial sector of a market-driven, global economy have been accompanied, and in many ways accelerated, by an increased availability of classified information as a result of:
>
> - Lax enforcement of export controls.
> - Relaxation of U.S. and Western export controls.
> - Growth in dual-use technologies.
> - Economic incentives to sell ballistic missile components and systems.
> - Extensive declassification of materials related to ballistic missiles and weapons of mass destruction.
> - Continued, intense espionage facilitated by security measures increasingly inadequate for the new environment.
> - Extensive disclosure of classified information, including information compromising intelligence sources and methods. Damaging information appears almost daily in the national and international media and on the Internet.[69]

A key concern is keeping high-technology industries economically viable. Former Secretary of Defense William Perry believed loosening export controls on computers actually helped DOD by keeping the industry healthy, with profits providing incentives to develop more powerful machines. For example, an item essential for the manufacture of advanced microprocessors ("steppers") is banned from export to China, although Japan is able to export to China without limitation. Japan's three stepper manufacturers (NEC, Nikon, and Canon) are flourishing, while the sole American manufacturer languishes. Industry representatives believe that the United States is in danger of losing its only indigenous manufacturing capability.[70] The substantial startup costs for this capability (approximately $8 billion) are such that government subsidies are not likely, and revenues without the benefits of exports will not sustain the enterprise. Similar experiences are occurring for products such as high-purity silicon wafers and ceramic packages, contained in components for U.S. Patriot, HARM, Tomahawk, Sidewinder, AMRAAM, Maverick, Sparrow, TOW, and Trident missiles, as well as for the Aegis and F–18 radar systems, B–2, B–52, Comanche helicopter, F–14, and M1–A1.[71] Overall, the American semiconductor industry claims that 40 percent of revenues come from exports. The aerospace industry attributes 31 percent of recent sales to exports, up 7 percent from 1989.[72]

Industry representatives state that to be effective, export controls should be

- Applied on a multilateral basis.
- Applied only to controllable and chokepoint products and technologies.
- Responsive to continual changes in technology and its availability.
- Implemented with regularized analyses of the impact of controls, taking full account of economic, competitive, and technology-related interests.[73]

In December 1999, the Defense Science Board Task Force on Globalization and Security released its report:

> The reality is that the U.S. capability to effectively deny its competitors access to militarily useful technology will likely decrease substantially over the long term . . . the utility of export controls as a tool for maintaining the U.S. global advantage is diminishing as the number of U.S.-controllable militarily useful technologies shrink. . . . Equally obvious, shutting U.S. companies out of markets served by foreign firms will weaken the U.S. commercial advanced technology and defense sectors upon which U.S. economic security and military-technical advantage depend.

Globalization has altered DOD dependence upon heavily subsidized, single-customer-oriented industries. Once relying upon government contracts, telecommunications firms now have vast private sector markets and are dependent upon these markets for investment/research capital. National security is intrinsically linked to the health of industries such as these. Nevertheless, denying dangerous technologies to rogues remains a valid concern.

Key Recommendations

Has globalization pitted the imperative of free trade against the imperative of national security? A close examination of the debate reveals that simple choices and solutions do not exist on the subject of export controls. The dilemma is not simply one of choosing between Adam Smith's and David Ricardo's ideals of free trade on the one hand and protection of militarily significant technologies on the other. Instead, it is one of degrees of restraints on trade or identification of critical chokepoints for particularized technologies and commodities based on cogent threat analysis. Nor are advocates for export control reform discretely divided along political or ideological lines. Industry comments that strangling of foreign export revenues endangers national security must be taken seriously but not be allowed to rule the roost when genuine national security interests are at stake. The commercial viability of the high-technology sector is a substantial part of national security because it promotes American technological competitiveness and self-sufficiency for key defense products. This is even more critical when American industries must compete with European and Asian industries receiving heavy state subsidies. This does not mean that the United States should adapt a similar national industrial policy approach, but rather that it should make an effort to level the playing field for American companies.

The interagency process provides a roughly balanced, albeit contentious, way to explore, determine policy, and implement export controls for dual-use items. To a degree, DOC represents industry, the State Department represents foreign policy interests, DOD represents national security concerns, and DOE represents a nuclear-centered policy viewpoint. The intelligence community participates in the process by providing data but does not function as a decisionmaker. The rough institutional balance of views can be influenced by the intervention of "external elements," such as the White House or Congress, whose agendas may steer export controls in one direction or another. In essence, this is the pluralist process of democracy at work, with both its positive and negative features.

Specific Policy Actions

The following actions are among those that can be considered in developing future policies.

Define the Mission. Establish a broad mission statement for export control policy that can serve as strategic guidance on specific goals, criteria, and policies. This document, perhaps incorporated in a Presidential Decision Directive, would recognize national security interests and the goal of preserving a robust and competitive American technology sector while preventing, as well as controlling, security-relevant technology transfers to certain entities when realistically possible. This policy document should recognize new post-Cold War realities: the change in the threat environment, trends toward globalization in business and security, and the Information Revolution that is driving commercially developed technologies faster than defense-developed technologies.

Define the Threat. A major problem is the failure to clearly define the threat or, put another way, to identify the specific states (or even nonstate entities) that may adversely affect U.S. national security. Although the Wassenaar Arrangement is vague in written form, it is generally understood that Iran, Iraq, North Korea, and Libya are the target countries of this agreement. The United States does not have a consensus with its allies over the threat posed from other states, particularly China. U.S. policy itself is ambivalent toward China, sometimes treating it as a partner, sometimes as a potential rival, and with no clear and consistent guidance for export control reviewers and enforcers. The European states and Japan recognize the vast market for high-technology goods that China offers. Is China a threat? In what ways should it be so treated? Consideration must also be given to sharing technology more equitably with U.S. allies and to cooperative development and production of new technology. Despite the recent initiatives, U.S. policy still does not allow many technological secrets to be shared with its allies.

Identify Critical Technologies. Some areas, such as cluster tools (improving the manufacture of wafers), lack sufficient nexus to strategically sensitive products. Conversely, export limitations may provide less control for the United States by denying intelligence (on importer capabilities) that may otherwise be unavailable and inaccessible. Although DOD-maintained MCTL does not necessarily feed into the Munitions List, a review of critical technologies requires significant consideration of this register. Efforts in this arena can ensure that criteria to identify critical technologies take into account all qualifying factors, such as international availability over time, availability of different technologies with comparable military capabilities, and the potential for third-party transfer and subsequent controls.

Develop Better Criteria to Delineate Military/Civilian End-use Technology. Because of rapid advances in many technologies, more specific and distinct criteria are needed to determine the current and future purposes of a technology and the time at which that technology may need to shift between critical lists (Munitions List and CCL) and controls.

Determine Critical Chokepoints for Technology. By focusing on certain technologies beyond which nations cannot develop adverse military capabilities, export controls can gain maximum effect for the effort. Chokepoints have worked well in the nuclear fields, where the technology is more than 50 years old, and in access to weapons-grade materials that are key to developing a weapon system. Chemical and biological technology chokepoints are far more difficult to define because some materials are used for routine purposes (for example, plant fertilizer).

Optimize Interagency Process. The competitive and dynamic current interagency process and its key participants should be maintained; however, a review should be undertaken regarding whether economic and intelligence information should be a required consideration for all participants and, if so, when such a review should be inserted into the review process. Also, GAO should examine the effects of legislative and executive interventions, which differ from the agencies' agreed-upon export controls decisions. The review might also look at ways to balance the licensing process, within and between agencies, so that lengthy appeals and resulting delays do not hurt American competitiveness.

Maximize a Consensus through International Forums. The lack of support by other nations for export control undermines U.S. controls and hurts U.S. industry. The latter and the Federal Government are in agreement regarding the clear-cut advantages of multilateral agreements and the near futility of unilateral ones. Greater priority should be given to achieving multilateral cooperation for export controls. Bilateral cooperation should be regarded as a base for multinational initiatives, not an end in itself. This could be proposed early in the bilateral negotiations.

Conclusion

The problem of developing sound export control policies is here to stay, and globalization is magnifying the troubles posed by it. This policy arena is a classic case where multiple objectives are at stake. These objectives are incommensurable in the sense that they are hard to evaluate in relation to each other and that they sometimes clash. Moreover, the task of analyzing policy options often is clouded by major uncertainties about the consequences of releasing advanced technologies abroad or of denying their release. These features make for a policy arena of thorny bushes—one that invites strong debates and bars the way to easy consensus building.

A sense of caution is necessary for the simple but powerful reason that the world remains a dangerous place whose turbulence is being intensified by proliferation of advanced military technologies, both nuclear and conventional. The United States clearly has a valid interest in stemming proliferation of destabilizing technologies to rogues and other countries prone to irresponsible conduct. Just as clearly, the United States has a valid interest in helping its allies remain militarily strong and in using high-technology exports to advance its own economic prosperity and competitiveness in global markets. The continuing challenge will be to strike a sensible balance among these disparate concerns.

Strong and clear policy guidance from the White House and Congress can help; however, because no simple policy formula can provide concrete guidance for all choices, decisions will have to be made on a case-by-case basis. These decisions will be made via a democratic process of pluralism that is both bureaucratized and often politicized. The continuing challenge will be to use this process in ways that lead to thorough analysis, a careful weighing of the tradeoffs, and wise decisions as often as possible. Perfection will be hard to achieve; however, if the United States succeeds in acting sensibly most of the time, it will enhance its prospects for having its cake and eating it, too (that is, promoting both security and prosperity).

Notes

[1] This chapter is based in part upon a study for the Institute for National Strategic Studies (INSS) conducted by Diana Kowitz and Charles B. Shotwell entitled "Export Controls: Balancing the Imperatives of National Security and Free Trade," written in February 1999.

[2] Members are Argentina, Australia, Austria, Belgium, Bulgaria, Canada, the Czech Republic, Denmark, Finland, France, Germany, Greece, Hungary, Ireland, Italy, Japan, Luxembourg, the Netherlands, New Zealand, Norway, Poland, Portugal, the Republic of Korea, Romania, Russia, Slovakia, Spain, Sweden, Switzerland, Turkey, Ukraine, the United Kingdom, and the United States.

[3] As adopted in plenary session, July 11–12, 1996.

[4] Michael Hirsh, "The Great Technology Giveaway? Trading with Potential Foes," *Foreign Affairs* (September/October 1998), 3.

[5] U.S. Department of Commerce, *Export Administration Annual Report of 1995*, 1–2.

[6] Many key appointees in the early Clinton administration, such as William Perry, John Deutch, and Ron Brown, favored liberalization of exports.

[7] Hirsh, "The Great Technology Giveaway? Trading with Potential Foes," 7.

[8] Secretary of Commerce Ron Brown, statement in Introduction to *Export Administration Annual Report of 1995.*

[9] Joseph C. Anselmo, "Industry Impacts U.S. Space Policy," *Aviation Week and Space Technology* (July 6, 1998), 34.

[10] Anselmo, "Industry Impacts U.S. Space Policy," 34.

[11] "Export Control Reform Ranks as Top AIA Issue for 2000," *Defense Daily*, February 2, 2000.

[12] William A. Reinsch, Keynote address to UpDate West Conference, February 9, 1999, 3.

[13] Hirsh, "The Great Technology Giveaway? Trading with Potential Foes," 6.

[14] Holman W. Jenkins, Jr., "Business World: High-Tech Noose Merchants?" *The Wall Street Journal,* January 20, 1999.

[15] U.S. Department of Commerce, *Export Administration Annual Report of 1995* and *1996 Report on Foreign Policy Export Controls*, 1–2.

[16] Jeff Gerth, "U.S. Agency Faults Study on Exports of Computers," *The New York Times*, September 17, 1998.

[17] Rodger Doyle, "By the Numbers: The Arms Trade," *Scientific American* (July 1998), 29.

[18] U.S. Department of Commerce, *Export Administration: Annual Report of 1997* and *1998 Report on Foreign Policy Export Controls*, III-3.

[19] Peter H. Stone, "A Clash Over Export Curbs," *National Journal* (January 23, 1999), 2.

[20] The White House, Office of the Press Secretary, press release, February 2, 2000.

[21] Ibid.

[22] John Markoff, "International Group Reaches Agreement on Data-Scrambling Software," *The New York Times*, December 4, 1998; Laura Wonnacott, "There are Exceptions of Encryption Export Controls That Can Stymie Your Business," *Infoworld* (January 1998), 2.

[23] Jeri Clausing, "Study Puts Price on Encryption Controls," *The New York Times*, April 1, 1998.

[24] Jeri Clausing, "House Panel Votes to Strengthen Export Controls on Encryption," *The New York Times*, September 10, 1997.

[25] "SEMI Export Control Proposal for Category 3-Wassenaar List Review," *Semiconductor Equipment and Materials International* (December 21, 1998), 2.

[26] Ibid., 3.

[27] Ibid., 7.

[28] Drew Wilson, "In for the Long Haul: Foreign Electronics Investors in China Look to the Future," *Electronic Business Asia* (February 1998), 25.

[29] Ibid., 24.

[30] Kenneth R. Timmerman, "Long Beach Missile Transfers," *The American Spectator* (September 1998), 48.

[31] Ibid., 49.

[32] Ibid.

[33] Laura D'Andrea Tyson, "Washington Can't Keep High Tech to Itself, So Why Try?" *Business Week* (July 6, 1998), 18.

[34] Jeff Gerth and Eric Schmitt, "Chinese Said to Reap Gains in U.S. Export Policy Shift," *The New York Times,* October 19, 1998.

[35] Timmerman, "Long Beach Missile Transfers," 49.

[36] Joseph C. Anselmo, "U.S. Reviews Plan to Lift Sea Launch Suspension," *Aviation Week and Space Technology* (August 17, 1998), 31.

[37] Anselmo, "Industry Impacts U.S. Space Policy," 34.

[38] Ibid.

[39] Joseph C. Anselmo, "Hughes Defends China Security," *Aviation Week and Space Technology* (July 6, 1998), 35.

[40] Hirsh, "The Great Technology Giveaway? Trading with Potential Foes," 6.

[41] Justin Brown, "Weapons Exports Will Get Less Scrutiny," *Christian Science Monitor*, June 16, 2000, 2.

[42] "Export Control Reform," 2.

[43] Hirsh, "The Great Technology Giveaway? Trading with Potential Foes."

[44] Vago Muradian, "New U.S. Export Policy to be Unveiled in June at NATO Summit," *Defense Daily*, March 27, 2000, 2.

[45] Cecil Hunt, "Overview of Export Controls," in *Coping with U.S. Export Controls 1998* (New York: Practicing Law Institute, 1998), 52.

[46] Reinsch, speech, 2.

[47] Hunt, "Overview of Export Controls," 52.

[48] Ibid., 43.

[49] Ibid., 47.

[50] This legislation was part of the National Defense Authorization Act for Fiscal Year 1999, October 5, 1998.

[51] Jeff Gerth, "State Department Has Final Say on Exports of Satellites," *The New York Times*, January 22, 1999, 1.

[52] Ibid.

[53] See the Arms Export Control Act, the Foreign Assistance Act (as amended), and the International Trafficking in Arms Regulations.

[54] The President's Export Council, *Unilateral Economic Sanctions: A Review of Existing Sanctions and Their Impacts on U.S. Economic Interests with Recommendations for Policy and Process Improvement* (Washington, DC: Government Printing Office, June 10, 1997), 1.

[55] Greg Schneider, "U.S. Will Relax Arms-Sale Curbs to Gain Greater Access," *The Washington Post*, May 24, 2000.

[56] "Cautious Kudos for Reform of U.S. Export Controls," *Aviation Week and Space Technology* (May 29, 2000), 66.

[57] Vago Muradian, "Allies Call on Albright to Reform Export Controls," *Defense Daily*, January 6, 2000.

[58] Vago Muradian, "New U.S. Export Policy to be Unveiled in June at NATO Summit," *Defense Daily*, March 27, 2000.

[59] "Defense Trade Security Initiative Announced," *Defense Daily*, May 25, 2000.

[60] Vago Muradian, "Officials: Export Control Reforms Signal New U.S. Government Stance on Cooperation," *Defense Daily*, June 1, 2000.

[61] Muradian, "New U.S. Government Stance on Cooperation."

[62] Tyson, "Washington Can't Keep High Tech to Itself," 18.

[63] The President's Export Council, *Unilateral Economic Sanctions*, 1.

[64] "Update U.S. Technology Export Controls," *Aviation Week and Space Technology* (April 10, 2000).

[65] Ibid., 2.

[66] The President's Export Council, *Unilateral Economic Sanctions*, 10.

[67] Jeff Gerth and Eric Schmitt, "Chinese Said to Reap Gains in U.S. Export Policy Shift," *The New York Times,* October 19, 1998.

[68] Ibid.

[69] *Commission to Assess the Ballistic Missile Threat to the United States*, Executive Summary (Washington, DC: Government Printing Office, July 15, 1998), 19–20.

[70] Interview with American Electronics Association, January 8, 1999.

[71] Undated AEA Japan Office leaflet, quoting U.S. Department of Commerce, "The Effect of Imports of Ceramic Semiconductor Packages on the National Security," August 1993.

[72] Brown, "Weapons Exports Will Get Less Scrutiny," 2.

[73] American Electronics Association, "AEA Principles for an Effective Export Controls Policy," undated.

PART III.
MILITARY POWER: THE CHALLENGES AHEAD

Chapter 17

Future U.S. Defense Strategy

Richard L. Kugler

What implications do globalization and its strategic consequences pose for U.S. defense policy and strategy? While the answer is complex in its particulars, it is simple in its basics. As globalization gains steam and interacts with other trends to alter security affairs in many places, U.S. defense planning likely will be affected in important ways. Not surprisingly, a changing world means that U.S. military affairs must change as well. These changes will affect U.S. forces, operations, and relations with allies and partners.

Dynamics of Change

Things will not be transformed overnight, but a decade from now, U.S. defense planning may be carried out in ways that differ from those of today in important ways. The task facing the United States is to anticipate these changes and pursue them wisely, not to make them at the last minute in a clumsy rush. This approach is the best way to ensure that U.S. forces not only retain their supremacy over opponents but also continue to support U.S. foreign policy and national security strategy in effective ways. What will remain constant is that defense planning must be guided by a keen sense of national interests and strategic priorities. Using diplomacy and economic aid to achieve overseas goals is one thing. Applying security commitments and military power in new ways is something entirely different.

Threefold Changes Ahead

U.S. defense policy and strategy should be anchored in strategic fundamentals, not in surface events and fleeting newspaper headlines. This chapter's thesis of impending changes to U.S. and allied defense plans rests on three key judgments about fundamentals. To a degree, they already apply today, and they will gain force in the medium term of 5 to 10 years as well as in the more distant future:

Richard L. Kugler is a distinguished research professor in the Institute for National Strategic Studies at the National Defense University. He formerly was a research leader at RAND and a senior executive in the Department of Defense. Dr. Kugler is the author of many books and studies including Commitment to Purpose: How Alliance Partnership Won the Cold War.

- Owing to globalization and other dynamics, the democratic community likely will make further progress, but major parts of the outlying world will continue to face turmoil, not only in politics and economics but also in security affairs. This especially is the case along the "southern belt," from the Balkans to Asia. There and elsewhere, tomorrow's opportunities, dangers, and threats often will be quite different from today's.
- As a result, U.S. national security strategy will be changing, and U.S. forces often will be required to perform different strategic missions than they do today. Moreover, some of these missions will occur at new places well removed from the bases and alliances inherited from the Cold War. This will be the case not only in crises and wars but also in peacetime, during which shaping the strategic environment will loom as an increasingly important and challenging mission.
- U.S. forces will themselves be changing, in response to new doctrines and structures, and to new information systems, weapons, and munitions. A decade or so from now, U.S. forces will operate much like Michael Jordan played basketball: at high speed and above the rim. The challenge will be to design and employ these ultrasophisticated forces so that they effectively perform not only their battlefield missions but also their new political and strategic missions.

Initial changes in all three areas are already altering the strategic framework for determining strategy, forces, programs, and budgets. As these changes intensify, they will put added strain on U.S. defense preparedness efforts—not only by elevating requirements to some degree but also by necessitating new approaches to using current resources. The task of pursuing new strategic purposes and priorities is difficult in itself. Equally difficult is creating new forces. Doing both will be even harder.

Because the world is changing rapidly, U.S. defense policy needs to be guided by a responsive sense of direction and purpose. For past several years, defense planning, that is, preparing strategy and forces, as opposed to actually using military power in crises, has been humming along quietly outside the glare of public debate. It has been operating on assumptions made shortly after the Cold War ended, making changes and improvements mostly at the margins. This tranquil setting is coming to an end. It is being supplanted by a growing need for deep thinking and creativity—in ways leading to a new strategic mentality. The future can best be addressed by mastering the coming period of change, not by clinging to the status quo.

Gauging Future Strategic Directions

This chapter's aim is to help illuminate the defense agenda ahead. It asserts that the United States can best shape future defense plans, old or new, by answering three key questions in ways that produce an integrated response:

- How should the United States appraise trends in geographical regions and strategic missions, and how should it craft national security policy and defense strategy in response to these trends?

- What planning standards should the United States use to size its military forces in order to support its strategy, and how should it go about improving those forces?
- How should the United States plan to employ its forces in peace, crisis, and war—in concert with its friends and allies?

This chapter's bottom line is that the United States will continue to need strong military forces not only to win wars and intervene in crises but also to help shape the strategic environment in peacetime. In providing insights in ways that analyze, not advocate, this chapter puts forth concrete ideas for how to act, so that effective strategies, plans, and forces are produced. These ideas should be evaluated carefully before being adopted. What matters most is their basic message. The United States has a viable option other than clinging to the status quo, retrenching from world affairs because it feels overloaded, or vastly increasing its defense resources in order to stay engaged. *Instead, it can stay heavily and fruitfully involved by using available resources wisely and by making sensible changes in its defense practices. The same applies to allies and partners. If all participants take these steps, they will stand a good chance of making a strategic success out of the coming decade.*

Toward New Strategy and Missions in Endangered Regions

Assessing future directions in U.S. defense plans begins by analyzing where geostrategic affairs, including the geography of coming dangers and conflicts, seem headed. Owing to globalization and other dynamics, the widening division of the world into two parts clearly has general implications for U.S. plans. With the democratic community progressing toward greater peace and strength, it will be freed to devote less worry to defending its borders in multiple places against direct attack by big conventional forces. Because the outlying world is changing and may be headed toward equal or greater turmoil than it is now, it is a different matter. In a manner that reflects a sound sense of strategic priorities, U.S. activity and power will have to be applied there, perhaps in growing ways, in order to defend U.S. interests and achieve key security goals. The implications of new geography, however, do not end with this general observation, for something more specific is taking place that will affect future strategy, forces, and operations in concrete ways.

Throughout the Cold War, the United States had a distinctly "northern" emphasis. It was focused intently on defending Central Europe and Northeast Asia, including both Japan and South Korea, against communist aggression, while managing relations with the Soviet Union through arms control. The United States not only permanently deployed 330,000 troops in Europe and more than 100,000 troops in Northeast Asia, but it had also backed up these formations with strong commitments for rapid reinforcement in a crisis. Especially after the United States withdrew from Vietnam in the mid-1970s, other regions mattered less in its defense plans. Defense of the Persian Gulf began gaining prominence only after 1980, and even then, few U.S. forces were stationed there. The Cold War's abrupt end swept away the threats to Central Europe and Japan, leaving only South Korea and the Persian Gulf still exposed to aggression. The Korean Peninsula's future remains uncertain, but in the coming years, both Central Europe and Japan seem likely to become even more immune than they are now from direct attack on their borders. As a result, U.S. defense plans increasingly will have the luxury of taking their physical security for granted. Although the threat of ballistic missile attack may grow in ways requiring missile defense, the United States will face few major military requirements to help defend it with big ground, air, and naval forces in a crisis. The United States still stations 100,000 troops in Europe and 40,000 troops in Japan. Sizable U.S. forces may remain there, but the main reason will be larger strategic and political considerations, not defense against local surprise attack.

In the outlying world, by contrast, a new southern belt of growing strategic instability and danger seemingly is evolving. This belt includes several diverse regions located side by side, united more by the growing heat of their unstable strategic affairs than by any similarity among them. This belt begins in the Balkans, moves southward through the Middle East and the Persian Gulf, extends across South Asia, and stretches along the Asian crescent from Southeast Asia northward to Taiwan, Okinawa, and ultimately, Japan. Sub-Saharan Africa is also an unstable region owing to poverty and troubled states, and although Latin America is now part of the democratic community, it still has significant problems, such as drug trafficking. Both regions will remain important considerations in U.S. foreign policy, and they will demand appropriate attention and resources; however, the multiple neighboring regions along the southern belt are acquiring growing strategic importance, not only because of their chaotic situations but also because of their potential impact on global stability and U.S. security involvements.

Why should this southern belt be fingered as a new hot zone of rising strategic troubles that in varying ways could draw U.S. military power into it? One obvious reason is that serious tensions there already have resulted in U.S. military forces becoming involved in ways that would have surprised most observers only a decade ago. Since the mid-1990s, the United States has deployed large forces into the Balkans: first to perform peacekeeping in Bosnia, next to bomb Serbia into leaving Kosovo, then to keep the peace there. In early 1991, the United States waged a major regional war to eject Iraq from Kuwait. The effort succeeded, but since then, the United States has remained deeply entangled in the Persian Gulf in ways necessitating a steady geographical expansion of its military missions. Approximately 25,000 troops are stationed there nearly full-time, and U.S. air forces regularly bomb Iraqi targets in enforcing United Nations (UN) mandates and no-fly zones. In Asia, U.S. forces still stand guard in South Korea, but a few years ago, carriers were sent southward in order to signal China to lessen its pressure on Taiwan, and growing U.S. military contacts are now being pursued with several Southeast Asian countries. Traditionally, U.S. forces have not operated in South Asia, but in 1998, cruise missile strikes were launched against terrorist camps in Afghanistan, marking an initial use of U.S. forces there.

Across the southern belt, frequent U.S. military involvements thus already are a fact of life. Current trends suggest they may increase in scope and frequency in the coming years, in unforeseeable but potentially significant ways. *A core issue is whether these operations should be mounted as an outgrowth of current U.S. national security strategy or should be accompanied by a change in the strategy itself.* Because the current strategy is still focused on Central Europe and Northeast Asia, it views the Persian Gulf as a primary concern but treats the rest of the southern belt as secondary (that is, as a place to apply military power only episodically and in modest ways). A revised strategy would alter this perspective in ways embodying a combination of continuity and change. In Central Europe and Northeast Asia, it would continue strongly pursuing national goals, meeting alliance commitments, deterring still existing threats, and safeguarding against the reappearance of old threats. Along the southern belt, it would continue defending the Persian Gulf in powerful ways, but it also would look beyond the Gulf to address the dangers and challenges of other southern regions where the strategic stakes are high. This new strategy would be acutely aware of the big differences among the various regions there, each of which will require a unique policy response, but it also would view the southern belt as a strategic zone whose regions are interacting and face common security troubles. As a result, it would create a strategic rationale for ensuring that U.S. forces and other instruments can operate there in appropriate ways, carrying out security missions that are viewed as primary, not secondary.

The case for a newly focused national security strategy stems from the judgment that much of the southern belt seems headed toward turmoil for a set of interacting reasons and in ways that menace Western interests. A core reason is the belt's strategic fragmentation and anarchy, the stubborn presence of outlaws and troublemakers, the vulnerability of weak countries to strong neighbors, and the virility of some of its political ideologies, including nationalism in the Balkans and Islamic fundamentalism in the Middle East and South Asia. Another reason is the presence of major powers in ways that magnify the southern belt's fault lines. If China begins asserting its geopolitical interests and growing power, the effect could be to destabilize Asia's already fragile security structure, which lacks the strong collective defense mechanisms of Europe. Both Russia and China are already involved in the Balkans and the Greater Middle East, in ways that create friction with U.S. diplomacy and complicate its search for stability there. In South Asia, the intensifying Indo-Pakistani rivalry does not take place in a cocoon, for the interests of the United States, Russia, and China are involved. The active presence of the big powers along the southern belt sets the stage for transforming purely local crises into escalating events with larger consequences.

Further endangering this precarious setting is the looming acceleration of weapons of mass destruction (WMD) proliferation along the southern belt. India and Pakistan already have exploded nuclear weapons and are building long-range missiles capable of carrying them. North Korea, Iraq, and Iran are also said to be pursuing WMD systems and missiles of their own, and they may succeed in deploying serious arsenals in the coming years. The prospect of these countries acquiring WMD arsenals is bad enough, but it could prove even more damaging if it triggers WMD proliferation elsewhere and further destabilizes local security affairs at key places. Added atop local instabilities and involved big powers, WMD proliferation makes the southern belt a dangerous hot zone of future geostrategic affairs—one that is capable of producing not only small conflicts but also bigger political confrontations and nastier wars possibly involving WMD weapons.

The entire southern belt is not irretrievably destined to go up in flames; nonetheless, much of it already is deeply troubled. If current downward trends intensify and the democracies do not respond wisely, its problems could worsen. The principal danger is not necessarily that a new strategic "near-peer" will rise to challenge the United States globally, or that a large anti-Western coalition will emerge anytime soon. Instead, the danger is that the multiple local problems along the southern belt and elsewhere will fester for reasons of their own, flare up in ever-shifting ways, and interact in a globalizing world to magnify each other. If so, the strategic effect could be to confront U.S. policy with many different, but interconnected, problems along a huge geographical expanse, and with no way to resolve them by influencing a single dominant source. During the Cold War, the United States faced global problems, but they mostly stemmed from a single source: the Soviet Union. The coming era will not produce a strategic situation nearly so simple or so readily manageable with a single-minded response.

The mounting turmoil along the southern belt and elsewhere thus creates growing pressures and incentives for the United States to examine whether and how to alter its national security strategy. This does not mean that U.S. strategy should abandon traditional areas, such as Europe and Northeast Asia, that will still require heavy U.S. engagement, leadership, and security commitments. *Rather, it means that U.S. strategy should upgrade the sustained attention that it gives to the southern belt, which has long been a zone of peripheral focus and spotty activity.* Aside from Persian Gulf oil and some other exceptions to the rule, U.S. interests along this long belt commonly have not been regarded as truly vital. Many of them, however, are now becoming highly important, and some are derivative of vital interests. Defending them will be necessary to prevent the emergence of serious threats to vital interests.

Clearly a selective approach anchored in priorities will be needed, but just as clearly, standing largely aloof seems infeasible. Along this belt and elsewhere in the world, progress will not be achieved unless strategic stability is first created. Although this task will fall heavily to diplomatic and political efforts, U.S. military power inevitably will be called upon to play a role, at least as much as today, perhaps more so, and in different ways from now. A principal hope is that U.S. military power, if properly embedded in a larger approach fully employing other instruments, could make an important strategic difference, not only by permitting the United States to resolve crises and win wars there but also by preventing military conflicts. Preventing war by acting wisely and strongly in peacetime has been a key strategic mission of U.S. military forces for decades. This likely will remain the case.

How would a revised strategy for the southern belt and elsewhere be composed? The United States cannot hope to solve all of the southern belt's festering problems, nor should it try to do so. Its aim should be to lessen those troubles that deeply menace critical Western interests and threaten to have widening consequences, breeding contagious and worsening instability elsewhere. What precepts would such an approach include? Worldwide, a revised U.S. national security strategy will still be carrying out today's three key precepts of "shaping, responding, and preparing"—or precepts like them. *A revised U.S. strategy should embrace a more proactive, integrated, and systematic approach to shaping, responding, and preparing at key places along the southern belt, as well as at other important places of similar turmoil.* Designing and carrying out such a strategy does not promise to be easy, for it will require synthetic thinking as well as careful handling of many complex nuances. Recognizing the need for a new strategy is the critical first step in the right direction. Examples of steps already being taken include talks with friends and allies about creating regional cooperative defense measures in response to WMD proliferation in the Greater Middle East and Asia. Progress on these counter-WMD initiatives, coupled with enhanced planning for conventional defense operations by U.S. forces and such alliances as the North Atlantic Treaty Organization (NATO), would reflect the type of systematic approach contemplated here.

Importance of Strategic Shaping Mission

How will U.S. military power and other policy instruments be employed in the southern belt in advancing national interests and pursuing high-priority goals? On occasion, U.S. forces may be used to intervene in crises or wage war (for example, to defend Persian Gulf oil fields and other key assets, to rebuff attacks against close friends, or to enforce critical norms of conduct). *But on a daily basis, the mission will be peacetime environment shaping for the strategic purpose of promoting favorable changes while dampening chaos and preventing damaging trends.* That is, U.S. forces and other instruments will be used to help pursue such political aims as (1) maintaining influence, reassuring friends, creating partnerships and coalitions, and pursuing outreach toward big countries such as Russia and China; and (2) establishing power balances, reducing tensions, discouraging arms races, signaling resolve, warning troublemakers, and deterring threatening behavior.

Strategic environment shaping is a servant of U.S. interests, but it does not mean the arrogant application of U.S. military power, in ways suggesting superpower dominion and disdain for the values and traditions of a region. Likewise, it does not mean crude balance-of-power politics in ways reminiscent of the late 19th century. What it means is collaborating with peace-minded countries, in consensual and constructive ways, to protect their security, to promote multilateral cooperation, and to enhance stability across their entire region. Strategic shaping is respectful of the legitimate interests of those countries that choose to remain outside this collaborative zone. It actively pursues cooperative military ties with former adversaries seeking productive relations with democracies. It applies coercion only against countries that use their own military power to advance illegitimate interests and to bully or conquer their peaceful neighbors. Rather than impose superpower domination, strategic shaping seeks to build stability from the ground up, by helping countries live peacefully and encouraging them to work together to pursue progress in ways that reflect their own values and visions.

This kind of strategic shaping has become increasingly important in recent years in all major theaters, including Europe, Asia, and the Persian Gulf. A main implication of a globalizing world, one leaving some critical regions tottering between progress and turmoil, is that the strategic shaping mission likely will become more important still, including along the southern belt. Indeed, it may play a critical role in determining whether wars are fought more often than now, or less often. *The heart and soul of strategic shaping is using military forces in peacetime to bring about stable conditions and constructive changes that likely would not evolve on their own.* Strategic shaping within the democratic community often is relatively easy because most countries are sympathetic to American goals, which normally serve their own interests. Strategic shaping in the outlying world will be harder because the political conditions are less easy to influence, and some countries have bullying agendas different from those of the United States and menacing to their neighbors. Dealing with such countries will require a firm and balanced response.

Recent experience shows that using military forces for peacetime shaping in difficult areas is an activity that must be planned carefully and carried out wisely. If done improperly, it can achieve little, or even backfire. Done properly, it can have a salutary effect: if not by wholly transforming the geopolitics of volatile regions, then by helping stabilize them in key ways. The amount of military power committed will depend upon the requirements posed by U.S. political goals in each region. Most often, a small dose of forces will be needed, but in difficult and dangerous situations, more may be required. Overall, the turmoil and instability of the large southern belt and elsewhere could necessitate more military power, sustained on a more regular basis, than is now the case. Exactly how much more is to be seen; however, it would most likely require more than the 25,000 troops now stationed in the Persian Gulf.

Across the southern belt and elsewhere, the common U.S. agenda of strategic shaping likely will be one of promoting stability and progress. Its specific goals and concerns will vary among the regions because their endangering conditions are so different from each other. In southeastern Europe, U.S. policy likely will focus on protecting Turkey and the eastern Mediterranean, dampening raging nationalism and ethnic rivalries in the Balkans, and reaching out to the turbulent, but oil-rich, Caucasus in limited ways. In the already hot Greater Middle East, protecting Western access to Persian Gulf oil will remain primary, but U.S. policy will face the bigger problem of dealing with outlaws, enduring tensions among several states, the Arab-Israeli conflict, and WMD proliferation. In South Asia, U.S. policy will focus on stabilizing the Indo-Pakistani rivalry in a nuclear age while discouraging tensions and proliferation there from infecting other regions. In murky Asia, the strategic challenge will be protecting the commercial sea-lanes along the Asian crescent, enhancing the security of allies and friends, and seeking cooperation with China while being prepared to deter it if it begins asserting its growing power on behalf of menacing goals. In different ways, similar judgments apply to Africa and Latin America. The challenge will be to use U.S. military power and other instruments, working multilaterally with allies and partners, to dampen these multiregion dangers and especially to prevent them from infecting each other in ways that could inflame the entire southern belt and elsewhere.

Future Directions in U.S. Military Strategy

If a revised national security strategy along these lines is adopted, it will need to be accompanied by an adaptive military strategy that is capable of supporting it. A revised U.S. military strategy likely will also embody a mixture of continuity and change. It will continue relying on strategic forces to deter nuclear attack on the United States and its allies. It will continue meeting defense commitments in such traditional areas as Central Europe, Northeast Asia, and the Persian Gulf through a combination of overseas presence and power projection from the United States. Military bases in these three regions will no longer function solely to support deployed forces and receive reinforcements in a crisis. They will acquire the new mission of themselves serving as regional hubs of power projection, so that U.S. and allied security involvements can be projected into outlying areas in peace, crisis, and war. A key purpose will be to provide assets for missions and operations along the southern belt and other endangered areas.

If a revised U.S. military strategy is to be adopted, it should continue providing ample scope for both unilateral and multilateral operations. The United States always will need to be capable of acting unilaterally in defense of its vital interests—for a superpower, this is a strategic constant. Yet in virtually all theaters, multilateralism has been a key practice in the past and will remain so in the future. This is the case for both political and military reasons. The twofold advantage of a revised strategy is that it can help produce better U.S. forces while motivating key allies and partners to create better forces of their own. The by-product can be better forces for both U.S.-only operations and combined operations with allies and partners.

The U.S. military strategy needed to carry out new missions in the southern belt and elsewhere will be different from that of the past. This will be the case not only because of the new geography and security challenges being addressed, but also because the nature of U.S. military missions and operations will be different. For the last several decades, U.S. military strategy has been primarily one of fixed positional defense through continental operations. That is, U.S. defense plans focused on defending Central Europe, Northeast Asia, and the Persian Gulf through a combination of stationary overseas presence there, backed by the capacity to send large U.S. reinforcements to these locations for local defense against direct cross-border aggression. The Army and Air Force were especially continental and stationary in their outlook; however, even the Navy, notwithstanding its wider maritime horizons, often found itself acting as the handmaiden of this strategy, including defending sea-lanes linking the United States to specific places.

By contrast, a new military strategy for the southern belt and elsewhere will be neither positional nor continental in its core features. Instead, it will focus on applying military power at ever-shifting locations, depending upon the needs of the moment. To apply this power, U.S. military strategy will need to rely more heavily on power projection, carried out flexibly and adaptively as conditions change and sometimes mounted in distant places that today might seem surprising. In peacetime, strategic shaping missions often allow U.S. forces to move at a deliberate pace. But when direct intervention in crises and wars becomes necessary, U.S. forces will need to project swiftly and operate decisively, sometimes in places where they have little experience and few advanced preparations.

Moreover, U.S. forces mostly will not be carrying out continental operations. Instead, their operations will be heavily littoral. That is, they will come from the sea and air, and they will operate near shorelines, rather than hundreds of miles inland. This especially will be the case in such critical regions as the Balkans and eastern Mediterranean, the Persian Gulf, South Asia, and the Asian crescent. Both the Persian Gulf War and the Kosovo conflict took the form of power projection missions conducted in mostly littoral areas. They likely will be forerunners of future crises and wars as well as of peacetime operations.

Joint forces clearly will be needed to pursue this military strategy while also carrying out modern U.S. military doctrine. Strategic shaping missions often will be performed by air and naval forces, which can move quickly from place to place, supported by ground forces as needed. Requirements for crises and wars will depend upon the situation, but in general, traditional calculations will apply. The Kosovo conflict shows how, in special cases, air power and sea power alone can win a war. But the bigger and more demanding Persian Gulf War shows that potent ground forces often will be critical, too. The key point is that U.S. forces should always retain the physical capacity to mount a robust joint response, for while they can always scale back by using only one or two services, they cannot swiftly send three services if only one or two are prepared to act.

In essence, this new military strategy will be a joint strategy of peacetime strategic shaping, swift wartime power projection, and decisive strike operations. Because this strategy often will come from the sea, it will have a strong maritime dimension, but it will need to be carried out by joint forces from all components. Whether such a revised military strategy for the southern belt and elsewhere will be adopted is to be seen. If so, it will be only one part, but a very important part, of an overall strategy that will include other missions and commitments. Like all strategy departures, this one should be studied and debated before it is adopted. What cannot be debated is that new U.S. military operations along the southern belt and elsewhere already are a fact of life and that they may grow. The U.S. military is amply capable of defending Central Europe, Northeast Asia, and the Persian Gulf, but it is not well prepared for operations elsewhere along the southern belt and similar distant places. U.S. forces possess most of the necessary structure and equipment, but they lack such critical accompanying features as a well construed overseas presence in key regions; a well distributed network of bases, infrastructure, and pre-positioning; and supporting alliances and coalitions. Creating such assets in the coming years will go a long way to determining whether, and to what degree, U.S. military operations achieve their strategic goals.

Regardless of the southern belt's exact role, the need for the U.S. military to stay fully prepared for wars and crisis interventions will remain a top priority. The act of determining how U.S. forces can best be used to perform peacetime strategic shaping also will be a constant challenge in the coming years. This mission will not only be important, but it will also be carried out in ways quite different from those used during the Cold War. Then, U.S. forces were used in peacetime to help manage the bipolar confrontation. Focused mostly on defending continental alliances, they primarily were guided by such familiar, well oiled precepts as containment, deterrence, forward defense, and flexible response. Their efforts were led by ground and air forces, with naval forces playing important but complementary roles. By contrast, today's strategic setting is not bipolar, and it is not even mostly continental. The old precepts cry out to be supplemented by new precepts that better spell out the relationship between military means and political ends in peacetime. Future shaping operations will be carried out by joint forces, but often they will be heavily maritime in nature, and naval forces will perform a more critical role than they did in the past. Precisely how shaping missions will be carried out on a worldwide basis is to be seen, and doubtless will depend upon how the future unfolds. What can be said is that this arena will impose strong new demands for fresh thinking about U.S. military strategy and defense plans in the coming years.

Creating New Force-Sizing Standards

What kind of military forces and capabilities will the United States require in the coming years in order to support its evolving strategy? Efforts to answer this important question should begin by acknowledging the major strides that U.S. forces already have taken to improve their capabilities for waging war and helping attain political goals. In the mid-1970s, in the immediate aftermath of the Vietnam War, U.S. forces were commonly judged to be in troubled shape. Morale was low, readiness was eroding, and the weapon systems of all three services were aging. Since then, U.S. forces have rebounded strongly to become, beyond question, the world's best in quality and combat power. High-quality people, better training, good readiness, and modern weapons have worked together to produce this turnabout. A major contributor also has been the progress made in creating better operational capabilities by each service component and by the services working together jointly.

Two decades ago, the operational capabilities of U.S. forces were considerably less impressive than they are today. In virtually all places overseas, initial defense plans were anchored in already deployed assets because the United States lacked the capacity swiftly to protect its large homeland-based forces in time to make a critical difference. U.S. air forces may have been able to win the air battle, but they lacked a strong capacity to help contribute to the land battle by destroying enemy forces and logistic support. U.S. ground forces were able to generate considerable stationary firepower, but they lacked the capacity to maneuver adroitly and otherwise show mastery of the operational art. U.S. naval forces were able to control the seas, but they lacked a capacity to contribute to helping the air and ground forces in major continental operations. These deficiencies, coupled with shortcoming in allied forces, resulted in justifiable worry about the capacity to defend Central Europe, the Korean Peninsula and Japan, and the Persian Gulf oil fields.

Since then, progress has been considerable. The U.S. military has greatly enhanced its power projection capacity by building impressive strategic mobility forces. The combination of increased overseas pre-positioning, strategic airlift, and strategic sealift has resulted in today's capacity swiftly to deploy nearly all U.S.-based active combat forces in a matter of a few weeks and months. U.S. air forces not only possess unchallenged mastery of the air battle but also can contribute heavily to the land battle with precision strikes against enemy combat formations, logistic support, and strategic infrastructure. U.S. ground forces—Army and Marines—now can fire and maneuver with high speed and powerful effect while conducting both offensive and defensive operations. This capacity allows them to defeat decisively larger, well armed enemy forces. U.S. naval forces not only dominate the high seas but also can bring their long-range firepower to bear to influence the land and air battles. Equally important, all three components are developing an improved capacity to operate together and to draw upon each other's strengths in dealing with a host of different military environments.

None of these developments means that today's U.S. forces are perfect or that all risks have been eliminated; however, the situation today is vastly better than that of 25 years ago. In the past decade, U.S. forces have been tested in two regional wars: the Persian Gulf and Kosovo. In both cases, they worked with allied forces to win decisively, with few losses to themselves. Dangers still exist at key regional hot spots; however, if war were to erupt in the Persian Gulf or Korea, U.S. and allied forces might encounter trouble at first, but they eventually would prevail. Their clear capacity to win decisively, perhaps quickly and easily, is a formidable deterrent to aggression—there or elsewhere.

This transformation did not occur easily. It came about as a result of hard strategic and military labor carried out consistently for more than two decades. Moreover, today's advantageous situation should not be taken for granted. Preserving it will require equally hard labor, backed by sufficient resources. The U.S. military will need to remain attentive to the shifting demands of remaining decisively superior in regional wars and other conflicts, including those erupting at unexpected places. Future opponents will be improving their forces with higher quality weapons, pursuing asymmetrical strategies aimed at slipping the U.S. military punch, and acquiring WMD systems. The U.S. military will need to retain and develop the capacity to prevail across a wide spectrum of future conflicts ahead. Even as the U.S. military continues to improve in operational terms, the U.S. Government will need to continue thinking insightfully about how its military power can best be used to exert advantageous political influence through strategic shaping in peacetime. Because the Cold War created a static, bipolar world, peacetime shaping was a straightforward process of supporting alliances and deterring enemies. Because the emerging era will be more multipolar and fluid, the shaping process will be considerably more complex, and doubtless demanding.

For military and political reasons, a high degree of U.S. military preparedness will continue to be needed. Even as the U.S. military remains prepared, it will have to undergo change, for it is experiencing its own internal transformation even as the world is evolving toward an unknown destination. Sound U.S. defense plans for employing forces overseas in peace, crisis, and war will be required. Forging them for today's situation and tomorrow's will be one of the most important challenges, for these plans will help determine not only how the U.S. military evolves, but also how it is employed to carry out national strategy.

In this context, a key issue arises. Regardless of whether new geographical missions are embraced fully or partly, U.S. national security strategy and military strategy likely will mutate in response to a changing, globalizing world of money and power. To what degree should the current force-sizing standard of being prepared for two major theater wars (MTWs) in overlapping time frames change along with them? The answer may not be apparent, but the question merits asking because the future will require a force-sizing standard that acts as part of the solution.

The role of a force-sizing standard is both to determine the size of the U.S. force posture and to explain the posture's strategic and military rationale in public. In less visible ways, it also has a major impact on defense programs, budgets, and force allocations among the key commands. The two-MTW standard has been playing this role since 1993, when it was first installed. Its positive contributions are severalfold. It has linked U.S. force levels to clear threats and plausible wars, while reducing calculations of force requirements to a simple numerical algorithm. By proclaiming the need for a two-war posture, not one war or three wars, it has boiled defense planning down to a single-point solution. It has helped build a broad political consensus for the current posture, establishing both a ceiling over the posture and a floor under it. The two-MTW standard achieves this end with arithmetic proclaiming that more forces would be superfluous and fewer forces would be inadequate. Seasoned military officers and operations researchers may blanch at this formula because they know reality is more complex, but the two-MTW standard thus far has gotten the job done in the public arena. Meanwhile, it has allowed the Pentagon to resolve its internal debates by focusing on two clearly defined wars whose postulated features have been developed in satisfying detail.

The two-MTW standard, nonetheless, apparently is now coming to the end of its useful life. Critics have faulted it on several grounds. One criticism is that the standard lacks credibility because it is anchored in the allegedly faulty premise that two big wars will occur concurrently. A second criticism is that it anchors the U.S. defense rationale too single-mindedly in fleeting threats: both the Iraqi and North Korean threats could fade from the scene, but others could remain or appear. A third criticism is that it ignores Europe and seems to relegate peacetime shaping missions, along with preparing for other crises and wars, to "back-burner" status. Yet another criticism is that the Department of Defense (DOD) does not take being fully prepared for two wars seriously in its own programming, even though failure to do so comes across as a major deficiency in U.S. defense preparedness. A final criticism is that the two-MTW standard makes it hard to prepare for other missions or allocate forces in a flexible manner when crises arise. A similar drumbeat coming from these criticisms is that DOD allegedly is too locked into a simplistic and rigid formula that, while performing valuable internal functions, no longer adequately looks outward at emerging requirements, priorities, and political necessities.

Regardless of how these specific criticisms are appraised, the core issue is whether the two-MTW standard continues to provide a sound strategic paradigm for viewing the future. *If a new standard is needed, the reason is to do a better job of measuring force needs in the coming era and offering a credible strategic rationale that can endure.* In order to perform both functions, a new standard must reflect how the strategic purposes of U.S. military power are changing. Defending the Persian Gulf and South Korea (the locations of the two MTWs) will remain important in shifting ways, but in the coming years, other strategic missions in other places—in peacetime and wartime—will be gaining prominence. A new standard should take these missions into account in ways that reflect the primary operations of U.S. forces and their emerging roles in national strategy.

The idea of creating new force-sizing standards is one that should be approached through careful study, for many issues must be considered. Broadly speaking, there are three alternatives: new contingency-based standards, capability-based standards, and strategy-based standards. Contingency-based standards would continue to size and design U.S. forces on the basis of wartime needs—for example, enough forces for 1.5 major theater wars or 2.5 major theater wars instead of today's 2.0 major theater wars. Capability-based standards would aspire to determine the force characteristics needed for a wide spectrum of operations—for example, sufficient land forces to provide a robust mixture of infantry, armored, mechanized, and air assault units. The same applies to air and naval forces. Strategy-based standards would look beyond wartime contingencies and combat capabilities to determine the forces needed to carry out the key precepts of national security strategy. All three options have advantages and disadvantages. The trade-offs need to be evaluated carefully before decisionmaking. The key point is that today's standard is not set in concrete. If another approach is deemed better, the door can be opened to adopting it.

Without pretending to settle the issue, this study reasons that strategy-based standards, supplemented by analysis of contingencies and capabilities, may work best. This approach's key advantage is that it would anchor force planning in a stronger strategic foundation. This approach was used successfully for most of the Cold War, during which U.S. forces were sized primarily to carry out national strategy with a broad spectrum of capabilities and secondarily to conform to the dictates of contingency plans. In this old-but-new approach, U.S. forces would be sized to carry out the three key precepts of national security strategy: shaping, responding, and preparing—or their successors. Once this key task is accomplished, forces can be fine-tuned to perform specific contingencies and provide a flexible portfolio of assets.

Illustratively, a strategy-based approach can be brought to life by anchoring U.S. defense plans in a nested hierarchy of three new standards that together provide a reliable measure of enduring military needs and a credible strategic rationale for the resulting posture. The first two standards are primary: the chief mechanisms for determining force needs for shaping, responding, and preparing because they focus on the most common strategic missions of U.S. forces and the highest probability events. The third standard is complementary, ensuring effective forces in more demanding, less probable events:

> Standard 1: Forces for Normal Strategic Missions. The purpose of this standard is to ensure that during conditions short of major war (that is, 95 percent of the time), the three major regional commands—U.S. European Command (EUCOM), U.S. Central Command (CENTCOM), and U.S. Pacific Command (PACOM)—always have enough forces assigned to them to perform their normal duties,

such as training, working with allies, performing peacekeeping, and responding to small-to-medium crises and conflicts. Such forces could include overseas-stated assets plus assigned units based in the United States. For example, this standard might allocate a posture of three divisions, five fighter wings, two to three carrier battle groups (CVBGs), and one amphibious ready group (ARG) to each command. In addition, it would withhold a sizable Reserve, under national command, for flexible use in these regions or elsewhere.

Standard 2: Forces for a Single MTW While Performing Normal Missions Elsewhere. The purpose of this standard is to ensure that U.S. forces can concentrate swiftly to win a single big regional war in varying places while not seriously denuding the other major commanders in chief (CINCs) of forces needed to carry out their normal missions. In the event of a Persian Gulf war, for example, this standard would allocate forces already assigned to CENTCOM plus the strategic Reserve in order to create an adequate wartime posture. Meanwhile, EUCOM and PACOM would retain control of most or all of the forces normally assigned to them. Thus, their normal operations would not be severely degraded. A similar calculus would apply to wars in other theaters.

Standard 3: Forces for More Wars, or Bigger Wars. The purpose of this standard is to ensure that in the event of more demanding wartime situations than those covered by Standard 2, U.S. forces would be adequate to the task if full use were made of the opportunity to concentrate them. This standard would examine force needs for two MTWs in overlapping time frames. It also would examine force needs should a bigger war—one much larger than today's MTWs—erupt. It would strive to concentrate enough forces to meet needs in these situations, albeit at the sacrifice of temporarily denuding other commands of their forces.

These new standards thus move to the forefront those missions that U.S. forces spend nearly all their time performing: normal operations and periodic waging of single regional wars. They are not blind to more demanding wartime situations, but their main effect is to ensure that defense plans address highest priority needs for Standards 1 and 2 and only then buy additional insurance for Standard 3—not the other way around. Their intent is to focus plans intently on the strategic missions of greatest activity and emphasis, and to explain publicly the rationale for the U.S. defense posture in these terms.

Initial appearances suggest that these standards do not call for force levels that are radically different from those required by the two-MTW standard. Instead, they provide a new and potentially better way to think about how existing U.S. forces are used and how they best can be improved. The current standard provides a single approach to planning: two large force packages for waging two MTWs. By contrast, the new standards provide a wide spectrum of valuable approaches. For normal conditions, they disperse forces by creating four medium-sized packages: three for the major overseas CINCs and one held in reserve. For dealing with a single MTW, they concentrate forces to provide a single big package, plus two medium-sized packages for use elsewhere. For dealing with more and bigger wars, they concentrate forces even more, to create two big packages or an even bigger single package. *Their common theme is that they focus on how to create appropriate force packages for the full set of purposes and missions ahead, not only for the low-probability event of waging two big wars at the same time.*

The effect of these standards will be to provide a fresh sense of priorities in ways that can enhance the U.S. military's flexibility, adaptiveness, and across-the-board performance. They will help provide alternative lenses for viewing candidate programs, and they will reward those that provide powerful strategic benefits in more ways than one. For example, they will cast a favorable light on measures for better infrastructure in outlying areas that help U.S. forces both to perform peacetime shaping missions and to wage major wars.

Like all standards, these standards should be applied sensibly, with their interplay in mind. Standard 1 should be employed not only for its own purposes but also to help create adequate capabilities for Standards 2 and 3. Likewise, Standard 2 should be broadly targeted, in ways that have positive effects on the other two standards. Standard 2 calls for being prepared to fight a single major war, but not only one kind of war in one place. Rather, it means that U.S. forces should be able wage different kinds of wars, varying in location, strategy, and operations. It mandates being prepared for single wars in Europe, the Middle East/Persian Gulf, Korea, and Asia. The flexible capacity to wage these different kinds of wars will provide an inherent capacity to wage more than one war at a time. Standard 3 no longer will rule the roost but will be used to identify cost-effective measures that help U.S. forces fight not only two wars but also one war. Examples include strategic mobility, command, control, communications, and computers, intelligence, surveillance, and reconnaissance (C^4ISR) systems, war reserve munitions, and stocks: areas where preparing for multiple wars still will make sense.

A guiding theme is that future defense plans should ensure that the goals of Standard 1 and 2 are solidly met, even as Standard 3's needs, as a still important insurance policy, are amply addressed. They should ensure that pursuit of Standard 3 measures does not result in loss of Standard 1 and 2 assets. Standard 1 and 2 programs can be tailored with the goal of also enhancing Standard 3 capabilities. When unique Standard 3 measures make sense for reasons of their own, they should be funded. *By prioritizing this way, DOD will build forces fully capable of meeting Standards 1 and 2, while preserving a robust capacity for Standard 3.*

The strategy-based approach that uses these three standards will be more complex and harder to explain than is contingency planning for two MTWs, but it is no more complex than Cold War thinking. *It would create a public rationale that rings true, and it would provide a force posture that reflects the full strategic purposes of national strategy.* It would help ensure that DOD programs and budgets flow in the direction of enabling the services and CINCs fully to carry out the peacetime and wartime missions that must be performed in today's world. It would reduce the risk that the Pentagon, in striving for a two-MTW posture, will leave itself inadequately prepared not only to fight one war but also to carry out normal duties that play a critical role in national strategy. Simply stated, this approach points toward a sound force posture because it is anchored in a balanced sense of strategic purposes and priorities.

An added benefit is that this approach would better enable DOD to develop plans and forces for performing new missions along the southern belt. It would relieve defense planning from being so fixated on big wars in the Persian Gulf and Korea that other conflicts and places might go unaddressed. It would allocate sufficient forces to the three major commands, all of which would be performing missions along the southern belt and elsewhere. It would free them from plans that employ only very large forces, thereby allowing them to develop plans for medium-sized projection and strike packages: the kind of forces that likely will be appropriate for most key missions there. In these ways, it would help facilitate the transition to a new military strategy that makes sense not only for the southern belt but also for all other endangered regions in the years ahead.

These three standards are put forth as illustrations, not a fixed blueprint. They illustrate that the recent past need not be prologue. The two-MTW formula is one option for navigating the future, but it is not the only viable option. Creative thinking can produce other approaches with attractions of their own. They can be articulated in enough detail to provide concrete guidance for sizing forces, allocating them among missions, and setting program priorities for improving them. The challenge is to develop a full set of options, analyze them, and choose one—not because it made sense in the past, but because it offers promise of working best in the future.

Building Flexible, Adaptive Forces

What kind of U.S. forces will be needed to carry out tomorrow's strategies, missions, and sizing standards, including those outlined here? Future U.S. forces will need to remain capable of waging two MTWs, should that improbable step become necessary; however, maintaining this capability will not be their most valuable characteristic. They will need to be highly capable of peacetime strategic shaping, especially in dangerous places where their presence can greatly enhance stability. They will need to be capable of responding swiftly and decisively to a full spectrum of crisis and wartime contingencies, from large to small, including peacekeeping, strike operations against WMD-armed opponents, and interventions against determined opponents who are skillfully employing asymmetrical strategies aimed at slipping the American punch. They also will need to have the capacity to perform strategic U-turns to switch to new missions and operations fast enough to deal with a rapidly shifting global setting.

These multiple assets add up to a strategic need for a flexible and adaptive force posture—one that can perform many different missions in frequently changing ways and thereby attain national goals. Future U.S. forces should not be designed with a single script in mind. Instead, they can best be preserved and built with an approach resembling that of an estate planner who assembles a diverse portfolio of stocks, bonds, and other investments in order to provide a robust combination of liquid assets, short-term growth, and long-term security. *In similar ways, U.S. forces can be tailored to provide a balanced portfolio of assets whose diverse subcomponents can be selectively brought together in ways that meet the needs of the moment as well as challenges of the future.*

Flexibility and adaptiveness come from a force posture that possesses diverse assets that can be combined and recombined to perform ever-shifting missions. To an impressive degree, these characteristics already exist in U.S. forces. As table 1 shows, this is the case partly because all service components have sizable assets. Together, they provide 13 active ground divisions plus similar reserves, 20 fighter wings, and 11 to 12 CVBGs, backed up by modern C^4ISR assets, large strategic mobility forces, and a well endowed infrastructure at home. The stationing of 235,000 troops, supported by the ability to deploy another 500,000 troops in a crisis, provides the U.S. military a flexible capacity to project sizable forces to many key corners of the globe.

Table 1. U.S. Defense Posture, 2000

Service Element	*Active*	*Reserve*
Army Divisions	10	8
Separate Army Brigades	—	18
Marine Divisions and Air Wings	3	1
Air Force Fighter Wings	12	8
Air Force Bombers	163	27
Navy Carriers	11 or 12	—
ARGs	12	—
Other Major Combatants	163	—
Active Military Personnel	1,350,000	865,000

Source: Data from Secretary of Defense William S. Cohen, *Annual Report to the President and Congress* (Washington, DC: Government Printing Office, 2000).

In addition, all services contain considerable diversity within their ranks. The Army has a mix of armored, mechanized, light infantry, airborne, and air assault forces. The Air Force has strategic bombers, air interceptors, and multimission aircraft that can perform deep-strike, interdiction, close air support, and reconnaissance roles. The Navy provides carriers, attack wings, cruise missiles, surface combatants, and submarines that can control the seas and project power ashore. The Marines provide integrated ground and air forces that can perform amphibious assault missions while working with the Army in sustained land operations. The growing capacity of the services to combine to perform joint operations, of course, provides considerable synergy and added flexibility. These characteristics allow DOD to get substantial mileage out of the current forces.

Nonetheless, the current posture is 30 percent smaller than it was during the Cold War, and its shrunken size limits the number of missions that it can perform. For temporary periods, it can surge its efforts, but if an abnormally fast pace is continued over an extended period, the posture will be stretched beyond its limits. Because quantity matters in the strategic calculus, the question arises: How many forces will be needed in a globalizing world? The same as today, less, or more? A few years ago, critics often said that the prospect of steady progress toward a stable world translated into an eventual need for fewer forces than now. Some argued in favor of force reductions to invest the savings into faster modernization. Recently, however, the prospect of world affairs becoming more turbulent has been giving rise to a reappraisal in many quarters. A growing number of observers are expressing alarm over the force posture allegedly being stretched too thin by current missions. They fear that these missions may become more numerous tomorrow. No consensus has yet emerged, but today's talk is mostly that the force posture should stay level, or even grow somewhat, to reduce mounting strains and/or perform new missions.

This chapter's three new force-sizing standards point toward a future force posture in the vicinity of today's model, not appreciably smaller or larger. This is the case for each standard considered individually. Sizable forces will be needed to carry out normal missions (Standard 1), to wage a single MTW while keeping other key theaters stable (Standard 2), and to provide a supplementary capacity to fight more and bigger wars (Standard 3). Their combined effects reinforce this conclusion, for they act together to erect three powerful barriers against steep reductions. Properly interpreted, these standards create no single-point requirement below which the remaining forces would be clearly inadequate, or above which added forces would be clearly superfluous. Yet even when an already existing posture is reasonably aligned with strategic requirements, small additions and subtractions often can make a big difference. While fewer forces can cause strategic damage, more forces can be beneficial because they provide added flexibility, missions, and insurance.

If a decision is made to enlarge today's posture, first priority likely will go to adding so-called low-density/high-demand (LD/HD) forces from all services. These are small units with highly specialized capabilities that are being stretched thin by growing requirements for using them in regular overseas operations, such as peacekeeping and crisis interventions. Examples include Air Force C^4I and defense suppression aircraft, Army military police and construction engineers, and Navy special operations forces. Adding assets in these critical areas could greatly enhance the U.S. military's ability to perform these missions while enlarging the total posture in only small ways.

As for major combat formations, the Army is unlikely to need additional active divisions and brigades. Priority already is being given to enhancing the readiness of 15 Reserve component brigades so that they can participate in major combat operations, if necessary. The Army may also need selective additions in special combat units, such as long-range fires, and in combat support and service support (CS/CSS) assets. More than one-half of the Army's CS/CSS structure is placed in Reserve component status. This could constrain the Army's ability to fight one major war, much less two wars at the same time. It already compels the Army to draw on Reserve component support units to perform lengthy peacekeeping roles, as has been the case in the Balkans. Selective expansion in these areas could enhance the Army's strategic responsiveness. The same applies to the Air Force, whose performance of new-era missions could be enhanced by adding active-duty pilots, mechanics, and support personnel. The Air Force's 20 fighter wings seem adequate for wartime missions, but the current structure of having only 12 active wings, with the other 8 in Reserve component status, is being stressed by overseas rotation and crisis response missions. Shifting two wings to active status, or even adding two active wings to the current posture, may make sense in the coming years.

The Navy posture is already the smallest in many years. The current posture includes 11 to 12 CVBGs, 171 surface combatants and attack submarines, 40 amphibious ships, and 75 mine warfare and logistic support ships. The total of 316 "battle force ships" is well down from the higher levels of 567 ships only a decade ago. The Navy's size seems headed further downward in the coming years, for although better quality ships are being built, their numbers are not adequate to offset retirements. The worrisome consequence is that the Navy already is hard-pressed to meet its training requirements, perform steady-state overseas presence in all major theaters, and react to growing missions for peacekeeping and crisis response.

Given the need for a large rotational base, current forces are meeting ARG deployment goals, but often fall short of CVBG goals. In 1998, a CVBG was deployed only 40 percent of the time in the Mediterranean, 67 percent in the Pacific, and 82 percent in Southwest Asia. In 1999, similar shortfalls were experienced in the Mediterranean and the Pacific. In 1999, the Navy responded to the Kosovo war by concentrating forces there, but this strained other theaters and missions. In the future, this situation of declining overseas presence and stressful concentrations could worsen at a time when requirements for strategic shaping, peacekeeping, and crisis response are not declining and even growing. Illustratively, adding an additional CVBG could elevate on-station time from 75 percent of current goals to 85 percent or better—a useful contribution to readiness and deployment rates. Short of this step, acquiring other combatants and support ships could lessen pressures on the Navy, while enhancing its responsiveness and ability to support national strategy.

The size of the future U.S. military likely will be debated in the coming years and its details analyzed endlessly, but the strategic bottom line seems clear. The current force posture was sized in 1993 on the basis of strategic assumptions that are now in flux and are headed toward an unknown destination that could call for equal or more forces, not less. If pressures for more forces continue to grow, they likely will come primarily not from major new warfighting requirements, but from the need to carry out a rising number of normal missions and operations around the world.

Today's U.S. forces are being stretched thin by the need to stay ready for major combat while carrying out missions for overseas presence, alliance commitments, strategic shaping, peacekeeping, and minor crisis interventions. Perhaps this trend can be dampened by setting strategic priorities more selectively, but the reality is that missions important to U.S. foreign policy and national security are hard to turn down. Today's missions and operations are being performed not for superfluous reasons, but because, after careful review, they were deemed critical enough to justify the expenditure of scarce resources. The same will be true tomorrow, and the number of these missions may increase before it decreases. The current practice of providing enhanced funds for readiness can help reduce shortfalls, but not endlessly. If U.S. forces become stretched to the point of snapping, which some observers judge already is happening, the need for more assets will no longer be debatable. *A big force expansion likely will not be necessary, but a modest, well planned expansion focused on critical assets might make a valuable contribution to future U.S. national security policy and military strategy.*

To a degree, the future need for forces as large as or somewhat larger than those of today could come into conflict with DOD budgetary pressures as the next procurement wave accelerates. If the situation is not handled well, plausibly decisions to emphasize fast procurement could compel contractions—if the DOD budget is not large enough to fund both adequate forces and modernization. Alternatively, insufficient procurement of new weapons could compel contractions if old weapons can no longer be operated. Only time will tell. Much depends upon future defense budgets and procurement plans, neither of which is set in concrete. DOD has faced similar problems before, and as it did then, it will have options at its disposal for ensuring that sufficient forces remain in the posture even as an adequate procurement effort is carried out. If unwise contractions become necessary, the result could be a paring back of U.S. defense strategy and overseas involvements. This step could damage U.S. security interests abroad and contribute to mounting dangers, if power vacuums emerge in key areas. History suggests that the wisest course is to fund adequate defense budgets and manage them carefully so that in size, readiness, and modernization, U.S. forces are capable of meeting future requirements in solid, well-balanced ways. If necessary, a booming American economy, and surpluses flowing from it, are making a somewhat larger defense budget a viable option in ways that could dispel lingering fears of a strategy-force mismatch.

The judgment that future U.S. force requirements likely will remain similar to those of today applies for the coming decade and somewhat beyond. Over the longer haul, much will depend upon how international conditions evolve and how they affect requirements. If the level of danger and threat remains similar to that of today, the required U.S. military posture likely will remain in the vicinity of today's force levels. The main task will be adjusting the existing posture in order to handle the ups and downs of ongoing changes abroad. If the international situation improves in major ways, force requirements likely will diminish and a smaller posture will suffice. If the global situation deteriorates markedly, a significant force expansion could be needed. The distant future is too uncertain to call. What can be said is that a modestly strengthened version of today's posture provides the assets to deal with the global situation at hand, while preserving the flexibility to contract or expand as the future warrants.

Setting Priorities for Higher Quality Forces

Regardless of decisions made about quantity, U.S. forces will be kept strong and improved through efforts to enhance their quality. Judged in relation to their demanding global missions, U.S. forces are not impressively large. Although they are called upon to help keep several turbulent regions stable, they total only 7 percent of military personnel around the world. Even when U.S. forces concentrate to fight wars, their opponents typically are as large as or larger than they are. High quality is what allows U.S. forces to shape events in peacetime and to win wars. They are the world's best by a wide margin. The challenge is to keep that status. Because adversary forces will be improving by acquiring modern weapons, information systems, and asymmetrical strategies, U.S. forces need to continue improving as well.

The current high quality of U.S. forces owes partly to their large amounts of training. To be sure, problems recently have arisen in personnel readiness because of high deployment rates that have taken some people and units away from their home bases for too long and too often. Likewise, shortfalls in some areas of materiel readiness—for example, depot maintenance and spares—are now being corrected. Lost in the clamor has been awareness that for active military servicemen, per capita spending on operations and maintenance today is 40 percent higher than it was in 1990 (in constant dollars), a year when overall readiness was judged excellent. The result is that U.S. combat forces train at high rates in ways that build impressive combat power. For example, U.S. tactical air combat pilots fly about 220 hours per year, mostly in training. This level is four times higher than that of most foreign air forces, especially those of potential adversaries. Navy ship steaming days for training meet DOD goals. Army tank miles per year are about 85 percent of DOD goals, but this level is far higher than that of most foreign armies. Indeed, many foreign armies train only at the company level, but the Army trains at the battalion level: a huge difference in combat power. U.S. forces also engage in joint training: perhaps not enough, but far more than other countries do, and the forces pursue training and exercises with key allies.

Another contributor is the high quality of U.S. weapons. Although DOD has been on an extended procurement holiday for some years, the weapons acquired in the 1980s are mostly still the world's best. This judgment clearly applies to U.S. fighter aircraft: the F–15, F–16, F–14, and F–18. It also applies to the M1 tank, Bradley Infantry Fighting Vehicle, and attack helicopters. As for maritime forces, no other Navy in the world has the big carriers, Aegis cruisers, destroyers, frigates, and submarines to launch major blue-water operations, much less contest the Navy for control of the seas. Overall, good people, advanced training, excellent weapons, joint operations, modern doctrine, good power projection assets, and other factors combine to make U.S. forces far better than any others. Some units doubtless are being called upon to do too many things: improvements are needed. Nevertheless, the idea that U.S. forces are steadily losing their fighting power in some wholesale way is bogus.

The primary vehicles for improving U.S. forces are the revolution in military affairs (RMA) and their new joint doctrine, recently *Joint Vision 2010* and *Joint Vision 2020*. The revolution in military affairs aspires to blend modern information networks with new weapons, munitions, and structures to create ultrasophisticated forces that can operate with greater speed, lethality, and punch than do current forces. *Joint Vision 2010/Joint Vision 2020* creates new doctrinal precepts for employing these RMA-enhanced ground, air, and naval forces in highly potent ways aimed at overpowering enemy forces quickly and decisively. Owing to the RMA and *Joint Vision 2010/Joint Vision 2020*, future U.S. forces will be able to disperse widely, but operate together through networking. They are to be capable of maneuvering expertly, engaging precisely from the air and ground, striking at long ranges, drawing on leaner logistic support, and protecting themselves from attack. All services are now designing new structures and practices that will allow them to work together in carrying out this doctrine. A good example is the Air Force's aerospace expeditionary forces, the Army's efforts to create fast-deployable brigades, and the Navy's emphasis on networking of dispersed assets. Meanwhile, DOD is gearing up for a major procurement effort to buy the new information systems, C^4ISR technologies, tactical combat aircraft, new land and sea platforms, smart munitions, theater missile defenses, and other assets that will be needed. It is hoped that steady progress will be made in the coming years. By 2010 to 2020, this overall effort is intended to culminate in greatly enhanced forces that take modern warfare to a new dimension and a higher plane.

Spending Funds Wisely

The speed and success of this effort will depend largely upon future defense budgets and how they are spent. The budgets of recent years—hovering at about $250 billion annually—were too small to permit a major improvement effort. Compounding the problem was the need to spend heavily on readiness, which combined with other dynamics to push DOD spending for operations and maintenance to $104 billion, or 40 percent of the budget. This was an all-time high compared with the normal level of about 30 percent. As a by-product, procurement fell to about $45 billion, which is barely enough to buy normal replacement stocks and not nearly enough to acquire new weapons. To help correct this problem, the defense budget has been increased by $112 billion for 2000–2005. The fiscal year (FY) 2000 budget is $280 billion. It will rise to $320 billion by 2005 and is likely to rise to a higher level later in order to offset inflation and perhaps provide modest real growth. Procurement spending is also rising: to $54 billion in 2000, $75 billion in 2005, and likely more later. This infusion of funds will permit DOD greatly to accelerate its acquisition of the new weapons, munitions, and other systems needed to bring the RMA and *Joint Vision 2010/Joint Vision 2020* to life. In particular, U.S. air forces will improve through acquisition of the F–22, Joint Strike Fighter, F/A–18 E/F, Comanche helicopter, and V–22 Osprey tilt-rotor aircraft.

Even so, the Pentagon likely will not be able to spend its way out of the age-old dilemma of setting priorities. About 95 percent of the funds likely to be available have already been committed. Future budgets, even larger than those now planned, likely will not be big enough to fund all plausible improvements. Pressures for new spending will be arising from multiple quarters: theater and national ballistic missile defenses, overseas operations and infrastructure, conventional force expansion, new force structures, personnel, readiness, and modernization. DOD will need to make hard decisions on what assets to acquire and what assets to forsake. Its actions will have a major bearing on how the future unfolds. The challenge will be to set priorities wisely so that the programs funded will produce the kind of improved forces most urgently needed by national strategy.

Setting priorities can begin by trimming secondary spending in the current budget and making better use of existing resources. Consolidating bases and infrastructure through base realignment and closure (BRAC) is one example already being pursued. Another is DOD pursuit of the revolution in business affairs. Possibly low-priority operations and maintenance spending can be pruned so that more funds can be spent on high-priority readiness measures. Consolidation of tri-service assets in such areas as medical care, C^4ISR, and administrative support can help, perhaps significantly so. As the revolution in military affairs results in streamlined combat and support formations, the freed personnel can be used to add new assets, such as LD/HD units. Finally, priorities will have to be set in determining how many funds to allocate among the multiple claimants for enhanced capabilities. The coming procurement wave offers an opportunity greatly to enhance U.S. air power. Fully finding it at a fast pace will be expensive, and there will be ample opportunities to spend scarce funds on other improvements, especially in building stronger force structures. *Most likely, a balanced approach will be best, but the point is that tough decisions about priorities should be subjected to careful analysis and planning.*

Using Forces Effectively

DOD will face a second, equally important challenge: to wisely organize and employ its improved high-technology forces so that they can effectively carry out the new missions of the future. History shows that gleaming forces are of little use unless they can act as potent instruments of strategy and fully perform the operations needed to achieve success. For example, the United States enjoyed a huge technological advantage in Vietnam, but still lost the war because its strategy was faulty and the outgunned enemy fought skillfully. Superb quality will matter in the future only if it is translated into winning performance and successful achievement of goals in peace, crisis, and war.

During peacetime, the act of wisely using U.S. forces will depend heavily on carrying out strategic shaping missions as effectively as possible. In each major theater, the United States will be employing a spectrum of defense assets on behalf of multiple objectives in a fluid setting. These multiple assets will include headquarters units, stationed combat and support forces, temporary deployments, committed reinforcements from the continental United States (CONUS), pre-positioned equipment, stocks, bases and facilities, and various types of security assistance. Together, these assets constitute an overall overseas presence program that must be integrated and blended with the other instruments of U.S. diplomacy and foreign policy. The successful performance of these assets and their cost-effectiveness are not to be taken for granted. Instead, the relationship between means and ends must be continuously studied and reevaluated in order to ensure that program resources are sufficient, adequately balanced and prioritized, and effectively applied in ways aimed at bringing about the desired political and strategic results. Because international conditions will be continuously in flux, the defense management agenda in this arena promises to be challenging and difficult in ways that mandate constant attention, plus a willingness to change when necessary. The future in this arena likely will be dynamic, not static, and the United States will need to react accordingly. In recent years, DOD has created the Theater Engagement Plans (TEP) system to help determine goals and priorities through overseas presence. Continued use of this methodology and further improvements to it will be an ongoing need.

In the coming years, the United States likely will face the need to reassess the strategic rationale for its current pattern of troop deployments overseas. In general, sizable overseas deployments offer important strategic advantages in maintaining American influence at high levels, training with allies and partners, and being ready to deal with emergencies. Nevertheless, there are countervailing considerations: the current overseas presence of about 235,000 troops costs about $10 to $15 billion annually, and DOD capacity swiftly to deploy forces from the United States means that rapid reinforcement now works effectively in many cases. Given this, large U.S. forces should remain deployed, not for continuity's sake, but because they serve clear strategic purposes, perform critical missions, and are a cost-effective way to spend scarce funds. The current distribution of forces has worked well during the past decade, but should not be seen as sacrosanct if a different, more appropriate presence becomes desirable. The continuing need for 100,000 troops in Europe likely will hinge not on NATO needs for border defense, but on whether the Europeans create improved forces for new missions that can act as partners with U.S. forces. In Asia, the need for 100,000 troops will depend heavily upon the situation on the Korean Peninsula. If tensions relax and Korea unifies, the United States may have reasons to seek a smaller Asian posture, one configured for mobile operations and regionwide missions. In Southwest Asia, growing dangers could increase the need for U.S. troop deployments, but political considerations currently bar this step.

Regardless of decisions on future force deployments, DOD will be best advised to rethink how overseas presence and power projection are blended in performing new-era missions in dangerous places. Current overseas bases in Europe and Japan will need to be reconfigured as regional hubs for power projection, rather than as mere reception facilities for reinforcements that operate locally. To the extent possible, steps can be taken to acquire new bases, facilities, storage, and equipment pre-positioning in distant areas where U.S. forces may be operating. Designing light but still strong units that can deploy rapidly is important. Added pre-positioning can help the Army make its heavy forces deploy faster. Airlift and sealift, critical to moving combat units swiftly, may need strengthening. Such practical steps, which often escape public attention, will have a major impact in determining whether future U.S. forces can serve as fully potent instruments of national strategy or are left gleaming but not succeeding. *Such measures should be given careful attention in DOD budgets, for they easily can be lost in the clamor over bigger things.*

In recent years, Armed Forces have been used to conduct peacekeeping missions, but their capacity to fight and win wars will remain their bellwether. Future crises and wars could come in many sizes and shapes, each requiring a tailored response that reflects force needs, military doctrine, and political goals. Flexibility is needed because small-to-medium crises and wars, in particular, could produce events that depart widely from commonly expected scenarios. In some cases, joint operations will be necessary in ways that require balanced contributions from all services; in other cases, one or another component may predominate. Normally, however, joint operations will be needed to some degree because each service brings uniquely valuable skills to war fighting. Simply stated, U.S. forces fight best as a joint team. Their capacity for jointness heavily accounts for their superiority on the modern battlefield.

Stripped of jointness, other assets—sophisticated technology, modern doctrine, and advanced training—become less significant.

For major theater wars, well endowed joint operations—that is, a robust combination of air, naval, and ground forces—will remain the standard. For such wars, a realistic scenario is a threefold operation in which small but potent U.S. forces rush to the scene of battle in order to halt an enemy attack in the early days, before valuable terrain is lost; larger U.S. forces are deployed over a period of weeks, during which enemy forces are degraded; and when their deployment is complete, U.S. forces launch a decisive counterattack aimed at destroying enemy forces, restoring lost territory, and attaining other political goals.

The task is to assemble a joint posture with the proper mix of assets to carry out operations in all three phases. Maritime forces provide an invaluable capacity for early availability, sea control, littoral operations from the sea, and forced entry. Clearly, air forces and other deep-strike assets will play major roles, especially in the initial halt and buildup phases, before large ground formations have had time fully to deploy. While the Air Force normally will deploy a large portion of these forces, the Navy and Marines provide fully one-third of total U.S. air power, and ship-launched cruise missiles provide added firepower. The Army contributes to deep-strike missions with attack helicopters and multiple-launch rocket systems and tactical missiles (MLRS/ATACMS). Blending these assets into a coordinated campaign, guided by a well construed targeting strategy, is key to success.

The ongoing acquisition of JSTARS, other C^4ISR assets, information networks, and such smart munitions as Skeet and BAT is greatly increasing the capacity of these long-range strike assets to attack targets in near real time, to destroy them with maximum effectiveness, and to inflict major attrition on enemy forces. In theory, they will possess the raw firepower and lethality to dominate many future wars while suffering few casualties. The mechanical application of attrition mathematics, however, is often a poor guide to judging the complex dynamics of war. Relying exclusively on deep-strike assets to defeat a well armed and wily enemy seems unwise because their effectiveness can be degraded by rugged terrain, bad weather, enemy tactics, and the sheer frictions of war. In addition, deep-strike assets cannot seize and hold ground, liberate cities, or physically eject enemy forces that are entrenched to the point of withstanding bombardment from the air. For these reasons, sizable numbers of ground forces often will be needed in order to conduct blocking actions during the defensive phase and to conduct swift, decisive counterattacks in the aftermath.

The exact number of ground forces needed will vary with the occasion. The key point is that numbers matter in determining how campaign plans are carried out. More forces broaden the tactical options available to commanders and thereby provide increased leverage over opponents. For example, two corps may possess more than double the combat power of only one corps—by a considerable margin. Two corps can allow a commander to conduct a dual "hammer-and-anvil" maneuver rather than a single-dimension operation, thus significantly enhancing prospects for defeating a tough enemy. In designing deployments and campaign plans, the proper approach normally will be to determine the missions that must be performed in order to win decisively and to tailor force commitments accordingly. This standard applies not only in determining total force levels, but also in selecting the mix of ground forces (that is, the combination of armor, mechanized, light infantry, airborne, air assault, amphibious, and artillery used on each occasion).

The combat operations of U.S. ground forces are undergoing major changes in response to new doctrines, technologies, structures, and practices. Their firepower and lethality are growing, frontages are widening, and speed of tactical mobility is increasing. Combat units are expected to strike deeper than in the past, and logistic support is improving while being streamlined. As a result, U.S. ground forces seem likely to preserve and upgrade their capacity to perform demanding missions in ways that keep their casualties low. In the final analysis, nonetheless, it is the joint nature of U.S. force operations that greatly elevates their combat power owing to the synergy, leverage, and fast tempo provided by all services working together on behalf of common campaign plans. Equally important, U.S. combat operations are being guided by a new military mentality aimed at capitalizing on the changing nature of modern warfare. Success at this endeavor promises to help keep U.S. forces superior to future opponents. If these gains are to be achieved, however, the necessary changes will have to be carried out, and future U.S. joint operations will need to be planned carefully in ways that reflect the mix of forces needed in each case.

U.S. defense plans also will need a clear understanding of force needs for carrying out specific new missions and operations in future crises and wars. In recent years, a prevailing assumption has been that U.S. military interventions will be either relatively small or quite big—for example, 10,000 troops for peacekeeping or, alternatively, 400,000 troops for a big major theater war. In some situations, one or the other of these polar-opposite models will still apply. In other situations, a quite different model may be needed: a swift and decisive medium-sized deployment of 75,000 to 150,000 troops. For example, the Kosovo conflict required about this number in directly committed air and naval units. *A sensible step would be to develop medium-sized joint strike packages for each of the three major commands: EUCOM, CENTCOM, and PACOM.* A joint package composed of the following units would provide a broad array of operational capabilities, including the capacity to conduct counterproliferation strikes against WMD-armed opponents:

- A CVBG, including a carrier, its air wing, and surface combatants armed with cruise missiles
- An ARG, with a Marine battalion and associated combat aircraft, backed by the capacity to build to one to two brigades
- For the Air Force, two to three aerospace expeditionary forces (AEFs), with a mix of interceptors, fighter bombers, bombers, reconnaissance, and other aircraft
- For the Army, one to two brigades capable of building to one to two divisions in a few weeks
- Advanced C^4ISR systems, information technologies, and smart munitions

Efforts to tailor appropriate force packages for crises and wars should be accompanied by careful thought about how U.S. force operations are to be integrated into the politics and diplomacy of each situation. Although the new U.S. military doctrines and forces will provide enhanced capabilities to inflict decisive battlefield defeat on opponents, the issues and stakes in many conflicts may be heavily political, rather than primarily military. The ability to win does not necessarily guarantee successful achievement of political goals. These goals often will be attainable only if military campaigns are tailored to support them and U.S. forces are employed accordingly. Because many crises and wars likely will grow out of murky politics, achieving such political-military integration of force operations may be one of the most important challenges confronting U.S. strategy in the coming years.

An equally weighty challenge will be learning how best to employ U.S. forces in WMD settings. During peacetime, a principal challenge will be reassuring a number of friends and allies who may be seeking U.S. nuclear deterrence coverage of the sort extended to NATO nations and to Japan. Extended deterrence worked in those places, but the numerous conditions for its re-creation may not be present along much of the southern belt and elsewhere. If this is the case, a different approach—one that adequately protects these countries and U.S. interests—will have to be found. Crafting it promises to be a demanding exercise in new strategic logic. The Cooperative Defense Initiative now being pursued in the Greater Middle East is an example of the new approaches likely to be needed. Another example is the U.S. effort to promote multilateral cooperation in Asia for a response to WMD threats.

During crises and wars, the challenge will be similarly difficult. Throughout the Cold War, U.S. forces faced an enemy with nuclear weapons in Central Europe, but since then, they have had the luxury of preparing for purely conventional conflicts. In contrast, future wars may see aggressors attacking with conventional forces, but holding WMD systems in reserve and being potentially willing to use them. Many important steps are under way to prepare for this development. Acquiring theater ballistic missile defenses will help protect deploying U.S. troops and other local targets. If a national missile defense system is built, the continental United States will be protected against limited attacks as well. Dispersing deployed forces can reduce their vulnerability. Acquisition of better strike assets, especially at long ranges in real time, will provide a capacity to degrade enemy WMD systems before their use.

While all of these steps will help in important ways, creating a sound political-military doctrine for force operations may be equally important. During the Cold War, the doctrine of forward defense and flexible response provided a path for initiating conventional operations, crossing the nuclear threshold, and gradually escalating in a politically controlled manner. Whether the same doctrine can be applied to the coming era of different strategic affairs is to be seen. What seems certain is that an appropriate doctrine will have to be created and implemented in ways that leave U.S. forces prepared to carry it out, not only through conventional operations but also through escalation when necessary.

Building Better Allied and Coalition Forces

Plans to enhance the quality of U.S. forces need to be accompanied by policies aimed at encouraging allies and partners to become better at power projection and new missions. Otherwise, U.S. forces will be left carrying too many burdens and so overstretched that they cannot be effective. For this reason, satisfactory progress in this arena may be fully as important as is enhancing the quality of U.S. forces. Owing to the Cold War heritage of defending only their own borders, allied forces are weak at performing new power projection missions. Whereas the United States can project about 750,000 troops from all services, the European allies could project only about 75,000 troops, and even then, slowly. Asian allies are even worse. As U.S. forces become more capable of swift power projection followed by RMA strike missions, the gap could grow so large that allied forces will not be able to operate with them even if political leaders want them to do so. If today's gap grows into a huge gulf, it could put a practical end to Western coalition defense planning.[1]

In 1998, there were few signs that NATO and the Europeans would respond effectively, but since then, matters have changed for the better in political terms. Initial signs of change were evident even before the Kosovo conflict erupted in early 1999, but when NATO initiated combat operations aimed at compelling Serbian troops to leave Kosovo, the experience turned out to be galvanizing. The conflict showed that wars could still occur in Europe and that NATO could muster the widespread resolve to win them. Kosovo also highlighted the shortfalls in European forces. Even though only air and naval forces were used, and operations were launched within range of NATO bases, the Europeans contributed only about 30 percent of the forces: the rest were provided by the United States. European forces performed their missions effectively, but deficiencies in such areas as C^4ISR, support aircraft, all-weather capability, and smart munitions became evident. When the Serbs withdrew in June, large U.S. and European ground forces entered Kosovo to perform enduring peacekeeping duties. In the aftermath, European leaders began voicing heightened awareness of the need to improve their forces, and U.S. leaders publicly urged them to act.

At its Spring 1999 summit in Washington, NATO adopted a new strategic concept. While this concept reaffirmed that NATO will remain a collective defense alliance for defending common borders, it also called upon the alliance to prepare forces for new missions—from peacekeeping to war fighting—outside its territory in the Euro-Atlantic area or beyond. At this summit, NATO also adopted its new Defense Capabilities Initiative (DCI), which encourages the Europeans to focus on swift power projection and decisive strike operations for new missions. This multiyear plan, now under way, calls for major improvements in such critical areas as RMA weapons, C^4I systems, multinational logistics, and strategic mobility assets. With the DCI under way, a few months later the Europeans announced parallel changes to their unification-oriented security and defense plans under the European Security and Defense Policy (ESDP). Their Helsinki accord broadened the ESDP beyond purely political steps to include efforts to build the types of improved military capabilities called for by the DCI.

These multilateral gestures have been accompanied by forward-looking steps by individual European countries. The United Kingdom defense review called for further measures aimed at improving British forces for power projection and modern strike operations. The French defense review did the same. Although these two countries always have been Europe's best at power projection, the Germans have begun showing signs of life by earmarking similar forces for new missions. In smaller ways, other countries, including Italy and the Netherlands, are doing likewise. Critics have derided these gestures as hollow because insufficient funds allegedly are being made available for fast progress. But at least the Europeans are now talking in responsive political language: in the past, such talk normally has been a sign of action to come.

The key issue now is whether the Europeans will act in sufficiently strong ways. The task facing them is far from Herculean. They already possess the basic assets needed to perform new missions if modest improvements are made. They have 2.3 million active troops under arms, and a force posture of about 53 mobilizable divisions, 3,350 combat aircraft, and 345 major naval combatants. This large posture—almost 50 percent larger than U.S. forces—arguably provides more formations than are needed to perform NATO missions, old and new. The chief constraint is lack of funds for new measures, but this problem seems solvable. Reducing current forces somewhat could free funds for investment: today, Europe's defense spending of $160 billion annually is mostly so consumed by personnel and operations that procurement efforts are too meager. If prudent priorities are set, the overall, 10-year cost of the DCI likely will be about $100 to $125 billion. This amount is only about 6 to 7 percent of Europe's planned defense spending for the coming decade. A combination of savings in current budgets plus modest increases—for example, 1 to 2 percent annually in real terms—could generate the flexible funds needed by the DCI and other improvement priorities.

The high-priority need is to improve European contributions to NATO rapid reaction forces (or similar formations) for new projection and strike missions. These forces number eight divisions, 600 combat aircraft, and 150 naval combatants. Currently, only about one-fourth of them can swiftly deploy outside NATO borders—a deficiency that was manifested in the Persian Gulf War and Kosovo. The biggest deficiency is lack of adequate strategic transport and logistic support assets for long-distance combat missions in austere settings. Fortunately, this deficiency can be remedied inexpensively: through using commercial aircraft and cargo ships and by acquiring limited amounts of special logistics equipment. The European forces already possess modern weapons and other platforms. If they are given improved C^4ISR assets, information systems and networks, smart munitions, and updated doctrines, they will be able to operate alongside RMA-capable U.S. forces in complementary ways. With better mobility and logistic support, they also will be able to deploy more rapidly than now and operate decisively with U.S. forces in the aftermath. In this way, NATO can preserve its capacity to perform combined U.S.-allied operations, not only inside Europe but outside as well.

Prospects in other regions are less bright, but modest steps can be taken as the political traffic permits. In Asia, Japan has agreed to new defense guidelines that enhance its forces for some new missions outside its borders, and other countries are expressing interest in collective military endeavors. In the Persian Gulf, U.S. partners have only small forces, but efforts to bring them closer together can enhance the region's self-defense prospects. Across the Greater Middle East, other countries, normally with bigger forces, can be brought together in a flexible web of coalition partnerships. Much will depend upon the Arab-Israeli peace process, but if major progress is made, the door may be opened for closer U.S. collaboration with various countries. In both regions, coalitions of the capable and willing, rather than formal alliances, likely will provide the main mechanisms for combined operations.

In all key regions, progress in this arena will be critical for both military and political reasons. Emerging security requirements are too big to be handled by U.S. forces alone: greater contributions by allies and partners are a military necessity. Politically, enhanced contributions are needed to maintain the bonds that tie the United States to its European and Asian alliances. Otherwise, allies will be defending their secure borders, while the United States struggles to defend common interests against serious threats and dangers elsewhere. Such a strategic imbalance will be unsustainable on both sides of the Atlantic and Pacific.

What the future will require is agreement on a new transatlantic defense and security bargain, and one for the Pacific as well. Such bargains will need to provide a common agenda for protecting mutual security interests, sharing burdens fairly, and ensuring that defense requirements are met through appropriate but flexible commitments of U.S. and allied forces. A strategic bargain of this sort sustained both alliances through the dark years of the Cold War and helped them emerge victorious. A similar but new bargain is needed now. If crafted, it will help enable the United States and its democratic partners perform the new and demanding missions of the future in ways that allow them to cope better with the problems and opportunities of a globalizing world.

Conclusion

This chapter has advanced several specific ideas for how U.S. defense planning in the coming era can be improved. These ideas will need to be evaluated on their merits. The underlying point is more important. The United States enjoys a favorable strategic situation around the world largely because, in the past, it created a strong defense posture and proved adept at using it effectively in peace, crisis, and war. With globalization now taking place and the international scene evolving in other ways, the same strategic effectiveness will be needed tomorrow. What marks today's scene as radically different from that of the Cold War is the scope and pace of change taking place, propelling events toward an uncertain destination. The central strategic challenge facing the United States is to influence how the future unfolds so that the ultimate destination proves healthy. Because the world is changing, U.S. foreign policy and national security strategy will need to change so that this demanding strategic mission can be accomplished. In more ways than one, the same judgment applies to U.S. defense planning. The United States will need to maintain strong, high-quality military forces. It will need to apply them wisely around the globe, in places dictated by U.S. interests and unfolding events. If the United States can perform both tasks, it will greatly enhance its capacity to deal with the international challenges ahead, regardless of how they unfold.

Notes

[1] For more detail, see David C. Gompert, Richard L. Kugler, and Martin C. Libicki, *Mind the Gap: Promoting a Transatlantic Revolution in Military Affairs* (Washington, DC: National Defense University Press, 1999).

Chapter 18

The Military in a New Era: Living with Complexity

Anthony H. Cordesman

Globalization is not a new phenomenon, nor is it easily defined in terms that are relevant for strategic and force planning. It is true that several key trends are reshaping much of global society. These include a far more integrated structure of trade and investment, the growth of multinational corporations, the integration of telecommunications and information systems, and a steady increase in the use of computer systems and automation.

At the same time, globalization can have a very different meaning in military terms. The world of the 21st century may be no more peaceful than the world of the 20th, or of any century before it. Progress is as likely to occur in the means of conflict as in the means of conflict resolution. Globalization can create new vulnerabilities and tensions as well as ease or transform old ones, and seemingly peaceful trends can cause violence with little or no strategic warning.

The problems that globalization creates for military force planners are also fundamentally different from those it creates for other analysts. Military planners do not need to plan for a future in which economic development ends a chief source of tension among nations. They do not need to plan for a world in which global information systems create a level of mutual understanding that resolves many past causes of conflict, or for a world that converges around democracy and shared values. Such a world is a world in which military planners can gradually go out of business.

Military planners do, however, need to plan for other global trends that are more threatening and are at least equally likely to shape the first half of the 21st century. The kind of regional, ethnic, and religious warfare that has characterized the early post-Cold War era can easily be equally characteristic of the next half-century. The United States may not face the kind of peer threats or ideological enemies it did during the 20th century, but it may well see the emergence of powerful regional powers and blocs that will sometimes be hostile to U.S. strategic interests.

Anthony H. Cordesman is a senior fellow at the Center for Strategic and International Studies. He previously served as assistant for national security to Senator John McCain. In addition, he has been a military analyst for ABC–TV and editor of Armed Forces Journal International. *Dr. Cordesman has also held positions in the Departments of Defense, State, and Energy.*

There are other global trends that may prove equally important and force the United States to plan for new threats and forms of warfare. These include:

- A world that has been, and remains, extraordinarily violent.
- The sheer complexity of a world in which so much change is occurring and in which overall economic development so far disguises a growing gap between rich and poor, both among nations and within them.
- A world in which unstable regional power blocs are mixed with a wide assortment of ethnic, religious, and racial tensions.
- A future in which the status of the United States as the world's only superpower is challenged by underspending, overcommitment, and the inability to commit resources that match the roles U.S. forces may be called upon to perform.
- A future in which these pressures will force the United States to adopt new forms of coalition warfare.
- A world in which technology transfer and shifts in the cost and availability of key technologies outpace the kind of developments that the United States is seeking in the revolution in military affairs. In such a world, the present edge that the United States preserves in conventional warfare may erode steadily because each improvement forces an escalation in marginal cost while producing diminishing returns in terms of effectiveness.
- A future in which nations that cannot challenge the United States and Western lead in conventional warfighting capabilities and technology increasingly turn to asymmetrical warfare.
- A world in which proliferation becomes the norm and a dominant form of asymmetrical warfare.
- A shift in the global economy that creates new patterns of vulnerability that match growing global economic interdependence and that have particular importance for maritime shipping, the flow of energy, and naval power.
- A world in which jointness and global engagement potential make the United States uniquely vulnerable to information warfare.
- The impact of changes in global media coverage and the battle for public and international opinion that has so far led the United States and the West to imprison themselves in a false image of perfect or bloodless war and that threatens to use the advantages the West can achieve through the revolution in military affairs to progressively limit the ways in which it can use force.

Living in Jurassic Park: The Problem of Complexity

Every new generation seems to invent reasons why history will end during the coming decades and to ignore the lessons of some 4,000 years of historical evidence. People look for an end to violence and seek reasons why it will end. It is useful in this context to consider a similar exercise in globalism and military planning toward the end of the last century. Imagine what a similar study on globalism would have found if it had taken place in the Royal United Services Institution in the late 1890s or early 1900s.

Such a study would have had perceptions remarkably similar to those that now influence much of the American thought about globalism. The British empire enforced a Pax Britannica throughout most of the world, although at the cost of an almost constant overdeployment of its land and air forces. The collapse of the French empire in 1870 had removed the only peer threat to British power, although the rise of the United States and Germany raised serious questions about the future. Lord Fisher's insistence on the construction of the *Dreadnought* and British pioneering of the submarine, advances in artillery and automatic weapons, and the promise of the airplane were creating a revolution in military affairs. The invention of the telegraph, the transatlantic cable, and early experiments with radio not only were making fundamental changes in the flow of information and world trade but also were creating the opportunity for information warfare.

The new power of mass media and global communications had helped trigger the Spanish-American War while appearing to put new limits on the ways in which wars could be fought as a result of media coverage of the Boer War. The rise of empire, the Industrial Revolution, and the vast expansion of world trade promised global development and new integration of the global economy. Economists and political scientists had begun a serious study of the impact of war that concluded that Western nations could no longer profit from wars in Europe. In fact, two Nobel Prizes were awarded in the years that followed the study proving the futility of war. Virtually the entire intellectual community of the Western world agreed that Western values would come to dominate and reshape the world—although there was little true consensus on what these values meant.

The problem with such perceptions is that they denied the true complexity of history. Like Jurassic Park, they were based on the false thesis that complexity theory is merely an annoyance to those who can identify clear and dominant trends. In the Jurassic Park movie, complex realities ruled over simple-minded designs: dinosaurs could not be tamed by creating a controlled setting for them. The same applies to world affairs. Complexity is, in fact, a key issue with terms such as *globalization*. According to this view of globalism, trees really do grow to the sky. The world is shaped by a few dominant trends and clear outcomes. There is no need to accept just how complex global trends really are, how rarely they are global in the sense of any broad symmetry in terms of their regional and local impact, and just how uncertain the future must be.

The Nonglobal Character of Globalization

One sign of this complexity is the fact that the global patterns in economic and technological change disguise great disparities in the level of development between rich and poor nations, within given regions, and within given states. The most recent report by the World Bank on *World Development Indicators* describes the following patterns and trends:[1]

- Demographics create major new pressures because of population growth.[2]
- The world's population grew from 4.4 billion in 1980 to 5.8 billion in 1997. It is projected to grow to 7.1 billion by 2015, and to 8.1 billion by 2030.
- The population of low-income nations will grow from 2 billion in 1997 to 3.4 billion in 2030 (66 percent growth). The population of middle-income states will grow from 2.9 billion to 3.7 billion (30 percent growth). The population of high-income states will change from 927 million to 981 million (6 percent growth).
- Basic shifts in the age of the population may exacerbate tensions. The percentage of people 14 years of age and younger in the low-income states is growing by 2 percent per year. It is growing by only 0.2 percent in middle-income states, and it is dropping by 0.6 percent annually in high-income states. The youth explosion in low-income states has reached the point where 40 percent of the population is 14 years of age or less while serious aging is taking place in the high-income states.[3]
- The average per capita income in low-income states is $350. It is $1,890 in middle-income states and $25,890 in high-income states. Low-income states make up about 35 percent of the world's 5.8 billion people, middle-income states account for 50 percent, and high-income states account for only 15 percent. (World Bank projections through 2050 show a rise in the percentage of the world's total population living in low-income states and a decline in the percentage living in high-income states.)
- There is little material evidence that low-income states are improving their position, in spite of the increase in many aspects of global economic growth. The average annual growth in the gross national product (GNP) in low-income states between 1965 and 1997 was 1.4 percent. It was 2.2 percent in the middle-income states, and 2.3 percent in the high-income states.
- Global trade favors the high-income and developed states. It makes up 40 percent of the GNP in low-income states, 50 percent in middle-income states, and 41 percent in the high-income states. But the volume for wealthy states is far higher than for low-income states.
- Regional trade blocs show a sharp growth in intraregional exports, relative to global markets. European Union (EU) exports within bloc rose from $76.5 billion in 1970 to $1,867.8 billion in 1997; North American Free Trade Agreement (NAFTA) exports rose from $22 billion to $496 billion.
- Global capital flows are not truly global.
- Foreign direct investment in 1997 totaled $10.6 billion in low-income countries, $160.6 billion in middle-income countries, and $233.9 billion in high-income countries.
- Private capital flows in 1997 totaled $17 billion in low-income countries and $268.9 billion in middle-income countries.
- Technology diffusion has so far favored richer and more developed states.

- The richest 20 percent of states control 74 percent of all telephone lines and have 91 percent of all Internet users.
- The top 10 telecommunications firms control 86 percent of the $262 billion global telecommunications market.

Other analysis further dramatizes the gap between rich and poor and the fact that globalization may not bring stability or reduce the threat of conflict. The richest 20 percent of the population controls 86 percent of world output and 82 percent of all world exports. Roughly 1.3 billion people live on less than $1 a day while the assets of the top three billionaires are equal to the GNP of all the "least developed" countries—with a total population of 600 million.[4] The impact of such differences on technology flows and sophistication is described in more detail in table 1.

Other data show that many positive trends are counterbalanced by serious problems and potential sources of conflict. For example, not only has globalization *not* brought world prosperity, democracy, and human rights, but also it has *not* brought something as simple as effective medical care. The infant mortality rate did drop from 76 to 58 per 1,000 births during 1990s. The percentage of 1-year-olds immunized rose from 70 percent to 89 percent. Access to safe water rose from 40 percent of the world's population to 72 percent. However, 160 million children remain severely undernourished, and 250 million are working in child labor. More than two-thirds of the developing world cannot afford to sustain health programs to deal with endemic diseases such as acquired immunodeficiency syndrome and malaria. Roughly 850 million people lack access to any health services, and 2.6 billion do not have access to basic sanitation.

These trends are only brief statistical snapshots of an extraordinarily complex set of changes. Nevertheless, they make it clear that globalization is extraordinarily complex and that any analysis must include any significant global trend that is relevant, not just those trends that are academically fashionable and politically correct. It is also clear that many global trends are potentially destabilizing or threatening.

Table 1. Technological Sophistication by Category of National Income (Total per 1,000 people)

	Income Category		
Devices	*Low*	*Middle*	*High*
Television sets	56	256	647
Telephone main lines	16	87	506
Mobile phones	1	15	189
Fax machines	0.2	0.9	49.7
Personal computers	2.2	15.8	264.4
Internet hosts (per 10,000 people)	0.10	3.96	374.89

Source: World Bank, *World Development Indicators, 1999* (New York: Oxford University Press for the World Bank, 2000).

Table 2. Patterns of World Conflict, 1945–1994

Area	Number of Wars: In Total	Number of Wars: Involving 10,000+ Dead	Number of Wars: With U.S. Military Action	Total Dead
Caribbean and Latin America	19	6	8	477,000
Mideast and North Africa	19	11	9	993,000
Sub-Saharan Africa	26	15	5	4,177,000
Europe	6	0	0	186,000
Central and South Asia	10	6	1	2,857,000
East Asia	34	17	6	10,396,000
Total	114	55	29	19,086,000

*Includes significant U.S. military assistance, covert action, demonstrative action, occupation, humanitarian efforts, combat, and emergency evacuations.

Source: International Institute for Strategic Studies, *Military Balance, 1998–1999* (London: Oxford University Press, 1998).

Table 3. Global Peacekeeping Activity

Operations	*Number of Activities*	*Some U.S. Involvement*	*Duration in Years: Over 2*	*Duration in Years: Over 5*	*10,000+ Peacekeepers Involved*	*Some Combat Activity*
Current UN	17	14	11	0	3	5
Past UN	27	23	6	5	7	7
Current Non-UN	6	5	1	1	3	2
Past Non-UN	5	2	1	1	4	1
Total	55	44	19	7	17	15

*Generally very low level or indirect involvement during fighting between principals.

Continuing Global Violence and Conflict

It is equally important to point out that military planning cannot be based on the assumption that there will be any kind of global clash of civilizations, between rich and poor states, or between "north" and "south," in the sense this means conflict between the developed and developing world. Such conflicts are always remotely possible, but unlikely.

Table 2 lists the most serious conflicts in a world that has had some 1,200 armed clashes and encounters since World War II.[5] It does show, however, that future conflicts *within* civilizations, regions, and nations are an ongoing certainty. The nature and frequency of these conflicts cannot be predicted, but there have been 20 to 30 ongoing regional civil wars and local conflicts every day since World War II, and a recent study found that there were 23 ongoing local conflicts in which 500,000 or more civilians were at risk.

It is also important to note that the existence of peer threats during World War I, World War II, and the Cold War tended to disguise the true nature of global violence. Figure 1 shows that such violence has always been dominated by intrastate killing, and that the kind of violence that leads to the peacemaking activity that now dominates U.S. and Western military operations is nothing new.

There is nothing new about this aspect of globalism or about the U.S. military involvement that follows. Work by Adam Spiegel of the Center for Naval Analyses found that the United States had overtly used military force more than 240 times before the end of the Cold War, excluding covert action and major military assistance efforts not involving an active combat presence. The real total would be well in excess of 300. These actions ranged from demonstrative actions to major wars, and they have very little in common. They are also almost impossible to categorize without getting into endless controversies over their context and definition.

The collapse of the Soviet Union and Warsaw Pact have scarcely brought global stability or peace, or an end to such U.S. military involvement. Instead, it has shifted the focus of military operations to peacemaking activities that have become something close to a new paradigm of globalism. UN peacekeeping and peacemaking activity is accelerating, and the United States alone has deployed troops 36 times since 1989—largely in peacekeeping missions. This compares with 10 times during the previous 40 years of the Cold War, including deployments for Korea and Vietnam. This trend has led to increased levels of U.S. military deployments even as U.S. forces have been cut. These engagements, which are summarized in table 3, are likely to remain key priorities for U.S. force planning indefinitely.

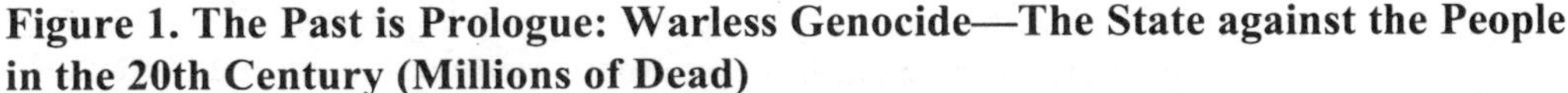

Figure 1. The Past is Prologue: Warless Genocide—The State against the People in the 20th Century (Millions of Dead)

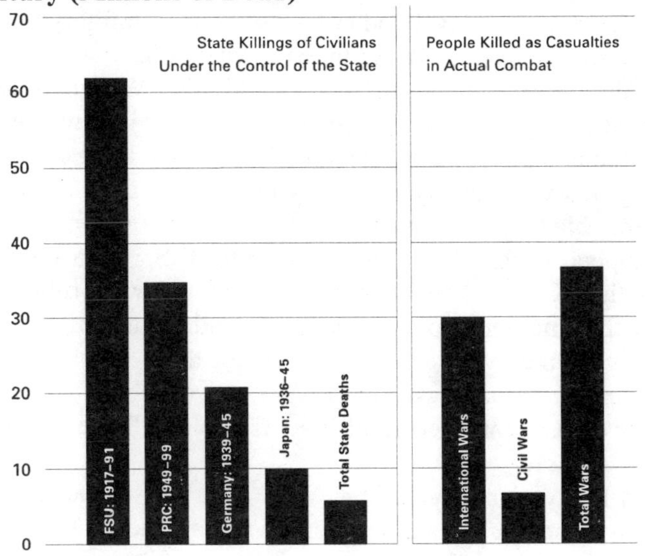

Source: Adapted from an estimate in *The Economist*, September 11, 1999, and Rudy J. Rummel, "Statistics of Democide."

It also seems realistic to warn that military planners cannot hope for any clear or constant criteria for determining what kinds of crises will involve military action. So far, the United States and its allies have dealt with each new crisis on a case-by-case basis. Vietnam may have appeared to lead the United States to reach decisions on such issues, but the years that have followed have shown that U.S. strategy documents and planning guidance failed to produce any clear doctrine or criteria for using military force. The legal constraints set up after Vietnam in the War Powers Act have been honored largely by evading any test of the act's provisions and constitutionality.

The United States has made an effort since Kosovo to define a Clinton doctrine for dealing with the commitment of military forces, but this "doctrine" so far consists of little more than a moralistic statements that, "If the world community has the power to stop it, we ought to stop ethnic cleansing" (June 20, 1999) and "If somebody comes after innocent civilians and tries to kill them en masse because of their race, their ethnic background or their religion and it is within our power to stop it, we will stop it" (June 22, 1999).[6]

Vacuous catch phrases, however, do not define real-world criteria for U.S. or Western military action, regardless of whether they are moral or noble in character. It is far easier to use terms such as *en masse* than to define them. While a phrase like "their race, their ethnic background or their religion" may seem noble, one does have to wonder why the level of suffering in a case like Cambodia should be excluded.

It is equally vacuous, however, to use seemingly pragmatic criteria such as vital strategic interest. The Weinberger doctrine's emphasis on such criteria has proved to be no more meaningful than the Clinton morality play. The United States simply cannot wait long enough to determine whether a crisis or problem involves a vital strategic interest. One awkward corollary of being a global superpower is that anything anywhere in the world involves at least a tenuous tie to some strategic interest.

The vast majority of low-level and crisis-driven U.S. military interventions during the Cold War did not involve any direct threat to vital U.S. strategic interests, and more than half had only a limited direct tie to the Cold War. Well over two-thirds did not involve significant strategic warning or occur under conditions where the United States could credibly predict and put clear limits on the ultimate level of its military commitments. In passing, it seems equally fair to say that in well over 70 percent of the cases, it would be impossible to get any consensus from U.S. foreign policy analysts over the level of moral imperative that these crises created for U.S. military action.

The fact is that U.S. and Western military action will probably continue to be event-driven by the emergence of a given crisis, and the use of force will then be determined by whether the event affects U.S. allies, there is major media concern, or those at hazard arouse political sympathy. As one ex-chief of staff of a U.S. military service said after the Clinton speech on June 22, "We will use our power if they look like us."

The same is likely to be true of the West as a whole, particularly now that the European Union is seeking to create a "crisis-management" force for contingencies that it has not bothered to define. Senior European officers have feelings similar to those of many U.S. officers. They believe that they increasingly are being asked to use military force to make up for diplomatic failures in a context where civil political decisionmakers pay far too little attention to whether military force can be effective, the risks involved, the ability to withdraw if military action fails, and the endgame in translating military victory into lasting political success.

The Regionalization of Power

The United States must also prepare for major regional conflicts, some of which could involve a major nuclear power and an emerging peer. These include the immediate risk of a major regional conflict in the Persian Gulf or in Korea and the longer term threats posed by Russia and China. They also include major regional wars against opponents such as North Korea and Iraq, and a wide range of opponents that may emerge with little warning.

The world now has nearly 200 nations, nearly 80 percent of which have emerged since World War II. About half of the emerging nations have serious ethnic and religious divisions or instability, and about 40 percent have disputed borders. It may be unfair to categorize some states as rogue or failed. At the same time, extremist regimes such as that in Libya are likely to emerge in many parts of the world. Continuing civil wars in states such as Burma/Myanmar, Sri Lanka, and Sudan are not likely to vanish. There is also a continuing risk of major regional wars that do not directly involve U.S. interests, but which could lead to U.S. intervention, at least on a humanitarian level. The nuclear arms race between India and Pakistan is perhaps the grimmest case in point.

It is not clear how these tensions and conflicts will interact with the emergence of regional blocs. It is clear, however, that U.S. military planning does face the need for power projection in a wide range of regions with very different force requirements and potential conditions for coalition warfare. U.S. planning must also consider the possibility of the emergence of the following new regional power blocs without being certain whether and when such blocs will be partners, rivals, or opponents:

- *The European Union and Europe versus the North Atlantic Treaty Organization (NATO) and Atlanticism:* The United States must face continuing uncertainty regarding Russia and other members of the former Soviet Union (FSU), and the possible emergence of a strategic relationship between China and Russia. At the same time, it may see NATO and Atlanticism erode as the European Union grows stronger, and economic and political rivalries distance Europe from the United States. Ironically, this may not reduce the implied U.S. military commitment to NATO or the level of U.S. peacemaking involvement in Europe.
- *Tense Middle East and Persian Gulf:* It seems unlikely that the United States will demonize Iran, Iraq, and Libya indefinitely. At the same time, there is little near-term prospect that the United States will not face the continuing risk of a major regional war in the Persian Gulf. It seems unlikely that even if an Arab-Israeli peace does involve all parties, the United States will not continue to have commitments in the Levant, and there is little near- to mid-term prospect that the United States can do anything more than slow the rate of proliferation in the region.

- *Divided Asia:* Asian economic development has brought a tenuous stability to Southeast Asia, although scarcely to Northeast Asia and South Asia. North Korea and the China-Taiwan issue currently seem likely to present lasting military problems, and China could emerge as a serious threat in regional terms. Even in Southeast Asia, the Association of Southeast Asian Nations (ASEAN) does little to bring stability to nations such as Burma/Myanmar and Cambodia, and the risk of a massive civil war in Indonesia is unlikely to be eliminated.
- *Unstable Africa:* It is far from clear that any part of Africa can cooperate as an effective region. North Africa, however, presents obvious problems in terms of immigration and transnational threats to Europe. The region is a major energy exporter, and it could affect naval traffic through the Mediterranean. So far, no Maghreb nation has demonstrated that it can develop fast enough to deal with its population growth. A large part of sub-Saharan Africa is already at war, and these wars are creating new and unstable regional power blocs. The increasing U.S. dependence on West African oil gives these problems growing strategic importance.
- *Unstable Latin America:* Like East Asia, Latin America has experienced significant economic growth in recent years. At the same time, economic and ethnic divisions still threaten to create new conflicts, and Colombia is already involved in a civil drug war of major importance to the United States.

It should be stressed that each region has its successes and the fact that things can degenerate in each region, in spite of globalism and more positive trends, is no indication that they will. U.S. military planning, however, is not concerned with regional successes. It is concerned with regional failures, and there are several major areas of potential regional conflict that involve nations fully armed for a future conflict. They include:

- Greece and Turkey
- Arab-Israeli
- Persian Gulf
- North and South Korea
- People's Republic of China and Taiwan
- South China Sea/Spratly Islands
- India and Pakistan
- Horn of Africa
- Sudan
- Congo

Reacting to a Violent and Uncertain World

Put simply, there is no meaningful prospect that the United States will face less need to plan for major regional wars during the next quarter century, or that any U.S. military service will face less need for global engagement, than it does today. The same is true of peacemaking activity, no matter what strategies and doctrines U.S.

political and military leaders may appear to agree on at any given time. Moreover, the very complexity of the national and regional problems in the modern world means that crises will emerge with only ambiguous strategic warning, that most U.S. scenario analysis and contingency planning will continue to have only limited success, and that the level of U.S. involvement will be contingency-driven. Strategy and doctrine that attempt to deny these realities have no chance of success and will almost certainly lead to planning that fails to properly prepare U.S. military forces for the future.[7]

It should also be clear that the risk of underestimating the true nature of the complexity of the trends that shape the modern world is particularly severe in the case of military forces. Conflicts and crises almost inevitably are random walks through history. They involve the cases in which the system does not work, and the trends that are perceived as dominant do not apply. This is true even in the case of the use of force to prevent conflict or when the United States and its allies attempt two politically correct oxymorons: crisis management and conflict resolution.

The true nature of globalism means that U.S. military action will remain event-driven. Neither the Clinton nor Weinberger doctrines will have a meaningful impact on this fact. Vacuous generalizations about treating the world as a morality play are neither a doctrine nor a policy. Statements about committing U.S. forces only to contingencies that involve vital strategic interests are strategically naïve to the point of being ridiculous. The United States will be unable to wait to determine whether a given crisis affects vital national interests.

Living as the World's Only Superpower

The nature of U.S. global military power adds more complexity to this situation. As much through an accident of history as anything else, the United States is now the world's only "superpower" in the sense that it is the only power in the world with major global power projection assets. Britain, France, and Russia can project power broadly, but only in limited amounts and with limited sustainability. At the same time, the United States is thrust into global roles that put serious strains upon its forces and that make it potentially vulnerable to shifts in regional military balances, proliferation, and asymmetrical warfare.

In summary, U.S. military globalism has the following strengths and weaknesses:

Strengths

- No peer threat likely during the time frame of this study; in any case have 5 to 10 years of warning.
- Superior base of conventional warfighting technology, and superior research-and-development effort.
- Lead in nuclear offensive technology and parity in weapons; lead in missile defense capability.
- Global power projection capabilities to support coalition warfare through the Army and Air Force power projection; independent global power projection capability through the Navy and Marine Corps.

- Superiority in space-based sensor and intelligence systems, overall superiority in intelligence and strategic reconnaissance.
- Major lead in strategic airlift and sealift, refueling capability.

Weaknesses

- Insufficient present resources to support current strategy of dealing with two near simultaneous major regional wars.
- Peacetime funding dynamic: only major new threat or near catastrophe will lead to major increases in military spending and force structure.
- Overdeployed, overcommitted, and overseas, as well as underfunded, underpaid, and undersupported.
  —Procurement problems: major dropout rate and slippage in programmed Quadrennial Defense Review force improvements.
  —Prolonged readiness problems.
  —Revolution in military affairs is unaffordable; the question is whether we can fund a slower "evolution" in military affairs.
- Growing global political constraints on the ways we can use force.
- Global proliferation.
- Globalization of asymmetrical warfare.
- Uncertainty and insufficient resources combine to force a reactive, event-driven strategy.
- Put differently, forces and resources are insufficient to support a consistent global policy. The United States must often say "no" and make hard decisions about its priorities and interests.

Perhaps the greatest single problem the United States faces in dealing with the global pressures described earlier is one of resources. Some studies indicate that the present U.S. force posture has been underfunded by some $100 billion and that the United States would need to spend roughly 4 percent of its GNP to adequately fund its current strategy and force goals.[8] This percentage compares with planned spending of 2.9 percent in fiscal year 2000, which will drop to 2.4 percent in 2010 and 2 percent in 2020.[9] There is strong evidence that the United States is not willing to spend the money necessary to meet its existing commitments, deal with continuing deployments for peacemaking and other unanticipated missions, develop and acquire a revolution in military affairs, and modernize its current mix of forces.

There is no way to predict whether the United States will increase defense spending to a level that matches its force plans and strategy in the future. If globalization continues to mean the lack of a peer threat and major wars, however, the United States is most likely to try to remain a superpower on the cheap. There will be a continuing mismatch between its strategy and force plans and the money it makes available. It is also likely that the declared foreign policy of the United States will continue to understate the real-world probability of U.S. interventions and peacemaking activity and consistently push the United States into overdeploying its forces.

No other power or international body is likely to fill this gap. Kosovo is living evidence of the fact that there is little near- to mid-term prospect that globalization will create meaningful international peacemaking capabilities under the United Nations. In fact, divisions in the Security Council make it likely that little effort will be made to create any kind of global norms for the use of armed force to intervene in humanitarian, peacemaking, and regional crises and conflicts. While Europe is creating a "crisis-management force" under the European Union, its members are simultaneously making major cuts in their military expenditures and forces. There is no other region where regional coalition partners are likely to create military capabilities that can greatly reduce the strain on U.S. forces.

This creates a strong prospect that the United States will find itself remaining the world's only superpower, largely because no peer will emerge to expose the limits of its military capabilities. Like Britain during the Pax Britannica of a century ago, the United States is likely to remain overdeployed in ad hoc operations and to make resource decisions that steadily compromise its military capabilities. The end result may be a cruel parody of an old joke about force planning, namely, the goal is to do more and more with less and less, until the resulting forces attempt to do everything with nothing.

The only way that the United States could avoid this would be to fund a capabilities-driven force rather than a requirements-driven force. The United States cannot now predict the timing or scale of the conflicts that will involve it in the future. All it can predict is that global interests will require global power projection capability, that major regional contingencies will remain a mid- and long-term requirement, and that the United States must at least consider the long-term emergence of some form of major peer threat and/or proliferator.

The U.S. Military Response: Living with Complexity

There is no way to predict whether or when globalization will intensify the need for U.S. military intervention, reduce it, or leave it at roughly its current levels. The most likely reality is that there will be no constant trend, and periods of relative quiet will be followed by high-stress cases such as major regional contingencies.

There are, however, a number of aspects of globalization that will almost always affect U.S. military requirements and planning. These include added reliance on coalition warfare, technology transfer, asymmetrical warfare, proliferation, shifts in maritime power and traffic, and new forces of war such as information warfare.

Coalition Warfare, Global Interoperability, and Global Engagement

The growth of regional powers and the limits to U.S. military capabilities mean that U.S. forces generally will have to fight on a coalition basis. Some of these coalitions will exist before a crisis and allow the development of interoperability and common force plans. Many, however, will not. The United States currently has a number of core partners. These include NATO, Australia, Britain, Canada, Egypt, Japan, Israel, Saudi Arabia, and South Korea. It is interesting to note, however, that virtually all of these partners now spend far less of their GNP on defense than the United States does, and most have steadily cut real defense spending since 1991. If there is an arms race among the main coalition partners of the United States, it is to cut military capabilities and take a peace dividend.

Kosovo has already demonstrated the risk involved if coalitions do not mean the growth of global interoperability among U.S. friends and allies. Secretary of Defense William Cohen stated in his speech to the International Institute of Strategic Studies on the lessons of the war:[10]

> We have all agreed to develop forces that are more mobile, beginning with the reassessment of NATO's strategic lift requirements for planning purposes. We need forces, we've agreed, that can sustain themselves longer; that means having a logistics system that will ensure they have the supplies when and where they need them. [We need] forces that communicate more effectively, I just touched upon that. We have to have a common NATO command and control structure and communication architecture by the year 2002, so we are working to develop that as well. [We need] forces that can engage more effectively; that means having the new advanced technologies such as greater stocks of precision-guided munitions and forces that can survive better against chemical, biological or nuclear weapons, and also information warfare.
>
> . . . What we now have to do is to measure up and to match the political commitment with actual deeds. There I would say the evidence is less encouraging. As I look around at the budgets of the members of the NATO Alliance I certainly see restructuring taking place as far as the size of the forces, and one cannot criticize that. But I also see a corresponding reduction in a commitment as far as the budget is concerned. So while there is a great sense of enthusiasm for what we have to do for the future to modernize NATO, to make it as effective as it needs to be, there is not at this point the kind of political commitment to actually carry it out. . . . [T]his is something that we must continue to point to; otherwise the gap that you have been reading and hearing about—the technological gap between the United States and the other NATO Allies—will continue to grow. If that disparity becomes deeper and more prolonged, that will carry political implications for the NATO Alliance itself.

The practical issues for the United States are: first, what to do if even Europe fails to develop the proper mix of force improvements and interoperability necessary to serve as an effective coalition partner; and second, what will happen in any future conflicts in the Persian Gulf, Korea, the Taiwan Straits, or any other area where coalition partners show even fewer signs of developing effective military capabilities. None of the other alliances and semi-alliances the United States has elsewhere in the world is growing stronger, with the possible exceptions of Israel and Japan. As a result, the United States may have to rely on a global coalition strategy that is

- Contingency-driven, and where the identity and commitment of the partners may be uncertain before, during, and after the contingency.
- Entangling and ally-driven, rather than serving U.S. policy.

- Largely regional and involving very disparate forces.
- Characterized by interoperability, which will almost invariably present major problems.

It is easy to talk about globalism as a trend in civilian technology, but there are few signs of any coherent globalism in coalition warfare. The end result may well be to force the United States into tailored "high-low" regional engagement strategies where the United States designs its command, control, communications, and computers, intelligence, surveillance, and reconnaissance (C^4ISR) battle management systems, tactics, and force employment strategies around the lack of allied capabilities and globalism.

Interoperability will often have to be unilateral. The United States will need training, tactics, and technology that allow it to rapidly integrate its forces in a wide range of unanticipated combinations of allies with little warning and preplanning. Access to bases is also likely to be a growing issue because of the contingency-driven and ad hoc nature of many coalitions. As a result, U.S. forces must be as expeditionary as possible, and they must be capable of projecting power faster and at longer in-theater distances. The value of deep-strike capabilities from the sea, sea-based missile defense, continental U.S.-based bomber forces, airlift/fast sealift deployable forces, and sea-based mobile pre-positioning will also increase with time.

These points reinforce another lesson that the U.S. military drew from Kosovo—the need to rethink joint warfare and military service planning to achieve what it calls "global force integration." The United States may not be able to structure any coherence behind its global coalition options, but it may be able to create "globalism" within its own force structure. The Department of Defense report on the lessons of the war in Kosovo notes that[11]

> Our ability to reach back and use capabilities in the continental United States to perform functions formerly accomplished only in the theater of military operations is one of the highlights of Operation Allied Force. Such capability improves responsiveness to urgent requirements in a conflict and reduces the amount of equipment and the number of personnel that must be transported to the theater. In short, the capability to integrate our force globally yields significant improvements in our ability to respond to crises, particularly during their initial stages.
>
> . . . Extensive growth in communications capacity enabled an unprecedented degree of reliance on U.S.-based forces to provide direct support for in-theater tasks. Targets in Kosovo and the Federal Republic of Yugoslavia were developed through the concerted effort of numerous agencies in the United States cooperating closely with commands in Europe. Planning and integration of cruise missile attacks by bombers operating from the continental United States and the United Kingdom and by ships and submarines operating in the Mediterranean were closely coordinated by commanders and planners who were widely separated geographically. Bomb damage assessments of strikes made against targets in theater were conducted by agencies and commands located in the United States in close support with efforts by commands in the European theater. This system of using geo-

graphically dispersed activities to perform and integrate bomb damage assessment (BDA) became known as federated BDA. Expert personnel located in the United States and Europe performed detailed planning of information operations. Kosovo operations continued a trend of increasing global integration of U.S. forces and commands to support operations in a distant theater.

Integration of global forces during Kosovo operations provides insight to the design of future exercises and training required for increasing our proficiency in the complex actions necessary for integrating a global force. While our focus is on theater operations, the Department must exercise the global capabilities required in support of theater operations. Additionally, the Department must recognize the need to deploy forces in a myriad of unpredictable scenarios requiring new levels of adaptability and flexibility in global interoperability and integration.

. . . our experience in integrating worldwide capabilities during Operation Allied Force highlights the importance of the joint operational architecture concept. This architecture would define the relationships between forces and commands involved in complex operations. A joint operational architecture would also serve as the basis for developing technical architectures to support warfighters' needs, and for prioritizing resources and training requirements. These technical architectures would be defined for the spectrum of global threats and would identify any organizational changes required to support the National Military Strategy.

It is far from clear that this kind of globalism can compensate for continued U.S. overcommitment and underspending or for the weaknesses in regional coalition partners. At the same time, it is clear that the United States cannot afford service- or theater-oriented force plans and strategies.

Arms Transfers and Transfer of Technology

For nearly a century, there has been a continuing shift in the global transfer of technology and in the flow of conventional arms. These trends are increasingly being affected by the transfer of many of the key aspects of the weapons and technology that make up the revolution in military affairs. They include the transfer of precision weapons, smart munitions, and C^4ISR systems that support the broad range of capabilities that currently give the United States its global edge in conventional warfighting capabilities. This mix of capabilities is as follows:

- *Unity of command*: The level of unity of command and "fusion" achieved during the Persian Gulf War was scarcely perfect, but it was far more effective than that possible in most states. Advanced powers have improved its unity of command and ability to conduct joint operations.
- *Jointness, combined operations, combined arms, and the "AirLand Battle"*: Advanced powers can use technology to train and integrate in ways that allow far more effective approaches to jointness, combined arms, and combined operations. They have developed tactics that closely integrate air and land operations.

- *Emphasis on maneuver*: The United States had firepower and attrition warfare until the end of the Vietnam War. In the years that followed, it converted its force structure to place an equal emphasis on maneuver and deception. This emphasis has been adopted by Britain and France, and by other advanced states.
- *"24-hour war"—superior night, all-weather, and beyond-visual-range warfare*: "Visibility" is always relative in combat. There is no such thing as a perfect night vision, an all-weather combat system, or a way of acquiring perfect information at long ranges. Advanced technology air and land forces, however, have far better training and technology for such combat than they ever had in the past, and they are designed to wage warfare continuously at night and in poor weather. Equally important, they are now far more capable of taking advantage of the margin of extra range and tactical information provided by superior technology.
- *Near-real-time integration of C^4I/BM/T/BDA*: New organization, technology, and software systems make it possible to integrate various aspects of command, control, communications, computers, and intelligence (C^4I); battle management (BM); targeting (T); and battle damage assessment (BDA) to achieve a near-real-time integration and decisionmaking-execution cycle.
- *A new tempo of operations*: Superiority in virtually every aspect of targeting, intelligence gathering and dissemination, integration of combined arms, multiservice forces, and night and all-weather warfare makes it possible to achieve both a new tempo of operations and one far superior to that of the enemy.
- *A new tempo of sustainability*: Advanced forces will have maintainability, reliability, reparability, and the speed and overall mobility of logistic, service support, and combat support force activity that broadly match their maneuver and firepower capabilities. The benefits of these new capabilities are already reflected in such critical areas as the extraordinarily high operational availability and sortie rates of Western combat aircraft and in the ability to support the movement of heliborne and armored forces.
- *Beyond-visual-range air combat, air defense suppression, air base attacks, and airborne C^4I/BM*: The coalition in the Gulf had a decisive advantage in air combat training, beyond-visual-range air combat capability, antiradiation missiles, electronic warfare, air base and shelter and kill capability, stealth and unmanned long-range strike systems, Identification, Friend or Foe (IFF) and air control capability, and airborne C^4I/BM systems such as the E–3 and ABCCC. These advantages allowed the coalition to win early and decisive air supremacy. Advanced forces will steadily improve the individual capability of these systems and their integration into "netrocentric" warfare.
- *Focused and effective interdiction bombing*: Advanced forces will organize effectively to use their deep-strike capabilities to carry out a rapid and effective pattern of focused strategic bombing where planning is sufficiently well coupled to intelligence and meaningful strategic objectives so that such strikes achieve the major military objectives that the planner sets. At the same time, targeting, force allocation, and precision kill capabilities will advance to the point where interdiction bombing and strikes are far more lethal and strategically useful than in previous conflicts.

- *Expansion of the battlefield (deep strike)*: As part of the effort to offset the Warsaw Pact's numerical superiority, U.S. tactics and technology emphasized using AirLand battle capabilities to extend the battlefield far beyond the immediate forward edge of the battle area. The coalition exploited the resulting mix of targeting capability, improved airstrike capabilities, and land force capabilities in ways during the Gulf War that played an important role in destroying Iraqi ground forces during the air phase of the war and that helped the coalition break through Iraqi defenses and exploit that breakthrough. Even in Kosovo, the United States and NATO were only beginning to employ advanced deep-strike targeting technologies and precision strike systems, and far more advanced systems are currently in development.
- *Integration of precision-guided weapons into tactics and force structures*: Advanced forces will exploit a technical edge in the ability to use precision-guided weapons with far more realistic training in using such weapons and the ability to link their employment to far superior reconnaissance and targeting capability.
- *Realistic combat training and use of technology and simulation*: During the Gulf War, the United States and Britain used training methods based on realistic combined arms and AirLand training, large-scale training, and adversary training. These efforts proved far superior to previous methods and were coupled to a far more realistic and demanding system for ensuring the readiness of the forces involved. They show the value of kinds of training that allow forces to rapidly adapt to the special and changing conditions of war.

So far, the United States retains a major global lead in most of these technologies, but the same trends that reduce the cost of virtually every other aspect of information processing may reduce the cost to other nations of acquiring similar capabilities, raise the cost to the United States of trying to preserve its current edge to unaffordable levels, or drive the benefits from any given aspect of the revolution in military affairs to the point of diminishing returns.

This particular form of globalism does not seem to be an imminent possibility. While many nations do possess important advanced arms and military systems, declassified U.S. intelligence scarcely indicates that there is a global, high-technology arms race.[12] The volume of global arms sales has dropped sharply in constant dollars since the late 1980s, and a detailed review of the equipment holdings in the 1999–2000 edition of the *Military Balance* indicates that the technology content of these arms transfers has been considerably less threatening than was estimated at the start of the Clinton administration.

The latest State Department estimate indicates that deliveries from world arms sales in constant 1996 dollars dropped from $84.4 billion in 1987 to $42.4 billion in 1996, and that sales to the developing world dropped from $58.3 billion in 1987 to $23.7 billion in 1996.[13] Work by Richard F. Grimmett of the Congressional Research Service includes data that are somewhat more up to date but covers only transfers to developing nations. These data indicate that new arms transfer agreements—which are a good measure of future trends in arms sales—dropped from $21.6 billion in 1991 to $13.2 billion in 1998.[14]

It should be noted, however, that these same sources do show a relatively high rate of transfer of high-technology weapons systems by the United States, Europe, and Russia in categories such as tanks, major surface combatants, guided missile patrol boats, supersonic combat aircraft, surface-to-air missiles, surface-to-surface missiles, and antiship missiles. For example, U.S. experts estimate that 420 major surface-to-surface missiles, 13,352 surface-to-air missiles, and 947 major antiship missiles were transferred to the developing world between 1991 and 1998.[15]

Arms and technology transfers are also extremely cyclical—with sudden massive bursts in the transfers of new forms of technology and arms. The decline in the current volume of global transfer, for example, has been heavily driven by a combination of factors that have favored the United States but that may not continue to do so in the future:

- The collapse of Russian arms sales and China's inability to manufacture competitive high-technology weapons for export.
- International sanctions against Iraq and Libya.
- Iran's economic problems, U.S. pressure not to sell to Iran, partial Russian cooperation, Iranian economic problems and Iran's decision not to attempt massive rearmament after its defeat in the Iran-Iraq War in 1988.
- Syria's poverty and inability to pay its massive arms debt to Russia.
- The economic collapse of North Korea.

Many of these constraints on world arms sales are easing or are likely to ease with time. At the same time, such constraints have not always helped lead to global stability. The inability to compete in conventional forces has unquestionably helped lead hostile states to pursue alternative options such as asymmetrical warfare and proliferation, and to increase their incentive to acquire lower cost and less constrained technologies, such as information warfare, for new types of wars and battles. Accordingly, the United States needs to be extremely careful in dealing with technology transfer and has strong incentives to limit the transfer of technology to potentially hostile states. It is also clear that it is far better and cheaper to deny technology transfer than to deal with its consequences.

At the same time, the United States should be very careful to conduct ongoing technological assessments to determine what rate of technology transfer will occur in spite of U.S. efforts, and it should not exaggerate the advantages technology gives U.S. forces. It seems fair to state that the United States has not deployed a single major military system on time, at cost, and with the promised effectiveness in the last quarter century and that it normally takes 3 to 5 years after initial deployment to modify and fix systems that were supposedly combat-ready in the first place.

The United States has a long history of exaggerating the effectiveness and useful life span of high-technology force multipliers, as well as of underestimating their life cycle cost and related training and sustainment costs. No element of the Department of Defense, U.S. defense industry, or the U.S. strategic studies community has an impressive rate of accuracy in such forecasting, and there is an almost universal history of advocacy analysis and special pleading. Given current global trends, a U.S.

technological edge, backed by transfers to friendly states, will remain a critical asset. The United States must, however, be extremely careful about exaggerating its requirements for technology and its effectiveness. The regular reexamination and iteration of requirements analysis will be vital to a successful high-technology strategy in a resource-constrained environment.

Asymmetrical Warfare

There is another aspect of military globalism that the United States must consider. Every reaction produces an equal and opposite reaction, and many hostile states have found two major counters to the kind of high-technology advantages that the United States can now exploit in conventional warfare. One is the use of asymmetrical warfare; the other, proliferation of weapons of mass destruction.

There is nothing new about asymmetrical warfare per se or about the fact that it poses a global threat to the United States. China posed a major asymmetrical threat to the United States in Korea by using deception, surprise, and human wave tactics. The United States was decisively defeated in Vietnam by asymmetrical warfare, even though it won virtually every conventional battle. The United States was driven out of Lebanon and Somalia and faced a major threat in Kosovo because of such methods of warfare.

The Department of Defense report on the lessons of the war notes that[16]

> in the Kosovo conflict, Serbia's Milosevic was unable to challenge superior allied military capabilities directly. His fielded forces were compelled to hide throughout most of the campaign, staying in caves and tunnels and under the cover of forest, village, or weather. He was forced to husband his antiaircraft missile defenses to sustain his challenge to our air campaign. Therefore, he chose to fight chiefly through asymmetric means: terror tactics and repression directed against Kosovar civilians; attempts to exploit the premium the alliance placed on minimizing civilian casualties and collateral damage; creation of enormous refugee flows to create a humanitarian crisis, including in neighboring countries; and the conduct of disinformation and propaganda campaigns.
>
> These tactics created several serious challenges for our forces, all of which we were able to overcome thanks to excellent training, leadership, equipment and motivation. Nevertheless, these challenges underscored the continued need to develop new operational concepts and capabilities to anticipate and counter similar asymmetric challenges in the future. Simply put, adversaries will use unconventional approaches to circumvent or undermine U.S. and allied strengths and exploit vulnerabilities. Milosevic illustrated very clearly his propensity for pursuing asymmetric approaches. He chose his tactics in the hope of exploiting the NATO nations' legitimate political concerns about target selection, collateral damage, and conducting military operations against enemy forces that are intentionally intermingled with civilian refugees.
>
> In the case of refugee flow, the time-scale was so rapid and the numbers so great that it initially overwhelmed the neighboring countries, particularly

> the Former Yugoslav Republic of Macedonia (FYROM) and Albania. The humanitarian crisis created by Milosevic appeared to be an attempt to end NATO's operation by "cleansing" Kosovo of ethnic Albanians, overtaxing bordering nations' infrastructures, and fracturing alliance cohesion. He failed, despite all these efforts, principally because NATO adapted to the changing circumstances. One general lesson learned is that similar attempts at asymmetric challenges should be anticipated in future conflicts as well.

There are numerous other examples of a shift toward asymmetrical threats. For example, Iran seems to have helped Serbia in some aspects of its asymmetrical strategy, and certainly Serbia learned from the Iranian experience. Chinese military literature shows a new interest in asymmetrical warfare, and Iran has shown considerable originality in using submarines, mines, unconventional forces, and antiship missiles to create a tailored asymmetrical threat to naval movement through the lower Gulf.

The United States is vulnerable to such forms of warfare in many ways and faces the full range of potential asymmetrical threats:

- *Sudden or surprise attack*: Power projection is dependent on strategic warning, timely decisionmaking, and effective mobilization and redeployment for much of its military effectiveness.
- *Saturation*: There is no precise way to determine the point at which mass, or force quantity, overcomes superior effectiveness, or force quality. Historically, efforts to emphasize mass have been far less successful than military experts predicted at the time. Even the best force, however, reaches the point where it cannot maintain its edge in C^4I/battle management, air combat, or maneuver warfare in the face of superior numbers or multiple threats. Further, saturation may produce a sudden catalytic collapse of effectiveness, rather than a gradual degeneration, from which recovery is possible. This affects forward deployment, reliance on mobilization, and reliance on defensive land tactics versus preemption and offensive defense.
- *Taking casualties*: War fighting is not measured simply in terms of whether a given side can win a battle or conflict, but in terms of how well the opponent can absorb the damage inflicted upon it. Many powers are highly sensitive to casualties and losses. This sensitivity may limit their operational flexibility in taking risks and in sustaining some kinds of combat if casualties become high.
- *Inflicting casualties*: Dependence on world opinion and outside support means some nations increasingly must plan to fight at least low- and mid-intensity conflicts in ways that limit enemy casualties and collateral damage to their opponents.
- *Low-intensity combat*: Low-intensity conflict makes it much harder to employ technical advantages in combat—because low-intensity wars are largely fought against people, not things. Low-intensity wars are also highly political. The battle for public opinion is as much a condition of victory as is killing the enemy. The outcome of such a battle will be highly dependent on the specific political conditions under which it is fought, rather than on revolution in military affairs-like capabilities.

- *Hostage taking and terrorism*: Like low-intensity warfare, hostage taking and terrorism present the problem that advanced technology powers cannot exploit their conventional strengths and must fight a low-level battle, primarily on the basis of infantry combat. Human intelligence is more important than conventional military intelligence is, and much of the fight against terrorism may take place in urban or heavily populated areas.
- *Urban and built-up area warfare*: Advanced military powers are still challenged by the problem of urban warfare. They do not perform particularly well in urban warfare. Most Western forces are not trained or equipped to deal with sustained urban warfare in populated areas during regional combat, particularly when the fighting may affect large civilian populations on friendly soil.
- *Extended conflict and occupation warfare*: Not all wars can be quickly terminated, and many forms of warfare—particularly those involving peacekeeping and peace enforcement—require prolonged military occupations.
- *Weapons of mass destruction*: The threatened or actual use of such weapons can compensate for conventional weakness in some cases and deter military action in others.

Asymmetrical warfare is not a one-way street. The U.S. use of carbon fiber weapons against power grids in Kosovo illustrates the fact that the United States can introduce new asymmetrical warfare techniques as well as its enemies can. Indeed, it might be useful to conduct a "what if" analysis of Kosovo to see how the introduction of other asymmetrical weapons now under development might have changed the course of the fighting.[17,18]

More broadly, however, the United States needs to give the ability to fight asymmetrical warfare the same priority that it gives to fighting conventional forces in documents such as *Joint Vision 2020*. It needs to examine Serbia's use of asymmetrical warfare in more depth to determine the merit of relative techniques and to examine worst cases in which the global spread of steadily more sophisticated forms of asymmetrical warfare accelerates.

The United States must recognize and reduce its key historical vulnerabilities in such forms of conflict, which include protracted conflict, urban warfare, guerrilla warfare, use of human shields, casualties, collateral damage, and failure to plan effectively for conflict termination. It also needs to understand that peacemaking almost inevitably means fighting asymmetrical warfare, and that a humanitarian crisis can easily turn into such forms of conflict. This places an especially high premium on avoiding casualties and collateral damage and on letting an enemy use the media to achieve political dominance of a conflict.

Proliferation

There is little present prospect of the effective globalization of arms control, and there is a near certain prospect of the globalization of weapons of mass destruction and long-range delivery systems. Hostile states will also acquire longer range, more lethal conventional weapons that they can use to strike with precision at critical strategic targets such as oil shipments and desalination plants.

The United States recognized this aspect of globalism in the bottom-up review that it issued at the start of the Clinton administration, which gave the development of counterproliferation capabilities its highest force planning and strategic priority. At the same time, the United States has been slow to develop coherent programs and acquire actual capabilities. Once again, this is partly because of the complexity and uncertainties surrounding the threats that the United States now faces.

Table 4 provides a rough estimate of the more visible forms of proliferation that are now reshaping global military capabilities. Many of the most hostile powers in this table, however, face international sanctions or are signatories to arms control agreements that provide a strong incentive to keep their efforts covert. The good news is that such constraints have often reduced their rate of activity and success and have sharply increased the cost of acquiring and deploying key threats like nuclear weapons. The bad news is that nations such as India and Pakistan have shown that such barriers do not block military change, and nations such as Iran, Iraq, and North Korea continue to acquire new technology and improve their capabilities.[19]

The United States also faces the risk of several paradigm shifts in the process of global proliferation that it must take into account in its force planning.

- *Making weapons of mass destruction an international norm*: As the Iran-Iraq War has shown, the present political barriers to the use of weapons of mass destruction are tenuous and can vanish under the pressure of war. The Gulf War showed that missile attacks against population centers and "horizontal escalation" are very real threats, and the course of the Gulf War might well have led to the widespread use of weapons of mass destruction if it had occurred several years later. There "is a serious risk that a new conflict using weapons of mass destruction—such as a nuclear conflict between India and Pakistan—could suddenly legitimize" both proliferation and the use of weapons of mass destruction in the sense that it could become a new norm for many developing countries.
- *Proliferating global breakout capabilities*: Proliferation has been slowed in the past by the difficulties in acquiring nuclear weapons and in designing chemical and biological weapons with real effectiveness. Some of these trends may continue. While most powers can now design fission and boosted weapons, there has been only limited progress in the technology needed to develop fissile material. This situation seems likely to continue, although the acquisition of high-speed centrifuge technology, the technology needed to build small reactors designed to produce plutonium, or fissile material from the FSU, presents continuing risks.
- Radically changing the present mix of risks that the United States faces would take the collapse of the political restraints enforced by the Nonproliferation Treaty and a major increase in supplier willingness to sell relevant technologies.

Table 4. Global Challenges: Who Has Weapons of Mass Destruction

	Type of Weapon			*Long-Range Missiles*	
Country	*Chemical*	*Biological*	*Nuclear*	*Theater*	*Intercontinental*
			East-West		
Britain	Breakout	Breakout	Deployed	Deployed	SLBMs
Canada	—	Technology	Technology	—	—
France	Breakout	Breakout	Deployed	Deployed	SLBMs
Germany	Breakout	Breakout	Technology	Technology	—
Sweden	—	—	Technology	—	—
Russia	Residual	Residual	Deployed	Technology	ICBMs/SLBMs
United States	Residual	Breakout	Deployed	Technology	ICBMs/SLBMs
			Middle East		
Egypt	Residual	Breakout	—	Deployed	—
Israel	Breakout Technology/ Booster	Breakout	Deployed	Deployed	
Iran	Deployed? Technology/ Booster	Breakout	Technology	Deployed	
Iraq	Deployed	Deployed	Technology	Technology	?
Libya	Deployed	Research	—	Deployed	?
Syria	Deployed	Technology?	—	Deployed	—
Yemen	Residual	—	—	—	—
			Asia and South Asia		
China	Deployed?	Breakout?	Deployed	Deployed	ICBMs/SLBMs
India	Breakout?	Breakout?	Deployed	Deployed	Technology
Japan	Breakout	Breakout	Technology	Technology	—
Pakistan	Breakout?	Breakout?	Deployed	Deployed	Technology?
North Korea	Deployed Technology/ Booster	Deployed	Technology	Deployed	
South Korea	Breakout?	Breakout	Technology	Technology?	—
Taiwan	Breakout?	Breakout	Technology	—	—
Thailand	Residual	—	—	—	—
Vietnam	Residual	—	—	—	—
			Other		
Argentina	—	—	Technology	Technology	—
Brazil	—	—	Technology	Technology	—
South Africa	—	—	Technology	Technology	—

Key: ICBM, intercontinental ballistic missile; SLBM, submarine/sea-launched ballistic missile.

Source: Adapted from estimates and data in National Intelligence Council, "Foreign Missile Developments and the Ballistic Missile Threat to the United States Through 2015," September 1999 (www.cia.gov/cia/publications/nie/nie99); NonProliferation Center, Director of Central Intelligence, "Unclassified Report to Congress on the Acquisition of Technology Relating to Weapons of Mass Destruction and Advanced Conventional Munitions 1 January Through 30 June 1999," ODCI/CIA, January 2000; National Intelligence Council, "Foreign Missile Developments and the Ballistic Missile Threat to the United States Through 2015," September 1999 (www.cia.gov/cia/publications/nie/nie99).

- Similar constraints do not apply, however, to chemical and biological weapons. The global spread of biotechnology, food processing facilities, fertilizer plants, and petrochemical plants is slowly giving a wide range of nations the ability to manufacture advanced chemical and biological weapons. In fact, far more countries have already begun research efforts than are shown in table 4. The U.S. intelligence community estimates that there are 25 to 35 such countries, although any list is classified. Moreover, the spread of missile warhead, cluster munitions, sprayer, and UAV technology is simplifying the creation of such weapons.
- *The risk posed by biotechnology*: Modern biological weapons can easily be as lethal as fission and boosted weapons. Biological weapons can also be used to attack in ways that incapacitate or threaten the agricultural sector, or modified—with or without genetic engineering—to defeat current vaccines and medical treatment. Globalization is making such weapons steadily cheaper and more accessible and is creating a wide range of national research and production capabilities that can mass-produce such weapons with only a limited chance of detection. There is a high probability that the threat of nuclear proliferation, which dominated the "globalism" of the last half of the 20th century, will be matched or surpassed by the threat posed by the globalization of biotechnology.
- *Long-range strike systems:* Nations such as North Korea, Iran, and Iraq are demonstrating that developing states can acquire the technology to produce missile boosters capable of launching weapons of mass destruction with enough accuracy to hit city-sized targets at ranges of more than 1,000 miles and eventually to attain intercontinental ranges. At the same time, the proliferation of GPS guidance systems and specialized commercial jet engines is greatly reducing the cost of developing and producing cruise missiles with ranges in excess of 600 miles.[20]
- *Weapons of mass destruction and asymmetrical warfare*: The technologies and weapons necessary to carry out covert and proxy attacks using weapons of mass destruction are far cheaper than those required to use ballistic and cruise missiles. They are also becoming available to nonstate actors such as terrorists and extremists. Such attacks offer the potential ability to attack without attribution.
- *Homeland and allied defense*: All of these risks combine to create a need for the homeland defense of the United States and allied nations that the United States has not seriously contemplated since the early days of the thermonuclear era. It is far from clear that emerging proliferators will have the kind of political leadership that is as subject to rational deterrence as is Russia. Certainly, Iraq and North Korea have been erratic enough in the past to create serious concerns about their conduct, and even a rational developing state might become involved in a process of escalation that ended in little restraint. The practical problem is that many forms of attack that could be used do not require an overt declaration of war or clearly identify the attacker, and the most costly forms of defense—national and theater missile defenses—deal only with the most costly and overt form of attack. As a result, effective counterproliferation may require a global shift to a broad mix of costly homeland defense measures ranging from missile defense and counterproliferation to response measures designed to limit damage and deal with its effects.

There are no certainties involved in any of these threats. It is impossible to assign reliable probabilities to their nature, timing, or effectiveness, but it is at least possible that diplomacy, political change, and economic development may reduce them, roll them back, or at least prevent the emergence of major paradigm shifts. It is equally possible, however, that these threats will interact to create the same broad changes in the global military environment as has asymmetrical warfare.[21]

It is clear from such changes that the counterproliferation program deserves high priority, and this will probably require broad changes in U.S. military deterrent, retaliatory, active defense, and passive defense capabilities. At the same time, it is important to point out several aspects of the response that the United States must make:[22]

- The United States cannot act as a global power if it does not provide counterproliferation capabilities for its allies and coalition partners. No nation is going to sacrifice itself for a defended America.
- Ballistic missile defense is only part of the problem and involves the most costly form of defense against the most costly form of attack.
- The nuclear threat is no more lethal than is the biological threat, and U.S. planning must give them at least equal vulnerability.
- The present maximum casualty level used for guidance in planning response measures for American homeland defense is 1,000 casualties. The existence of the biological threat alone means that far higher thresholds of damage must be considered.[23]
- The threat of retaliation and extended deterrence will probably have to be redefined to deal with these problems.
- Arms control and limits on technology transfer are the cheapest methods of counterproliferation *if* they can be made effective. To paraphrase Clausewitz, they must be regarded as "an extension of war by other means."
- The United States must rethink its doctrine, tactics, technology, training, and C^4I/BM/SR to fight in a regional and low-level NBC environment as well as rethinking force protection and coalition defense capabilities.
- The United States must also rethink its global vulnerabilities. For example, sea power can minimize vulnerability and incentive to strike at U.S.-coalition forces in some circumstances, but it also often requires extended strike and deployment ranges. At the same time, ports, bases, and over-the-beach assembly areas become potential critical targets that give both sea power and the maritime economy a new level of vulnerability.

There are no rules or precedents that the United States can afford to trust in shaping this response, and it presents a further major potential drain on already inadequate defense resources. It will also ultimately prove at least as important to the future of an effective strategy for global coalition warfare as any of the lessons of Kosovo.

Shifts in Economic Interdependence, Air and Maritime Traffic, and Related Information Systems

The analysts of the economic aspects of globalism often focus on its benefits and not its vulnerabilities. It is clear, however, that economic interdependence makes the U.S. military more vulnerable with time. This is a function not only of the increase in the volume of U.S. trade but also of the increasingly specialized nature of trade, which means that the United States obtains most of many specialized products and components from overseas and has only a limited industrial base to provide substitutes in an emergency.[24]

There are few tangible data on such vulnerabilities, which are far more complex than the kind of dependence on strategic raw materials that was the subject of analysis during the Cold War. It is clear, however, that U.S. dependence on trade is growing steadily, as is its dependence on the overall health of the world economy. In fact, the International Trade Administration of the Department of Commerce indicates that the volume of U.S. trade more than doubles in value in constant dollars every decade.[25]

The latest Central Intelligence Agency estimate of U.S. trade indicates, however, that American exports totaled $663 billion in 1998 and that the chief importers were Canada, 22 percent; Western Europe, 21 percent; Japan, 10 percent; and Mexico, 10 percent. American imports were a much larger $912 billion and were equally diverse in nature and source. The main imports included crude oil and refined petroleum products, machinery, automobiles, consumer goods, industrial raw materials, food, and beverages. The main sources of American imports were Canada, 19 percent; Western Europe, 18 percent; Japan, 14 percent; Mexico, 10 percent; and China, 7 percent.[26] The total volume of world trade totals about $5 trillion annually in both imports and exports.

This dependence on the globalization of world trade has been accompanied by changes in management and information systems that can provide a steadily improved capability to reduce inventories and stockpiles, and to manage much more complex flows of interrelated imports and exports. As a result, both the volume and "fragility" of trade increase with time. The tangible impact of such shifts is a steady series of increases in interdependent ship and air cargo movements and capacity and in the growth of specialized ports, airports, and trade-related facilities. Moreover, the growing U.S. strategic dependence on overall health of the world economy means that the United States must consider increasing the security of the trade and imports of other states.

U.S. energy imports are a good case in point. The level of U.S. dependence on oil imports increased from 6.3 million barrels per day (mbd) in 1973 to 10.5 mbd in 1999.[27] Projections by the U.S. Energy Information Agency indicate that petroleum imports could reach around 15 mbd by 2020.[28] This may seem like a massive increase in the volume of a critical aspect of world trade, but it is only part of the story.

United States dependence on oil imports consists of both direct and indirect imports. American trading partners need to produce their exports to the United States and to sustain their economies in ways that allow them to finance imports from the United States. Globalism means that data that report only on the direct level of

American dependence on oil imports are obsolete and misleading. As a result, it is the overall volume of the increase in world oil exports between today and 2010 that matters, and the U.S. Energy Information Agency projects that these imports will rise from around 37.1 mbd to 66.0 mbd by 2020.[29] It is also interesting to note that the flow of trade is changing strikingly as well and that the flow of exports to Asia is projected to shift from 11.8 mbd in 1995 (32 percent of world imports) to 23.2 mbd (36 percent of world imports).

The end result is that globalization will alter how the world's sea-lanes are used. Long-range strike systems will pose a greater menace to key chokepoints, which themselves will be used by growing maritime traffic carrying specialized products that must be delivered quickly. The same will be true of air cargo, which cannot handle anything like the volume of maritime traffic, but which is often even more time-sensitive in terms of the efficient operation of world trade.

As a result, the United States will have to react to the globalization of trade, maritime and air traffic, and changes in the way in which trade is managed at a time when technology is also changing the ability of states to use long-range antiship missiles, mines, submarines, and antiair systems to vastly increase the range at which they can strike at the world's chokepoints. There has been so little analysis of these aspects of globalization, however, that the starting point for force planning has to be to establish a suitable analytical base.[30] This means that the U.S. military must:

- Analyze the changing patterns in trade flows in depth.
- Reanalyze dependence, interdependence, and vulnerability.
- Evaluate capability to protect a greatly expanded number and regional areas of chokepoints.
- Consider the impact of proliferation and asymmetrical threats on chokepoints.

Out of the Box: New Forms of Warfare

The United States must also plan for the impact that the same trends that create globalism will have in creating new forms of warfare. The most obvious of these forms of warfare is information warfare, which has a major potential impact in attacking both civil society and military forces. While it can be argued that many forms of information warfare are simply a new form of electronic warfare and asymmetrical warfare, the level of technology involved is so different, and its importance is growing so rapidly, that military operations must plan for information warfare on a global basis.[31]

Thought must also be given to the risk of new forms of environmental warfare (for example, oil spills in the Gulf War) and economic warfare directed at critical economic and civil systems such as land-based pipelines, desalination plants, and electric power plants. The globalization of precision strike capabilities and the growing complexity and vulnerability of modern societies are redefining strategic vulnerability, particularly for U.S. allies and coalition partners in theaters and regions where such capabilities become common.

At the same time, the United States almost certainly needs to rethink the way in which it deals with the global media and the fact that war is now a real-time televised event. "Information dominance" is scarcely a matter of battle management in today's world, a point that is clearly recognized in the Department of Defense report on the lessons of Kosovo:[32]

> The first political-military plan on Kosovo, completed in the fall of 1998, focused on using the threat of NATO air strikes to achieve a political-military settlement. After this threat of force convinced Milosevic to garrison most Serb forces in October 1998, interagency planning efforts focused on deploying the OSCE's Kosovo Verification Mission, facilitating humanitarian assistance, and responding to possible Serbian noncompliance. During Operation Allied Force, two interagency planning efforts occurred simultaneously. The first involved the development of a strategic campaign plan designed to ensure that wider U.S. and allied diplomatic, economic, and information efforts were integrated with our military operations.
>
> As it became clear that Milosevic hoped to outlast the alliance, more attention was paid to other ways of bringing pressure to bear. The second effort involved planning for a NATO-led peace implementation force in Kosovo and an international civilian presence for the UN Mission in Kosovo (UNMIK) after NATO's military campaign had achieved its objectives.
>
> This experience has taught us that our planning must better reflect the full range of instruments at our disposal, including the use of economic sanctions, public diplomacy, and other information efforts. Our initial planning focused on air strikes and diplomacy as the tools to achieve U.S. and NATO objectives. To ensure comprehensive planning and high-level awareness of the range of instruments available to decisionmakers, we believe it is important that senior officials participate routinely in rehearsals, gaming, exercises, and simulations.
>
> Successfully conducting operations to disrupt or confuse an enemy's ability to collect, process, and disseminate information is becoming increasingly important in this "information age" of warfare. The importance of such capabilities was recognized fully during Operation Allied Force, but the conduct of an integrated information operations campaign was delayed by the lack of both advance planning and strategic guidance defining key objectives. The Department will address this problem by developing the needed plans and testing them in exercises.

There is good reason to address the problem. One of the most striking aspects of any review of the propaganda campaign conducted by both sides is how inept many portions of the campaign were, how unconvincing many media and propaganda statements were, and how often the content lacked the depth to be convincing. In many cases, the statements also seemed to ignore the different values and perspectives of the other side and may have done more to reassure those issuing the statements than to influence either the enemy or world opinion. Although NATO certainly did a better job than Serbia did, the former had far more means and a far better case. It also did not avoid overselling in shallow ways that alienated a considerable amount of the media and created a major credibility problem.

There are two broader problems that emerged in Kosovo that the United States will also have to address if it is to exploit information warfare and effectively exercise military power:

- The most serious is the de facto decision that the sensitivity of the global media is so great that each advance in U.S. military technology means that the United States must use those advances to virtually eliminate American and friendly casualties and to reduce collateral damage and even enemy casualties to an absolute minimum. It is one of the ironies of the real-world impact of the revolution in military affairs, and the current U.S. approach to the globalization of the media, that the U.S. military tries to create an image of perfect war that is so demanding that every bit of friction becomes a potential political disaster. The possibility of using force to achieve shock and awe has been minimized by a military culture that fails to warn that collateral damage and casualties are as inevitable as are mistakes, weapons failures, and the fog of war, and that the political cost of every mistake, failure, and casualty has been exaggerated.
- The United States talks about offensive information warfare but does not seem to be able to fight it. Kosovo showed that U.S. information warriors must find some way to overcome the longstanding objections by the CIA and the National Security Agency to direct attacks on enemy computer systems that are prime sources of intelligence. Furthermore, the Department of Defense encountered major legal objections during Kosovo to attacks using international links that might affect public and financial systems. Lawyers raised strong "law of war" arguments that information warfare can be used only against dedicated military systems, and the General Counsel's office of the Department of Defense ended up issuing some 50 pages of complex guidelines on the legal issues involved.[33]

Living with Uncertainty

Globalization will not reduce the challenges that U.S. military forces face in the future. It may not make them worse. This depends on the unpredictable emergence of threats whose capabilities evolve faster than those of U.S. forces and U.S.-led coalitions. It will make them more complex and—in some cases—require significant changes in the way that the United States plans to use military power.

It is also clear that globalization involves different trends from a military perspective than it does from one focused on the civil economy. In particular, U.S. strategy must look beyond "jointness" to a true focus on global engagement that cuts across service and command lines. It must redefine its approach to coalition warfare in ways that take account of regional differences and the need for a new approach to global interoperability.

U.S. force planning must also take account of the globalization of new threats and vulnerabilities. The most immediate of these threats are technology transfer, asymmetrical warfare, and proliferation. More broadly, however, the United States must also prepare for the fact that the globalization of trade, information systems, and the media creates both new vulnerabilities and new criteria for military operations.

There are three cultural challenges that the United States, and the U.S. military, will face in making the necessary changes. The first is to accept the true complexity of the future that the United States faces, and the near certainty that it will be just as violent and uncertain as the past. The second is to understand just how serious the present problem caused by insufficient resources will be in limiting the level of military modernization and change necessary to meet the new pressures and threats created by globalization. The third will be to transition as quickly as possible out of the conventional wisdom that shaped U.S. military strategy and planning during the Cold War and to respond flexibly and rapidly to new emerging new threats.

No one can really define "globalism" in military terms with any precision, much less predict the impact given trends will have at any given point in the future. It is clear, however, that the narrow conventional warfighting mindset set forth in *Joint Vision 2020* must be replaced with a far more flexible and adaptive approach to strategy and force planning. It is equally apparent that globalization is already challenging enough to require substantially larger forces and resources than have been considered under the Quadrennial Defense Reviews or are programmed in the Five Year Defense Program. The United States became the world's only superpower largely through a series of historical accidents. It will remain a preeminent power only through deliberate planning.

Notes

[1] World Bank, *World Development Indicators, 1999* (Washington, DC: World Bank, 1999).

[2] These seem to be relatively optimistic projections. Older and more independent World Bank projections were considerably more pessimistic. See Eduard Bos, My T. Vu, Ernest Massiah, and Rodolfo A Bulatao, *World Population Projections, 1994–1995* (Washington, DC: World Bank, 1996). The World Bank ceased publication of these projections from The Johns Hopkins University after 1996, evidently because they felt the projections were not optimistic enough.

[3] For further background, see Walter Mondale, Ryutaro Hashimoto, and Karl Otto Pohl, *Global Aging: The Challenge of the New Millennium* (Washington, DC: Center for Strategic and International Studies-Watson Wyatt, 2000).

[4] Erik R. Peterson, *Our Divided Future* (Washington, DC: Center for Strategic and International Studies, January 29, 1998).

[5] This estimate is based primarily on work by Herbert J. Tilemmar in trying to summarize the history of such violence since World War II.

[6] For an interesting discussion of the issues involved, see Andrew J. Bacevich, "Policing Utopia," *The National Interest* 56 (Summer 1999), 5–13.

[7] For additional reading, see Tom Czerwinski, *Coping with the Bounds: Speculations on Nonlinearity in Military Affairs* (Washington, DC: C[4]ISR Cooperative Research Program, 1998), Zalmay Khalilzad and Ian O. Lesser, *Sources of Conflict in the 21st Century* (Santa Monica, CA: RAND, 1998), and David S. Alberts and Tom Czerwinski, *Complexity, Global Politics, and National Security* (Washington, DC: National Defense University Press, 1997).

[8] For a detailed analysis, see Daniel Goure and Jeffery M. Ranney, *Averting the Defense Train Wreck in the New Millennium* (Washington, DC: Center for Strategic and International Studies, 2000). Also see Harlan K. Ullman, *In Irons: U.S. Military Might in the New Century* (Washington, DC: National Defense University Press, 1995).

[9] Jeffery M. Ranney, testimony to the Senate Armed Services Committee, February 4, 2000.

[10] William S. Cohen, speech to the International Institute of Strategic Studies, San Diego, CA, September 9, 1999, <www.defenselink.mil/speeches/1999>.

[11] U.S. Department of Defense, *Report to Congress: Kosovo/Operation Allied Forces After-Action Report* (Washington, DC: Department of Defense, January 31, 2000), 122–125.

[12] There are two primary sources of such declassified intelligence data. One is the annual work of Richard F. Grimmett of the Congressional Research Service in *Conventional Arms Transfers to the Developing World.* The other is the annual edition of *World Military Expenditures and Arms Transfers*, which is available at the State Department Web site under the reports section of the Bureau of Arms Control.

[13] See the Web site edition of World Military Expenditures and Arms Transfers, 1997, table II.

[14] Richard F. Grimmett, *Conventional Arms Transfers to the Developing World, 1991–1998*, CRS–44 (Congressional Research Service RL30275, August 4, 1999).

[15] Grimmett, *Conventional Arms Transfers*, CRS-69.

[16] U.S. Department of Defense, *Report to Congress: Kosovo/Operation Allied Forces After-Action Report*, 6–7.

[17] *New York Times International*, May 4, 1999, A12.

[18] *Jane's Defense Weekly*, May 12, 1999, 4.

[19] For recent reporting, see National Intelligence Council, *Foreign Missile Developments and the Ballistic Missile Threat to the United States Through 2015*, September 1999, <www.cia.gov/cia/publications/nie/nie99> and Non-Proliferation Center, *Unclassified Report to Congress on the Acquisition of Technology Relating to Weapons of Mass Destruction and Advanced Conventional Munitions 1 January Through 30 June 1999* (ODCI/CIA, January 2000).

[20] National Intelligence Council, *Foreign Missile Developments and the Ballistic Missile Threat to the United States Through 2015*, September 1999, <www.cia.gov/cia/publications/nie/nie99>.

[21] For an interesting discussion of some of these issues, see Michael E. O'Hanlon, *Technological Change and the Future of Warfare* (Washington, DC: The Brookings Institution, 2000), 160–166.

[22] For further discussion, see Barry R. Schneider, *Future War and Counterproliferation: U.S. Military Response to NBC Proliferation Threats* (Westport, CT: Praeger, 1999).

[23] U.S. General Accounting Office, *Combating Terrorism: Need for Comprehensive Threat and Risk Assessments of Chemical and Biological Attacks* (Washington, DC: GAO/NSIAD-99-163, September 1999).

[24] Interestingly enough, even many books on the future of seapower largely ignore these issues. For example, see the essays in Pelham G. Boyer and Robert S. Woods, *Strategic Transformation and Naval Power in the 21st Century* (Newport, RI: Naval War College Press, 1998) and Center for Strategic and International Studies Working Group, *The Role of Sea Power in U.S. National Security in the Twenty-First Century* (Washington, DC: Center for Strategic and International Studies, March 1998).

[25] International Trade Administration, U.S. Department of Commerce, Office of Trade and Analysis, *U.S. Trade In Perspective*, online editions.

[26] CIA, *World Factbook, 1999*, <www.odci.gov/cia/publications/factbook/us.html>.

[27] U.S. Department of Energy, "Table 1.8," *Overview of U.S. Petroleum Trade*, <www.eia.doe.gov/pub/energy.overview/monthly.energy/mer1-8>.

[28] Energy Information Agency, *International Energy Outlook, 1999*, DOE/EIA-0484 (99) (Washington, DC: U.S. Department of Energy, March 1999), 32.

[29] U.S. Department of Energy, "Table 1.8."

[30] The author could only find unclassified vulnerability analyses that focused solely on existing trade flows and which were not linked to analyses of global economic interdependence. For example,

see John H. Noer with David Gregory, *Chokepoints: Maritime Economic Concerns in Southeast Asia* (Washington, DC: National Defense University and Center for Naval Analyses, 1996).

[31] For a broad review of the issue, see Zalmay M. Khalilzad and John P. White, *The Changing Role of Information Warfare* (Santa Monica, CA: RAND, 1999).

[32] William S. Cohen and Henry H. Shelton, prepared joint statement on the *Kosovo After-Action Review* presented before the Senate Armed Services Committee, October 14, 1999. For legal details, see Lawrence T. Greenberg, Seymour E. Goodman, and Kevin J. Soo Hoo, *Information Warfare and International Law* (Washington, DC: National Defense University/C^4ISR Cooperative Research Program, 1998).

[33] *The Washington Post*, November 8, 1999, A1, A10.

Chapter 19

Transforming the Armed Forces: An Agenda for Change

Paul K. Davis

Since 1997, the Department of Defense (DOD) has placed a great deal of emphasis on transforming the force. This emphasis first appeared in the Quadrennial Defense Review (QDR). It was further encouraged by the National Defense Panel (NDP), which was commissioned by Congress to review the new strategy. Although the initial DOD treatment was essentially rhetorical, with no immediate influence on programs or budgets, much of the groundwork has subsequently been laid for turning that rhetoric into substance. Depending on choices made in the Bush administration, events over the next 3 to 10 years may indeed prove to be transformatory.[1]

This chapter begins with background on why transformation is needed, what some of its main features are, factors in achieving it, the current status of change within the United States, and some key issues. Some issues are for the United States alone, but it is appropriate in this volume on globalization to highlight two points. The first is that participants in future coalitions will have widely varied capabilities. The second is the importance of developing a consensus among friendly nations worldwide about how to increase the effectiveness of multinational political, economic, and military instruments for extended versions of deterrence and compellence.

Background

Why Transformation Is Needed

Military transformation is not an end in itself, but it is needed for reasons of both opportunity and necessity.[2]

Opportunity. In the relatively near term, America's forces can exploit modern technology to maintain their ability to overmatch opponents. Moreover, for most missions, it will be possible to be more militarily effective than today, even with smaller forces than would have traditionally been used for those missions. This reflects the

---

Paul K. Davis is a research leader for defense and force transformation planning at RAND. He also teaches in the RAND Graduate School of Public Policy and formerly served as a senior executive in the Department of Defense. Dr. Davis is the author of 1000 Decisive Battles: From Ancient Times to the Present.

traditional process of substituting technology for labor. There are limitations to what can be accomplished here, since some missions (for example, combat, even peace-keeping, in troublesome urban areas) are inherently manpower-intensive and U.S. forces are being called upon to do more missions than in years past. Nonetheless, modern technology can allow the United States to get a good deal more mileage than otherwise from whatever forces it finds necessary and affordable.

Necessity. In the longer term, many nations' forces will use aspects of the new technology. Indeed, much of the requisite technology is or will be commercially available. As a result, traditional forces will no longer be viable. For example, forces will need to disperse substantially because of the extreme vulnerability of fixed targets. For related reasons, they will need to maneuver over longer distances, to maneuver much more quickly and with much less physical concentration of forces themselves, and to operate with greatly reduced logistical footprints. In addition, they will need to defend themselves from a variety of missiles, including those carrying weapons of mass destruction (WMD). In the longer run, it is not clear how the measure-countermeasure race will play out. Aircraft and ships will become more stealthy, but remotely piloted aircraft and space-based surveillance will improve, as will missiles to attack those aircraft and ships. Active defenses will improve, but may be overcome by sheer numbers. New forms of active defenses, such as beam weapons, will perhaps be less prone to saturation. The war in cyberspace will likely be increasingly important. There is no end in sight to the changes that may occur.

Implications: Change Is Required. With this combination of near-term opportunity and daunting, longer term challenges, there should be little question about the need for major changes. Many of those changes will be inexorable consequences of the same information technology that has transformed modern business practices and day-to-day life. Others will be more uniquely related to the increased precision of weapons, superb navigation, WMD systems, and information warfare.

A Two-Era Framework for Discussing Transformation

In discussing issues of transformation, it is useful to adopt a two-era framework (see figure 1). Era A is from now until roughly 2010; Era B takes up thereafter. The distinction between the two eras is not clear-cut in time. Moreover, it does not correspond neatly to the distinction between opportunity and necessity because many of the problems that will be quite serious in Era B are already becoming matters of concern today. These include the potential for adversaries to use short-warning attacks; tactics and strategies that would delay U.S. access to regional bases; commercial satellites providing high-resolution intelligence; some highly lethal conventional weapons; cyberspace attacks; and even small numbers of mass-casualty weapons.[3] The shading in the figure suggests that these problems exist and are worrisome now but will become major features of the landscape over time.[4]

Figure 1. A Two-Era Framework for Discussing Change

ERA-A (now until 2010?)

Exploit *within-reach* technology for opportunities and problems visible now:

- Attaining lopsided advantage
- Reengineering for more capability at less cost
- Dealing with Achilles' heels (asymmetric strategies access, WMD,...)

ERA-B (post 2010?)

Prepare for *long-term* problems:

- Widespread proliferation of missiles and WMD
- Advanced threats to naval surface forces, forward operating bases, and concentrated forces
- Enemies with some precision weapons and reconnaissance capabilities
- CyberWar
- Emergent China
- Threats to U.S. homeland

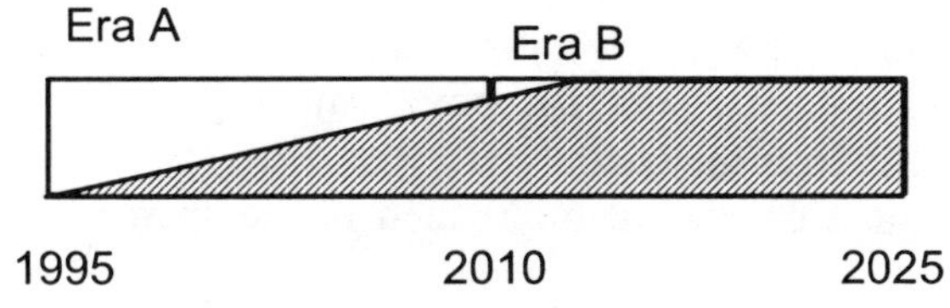

Transformation and the Revolution in Military Affairs

The discussion so far has avoided deliberately any reference to the revolution in military affairs (RMA), but the linkage is often made. Sometimes this linkage is useful because it raises enthusiasms, but when it encourages hype and engenders endless debates about what constitutes a revolution in military affairs, it is counterproductive. Another problem is that too much emphasis on revolution turns the best into the enemy of the better in the budget process: any system real enough to be given a name, a program, and a budget will be seen by some as a dinosaur. Yet another problem is that RMA advocates sometimes act as though epochal changes can occur overnight, whereas revolutions often are, and need to be, the result of evolutionary processes over many years. Despite these problems, the revolution in military affairs is a useful concept and is defined as follows:

> An RMA is a major change in the nature of warfare brought about by the innovative application of technologies, which, when combined with dramatic changes in military doctrine and operational concepts, fundamentally alters the character and conduct of operations.

There have been many revolutions in military affairs over the millennia.[5] Examples are associated with the introduction of the crossbow; the emergence of navies with shot and sail; the introduction of gunpowder; Napoleon's innovations in logistics and military organization; the transition of navies to steam, steel, and submarine; carrier aviation; blitzkrieg operations; and nuclear weapons. In all of these, technology played an important part, but the revolution required a retooling of organization and doctrine.

Everyone agrees that major technological changes are occurring. However, it remains for future historians to judge whether and when the United States and other nations harnessed that technology, combined it with the new concepts and organizations, and achieved fundamental change. One or more RMAs seem almost certain, but they may occur decades from now after a disastrous war, rather than as the result of more rational processes today. Or perhaps America will squander opportunities, while her future adversaries exploit inexpensive technology to undercut major U.S. capabilities. In any case, when the revolution occurs, we should expect it to affect only some aspects of warfare dramatically. Armored invasions over deserts may have become infeasible, but life may be similar to that in years past for infantry fighting in cities, urban sprawl, forests, and jungle.[6] Much is yet unclear.

With these cautions expressed, let us now proceed more bullishly in discussing transformation challenges and prospects. Because of the omnipresence of the information revolution in our everyday lives and economy, it is unthinkable (that is, too painful to contemplate, rather than unimaginable) that America will not achieve comparably substantial changes in military affairs. Moreover, much groundwork has been laid. If the new Secretary of Defense includes "getting on with transformation" on his short list of action items, much can be accomplished in the span of 3 to 10 years. But it will not be easy.

Moving to Transform the Force

A Strategy for Transformation

U.S. difficulties in mounting and executing a successful transformation strategy are considerable. DOD lacks such advantages (for this purpose) as an imminent threat or bankruptcy, a recent debacle, or an operational and a budgetary slack. Thus, developing its strategy, the Pentagon has focused on a great strength for change that it does possess: the professionalism of its officer corps. Members of the American military know well from their daily lives how dramatic the impact of modern information technology can be. Moreover, they consciously see themselves in learning organizations. Also, in both Operation *Desert Storm* and the Kosovo affair, they saw tangible indications of why the new ways are so needed.

DOD also benefits from having many organizations to help stimulate innovation and change.[7] As a result, there is no shortage of good ideas, initiative, and motivation for change. The obstacles to change lie elsewhere, particularly in the large, ponderous organizations and existing ways of doing business. As demonstrated by industry, however, large organizations can change.[8]

Keys to transformation strategy include providing appropriate visions, defining suitable organizational responsibilities and authorities, providing more specific objectives and requirements, providing funding for research, including experimentation, and tying transformation into the routine functioning of the department's planning, programming, and budgeting system (PPBS) and acquisition system. This effort is still a work in progress.[9]

A Two-Era Model for Thinking about Transformation

The two-era model of figure 1 suggests a two-track approach, as seen in table 1. The reason is that the kind of planning and activity, and the management thereof, needed for Era A and Era B work are significantly different. Indeed, the efforts can even be in opposition unless carefully protected from each other.

Table 1. Differences Between Changes for Era A and Era B

Changes for Era A and the Start of Era B	*Changes for the Longer Run in Era B*
• Though surprises are likely, outcomes and outputs can be reasonably visualized. • Operational challenges can be posed and decomposed. • Responsibilities can be assigned and success assessed. • Valuable mid-term measures can set stage for longer term. • Mainstream organizations can and should make them work.	• Nature of long-run changes is such that fresh, out-of-the-box thinking is essential. • Much discovery is needed. • Outcomes are at best dimly understood. • Highly structured management is counterproductive. • Major surprises and changes of concept are likely. • Mainstream organizations are likely to actively oppose them.

Era A work lends itself to revolution by vigorous evolution driven by well-defined and relatively tightly managed programs that can be organized around discrete operational challenges that are particularly important, enduring, stressful enough to demand use of the new technology and a rethinking of doctrine and organization, and unequivocally output oriented. One example of a challenge from the Secretary of Defense might be, "Develop the capability to halt an armored invasion within days, thus rendering obsolete the classic 20th-century route to conquest"; another might be, "Develop the capability for rapid and decisive interventions in relatively small-scale conflicts, using only the small forces that could realistically be made available within the first days and weeks of need."[10]

Such missions or operational challenges are very useful. They can be understood by the organization as a whole and can be used pragmatically by managers, who can decompose the challenges into subordinate requirements for building-block capabilities and the rapidly adaptive command and control to integrate those capabilities as needed. Responsibilities, authorities, and technical requirements can be established and tests accomplished as the capabilities emerge after conceptual work, research, experiments, and iteration.

Of particular importance is the fact that Era A activities are well suited for the enthusiasms and talents of mainstream organizations and their leaders, including specifically those who seek accomplishments during their relatively short tours of duty. Thus, it should not be necessary to destroy or bypass these organizations to reform them.

A remarkable feature of the landscape highlighted in the model depicted in figure 1 is that because the beginnings of Era B problems are already visible and troublesome in their theaters, current regional military commanders can be expected to support—and even to demand—changes that might otherwise not occur for many years. That is, even regional commands or their component commands can be engines of change. In contrast, in traditional defense planning it was thought that they were so mired in the present as to be either disinterested in, or opposed to, changes in technology and doctrine.

With proper organization and top-level leadership, DOD can reasonably hope to have the military services and the joint interservice world working together vigorously on Era A developments. If this vigorous evolution-to-revolution succeeds, it will be quite a tribute to the defense establishment.

As table 1 suggests, Era B work requires a different style of work and a different style of management and financial support than does Era A work.[11] The former needs to be more exploratory with multiple paths, multiple knowledge-building experiments, and more failures than the latter. The time scale must necessarily be greater than the tours of typical military leaders or even defense secretaries. Work for Era B will require supporting and protecting special people (so-called worriers and conceivers), perhaps in skunk works devoted to exploration and advanced development. As illustrated by the way in which carrier aviation was developed, path-breaking work must go beyond studies to include experiments and prototypes with which to discover and to learn—not just demonstrate or verify.[12]

Reforming the Way Forces Are Conceived

Another challenge for DOD is to rethink the very objects on which it chooses to focus its managerial and programmatic attention. In particular, it has been evident for some time that the current tokens of defense capability (for example, numbers of classic versions of divisions, wings, and carrier battle groups; or, worse, end strength) are rapidly becoming less relevant, while smaller but highly capable units and globally netted command, control, communications, computers, intelligence, surveillance, and reconnaissance (C^4ISR) are becoming dominant factors.[13]

To be sure, the United States will also need new platforms (such as aircraft with greater range and stealth, unmanned combat aerial vehicles, relatively stealthy surface ships with small crews, lighter and faster combat vehicles). New varieties of short-takeoff-and-landing aircraft and advanced weapons are also needed. New weapons, such as those with greater standoff range and accuracy, will also be needed. Many of the most fundamental changes, however, must be organizational and doctrinal—primarily driven by information technology. It remains to be seen whether the power baronies associated with platforms and traditional units will give way to something more suitable.

Does the Modernization of Era A Create Shiny Dinosaurs?

The possibility exists that the advanced concepts and systems of Era A will come into being just about the time that we are better able to appreciate what will be needed in Era B. Some observers worry that modernizing with new platforms that are arguably just better versions of the platforms that they replace will stand in the way of more fundamental reform. To them, the F–22 is just another manned fighter aircraft—an outrageously expensive one, to boot. They have similar quarrels with advanced surface ships.

These critics have a point, but it can also be overdone. It is particularly important to note that much of Era A transformation is about information technology. Can anyone doubt that prowess in the application of information technology will be a central element of whatever eventuates in Era B? And, to take an analogy, should we forgo buying desktop computers and Palm Pilots today because, in 5 years, they will be overtaken by newer products? The question is not purely rhetorical. After all, it was only about 15 years ago that many organizations made huge investments in mainframe computers that would be rendered obsolete well within their expected lifetimes. The answer to the question is that to be effective now, we need to make the investments in what can be obtained now. At the same time, we do not want to make long-term obligations that we may later regret.

In the same spirit, Era A modernization should generate platforms, weapon systems, and command-and-control systems that are designed from the outset with the expectation of frequent and sometimes massive changes in everything resident on the platforms. Furthermore, it may be that the numbers of new, top-of-the-line platforms procured should be fewer in number than in earlier years, so as to leave room for experimental systems and iteration. The concept of a strategic pause is no longer valid, but the concept of reverting to old-style massive buys with the expectation of 20-year lifetimes, with only minor changes, could be disastrous.

Recent Developments

U.S. Joint Forces Command

The jury is still out on transformation, but as indicated above a good deal of groundwork has been laid in the last few years. Most important, U.S. Joint Forces Command (JFCOM), which replaced U.S. Atlantic Command, is oriented heavily toward transformation.

JFCOM has the roles of joint trainer, integrator, and provider. Perhaps most relevant, it has been given prime responsibility for joint experimentation, an unfortunate rubric used for many transformation-related activities.[14] Many important details are still evolving, and many issues remain, such as how much funding JFCOM should have and for what purposes. Even with today's responsibilities and authorities, however, JFCOM has a great deal of opportunity to move the transformation effort forward. Success depends, of course, on the strong support of the Secretary of Defense and the Chairman, but Commander in Chief, U.S. Joint Forces Command, indeed has that support.[15] Moreover, JFCOM now plays a more explicit role in the critical requirements-setting process. In addition, the Joint C^4ISR Battle Center does rigorous testing of interoperability for selected systems.

JFCOM work on joint experimentation is beginning to gain momentum after a fairly lengthy period of startup during which it was ill-staffed for its new mission and deluged with miscellaneous expressions of miscellaneous needs. It has now focused its work considerably and organized accordingly. As of summer 2000, its focus areas were:

- Command and Control
- Combat Identification
- Intelligence Surveillance and Reconnaissance
- Attack Operations Against Critical Mobile Targets
- Joint Deployment Process
- Joint Simulation System
- Unmanned Aerial Systems (for Battlefield Awareness)
- Deep Theater Air and Missile Defense
- Strike and Battlefield Interdiction

A significant feature of these focus areas is that they are all quintessentially joint and unquestionably important. Moreover, they relate to relatively high-level military functions. This is not accidental since JFCOM has been careful to focus its energies on these matters, rather than to redundantly attack problems that are already being pursued by the individual services or define tasks at too low a level. There are many reasons to believe that the greatest leverage in increased jointness, as well as exploitation of modern technology, is in the higher level functions of particular concern to CINCs, Joint Task Force commanders, and their subordinate commanders.

In related developments, joint experimentation work by JFCOM is now organized around what amount to two large integrating concepts: Rapid Decisive Operations (RDO) and Attack Operations Against Critical Mobile Targets. Closely associated with these are such subordinate subjects as joint interactive planning; assurance that commanders have a common relevant operational picture; adaptive joint command and control; information operations; focused logistics; forcible entry operations; and strategic deployment.

Figure 2 is a useful depiction of how one can look at the RDO issue, variants of which have been urged for several years.[16] In this depiction, the RDO concept depends on four key subordinate attributes of the force: strategic and operational agility, full-dimensional force protection, multidimensional precision, and operational decision superiority. These correspond, with some name changes, to themes of the influential *Joint Vision 2010.*[17] Moving outward in the figure, one sees a ring of enablers, such as agile interdependent joint forces (top center).

The RDO concept is being explored in the JFCOM Millennium Challenge '00 activity. The study of this concept involves everything from brainstorming to human war gaming, more extensive computer simulation, and field experiments. A similarly broad range of work is needed for the critical mobile target problem. A significant start on the simulation work was accomplished by JFCOM in 1999, with major help from the Institute for Defense Analyses (IDA). Stimulated in part by earlier work of the Defense Science Board,[18] the research involves state-of-the-art, man-in-the-loop synthetic theater of war tools, which evolved from SIMNET work pioneered earlier under the Defense Advanced Research Projects Agency. In the 1999 work, IDA examined the significance of alternative command and control relationships, as well as new sensors and weapons for attacking mobile targets. Some conclusions were highly significant and, equally important, convincing to participating services.

Figure 2: Rapid Decisive Operations: Its Primary Components and Enablers

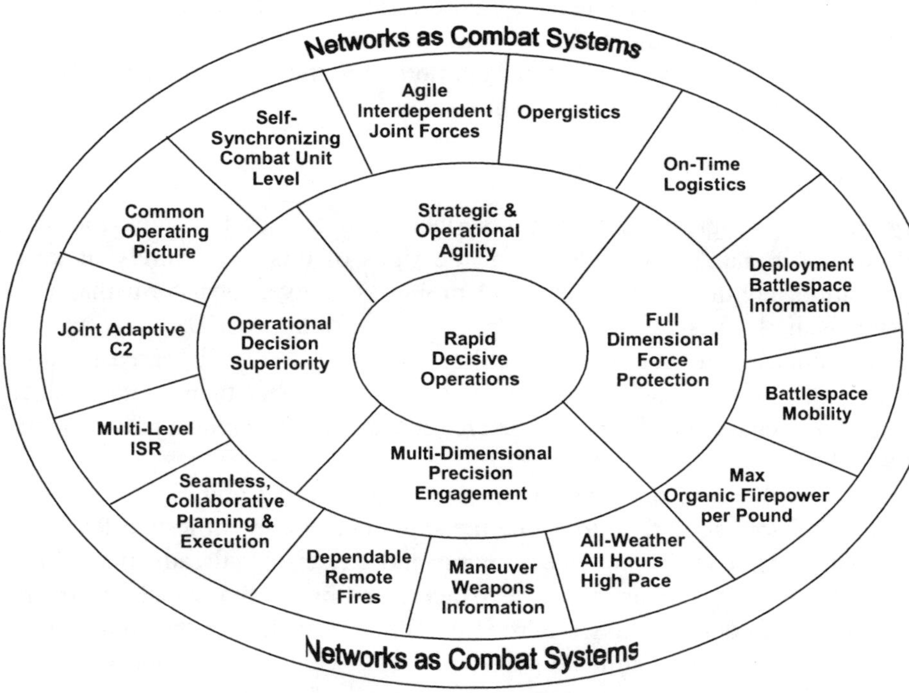

Source: Adapted from a briefing by General Lawrence G. Welch, USAF (Ret.)

In summary, JFCOM has been stood up, funded, and anointed to lead the transformation effort. It is now well under way, and one may hope to see significant accomplishments over the next few years.

The Crucial Role of the Services

Although transformation is often seen as a joint matter, and thereby tied to US JFCOM, it is important to emphasize that the vast majority of changes in a successful transformation will in fact be accomplished within the separate services. The American military system is built around the services, and it is in the services that one finds not only long traditions but also great depth of expertise in matters ranging from research and development on systems to both current doctrine and potential innovations. Moreover, the services have been remarkably vigorous in recent years. Navy emphasis on network-centric operations, Air Force moves toward becoming an Expeditionary Air Force, Marine Corps continuing experiments with new doctrinal concepts (for example, Desert Warrior, Urban Warrior), and, most recently, announced Army effort to develop medium brigades with increased responsiveness and flexibility are all important activities that will be at the core of transformation—if these efforts bear fruit as intended. Although there is always a basis for skepticism, and indeed many initiatives over the years (for example, the Navy Arsenal Ship and the Army Strike Force) have petered out, guarded optimism appears to be more appropriate. Not only are there many talented, vigorous, and forward-looking people at work in the services, but also the great accomplishments in private industry—driven by transformational strategies—are a constant motivator and a constant basis for them to argue in favor of the changes that they advocate.[19]

Shortfalls

Despite this progress by both the services and the joint system, the status of transformation remains spotty. Some of the signs of this are severely underfunded modernization; continued Achilles' heel problems in even near-term major theater wars (for example, base access problems, short warning, WMD); slow and uneven changes of doctrine; a programming and budgeting system still geared toward marginal decisions about classic measures of capability, rather than strategic decisions focused on the character of future warfare; and continued preoccupation of the services with budget share and end-strength.

Another problem is that the quantity of joint training and exercising is not as large as it probably should be to refine the skills needed, much less to learn from iteration. The reason is that service training and exercising already place great demands on the forces—demands that are exacerbated by the many calls for them to be employed in real contingencies. There is no simple remedy for the shortage of joint activities, but more joint command post exercises—which are less demanding of personnel, travel, and time—can accomplish a good deal. Also, joint overlays on what are essentially service exercises are often proving useful. In any case, there is much still left to be done on transformation. The process has only begun.

Next Steps for the United States

The Bush administration will have a historic opportunity. No one can predict confidently what that administration will in fact do, but it is surely plausible that the newly appointed Secretary of Defense will, early in 2001, construct a short list of action items for special attention during his tenure. It is also quite plausible that getting on with transformation will be on that list. If so, and if the many stars in the heavens are properly aligned, then much can happen within 3 to 10 years. Some priorities should include:

- Redefining the building-block forces that determine U.S. and coalition military capabilities (for example, moving from a division-centric Army structure to a more brigade-centric structure with brigades that are substantially smaller but more capable—for most missions—than are current brigades).
- Adopting a mission-system view in conceiving, evaluating, and implementing programs, which will require significant changes in how the PPBS is conducted.[20]
- Fielding initial versions of these building-block forces and beginning the lengthy process of perfecting them and transitioning force structure, personnel systems, and doctrine.
- Implementing network-centric operations, with its implications for command and control and the acquisition processes in defense planning.[21]
- Fielding modest but significant missile defenses.

These may need to occur during the same decade in which U.S. global military posture adjusts to changes in the strategic environment. This chapter is not the place to discuss such adjustments in detail, but the warming relationship between North and South Korea reminds us that the presence of U.S. ground forces in the middle of Korea is hardly a natural and permanent matter. Nor, for that matter, is the presence of U.S. ground forces natural in the middle of Europe, or even in the chronically troubled Persian Gulf. Such presence may prove desirable to those affected and therefore persist for a very long time, but this is by no means a foregone conclusion. It is arguably more likely that the global U.S. force posture will come to depend increasingly on naval forces, air forces, and small but rapidly projected and highly capable ground forces—coupled with both permanent and ad hoc networks of systems for intelligence, reconnaissance, and surveillance, and with networks of systems for theater missile defense.

Allies Are a Core Requirement, Not a Necessary Annoyance

It has been observed that American military planners would often prefer that allies just stay out of the way, especially in combat operations. Operational planning is difficult under the best of circumstances, but more dramatically so when encumbered by major disparities in capability, interoperability, and detailed targeting and rules of engagement. So, also, transformation is difficult enough for the United States without worrying about allies.

Despite all this, even the most rudimentary analysis of future scenarios and missions demonstrates that allies will be at the core of many and probably most operations. U.S. forces will be neither defending empty territory nor attempting to deter adversaries from threatening empty territory. On the contrary, operations will be conducted in support of others and involve numerous countries.

If we move to more specific matters, allied issues also loom large. The reasons include the following:

- As discussed below, deterrence or timely action in defense of friendly countries will typically depend on having appropriate U.S. military capabilities in place before crises occur. This, in turn, will be possible only with long-term relationships and presence agreements.[22]
- Employment of U.S. ground forces and ground-based air forces will continue to depend critically on working relationships with host countries.
- Interventions (or threatened interventions) on the ground will prove necessary because there are too many circumstances in which air forces and missiles simply cannot accomplish the key missions (for example, stopping the killing in places such as Kosovo during the Serbian period of ethnic cleansing). Although U.S. ground forces will be involved, their numbers may be modest in percentage terms. This will be especially so for manpower-intensive operations in urban areas, forests, or jungles.
- Theater missile defense systems will depend for their effectiveness on layering and networking. Although some components will be naval, others will need to be located in friendly countries. Overall defense systems will need to be integrated during operations to achieve high effectiveness and to avoid fratricide.
- U.S. forces are probably not suitable for many key operations on the ground. The reasons include perceived legitimacy, language gaps, cultural naïveté, and inhibitions in periods when ruthlessness is required. U.S. forces may make for good SWAT teams and may be ideal for rapid and decisive operations, but they will not be suitable for others.

A contrasting military-technical view is that threats from WMD, delivered by missiles of increasing range, will drive U.S. forces to greater range and, eventually, to disengagement and a fall back to the United States itself. The preferred systems in the future, according to this view, will be long-range bombers, submarines with long-range missiles, and dispersed surface ships well distant from shore. This image is misleading to the extent that it encourages a pullback of U.S. forces and a lessening of military engagement. Ultimately, the strength of the international security system depends on continued close engagement. Moreover, as noted above, the ability of the United States to react decisively in crisis, and the ability of defended allies to risk requesting such assistance, may depend on U.S. forces already being in those territories. It is one thing to imagine a President and the ally's leader agreeing to a decisive reinforcement; it is quite another to imagine a fresh intervention when, from the viewpoint of cautious Americans, the United States has no vital national interests at stake and the risks are high—as they might be if the aggressor threatened to start using missiles and weapons of mass destruction if U.S. forces began to deploy. The aggressor might make similar threats to prevent reinforcement of forces already in place, but the decision dynamics would be quite different because the U.S. imperative would be to reinforce its troops.

Must Allies Also Transform Their Forces?

Peacemaking, Peacekeeping, and Interoperability

On the one hand, it can be argued that most nations do not need military forces with high-tech firepower and maneuverability. They primarily need forces suitable for peacekeeping and some moderately stressful peacemaking.[23] For them, the best transformation might look more like drastic reductions in the size of forces, plus increased capabilities for projecting and supporting peacekeeping/peacemaking forces, rather than a high-tech revolution. Key elements might be mundane trucks rather than top-of-the-line weapons. More generally, there is a requirement for power projection logistics, which is needed for combat operations as well as peacekeeping and peacemaking. The logistics shortfall includes strategic mobility.

The conundrum is that if coalition operations are to succeed, then it would seem necessary that U.S. and allied forces be reasonably compatible. That line of reasoning suggests the need for allies to modernize their forces. Otherwise, as in the conflict with Serbia over Kosovo, only U.S. air forces will be militarily effective. In a war involving ground forces, similar disparities would arise. U.S. forces would aspire to sudden and decisive dismantling of enemy units, whereas allied units might be condemned to classic close combat and extended dirty operations.

Preparing for Strategic Adaptations

A third consideration is that many nations must be concerned about maintaining a high level of military expertise so that, in the event of drastic changes in the strategic environment, they will be able to field competent and sizable forces for large-scale war. And, of course, professional military officers are often more interested in maintaining such expertise than in specializing only in peacekeeping operations.

Priorities for the High-End Component of Allied Force Adaptations

What are the consequences of these considerations? There is no single, one-liner strategy: each nation will need to have a relatively complex strategy dealing to some degree with all of the above considerations. From the perspective of the United States and future coalition operations, however, the high-end component of allied efforts should set a high priority on the following:

- Higher level joint and combined command and control (for example, excellence of common situation assessment, common understanding of all major unit missions and rules of engagement).
- True network-centric capabilities for joint/combined air and missile defense.

The first of these stems from the observation that the primary tool of coalition planners for avoiding problems has been, and will continue to be, separation of areas of responsibility. Individuals at the platoon level of one nation simply do not need to know what their analogues from other nations are doing. Moreover, if units deployed by nation X are much more effective than those of nation Y and that fact is known to commanders, then so be it. The coalition can cope in any case. The same is not true at the operational level. Commanders at this level need to have common operational pictures and the ability to avoid fratricide due to inadvertent maneuvers. Unfortunately, today there are severe operational-level problems in coalition operations unless months exist to hone the related command-and-control systems.[24]

The second item reflects the fact that missile defense is fundamentally different: the time scales are short, and defense effectiveness will likely depend critically on coordinated layering. The mathematics here are compelling. If one has three defense systems, each with a 70 percent probability of intercepting a given missile, then the combined effectiveness can be 97 percent—but only if the systems are independent and all operate against that missile. In contrast, if a missile going through one portion of the theater can be attacked by only one of the systems (that is, the sky has been divvied out among systems), then effectiveness will be only 70 percent. If missiles have chemical, biological, or nuclear warheads, then such an effectiveness is likely to be unacceptable. Similarly, if there are three defense systems with limited capacities against multiple targets and decoys, any one of the systems could have zero-effectiveness for later missiles in a salvo attack on a critical target. However, if properly networked, the overall system might be a good deal more effective. It follows that very high standards of network-centric efficiency will be needed.

To summarize, differences in U.S. and allied systems and capabilities are indeed a matter of concern. However, some are much more important ultimately than others (figure 3). It is to be hoped that priorities develop accordingly.

The Multiplicity of Instruments

Most of this paper has dealt with military transformation, but in a volume devoted to globalization, it seems appropriate to emphasize that future success in international security work requires much more. Military instruments are uniquely powerful for some purposes, but it is the overall system of power and related instruments that matter. Indeed, as figure 4 suggests, the power of good international relationships is greater than the power of general deterrence, which is substantially greater than the power of immediate deterrence (crisis action), which is in turn substantially greater than various compellent actions associated with actual force employment. The primary task in international security is not so much to win the Nation's wars and lesser scuffles, but to make such events unnecessary.

Figure 3: Not All Interoperability Is Equally Important
Transforming Political-Economic-Military Doctrine

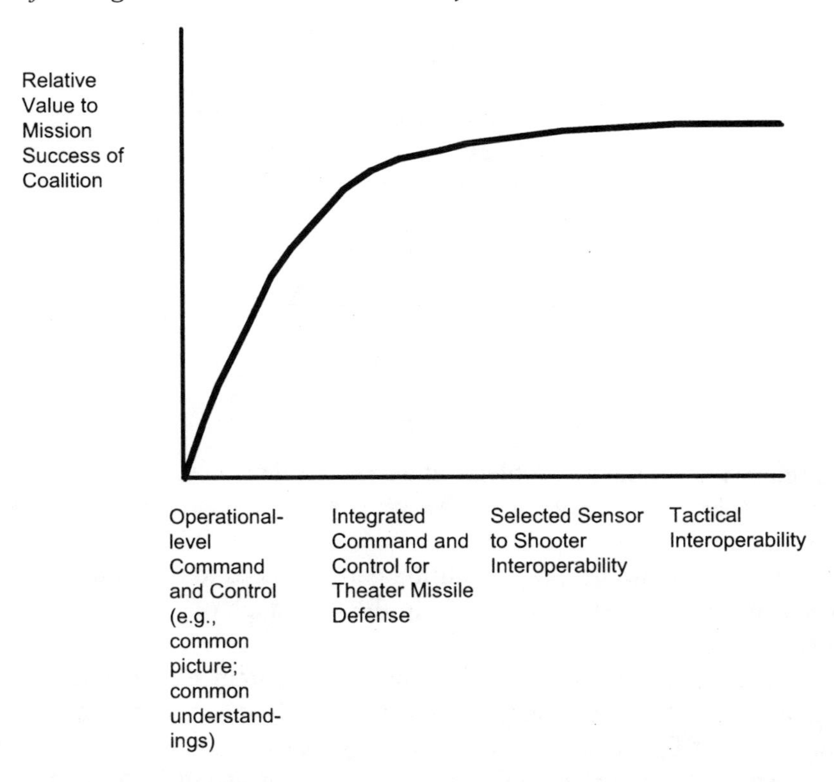

Deterrence and Compellence Often Require Coalition Unity

The folly of depending too much on the upper levels of the pyramid in figure 4 becomes evident when we look at the historical record and acknowledge that the history of multinational interventions is not a happy one. Consider, for example, the bluntness and ineffectiveness of the North Atlantic Treaty Organization (NATO) strategy in dealing with the Kosovo crisis and its antecedents. Although NATO prevailed eventually, it failed to head off the crisis in the first place, to prevent ethnic cleansing, or to substantially reduce the capabilities of the Serbian Army. This was so despite overwhelming NATO military superiority. The Kosovo affair is still recent, but we might think also of the debacle in Somalia, the dubiousness of results overall in Bosnia, or the results of many other UN interventions. There simply is no basis for optimism as we look to the future unless something changes.

Figure 4. Relative Effectiveness of Security Factors
Effectiveness decreases with area of layer in figure

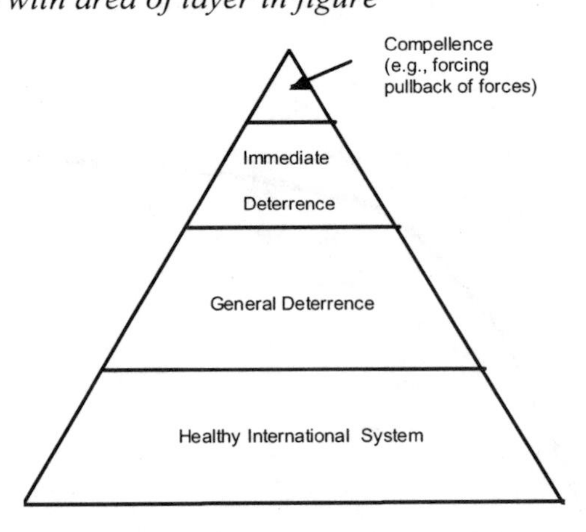

The first principle is to address problems at a more fundamental level and head off the crises in the first place. Arguably, three other principles should also be followed:

- The United States and its likely coalition partners need to develop consensus views ahead of time on how to deal—using the full range of instruments—with potential regional crises.
- This consensus should be forged around the requirement for effectiveness rather than ad hoc political expediency. This will imply much more emphasis on prior expressions of firm intent, in response to aggression, to apply strong, long-term political and economic sanctions; and prior expressions of firm intent, in response to aggression, to use military means in limited but decisive ways—even at the cost of some innocent lives and some casualties to service personnel.
- These intentions should be made known in ways that undergird deterrence and increase credibility in situations of immediate deterrence or attempted compellence.

Adopting and executing these principles would be very difficult: in many respects they fly in the face of natural political-level thinking. However, at some point, the world's nations must recognize that unusual measures such as these are needed if crises are to be averted or dealt with effectively when they arise. Deterrence and compellence are very difficult and are undercut by the natural phenomena of ambiguity, indecision, and divisiveness among allies.[25]

Illustrative Implications

If accepted, the principles just described would have many implications. For example, although many nations would prefer a strong U.S. military presence over the horizon (but not in their immediate neighborhood), the quality of general deterrence and immediate deterrence is sometimes far higher with more immediate presence.

This is due not only to the increased and visible military capability that may be achieved, but also to the fact that having forces already in place simplifies and toughens decisionmaking for the United States and the allies that it would defend. Presence implies commitments, whereas failures of deterrence often occur because of a perceived lack of commitment or resolve.

As a second example, consider implications for force employment planning. As a preface, we might compare the experiences of *Desert Storm* with those of Kosovo. In *Desert Storm*, the fighting war was measured in tens of hours rather than months—in large part because of the comprehensive, focused, and creative manner in which the offensive was conducted (and the enormous effects of the preceding air attack). The contrast with the Kosovo operation is stark. Immediate objectives were not achieved, and many innocent people died as a result of ethnic cleansing begun in earnest after NATO began its operations. NATO forced Milosevic to back down eventually, but at an extraordinary cost. Dealing with a fourth-rate nation required a substantial fraction of U.S. and allied air forces and months of time. The price of self-imposed NATO constraints was high.

What lessons should be learned, and to what extent will future political-economic-military doctrine be different? Will leaders again talk themselves into believing that modest strikes virtually designed to avoid harm will accomplish compellent goals or that the threat thereof will deter aggression in the first place? Will they be so convinced on the matter as not even to develop full-scale contingent options to execute if needed?

We cannot rerun history, but it is legitimate to argue that the likelihood of an early success that would have prevented ethnic cleansing might have been much higher had the alliance visibly prepared for the immediate use of ground forces and the potential for a subsequent full-scale invasion of Serbia, and struck air and missile targets initially with far greater intensity and fewer constraints (albeit at the price of some casualties to NATO pilots and many more civilian casualties in Kosovo and Serbia). The lessons learned would seem to support the principles suggested above.

The purpose here is not to second-guess the decisions of anguished NATO political leaders but to emphasize that there are lessons to learn and that those lessons tend to call for increased decisiveness and, in some cases, casualty tolerance and use of ground forces. That, in turn, calls for extensive efforts in peacetime to bring about the changes in attitude within alliances that would make such decisiveness possible in sufficiently serious crises. Regrettably, many officials emerged from the Kosovo experience believing that it was ultimately a success, which is not the case.

As a third example of how the principles might apply, consider the dismal history of attempting to use political and economic threats for deterrence and after-the-fact compellence. The sanctions have often had many profound effects, but most typically the innocent have suffered and objectives have not been achieved. Among the reasons are that, in a crisis, a miscreant leader who is the object of deterrence or compellence may believe that sanctions may not actually be applied, since the relevant nations disagree about them; that even if they are applied, they will be leaky, spotty, and temporary; and, finally, that so long as he remains in power, he will be able to allocate whatever resources remain after sanctions to his own purposes.

A Modest Proposal

To conclude, I note that one of the most traditional American images has been that of the hero who is reluctant to accept a fight, but who acts suddenly and decisively when the threshold is crossed. A version of the image was Theodore Roosevelt's adage, "Speak softly, but carry a big stick." Sometimes folk wisdom has merit. The United States and its many allies worldwide need to develop a comparable doctrine, and they need the underlying consensus and the physical and doctrinal capacity to carry it out. Without this, the value of military transformation will be much reduced.

Notes

[1] William S. Cohen, *Report of the Quadrennial Defense Review* (Washington, DC: Government Printing Office, 1997). See also National Defense Panel, *Transforming Defense: National Security in the 21st Century* (Washington, DC: Government Printing Office, 1997).

[2] Paul K. Davis, David C. Gompert, Richard Hillestad, and Stuart E. Johnson, *Transforming the Force: Suggestions for DOD Strategy*, RAND Issue Paper (Santa Monica, CA: RAND, 1998).

[3] Such problems were highlighted in a 1995 Defense Science Board study led by John Foster. See also Cohen, *Report of the Quadrennial Defense Review* and National Defense Panel, *Transforming Defense.*

[4] This is used by Andrew W. Marshall, the Pentagon Director of Net Assessment. See Jeffrey Barnett, *Future Warfare: Assessment of Future Aerospace Campaigns 2010* (Maxwell AFB, AL: Air War College, 1996) for a good survey on the subject that reflects much work done by Marshall's office. Other mid-to-late 1990s discussions of the revolution in military affairs can be found in Cohen, *Report of the Quadrennial Defense Review*, Joint Chiefs of Staff, *Joint Vision 2010* (Washington, DC: Department of Defense, 1997), Joint Chiefs of Staff, *Joint Vision 2020* (Washington, DC: Department of Defense, 2000), Andrew Krepenevich, "Cavalry to Computer: The Pattern of Military Revolutions," *The National Interest* (Fall 1995), Stuart E. Johnson and Martin C. Libicki, eds., *Dominant Battlefield Knowledge: The Winning Edge* (Washington, DC: National Defense University Press, 1995), James A. Blaker, *A Vanguard Force: Accelerating the American Revolution in Military Affairs* (Washington, DC: Progressive Policy Institute, 1996), and Institute for National Strategic Studies, *Strategic Assessment 1996* (Washington, DC: National Defense University Press, 1996).

[5] See Stephen Peter Rosen, *Winning the Next War: Innovations and the Modern Military* (Ithaca, NY: Cornell University Press, 1991), Krepenevich, "Cavalry to Computer," Jeff Isaacson, Christopher Layne, and John Arquilla, *Predicting Military Innovation*, RAND DB–242–A (Santa Monica, CA: RAND, 1998), and Richard Hundley, *Past Revolutions, Future Transformations: What Can the History of Revolutions in Military Affairs Tell Us about Transforming the U.S. Military* (Santa Monica, CA: RAND, 1999), for interesting discussions.

[6] For discussions of urban issues, see Russell W. Glenn, ed., *The City's Many Faces*, CF–148–A (Santa Monica, CA: RAND, 2000) and Alan Vick, John Stillion, David Frelinger, Joel Kavitky, Benjamin Lambeth, Jefferson Marquis, and Mathew Waxman, *Aerospace Operations in Urban Environments: Exploring New Concepts* (Santa Monica, CA: RAND, 2000).

[7] Examples include the Office of Net Assessment, the Defense Science Board, services science advisory boards, and think tanks.

[8] See David C. Gompert and Irving Lachow, *Transforming the Force: Lessons from the Wider Revolution*, RAND Issue Paper (Santa Monica, CA: RAND, 2000), for lessons to be learned from industry's information revolution.

[9] Leadership for DOD effort has come from Assistant Secretary of Defense Edward Warner and his office and from two Chairmen, General John M. Shalikashvili and General Hugh H. Shelton, and their staffs.

[10] The value of such mission orientation and system thinking is emphasized in Davis, et al., *Transforming the Force*, Paul K. Davis, James H. Bigelow, and Jimmie McEver, *Analytical Methods for Studies and Experiments on "Transforming the Force,"* DB–278–OSD (Santa Monica, CA: RAND, 1999), Gompert and Lachow, *Transforming the Force*, and the National Research Council, *Network Centric Naval Forces: A Transition Strategy for Enhancing Operational Capabilities*, Naval Studies Board (Washington, DC: National Academy Press, 2000).

[11] This section has benefited from discussions with colleague Richard Hundley.

[12] Hundley, *Past Revolutions, Future Transformations.*

[13] Paul K. Davis, *New Challenges in Defense Planning: Rethinking How Much Is Enough*, chapter 2 (Santa Monica, CA: RAND Compendium, 1994).

[14] Some enthusiasts for change apparently believed that the panacea was large joint field experiments, whereas what is needed is a multifaceted, iterative effort involving a combination of brainstorming, laboratory research, modeling, simulation, and gaming, as well as field experiments (Davis, Bigelow, and McEver, *Analytical Methods for Studies*). U.S. Joint Forces Command now embraces this view.

[15] William F. Kernan, who currently heads the Army's prestigious XVIII Corps, succeeded Gehman in early autumn 2000.

[16] See Defense Science Board, *Tactics and Technology for 21st Century Operational Superiority, Office of the Under Secretary of Defense for Acquisition and Technology* (Washington, DC: Department of Defense, 1996), Defense Science Board, *Joint Operations Superiority in the 21st Century: Integrating Capabilities, Underwriting Joint Vision 2010 and Beyond*, 2 vols. (Washington, DC: Office of the Under Secretary of Defense for Acquisition and Technology, 1998), and Harlan K. Ullman and James P. Wade, *Shock and Awe: Achieving Rapid Dominance* (Washington, DC: Government Printing Office, 1996). A related concept that is now under study by direction of the Office of the Secretary of Defense is that of a Joint Strike Force (JSF). The Institute for Defense Analyses is currently doing an OSD–sponsored JSF study, working with JFCOM's staff engaged in the Rapid Decisive Operations effort.

[17] Joint Chiefs of Staff, *Joint Vision 2010.*

[18] Defense Science Board, *Tactics and Technology and Defense Science Board, Joint Operations Superiority in the 21st Century.*

[19] The services' initiatives are described briefly in vision documents that can be found at their Web sites, all of which can be reached from <http://www.defenselink.mil>. See also the brief accounts in the annual defense report; for example, William S. Cohen, *Annual Report to the President and Congress* (Washington, DC: Department of Defense, 2000).

[20] As one example, developing the operational capability to halt an invading army *early* depends on a whole system of subordinate but integrated capabilities. Missions can fail even with superb weapons because of a number of weak points in the system. Perhaps most obvious is command and control. There is little precedent for complex command and control, as would be required for early-halt operations, to work immediately and from a standing start. For discussion of such matters and the system perspective, see Davis, Bigelow, and McEver, *Analytical Methods for Studies.*

[21] National Research Council, *Network Centric Naval Forces*; David Alberts, John J. Garstka, and Frederick Stein, *Network Centric Warfare* (Washington, DC: National Defense University Press, 1999).

[22] Some of these arrangements will involve access to bases (for example, for servicing of ships, even "homeporting"), pre-positioning, and prior discussions about potential needs during crisis operations.

[23] See Reiner Huber and Bernhard Schmidt, *The Challenge for Defense Reform in Europe* (McLean, VA: Potomac Foundation, 2000), for a discussion of European force needs and priorities.

[24] See Michele Zanini and Jennifer Taw, *Multiforce Compatability: Lessons from Past Operations* (Santa Monica, CA: RAND, 1998).

[25] See National Research Council, *Post Cold War Conflict Deterrence* (Washington, DC: National Academy Press, 1996), Appendix J, for my own views on deterrence, which reflect an analysis of past crises and counterfactual versions using psychologically realistic models of decisionmakers, such as Saddam Hussein.

Chapter 20

The Navy and the New Strategic Environment

Bradd C. Hayes

It's hard to forecast, especially about the future.
—*Casey Stengel*

This chapter discusses major global trends that are altering the security environment and posits how those changes might affect the roles and missions of the services, specifically the Navy. It does not attempt to cover either the breadth or depth of the subjects dealt with elsewhere in this book; rather, it skims over some of the most significant trends in a variety of areas, including security, economics, technology, social affairs, and the physical environment. Of these, economics, technology, and social affairs are perhaps the most important.

As Francis Fukuyama has noted:

> There are two separate motors driving the historical process. The first is economic. What gives History its fundamental directionality and progressive character is modern natural science. . . . The progress of science and technology . . . creates a frontier of production possibilities and thus an economic order. . . . The second motor is what Hegel called the "struggle for recognition." Human beings desire not just material well-being; they seek recognition of their dignity and status on the part of other human beings, and this demand for recognition is the fundamental passion that underlies politics.[1]

Hence, a survey of historical trends affecting the military can be too narrow, but seldom too broad. This chapter deliberately raises more questions than it answers because the future is not linear and the ultimate effects of globalization have yet to be seen.

The fact of the matter is that "today's wave of technological change seems destined to transform life over the next 20 to 30 years."[2] It is inconceivable that such changes will not result in a new security paradigm. The new economy and the new security paradigm will prove to be linked more closely than the military and the economy have been at any time during the past 100 years; unfortunately, the links will not be overt. The reason is that military support for the new economy will be

---

Bradd C. Hayes is a professor and senior researcher in the Decision Strategies Department at the Naval War College. His publications include The Politics of Naval Innovation: Naval Rules of Engagement, Transforming the Navy: A Strategy for the Secretary of the Navy, Beyond Traditional Peacekeeping, *and* Doing Windows: Non-Traditional Military Responses to Complex Emergencies.

much different than it was in the past and will require a more subtle and holistic approach to security. This will inevitably provoke cries of "mission creep," and those cries will be wrong.

Security Environment Threats

The End of Major War?

After 50 years without a conflict pitting great powers against each other, speculation is rising that we have seen the end of major wars. Because no one can confidently predict that major war will never occur again, especially if, as some believe, we are doomed to repeat historical cycles, the U.S. military must continue to field a hedging force against such an eventuality.[3] Most analysts believe, however, that major war, although possible, is unlikely. Hans Binnendijk noted that the Cold War ended without global conflict "because nuclear weapons created too dangerous a prospect for major war."[4] Michael Mandelbaum defines major war as "a war fought by the most powerful members of the international system, drawing on all of their resources and using every weapon at their command, over a period of years, leading to an outcome with revolutionary geopolitical consequences including the birth and death of regimes, the redrawing of borders and the reordering of the hierarchy of sovereign states."[5] Donald Kagan agrees with Binnendijk that "the deterrent offered by nuclear war works toward" making major war obsolete "and that the growth of trade, democracy and economic interdependence assists that prospect." But he accompanies this observation with a warning that "peace in the future depend[s] on the decisions and the actions taken by people and these, as always, provide no guarantee against war—even 'major' war as Michael Mandelbaum has defined it."[6]

How Great a Hedge?

Since the consequences of major war are so catastrophic, fielding a hedging force against its eventuality is the sine qua non of defense policy. The question is, How large a force is necessary, and what else should it be able to accomplish? If the likelihood of using such a force is truly minimal, how much are U.S. taxpayers willing to spend for such an insurance policy? Probably less than the current 3 percent of gross domestic product (GDP) that is spent on defense. The answer to this conundrum would appear to be the fielding of a dual-purpose force that serves as a hedge against major war and at the same time is capable of responding to lesser crises. Thomas Barnett argues, however, that these missions are so different that trying to field a force for both has created a military schizophrenia that is good for neither the military nor the Nation.[7] He argues that the Navy should return to its roots as a guarantor of U.S. commercial interests, helping ensure that goods and services can freely move around the globe through the mediums of sea, space, and cyberspace. With the notable exception of strategic nuclear submarines, Barnett would leave the care and feeding of the hedging force to the Army and the Air Force.[8]

Sorting Out the Threats

Ashton Carter offered a typology for thinking about America's security threats, placing them on an A-, B-, or C-List (figure 1).[9] Although Carter's typology is theoretically sound, he recommends that the active military assume some challenges better assigned to the National Guard or law enforcement agencies. The A-List (military) challenges presented by Russia and China are subject to continuing scrutiny by the military, but Carter recommends adapting a "preventive defense" strategy that requires "defense by other means." By this he means engaging in activities other than preparing for and fighting America's wars. "Preventive-defence measures range from policies to influence the strategic direction of the Russian and Chinese militaries, to initiatives such as the Nunn-Lugar programme to prevent Russian 'loose nukes,' and intelligence innovations to detect transnational 'catastrophic terrorism.'"[10] While some of these "other means" are critical, if they fail and traditional military missions have been ignored, the country truly will be in peril. Carter rightfully points out that in the absence of a peer competitor, today's military is building its force structure to meet B-List challenges. He fails, however, to note why such a force, if it continues to modernize, will be unable to meet any rising Chinese or Russian challenge. He also fails to explain how these countries are going to achieve superpower status when the United States continues to outspend them at an astonishing rate. Having said that, his typology is nonetheless useful for thinking about which challenges the military must prepare for.

Figure 1: Typology of Threats

A-List	*B-List*	*C-List*
Potential future problems that could threaten U.S. survival, way of life and position in the world; possibly preventable	Actual threats to vital U.S. interests; deterrable through ready forces	Important problems that do not threaten vital U.S. interests
• "Weimar Russia" • Loose nuclear, chemical, biological weapons • A rising China that spawns hostility • Proliferation of weapons of mass destruction • Catastrophic terrorism	• Major Theater War in Northeast Asia • Major Theater War in Southwest Asia	• Kosovo • Bosnia • East Timor • Rwanda • Somalia • Haiti • ...

Source: Adapted from Ashton B. Carter and William J. Perry, *Preventive Defense: A New Security Strategy for America* (Washington, DC: The Brookings Institution Press, 1999)

A-List: Missions Other Than War

Many of Carter's A-List missions are not lesser included cases of preparing for a major war, which means that hedging forces are not suited to accomplish them. Carter would divert funding and attention from the hedging force to preventive activities for which hedging force infrastructure is ill suited. Although some of his "defense by other means" activities could play a significant noncombat role in B- and C-List missions, for the most part, traditional military forces are going to be required to respond to them. Although most discussions surrounding the proliferation of weapons of mass destruction have centered recently on chemical and biological weapons ("poor men's nukes"), *The Economist* asserts that "the chances of a smaller nuclear exchange may have already increased, or be about to. There are three factors which govern the chances of nuclear war: the number of nuclear powers; the likelihood that one of those powers will reach a point where it sees the use of nuclear weapons as its best option; and the possibility of mistakes. Together they make nuclear war seem quite possible, even likely, in the next half century."[11] This assertion was supported by the Naval War College South Asia Proliferation Project, which ran a series of decision events looking at the possibilities for and consequences of a nuclear exchange between India and Pakistan.[12] The problem is that the U.S. strategic nuclear force is not a credible deterrent against such exchanges.

B- and C-List Missions Remaining the Norm

Some pundits have argued that "superpowers do not do windows." Chester Crocker counters that "the United States cannot disavow all strategic responsibility and expect to remain a great nation, a nation that will lead and be accepted by others as a leader."[13] On occasion, he says, the U.S. military must "volunteer to walk between dogs and lamp posts." He goes on to say, "The way we Americans are thinking about war these days is deeply disturbing. We seem to believe that we can prepare for the wars that we want to fight while remaining ill-equipped for, and uninterested in, the kinds of challenges we will most likely face."[14] Bernard Trainor agrees with Crocker: "There is a tendency on the part of the Pentagon to wish all of this (that is, C-List missions) would go away and say that 'We just do classical wars' and that the purpose of the military is to fight the Nation's wars. Well, that's very nice, but they're liable to find themselves as hangar queens in the future, in that classical war on the horizon doesn't seem to be very likely, but these dirty little messy things, like Bosnia, seem to be a constant."[15] If Crocker and Trainor are correct, the implications for military roles, missions, organization, infrastructure, and training are significant.[16]

Implications of Carter's Threat Typology for the Navy

Dealing with Carter's A-List Threats

The military, including the Navy, must maintain a hedging force against the emergence of a belligerent peer competitor (China and Russia being the primary concerns), but head-on conflict is an unlikely eventuality. The hedging force should concentrate on applying appropriate force during conflicts on the periphery, since major ground operations either in China or Russia are remote. The exception, of course, is maintaining a credible nuclear deterrent force. For a number of reasons, the centerpiece of the Navy hedging force will remain the aircraft carrier battle group. First, carriers, like other navy ships, are long-lived. The USS *Midway*, for example, was retired after 50 years of service. Second, although alternatives to manned aircraft are being developed, their capabilities will not be sufficiently robust to replace manned carrier-based aircraft before the next class of carrier is built. Hence, the United States will have carriers in its inventory for at least the next 70 years. Third, air superiority will remain an essential element of warfare, and manned aircraft will be required to achieve it well into this century and possibly into the next. Finally, the ability to linger offshore with a powerful air force will remain an important source of leverage during times of growing tensions.

The big question is, How many carriers are enough? The Navy rushed a half-dozen carriers into the fray during *Desert Storm*.[17] When the Department of Defense (DOD) developed its two major theater war requirement for force sizing, the Navy used this fact to back its claims that it needed a dozen carriers. That measurement, developed during the Clinton administration, will disappear and the Navy will be left looking for new arguments to sustain its force structure numbers. Those arguments will be difficult to find. During most Cold War crises, U.S. administrations were quick to ask, "Where are the carriers?" Today, they are more likely to ask, "Where are the Tomahawk shooters?" Twelve carriers may be the correct quantity for the future, but the Navy may not be able to afford that many if it is to meet its other surface combatant requirements. Fiscal constraints could drive the Navy, after much kicking and screaming, to retain between 8 and 10 carriers and a matching number of amphibious-readiness groups. This size of a force will require the Navy to be extremely creative in meeting its forward engagement missions.

Complementing the carrier's power projection capabilities, and integral to any future battle group, should be a surface combatant with a sea-based theater ballistic missile defense system. The Nation will be far better served developing a sea-based missile defense system than in pursuing the land-based continental system currently under consideration. Historically, the strategy of the United States has been to fight wars as far from its shores as possible. Sea-based missile defenses fit well into this traditional strategic paradigm, and they offer leverage that the United States could use to encourage coalition partners to join with it and stay the course. Thus, future carrier battle groups should include three types of capital ships: aircraft carriers, ballistic missile defense ships, and submarines. All three types offer unique capabilities, and each is a power projection platform. Unfortunately, they are all extremely expensive.

Depending upon the budgets, expensive ships could mean a smaller force. The irony is that the smaller the hedging force becomes, the more likely it is to be used belligerently—*if* that is the *only* force acquired by the Nation. No country with far-flung international interests has ever been able to protect them using garrisoned forces and a surge strategy. Nevertheless, the smaller the force, the more garrisoned it becomes, for the simple reason that there will not be enough resources to deploy effectively on a routine basis. For the Navy, a mixture of high- and low-end ships is needed to overcome this conundrum.

Increased attention should be given to intelligence collection and analysis aimed at thwarting proliferation and terrorism. Ehud Sprinzak asserts that

> the intelligence community should naturally assume the most significant role in any productive campaign to stop chemical and biological terrorism. However, new early warning CBW (chemical/biological weapons) indicators that focus on radical group behavior are urgently needed. Analysts should be able to reduce substantially the risk of a CBW attack if they monitor group radicalization as expressed in its rhetoric, extralegal operations, low-level violence, growing sense of collective paranoia, and early experimentation with chemical or biological substances. Proper CBW intelligence must be freed from the burden of proving criminal intent.[18]

The military, including the Navy, has a role in such a scheme, but the bulk of intelligence gathering and analysis is beyond the scope of the operating forces.

The proper role for the military is to respond as directed to terrorist acts and to punish terrorist groups and states that sponsor or permit terrorist organizations to operate within their borders. The military should be wary about accepting roles dealing with terrorism in domestic settings. Just as DOD has been given an extensive, if unwanted, role in the "war on drugs," there will be increased calls for it to get involved in the war on terrorism. Terrorist organizations such as the one run by Osama bin Laden, whose primary aim is to punish the United States for its decadence, will keep terrorism high on the political agenda.

Dealing with Carter's B-List Threats

Major theater war remains the likeliest setting for high-intensity conflict involving the deployment and buildup of significant U.S. forces. These conflicts will occur suddenly and require the military to deploy quickly and execute operations rapidly. Hence, the emphasis for the Navy should be on forward presence for its own forces and fast sea lift in support of other services' forces. Hedging forces will prove extremely useful during these conflicts and will justify taxpayer confidence in maintaining them. These conflicts will confront the Navy with asymmetrical challenges and the concomitant risks of operating in the littorals. Access to conflict zones will be the issue.

The Navy must continue to explore strategies to ensure that it can execute operations in the littoral. Access challenges can be handled in a number of ways. The best way is by adopting a strategy aimed at blinding an opponent. An enemy cannot hit what it cannot see. Unfortunately, this ideal is difficult, if not impossible, to achieve. Severely blurring an adversary's vision, however, is possible. Stealth is part of the answer, but its primary benefit is forcing an opponent to invest in large, powerful counterstealth systems (so large that they can be identified, located, and destroyed). Decoys and operational deception also play a role, as do size (the smaller the better) and speed. A debate rages within the Navy about the effectiveness of developing a new class of small, fast ships that could be built at less cost (therefore in greater numbers) and that are capable of operating in restricted access environments. Dubbed "streetfighters" for their ability to get in close and mix it up with the enemy, these ships would be highly dependent on a robust sea base (a so-called mother ship or mother fleet) or on nearby ports. They would be complemented by a new class of mini-sub designed for operations in the littoral. For autonomous operations, "marsupial battle groups," consisting of a mother ship (carrying a number of streetfighters and mini-subs in a large well deck), and a couple of escort ships could prove extremely useful against most B- and C-List challenges. These concepts, however, exist only on paper, and they will stay that way until more detailed cost estimates and feasibility studies are available. Marsupial battle groups, if they are built, could help resolve the problem of numbers.

Numbers matter, and streetfighters could help get the Navy's numbers up. Without some kind of low-end ship, budget realities could drive the Navy to an overall fleet of 200 to 300 ships (probably closer to 200 than to 300). That level is too low to handle the number and range of missions the Navy *should* be tasked with. (I emphasize "should" because the United States needs to continue an active role in maintaining world stability and that means tackling a lot of C-List threats.) Streetfighters could be useful in satisfying many of the peacetime forward presence missions demanded of the Navy.

Figure 2. Economics and Security

1. The global energy market has the necessary resources . . .
2. But no stability, no market
3. No growth, no stability
4. No resources, no growth
5. No infrastructure, no resources
6. No money, no infrastructure
7. No rules, no money
8. No security, no rules
9. No Leviathan, no security
10. No U.S. military, no Leviathan—*so the military-market connection must be understood*

Dealing with Carter's C-List Threats

The U.S. military will continue to respond to these kinds of threats, although crisis fatigue or different policies could result in fewer responses in this decade than in the 1990s. Failure to respond often enough, however, will result in informed and influential people continuing to ask the same question as did Secretary of State Madeleine Albright: "What's the point of having this superb military that you're always talking about if we can't use it?"[19] Or, as former Assistant Secretary of State for Human Rights Patricia Derian, put it, "Wait a minute. If the soldiers don't want to fight, what are we paying them for?"[20] Forward presence will remain critical if the Navy and Marine Corps are to maintain their traditional roles as America's emergency response forces. The Department of the Navy's budget will likely be tied more closely to its capabilities to respond in this area than in any other. Hence, the probability that C-List missions will continue to engage the military should be viewed as good news for both the Navy and the Marine Corps.

For most people, the gut reaction to hearing that the United States is the world's police force is immediate and negative. Yet, in effect, that is exactly what is required to maintain future peace and prosperity. The investment required to meet C-List challenges is a bargain—especially since most of the world's problems, from the U.S. point of view, are virtual crises, in that the United States has the luxury of choosing the crises to which it will respond. The rationale for remaining the world's police force is best summed up in the attached decalogue developed by Thomas Barnett (figure 2). It is drawn from lessons learned during an economic security exercise that he conducted on

Wall Street that looked at Asia's energy future. Although the decalogue discusses energy markets, it holds true for the global economy as well. The bottom line, to borrow a cliché from Wall Street, is that the cumulative effect of unconstrained C-List crises is as problematic for U.S. interests as any threat on Carter's B-List.

National Security Strategy

Some critics continue to bemoan the fact that a U.S. grand strategy has not emerged since the end of the Cold War.[21] They are looking for what cannot be found. There is no grand strategy because there is no grand threat. Regional threats now dominate the security landscape, and with them should come a series of regional strategies. Hugh De Santis calls this approach "mutualism." He writes that "mutualism is an interest-based rather than a norm-centered concept of international cooperation. It emphasizes regional rather than global approaches to international cooperation, recognizes the continued importance of the nation-state, and is ipso facto a nonhegemonic approach to international security."[22] The logical result of such thinking is the establishment of a series of regional security relations, equivalent to NATO, but not formal alliances. Adopting this approach would require that the military spend more time and money than it now does on overcoming the challenges of coalition operations.

Toward Regional Strategies

De Santis is not alone in believing that regionalization will be the hallmark of the future. For several years, Robert Kaplan has been describing a new world in which regions (sometimes defined as "vast city-states") will be the main political organizations.[23] Such a development may seem counterintuitive to globalization, but it is not. Kaplan argues that geography will once again matter as regions, regardless of borders, will find that they have much in common and that working together can better promote their economic interests in the global marketplace than working through national capitals. Regionalization also complements another trend—urbanization.

As the trend for regionalization becomes more pronounced, the importance and influence of U.S. regional commanders in chief should also increase. Eventually, they may have a greater input into what kinds of forces and equipment they receive, as well as into how deploying forces are trained. Such a development will have a profound impact on the services.

Two aspects of the national security strategy, or the lack of one, will continue to affect the military. The first aspect is that over the course of the 1990s, "Force has become the preferred instrument of American statecraft."[24] Whether this trend proves irreversible remains an open question, but it does signal that the military will remain engaged in messy intervention situations. The second aspect is the regionalization of strategy. This trend naturally leads to regional security arrangements that offer transparency and cooperation as a path to peace. Because of its prominent geographical and political positions, the United States will likely seek to be a part of most, if not all, of these arrangements. This will have an enormous bearing on the required infrastructure for both the Navy and the Marine Corps. Being a part of these arrangements means being deployed to areas where they will operate. How many ships one needs can be directly correlated to how many places one wants to be.

Implications of National Security Strategy for the Navy

The naval services should work more closely with regional combatant commands to develop regional strategies for the use and deployment of forces. Continued attempts to develop separate service strategies in hopes that unified commanders will adopt them will result in a mismatch between strategy and forces, and the political backlash will reduce the influence of the services. The Navy may end up floating three or four different kinds of fleets: so what? The Information Age brought with it a new economy, but less well understood is that it brought with it a new security paradigm as well. National security is no longer the private domain of the Departments of Defense and State. Neither the regional commanders nor the services have fully adjusted to this new reality.

As a result of this new security paradigm, regional unified commanders should go beyond examining their warfighting capabilities and develop a new approach to theater engagement. The Commander in Chief, U.S. Naval Forces, Europe (CNE), is developing a new cross-sector approach to engagement that has much to offer. During a period of decreasing force structure and constrained budgets, the CNE believes that it makes sense to preserve scarce resources through preventive actions. A truism accepted by everyone is that peace is cheaper than war—peace is also easier on personnel and equipment. Nevertheless, the military has concentrated its efforts on planning for crisis response and has woefully ignored how it might assist in crisis prevention. Past peacetime engagement activities have relied for the most part on military-to-military relationships, exercises, educational opportunities, and port calls. The last activity is good for bar owners and other ancient professions, but not much good for sustainable development or crisis prevention. The CNE staff asked, "What organizations are involved in sustainable development activities (that is, crisis prevention), and what can the military do to assist them?"

Figure 3. Security and Economics

1. International security is based on a single global rule set (free markets)
2. No regional security, no single global rule set
3. No internal stability, no regional security
4. No increased consumption, no internal stability
5. No energy growth, no increased consumption
6. No infrastructure, no energy growth
7. No money, no infrastructure
8. No rules, no money
9. No reform, no rules
10. No economic downturn, no reform—*an Asian downturn puts at risk the single global rule set*

Sustainable development per se is not the military's business, but the military will continue to make port calls and country visits, so why not make the most of them? The CNE is realistic in what the military *can* do in this area (not much), but its new approach is an attempt to leverage military assets in order to get the most out of what little it *does* do. The CNE's approach is cost-effective, sensible, and well conceived. It also helps align the new security with the new economy.

Economic Environment

This book serves as testimony to the fact that no trend has been more discussed than globalization. As one author noted, "Although the pace and structure of globalization are still open to debate, the phenomenon of globalization is a fait accompli."[25] There is perhaps no greater indicator of this phenomenon than the increase in foreign direct investment around the world, which increased fourfold between 1982 and 1994.[26] This begs the question of what it means for the military to protect U.S. property and investments overseas. Fears raised about globalization generally focus on its negative impact on nation-states and local cultures.[27] The Seattle riots that exploded in early 2000 during the meeting of the World Trade Organization are an early warning of the backlash that globalization is likely to engender. While globalization may make major war less likely, it will probably increase the number of local conflicts that will involve U.S. global interests. As a result, national governments will have to deal with the phenomenon that Thomas Barnett calls "glocalization"—the need to engage globally while protecting interests locally. Nevertheless, "there remains no viable alternative development model that promises better results than globalization."[28]

As mentioned earlier, economic growth relies on the benign (and sometimes compelling) presence of military might. In areas outside Europe, one could go even further and say that economic growth relies on the military might of the United States. The global economy does not run on money—it runs on trust that is developed through transparency and stability. Markets provide the transparency, and the military helps provide the stability. Thomas Barnett's companion decalogue to the one shown earlier demonstrates how today's rosy economic picture could go awry in a big way—especially in Asia. Its logic underscores the important connection between the new economy and the new security (figure 3).

Implications of Globalization for the Navy

Some people view the Federal budget as a zero-sum game. Representative Barney Frank (D–MA) represented the views of these people when he stated, "Every dollar spent for the military is a dollar that cannot be spent to alleviate poverty, to fight against crime, to improve our environment." He further commented, "The biggest threat to the American way of life now, in many ways, is the globalization of the economy. . . . How can we maintain our standard of living, our environmental standards, our wages, our working conditions, in a world in which we are competing with people who do not follow those standards, who have a much lower standard?"[29] Representative Frank's argument can be turned on its head, allowing us to view defense budgets in a new light. The congressman is really complaining about the fact that the global economy is not operating according to a single rule set, not about globalization per se. From that perspective (and accepting Barnett's two decalogues), defense appropriations are not a zero-sum game, but an essential investment in America's economic future. Unfortunately, the connection between defense budgets and prosperity is neither as direct nor as immediate as one would hope in order to capture the public imagination. As a result, defense budgets are not going to grow dramatically. On the other hand, neither should they decline dramatically.

There are, of course, alternative scenarios that could result in dramatic increases in defense spending—for example, threats from an expansionist and well-armed China[30] or from a resurgent Russia. As mentioned earlier, Ashton Carter's "preventive defense" program is aimed at ensuring those futures never mature. That begs the question about whether the current level of defense spending is enough. As of this writing, defense spending is scheduled to decline every year after 2004. At the Naval War College Current Strategy Forum 2000, Ron O'Rourke noted that efficiency efforts would not pay the bills in the future. Daniel Gouré and Jeffrey M. Randy refer to this recapitalization shortfall as a "train wreck."[31] To avert it, they argue, defense spending must increase significantly, force structure must reduce significantly, or technologies must be applied in a way that they drastically reduce the cost to procure, operate, and maintain forces so that their numbers can be maintained at required levels.

Neither the defense budget nor the Navy's share of it is likely to increase or decrease dramatically. That being the case, the Navy must make some difficult choices between readiness and modernization. To date, it has chosen readiness over modernization. This is fine in the short run, but in 20 years this policy will result in a dramatic decline in the number of ships that can be forward-deployed and tasked with engagement activities. The most drastic result of this policy could be the curtailment of capital ship construction in order to pump out larger numbers of low-end ships just so the American flag can continue to be shown around the world. That is not the balance required to keep the Navy the world's best. A low-end ship program needs to begin now so that future required capital ships are not held hostage to low fleet numbers in 20 years. Aircraft modernization is in better shape, but all of the aircraft types desired by the military are unlikely to be acquired and, if they are, it certainly will not be in the quantities desired.

Implications of Regionalization for the Navy

As noted earlier, globalization and regionalization are not inconsistent concepts. For years, the economics of competition has created pockets of associated businesses. Michael Porter calls these pockets "*clusters*: critical masses—in one place—of unusual competitive success in particular fields." He goes on to note that "enduring competitive advantages in a global economy lie increasingly in local things—knowledge, relationships, motivation—that distant rivals cannot match."[32] As these clusters develop, some of them may be critical to the continued economic well being of the United States (that is, they become new-economy Persian Gulfs). This notion also supports Kaplan's prediction that geography will remain important in the future.

The new economy is going to be a major driver in determining where naval forces deploy and for what purpose. The Persian Gulf region will remain important over the next half-century because gas and oil will continue to power the global economy. Interestingly, however, the United States will remain there for different reasons. Instead of being there to protect Western (American and European) interests, the United States will be there primarily to protect Asian (Japanese, Korean, and Chinese) interests as well as its own—not its oil interests (since up to 90 percent of the oil will be going to Asia), but its economic interests. Economic analysts are predicting that the largest massing of capital in history will occur in Asia over the next 50 years. The money will be invested primarily in Asian energy infrastructure in order to keep the global economy moving forward. That money will come mostly from the West, and the U.S. military will be expected to protect that investment by helping to maintain a secure and stable environment.

In addition, South and Southeast Asia will play much larger roles than they have in the past because they are areas of enormous tension and unrest. The tensions between India and Pakistan are well documented, as is China's interest in Southeast Asia. Less studied is the effect that a breakup of Indonesia would have on Asia and the rest of the world. Indonesia has global ties in economics and religion, and its fate is of no small concern. New forward presence challenges like these may be met not only with new ships but also with new deployment patterns. The Navy will not have the luxury of tethering ships to a single area, such as the Northern Arabian Sea, but will have to swing them through several areas during the course of a single deployment. By purchasing smaller, but much faster, ships (with transit speeds exceeding 40 knots), maritime action groups could dash between these spots and linger in place longer than is possible using today's force—thereby helping create the stable security conditions needed for economic progress.

For years, analysts have warned that the economic gap between the developed and developing worlds is growing and could lead to unrest and instability.[33] The rapid transition by the industrialized world into the Information Age is exacerbating this trend, with the economic gap between connected and unconnected nations increasing dramatically. Michael Porter asserts that this will continue as long as poor countries try to "compete in the world market with cheap labor and natural resources. To move beyond this stage, the development of well-functioning clusters is essential."[34] If these areas of specialization emerge and the global economic gap begins to narrow, a new definition of U.S. interests might also develop as new hubs become essential to the Nation's well being. Hence, whether the gap widens or narrows, the military must pay attention to what happens because it will affect deployment patterns and requirements.

Globalization refers most often to the world economy—an area of limited involvement for the military until unrest spawned by poverty erupts into violence. As noted earlier, the CNE cross-sector approach utilizing partnerships with other U.S. Government departments and agencies, as well as with those in the nongovernment and private sectors, offers a new and innovative process for leveraging limited military resources and promoting sustainable development and peaceful change. As Michael O'Hanlon notes, "In today's world, the United States should sustain a defense strategy emphasizing forward presence operations, exercises with allies and neutrals, military-to-military exchanges, peacekeeping missions, and response to crisis when necessary. . . . Nonmilitary tools of foreign policy, such as foreign aid, also have an important role in this broader security policy and are being underfunded."[35]

For greatest effectiveness, this approach needs to be undertaken on a regional basis with the full involvement of all services and U.S. country teams. The naval services should support this approach, since its success could preserve scarce military resources and support U.S. foreign policy objectives. Military-to-military engagement programs using traditional avenues such as UNITAS or West Africa Training Cruises should continue (with other regions adopting similar approaches). These rolling exercises cover large areas and engage a number of countries while fostering interoperability and cooperation.

Technological Environment

Much has been written concerning the benefits of and fears about the Information Age. The up side seems to be much larger than the down side, especially when considering the international security environment.

Information Age

As Joseph Nye has written, "The ability to disseminate information increases the potential for persuasion in world politics. NGOs [nongovernmental organizations] and states can more readily influence the beliefs of people in other jurisdictions. If one actor can persuade others to adopt similar values and agendas, that is soft power. Free information and soft power can, if sufficiently persuasive, change perceptions of self-interest and thereby alter how hard power is used."[36] The implication for military operations of Nye's assessment is profound. Information warfare takes on an entirely new meaning, and how the forces equip themselves to conduct it needs thorough review. There is a down side to this. Democratic states are vulnerable to cyberterrorism, and their leaders are more susceptible to being swayed by persuasive, if flawed, arguments. The result, according to Nye, is that democracies will have difficulty maintaining "a coherent ordering of foreign policy."[37]

Speed and Flexibility. According to Larry Carter, chief financial officer of Cisco Systems, in the Information Age, "it's no longer about the big beating the small, it's about the fast beating the slow."[38] This is just as true in the security sector as it is in the commercial. The critical factor is not technology, but how one organizes to take advantage of its opportunities. "The technologies of the late twentieth century," asserts Fukuyama, "seem to encourage flexibility and decentralization."[39] Although some attention has been given to this subject, more emphasis needs to be made concerning what organizational and cultural changes the military is going to require.

Computing with Light. Optical computers that use light instead of electricity probably will enter the marketplace in the next 20 years. They are expected to operate 1,000 times faster than electronic computers do. Currently, there are "more than 3,000 companies . . . hard at work in a virtual 'Photon Valley' to develop optical computers. Much of the infrastructure for computing with light is already in place. Fiber-optic cables provide high-speed lines, lasers serve as modulating devices, and CDs [compact disks] allows high-capacity optical storage. . . . Ultimately, a single fiber should be able to transmit 200 terabits, equivalent to the entire Library of Congress, in one second."[40] Coupled with anticipated breakthroughs in artificial intelligence, smart software, and robotics, many activities currently conducted by humans may be carried out by robots or virtual assistants. This trend holds the promise of drastically reducing personnel requirements aboard ships.

Digitization of Communications. Michael O'Hanlon points out that "today's information and communications systems are largely service-specific and analog. In the years ahead they will be integrated between military services. They will also be digitized. Digital radio can transmit impressive amounts of data among a large group of weapons platforms or soldiers."[41] This is extremely important because aircraft, tanks, and ships cannot use fiber optics to connect to other platforms. Hence, data will still have to be forced through slower and more limited radio links. As a result, future conflicts may well be characterized as battles of bandwidth. One example of how digitization and compression technologies can drastically improve performance is found in the world of popular music, where MP3 files will soon overtake cassette tapes and CDs as the medium of choice. An MP3 player similar in size to a portable CD player can hold the equivalent of 100 albums.

Implications of the Information Age for the Navy

Left to their own devices, the services will continue to support legacy systems and favor homegrown data links over developing the ability to connect with others. The first job for the Joint Staff is to establish mandatory standards to which all the services must conform when building future systems. These systems must be digital and, where possible, take advantage of fiber optics in order to maximize their effectiveness and provide the infrastructure foundation for further modernization. The Navy has an even bigger challenge: to communicate through the ocean itself. The technological challenges are daunting, but no other service has reason to devote resources toward this challenge. Until the submarine force can be netted in a significant way to the rest of the force, the full promise of network-centric warfare will remain unrealized.

Alternative Fuels

The end of the oil era is just around the corner, and alternative fuel sources need to be developed. There are predictions that over the next 5 years, companies involved in fuel-cell technology will start turning a profit. Fuel cells turn hydrogen and oxygen into electrical power and water, offering pollution-free power generation using an inexhaustible source of fuel. "The technology seems likely to become more efficient and less expensive than traditional power sources."[42] Some biomass fuels (such as ethanol) also hold promise as substitutes for current oil products. Nuclear power remains an option, but it comes with a high political price tag.

The services should begin now to study how to deal with the energy problems of the future.[43] The Navy may very well be building its last few classes of surface combatants that rely on carbon-based fuel. The decision to pursue electric-drive propulsion takes the Navy one step down this course. Complementing this decision, Congress has funded an Energy Systems Analysis Consortium, led by engineers at Purdue University and the University of Missouri. They are working on a system that automatically reroutes ship power in case one part of a ship is damaged during a conflict. This automated system, which should be in service by 2010, will help reduce the number of personnel aboard new ships by half.[44] Robust electrical systems are required if electric drive and future weapons systems, such as electromagnetic rail guns, are to be fielded. If fuel-cell technology develops as anticipated, it would be the final step to an all-electric fleet. The advantage that fuel-cell technology has over nuclear power is that it promises pollution-free transportation without the waste problem. As the White House Office of Science and Technology stated, "Fuel cells will take us beyond the age of fire."[45] The use of hydrogen fuel cells would encourage the development of hydrogen gas guns as well. Obviously, establishing an energy policy and supporting a robust research and development program should be at the top of the services' agendas.

Nanotechnology

Science fiction writers over the past 100 or so years have correctly predicted many of the discoveries that we now enjoy—from nuclear power to computers. They all failed to predict, however, how miniaturization would influence our lives. With scientists now capable of manipulating individual atoms, our minds no longer suffer from a lack of imagination when it comes to picturing how small useful gadgets can become. Miniaturization will allow us and everything we use to connect to the *evernet*, to use Thomas Barnett's term.[46] Unless we choose to unplug ourselves, the day will come when we have constant connectivity to everybody and everything that is important in our lives. Our appliances will tell us when we are running short of milk, as well as when they are in need of repair. We will download books onto electronic paper. Implants will monitor our health the same way that imbedded chips now monitor the condition of machinery. William Halal calls this "teleliving," and he believes a new lifestyle will "emerge around the use of information devices and the Internet for shopping, working, learning, playing, healing, praying, and conducting all aspects of life seamlessly."[47]

Smaller generally means "cheaper," which means things can be bought in greater numbers for the same cost. This will be extremely important for sensors because more is better. Technology should offer improved sensors of all types—for example, sensors to monitor equipment, sensors to help navigation, sensors to detect targets. Improvements in target location and marking will have greater impact on weapon efficiency than any other course that can be taken. The Navy should field a full array of expeditionary sensors. Some can be carried by long-endurance unmanned aerial vehicles (UAVs) that can be launched as a virtual satellite constellation, providing both surveillance and communications capabilities for theater forces. Not all sensors need to be indigenous to the fleet. The Navy should work closely with the Air Force to develop theater- and space-based sensors that can benefit sea, land, and air operations. If urban operations become prominent, sensors that can continuously monitor swept buildings or that can conduct autonomous reconnaissance missions in high-risk areas will need to be developed.

The flip side of the sensor story is that sensors will also become available to potential adversaries, making access a problem for the military. Learning to blind or degrade these sensors will become an increasingly important, but difficult, challenge. "The popular notion of information dominance, voiced by most RMA [revolution in military affairs] proponents and repeated in the Pentagon's *Joint Vision 2010*," concludes Michael O'Hanlon, "simply goes too far, as does the concept of dominant battlespace knowledge."[48] The technology is simply not available in either the offensive or defensive arenas to achieve these ends.

The value of small computer chips for the Navy is that they should allow off-site managers to monitor the status of shipboard equipment as well as the level of afloat supplies. Savings should result from reduced stockpiles, similar to those achieved by Wal-Mart, and readiness should improve, since systems could remain online until sensors indicate a problem is developing. The use of virtual assistants or long-distance, over-the-shoulder supervision should help reduce personnel requirements aboard ships.

Biotechnology Breakthroughs

For 200 years, people have been saying that mankind has discovered all the significant things that need to be discovered—and for 200 years, scientists have continued to prove them wrong. We now stand on the cusp of a new era of biotechnologies that promises again to transform the world. The possibilities range from growing our own replacement organs from stem cells to harvesting replacement human organs from swine. The human genome has been fully mapped, promising to help rid the world of genetic flaws within the next 25 years. Biomedical breakthroughs will also spawn "what promises to be the largest industry in the world: the life-science industry."[49] Fukuyama says, "Just as the twentieth century was the century of physics . . . the twenty-first promises to be the century of biology."[50] Dramatically increased life expectancies (at least for those who can afford proper medical treatments) will be possible in the next 50 years.[51] William Halal predicts that by midcentury the average life expectancy in developed nations will rise to 100 years.[52] Sanguine as all this sounds, this biomedical revolution will not be available to everyone and will change the economic and social landscapes as we now know them. Fukuyama goes so far as to predict that "the ultimate implication of this is that biotechnology will be able to . . . bring about a new type of human being."[53]

Advances in biotechnologies with their promises of increased life expectancies will have a profound effect on the military. Robert J. Samuelson, among others, has noted, "Most European countries, Japan and the United States face rapidly aging populations that will compel them to reduce sharply welfare benefits for their elderly or face the prospect of much higher taxes or budget deficits—developments that could endanger their economies."[54] As populations age, the able-bodied workforce, in relative terms, decreases, placing a premium on the worker. This will ultimately result in increased compensation. For business, increased wages mean reduced profits. For the military, it means that a greater percentage of its budget will be spent on personnel, which, on top of increased fuel prices, could drastically curtail readiness, modernization plans, and force size. No one can argue persuasively concerning the future size of the defense budget. The graying of America, however, could present a double blow to the budget, as defense dollars are siphoned off to pay welfare bills and the American economic growth rate suffers.

The graying of America will make recruitment more difficult and should have a far-reaching effect on service personnel policies. For example, as people live longer and healthier lives, current "up-or-out" policies will make less sense. As the services attempt to compete for the same skill sets from a diminishing pool of qualified individuals, they may have to consider a mixture of career personnel and temporary hires to fill specific deployment gaps. All this will require careful analysis and the cooperation of Congress.

Personnel numbers (and/or retirement entitlements) must be reduced drastically or long-lived retirees will consume a greater share of the services' budget as their numbers continue to grow. Technology applications that slash personnel requirements must be a top priority. One unintended, but certain, consequence of fewer military personnel, however, will be that the gap between them and the U.S. public will continue to grow as fewer and fewer civilians have knowledge of or experience with the military. Pension systems will have to become more similar to (and interchangeable with) those in the private sector. An active preventive health care system for retirees should also be put in place in order to reduce medical costs. Today's health care system is reactive, not proactive.

Implications of New Technologies for the Navy

The Navy will face several challenges in this area. First, maintaining a technological edge will be more difficult because information technologies have released a genie that permits the free flow of data around the globe, and that genie cannot be put back in the bottle. Another challenge will be to adapt information technologies in such a way that they increase warfighting capabilities and yet reduce costs through reduced personnel, better maintenance, and more efficient sustainment. Finally, managing the rate and direction of technological change will not be easy. A debate already swirls around the direction and rate of Navy transformation. Some analysts believe that the Navy is moving too fast and as a result is outpacing its ability to form meaningful coalitions. Others believe that the Navy is transforming too slowly and will end up with a traditional, albeit smaller, maritime force.

The Transformation Task Force formed at the Naval War College, in responding to the Secretary of the Navy, favored an evolutionary, not revolutionary, approach to transformation.[55] A *Harvard Business Review* article cautioned, "If an organization faces major change . . . the worst possible approach may be to make drastic adjustments to the existing organization. In trying to transform an enterprise, managers can destroy the very capabilities that sustain them."[56] Such an outcome could prove fatal for both the Navy and the Nation. The task force recommended a peripheral transformation strategy that involved the establishment of an experimental squadron and "operational" strategic studies group to examine new hardware and concepts. Its mission would be to introduce the best, not the riskiest, of these into the fleet. The task force supported the robust use of prototypes and concept demonstrations as part of the strategy. Although transformation would take longer following this path, it would be more affordable and less risky. It would also face less opposition.

Just as important as adapting technological advances into war fighting is organizing properly around them. Taking Fukuyama's and Carter's points, a cultural clash between traditional hierarchical military structures and Information Age flexible and decentralized structures is inevitable. This will come to a head when optical computers and artificial intelligence progress sufficiently to allow some target-designation and weapon-assignment tasks that now require a human in the decision loop.

Social Environment

Although early dire predictions about overpopulation have had to be reevaluated, Bill McKibben notes that "the world is still growing, at nearly a record pace—we add a New York City every month, almost a Mexico every year, almost an India every decade."[57] The most depressing of the world's augurs predict that overpopulation will lead to massive famines, which will lead to the spread of disease, which will lead to political instability, which will lead to the proliferation and use of terror weapons by desperate nations. The ultimate result will be widespread death. "The temptation in the 21st century will be to lock the gates and let the neighbours kill and die."[58] On the other hand, some pundits rejoice over the population growth, insisting that "population growth . . . is a driving force for democracy and prosperity, the true long-term threat comes from declining population."[59]

The United Nations estimates that the total population living in towns and cities will double by 2030, and that 6 billion of the 9 billion people on the planet will be living in urban areas.[60] People are drawn to the cities primarily out of economic necessity. Once there, however, they generally find only poverty and hopelessness; in fact, they find themselves contributing to both conditions. The trend toward urbanization is actually gaining speed. In China, it is being exacerbated by the Three Gorges Dam project being built on the Yangtze River. The project will force the migration of approximately 3 million people and has encouraged the Chinese government to draw up plans to move as many as 300 million people into tens of thousands of new towns.[61] The Chinese believe that this unprecedented urbanization plan will stimulate economic growth and keep it moving toward a consumer-based economy, as new urbanites buy refrigerators and television sets. Even without this plan, "megacities—those populated by at least 10 million people—are projected to double by 2025."[62] There are presently 21 such cities. Recent studies have shown that megacities present other problems for the planet besides unhealthy living conditions and poverty. Such cities "increase temperatures by up to 12°F relative to the surroundings."[63] The result is increased smog and thunderstorms and reduced land productivity. Not everyone laments this trend. Lawrence Solomon has pointed out, "In modern times, no nation has maintained high per-capita increases in income without having urbanized. Cities consume far less resources to get work done, and generate far more wealth in the process."[64]

War, weather, and the search for wealth have combined to create nearly 100 million migrants worldwide.[65] The growth of this group shows no sign of abating. Refugees generally become regional problems since they "become economic liabilities, have increased health risks, and form the core of politically discontent groups."[66] In other words, the more refugees, migrants, and displaced persons at large in the world, the more pronounced the crisis that fostered them will become. For the military, this means that humanitarian interventions are likely to continue to consume both time and resources.

Continued population growth and urbanization mean that an increasing number of crisis responses will be undertaken in metropolitan settings. Human intelligence, along with the sensors discussed earlier, will be critical for operational success in these settings. Precision and nonlethal weapons will also be essential for these missions. As discussed elsewhere, preventive engagement activities must be adopted as part of the military's arsenal. United States casualties are predicted to be high in any urban conflict; thus, preventing such conflicts is in the U.S. interest.

If the United States does get involved in urban conflict and if recent experience holds, casualties will make sustained operations difficult. To minimize casualties, UAVs, unmanned sensors, and autonomous reconnaissance robots must be developed.

Health

The human immunodeficiency virus and acquired immunodeficiency syndrome are ravaging the African continent and may intensify on other continents in the future. In addition, virulent strains of tuberculosis are on the increase (including in Russia, one of Carter's A-List countries of concern). The devastating results for involved regions include millions of dead and disabled people who require countries to divert development money to health care. This "double whammy" of a weakened workforce and decreased development money could result in increased unrest and migration.

Health risks to U.S. military personnel during crisis response, over and above the chemical and biological threats that capture most of the headlines, will increase as a result of operations conducted in unsanitary conditions among unhealthy populations. If these interventions, as some predict, increase, then pre-crisis programs dealing with these health issues are a national security issue. That does not mean that the primary responsibility for conducting them belongs to the military, but the military should certainly be supportive of such programs.

Democratization

Since the end of the Cold War, U.S. foreign policy has rested in large part on the presumption that democracies do not fight one another. The logical conclusion of this hypothesis is that expanding the circle of democracies is good for the United States as well as for the world. Fukuyama asserts, however, that "it is liberalism more than democracy that is the true institutional basis for so-called democratic peace."[67] This distinction, if understood by senior service leaders, will help them achieve better results during their engagement activities with states whose systems we are hoping to transform. The importance of these military-to-military (or military-to-political) contacts should not be underestimated. Following the collapse of the Cold War, both military and political leaders were anxious to meet with senior U.S. military commanders.

The realpolitik school of international theory would never have predicted that Russia and its Warsaw Pact allies would have unilaterally disarmed (that is, reduced their forces) after 1989. As Fukuyama notes, they did this on "the basis of an *internal* change in regime type, rather than a change in the external balance of power."[68] Not only is there a strong correlation between peaceful relationships and democracy, but also there is a correlation between democracy and economic development, another important factor resulting in stability.

The onset of the Information Age almost guarantees that global democratization will continue. As Joseph Nye has noted, "Not all democracies are leaders in the information revolution, but many are. This is no accident. Their societies are familiar with the free exchange of information, and their systems of governance are not threatened by it."[69] States aspiring to global leadership (such as China and Russia) will discover that they have to transform themselves into more open societies or find themselves falling behind those that do. India, for example, is in a position to take advantage of the Information Revolution.

The largest down side to democracy comes from the concomitant concept of self-determination. The problem is that "the number of established, recognized states seems ready to grow at a dizzying rate."[70] Every ethnic group now sees its best hope for the future in establishing its own state. With "roughly 5,000 such groups on earth, it is easy to understand the baneful effects of an untrammeled application of the right of self-determination."[71] The distressing war in Chechnya amply demonstrates the devastation that can result when ethnic groups opt for secession rather than union. Of the A-List states that the United States should concern itself with, Russia is not alone facing the problems of breakaway regions. Indonesia will continue to face problems, as will India (Kashmir) and China (Tibet, Xinjiang, and Inner Mongolia).[72]

In support of U.S. foreign policy objectives, military engagement programs need to be structured to encourage the adoption of liberal principles within target states. This has been a primary focus of the Partnership for Peace program, especially in the area of civil-military relations. These programs should also continue to foster interoperability and military cooperation so that coalition building becomes easier in times of crisis. Michael O'Hanlon is correct when he points out that "these are the tools with which alliances are kept credible and cohesive, and potential adversaries are contained or deterred."[73]

Religion

Samuel Huntington's *The Clash of Civilizations* brought religion to the forefront of international security discussions.[74] Not everyone agreed with his assessment, and many felt it set back relations with the Muslim world; nonetheless, the debate it spawned was important. Two trends have appeared in almost all religions over the past 50 years. First, scientific materialism has caused most developed countries to become decreasingly religious. Second, countries that have tried to preserve their religious heritage (and denominations facing the same dilemma in more secular states) have turned increasingly fundamental. Often, this fundamentalist fervor has complemented growing nationalist movements.

The problem with the first trend, as described by E.O. Wilson, is that it leaves states with no ideological authority or clear transcendent alternative to guide their actions.[75] Some analysts note that this loss of belief has been accompanied by the sexual revolution and the breakdown of the traditional family. The problem with the second trend is that fundamentalism and nationalism are often the traveling companions of militarism. Zealots of any persuasion can be (and generally are) trouble.

A robust foreign area officer program is required to prepare fighting forces for dealing with cultural problems, including religion. Navy chaplains also are being trained to understand how religious leaders and communities of faith can be used during crisis responses to promote a peaceful and lasting solution.[76]

Physical Environment

While some analysts are concerned that the Information Age will usher in a borderless (almost anarchic) world, others, such as Robert Kaplan and Joseph Nye, have asserted that geography will continue to play an important role in international relations. If true, the world's most prominent geographical feature—its oceans—should play a leading role. Following through on that logic, things maritime, including naval forces, should play a larger part in world affairs in the future.

Energy

Everyone knows that Americans are huge consumers of resources. The average global energy consumption per day per individual is about 31,000 calories. Those who live in the United States consume six times that much.[77] As a result, the United States is also the largest single producer of wealth in the world. The avowed policy of the United States—to help others achieve a sustainable level of development by engaging them in the global marketplace—takes energy, and lots of it. The United Nations has determined that the economies of developing countries need to be 5 to 10 times larger in order for them to rise to an acceptable standard of living. Thus, competition for all sources of energy will be a major salient in the future. Demand for energy in Asia alone is predicted to increase by 9 million barrels a day by 2010—equal to the current daily output of Saudi Arabia. Drafting and implementing, as well as helping others draft and implement, reasonable energy policies will become an important national priority.

There is an interesting hypothesis being investigated that, if proved correct, increases the incentive for the developed world to help the developing world improve its standard of living as quickly as possible. "Two Princeton University economists found that after a country reaches a per capita income of $8,000, further increases in income cause pollution to decline."[78] The data show that for specific pollutants, the required level of per capita income varies from around $2,000 to $12,000 before decreasing. When this observation is paired with the observation that "above a level of $6,000 per capita GDP in 1992 parity purchasing power, there is not a single historical instance of a democratic country reverting to authoritarianism,"[79] the importance of promoting sustainable development becomes obvious.

Security threats are anticipated to rise as competition for resources increases and as detrimental environmental effects, caused by a doubling of carbon-based fuel consumption in the developing world, affect the lifestyle and health of neighboring states. The military will undoubtedly find itself embroiled in such tensions.

As the availability of oil diminishes (later in the coming decades) and energy costs increase, the naval services will be confronted with a real dilemma. For surface ships, nuclear power offers one possible, if currently unattractive, option. Alternatives for aircraft propulsion are not as obvious. How do you fly when the oil is gone? Two potential sources of energy are being touted as future solutions for most energy needs—hydrogen and ethanol. Hydrogen is the most abundant element in the universe, while ethanol is derived from plants and is renewable. The drawback to hydrogen/oxygen systems is that producing pure hydrogen is expensive. Platinum-coated membranes are needed to separate hydrogen into the protons and electrons necessary to produce electrical energy. As discussed later, platinum is a strategic metal not readily abundant in the United States. Hydrogen/oxygen systems might prove useful in powering surface ships, but not aircraft. Ethanol appears to be a more promising solution. If biotechnology continues to progress as quickly as predicted, plant genomes may be "engineered in a way that enable[s] their starches to be transformed into alcohol at higher volumes," allowing oil companies to "produce economically attractive gasoline substitutes."[80] The down side to ethanol production is that with the world's population continuing to increase, growing crops for fuel, instead of food, may create new challenges. For this reason, recent research has focused on producing bioethanol from waste products.[81]

The greatest near-term impact on the military will be a sharp increase in oil prices that eats up increasingly large segments of the budget and sharply reduces at-sea time and flying hours. The Coast Guard found itself with just such a dilemma in mid-2000 and had to curtail some of its activities. High oil prices are inevitable, as is the decreasing availability of oil. The longer term problem will be to develop propulsion systems that are not reliant on fossil fuel. Other complementary actions should be pursued, such as procuring smaller ships, developing drag-reducing hull materials, supporting research involving fuel-efficient engines, and exploring crew rotation schemes that could reduce fuel-consuming transits while maintaining more of the force structure forward to conduct engagement operations.

Water and Land

Today, "20 percent of the world's population lacks access to potable water, and fights over water divide many regions,"[82] including regions in the United States. There is hardly a region in the world that is not worried about having access to sufficient water. Water problems go beyond access, however, to infrastructure. Eighteen of the world's 21 megacities suffer from "leaky water systems which … hemorrhage as much as half their precious freshwater reserves."[83] International conflicts over water rights will increase in the years ahead.

Conflicts over arable land will likely erupt over the coming decades, as will claims over ethnic territories. Revanchist claims will continue to be sources of tension (for example, in the South China Sea). One overlooked source of conflict, however, is strategic minerals. Robert Mandel noted that "of all types of resources . . . nonfuel minerals are the least publicized and the least widely understood." He goes on to note that "the industrialized Western nations are far more heavily dependent on foreign sources for a number of nonfuel minerals than for crude oil."[84] The military's particular concern has been with so-called strategic minerals (those required to build modern weapon systems).[85]

Tensions over access to water and land, like rising competition for fuel, will continue to engage the military in the future. Aside from strategic minerals, the challenge with nonfuel minerals is one of distribution, not availability, and virtually all minerals are shipped by sea. Currently, no open ocean threat to shipping exists, but the importance of the shipping lanes to the economic well-being of the United States cannot be overstated. Ensuring that threats to those lanes do not emerge will remain an ongoing mission for naval forces. A growing concern is the vulnerability of distribution at the superports (or megahubs) that are used to load and offload ships (particularly large container ships). This is another reason that a sea-based missile defense system should be pursued.

Changing Weather Patterns

With all the talk of global warning and *el niño* effects, people are starting to understand that it is not only the Cassandras who are raising an alarm. Environmentalists look at direct manifestations of widespread and long-term warming trends such as heat waves and periods of unusually warm weather, sea-level rise and coastal flooding, glacial melting, and Arctic and Antarctic warming. They also track events that they believe are directly related to and foreshadow the impacts of global warming. These events include spreading disease, earlier arrival of spring, plant and animal range shifts and population declines, coral reef bleaching, downpours, heavy snowfalls, floods, droughts, and fires.

Catastrophic changes in weather can affect the military in two ways. First, bad weather in the United States could result in a dramatic economic downturn. Such a downturn could halt any modernization plans under way by the military and drastically affect readiness as well. Bad weather overseas could increase the demand for military humanitarian disaster response (the consequences of famines and floods, for example), which could accelerate the wear and tear on aging equipment and divert scarce resources to pay for the operations. Analysis should be undertaken to determine how the services could best prepare for this eventuality so that its effects can be minimized.

If the Navy develops a strategy that relies on increased transit speeds to meet mission requirements, global severe weather could have some impact if speeds had to be reduced to cope with extreme conditions.

Resolving the problem of global warming is certainly not a military responsibility. The military can, however, behave as a responsible global citizen and support others in their efforts to understand and counter this phenomenon.

Conclusions

This *tour d'horizon* has looked at a few future trends associated with globalization and has surmised how they might affect the military. The trends are fairly accurate, their effects on the military less so. Nevertheless, there is much food for thought.

For the naval services to avoid becoming "hangar queens," they should limit their hedging force infrastructure to nuclear deterrent forces and deliberately concentrate on developing force structure and doctrine for responding to missions in Carter's B- and C-Lists. The sea services should concede the heavy lifting hedge forces to the Army and the Air Force. Building a large hedging force that is capable of meeting a threat from a peer competitor (that is, a country that has opted to match U.S. might) is, at any rate, more a matter of political will than of military planning. Focusing on B- and C-List missions will require a reevaluation of the warrior ethos that drives so much of the planning and rhetoric in the military (that is, the attitude that the only good fight to plan for is one against somebody your own size). No respectable war fighter wants to police the world, keep the peace, or be known primarily as a tree hugger or a humanitarian. Nonetheless, in light of the global trends discussed earlier, a slight reorientation in that direction will prove both prudent and productive.

This change in thinking is not as controversial as it may at first appear. Many of the decisions made by the naval services have been moving them in this direction since the introduction of *Forward . . . from the Sea*. That document clearly indicated that the naval services should plan for dealing with B- and C-List challenges. Tomorrow's security environment will require that more attention be focused on peacetime missions such as engagement, humanitarian assistance, and coalition operations. The aim of peacetime engagement activities should be to help target states build institutional capacities and foster peaceful change. This is not mission creep, but essential mission. We need to reinstill pride in being a soldier-statesperson.

The naval services should focus on assimilating information technologies in ways that increase connectivity, reduce decision time, permit workforce reductions, enhance sustainability, and improve maintenance practices. This will require changing the leadership culture of the services into one that is comfortable with greater decentralization and autonomy of their forces. The naval services will also have to reevaluate their personnel policies. Working with Congress, they should eliminate "up-or-out" policies and restrictions on length of service. They should examine ways of permitting lateral hires and flexible retirement packages that permit some military personnel to change jobs as frequently as their private sector counterparts. A small cadre of "career" military officers and enlisted personnel are probably all that is required. The Marine Corps is well along this path; 75 percent of its enlisted personnel are short-term hires.

This refocusing of the Navy and the Marine Corps effort helps them move together strategically into the future with a plan that is affordable, understandable, and supportable.

Notes

[1] Francis Fukuyama, "Second Thoughts: The Last Man in the Bottle," *The National Interest* 56 (Summer 1999), 17.

[2] William E. Halal, "The Top 10 Emerging Technologies," *The Futurist, Special Report* (July/August 2000), 2.

[3] "Is Major War Obsolete? An Exchange," *Survival* 41, no. 2 (Summer 1999), 139–152; Hans Binnendijk and Alan Henrikson, "Back to Bipolarity?" *Strategic Forum*, no. 161 (May 1999), 1.

[4] Binnendijk and Henrikson, 2.

[5] "Is Major War Obsolete?" 139.

[6] Donald Kagan, "History is Full of Surprises," *Survival* 41, no. 2 (Summer 1999), 140.

[7] Thomas P.M. Barnett, "Life After DODth or: How the Evernet Changes Everything," U.S. Naval Institute *Proceedings* (May 2000), 48–53.

[8] Donald C.F. Daniel and Bradd C. Hayes, *The Future of U.S. Sea Power* (Carlisle Barracks, PA: Strategic Studies Institute, 1993).

[9] Ashton B. Carter, "Adapting U.S. Defence to Future Needs," *Survival* 41, no. 4 (Winter 1999/2000), 101–123.

[10] Ibid., 105.

[11] "The Ostrich's View of the World," *The Economist* (December 19, 1998), 70.

[12] Bradd C. Hayes, *International Game '99: Crisis in South Asia,* DSD Research Report 99–1, and Paul D. Taylor and Andres Vaart, *Economic Security Exercise: South Asia Proliferation Project,* DSD Research Report 99–2 (Newport, RI: Center for Naval Warfare Studies, 1999).

[13] John F. Hillen, Jr., "Superpowers Don't Do Windows," *Orbis* (Spring 1997).

[14] Chester A. Crocker, "How to Think about Ethnic Conflict," 1999 Perlmutter Lecture on Ethnic Conflict, Foreign Policy Research Institute, *Wire* (September 1999).

[15] Council on Foreign Relations, *Policy Impact Panel on U.S. Defense Priorities*, October 27, 1995, 8, <http://www.foreignrelations.org/studies/transcripts/951027.html>. A *hangar queen* is an aircraft that never flies but is kept in the hangar and cannibalized for spare parts.

[16] Bradd C. Hayes and Jeffrey I. Sands, *Doing Windows: Non-Traditional Military Responses to Complex Emergencies*, DSD Research Report 97–1 (Washington, DC: C^{4}ISR Cooperative Research Program, 1998).

[17] At the start of the crisis, the USS *Eisenhower* and USS *Independence* were the first carriers to respond. As plans for offensive operations proceeded, additional carriers were deployed to the theater. They were USS *Midway*, USS *Ranger*, USS *Theodore R. Roosevelt*, USS *John F. Kennedy*, USS *Saratoga*, and USS *America.*

[18] Ehud Sprinzak, "The Great Superterrorism Scare," *Foreign Policy* (Fall 1998), 121.

[19] Andrew J. Bacevich, "Policing Utopia: The Military Imperatives of Globalization," *The National Interest* (Summer 1999), 7.

[20] Council on Foreign Relations, *Policy Impact Panel*, 21.

[21] For example, Hugh De Santis laments, "From the Bush administration's vacuous 'new world order' rhetoric to the 'engagement and enlargement' effluvia of the Clinton administration, the United States has substituted slogans for strategy." Hugh De Santis, "Mutualism: An American Strategy for the Next Century," *Strategic Forum*, no. 162 (May 1999), 1.

[22] Ibid., 2.

[23] Robert D. Kaplan, "Could This Be the New World?" *The New York Times*, December 27, 1999, A23.

[24] Bacevich, "Policing Utopia," 5.

[25] Stephen J. Kobrin, "The MAI and the Clash of Globalizations," *Foreign Policy* (Fall 1998), 99.

[26] Kobrin, "The MAI and the Clash of Globalizations," 100.

[27] Henry Wai-chung Yeung, "Capital, State and Space: Contesting the Borderless World," *Transactions of the Institute of British Geographers* 23, no. 3 (1998), 291–301.

[28] Fukuyama, "Second Thoughts," 22.

[29] Council on Foreign Relations, *Policy Impact Panel*, 5–6, <http://www.foreignrelations.org/studies/transcripts/951027.html>.

[30] Sinologists are quick to note that, with the exception of Tibet, China does not have an expansionist history.

[31] Daniel Gouré and Jeffrey M. Randy, *Averting the Defense Train Wreck in the New Millennium* (Washington, DC: The Center for Strategic and International Studies Press, 1999).

[32] Porter, "Clusters and the New Economics of Competition."

[33] World Resources Institute, *World Resources 1996–97: A Guide to the Global Environment*, August 19, 1998, <www.wri.org/wri/wr-96-97/ei_txt4.html>.

[34] Porter, "Clusters and the New Economics of Competition," 86.

[35] Michael E. O'Hanlon, *Technological Change and the Future of Warfare* (Washington, DC: The Brookings Institution Press, 2000), 171–172.

[36] Joseph S. Nye, Jr., "Responses to Fukuyama," *The National Interest* 56 (Summer 1999), 43.

[37] Nye, "Responses to Fukuyama," 44.

[38] Cisco@speed, *The Economist*, June 26, 1999, survey on "Business and the Internet," 12.

[39] Fukuyama, "Second Thoughts," 27.

[40] Halal, "The Top 10 Emerging Technologies," 9.

[41] O'Hanlon, *Technological Change*, 52.

[42] Halal, "The Top 10 Emerging Technologies," 4.

[43] Colin J. Campbell and Jean H. Laherrère, "The End of Cheap Oil," *Scientific American* (March 1998), 78–83.

[44] "Automated Warships," *The Futurist* (July/August 2000), 13.

[45] Halal, "The Top 10 Emerging Technologies," 4.

[46] Barnett, "Life after DODth."

[47] Halal, "The Top 10 Emerging Technologies," 5.

[48] O'Hanlon, *Technological Change*, 67.

[49] Juan Enriquez and Ray A. Goldberg, "Transforming Life, Transforming Business: The Life-Science Revolution," *Harvard Business Review* (March/April 2000), 97.

[50] Fukuyama, "Second Thoughts," 28.

[51] Stephen S. Hall, "Racing Toward Immortality," *The New York Times Magazine* (January 20, 2000), 32–35, 46, 74–79.

[52] Halal, "The Top 10 Emerging Technologies," 9.

[53] Fukuyama, "Second Thoughts," 28.

[54] Robert J. Samuelson, "Responses to Fukuyama," *The National Interest* (Summer 1999), 42.

[55] Bradd C. Hayes, Lawrence Modisett, Donald C.F. Daniel, and Hank Kamradt, *Transforming the Navy: A Strategy for the Secretary of the Navy*, DSD Report 00–3 (Newport, RI: Center for Naval Warfare Studies, 2000).

[56] Clayton and Overdorf, *Harvard Business Review*, 68.

[57] Bill McKibben, "A Special Moment in History," *The Atlantic Monthly* (May 1998), 56. He does note, however, that "new demographic evidence shows that it is at least possible that a child born today will live long enough to see the peak of human population."

[58] Doug Beazley, "A Bleak Look into the Distant Future," *The Edmonton Sun*, Opinion, 11. [Lexis/Nexis]

[59] Lawrence Solomon, "Six Billion Reasons for Hope," *Financial Post,* October 5, 1999, C7. [Lexis/Nexis]

[60] United Kingdom Department for International Development, "Clare Short Sets the Challenge to Improve the Lives of the Urban Poor around the World," January 26, 2000 [Lexis/Nexis].

[61] Damien McElroy, "China to Resettle 300 Million," *The Ottawa Citizen,* November 14, 1999, A1. [Lexis/Nexis]

[62] Mitch Potter, "Water Fight Looms for Megacities," *The Toronto Star,* March 20, 2000. [Lexis/Nexis]

[63] Roger Highfield, "Mega-Cities Form 'Isles of Heat' around World," *The Daily Telegraph* (London), February 23, 2000, 12. [Lexis/Nexis]

[64] Solomon, "Six Billion Reasons for Hope."

[65] Myron Weiner, *The Global Migration Crisis: Challenge to States and to Human Rights* (New York: HarperCollins College Publishers, 1995).

[66] Hayes and Sands, *Doing Windows*, 88.

[67] Fukuyama, "Second Thoughts," 18.

[68] Ibid.

[69] Nye, "Responses to Fukuyama," 43.

[70] Pascal Boniface, "The Proliferation of States," *The Washington Quarterly* 21, no. 3 (Summer 1998), 111.

[71] Ibid., 112.

[72] "The Ostrich's View of the World," 67.

[73] O'Hanlon, *Technological Change*, 171.

[74] Samuel P. Huntington, *The Clash of Civilizations and the Remaking of World Order* (New York: Simon and Schuster, 1996).

[75] E.O. Wilson, "Responses to Fukuyama," *The National Interest* (Summer 1999), 35.

[76] Douglas Johnston, "Religion and Foreign Policy," in *Managing Instability: A Pre-Crisis Approach*, DSD Research Report 00–4 (Newport, RI: Center for Naval Warfare Studies, 2000), 23–33.

[77] McKibben, "A Special Moment in History," 57.

[78] National Center for Policy Analysis, "Third World Pollution," 1996, <http://www.ncpa.org/ea/easo94/easo94m.html>.

[79] Fukuyama, "Second Thoughts," 18.

[80] Enriquez and Goldberg, "Transforming Life," 101.

[81] Stanley R. Bull and Lynn L. Billman, "Renewable Energy: Ready to Meet Its Promise," *The Washington Quarterly* (Winter 2000), 234. According to the authors, jet fuel is closer to kerosene than gasoline, but a bioenergy source more closely matching current jet fuels is possible. Diesel fuel, a step closer to jet fuel, "is being produced in limited quantities from soybeans. Research has shown that diesel fuel can also be produced from less costly and more abundant sources, such as natural oils occurring in algae and the pryolysis of biomass. A diesel substitute, dimethyl ether, also can be produced from biomass."

[82] McKibben, "A Special Moment in History," 60.

[83] Potter, "Water Fight Looms for Megacities."

[84] Robert Mandel, *Conflict Over the World's Resources* (New York: Greenwood Press, 1988), 75.

[85] Historically, the four most important groups of strategic minerals have been chromium, cobalt, manganese, and platinum, a majority of which comes from Africa.

Chapter 21

Security from the Oceans

Sam J. Tangredi

> *This, with the vast increase in rapidity of communication, has multiplied and strengthened the bonds knitting the interests of nations to one another, till the whole now forms an articulated system, not only of prodigious size and activity, but of an excessive sensitiveness, unequalled in former ages.*
>
> *— Alfred Thayer Mahan*[1]

Surprisingly, these are not the musings of a recent commentator on the 21st century phenomenon of globalization. They are, in fact, the words of the (frequently lionized, but more recently disparaged) philosopher and prophet of sea power, Alfred Thayer Mahan, writing at the turn of the century.

Therein lies the clue to clarifying the thus far unexplored relationship between naval power and globalization. Like other elements of military power, naval forces—and specifically the forces of the United States Navy—contribute to the international security function of protecting the mediums and markets critical to the increasing international exchange known as globalization. Indeed, the very nature of navies makes their protective role *uniquely attuned* to the new era dynamics created by globalization. Moreover, because the United States Navy is the sole global navy in existence today, it plays a vitally important role in the globalization process. The Navy is both a globalized and globalizing force. This has been the case for at least the last 50 years. It will remain true for the future in growing and changing ways.

To understand this role, we must understand not simply the effects of globalization on navies—and the Navy in particular—but also the influence of navies and sea power (of which naval power is an element) on globalization itself. With these dual effects in mind, the purpose of this chapter is threefold. First, it seeks to explain the relationship between sea power and globalization and why they are interlocked. Second, it identifies the role that the Navy plays in the globalization phenomenon, including the influence of the Navy on globalization, as well as the influence of globalization on the Navy. Third, it examines the shape and force structure that the Navy might need to maintain in order to ensure that globalization remains a process that benefits the United States. The underlying premise is that the elements constituting the traditional concept of sea power are so similar to those of the 21st century

---

Captain Sam J. Tangredi, USN, is a senior military fellow in the Institute for National Strategic Studies at the National Defense University. He commanded USS Harpers Ferry *and served on the Joint Staff as well as in both the Office of the Secretary of the Navy and the Office of the Chief of Naval Operations.*

concept of globalization as to make the Navy uniquely positioned to influence the outcome of today's globalization process. This is a premise that even Rear Admiral Mahan, an unabashed Victorian era nationalist, could understand.

What Is a Navy?

Why are navies functionally attuned to the process of globalization? The answer lies within the very nature of naval power. What exactly *is* a navy? The obvious, but only partially correct, answer is that a navy is a military force that operates primarily at sea. However, there is a significant difference between the functioning of navies and that of land-based military forces. Unlike other forms of military power, naval forces are primarily and uniquely designed to control the flow of commerce through the dominant mediums of commercial interaction, rather than to directly control territory or areas of human habitation. In short, armies are designed to control *territory*; navies are designed to control *access* to territory and interaction with the international system.

Operating in a multiplicity of mediums—the undersea depths, the surface of the sea, the air, littoral regions, space, and the infosphere—navies contest for the control of political and economic interactions, rather than for the control of populations. The classic naval struggle for sea control is for dominance of oceans—which are, in fact, mediums that humans use, but cannot permanently inhabit. Once dominated, these oceans (not all of them consisting of water) can provide access to the areas where humans live as well as control of links between these areas and the rest of the globe.[2]

If, as previously defined, globalization is a "process of expanding cross-border networks and flows,"[3] then naval forces, broadly defined, are both protectors and inhibitors of this process. The traditional language of sea power—with its concern for the sea lines of communications (SLOCs), blockades, fleets-in-being, and naval presence—may seem like a quaint legacy to those schooled in information technology and e-commerce. But though it may not use the same grammar, it uses the same logic of carrying out and influencing access.

The traditional goal of sea power is unfettered *access* to the world's common transportation routes for raw materials and manufactured products, as well as access to the actual markets and sources of materials themselves. The emerging concept of the new economy revolves around *access* to the world's common information routes—such as the Internet—and to the sources of information, as well as to the potential markets for value added to the information. The Internet is both a facilitator and a product of the globalization phenomenon; its impact parallels the advances of maritime commerce that fueled the Colonial Period of the years 1400 to 1900. It is reshaping the economic and political world. But like every other such shaping process, globalization, at its very heart, involves a struggle for economic and political power—a struggle for access to the sources and the fruits of the process.

This struggle includes access to the infosphere, access to financial markets, access to raw materials (of which information is one), access to the means of production, and access to markets. Just as a hacker can use information warfare to delay, disrupt, distort, or deny access to the infosphere, more traditional military forces can deny access to the physical sources of the production of wealth. The maintenance of a navy is a form of insurance that such physical access could not be cut by military force—at least not without a physical struggle. Equally true, navies themselves can be used as very effective means of access denial to opponents or rivals. They do so while operating with the global commons of the sea, their movement protected and sanctioned in peacetime by international law.

As noted above, armies are designed to control *territory*; navies are designed to control *access*. If globalization is really breaking down the territorial barriers of our world—which is what most of the contributors to this volume suggest—then access to information, markets, and resources is becoming even more important to the world's political economy than is control of territory, no matter how fertile or resource-filled, and populations, no matter how productive. Arguably, this reality means that naval forces—broadly defined—are becoming even more important as well.[4] In the real world, unlike the utopia many would prefer, there are forces that would deny or restrict our access. Even those who view globalization as a beneficial force that will eventually result in a more politically integrated, economically balanced, just, and peaceful world must admit that the process appears a potentially dangerous voyage.

In summary, a navy is the portion of military forces that *operates in the fluid mediums that humans use for information, transportation, and exchange but cannot normally inhabit*. Its prime purpose is to *ensure or deny access*. Its effect on territories and population is generally indirect. However, the freedom of operation that the law of the sea allows in the international commons of the oceans provides for independent and direct effects in the littoral regions to the ever-increasing range that technology allows naval weapons (which includes sea-based aviation) to reach.

Comparing 1902 and 2002

The interlocking nature of sea power and globalization becomes evident in comparing the worlds of 1902 and 2002. In essence, 1902 was also an era of globalization. Then, the process of expansion of cross-border networks and flows was more commonly referred to as colonialism or imperialism. The world's great powers competed for access to the raw materials and markets of the rest of the world. To traverse the oceans in economic terms required naval power to ensure maritime security. As Mahan defined it, sea power included the totality of a nation's maritime capability—its merchant trade and exploitation of sea resources, as well as its naval might. But economic commerce also required—at least as it was then understood—direct political control over foreign access, in other words, colonies. With the invention of manned aviation still a few years away, the oceans remained the sole medium for international trade, and though armies were needed to maintain colonies, access relied exclusively on sea power. At the height of the colonial era, most international trade traveled by sea.

In the early 21st century, we live in an era in which information can travel instantaneously on the Internet. Small packages can be flown overnight to cities on the other side of the globe. Human reach extends into space. Yet, often forgotten is the fact that

90 percent of international trade still travels by sea, for the very same physical reasons that it did in 1902. The sea remains the most efficient and cheapest means of transporting bulk materials. There appears to be no impending technological breakthrough to change this situation in the near future. The traditional sea power term *SLOCs* may prove a confusing concept to generations more familiar with the many other mediums for personal communication. But replacing it with the term *sea lanes of commerce* may get the point of their continued importance across. SLOCs even have numerous indirect effects on the shape of the infosphere. Most global telecommunication is conducted along the traditional maritime trade routes. And with rare (and expensive) exception, overseas manufactured components for even the personal computers that allow individual access to the Internet arrive in the hulls of ships.[5]

This means that a hostile navy (or air force, operating in a navy-like interdiction mode, rather than conducting strategic bombing) could exert considerable influence on the flow of the manufactured goods that ultimately determine the success of globalization. There are three reasons that people today often do not worry about such flows being disrupted. First, of course, is that people often forget how dependent international trade is on maritime commerce. Second, they assume—quite correctly—that most everyone else in the world wants to trade with the United States (and other industrial powers) and has no sane interest in curtailing such trade. Finally, the United States is the only Nation that still possesses a global navy.

Ultimately, the possession of a global navy by a nation committed to global trade allows for the international access that underlies today's globalization. If international trade is secure from threats to its disruption, trade can expand. Economic confidence and creativity are thereby energized. Participants in the globalization process have a reduced sense of fear—and therefore reduced potential hostility—in an assured security regime for international exchange. Local conflicts can break out, but in a world without rival or hostile sea powers, they remain relatively local.[6] The freedom from a threat of denial of international access allows for the flow of economic commerce and the growth of prosperity. Perhaps it even furthers the internationalization of world citizenry and the increasing cosmopolitanism that may presumably make armies and navies some day obsolete.

In any event, the economic dreams of globalization advocates parallel those of the traditional sea power advocates: a world with assured access to the lines of communications and commerce that provides for prosperity. The linkage between modern globalization (seen as a beneficial process) and sea power is perhaps most evident in this common objective of keeping the sea lanes of commerce open. Sea power can have another important political impact. By creating a climate of assured security, it can help bind nations together in cooperative relationships that begin in the military arena, but spread outward to the political and economic arenas. The Asia-Pacific is a vast region where naval interactions play a major role in determining security conditions, but the same principle applies elsewhere. Because the Navy's presence encourages stable security affairs, it helps set the stage for diplomatic and political cooperation to develop and for economic markets to take hold.

From Global to Globalized Navy

Like the U.S. dollar in international commerce and the use of the English language in the development of information technology, the Navy has become the benchmark and dominant standard for all things naval. In today's world, all other navies are essentially regional or coastal, with the exception of the fleets of the United Kingdom and France, both long-term U.S. allies.[7] Even these two oceangoing navies are shadows of their former selves, capable of extended deployments in relatively small numbers. The former Soviet fleet, once sole challenger to U.S. sea power, is a defeated and ruined hulk. Its successor, the Russian Navy, is left with but a handful of seaworthy vessels. Other countries, notably China and India, are building up their naval capabilities, but sustained out-of-area operations currently are far beyond their reach. Like Rome or Britain in former days, the United States is—militarily—sovereign of the seas.

But in what can only be considered an apt metaphor for the overall phenomenon of globalization, U.S. "rule" is over an internationalized ocean open to the commerce of all nations and subject to the legal authority of no one state. The law of the sea, by treaty and custom, allows anyone to use the oceans as the grand highway of trade and—subject to limits on pollution and overfishing—as a source of "free" resources. All that is needed is the physical means to do so, making the sea a truly open market. By protecting access to this open market to all those who accept international law, the Navy performs a common security function on a global basis. In reality, it provides the protocols and security structure of the "maritime internet," which, in terms of international trade in goods, remains the ultimate internetted exchange.

That is why the Navy can be considered a globalized as well as a global navy. In essence, it is no longer solely the U.S. Navy; it has become the world's navy—delivering the security of access function across the entire world system. When the Asian tiger economies—such as that of Taiwan—are shaken by the bellicose posturing of a neighbor, it is the movement of U.S. naval forces into the region of potential crisis—such as the Taiwan Strait—that provides the prime means of psychological restabilization. In attempting to quantify this stabilization effect on markets, recent studies have identified the positive impact of such naval deployments.[8]

Moreover, with the exception of the "states formerly known as rogues,"[9] which seem ideologically opposed to globalization, as well as the Chinese Communist Party, which appears to want only those globalization effects that would allow for continued authoritarian rule within its domain, no one expects any harm from the Navy. Japan, which is sometimes an economic competitor of the United States, even allows the Navy to homeport both a carrier battle group (CVBG) and an amphibious ready group (ARG) in its own port cities—and pays for the infrastructure to do so. When building its own ships, Japan routinely licenses technology used by the Navy. Russia, with a military still often suspicious of the West, has conducted post-Cold War exercises with the North Atlantic Treaty Organization (NATO) and U.S. naval forces. It would probably conduct more exercises, were it not for the disastrous state of its navy and the desire to hide its weak readiness (made evident in the *Kursk* rescue attempt). The Navy is welcomed in ports around the globe, and the forward naval presence of U.S. warships is readily accepted—often advocated—by most nations as a sound policy for maintaining regional security.

This naval presence gives the United States certain advantages in the same way that the internationalization of the dollar or the U.S.-led computer industry does in other markets. It allows the United States—as a society, if not as a government—to set the rules and protocols of yet another slice of the expansion of cross-border networks and flows. As a globalized service, the Navy can—within certain limits—determine the when, where, and how of the world's maritime exchanges. This represents the direct influence of U.S. sea power on the overall globalization process. Because of the U.S. commitment to global trade and open access, what is good for the United States is generally good for all other trading states. The day-to-day impact of U.S. sea power on globalization thus appears transparent. If push came to shove, however, there would be no alternative maritime security service. The Navy simultaneously operates major fleets in the Mediterranean, Arabian Sea, and Western Pacific, and it has individual ships and squadrons in almost every major locale. This ensures that U.S. influence can never be easily outvoted. From the perspective of realpolitik, "It is good to be king"—especially of the sea: U.S. naval presence influences not only economic commerce but also the new era geopolitics of regions in stabilizing ways.

Participant in the Globalizing Function

In addition to being a globalized navy, the Navy facilitates at least four key globalization functions. As previously discussed, it provides the world standards for naval operations. Second, it conducts direct interactions—such as combined training and exercises—with almost every other national fleet. Such interactions, which the U.S. Department of Defense (DOD) refers to as engagement, are expected to promote the existing and future policies of the engagement and enlargement of global democracy. Third, it carries out the long-term mission of naval forward presence (that is, the continual deployment of naval forces to potential regions of crisis in order to provide stability and deter hostilities). Fourth, it provides naval weapons technology to selected foreign navies—a globalization, so to speak, of naval power. All of these functions contribute in important ways to the expansion of cross-border networks and flows.

Since the end of World War II, the Navy has replaced the British Royal Navy in providing the world standards for naval operations. With the exception of Russia, China, and states formerly known as rogues, such as Iran and North Korea, almost all national navies use concepts of operations and procedures derived from or similar to those of the Navy. This ensures a considerable degree of interoperability. Even those navies that do not have the technology to establish electronic links with U.S. tactical information networks are generally well versed in *Allied Tactical Publications 1,* the NATO signal book for naval operations. The signals and tactics of the United States and NATO have become global; they are used to facilitate naval communications and tactics throughout the world.

This degree of interoperability is solidified and enhanced by combined exercises and operational training around the globe. The Navy routinely conducts combined exercises and operations, as well as policy discussions, with most other fleets. Operations range from highly integrated Standing Naval Forces Atlantic (STANAVFORLANT) and Standing Naval Forces Mediterranean (STANAVFORMED); to frequent exercises with Latin American and Asian navies and with that of Australia; to passing exercises with friendly coastal navies, such as that of Oman; to occasional exercises with Black Sea navies, including that of Russia. A biannual seminar, the International Seapower Symposium, brings high-level representatives from almost every naval staff—including those of Russia and China—to the Naval War College in Newport for discussions of naval policies. The location is familiar because many of the flag officers of the world's navies are graduates of the Naval War College. Bilateral talks between the staff of the Chief of Naval Operations and its foreign counterparts are also routine.

As a primary mission of U.S. naval forces in peacetime, forward presence—the continual deployment of naval forces to potential regions of crisis—places the Navy in the forefront of the proverbial "global security market." Like the best of global corporations, the Navy maintains representatives in the immediate vicinity of its significant customers. Not a day goes by in which U.S. naval forces cannot strike in some fashion at the forces of Saddam Hussein, ethnic cleansers, international terrorists, or maritime drug traffickers, to name but a few potential threats to global and U.S. security. Most national decisionmakers express their support (privately, if not publicly) for the Navy to continue performing this regional deterrence and peacekeeping function.[10] This is a de facto globalization of a common concept of deterrence and security.

Finally, the Navy provides naval weapons and technology to selected foreign navies, and it includes foreign weapons systems on board some of its own ships and aircraft. Examples of the former include the AEGIS air defense system outfitted on destroyers of the Japanese Maritime Self-Defense Force; examples of the latter include the German-American rolling airframe missile (RAM) ship self-defense weapon, UAV prototype systems from Canada and Israel, and the Italian OTO Melara 76-mm gun on U.S. FFG–7 class ships. This exchange of systems, which the United States dominates by virtue of its robust defense industrial sector, increases the level of global naval interoperability.

Effects of Globalization on the Navy

Globalization is a multidirectional process. Several obvious globalization trends have a direct operational impact on the Navy of today and will have implications for future naval policy and force structure.[11] Five of these trends are (1) proliferation of advanced antiaccess weapons, (2) proliferation of information systems and sensors, (3) increases in maritime trade and traffic; (4) increased involvement in smaller scale contingencies, peacekeeping, and peace enforcement, and (5) emerging concerns about economic security.

Antiaccess Weapons Proliferation

A key trend is the proliferation of advanced weapon systems and sensors, particularly to the few nations—mostly "states formerly known as rogues"—that might seek to challenge U.S. military power. Although the United States does share military technology with selected nations, advanced technology from the former Soviet Union (some of it in continued Russian production, and some of it surplus) has also emerged on the world market.[12]

The technology being marketed includes weapons that the Soviet Union would not export to other Warsaw Pact states during the Cold War. A primary example is the SS–N–22 Sunburn (Russian name *Moskvit*) antiship cruise missile, which was considered one of the most potent ship killers of the Cold War. Initially reluctant to sell the missiles, Russia included them as the main armament in the sale of four *Sovremenny* class destroyers to China in the late 1990s. This sale was a disappointing development since, according to reports, the United States had attempted in the mid-1990s to buy the entire former Soviet inventory of 841 Sunburn missiles from Russia before they could reach the global market.[13] The attempt failed. This transfer could presumably make U.S. naval forces more vulnerable if China becomes a potential opponent.[14] It is also possible that China could produce a reverse-engineered version for additional export.

The proliferation of advanced military systems—such as intelligence, surveillance and reconnaissance sensors, ballistic and cruise missiles, submarines, sea mines, and weapons of mass destruction (WMD)—parallels the intellectual proliferation of a post-Gulf War operational concept on how to defeat U.S. forces, known as antiaccess or area denial strategy. This strategy recognizes the difficulty in defeating U.S. power projection forces after they have entered the region of conflict and are ready for combat. Instead of fighting U.S. forces on a regional battlefield (where the results might be similar to those of the Gulf War), the potential opponent could attempt to prevent U.S. forces from entering the region at all. In the logic of the antiaccess approach, a potential opponent would initially seek to destroy any forward-based U.S. forces stationed in the region, and then seek to block U.S. maritime and air forces from entering and bringing troops into regional littoral waters and territory by massive attrition attacks using the proliferated weapons systems.[15]

According to this construct, if there were to be threats to U.S. naval operations, they would come from asymmetrical weapons systems designed to deny U.S. passage through maritime chokepoints or the ability of the Navy to conduct operations near land.[16] Both the Office of Naval Intelligence and the Office of Net Assessment within the Office of the Secretary of Defense report the steady proliferation of such weapons as ballistic missiles, cruise missiles, diesel-electric submarines, sophisticated naval mines, and fast patrol craft.[17]

In other words, the Navy may not have to face another globalized navy in the future, but it may have to face globalized antiaccess weapons. In an antiaccess scenario, with regional land bases capable of supporting U.S. forces destroyed and littoral access denied, the opponent may have effectively extended its defenses out to the entry points of its region. The United States could find itself in the position of having to undertake potentially costly forcible entry operations. This would be the modern equivalent of the D-Day invasion of Nazi-occupied Europe, but with both sides having access to a range of high-technology weaponry.[18] Even in this war of attrition, it is likely that the Armed Forces would eventually breech the antiaccess defenses, both through naval operations and the use of standoff weapons stationed outside the region or in the continental United States. However, the real goal of an antiaccess strategy is to convince America and its allies or coalition partners that the cost of penetration is simply too high.[19] Hostilities could thereby be ended via a diplomatic agreement that, in effect, grants the regional power its wartime objectives. Such an agreement might be encouraged by international organizations that traditionally advocate negotiated peace. In these ways, an adversary whose military forces are inferior to those of the United States might still be able to attain its political objectives notwithstanding the opposition of U.S. forces.

Proliferation of Information Systems and Sensors

Another likely effect of economic globalization is a continuing increase in the capability and proliferation of high-speed information systems and remote sensors. Of particular concern to naval forces is the increasing availability of commercial satellite imagery, as well as satellite communications and navigation systems. Satellite imagery is the key element in military reconnaissance and targeting. Satellite navigation systems allow for accurate attacks. Space-based communication systems are more difficult to jam and allow communications between units in difficult operating terrain, including urban terrain.

As part of a revolution in military affairs, many sources claim or imply that naval forces will be more detectable in the future because of the proliferation of space-based imagery. The Office of Net Assessment has sponsored a number of briefings at which it has been argued that surface vessels have become vulnerable to detection and strike by antiaccess weapons, particularly in littoral regions, and are no longer viable warfighting platforms. This argument is challenged by sources pointing out the inability of most potential opponents to strike moving targets, particularly at sea.[20] An additional debate concerns the continued use of commercial satellite imagery, navigation, and communications during actual hostilities. The availability of such information to potential opponents of the United States during time of war remains doubtful.[21] But whatever the actually survivability of U.S. surface ships may be, the reality of commercial targeting data becoming widely available is of considerable concern and is a globalization trend that should be taken into consideration in naval planning.

Increases in Maritime Trade and Traffic

A key effect of economic globalization is the continuing increase in maritime trade and traffic. While the new economy that helps fuel globalization is knowledge-based, the fact is that knowledge needs to be transformed into goods and services. These goods and services need to be transported internationally. While personnel may travel by air, most goods can travel economically only by sea. If globalization indeed results in an increase of world trade and cross-border networks and flows, it will necessarily result in an increase in maritime traffic.

At the same time, ongoing trends could make maritime trade more vulnerable to disruption. Modernization of maritime off-load and on-load is being consolidated in a handful of megaports or hub ports such as Rotterdam, Singapore, Kobe, Vancouver, and Long Beach. The impact of future crises near these megaports—or the sea lanes of commerce leading to them—will have a greater overall effect on international trade than it had in the past, when there were many more ports open to the most modern ships.[22] Obviously, this increases the potential workload of the Navy in providing the maritime security function, whether against bellicose states or against piracy and international crime.

The impact of a global navy is directly related not only to its workload but also to the perception of stability that it brings to the international environment. This would argue that the requirement for naval forward presence—naval forces operating within the regions of potential crises—will become even more important under continuing globalization. Indeed, the demand for forward presence forces could increase sharply with an increase in the number of small-scale contingencies (SSCs), and peace enforcement and peacekeeping operations in which the United States and its military become involved.

Involvement in Peace Operations, SSCs, and Regional War Fighting

In their foreign policies of engagement and humanitarian intervention, the post-Cold War Bush and Clinton administrations greatly increased U.S. military involvement in many world crises. Supporters of these policies argue that the end of the Cold War lifted the lid off many national and ethnic conflicts, and that the United States can make positive steps to contain and reduce them. Opponents argue that such conflicts have been steady throughout history and that U.S. involvement, while worthy and effective in certain cases, is akin to bailing water from the sea. Whatever position dominates, one effect of globalization is to make it appear that such crises have greater effects on the rest of the world than they did in the past. Thus, there is a perception that the increase in cross-border networks and flows necessitates international involvement in the internal crises of far-off nations, to include such supposedly smaller scale contingencies as NATO bombing of Serbian forces, and peace enforcement and peacekeeping in a variety of locales.

Although much of the actual peace enforcement and peacekeeping involves ground forces, strong support from air and sea is often a prerequisite. As a part of the Department of the Navy, the Marine Corps is a naval service, thereby bringing direct naval involvement to day-to-day peacekeeping on the ground. The Clinton administration also increased the use of sea-based force in such peacetime SSCs, even using sea-launched Tomahawk land attack missiles (TLAMs) to strike terrorist targets in landlocked countries. Additionally, naval forces have direct involvement in enforcing international sanctions, such as those against illegal maritime traffic with Iraq and the southern no-fly zone. If globalization continues to increase, along with the perception that such missions are a vital American responsibility, the Navy operational tempo may continue to increase. This would have a significant impact on the numbers and types of naval forces required for such contingencies.

Navy and Marine forces, of course, will also continue to play important roles in defense strategy for waging major regional wars. The Marines provide about 25 percent of the Nation's active duty ground forces. Together, the Navy and the Marines generate about 40 percent of the Nation's tactical air power, including the capacity for precision strikes. They play a key role in joint doctrine. Often, the Navy and the Marines will be among the first U.S. forces to converge on the scene of a war, where they will play an important role in halting enemy attacks in order to provide time for larger U.S. forces to converge on the scene. Once the U.S. buildup is complete, they will contribute importantly to counterattack plans and ultimate victory. Should some future conflicts be primarily maritime events, their role will be even larger.

Emerging Concerns about Economic Security

The proliferation of weapons of mass destruction, potential threats to commerce, potential denial of access, and erupting national conflicts have created emerging concerns about U.S. economic security. Homeland security, rarely a topic of popular discussion, is of increasing interest to political, business, and economic leaders. Of particular concern is the potential for terrorist use of chemical or biological weapons on U.S. soil. While the effects on individuals are frightening to contemplate, there are also concerns as to what impact the very existence of such an ever-increasing threat may have on U.S. prosperity. Can the United States be truly open to the beneficial aspects of cross-border networks and flows without becoming more vulnerable to terrorist and hacker attacks on individuals, infrastructure, and computer networks?

At the same time, there are emerging concerns as to whether American or multinational businesses operating overseas can be protected against what appears to be an increasingly chaotic world filled with WMD-capable terrorists, disgruntled ethnic groups, and increasingly sophisticated international criminal groups. Demands for increased homeland and overseas protection could have significant impact on naval forces.

The Composition and Disposition of the Future Navy

The overarching questions concerning naval forces and globalization revolve around whether today's Navy is configured so as to be able to deal with the challenges just described. Does it need to make significant changes in order to support the beneficial aspects of globalization or protect us from hazardous trends? If globalization is a continuing phenomenon, how should the Navy adapt? Are the Navy's future programs designed to deal with future globalization effects? Are other platforms, platform mixes, and operational concepts needed? How "joint" do naval forces need to be, and how much jointness is needed to deal with the maritime effects of globalization?

It is difficult to link recommendations on naval force structure directly to the globalization process because force structure choices are presumably based on the anticipated threat and related military requirements. Globalization, as it is currently construed, is a recent and not fully understood phenomenon. Nonetheless, it is possible to suggest how current, planned, and proposed naval systems might fit in a globalized world. Where the basis for concrete suggestions may be lacking, questions for future analysis at least can be posed.

Size of the Fleet

One of the current concerns expressed by both Congress and DOD leadership is the overall size of the Navy and the number of ships in the fleet. With the end of the Cold War, the Navy, along with its sister services, faced substantial reductions. Overall U.S. defense spending was reduced by more than one-third. Depending on how one calculates fleet size, the Navy was reduced by almost one-half. During the 1980s, the Reagan administration aspired to a 600-ship Navy; although that actual number was programmed, it was not reached. The latest defense structure review, the Quadrennial Defense Review of 1997, called for a fleet size of slightly more than 300 ships (current size is 316), which was deemed sufficient until 2015.

However, the significant number of SSCs and other operations in which the U.S. Government has chosen to become involved has increased the operational tempo of the services sharply enough to cause great strains in the force. A fleet of 316 ships does not have a sufficiently large rotation base to provide a CVBG and an ARG for all three of the critical theaters of interest (Mediterranean, Arabian Gulf, Western Pacific) simultaneously, as requested by the commanders in chief (CINCs) of the Unified Commands. While almost one-third of the Navy is forward-deployed for a period of 6 months, the rest of the fleet is in overhaul or training for deployment. Instead of being able to provide this 3.0 presence (1 CVBG and 1 ARG per theater), today's worldwide presence varies between 2.5 and 2.7 ships. According to a recent study, a 3.0 presence would require a fleet of approximately 360 ships.[23]

The fleet reduction was achieved by decommissioning ships early in their life spans and reducing the ship construction budget. The current ship construction level can no longer replace ships that are reaching their normal decommissioning age. If ship construction is not increased, the Navy will inevitably fall below 300 ships by 2010.[24]

This shortage could become acute if globalization trends increase the requirements for naval presence, engagement, and contingency operations.[25] Although it may be possible to increase the length of ship deployments and reduce their maintenance time, this step has a deleterious effect on both equipment readiness levels and personnel retention. Secretary of Defense William Cohen endorsed the Navy's proposal for a 360-ship fleet;[26] however, currently there is no strong Congressional support for the budget increases required.

Though globalization does seem to increase the value of naval forward presence, the question remains as to what increase in fleet size is actually required. Some argue that the United States maintains sufficient joint service forces to substitute air or land forces for naval presence. To a considerable extent, this is the logic behind the Air Force's recent decision to organize itself into Air Expeditionary Forces (AEFs).[27] But if a globalized security environment is characterized by effective antiaccess strategies, a choice to become *more* dependent on overseas land bases for joint operations would seem illogical. In fact, the Navy's independent capability to operate at sea without a significant overseas logistics footprint would appear a great advantage. Whereas the United States has air bases in Europe and Northeast Asia, plus conditional access in the Persian Gulf, it lacks comparable facilities elsewhere, including virtually all of Asia south of Okinawa. Using the seas, by contrast, U.S. carriers can reach many of these places.

Issues Concerning Current Force Structure

Perhaps fleet size is ultimately less critical than its actual composition. A large fleet of smaller, less capable ships is not necessarily as effective as a smaller fleet of more powerful ships. Additionally, individual ship characteristics need to include increased levels of protection against weapons of mass destruction (primarily chemical and biological weapons) as these weapons proliferate. The current configuration of the Navy seeks to balance combat firepower with multimission capability and the requirements for naval forward presence. However, the downsizing of the 1990s resulted in the divestiture of naval capabilities on the low end of the spectrum. The search for a capabilities-size balance in a globalized world would require an assessment of desired ship characteristics and might indicate the value of new ship concepts. The following short survey barely scratches the surface of issues that require considerable detailed analysis.

Aircraft Carriers. The large through-deck carrier capable of operating conventional takeoff and landing aircraft is a virtual U.S. monopoly. No other nation operates such ships, although all other potential blue-water navies aspire (whether driven by future plans or wishful thinking) to do so.[28] However, critics—focused on the enormous cost of building and operating such floating airfields—question their survivability in an antiaccess environment.

While the expense of constructing carriers is undeniable, their survivability in an antiaccess environment would seem much greater than that of overseas land bases (assuming prudent employment), and their capability to remain on station is obviously much greater than that of long-range aircraft. If direct engagement and presence are required in a not-yet-hot-war environment, carriers are unparalleled assets. Their key advantage is great flexibility—they provide airfields that can move at relatively high speeds and defend themselves by maneuver as well as strike operations. An aircraft carrier is relocatable U.S. territory that is readily usable in demonstrating U.S. interest and resolve. Its disadvantage is its vulnerability to submarines—a problem that existed under previous conditions and can be mitigated only through the combined-arms operations that have been the existing fleet's concept.[29] The type of aircraft that can be operated and their sortie rates are less than that of overseas land bases, but a combination of carrier operations and long-range aircraft (Air Force bombers) would seem to provide the greatest capacity for probing and breaking through antiaccess defenses. The bottom line is that while U.S. carriers might seem vulnerable at first glance, they are well defended and are far from easy to sink. Indeed, none has been lost since World War II even though they were heavily employed in three regional wars over the past 50 years.

The recent Navy report to Congress calls for a force of 15 carriers to provide 3.0 worldwide peacetime presence. Such a force could not be built or maintained without a substantial increase in the Navy's budget. The bottom line appears to be that evolutionary improvements in carrier design make such a platform desirable in a globalized future, but adequate funding—for what are self-sustaining overseas air bases—seems problematic. Short of adding more carriers, the most substantial increase in efficiency could come about by using them as command-and-control centers for overseas joint operations.

Aviation Squadrons. The overall Navy aviation program has focused on improving relatively short-range strike aircraft, such as the F/A–18. A globalized antiaccess environment would appear to call for longer range and greater relative stealth in such aircraft. Additionally, internetted defenses would seem a prime target for electronic warfare aircraft, an expertise that primarily resides in the Navy and Marine Corps EA–6B Prowler squadrons.

Recent regional interventions have made the shortage in existing EA–6Bs very evident. It is surprising that the Navy has not pursued an increase and enhancement of electronic warfare aviation systems with greater alacrity or apparent interest. To be effective in regional conflict in a globalized world, electronic warfare/cyberwarfare cannot be confined only to space or ground assets—at least not without giving up a certain degree of precision and local effectiveness. Adequate aircraft, including naval aircraft, are necessary.

Attack Submarines.[30] With the end of the Cold War, the U.S. nuclear attack submarine (SSN) inventory was cut dramatically from a force of about 100 to a planned force slightly above 50. This step stemmed from the perception that the former Soviet submarine force of Russia—much of which is no longer operational—represented a much reduced threat. Recently, however, the Navy has argued that the planned submarine force will not be large enough to carry out all the engagement and intelligence operations required by the CINCs, along with providing two submarines as part of every deploying CVBG. (The latter is an organizational choice by the Navy, rather than a joint requirement.) Studies of joint requirements have specified the number of 68 SSNs as the desired force level.[31] Due to their stealth and flexibility, submarines would appear to be a priority asset for a globalized world, particularly in the intelligence, surveillance, and reconnaissance (ISR) role as well as blue-water sea control.

Surface Combatants. During the Cold War, *surface combatants*—the generalized term used for cruisers, destroyers, and frigates—were multipurpose designs optimized for war *at* sea, as opposed to land attack or strikes against land targets—which could be considered war *from* the sea. With the absence of a global naval threat, surface combatants are currently prized for their capability to launch TLAMs and their developing capability of theater ballistic missile defense (TBMD).

Both missions retain their relevance in a highly globalized world. In fact, TBMD could become the greatest asset in demand during future periods of potential crises. The advantage of naval TBMD is that it is rapidly and highly mobile, with near indefinite on-station time, and that it uses an already existing air defense combat system capable of future upgrades for cruise missile defense.

The current Navy program includes the development of DD–21, a destroyer-sized platform designed specifically for land attack. As conceived, DD–21 would require a drastically reduced crew size compared with the current DDG–51 class, would possess only a modest self-defense capability, and would take much of its targeting data from off-ship sensors. But with its relatively large size, DD–21 would appear to be giving up survivability without a dramatic improvement in strike capability. An alternative in a dense antiaccess environment might be a significantly smaller vessel with similar characteristics, such as the streetfighter proposal described below.

Amphibious Warships. When the Navy shifted from its Cold War maritime strategy to the littoral-focused "Forward . . . from the Sea" strategy, greater emphasis was placed on modernization and new operating concepts for the amphibious fleet. This, in turn, seemed to herald an ever-increasing integration between the Navy and the Marine Corps. These developments have cooled recently, reflecting a return to the Navy's traditional reluctance to prioritize assets for a Marine fleet. Modern assets such as the LPD–17 class are being developed to replace older, more specialized amphibious ships (most of which are already decommissioned) and to achieve the 2.5 Marine Expeditionary Brigade (MEB) lift requirement mandated by Congress. Certain previously held capabilities, such as the ability to pump fuel directly to forces operating ashore, are being quietly discarded. If a globalized world requires a greater number of interventions in the littoral regions—where most of the world's cities are located—it would seem prudent to increase rather than decrease such combat-capable maritime support for land operations.

Another capability that has been quietly discarded is the inclusion of vertical launch tubes in the LPD–17 class. Such tubes could have been stocked with TLAMs, substantially increasing the number of Tomahawk shooters in the fleet. The tubes could also be used for enhanced air defense weapons or for shorter range fire support missiles to provide fires for troops engaged in combat ashore. Ostensibly a cost-reduction decision, the elimination of vertical launch capabilities in the amphibious fleet was a missed opportunity for enhancing fleet striking power at a modest overall cost. A potential alternative is the littoral supremacy ship proposal described later.

Counter-Mine Warfare. Beyond any doubt, counter-mine warfare is the weakest capability in the U.S. fleet inventory. During the Cold War, the mission was relegated to allied navies (particularly NATO allies) that could not afford to construct large oceangoing ships, but could spend their resources by specializing in this function. With the Cold War over, this "specialization agreement" is in doubt because European military assets are declining. Moreover, the Navy operates in regions in which NATO allies may not venture.

Since sea mines are among the cheapest antiaccess weapons readily available on the open market, recent trends seemingly require the Navy to re-formalize the counter-mine specialization agreement or increase its capability at mine hunting and clearing, a capability that was sorely taxed in the Gulf War. This issue is not a pressing one for a navy that operates in the deep blue water of the oceans, where mines cannot normally be placed, but it becomes critical as a prerequisite for littoral operations. The Navy's counter-mine capability has not increased at the same rate as has the Navy's interest in and commitment to littoral warfare.

Future naval programs are focused on developing organic mine-hunting capabilities that could be added to multipurpose surface combatants and submarines. But this adds yet another mission to ships that are already tasked with strike, TBMD, antisubmarine warfare, and fleet air defense. Unless a significant increase in surface combatants and submarines is programmed, it would seem prudent to make a comparatively modest investment in additional specialized surface and air mine-hunting and mine-clearing platforms. In order to develop a long-term advocate for this critical mission, it may be appropriate to assign this mission to a community other than surface or submarine warfare, such as to explosive ordnance disposal (EOD).

Patrol Aircraft. Navy patrol aircraft, such as the P–3 Orion, have proved their value as the most rapid and long-range antisubmarine warfare platform for blue-water operations; however, they appear particularly vulnerable in an antiaccess littoral environment. As the Cold War ended, the number of patrol squadrons was greatly reduced. Unless survivability of such aircraft can be increased or new concepts of operations developed, retaining this capability in modest numbers would seem appropriate for the current reduced oceangoing submarine threat.

Patrol Combatants. Since they are not independent or seagoing, and possess only very light armament, small patrol combatants cannot readily be deployed to theaters of crisis in a timely fashion. Used almost exclusively as special operations force (SOF) assets, patrol combatants are not integrated into fleet littoral operations. But if a globalized world requires greater near-shore engagement, such vessels would seem to have a significant role. Two possible solutions for increasing this capability would be constructing patrol combatants to be able to fit in the well decks of the current and future amphibious fleet, or developing a more lethal, more survivable combatant with greater seakeeping capabilities—similar in concept to the streetfighter described below.

Combat Logistics Ships/Military Sealift Command. As part of its downsizing, the Navy elected to convert most of its logistics assets into civilian-manned ships operated by the Maritime Sealift Command (MSC). The long-term cost reductions may be modest; in the near term, this reduces direct costs to the Navy budget, particularly military personnel costs. Although the legal status of these assets in a major theater war scenario still requires some scrutiny, there seems no pressing need in a globalized world to remilitarize them.

However, one area of significant reduction that could limit independence of operations in a globalized world is the complete elimination of destroyer tenders and repair ships, as well as most submarine tenders. The logic of this move was that repair of forward-deployed ships could be performed in overseas ports using foreign assets. But the availability of such foreign assets during wartime is uncertain, and much of the specialized repair needs of U.S. warships can be obtained only at relatively high cost. Another concern was that the decommissioned tenders were potentially the only means of reloading vertical launch tubes in forward-deployed forces. As of today, expended magazines require surface combatants to steam back to the United States for reload. This may create a considerable bottleneck to long-range land attack missions in an extended conflict.

New Force Structure Concepts

A number of new concepts may prove useful adjustments to fleet structure in order to meet the requirements of a globalized world. With the exception of network-centric warfare, which has been frequently discussed, but is still in the conceptual stages, these proposals have not been adopted in future Navy programs.

Arsenal Ship/Arsenal Submarine. An arsenal ship, consisting primarily of a large number of vertical launch tubes and a small crew and requiring targeting data and protection from other naval platforms, was a proposal particularly intriguing to the late Admiral Jeremy M. Boorda, a former Chief of Naval Operations. Although official scrutiny of the proposal did not long survive Admiral Boorda's demise, a variant that has gained increasing popularity among defense analysts and Congress is the arsenal submarine. The prototypical variant is a converted Trident nuclear ballistic missile submarine (SSBN) that replaces its ballistic missile tubes with multiple cruise missile tubes capable of firing TLAMs. Although arms control treaties create some complications, the use of an existing submarine hull could provide such an SSGN at a much lower cost than new construction. The advantage of an SSGN over a surface arsenal ship is its stealth characteristics, which would seem valuable in a globalized world/antiaccess environment. The recent *Report to Congress on Naval Vessel Force Structure Requirements* identifies the SSGN proposal as being under consideration.

Network-centric Warfare. A widely discussed proposal, the concept of network-centric warfare could be described as a shift in focus away from platforms to networks.[32,33] Network-centric operations promise to increase the value of individual units by providing more effective information linkage and a common operational picture that, in turn, allow for the optimum, coordinated use of weapons and effects. Conceptually developed by Vice Admiral Arthur K. Cebrowski, the current President of the Naval War College, network-centric warfare clearly responds to the information era. One area of concern is the increased vulnerability that a tight tactical Internet could experience if any of its access nodes are penetrated by an enemy.

Littoral Supremacy Ship. Suggested in the writings of retired Admiral William Owens[34] and elaborated upon by others,[35] the littoral supremacy ship is a proposed combination of surface combatant and an amphibious warship that is optimized for land attack. The advantage of this idea is the potential for reducing the number of different ship types assigned to the fleet, thereby achieving economies of scale in construction, maintenance, and training. Although still a vessel of considerable size, capable of operating vertical or short-takeoff-and-landing (VSTOL) aircraft, the littoral supremacy ship would sacrifice blue-water warfighting capability for land attack and self-defense weaponry. The choice to construct these ships is postulated on the belief that the Navy will remain unchallenged in the oceans.

Mobile Off-shore Base. First proposed in the late 1960s, the concept of a mobile off-shore base, consisting of a series of connected off-shore oil platform-like structures, has been periodically reexamined. It recently attracted renewed interest through Admiral Owens and studies developed by potential mobile off-shore base builders.[36] The technological difficulties of linking oil platform structures in relatively moderate sea states are challenging, but not insurmountable. The goal would be a composite platform capable of being used as an air base for operations by almost all aircraft in the Navy and Air Force inventory. In contrast to the 80 to 100 marinized aircraft that can be operated off today's largest aircraft carriers, the proposed mobile off-shore base might be capable of operating more than 300 aircraft, including large transports requiring a long runway.

Mobile off-shore bases would be constructed at sea at the major deployment hubs or in nearby areas of long-term crises. In effect, they would provide the same capacity as an overseas air base ashore without the force protection requirement (such as antiterrorism defenses) or the vulnerability of a fixed land target. Unlike an aircraft carrier, the mobile off-shore base could move only at very slow speeds (less than 5 knots) and would probably require disassembly to make a major relocation.

The advantage of the mobile off-shore base proposal is the vast size and high aircraft sortie rate it could bring to areas of long-term U.S. commitment. It would be an asset that satisfies numerous joint service requirements. However, it would probably still require naval battle group assets for its defense, and it obviously lacks the flexibility and survivability characteristics of an actual carrier. If a globalized world requires a continuing U.S. presence in an area where land bases are not readily available or subject to an antiaccess threat, the mobile off-shore base could prove a viable alternative to land basing.

Streetfighter. Another recent concept championed by Admiral Cebrowski, streetfighter would be a small surface combatant optimized for near-shore land attack.[37] Under the proposal, streetfighter would be an offensive platform with a small crew and would rely on speed, stealth, and point-defense weaponry for self-protection. Such a ship could be purchased in large numbers, thereby allowing it to be more expendable than are larger, capital ships. The historical analogy is World War II patrol torpedo (PT) boats that operated in the Pacific island archipelagoes. Much more technologically sophisticated than their predecessors, streetfighters would be armed with land attack missiles and possibly long-range guns, rely on remote targeting data for strikes, and be supported for logistics and repair by a seagoing mother ship (possibly similar to the littoral supremacy ship). Thus far, streetfighter has received a lukewarm reception by the majority of naval leaders.

Evaluating the current force structure and the above alternative concepts in terms of their effect on globalization and their relevance in a globalized world would be a most complex but worthy challenge. Perhaps it is a task that the dominant staff of the Office of the Chief of Naval Operations cannot handle alone, but is best achieved by commissioning competing analyses from a range of naval organizations including the Naval War College, Naval Postgraduate School, Office of Naval Research, and the systems commands of Naval Sea Systems Command, Naval Air Systems Command, and Space and Electronic Warfare Command, as well as the analytical organizations of the Marine Corps. Ultimately, such analyses come down to two basic questions: Which naval systems best achieve our objectives in a globalized world? and If the globalized world does not evolve as we expect it will, which systems are the best hedges against uncertainty?

Conclusions: The Leverage Called Sea Power

Since naval forces are structured to ensure or deny global access and interactions, they have the potential to provide leverage to the positive aspects of globalization as well as protection from some of the negative aspects.[38] While this contribution may not be apparent to those who think Internet or foreign stock market every time they hear the term *globalization*, it becomes evident once the trappings of the globalized economy are seen through and the question "What provides stability?" is asked.

The Nation is in the unique position of being sole possessor of a global navy. This position provides considerable leverage for a pro-democracy, pro-free market emphasis on globalization. It also allows the United States to act as underwriter for the security of international trade, which is both a burden and an advantage. In effect, the United States Navy has become the world's navy, with no serious challengers to the claim. A strong instrument of military power, the Navy seems to be viewed with little jealousy, fear, or animosity by most countries. In part, this is due to a view of the United States as an honest broker, but it is also buttressed by acceptance of the law of the sea and a perception that naval power is less a direct threat to sovereignty than are armies stationed overseas. The very size of the U.S. fleet dissuades potential competitors from even attempting to build a seagoing fleet.[39]

This happy state of affairs may not last forever, or even a few decades. Antiaccess weaponry is multiplying. Unsatisfied states such as China are slowly increasing their sea reach. The United States has an underfunded shipbuilding program, and its fleet will eventually age. Rather than apply the criteria of the past, it may be in the best interest of the United States to reshape naval assets toward managing a more globalized future. This is a thought that the Navy should analyze seriously if it expects to remain a dominant force in a globalized world.

The future of globalization cannot be foreseen. Perhaps globalization will make war between great powers obsolete, even while exposing the tensions between the haves and have-nots. However, the prospect of war—whether global, regional, or local—is never something to dismiss lightly. Sir Francis Bacon once remarked that a nation with sea power could "take as much or as little of war as it desires." It may be that such a nation cannot avoid taking a good dose of globalization if it wishes to remain relevant in the world economy. But a sea power nation comes to the process with a leverage that others do not possess. To paraphrase a common optimistic saying: the rising tide of globalization may truly "lift all boats." If most of the boats are yours, it is a fine tide indeed.

Notes

[1] Alfred Thayer Mahan, "Considerations Governing the Disposition of Navies," *National Review* 39 (July 1902), 701–719, reprinted in John B. Hattendorf, ed., *Mahan on Naval Strategy* (Annapolis, MD: Naval Institute Press, 1991), 284.

[2] Recent criticisms of the writings of Mahan focus on his supposed fixation on decisive fleet-on-fleet engagements as the means of establishing sea power and dominating the oceans. It seems more likely that his emphasis on decisive engagements was simply a concern as to the prerequisite for domination in an era in which there were competing navies of comparable strength. Mahan also discussed other means of establishing sea control, but, more importantly, he did not foresee the post-Cold War

world in which there are effectively no global navies other than that of the United States. In effect, the decisive fleet-on-fleet engagement was the Cold War, which was settled without blue-water combat.

[3] For further discussion, see chapter 2.

[4] This broad definition includes military operations in space and cyberspace, both of which are mediums of communications, transformation, and exchange similar to the oceans. Admittedly, the current division of roles and missions of the U.S. Department of Defense assigns significant or primary responsibility to joint commands or services other than the Navy. However, that in no way lessens the fact that operations in those mediums are essentially *naval* in nature. See discussion in Sam J. Tangredi, "Space Is an Ocean," U.S. Naval Institute *Proceedings* 125, no. 1 (January 1999), 52–53.

[5] Obviously, components built in Canada or Mexico, as well as in the United States itself, are exceptions.

[6] It is possible that the possession of nuclear weapons by two regional belligerents could cause the conflict to become quite global. However, the traditional logic of nuclear deterrence holds that such weapons are quantitatively different from other forms of military power, and presumably would not be used to expand a local conflict to nonbelligerents.

[7] An illustration of this absolute dominance is the fact that the United States possesses its own coastal navy, the United States Coast Guard, which itself is larger than the naval forces of most nations.

[8] See, for example, Ron Brown et al., "Forward Engagement Requirements for U.S. Naval Forces: New Analytical Approaches," Report NPS–OR–97–011PR (Monterey, CA: Naval Postgraduate School, July 23, 1997).

[9] *The Washington Post* reported that on June 19, 2000, Secretary of State Madeleine K. Albright announced that the Clinton administration would no longer use the term *rogue states*, but that "henceforth, nasty, untrustworthy, missile-equipped countries would be known as 'states of concern.'" This would appear to be a reaction to a recent meeting of the South and North Korean heads of state. See Steven Mufson, "What's in a Name? U.S. Drops Term 'Rogue State,'" *The Washington Post*, June 20, 2000, 16. However, the term *rogue state* is ubiquitous within the analytical literature.

[10] See discussion in Sally Newman, "Political and Economic Implications of Global Naval Presence," in *Naval Forward Presence: Present Status, Future Prospects* (Washington, DC: Center for Strategic and International Studies, 1997), 48–50.

[11] Other trends, including indirect impacts on naval forces, are discussed in chapter 3.

[12] Additionally, numerous Western European nations—notably Sweden, France, and Italy—sell advanced naval systems. China is the original source for many weapons that emerge in the hands of "states formerly known as rogues." North Korea has a re-engineer and re-export network with other states, such as Iran.

[13] Norman Friedman, *World Naval Weapons Systems 1997–1998* (Annapolis, MD: Naval Institute Press, 1997), 243–244.

[14] However, in April 2000, it was reported that the U.S. point defense system rolling airframe missile (RAM) had successfully engaged a simulated SS–N–22 conducting a high-speed weave. Report in "RAM Passes OpEval," U.S. Naval Institute *Proceedings* 126, no. 4 (April 2000), 6.

[15] The term *asymmetrical* includes weapons designed to attack U.S. weaknesses and take advantage of the geographical features of the region, such as straits and narrow passages. From the naval perspective, these weapons can be considered asymmetrical because the Navy is largely configured for open-ocean operations. But historically, use of such weapons or their antecedents might be considered a *normal* aspect of naval warfare in narrow seas. An excellent study of the historical and environmental factors influencing near-shore naval operations is Milan N. Vego, *Naval Strategy and Operations in Narrow Seas* (Portland, OR: Frank Cass Publishers, 1999).

[16] A good discussion can be found in Tim Sloth Joergensen, "Navy Operations in Littoral Waters: 2000 and Beyond," *Naval War College Review* 51, no. 2 (Spring 1998), 20–29.

[17] Detailed in Office of Naval Intelligence, *Challenges to Naval Expeditionary Warfare* (Washington, DC: ONI, 1997).

[18] The most detailed discussion is Theodore L. Gatchel, *At the Water's Edge: Defending Against the Modern Amphibious Assault* (Annapolis, MD: Naval Institute Press, 1996).

[19] Thomas G. Mahnken, "America's Next War," *The Washington Quarterly* 16, no. 3 (Summer 1993), 171–184; Thomas G. Mahnken, "Deny U.S. Access?" U.S. Naval Institute *Proceedings* 124, no. 9 (September 1998), 36–39.

[20] See discussion of this debate in Sam J. Tangredi, "The Fall and Rise of Naval Forward Presence," U.S. Naval Institute *Proceedings* 126, no. 5 (May 2000), 29–32.

[21] See discussion in Sam J. Tangredi, *All Possible Wars? Toward a Consensus View of the Future Security Environment*, McNair Paper 63 (Washington, DC: National Defense University Press, November 2000).

[22] From discussion in Daniel Y. Coulter, "Hub Ports and Focal Points: New Entrants in the Maritime Security Lexicon" (unpublished paper, circa July 1998), many points from which are contained in an unclassified Office of Naval Intelligence briefing entitled "Global Commercial Maritime Environment," Dan Coulter, presenter.

[23] U.S. Department of Defense, *Report to Congress on Naval Vessel Force Structure Requirements* (Washington, DC: Government Printing Office, June 26, 2000), 4.

[24] Chuck McCutcheon, "The Navy Pushes for More," *Air Force Magazine* 83, no. 7 (July 2000), 57.

[25] The total Navy is composed of units other than ships and aircraft squadrons, such as naval construction battalions (Seabees), explosive ordnance disposal (EOD) units, sea-air-land (SEAL) commando teams, and others. They will not be addressed in this chapter.

[26] "Cohen Admits Navy's Force Size Is Stressing Sailors and Marines," *Inside the Pentagon* (June 29, 2000), 1.

[27] Tangredi, "The Fall and Rise of Naval Forward Presence," 30.

[28] The Soviet Navy built smaller carriers and eventually constructed several large carrier hulls but was unable to perfect comparable carrier operations. The French Navy has recently constructed a large nuclear-powered aircraft carrier, the RFS *Charles De Gaulle*. However, she has had numerous design and construction problems, and sea trials indicate she is not yet operational.

[29] Critics maintain that carriers are also vulnerable to ballistic and air- or ground-launched cruise missiles, but these are easier to defend against by combined arms fleet operations. Unless ballistic missile warheads were enhanced with terminal homing—a major technological advance—or massive saturation attacks were directed against individual ships—a costly and inefficient strategy—conventionally armed ballistic missiles would not be serious threats against maneuvering warships. Obviously, nuclear weapons are a greater magnitude of threat, as they would be against any target. Cruise missile attacks at sea require real-time targeting data or proximity, both of which are difficult to obtain against an alerted fleet.

[30] SSBNs, which are national deterrence assets subject to arms control limitations, are not addressed in this chapter.

[31] "Cohen Admits Navy's Force Size Is Stressing Sailors and Marines," 1.

[32] Arthur K. Cebrowski and John J. Garstka, "Network-Centric Warfare: Its Origin and Future," U.S. Naval Institute *Proceedings* 124, no. 1 (January 1998), 28–35.

[33] David S. Alberts, John J. Garstka, and Frederick P. Stein, *Network Centric Warfare: Developing and Leveraging Information Superiority*, 2d ed. (Washington, DC: Department of Defense C^{4}ISR Cooperative Research Program, August 1999).

[34] William A. Owens, *High Seas: The Naval Passage to an Uncharted World* (Annapolis, MD: Naval Institute Press, 1995), 166–169.

[35] See discussion in Sam J. Tangredi, "A Ship for All Reasons," U.S. Naval Institute *Proceedings* 125, no. 9 (September 1999), 92–95.

[36] Owens, *High Seas*, 162–166.

[37] See public discussion in Arthur K. Cebrowski and Wayne B. Hughes, "Rebalancing the Fleet," U.S. Naval Institute *Proceedings* 125, no. 11 (November 1999), 31–34; Dave Weeks, "A Combatant for the Littorals," U.S. Naval Institute *Proceedings* 125, no. 11 (November 1999), 26–30; and Wayne B. Hughes, "22 Questions for Streetfighter," U.S. Naval Institute *Proceedings* 126, no. 2 (February 2000), 46–49.

[38] The concept of leverage is adopted from Colin S. Gray, *The Leverage of Sea Power: The Strategic Advantage of Navies in War* (New York: The Free Press, 1992).

[39] Secretary of the Navy Richard Danzig discusses the concept of dissuasion in Richard Danzig, *The Big Three: Our Greatest Security Risks and How to Address Them* (New York: Center for International Political Economy, February 1999), 22–24.

Chapter 22

Influencing Events Ashore

Harlan K. Ullman

The thrust of this study is to assess how globalization and its impact are likely to affect national security strategy and, in turn, what this will mean for the naval forces of the United States. The simple answer is that U.S. naval forces will be powerfully affected by globalization and the phenomena associated with it. But, as with most answers to difficult and complex questions, some of the devil will rest in the detail. And more will rest in how Congress responds to its constitutional mandate to "provide and maintain a Navy" and how the President, as Commander in Chief, carries out those responsibilities. Three observations and findings are particularly relevant to this line of inquiry and the impact of globalization on naval forces.

First, globalization is having and will have profound effects on states, regions, and people. For example, as China joins the World Trade Organization, its society, culture, and political systems will be buffeted and battered simply by virtue of having to deal with rules, regulations, and agreements largely foreign to its historical experiences, but standard and essential to the way that the world conducts its commerce and business. However, predicting specific consequences and impacts of the force and power of globalization will not follow automatically or easily.

Second, naval forces (along with everyone else) will have to deal with two revolutions that are both symptoms and causes of globalization and its associated phenomena. These are the revolutions in knowledge and in people. About the first, perhaps well before the 21st century ends, more new knowledge will be invented and created than has existed for all of previous history. In essence, knowledge will become extraordinarily inexpensive, provided one knows where to look. The great enabler of this first revolution is the second. It has been the empowerment and indeed the liberation of unprecedented numbers of people that form this revolution and a principal driving force behind globalization. Exploiting and mining the knowledge revolution must and will remain dependent on people and their capacity to act.

Third, globalization, along with other realities of international politics, particularly the absence of a comparable naval threat, is linking U.S. naval forces even more intimately with events ashore and the traditional role of influencing and affecting those events. Thus, U.S. naval forces will be faced with a double challenge: shaping this capacity and potential to tasks that are likely to be highly political, psychological,

---

Harlan K. Ullman is both chairman of the Killowen Group and co-chairman of the Rapid Dominance Group. He chairs the senior seminar program at the Center for Naval Analyses. Dr. Ullman has held positions at the Center for Strategic and International Studies and served as a professor at the National War College.

and perceptual in nature, *while* retaining sufficient warfighting means both to be credible and to be prepared for whatever circumstances necessitate the use of force in anger. Globalization will demand changes in the roles, missions, and operations of naval forces. The future measure of the effectiveness of U.S. naval forces will be how these challenges are met in responding to globalization and the other realities and uncertainties of the new century.

Changes Ahead for the Navy and the Nation

Few people taking part in this study would disagree with the proposition that the forces and factors that are part of the phenomena of globalization will have a profound impact on the future. Nor would many contradict the view that even 30 years from now the world will be a very different place. This future may or may not be one of wider peace and prosperity. However, what can be done now, today, that will make this transition safer and more secure for the United States and its allies? The Navy provides two examples.

During the late 1950s and early 1960s, the Polaris fleet ballistic missile program went into overdrive to deploy a ship as soon as possible. The first patrol began in December 1961, and Polaris' successor, Trident, remains on station today. A small, relatively obscure annex to the Polaris program was called Project Michelson, in honor of Albert Michelson, the Naval Academy graduate and Nobel Prize winner who first measured the speed of light in 1886. Through Project Michelson, the academic community was challenged and commissioned to examine the fundamental questions of war and peace in the Nuclear Age. Because of this project, a great deal of the intellectual work that went into defining and better understanding the meaning of war and peace and defense and deterrence in the Nuclear Age was conducted. Given the effect of the knowledge revolution, it is possible that we are entering an era that in some ways will be as profoundly different as were the worlds before and after these weapons of mass destruction (WMD) were first created. Perhaps globalization will necessitate a new Project Michelson in order to understand better this new and evolving world and the effects of globalization.

Second, when Admiral Elmo Zumwalt became Chief of Naval Operations in 1970, he initiated Project 60. That project, meant to be completed in 60 days, was to be the design and blueprint for a new Navy. While it took nearly an additional month to finish, the blueprint was created that reshaped the Navy, moving it from a largely World War II posture with over 900 ships ultimately to a modern, combat-ready force about half that size. If the impact of globalization turns out to be as profound as some expect, then a modern-day Project X may be needed. A hybrid of Projects Michelson and 60 could be one possibility.

Over the next 30 years, the effects of globalization on naval forces will be to expand the geostrategic and political-military requirement to influence events ashore. This requirement will extend well beyond seeking and winning command of the seas by sending enemy fleets to the bottom, and beyond projecting naval power on the littorals and nearby oceans in wartime. The peacetime use of naval force will matter more than simply keeping the ability to place ordnance on target in determining how this future evolves. Future naval operations will encompass conflict, crisis, and peace, and extend across the political-military spectrum from war to defense diplomacy and routine overseas presence. Responses will range from new forms of deterrence, prevention, and containment of dangers and potential threats to building political-military relationships and inroads in selected littoral states and with a broader array of governments and nongovernmental organizations.

This enhanced link with the shore will create a great tension. Naval forces, of course, will have to remain fully prepared in their core competence of fighting and winning the Nation's wars, as they have been since the Continental Navy and Marine Corps were created more than 200 years ago. But the spectrum of naval missions is broadening as new political-military operations gain greater frequency—for example, military operations other than war (MOOTW); law enforcement for combating terrorism, crime, and drug trafficking; humanitarian interventions such as that in Kosovo; peace operations. Even as this spectrum increases in width, traditional concerns are narrowing; for example, deterrence is becoming more selective and focused, and prevention of dangers, crises, and instability is being aimed at particular groups of state and nonstate actors. Iraq and North Korea fall into the first category; terrorists such as Osama bin Laden, into the latter.

The simultaneous broadening and focusing of certain tasks, coupled with the inherent tension between the demands of maintaining core competencies while conducting newer missions, have immediate consequences. Absent a major military threat, and in spite of the countervailing technological potential, the tensions between war fighting and influencing events ashore are likely to be made more pronounced by globalization. Owing to the new century's dynamics, wars likely will be fought and military force applied in different contexts and settings. The (unprecedented) intervention of the North Atlantic Treaty Organization (NATO) in Yugoslavia in 1999 is one such example. As national policies respond, naval forces will have to retain an inherent flexibility in concept and structure to accommodate the political and strategic demands. Regardless of whether military operations are unilateral, bilateral, or multilateral, naval forces will have to be prepared to respond to each challenge, perhaps with little warning time to prepare and rehearse.

As the strategic mission of affecting and influencing events ashore grows in importance, sailors and marines will need a bigger tool kit that will enable them to understand their roles and responsibilities. Seeking influence ashore will require naval forces to closely coordinate with other military services and agencies of government with national security responsibilities. The tools will extend beyond the familiar weapons of war (for example, satellites, bullets, bayonets) to include less familiar civilian tools. These include rendering humanitarian aid and assistance, training and educating foreign militaries, exploiting cyberspace and other commercial technologies, and building influence by promoting understanding and knowledge among countries and societies having the common bond of the sea. Fostering an effective synergy among these tools (and across services and departments) will require an extraordinary amount of training and education. In addition, understanding how to influence events ashore will require development of an effects-based and nodal analysis targeting methodology that focuses on political perceptions and will without necessarily having to resort to the traditional threat or use of force.

Even as naval forces become more adept at performing these new missions, they will have to master the demanding agenda of continuing to transform themselves internally. Contributing to this enterprise are the knowledge revolution and the people revolution, both of which are intensified by globalization. Whereas the former is greatly enhancing human intellectual capacities, the latter is empowering individuals and altering American society. Together, the two revolutions create opportunities and challenges for naval forces and their senior leadership to exploit. In order to deal with these concurrent revolutions, changes to doctrine, organization, training, and equipment will be mandatory. As the Navy adapts to changes ahead, one overarching challenge will be recruiting and retaining skilled personnel. Training and educating this cadre will be made more demanding by the changing demographic and vocational makeup of American society. Currently, the Department of Defense (DOD) is focusing on quality-of-life issues. While attending to them is necessary, this will be far from sufficient in confronting the demographic and vocational realities ahead. Future military systems will certainly be more technologically sophisticated, and every sign suggests that future military tasks will be broader. These realities will pose fundamental challenges in recruiting and retaining the necessary numbers of able people to man the units that will form tomorrow's naval forces.

In addition to maintaining extremely able people, naval forces will have to continue modernizing ships, aircraft, sensors, information systems, weapons, munitions, and other contributors to combat capability. While there may be no global military threat to U.S. interests for some time to come, the need to prepare for advanced military technology, information systems, and asymmetrical strategies capable of deployment against U.S. forces will be a critical priority. While tomorrow's naval forces will be performing new missions, including substantial transformation with a view to enhancing their own potential, these forces will have to retain a proficient fighting capability for the wars of tomorrow, and against the enemies of tomorrow, who doubtless will be better armed than those of today.

How U.S. naval forces are organized, provided for, trained, equipped, and used in a globalizing world will require fresh ideas, new perspectives, and innovative policies. These functions are the legal responsibility of DOD civilian and military leaders. Innovation is one of the intellectual scantlings on which the future course of the Department of the Navy is set. It is clearly the consensus of past and present naval leaders that the ability to embrace change is essential to dealing effectively with the changing security environment. The overwhelming challenge will be to understand what the new century will demand for and from national security strategy, and then to display the intellect and courage needed to examine alternative courses of action, including some that may seem radical or unconventional.

The findings, observations, and recommendations of this chapter are directed to the Secretary of the Navy and ordered according to the responsibilities for organizing, training, equipping, and providing for the forces as enumerated in Title 10 of the U.S. Code. The results are intended to help inform the debate about the Navy's future and to assist decisionmakers in determining future courses of action.

The Legacy of the Past

It can be argued that it is the inherent ability of naval forces to strategically and politically affect and influence events ashore that will matter most in a future that extends out perhaps as far as 2030 and in which globalization continues to exert great influence. Such an argument is justified by an understanding of how the role of naval forces has evolved since the first iron men went to sea in wooden ships and how the future naval forces of the United States are likely to be designed, manned, and employed. In practical terms for naval leadership, the main challenge will be in organizing, training, equipping, and providing for those forces in a future that will be decidedly different from that of today's setting. And this will of course require an understanding both of what is different about the impact of globalization and what remains valid from the lessons of the past.

A Changed Navy Role: Political Influence Born of Strategic Reach

For centuries, the principal purpose of naval forces was popularly perceived as resting in the ability of great men-of-war, called capital ships, to win command of the seas and oceans. Alfred Thayer Mahan, the godfather of sea power advocates, concluded on economic grounds that, in order to sustain growth, modern states would need access to colonies both for resources and for larger markets. In gaining access to, and control of, these colonies, states would come into conflict with other states embarked on similar missions. Navies would be needed to seize and defend colonies and foreign bases to ensure access and control and to destroy rival navies bent on doing the same. In this maritime competition, as envisaged by Mahan, great, decisive sea battles would be fought between capital ships to win command of the seas and control of the wide ocean commons.

Lesser navies, measured in the currency of those distant days, possessed fewer or inferior capital ships. Therefore, these weaker navies had no alternative but to attempt to deny command and control of the sea, to fight limited actions in which surprise or some other tactic could compensate for inherent weakness in capital ships and therefore in collective naval power, to concentrate on destroying commerce to impose a heavy economic price on hegemonic enterprise, or to serve a coastal defense role. But, as will be argued, the broader strategic and political utility of naval forces lay in the ability to affect and influence events ashore. Sinking enemy fleets and conducting combat operations at sea would ultimately prove relevant and successful only when those actions led to achieving the policy objectives of the war or conflict.

Technology encouraged and intensified this strategic relationship between naval forces and political objectives ashore. Modern air power and aircraft, electronic systems (for example, radio, radar), and the submarine redefined the meaning of naval strategy and tactics, and even that of the capital ship. Aviation was the classic example of extending the strategic reach of naval forces beyond the range of naval guns and therefore influencing events ashore from a greater distance. The Japanese believed that the surprise air attack against Pearl Harbor in 1941, while sending much of the Pacific fleet (temporarily) to the bottom, would shock the United States into passivity and inaction, allowing Japan freedom to expand its Greater East Asian Co-

Prosperity Sphere. Indeed, they were quite wrong. This event provoked just the opposite reaction, and the effects and influence were to catalyze the United States into declaring war and ultimately forcing Japan to accept unconditional surrender. In the aftermath of World War II, nuclear weapons, nuclear power, and intercontinental missiles would produce another revolution in politics and strategy that had profound implications for military and naval forces and that would reinforce the central importance of naval forces in affecting and influencing events ashore.

More from the Past: A Primer on Geopolitics and Naval Forces

From the days of Alfred the Great and the birth of the Royal Navy until today, why had the strategic, political, military, and operational value and virtue of naval forces inherently rested in their ability to affect and influence events ashore even though winning command of the seas was widely perceived as the core purpose? Why was the reality of naval operations more complex than the popular mythology? The reasons, relating to geography and society, are so obvious that they are often overlooked. Society is shore-based. The seas and oceans provide access to, and transport of, resources and peoples. The oceans are the broad commons on which the bulk of commerce flows. But the seas and oceans are transitory, in that they may be used but can never be permanently occupied. They are not the places and regions where people live, society functions, and political decisions are made. That is on land. Hence, naval forces are of strategic and political value only when their use has effect and influence on what happens ashore. If sinking enemy fleets is relevant to that purpose, then naval forces provide strategic value. A historical example is the destruction of Phillip II's great armada in 1588 by a combination of English "seadogs" and devastating Channel storms, saving England from invasion and possible occupation by Spain.

Naval forces can achieve effect and influence in various ways. Mahan, among many naval strategists, saw the threat of a direct attack to destroy a state's navy and its other means of defense, to impose an economic blockade, or to launch an invasion as the basis for naval power and strategy. The corollary was the notion of the superior fleet in being, with the implicit and potential power to bombard, invade, and inflict substantial damage on an adversary, thereby deterring or preventing specific actions by that adversary.

Still, naval commanders relished the prospect of scuttling an enemy fleet whether at sea or at anchor. Before the Battle of Copenhagen, Lord Nelson told his "band of brothers," "No captain can do wrong if he brings his ship alongside that of the enemy." Yet, when Nelson finally swept the combined Franco-Spanish fleet from the seas at the Battle of Trafalgar on October 21, 1805, Napoleon still fought on for another decade until he finally met defeat at the great land battle of Waterloo. The seas may have belonged to England, but it was the European continent on which victory or defeat would be determined.

Despite the attraction of commanding the seas, in fact, the seas were and are generally uncommanded. One side could use the seas if it avoided direct confrontation with its adversary and if time was not an important factor. The question to be answered is, "If command, then for what?" The "for what" is often forgotten. Yet it relates to influencing events ashore and projecting or applying naval power and force for political purposes of one kind or another. Interestingly, in its earliest days, because it possessed no true capital ships, the Navy limited its wartime roles to harassing enemy commerce and defending the coastlines (along with Army coastal artillery defense forces).

Mahan and Halford Mackinder collided over whether the great ocean commons or the heartland of Eurasia was the strategic center of greater gravity. Mackinder argued that whoever controlled the heartland of Eurasia would control the world. This was a land-centric, geopolitical formulation for strategy. The two competing strategic theories found homes and followers, and eventually there were attempts to put each into practice. The great sea battles and naval actions of World War I (despite the deep frustration of the Royal Navy in failing to sink the High Seas Fleet at Jutland in 1916) and of World War II were events that seemed to shift the argument in Mahan's favor. However, it was nuclear weapons that would dominate the strategic calculus of the second half of the last century, certainly for the United States and the Europe-centered world.

Nuclear and thermonuclear weapons transformed the strategic calculus for a simple reason. Their destructive power threatened the existence of society at large. A thermonuclear war between the Soviet Union and the United States could conceivably and very likely have destroyed both. For the first time in history, the prospect was real that there would be no distinction between winners and losers in a war. Avoidance of war had to be made the strategic priority. Deterrence was the foundation for strategy, even though the balances between offensive and defensive systems and between nuclear and conventional forces were hotly debated.

Of the consequences of the strategic nuclear revolution, two are relevant. First, the Cold War and the long nuclear standoff between the superpowers and their allies reaffirmed what mattered most. Deterrence required that the targets for effect and influence were political and resided in the various leaderships. The ambitions and intentions of the Soviet leaders in the Kremlin were to be contained. Allies and the American public became concerned, and occasionally frightened, if the Soviets seemed to be gaining or winning some advantage. Of course there was no quantitative measure of knowing with certainty what actually deterred and what did not. It took years to arrive at a state of mutual deterrence that was acceptable to both sides and that facilitated stability in the superpower relationships. Second, throughout this strategic stalemate, and perhaps because of it, the goal of commanding the seas became increasingly irrelevant, at least in actual practice.

During the Cold War, from Korea in 1950 through Vietnam two decades later, the October 1973 Middle East Crisis, the Yom Kippur War, and Operations *Desert Shield* and *Desert Storm* in 1990 and 1991, the fact was that the United States and its allies controlled (or commanded) the seas all of the time. But control did not guarantee success. In those conflicts, and despite its naval dominance, the United States won some and lost others. However, strategically, the theories of neither Mahan nor Mackinder were substantiated. Strategic, political, and operational considerations other than the importance of the oceans or the heartland, including limits on the use of force and the risk of nuclear escalation, produced the particular outcomes in Korea and Vietnam. Neither argument won. And, especially now, when there is no navy or naval force even on the distant horizon that could challenge that of the United States, a framework beyond that of Mahan and Mackinder is needed.

A Strategic Assessment for the Era of Globalization

Globalization might have little impact on U.S. naval forces if it were taking place only in the United States, Europe, and other continental land masses. But that is not the case. Indeed, globalization's dynamics are especially vigorous in regions dominated by oceans, islands, and littoral urban areas: Asia, the Mediterranean, the Greater Middle East and Persian Gulf, the Caribbean, and Latin America. The politics, economics, and security affairs of most of these regions are being transformed by globalization. Of special significance is that many of these are regions where U.S. naval forces operate and play a leading role in carrying out U.S. national security policy and defense strategy. The strategic challenge is twofold: adapting U.S. naval forces to new missions being created by globalization, *and using these forces to help guide globalization in ways that serve U.S. interests and goals.*

In these and other regions, key features of globalization are noteworthy because they create a framework for thinking about the potential contributions of U.S. naval forces. Globalization

- Is a relentless and mainly inexorable force largely driven by the knowledge revolution and the people revolution.
- Is likely to have profound effects on virtually every state and society.
- Is uneven and uncertain in impact, and difficult to predict.
- Creates forces of both integration and disintegration.
- Expands strategic reach in both breadth and scope.
- Blurs and bypasses political, economic, legal, and cultural boundaries.
- Creates new security challenges that are horizontal in nature, cutting across many boundaries, and challenges structured international institutions, national governments, and other bodies for vertical solutions.

What should be the basis for an assessment of the role of naval forces in an era of globalization? As much as any symbol of globalization, the ubiquitous Golden Arches of McDonald's provide a starting point for an alternative strategic construct. That the staples of the American diet—cheeseburgers and french fries—are becoming parts of the global diet is no longer a surprise. A similar ubiquity cuts across the commercial world, providing American products and culture extraordinary, and not always welcomed, access around the world. Globalization is transforming international, regional, and local economies. Ownership, access, and the flow of business, commerce, and finance have been redefined in this new, dynamic global economy.

The realities of the global economy must be assimilated as part of the new security environment. For nearly a century after Mahan, economic dependence on the seas and oceans for trade and commerce was absolute. Over 95 percent of all trade and overseas commerce was by sea, for the simple reason that other forms of transportation were too costly and uneconomical. This situation became one of the prime contributors to the argument that naval forces should be used to protect sea-lanes from interruption and otherwise help promote economic stability. But the effects of globalization have transformed the relevant economic factors of the past. In gross tonnage and total volume, sea-borne trade is still dominant. Yet in terms of dollars and other assets that express wealth, today's financial transactions flow through electronic networks and the ether of the atmosphere, whether by landlines or satellites. In terms of commercial wealth and dollar value, cyberspace has eclipsed Mahan's ocean commons. It is unclear how cyberspace can be protected by military forces in the manner that navies once stood astride ocean sea-lanes, keeping safe the oil, goods, and food that sailed from state to state and from continent to continent.

Another consequence is that the equation for access is changing. Ensuring access to economic resources has always been a significant rationale for military forces, especially naval power. There has been an enduring need for access—to oil, natural gas, bases, allies, adversaries, and key regions—and for keeping navigation unfettered and maintaining overall freedom of the seas. But all the military forces in the world had no leverage or effect in maintaining access to Persian Gulf oil in 1973–1974, when the Organization of Petroleum Exporting Countries (OPEC) cut the flow of oil to the United States. Today, with gasoline selling at $2.00 per gallon, military power will not reverse that hike. The new reality is that currency flows, devaluations, and devastating speculation can close access to markets in the time it takes to move money electronically. Military forces cannot be used to buffer or constrain these financial flows and transactions. Globalization has created economic transactions that overshadow access and that cannot be countered with military power or other usual instruments of national policy.

The Mahanian economic argument for naval forces no longer applies in a period when there is no major danger to sea-lanes, and military force cannot be used to deal with the new electronic means of economic transactions. Naval forces are likely to have an indirect role in ensuring that the economic conditions for stability and prosperity are protected. But it will not only be sea-lanes and ocean commons that will have to be protected, certainly for the short term, for there are many littoral dangers, including piracy, mines, and cruise missiles. The indirect role resides in the underlying capacity for projecting force in ways that reassure friends and perhaps restrain those with unfriendly intentions. Building military-to-military relationships, especially with states for which the military serves as a guarantor of stability, will also reinforce this assurance.

Beyond this, globalization is occurring in a world with many middling or smaller powers that have little ability or desire to challenge the United States in a face-to-face military confrontation or take on the Navy and Marine Corps on the high seas and littorals. Happily, for the time being, global wars are of historical and not current concern. Moreover, the prospect for major regional wars may be waning. A new peer-rival to the United States could emerge in the distant future, but not tomorrow. Despite the continuing presence of Saddam Hussein and North Korea, plus a nuclearized South Asia, the reality is that other conventional threats have diminished. In their stead, a new or different type of danger loosely termed asymmetrical has emerged. This term suggests that future adversaries most likely will seek to avoid a direct clash with the United States by using indirect means to obtain their objectives. These instruments could include information or cyberspace war, or biological and other WMDs, backed by long-range missiles—in essence, responding outside the rules to extract force multiplier strategies. These new and more relevant threats arise as much from uncertainty about the impact of change as from well-armed and technologically capable states that wish the United States ill. This faceless, diaphanous nature of security in a globalized world will pose challenges that are more perplexing than those of the past, although of lesser absolute danger.

Irrespective of specific military threats and any consensus on what this term implies for specific policies, the political leadership of the United States still regards and considers the Nation as the sole remaining superpower. This position implies unique capabilities and worldwide responsibilities that make isolationism both impractical and unlikely. These responsibilities entail responding to so-called asymmetrical threats, mounting humanitarian interventions, and shaping the strategic environment to encourage stability. Political pressures forcing U.S. military forces into law enforcement roles are also growing. Countering terrorism and drug trafficking are two of the better known activities. Countering the proliferation of nuclear, chemical, and biological weapons also has a strong law enforcement component.

As globalization continues to impose change and transformation, these fresher, nontraditional tasks seemingly are emerging as the newest drivers for determining where, how, and how often U.S. military forces are likely to be used in the future. If so, perhaps the most interesting and perplexing question for the long term will be how the core competencies required for fighting and winning big wars, which have been the traditional drivers of force structure and doctrine, will be balanced with these other less traditional and non-warfighting missions. The task of quantifying and measuring military threats in order to set requirements for U.S. forces and capabilities will be more difficult than in the past. The impact of globalization on an already changing world will pose a major challenge for DOD in identifying and justifying the forces that the Nation is likely to need.

What does this strategic assessment mean for the Nation's naval forces? The critical challenge during the 20th century was to deter, fight, and win the Nation's wars on the high seas and littorals. In the early 21st century, absent a maritime rival, there will not be wars, or even big military rivalries, on the high seas. The most pressing new challenge will be to work with other military services and U.S. agencies to prevent potential instabilities, threats, and enemies from becoming actual dangers to U.S. and allied interests. Former Secretary of Defense William J. Perry has called this "preventative defense." If prevention and containment of conflict, instability, and other dangers have become drivers of defense planning, the key challenge for the Navy and Marine Corps and other services will be determining how to use military forces to affect and influence those events ashore that have an important bearing on U.S. interests and goals. Applying power ashore for new era purposes thus will be a principal subject on the strategic agenda.

Future Naval Missions: How to Influence Events Ashore

Charting the future course begins by understanding the legal basis for DOD and Navy authority in building and operating military forces. The Law of the Land, explicit in Title 10 of the U.S. Code and the National Security Act of 1947, sets responsibility for conducting "prompt and sustained combat incident to operations at sea" as the legal and operational basis for naval forces. Whereas during the Cold War the Navy and the Marine Corps mostly operated as individual and separate services under the Department of the Navy, today they operate as a single composite team. Moreover, great emphasis is being placed on joint planning in order to integrate the efforts of all four services. The actual employment of forces from all services is the responsibility of the Secretary of Defense, the Chairman of the Joint Chiefs of Staff, and the commanders in chief (CINCs) of the various services. But organizing, training, equipping, and otherwise providing for naval forces is the legal responsibility and authority of DON and its secretary. DON prepares the budgets, programs, and investment strategies for building the naval and marine forces of today and tomorrow.

The Navy is manned with about 543,000 active duty sailors and marines, plus about 130,000 uniformed reservists, and 190,000 civilians. In the 2001 DOD budget, the Navy receives about $92 billion that must be allocated among military personnel; operations and maintenance; procurement; research, development, testing, and evaluation; and other categories. Guiding this spending not only each year but also over extended periods of 5 and 10 years is a big and important challenge. An interesting issue will be whether the legal authority of the Navy Department under Title 10 and related Federal directives should be expanded to take greater account of non-wartime missions and operations. In any event, clarity on missions and priorities is key to charting the future wisely.

What are the Navy's missions? In 1970, Admiral Zumwalt defined four general missions: deterrence, sea control, power projection, and presence. While these missions often were recast and redefined to reflect the outlook of particular administrations and naval leaders, they remain valid for today and tomorrow. But in contrast with the Cold War, the priorities and means for accomplishing these missions have been greatly transformed. Because deterrence and sea control are now more certain today than then, emphasis has shifted to new variants of power projection and peacetime presence to support U.S. interests.

Deterrence has shifted from managing the nuclear standoff between the superpowers. Applying deterrence against weaker but potentially hostile states, such as Iraq, will require more thought. Here the notion of preventive deterrence may fit. Preventing, as opposed to deterring, suggests a proactive strategy that requires more than the threat of overwhelming retaliation. Sea control has become a lesser mission—one that is part of littoral warfare and projecting power, along with antimine, antimissile, and antisubmarine warfare in confined sea areas. Until a major maritime threat emerges, sea control will have less importance. Similarly, projecting power is mutating. Preparing to project naval power during wartime will remain a central planning task. But this mission can no longer be defined solely in terms of strikes against the shores with missiles or marines. The notion of power has been extended to what Professor Joseph Nye of Harvard has called "soft power," that is, the use of nonmilitary, nonforceful instruments of policy to achieve preferred outcomes.

As for "hard power" missions, the Navy seemingly will acquire new responsibilities as the United States moves to deploy ballistic missile defense systems in the coming years. A particular Navy responsibility will be to take part in the construction of theater air and missile defenses (TAMDs) for protecting deployed U.S. and allied forces, as well as allied countries needing protection from WMD proliferation. Currently, the Navy has two TAMD systems under development: a lower tier Navy area defense system and an upper tier Navy theaterwide program. The idea is to fit defensive missiles aboard different classes of surface warships and submarines, thereby providing considerable mobility for quickly concentrating defense screens at places of critical importance. The Navy's role in any future national missile defense program will depend on the technologies fielded. In addition, the United States will be taking steps to upgrade its homeland defenses against terrorism, attacks on its information systems, and other threats. The Navy will be playing roles in these efforts, which likely will have a significant impact on all four services. If homeland defense and missile defense emerge as growing national security concerns, the reach of naval forces in other than a defensive capacity may become important—for example, their capacity to threaten retaliation and pre-emptive attacks.

Presence is perhaps the mission that will be the most completely redefined, and the most useful. The Navy regularly keeps three carrier battle groups and amphibious ready groups deployed in the Mediterranean Sea, the Persian Gulf, and the Asia-Pacific region. In addition, nearly a full marine division is stationed on Okinawa. Periodically, other naval and marine units deploy overseas to meet shifting demands for presence. There and elsewhere, the purpose of naval presence is not only to provide readily available options for crisis response but also to influence peacetime political and military affairs. Presence implies the ability to support the role of affecting and influencing, provided it is done in ways that will achieve those aims. Doing so will require new or at least more intensive and rigorous analytical approaches to understanding the limits of what can and cannot be achieved through various forms of presence.

For some time to come, it is unlikely that naval forces will have to fight great sea battles such as those of the past or conduct sweeping assaults on enemy beaches. However, the strategic reach of naval forces in peacetime will become more global, extending to political and economic relationships that traditionally were viewed as nonstrategic and entirely commercial. *One result is that the very presence of naval forces in distant parts of the globe can contribute to economic and political stability, and in ways that serve to significantly facilitate peace, prosperity, and progress.* In the coming years, then, the act of influencing events ashore will involve shaping not only the geopolitics of key regions but also their economic dynamics. There must be a sufficient understanding of how to employ naval forces to achieve these ends. Developing this understanding is becoming one of the central challenges of the future, and meeting that challenge will profoundly change the qualitative face of naval forces. *The relationship between naval forces and economic and political stability, and even peace and progress, could become the basis for a new strategic rationale for, and realignment of, naval missions.*

Effects-based targeting and nodal analysis are useful methods for assessing how naval forces can be used to influence events ashore. While effects-based targeting was discredited in the 1960s as part of the failed strategy of gradual escalation in Vietnam, it has since become part of the planning process for wartime operations. Its core idea is that instead of destroying an entire target system or complex, a bombing campaign should focus on disabling key nodes and subelements in ways that have identical effects at the cost of far fewer sorties. Knocking out a single, largely irreplaceable transformer or junction box can have the same effect as destroying an entire power generation facility. Hence, nodal analysis is crucial to deriving the basis for targeting. A generation ago, effects-based targeting was hard to carry out because U.S. aircraft lacked the capacity to deliver ordnance with the necessary accuracy. But the arrival of smart munitions has made it a far more feasible proposition. Indeed, it has produced not only greater lethality and effectiveness but also a need for fewer aircraft and personnel in carrying out air bombardment missions.

The emerging need is to broaden effects-based targeting for use also in peacetime, specifically, for the purpose of influencing political events ashore. Just as munitions are employed to strike military targets in wartime, naval forces are employed in peacetime and individual crises for the purpose of achieving political and economic goals. By learning how to employ them in highly focused ways, on the targets that matter, the United States should be able to gain more mileage and effectiveness out of its naval forces and other military assets when they are employed in such missions. An added benefit will be to help reduce the currently growing pressures for committing greater amounts of military personnel to such missions as peacekeeping, law enforcement, humanitarian assistance, defense diplomacy, and others. The key point is that effects-based targeting can improve the effectiveness and efficiency of political and diplomatic missions of U.S. naval forces.

Regardless of the specific approach used, the act of understanding how to employ U.S. military forces to shape the political will and perceptions of foreign actors at a variety of levels will be of critical importance in the 21st century. In all likelihood, transition to the use of naval forces in this way will require changes in how they are organized, trained, and equipped. It also will require the adoption of new intellectual and operational approaches. What will be needed is a new mentality and way of thinking that goes beyond traditional war fighting and its professional skills.

Learning how to influence events ashore in a world committed to globalization will have even greater implications for how the U.S. Government makes foreign policy and carries out its efforts overseas. A key effect of globalization is that boundaries between states, business corporations, NGOs, and other institutions are blurring. This development makes it harder for all of them to operate independently in their once separate spheres of activity. To a great degree, they must now take each other into account and often coordinate their activities with one another. Government institutions in particular face trouble adjusting because they normally are organized vertically to preside over limited spheres of activity rather than to integrate policies across several functional areas. The institutions that worked during the Cold War were not configured to fit this globalizing world either internationally or nationally. This particularly applies to the United States because its global involvements and multiple policy instruments, as noted by Ellen L. Frost in her chapter, create a greater need to think on an integrated basis while magnifying the negative consequences of failing to do so. Reorganizing staffs and operations both in Washington and in the field likely will be needed if U.S. foreign policy and national security strategy are to handle the pressures *and opportunities* of exerting strategic influence in a globalizing world.

Transforming the Naval Forces

The Navy's current size of about 320 warships is partly a product of history. In 1970, when Admiral Zumwalt became Chief of Naval Operations, the Nation's naval forces numbered more than 900 ships, most of them of World War II vintage and designed for threats and dangers of the past. DOD had over three million troops in uniform, more than double the number in service today, and its budget commanded six percent of the gross domestic product (GDP). The war in Vietnam was destroying the Nation, and the Nixon administration was beginning a slow drawdown under the banner of Vietnamization of that war by assigning more responsibility to the local forces.

Zumwalt reached several conclusions. First, he believed that the war was causing a crisis over race within the Navy that, if unchecked, could destroy the service. Second, he concluded that the Navy had to be modernized if it was to deal with the emerging Soviet threat. And third, he calculated correctly that the Nation had the time to make this transition. As a result, Zumwalt was able to cut the size of the Navy nearly in half, thereby freeing up additional resources for modernization. He also put in place controversial personnel policies to cope with what he saw as the largest and most immediate threat to the Navy: racism and prejudice.

Ten years later, in the waning days of the Carter administration, the Navy stood at about 480 warships, including 13 aircraft carriers, 188 surface combatants, 79 attack submarines, and 66 amphibious ships. In response to what seemed to be a growing Soviet threat, the Carter administration began, and the incoming Reagan administration expanded, a huge defense buildup in 1981 that included an ambitious shipbuilding program to reach a goal of 600 ships and 15 aircraft carriers. The goal of a 600-ship navy was never attained, but, a decade later and by the end of the Cold War, the fleet numbered 580 warships. Subsequently, both the Bush and Clinton administrations conducted reductions in forces, reducing active duty levels to about 1 to 1.4 million service personnel[1] and the following battle force ships (projection for 2001):

Ballistic missile submarines	18
Aircraft carriers	12
Attack submarines	55
Surface combatants	116
Amphibious ships	40
Mine warfare ships	16
Logistics force ships/support forces	59
Total	**316**

Today's total force ostensibly is sized to support overseas presence as well as to carry out two major theater wars (MTWs) nearly simultaneously. Higher force levels for each of the services will be approved only if a serious new threat emerges. But no such threat is foreseeable either at sea or elsewhere for at least the coming decade. For the following reasons, the 10-year rule once followed by the British government could become a good rule of thumb for gauging future force levels.

- This is about the length of time for a new threat to emerge and for a counter to be put in place.
- DOD is in a procurement cycle that emphasizes modernization, not greater force levels, but a cycle that is substantially underfunded.
- Today's shipbuilding program for the coming 5 years includes 39 ships, 17 of them combatants. Given a warship's life expectancy of 35 years, this plan is headed toward a 200- or 250-ship navy at best unless the shipbuilding plan is considerably augmented or life expectancy lengthened.

Although the DOD budget is edging upward, it remains around 3 percent of GDP. And much of this increase is largely to offset inflation, so its significance should be kept in perspective. Where the Nation will be in regard to its security and military force structure in 30 years is not knowable. If the current focus and resource expenditures on law enforcement and humanitarian missions (for example, Yugoslavia) continue, and the need for war fighting does not increase, then a straight-line projection from 1970 through 2000 to 2030 establishes a bottom line for a future level of defense capability and spending at around 2 percent of GDP. At that level, DOD resources would include less than 1 million active duty servicemen and a Navy and Marine Corps of perhaps 200 to 250 ships or less organized around 10 to 15 battle groups and amphibious forces. Of course, a threat or a crisis could arise and change the Nation's course, mandating a larger force. Or, assuming the Federal budget and spending practices permit, the Nation may choose to keep the current posture indefinitely. The future is uncertain, but the full range of possibilities needs to be kept in mind in gauging how the Navy should prepare for the coming era.

The key to keeping well-prepared naval forces is no longer strictly through enhancing quality and ensuring greater ability to perform future missions. Better quality can be achieved partly by buying new weapon systems, munitions, and command, control, communications, computers, intelligence, surveillance, and reconnaissance (C^4ISR) systems. But something more profound and underlying applies. The differences between naval forces of today and well into the future may not be defined in terms of platforms. There will still be aircraft carriers and sleek aircraft, guided missile cruisers and destroyers, submarines, and versatile amphibious ships, although of far higher quality. Instead, the main difference will be their missions, their uses, and the impact of knowledge that will bring about a profound, qualitative transformation. It is with the serving people—sailors, marines, and civilian employees—that this transformation and the influence of the knowledge revolution will have its greatest impact.

Exactly what is meant by the knowledge revolution and the people revolution? As seen by many, the knowledge revolution can be defined as the creation, during this century, of more new knowledge than has been generated in all of human history. Consider that in the last 100 years, new knowledge has produced such inventions as penicillin, the artificial heart, automobiles, airplanes, nuclear power, jet and rocket propulsion, radio and television, the computer, the Internet, and air conditioning. The Human Genome Mapping Project and molecular and distributed computing are leading examples of the potential for greater advances and the extraordinary impact that these knowledge-driven advances will hold for humankind. The consequences are beyond comprehension. How all this extraordinary knowledge will be put to use remains a penetrating question. To cite one example of the prospects ahead, computing power will be orders of magnitude greater than now, and it will be essentially free of cost. Putting this capacity to work will provide opportunities that simply have not been thought about yet, and they will be mind-bending. The knowledge revolution is taking place mostly in the scientific community and the commercial sector, but it will affect the defense arena as well, creating changes that will be no less profound than those brought about by the nuclear era.

The people revolution can be defined in terms of changing attitudes, capabilities, needs, and expectations of American society. It is the consequence of two factors. One is the extraordinary empowerment of individuals in terms of how they live their lives, and the second is the changing demographics of American society. Creativity and productivity have been enhanced. Access to ideas, information, and the means of making a living have been opened and expanded. In all modern states, social and cultural norms—reflecting work, values, education, and rewards—are being redefined to keep pace with these changes in empowerment. Concurrently, demographic and vocational patterns are changing dramatically. In the United States, people will live longer, perhaps marry and have children later, and both spouses likely will work. People may hold dozens of jobs, not just one or a few, during their careers. The Nation is also graying, and several of today's ethnic minorities will become future majorities in major cities and regions. Given these extraordinary changes, the military services will have to adjust, perhaps in ways that are seen today as revolutionary, in order to attract, recruit, retain, reward, train, and educate the future military cohorts.

Empowered by technology and free markets, people are the creators of the knowledge revolution and the whirlwind of globalization. In addition to the freedom, flexibility, and opportunity created by the knowledge revolution, people have become more valuable as resources, if such a distinction exists. Consider a few of the implications for naval personnel in recruitment, manning, and retention. Given the reduced manning needs of new ships such as the Elmo Zumwalt class of destroyers (the DD–21), the problems of recruiting large numbers of sailors for shipboard duty may be lessened. However, there is a more difficult side to the personnel issue. Fewer sailors may be needed, but they will have to be highly intelligent, well educated, and superbly trained to operate the advanced systems of the future. How can such people be recruited and kept on active duty long enough to justify the costs of training them over a period of many months or longer? Will tomorrow's personnel need to be older and more experienced than now? How will this need square with the reality that for most enlisted people and many officers, military service is performed at a young age and lasts only a few years? If tomorrow's sailors are older, will they be equally able to handle the rigors and stresses of military life, which commonly are regarded as being best experienced at a young age? Indeed, how do the services deal with the personnel cohort when average life expectancies approach 100 years? What happens when people hold perhaps 20 completely different jobs during their careers, and work until their 70s, 80s, and even 90s? What happens when working spouses and married couples delay childbearing into middle age and beyond? Each of these issues will have profound consequences for how naval forces are recruited, trained, manned, organized, and retained.

The crucial and exciting challenge will be that of blending the knowledge and people revolutions with new military technologies in order to produce the transformed force of tomorrow. Clearly, this transformation should aim at enhancing the combat power of the Navy and Marine Corps, and at strengthening their capacity to contribute to CINC war plans. In all likelihood, the Navy and Marine Corps will play the critical role of providing a highly mobile force that can be deployed quickly in a crisis, especially to littoral areas that lack prepared bases and infrastructure. They may be called upon to lead the way in halting enemy aggression so that later arriving U.S. forces from other services have the time and opportunity to deploy. Even after all U.S. forces are fully deployed, the Navy and the Marine Corps will provide a major portion of the joint force's total combat power and thereby will contribute importantly to its ability to strike precisely, maneuver in dominating ways, support its operations leanly, and protect itself from enemy attack.

In addition to enhancing combat power, transformation must address how to enhance the capacity to exert political influence ashore during peacetime. There will have to be organizational and institutional changes beginning at the national level and working their way down to small units in the field. Unified commands will require more knowledge and information about how to deal with the local political and economic affairs of each region. Perhaps mini-National Security Council staffs will be created that reflect the cross-cutting nature of issues in each region. Such staffs might be installed at the unified and specified commands. For naval forces, operational commanders at the numbered fleet, fleet Marine force, and even battle group may need such staffs. Regardless of the exact staff arrangements, much of the necessary analysis will be done at the regional and local levels. This means that foreign area experts, officers and enlisted, will be needed—the kind now being provided by the Navy and the Marine Corps through expansion of their foreign area officer programs. With improved data and knowledge, there will have to be modeling, simulation, experiments, and exercises to test and challenge the various ways to exert influence and pursue national goals. The key point is that the act of exerting influence should receive as much analytical attention as fighting wars.

For military and political reasons, naval deployments also are likely to change. Alternatives should be investigated now. Permanently deploying ships, aircraft, and submarines is a possibility, as is using rotating crews. Going to cruising squadrons and deployment on warning are other options. Altering port visits in order to increase time ashore is another attractive idea, for it could help enhance influence. Naval leaders also should consider assigning far more officers and enlisted men to foreign states as advisors, observers, ship's company, or staff aids in order to build up the interchange among militaries. Over time, expertise in foreign affairs could become as important to promotion as joint duty has been in the Goldwater-Nichols era.

If current trends continue, the integration of ship's companies with marines and Coast Guard personnel, and perhaps airmen and soldiers too, may make sense as a way to increase the Navy's capacity for its new missions. On a frigate or destroyer, a reinforced platoon of marines as ship's company or a unit of Coast Guard personnel could become the standard. These personnel would be trained for law enforcement, intervention, and other tasks that may require the equivalent of landing the landing force to protect U.S. citizens and friends in hostile areas. While the Reserve component forces are used differently by the Navy and Marine Corps than by the Army, options for employing them effectively should be examined. In the future, new ships that replace both the aircraft carrier and the amphibious assault ship, as well as other old ships in service, could have this mixed manning scheme. Future crews might include a blend of active, Reserve, and virtual members from the other services. Two centuries ago, marines were stationed onboard Navy ships in rather large numbers. The past here may become prologue.

The consequences for platforms and force structure are still in the formative stages. Clearly, improved information and knowledge systems will result with or without the help of globalization. It is the volume and carrying capacity of ships rather than specific systems that could become more important as the spectrum of missions broadens. Each battle group might be task-fitted for particular missions and even trained en route to the region of interest. If the wartime capacity of naval forces increases greatly in lethality and battlefield punch, as appears likely, logic suggests that fewer units and fewer personnel will be needed in many contingencies. Assuming this holds true, will the bureaucratic and political process permit this type of rational planning to take hold? This is a question that applies with equal relevance across the other services and DOD as a whole.

Globalization also has important consequences for the defense industrial base inherited from earlier times. Largely composed of private companies that sell goods and services to the armed services, the defense industrial base is in the midst of a major transformation and compression. The public- or government-owned components—national laboratories, research and development establishments, and supporting infrastructure—are also vast. In many ways, they have become competitors with the private sector for scarce resources. Owing to shrinking budgets, the past decade has seen the defense industrial base shrink from about a dozen large aerospace and defense companies down to basically four: Lockheed Martin, Boeing-McDonnell Douglas, Northrop Grumman, and Raytheon. The maritime industries, for both defense and commerce, have been compressed and reduced even more so. To a degree, what happened to the American civilian maritime industry—the private shipping companies and shipbuilding yards—is instructive. Since the 1980s, the United States has not had a commercial fleet flying under its flag, and its shipyards build almost solely for the Navy and the Department of Defense. For the entire defense industry, the growing risk is that there will not be enough demand and money to buy ships, aircraft, and other major platforms to sustain even the current capacity.

For defense industries, it will be the production of components and subsystems of platforms that sustain them and that play a lead role in determining the modernization of U.S. forces. Especially for information technology, globalization is spreading the numbers of private sector, nondefense firms that could become capable of producing such subsystems for defense. Given the restrictions of law, regulations, oversight, and profit limits, however, many of these nondefense firms will have no incentive to work for the government. For their part, the current defense firms are so dependent on a few huge projects—for example, the F–22, the Joint Strike Fighter, and the SSN–21 submarine—that they will have little flexibility to shift to other lines and products. For these reasons, the defense industry faces a troubled future. Guiding it to a safe landing will be difficult, but this is a task that must be done, for a globalizing world will be one in which high technology counts for a lot, especially in the military arena.

The Distant Future: Few Big Wars, Many Other Missions?

Clearly, a major military and naval transformation will occur. The process by which this transformation is unfolding can be portrayed in distinct terms. But what is the ultimate destination: not necessarily the size of the Nation's naval forces, but the qualitative characteristics and mission orientation? What kind of naval forces should emerge: not just in 5 to 10 years, but in the longer term, 20 to 30 years from now, when the transformation will be complete? Peering into the distant future is a precarious exercise, but it also can be an instructive way to help think about how U.S. naval forces are evolving.

A good way to begin is by asking this question: If Mahan and Mackinder were alive today, what might they predict that the Navy would do or look like in 30 years' time? An admiral in Mahan's day, circa 1910, would not have been shocked to see the fleet in 1940, with its battleships and subsequent island-hopping strategy against Japan. While he might have been surprised by the role of carriers, submarines, and amphibious operations, he would have adjusted quickly. An admiral of 1940 would have been shocked, however, by the Navy of 1970. While he might recognize the silhouettes of some ships, he would have been astonished by jet aircraft, missiles, nuclear weapons, operational patterns, and even the Navy's personnel and culture. How might an admiral of today react if he or she were to be granted a preview of the Navy of 2030? The question is unanswerable, but because so many changes are occurring in technology, geopolitics, and other arenas, the outer reaches of possibility should be kept in mind in trying to judge where the Navy may be headed in the coming decades.

Three possible scenarios illuminate different directions in which the future might evolve in response to globalization and other dynamics. At one extreme is a world made quite stable, peaceful, and prosperous by the positive and integrative forces of globalization. Some conflict and violence would exist, but would be mostly contained to minor or local levels, and the prospect of world war among developed states would be virtually unimaginable. At the other extreme is a world torn apart by globalization. This is a competitive world, as Mahan might have predicted, in which states compete over territory and resources. In this more contested world, the emergence of a rival peer or coalition to challenge the United States, and thus the potential for serious war, would remain a persistent threat. Between these two extremes is a world in which globalization has brought about both positive benefits and negative backlashes. In this third scenario, the interconnectivity of markets, communications, commerce, and finance would make many countries prosperous, but also would produce painful dislocations, widening the gap between haves and have-nots. Global wars between developed countries would be highly unlikely in this third scenario, and even the likes of today's major regional wars would be reduced in frequency. But a great deal of conflict and violence still would exist in unstable areas, as would other dangers such as WMD proliferation, asymmetrical threats, ethnic turmoil, humanitarian catastrophes, terrorism, and organized crime.

Each of these worlds could mandate a quite different U.S. national security strategy and require naval forces to perform different missions. In today's parlance of shaping, responding, and preparing, the first world of fewer and lesser threats would require naval forces to focus on preparing and shaping in order of priority, with little responding. The second world, of greater chaos and danger than now, would require naval forces to respond and shape, with little time left over to prepare for the future. In the third world of mixed geostrategic trends, shaping would emerge as the priority mission, with responding and preparing as subordinate, coequal tasks. In this world, naval and all U.S. military forces might not have major regional wars that they could single out as a clear justification for defense planning. But they would have many demands on their hands in terms of humanitarian missions, broad law enforcement, homeland defense, peacetime shaping and defense diplomacy, and low-level crisis intervention.

In the first world, the demand for naval and other forces would be significantly lower than it is today. Defense forces would be focused on traditional war fighting as insurance against some future threat or contingency. But they would be a less used instrument of national policy, presumably assuming detached roles similar to those of the 1920s and early 1930s. In the second world, the demand for U.S. forces might be as great or even greater than now if China, Russia, or some large coalition emerges as an adversary. Regardless of their size, they would be focused on fighting major wars, not performing peacekeeping and intervening in small crises. In many ways, the third world, in the middle of the spectrum, is the most interesting for, and demanding of, the services—for reasons that go beyond its ready plausibility (it would, after all, represent a less tense extrapolation of today's world). This is a world in which military force would still play an important role, but budgets would be tight in ways that imposed difficult trade-offs and choices. There would be no overarching threat on which to base claims for money and capabilities, but there would be many challenging missions creating a broader spectrum of demand on the services' skill and competence. They would need to remain prepared for war fighting—most likely a single MTW at a time—and, simultaneously, for a wide range of lesser missions that could have a substantial cumulative impact on the military's time, attention, and scarce resources.

The political-military geography of such a world is instructive. In contrast to the Cold War, Europe would no longer be a zone of political confrontation and conflict with the ever-present threat of nuclear war. Instead, Europe likely would become a zone of peace, brought together by globalization and the European Union, and carrying out business-like relations with Russia. East Asia likely would turn out to be a zone of political and economic stability in ways encouraged by globalization. Korea likely would have unified, Japan would continue its constructive ties with the United States and other democracies, and China would be less authoritarian and integrated into the world economy, pursuing a modus vivendi with Taiwan. Overall, the Middle East and Persian Gulf likely would be less tense than now, with Iraq remaining a pariah, but Iran pursuing a moderate path and integration with the globalizing world economy, and the Arab-Israeli conflict largely settled.

If the three most important geostrategic regions seem likely to be made more stable by globalization, where will the zones of chaos and instability lie? One unstable zone will be the Balkans and the oil-rich Caucasus-Caspian Sea region. South Asia will remain troubled by Indian-Pakistani rivalry, WMD proliferation, religious fundamentalism, and backlash against globalization. Partly owing to its inability to profit from globalization, sub-Saharan Africa seems destined to become the Balkans of the early 21st century, torn apart by political incompetence, poverty, disease, and conflicts over resources in ways necessitating regular outside help and intervention. In Latin America, the combination of uneven economic development and a narco-technical culture could lead to greater threats to the northern tier, particularly the Andean states and parts of Central America drawn into drug trafficking. Mexico could become nearly ungovernable, resulting in refugees and illegal immigration posing a crisis for the United States.

Clearly, this global scenario could evolve in many ways far different than portrayed here, with some regions becoming unstable and others succumbing to more extreme forms of violence and chaos. But the point is that this scenario, irrespective of exactly how it unfolds, could produce a future in which conflict and violence will not automatically disappear. In the world of 2030, globalization will produce challenges and demands for ensuring security that may well be far broader and more complicated than now. Progress will be made by the inexorable spread of the rule of law, accepted commercial standards of conduct, and greater emphasis on humanitarian issues. While pursuit of peace, stability, and progress will become the goal of most states, there will remain a wide divergence of opinion about specific ends and the means to achieve them. As a consequence, U.S. military forces could be stressed by new challenges and requirements, as well as by the constraints on resources in the absence of a major new threat or danger.

How will the U.S. military be affected as a whole, especially if the future produces a world in which concern about big war is less prevalent than now, but demands grow for using forces to deal with a wide variety of other tasks—for example, handling messy local situations, building partnerships with new countries, and reassuring others of their security? While this scenario is not certain, thinking about its likely impact is instructive. Clearly, the U.S. military will need to remain capable of fighting major regional wars, but most likely not two at the same time. Through changes in technology and doctrine, front-line personnel requirements for waging such conflicts seem likely to decline. This is the case because modern weapons will make U.S. combat forces more lethal and mobile, and because the modern battlefield itself is spreading out, becoming less dense.

In this world, however, the widening spectrum of other missions seems likely to become more personnel-intensive and resource-demanding. Whether interdicting Liberian drug runners at sea, providing forces on the ground for stability in Central Asia, or pursuing an upsurge of partnership activities in multiple regions, the daily chores of the U.S. military will become less susceptible to technological fixes while requiring more manpower. As personnel with these skills become increasingly difficult to recruit and retain, pressures will grow to reduce the numbers committed solely to warfighting missions. Especially if the U.S. defense posture contracts below the current level, striking a sound balance between manpower levels for warfighting and levels for these other missions will be a difficult management challenge.

To the extent that this scenario transpires, all services seem likely to be affected by the accompanying challenges and by the need to alter their force structures. The Army is designed almost totally for fighting two MTWs; its 10 active divisions, support assets, and multiple Reserve component forces are organized in ways that provide few assets and personnel for the nontraditional missions that may lie ahead. While it is trying to become more mobile and agile, it likely will be pushed in the direction of making broader reforms in order to align itself with future requirements in a world of fewer wars, but many other missions. The Air Force faces similar constraints, for its own forces are oriented to carrying out traditional warfighting missions: air defense, tactical support, interdiction, and strategic bombardment. It will be able to perform some new missions, but not the full spectrum of them. How these two services will cope with their future challenges remains to be seen. What does seem apparent is that while the Navy and Marine Corps are not fully prepared, they are the best situated to deal with the new environment and the role of influencing events ashore by performing the new missions. The Marine Corps has the necessary focus on expeditionary missions, with light and agile, but potent, forces. Naval forces have the mobility and flexibility to deploy to many places, to influence the critical littoral areas, and to organize regional security affairs around cooperative maritime concepts, in ways reflecting NATO's Partnership for Peace. Working as a team, the Navy and Marine Corps have the mobility, agility, and lethality demanded by tomorrow's globalized world.

Even so, naval forces will have to make important changes in order to become properly configured and prepared for the future. To fully exploit the knowledge revolution, it will have to pursue new technologies, systems, and ship designs. For example, several ballistic missile submarines no longer needed for strategic deterrence might be converted to new hybrid roles of carrying both troops and tactical or antiballistic missile systems. Personnel demands will require new and innovative forms of service, compensation, and training. Outsourcing of many tasks that were once performed by military personnel will be needed. Maintenance, supply, logistics, health care, communications, and even intelligence fall into this category. In strategy and doctrine, naval forces will have to resolve the dilemma of preserving core competencies by maintaining a credible warfighting capacity, but with a different force than now. In many ways, the view of the three-block war expressed by the Marine Corps in the 1990s provides a model to follow. These blocks include warfighting, peacekeeping, and humanitarian assistance, to include operations in cities and highly populated areas. Added to these blocks will be new missions for protecting the environment, adjudicating legal and international settlements, providing closer links with other navies and countries, and performing other assorted assignments to help influence a broader range of events created by globalization.

The U.S. military posture in 30 years will depend heavily on political decisions made about strategic requirements, defense budgets, and manpower levels. If DOD military manpower remains at its current level of about 1.4 million soldiers, sailors, and airmen, the future size and mix of key forces might not differ greatly from now. But if manpower is reduced to about 1 million personnel as a byproduct of this scenario, there will have to be significant reductions. In any event, emerging technologies and new missions create added reasons for thinking in nonlinear, innovative ways about future force structures. Clearly, detailed analysis, unconstrained by past assumptions and paradigms, will be required to determine force structures and distribution among the services appropriate to these technologies and emerging missions. However, if DOD manpower were to decline to this level, the Navy might have to consider more radical restructuring. The issue is not predicting the future, but preparing for future international environments that could be affected by these personnel trends and the effects of globalization.

Naval Forces for a World Similar to Now

Between the poles of global peace and global confrontation, the type of middle-ground world discussed earlier is not the only way in which the future could evolve. An alternative is a world security system not radically dissimilar to today's. In this scenario, the effects of globalization will have less geostrategic consequence than in the others. Despite this strategic continuity, however, U.S. military forces will still face important pressures to change. This future military environment likely will be characterized by five general categories of threats and U.S. force operations that will drive defense planning:

Direct traditional threats. From major theater wars to ballistic missile defense, these will represent clear military threats to the United States and its vital interests. Preparation for these threats is preparation for serious warfighting tasks.

Traditional MOOTW. These operations include, for example, peacekeeping and the evacuation of U.S. citizens from dangerous overseas situations. Long part of the lesser included contingencies of the U.S. military, these requirements typically have affected policy and procurement on the margins.

Direct asymmetrical threats. These threats could range from cyberwarfare to terrorist use of nuclear, biological, and chemical weapons in the United States. Whether by individuals, organizations, or nations, these threats will reflect direct attempts to hurt the United States, its citizens, and its interests. These threats seek to counter U.S. capabilities in traditional war fighting by moving warfare into a different domain, where U.S. advantages might not be so disproportionate.

Implicit threats. These are not threats whose main motivation is to attack the United States or defeat its forces. Instead, they fall into the category of transnational threats. The clearest example is globalized criminal activity, especially drug trafficking and illegal immigrant smuggling across national boundaries. Illegal financial flows and environmental crimes (for example, illegal fishing, pollution at sea) fall into this category as well.

Globalization challenges. A wide range of developments could menace U.S. interests and goals, as well as those of the international community. Challenges could include genocidal actions in Rwanda, famine in Ethiopia, floods in Mozambique, chemical spills in European waterways, environmental strains (for example, global warming, a decline in fishing stocks), the election of nationalist leaders who challenge international order, and tensions created by a divide between haves and have-nots. These challenges will arise not necessarily due to any conscious action or intention to harm U.S. interests, but they are capable of directly or indirectly causing such harm. The changes in strategic reach due to globalization suggest that any or all of these developments have the potential to engage the United States. Many could make demands on U.S. military forces for responses that fall well outside the traditional province of war fighting, and they present opportunities for preventive shaping.

All five of these categories create fundamentally dissimilar rationales for the use of U.S. military forces and radically different environments in which they will be operating. For many in the U.S. defense policy community, the comfort zone for military planning and procurement remains mainly in the first category and, marginally, in the second. The reality is that in the future, U.S. forces will be used most frequently in the last four categories, not the first category of fighting major wars. In addition, U.S. forces will be regularly called upon to *participate in the shaping of international trends and dynamics through their overseas presence and political-military interaction with the forces and governments of other countries.* Peace maintenance will be a sixth category of operations, and it too will fall outside the domain of preparing for wars and create demanding challenges of its own.

In addition to performing these operations in a fluid setting over the coming 30 years, U.S. forces will be undergoing changes of their own, as will the entire U.S. national security structure. How will U.S. naval forces be affected? The likely result will be a mixture of continuity and change. Physical realities will produce the appearance of dominating continuity. The vast majority of DOD weapons and infrastructure have already been built, are now being constructed, or are in the finished design stage. Aircraft carriers will still sail the world's oceans, though they may look different and carry a smaller air wing made up of different aircraft than are deployed today. Marine Corps combat units may have fewer people than now, but they will rely on MV–22 Ospreys and advanced amphibious assault vehicles for far better mobility moving from ship to shore and shore to shore. The same trends of fewer forces but more capability will apply to the other services. The Air Force will fly F–22 and Joint Strike Fighters, but probably in reduced numbers. The largest uncertainties, however, will apply to the Army and whether it relies on the M1 tank or a vehicle like it or whether it can make the transition to a lighter, more mobile system. The Pentagon, 90 years old in 2030, likely will still be the headquarters of the Department of Defense. But behind this surface appearance of continuity, a great deal of change is likely, including change in the naval forces.

Virtual command centers likely will dominate the entire U.S. military, down to tactical levels. In a ship's Combat Information Center, the officer on duty will have instant access to multiple offices, staffs, and data banks from around the world, receiving advice ranging from intelligence analysis of ongoing events in a region to assessments of how to deal with a radar system in a dust storm. Artificial intelligence aids and systems will have taken over many of the duties performed by humans today, and they will be augmenting tomorrow's decisionmaking. Virtual command centers, remote staffing, and artificial intelligence tools will have combined to greatly reduce the number of military personnel that will have to be put into harm's way in order to provide effective command and control of forces. The Marine Corps will be able to deploy a fully functional Joint Task Force (JTF) headquarters using only two big air transports to carry all of its equipment and a fraction of its personnel. These few personnel will perform three functions: direct support of the commander, liaison with other organizations, and systems operations. Everything else will be handled via remote staffing and virtual personnel.

Virtual activity may come to dominate much of military training and exercises. Already today, powerful constraints on training have arisen, including environmental effects and public opposition. These constraints likely will intensify, as fewer areas on land and at sea remain sufficiently open to allow for military operations. Another factor will be the growing capacity of information systems and simulators to provide much of the necessary training with the high-technology weapons of the future. Major field deployments may be necessary less often than today. If so, the cost of operating forces and keeping them ready may diminish in some respects.

Fleet structures will change greatly. While fleet commands will still exist, they likely will be shore-based, with the vast majority of personnel and skills shared between fleets and organizations in the United States. Fleet staffs will include only a handful of personnel who provide the admiral a core team. Admirals will be shore-based, but will be able to move aboard essentially any ship while still maintaining connectivity and staff support. In practice, fleet commanders will be far more relevant to conducting missions of political suasion through theaterwide travels than to actually commanding their forces from the windswept bridge of a warship. Indeed, CINCs will increasingly rely on JTFs for operations, and naval forces will report directly to the JTF commander rather than to fleet commanders. Deployments will be both more standard and more variable. About a quarter of the Navy's ships may be either home-ported outside the United States or on extended, multiyear deployment supported by rotating crews. Similar to pre-positioned ships of today, a sizable share of the Navy's warfighting capability will be carried aboard civilian ships with minimal crews and only a few assigned Navy personnel to monitor combat systems; thus, black hulls may be as likely to shoot the decisive missile as gray hulls.

Naval warships themselves will have fewer personnel than now. The number of personnel per ton aboard each ship likely will be a fraction of today's total. Each and every sailor aboard ship will be individually selected in order to enhance the ship's functioning. Everything likely will be done not only to minimize the number of deployed sailors but also to ensure that each sailor and marine has a clear understanding of why his or her presence and personal skills are needed. Technical skills will rule assignments, not old-style labor. While Navy ships will still be more heavily manned than civilian ships, chipping paint and swabbing decks will no longer be shorthand for the deck hand's daily responsibility.

Aboard ship, the makeup of crews will be different than now. No longer will age be a clear determinant of an individual's status in either the enlisted ranks or officer corps. With personnel moving between military and civilian jobs, specialty skills and relevant experience will play a larger role than age and longevity in determining status. By age 20, some personnel already may be senior limited-duty officers due to their mastery of computers and information networks. Some aviation squadrons may have lieutenants in their 40s, with thousands of hours in the cockpit, who value the opportunity to fly above the allures of command. With biotechnology fostering longer life spans, an intelligence specialist might be over the age of 70, with decades of experience in understanding regional affairs. Perhaps one of the most unusual changes will be the common deployment aboard ships of personnel from other U.S. Government agencies, foreign countries, the United Nations, and even nongovernmental organizations. These personnel will be integrated into staffs and crews, especially in cases where efforts are being made to launch effective international responses to disintegrating nations or environmental disasters.

When wars or conflicts occur, naval forces will be able to orchestrate combat operations at sea from any and all of its platforms and command centers. The ability to make war from shore-based command centers such as Cheyenne Mountain will be matched by a similar capability aboard a range of combatants from the LPD–17 class amphibious ship to carriers and cruisers. Key naval assets for war will include ballistic missile defenses and hybrid ships that could have as few as 25 crew members. Weapons systems will be capable of being engaged either by senior leaders ashore or relatively junior personnel aboard ship or in the area of action. For the Marine Corps, what a former commandant termed a "strategic corporal" will have the capacity to bring all or much of the Nation's capability to bear on specific targets. For the Navy and Marine Corps, this extended range of warfighting command capacity will require greatly increased training, education, and technical expertise. Every sailor and marine will be viewed as an expert, empowered to make important decisions in ways that produce lateral organizations of networked assets rather than the vertical military hierarchies of the past. The effect will be to make the Navy and the Marine Corps more capable of employing their high-technology weapons, advanced information systems, and modern doctrines with great effect on the battlefield. How often serious wars will occur three decades from now remains to be seen, but when they occur, the Navy and Marine Corps will be able to marshal impressive combat capabilities to wage them.

Conclusion: Charting the Navy's Future

Clearly, the impact of globalization is changing the world. Naval forces will need to change in order to remain important policy instruments. Although the future is impossible to predict beyond generalities, certain changes now under way within the realms of both international and U.S. defense establishment politics lead to important conclusions for naval forces in the near and longer terms. Naval forces will be performing missions that are untraditional and, by today's standards, new or unconventional. These forces will not only be preparing for war, but they will also be taking roles in influencing events ashore and otherwise shaping the peacetime geostrategic environment. Naval forces will themselves undergo major changes as new doctrines, technologies, information systems, ships, weapons, people, and organizational cultures become the actual resources for response to these future challenges, realities, and needs.

The task facing the current and future leaders of DOD and the Navy will be to anticipate and to implement these changes so that future naval forces remain fully effective in conducting national security policy and defense strategy. But does DON have the proper legal authority to carry out these important transformations and responses to the demands of globalization? Currently, Title 10 of the U.S. Code and related Federal directives provide DON the full authority to prepare naval forces for prompt and sustained operations incident to combat at sea. But while the law and directives permit conducting and preparing for these non-warfighting tasks, the authority and language lack the emphasis, clarity, and detail that are likely to be needed. The implication of the current statutes is that being prepared for combat operations is not only more important than these other missions, but that such preparation is also sufficient for these lesser tasks. This language made sense in the past, but no longer; because noncombat missions are already important, and seem likely to become even more important in the years ahead, they no longer can be treated as a backwater concern. A strong case can be made for rewriting the relevant codes and directives to ensure that the necessary legal authorities are beyond question. The need to create proper legal authority to prepare for new missions, of course, must be accompanied by sensible decisions in allocating Navy funds, personnel, and other resources so that adequate capabilities for new missions are created.[2]

A set of additional recommendations for naval forces also can be advanced. Naval forces must continue to develop a sound understanding of how to employ assets in peacetime in order to influence political, economic, and military events ashore and in surrounding waters. Owing to globalization, the agenda ahead in this arena may be different from now, yet it is reminiscent of how the British Navy was used in the 19th century and earlier as an important instrument of diplomacy and strategic policy. The key point is that action consistent with this agenda must be carried out with care and precision if it is to succeed; there are good ways to use naval power for this purpose, but also bad and ineffective ways. Naval forces also will have to develop a keen understanding of the wide spectrum of other missions short of war fighting—for example, peacekeeping, humanitarian operations, and partnership building with foreign militaries. The key point is that the Navy will need not only to understand how to perform these missions expertly but also to have the physical assets to do so. These assets will exist only if conscious decisions are made to fund them in Navy programs and budgets. The same applies to the need for new overseas bases, facilities, and infrastructure. Because naval forces likely will be called on to operate in new geographical areas, it will require necessary shore-based support assets. Such requirements must be identified, funds allocated, and the necessary arrangements made with friendly foreign countries.

The future will depend upon how the incoming administration and the Congress decide to act. Public opinion seemingly favors a still strong military, but there is no widespread enthusiasm for major spending increases. Modest spending hikes, however, may be forthcoming. If carried out annually, they can gradually elevate the DOD budget over the coming decade, thereby broadening investment options. In any event, priorities set by DOD and the Navy will have a major impact on determining the future naval force posture, its capabilities, and its mission orientation. Careful planning will be needed.

In the spirit of Projects Michelson and 60, the Navy would be well advised to institutionalize a planning cell to deal with future eventualities and with the long-term effects of globalization, the knowledge revolution, and the people revolution. The immediate task is to get started on this enterprise, for developing a better understanding of the changing environments at home and abroad is essential to maintaining the intellectual basis and flexibility needed to deal with the challenges that certainly lie ahead.

Notes

This chapter, and indeed the entire project, were inspired by Admiral Elmo Zumwalt, who died recently. Much of its content is drawn from his wisdom and experience. Adam Siegel also made a significant contribution. The term *naval forces* applies principally to the Navy and Marine Corps. However, the roles of the other major military services—especially as joint operations expand—and the Coast Guard are also important ingredients in the overall power and effectiveness of naval forces.

[1] This includes a Marine Corps of about 175,000 organized into three active and one Reserve division.

[2] See DOD Directive 5100.1, *Functions of the Department of Defense and Its Major Components*, September 25, 1987.

Chapter 23

Formative and Operative Engagement

Stephen Benson

Although the definition of globalization is still evolving, this volume accurately portrays it as a powerful process of integration that is rapidly becoming a major consideration in U.S. foreign policy. Concurrently, engagement is undergoing its own evolutionary process. To senior naval strategists, the word *engagement* may first evoke the image of blue-water battle as in the campaigns of the Pacific during World War II. To a newly promoted lieutenant junior grade, engagement may connote hors d'oeuvres on the flight deck with the ambassador and his guests. These are two extremes that exist today. They bracket a spectrum of thought and activity that defies limitations and consumes military resources. The engagement mission has grown beyond earlier boundaries and now needs greater definition. This new definition should be based on a fundamental understanding of the global condition and the unique capacity of a strong and credible naval force to positively influence that condition. Achieving the necessary balance and focus in an environment of globalization is the imperative of engagement.

All engagement by U.S. military forces during peacetime should reflect a commitment to a more secure, stable, and less risky international environment, lest the force serve merely as a strategic tripwire. What has become clear in studying engagement is that the commitment exists, but the concept itself and the global environment in which it is applied have both undergone a dramatic, bifurcated development since the end of the Cold War and its containment strategy. The armed services face an engagement conundrum in which the proper application of preventive and corrective approaches to unstable conditions presents an ever-widening dilemma. Further, global development in this technological age is separating the world into the political, economic, and military haves and have-nots. A conceptual framework for engagement is needed—one that leverages the unprecedented power and precious resources of U.S naval forces.

U.S. naval forces protect U.S. national interests. The threats to those interests have come to demand a reliable and continuous global naval force presence at high readiness levels. The Navy and the Marine Corps have successfully met many chal-

---

Commander Stephen Benson, USN, has held a Federal executive fellowship at the Center for Strategic and International Studies. He also has served as a regional strategy officer for the Commander in Chief, U.S. Naval Forces, Europe, and as chief staff officer for CJTF Silver Wake *and CJTF* Guardian Retrieval.

lenges both unilaterally and in joint operations over the past decades. Occasionally, augmentation by standby forces has been necessary to reinforce the deployed units. These occasions have included primarily operations of limited duration—usually no more than a year. Residual tasking from these contingency response actions has employed some specialized naval capabilities over longer periods. However, the Navy and Marine Corps have always managed to minimize the impact of these operations on the continuum of global naval force presence. The emphasis has been on the capability to respond on short notice; the hot spots of the world have seldom been without a naval force on at least 96-hour alert. Even through a decade of declining resources, the expeditionary rhythm of the force has been preserved.

Through peak Cold War tensions and well past the end of the containment mission, regional commanders in chief (CINCs) have placed a premium on naval force presence, the highest priority being the availability of carrier battle groups and amphibious ready groups. Their requirements did not decrease with the demise of the Soviet Union. Instead, they increased with the emergence of new threats and the growing uncertainty in an increasingly interdependent world. A shift in naval strategy placed new emphasis on projecting power from the sea into the contested littoral and heartland regions. Inspired by new and innovative over-the-horizon warfighting concepts, naval forces have become more relevant to combat in these regions.

Nevertheless, few innovations or inspirational concepts have emerged to guide the forward-deployed naval forces in deliberate engagement planning and execution. Basic accounting procedures have been established in the new theater engagement planning process. Yet there is no method for ongoing examination of the impact of engagement, nor is there a valid process for establishing priorities. Strategy documents, in their quest to be globally inclusive, forgo the detail and clarity necessary to foster a more discriminate and deliberate approach. Declining resources fall victim to a high-level penchant for ephemeral issues rather than enduring priorities. Naval force employment remains conceptually wedged between Cold War containment constraints and the boundless possibilities of post-Cold War globalization. Recent fleet efforts to proactively assert the naval force role in engagement attest to the profound change in the course of political, economic, and military affairs. These efforts are the beginning of a peacetime naval force contribution unmatched in U.S. history.

The engagement role of the U.S. naval forces in the rapidly changing global environment can be defined from three perspectives: the scope of the National Security Strategy and its "imperative of engagement," examined within a new construct of "formative and operative engagement"; key trends in globalization that impact the way naval forces influence the international environment; and U.S. naval force engagement during a similar period in U.S. history.

It is a primary assumption that naval forces can be more effective in the engagement role without increasing operational tempo, decreasing quality of life, or affecting readiness. Another is that U.S. naval forces can better serve national security interests by providing critical support to other elements of national power. Hopefully, the observations and recommendations of this paper will inspire movement toward realizing the full potential of a naval force that will be forward and present in the new millennium.

Engagement: An Imperative

To subdue the enemy without fighting is the acme of skill.
— *Sun Tzu,* The Art of War

Perhaps the most vivid realization of Sun Tzu's philosophy was the demise of the Soviet Union after almost a half-century of Western political, economic, and military maneuvers. During this time, the sustained commitment to containing communist expansion was not only a singular rallying point for U.S. interests, but it also brought together an international community to serve common interests and reinforce the commitments of nations. When the Soviet Union dissolved, so did the monolithic threat, and thus the singular rallying point. The aftermath of that dissolution was dominated by two conspicuous trends: a destabilizing reemergence of historical national and ethnic tensions that had been suppressed by the Soviet Union or managed within the Cold War's bipolar alignment; and an increase in global interdependence, and with it the growing certainty that U.S. prosperity, indeed the very expectations of the American people, depended on a stable international environment. The uncertainty as to the scope and volatility of these trends prompted the maintenance of Cold War-like U.S. naval force deployment patterns and readiness postures.

The 1986 Goldwater-Nichols Act mandated that the President develop an annual security strategy addressing at a minimum: vital global interests and objectives, proposed short- and long-term use of all elements of the national power to achieve U.S. objectives, and the commitments and defense capabilities required to deter aggression and implement the strategy while achieving a balance among all elements of power.[1] Over the past 14 years, this National Security Strategy has elevated engagement from a footnote to a strategic pillar. Bush administration documents turned the corner from containment to engagement with the deliberate focus on "collective engagement."[2] The Clinton administration followed by adding "enlargement" to the strategy. Expansion of U.S. influence through growing involvement in international affairs was the end, and it appeared that the U.S. military would be a primary means to that end.

To engender momentum toward a more stable world and to maintain influence and play a leadership role, the National Security Strategy and National Military Strategy of the 1990s consistently embraced the importance of engagement. One can develop an appreciation for the scope and complexity of strategic tasking by reviewing the phraseology typical of the national strategy documents of that decade:

- National Security Strategy phraseology
  —Engage actively *abroad*
  —Enhance *global* security
  —Bolster prosperity around the *world*
  —Construct *global* institutions
  —Harness *global* forces of integration
  —Leadership for *international* response
  —Dynamism of the *global* economy
  —The United States must lead *abroad*

—Advance U.S. leadership around the *world*

- National Military Strategy phraseology
  —Armed forces engaged *worldwide*
  —*Global* competition
  —*Global* responsibilities require global capabilities
  —*Global* command and control
  —*Worldwide* security interests
  —Continue *global* engagement
  —Prosper in the *global* economy
  —Actively engaged in the *world*

The language commits the U.S. military to a growing worldwide engagement effort. American political and economic health increasingly relies on the foundation of a secure and stable international environment, one that can accommodate an agenda of integration. In this pursuit, limited resources are at work in regions where Cold War barricades, together with imposed order, have been removed. The U.S. military is now exposed to a much broader array of unstable situations that have effectively blurred the distinction between the front, the rear, and the flanks. They engage to buttress flagging security conditions and reassure fledgling democracies in areas where national interests mingle with the interests of an increasing number of legitimate transnational benefactors as well as malefactors. This requires extraordinary coordination and synchronization of effort, as it is an extraordinary environment in which to engage.

Certain successes can be attributed to the strategy of remaining forward, present, and engaged in the world—for example, new democracies, burgeoning free markets, a growing observance of international law. These successes, however, have not lessened the engagement workload for the military. Even more is required now that many countries of the developing world are at critical junctures. Those that desire and have the potential to transition to modern societies with connected economies often are in bad neighborhoods and under extreme political pressures. U.S. support has, in many cases, been the defining factor in always tough political decisions to break with old ways and regimes, and to pursue independence and statehood. For many of these vulnerable countries, reassurance comes only through sustained U.S. engagement.

This increased workload has also brought more scrutiny to the allocation of resources. Resources for military engagement are limited, and the competition for those resources was in part responsible for institution by the Joint Chiefs of Staff (JCS) of a formalized accounting process. The theater engagement-planning process was designed to track all military engagement activity by area of responsibility. CINCs were charged with the responsibility of developing theater engagement plans (TEPs) that linked activities and resources to prioritized regional objectives. The plans include annexes that detail activities over 5-year periods. Recognizing the scope of activity that this process now encompasses is important. It accounts for all engagement with the developing countries mentioned earlier—and other underdeveloped countries with less strategic value—but more importantly with the reliable and militarily sophisticated allies of the United States. Along with combined exercises and a host of foreign military interactions, the TEP is required to report as engagement those routine and continuous operational activities to which U.S. forces are committed for the long term, whether they began as a scheduled activity or are the result of ongoing operations.[3] The TEP attempts to track the complete range of global military activity short of the initial crisis response actions and the war fighting itself. Initial versions of the TEP submitted by CINCs were in most cases 500-page documents.[4]

Engagement: A Military Conundrum

For the U.S. naval force, indeed the entire military, the meaning of the word *engagement* is not well understood. It is as vague today as the term *security* has been through the ages. Perhaps no other word had quite its capacity to infiltrate post-Cold War military lexicon. The *Chairman of the Joint Chiefs of Staff Manual* (CJCSM 31130.10) published February 1, 1998, defines *engagement* as "all military activities involving other nations intended to shape the international environment in peacetime." Here a vague phrase is used to define a vague concept. Ideally, engagement would shape (nurture) the international environment with the values of democracy, prosperity, and security. On the one hand, it seems that injecting these three ingredients into underdeveloped regions that exist beyond the margins of globalization would require a certain concept of engagement. On the other hand, sustaining these three ingredients in the mature, wealthy democracies of the developed world would require a fundamentally different concept of engagement. Yet strategy documents and vision statements to date reflect no conceptual distinctions regarding engagement.

The mind of the military strategist, while laboring to embrace the geostrategic breadth of the engagement mission, is further challenged as it plumbs the professional depth of its role in engagement. In the U.S. naval force, engagement has traditionally been viewed in a warfighting or response context (closing with the enemy in battle at sea). After the fall of the Berlin Wall, naval strategy added a landward focus, deepening the response context of engagement. New tactics like precision engagement and overland engagement are now set within this response context.

Furthermore, successive iterations of the National Security Strategy have increasingly emphasized the imperative of engagement in the peacetime or shaping context. Engagement, with its many modifiers, has fully penetrated the professional lexicon in both the shape and respond contexts. In one high-level document, the phrase *cooperative engagement* refers to coordinating efforts to shoot and kill the enemy and, in the next chapter, to the coordinated but benign activities designed to build relations and stabilize the international environment. Little discipline has been exercised in the development of the language of this strategic imperative.

It is useful to examine how the shape and respond aspects reveal themselves in the current strategy documents. Table 1 lists the term *engagement* and its modifiers as used in recent strategy and vision documents and posture statements from the Department of Defense (DOD) and its subordinate organizations. In the 263 instances in which the word was used, the context was either one of peaceful interaction (shaping) or war fighting (responding). In a few cases, the word served in both contexts. This theme runs completely through DOD organizations.

Other agencies and departments with significant international responsibilities and activities—the Departments of Agriculture, Commerce, Energy, Justice, and Transportation—do not use the word *engagement* in their key documents. Despite its status as an imperative in National Security Strategy, with the exception of the U.S. Coast Guard, none of the non-DOD organizations examined make reference to engagement in their strategic plans or vision statements. In over 1,000 pages of high-level documents, the word is absent. This is not to say that the imperative of engagement has been overlooked in these organizations; they are involved in international activities. It does, however, reveal inconsistency at the highest levels.

When it became clear that the word *engagement* was not used in high-level Department of State documents, examination of lower level documents was undertaken. The motivation for a deeper look at these guiding documents came from the realization that the State Department's field organizations (embassies and consulates) had the charter to oversee and regulate U.S. military interaction with their host countries. Furthermore, an ambassador, the direct representative of the President of the United States, would presumably place emphasis on any imperative set by his or her superior. The current Mission Performance Plans of the U.S. embassies in the United Kingdom, Turkey, and Tunisia were selected. Review of the Chief of Mission Statements encompassing embassy goals, interests, strategies, objectives, and assumptions in these three important and diverse countries revealed the word *engagement* used once.

Another element of inadequacy stems from the failure of the official definition of engagement to include that portion of engagement that is not focused on shaping the international environment. This is a matter of emphasis. Naval engagement with England, Germany, and Japan is not meant primarily to shape, but rather to reassure allies of U.S. commitment and to maintain the military access and interoperability that allows a strategy of engagement and enlargement to exist. These countries are, for the most part, shaped. They have democracy, prosperity, and security—in some instances, above U.S. levels. The emphasis here is on response-oriented engagement, engagement that focuses on complex war fighting and does not necessarily require

Table 1. Use of the Term *Engagement* by the Department of Defense

Shaping Context	Response Context	Both
Theater engagement	Multiple engagement	Engagement
Proactive engagement	Maritime engagement	Global engagement
Peacetime engagement	Overland engagement	Regional engagement
Military engagement	Precision engagement	Cooperative engagement
Environment engagement	First-round engagement	
International engagement	Long-range engagement	
Commercial engagement		
Sustained engagement		
Collective engagement		
Selective engagement		
Committed engagement		
Subregional engagement		

coordination with other political or economic engagement. It is perhaps disingenuous to consider naval engagement with France for the purpose of shaping the country or its international affairs. This must be considered less important than engagement for the purpose of enabling combined response to crisis or interoperability in war fighting. Hereafter, this type of engagement—that is, engagement with an operational focus—will be referred to as *operative engagement.*

On the other hand, military engagement with new and developing nations like Romania, Tunisia, or Algeria focuses on nurturing the internal and regional security environment and encourages rational defensive ambitions and capabilities. Naval engagement with new and developing nations will have an important but limited military agenda and in almost all cases will benefit from close coordination and balance with the political and economic elements of U.S. national power. This type of engagement targets fundamental security issues in unstable regions and hereafter will be referred to as *formative engagement.*

Engagement in this manner is a necessity brought on by the way that the United States routinely pursues its security objectives. The end of the Cold War did not bring the spoils or the subjugation of peoples that would normally accrue from victory. Instead, the United States has sought to embrace, not to occupy, and to influence, not to control. The emphasis has been on incorporating countries into a growing group of friends and allies committed to democracy, and on a law-bound international order. As Henry Kissinger points out, this approach has resulted in a "triumph of faith over experience."[5] U.S. engagement strategy has as its underlying objective international order through enlargement of the group of responsible international actors, and that strategy is in all particulars noncoercive.

Thus, the U.S. naval force enters the 21st century exposed to a much wider spectrum of engagement. Figure 1 illustrates this in one dimension. Consider the military activities, competencies, and force postures that ensured a successful strategy of containment and place them on a spectrum that begins with the tense peace of the Cold War and ends in a major theater war. The strategic shift from containment to engagement mandated new activities, competencies, and force postures to supplement the old, most of which remain relevant and in place. The engagement spectrum extends beyond that tense peace of the Cold War, which today is merely a strategic placeholder with a particularly stubborn and perhaps permanent structural component of crisis. The spectrum now extends to an undefined point that could be characterized as an optimum combination of prosperity, democracy, and security. For the lack of any adequate military terminology, this point will be called *Har,* short for *harmony*—in a practical sense, the union of distinctly different parts to make a more stable and secure environment for change. Unfortunately, going to Har is not like going to War. Where War has primarily a military end state, Har has primarily a socioeconomic one. Where War requires that the United States maintain a unilateral capability, Har demands a multilateral approach. Where War focuses on the order of battle, Har focuses on international order. And finally, where War increasingly relies on over-the-horizon sanctuaries, Har depends on closing with the willing at the margins of stability. Such is the broad and contrary nature of the Har-to-War engagement spectrum.

Figure 1. Peacetime Engagement Spectrum

The challenge of understanding the impact of a wider role in engagement is great. The combined strategy goals of enhancing security, bolstering prosperity, and promoting democracy do not attain the same clarity for the strategists as does the objective of winning the Nation's wars. Further, engagement for the purpose of shaping the international environment is not an objective that easily translates into action by way of traditional, formalized military planning tools or intelligence methods. Simply put, engagement by the military in peacetime has traditionally focused on preparing the force so as to reduce the risk *in the fight* (Peace $\Rightarrow$ War). Since the end of World War II, the military has become more directly involved in reducing the risk of *having to fight* (Har $\Leftarrow$ Peace), and it should be developing core competencies in this new dimension as economy of force measures.

In a more practical sense, engagement activity to the right of Peace should be operative in focus, with priority on enhancing war fighting and crisis response with the reliable, ready, and modern militaries of allies and friends. This should be a more exclusive group of developed countries, given the short list of reliable, ready, and modern naval forces, as well as the level of national commitment necessary to build and maintain a naval force. Engagement activity to the left of Peace should be formative in focus, with priority on those developing countries whose potential to positively impact regional stability is high. This, too, should be a more exclusive group, given the minimum level of physical and organizational infrastructure necessary to realize a benefit from naval engagement and the rare political potential for gathering regional support for peaceful conflict resolution. The other important aspect of formative engagement is incorporating a host of nontraditional actors from across key sectors of society. This should be an interdisciplinary effort that would often cast the U.S. naval force in the supporting role.

Formative and operative engagement act together in lessening the need for, and increasing the effectiveness of, actions like the gunboat diplomacy that occurred between the United States and China in the Taiwan Straits in 1996. There, Navy carrier presence helped calm the tensions and stay the geopolitical brinkmanship between China and Taiwan. Increasingly, this type of unilateral, geopolitical engagement exists along the Har-to-War spectrum in the gray area of crisis. In the future, its success will depend on the effectiveness of the formative and operative engagement that precedes it.

From Har-to-War, the U.S. naval force is now exposed to a broader set of missions that stress its resources and professional culture. The force has adjusted well to extensions of its mission, including nontraditional national security threats (for example, environment and health).[6] Yet without a coherent conceptual framework for engagement, one that taps its potential but also sets limits, the U.S. military may not control its destiny.

Engagement: The Global Dimension

When thinking about the imperative of engagement across the Har-to-War spectrum, one is compelled to consider the following examples of the new dynamic of globalization—that is, the vast changes in the traditional linkages of power and influence:

- A retired Army Colonel, John Kronkitis, and a retired Air Force Colonel, Rom Kilikauskas, serve as the Minister of Defense and the Deputy Chief of Defense, respectively, for Lithuania.
- Greenpeace, whose followers have attempted to block Navy ship visits in various ports around the world, now has "prominent industrialists, including BP Amoco, Enron and Unilever"[7] appearing at their conferences, and the eco-organization is listed in the Mission Performance Plan of the U.S. embassy in Tunisia as the nongovernmental organization (NGO) for consultation on fisheries issues.
- In 1998, Daimler-Benz of Germany acquired U.S. carmaker Chrysler in, at that time, the largest ever takeover of an American company by a foreign company. In World War II, the armaments produced by these two flagship industrial groups closed in battle.
- On May 3, 2000, the merger between the London Stock Exchange and the Deutsche Börse was announced, ending 200 years of London Stock Exchange independence. The new body immediately signaled an alliance with the National Association of Securities Dealers and Quotations (NASDAQ).

Traditional linkages of power and influence are changing. National borders now seem to be more pliable and, in some cases, to have disappeared altogether. Traditional linkages are being broken down, and new linkages are forming. At a recent high-level meeting of a globalization study group, an official from a major American media corporation repeatedly emphasized that it was not "American," but rather an international entity. He added that efforts were made to ensure that it was not seen as an American corporation—linkages breaking down. At the same time, the phenomenon of dollarization, by which a country's monetary policy independence is sacrificed for the stability of direct ties to the U.S. dollar, has placed sovereign states under the policy arm of the U.S. Federal Reserve—new linkages forming.

The 21st century began amid a growing global transition of power and influence. That transition affects all sectors of society, and it appears to the developed world to be changing the entire earth. Worth noting, however, is the fact that the transition is not yet all-encompassing. Three-quarters of all business and social transactions still take place on paper, and only five percent of companies have made the transition to modern technologies. Almost half the world's workers remain in the agricultural sector, and half the world's people have yet to place a telephone call.[8]

The year 2000 National Security Strategy states that globalization is "the process of accelerating economic, technological, cultural and political integration." Achieving National Security Strategy objectives will increasingly depend on the degree to which states, regions, and superpowers can reconcile their growing integration. The forces of integration or globalization are powerful. They have been with us before, but never in such an accelerated or pervasive fashion. Understanding the impact of this process is a necessary albeit complex task, akin to capturing the societal and cultural impacts of the Agricultural Revolution and the Industrial Revolution occurring simultaneously and in double-time.

Some experts see globalization as growing interdependency across national boundaries with an attendant slow deterioration of the nation-state. One economist emphasizes a more routine yet pronounced cyclical rise and fall of pivotal commodities.[9] John Gray, another economist, and former advisor to Margaret Thatcher, calls the emerging global free market (the proximate cause of globalization) "a product of artifice, design, and political coercion that is short lived in any democracy."[10] Contrarily, in his book *The Lexus and the Olive Tree*, the popular journalist Thomas Friedman refers to globalization as an enduring and dynamic process involving the "inexorable integration of markets, nation-states and technologies to a degree never witnessed before."[11] International financier George Soros warns of global crisis when he writes that globalization under the current capitalist system is fundamentally unstable, as there is no global society to temper to the global economy.[12] Leading professionals from all disciplines are thinking in terms of a new global dynamic.

James N. Rosenau, a professor of international affairs, sees our epoch as a time of contrary trends and episodic patterns, a period of commonplace anomalies. He highlights an underlying erosion yet a still vigorous assertion of state sovereignty, loss of government influence while government resources grow, and soaring corporate profits in a time of stagnant wages. Rosenau asserts that tradition and history are being redefined amid these contradictions, but points out that we are ill equipped to deal with the changes because the vocabulary does not exist. Professional military strategists would agree with this statement, as it would appear that recently DOD has become a clearinghouse for the difficult act of dealing with the downsides of these contrary trends: organized crime, contagious disease, environmental degradation, and a host of other transnational dangers and semi-dangers.

Engagement: The Themes

It can be argued that, as far as U.S. naval forces are concerned, there are three central and cross-cutting realities, or themes, of globalization: transnationalism, privatization, and decline in hierarchical authority. It is changes of these kinds that, in fact, will necessitate a reexamination of the way U.S. naval forces can influence the international environment.

Transnationalism

Globalists have their many unique perspectives. A reasonable one is that of transgovernmentalism. First observed by political scientists Robert Keohane and Joseph Nye in the 1970s, transgovernmentalism has become widespread. More recently, it has been paralleled in NGOs that no longer feel constrained by national boundaries—for example, labor unions, professional associations, special interest groups, and lobbyists. The broadening of Government or nongovernment activities and associations with foreign interests continues.

Significant nongovernment aspects expand transgovernmentalism to the more complex and pervasive notion of transnationalism. More than a vision of the future, transnationalism is happening now and is having fundamental impact on the "New World Order." Transnationalism brings about a state's disaggregation or fragmentation into separate, functionally distinct parts. Courts, regulatory agencies, executives, legislatures, labor unions, and even military and paramilitary organizations are networking with their counterparts abroad, creating a dense web of relations that constitutes a new transnational order. Today's expanding national security challenges—for example, terrorism, organized crime, environmental degradation, money laundering, proliferation of weapons of mass destruction (WMD), bank failure, securities fraud, contagious diseases—create and sustain these relations.[13]

Transnationalism in the private sector can be adequately illustrated by further examining the Daimler Benz-Chrysler merger mentioned earlier. Roughly a year after the merger, in October 1999, a formal agreement established the European Aeronautics, Defense and Space (EADS) Company. EADS was the result of the merger between DaimlerChrysler Aerospace (DASA) and the French firm Aerospatiale Matra. The merger was called a political milestone in that it marked the restoration of the traditional privileged relationship between France and Germany. It was characterized as the "first truly cross-border, fully integrated aerospace and defense company in Europe"—the world's third largest aerospace company and the leader in the helicopter and commercial space launcher sectors. The ownership structure formally acknowledges DaimlerChrysler as the single largest shareholder. However, the French state maintains prerogatives that effectively give it the right to veto future strategic decisions. Additionally, immediately following the creation of EADS, a merger between Aerospatiale Matra, Matra, the British firm BAe, and the Italian firm Finmeccanica brought together the main European missile producers under a new Matra BAe Dynamics entity. This entity controls 30 percent of LKA, a German missile company, which is controlled by DASA.[14]

Consolidation of the European defense industry is ongoing and complex. Yet the impact of transnational defense industrial integration on the major European powers and the United States is up for debate. Some would focus on the loss of a U.S. flagship company like Chrysler to European control or, in other instances, the potential for unauthorized direct or third-party transfer of sensitive military technology. Others can see an enhanced North Atlantic Treaty Organization (NATO) through greater system interoperability or greater burden sharing in system development and production. A recent study by the Defense Science Board examined the potential risks of cross-border defense linkages and found them neither new nor compelling in view of the potential benefits.[15]

Examination of this phenomenon at the working level, in fact, discloses benefits. Soon, instead of a team of technical experts flying from Norfolk, Virginia, to Sigonella, Italy, and then out to a Navy ship to troubleshoot a critical weapons system, a team of French and German technical experts could embark from Marseilles, France, and be back home the same day.

Capital-intensive commercial industries have been impacted by transnationalism throughout the 1990s. Changes have been market driven and have substantially affected company control and ownership. Firms with international supplier, product, and investment bases are responsible for more than half the world's industrial output, and the advanced technology sector depends on a worldwide supplier network and labor pool. In this commercial metamorphosis, the characteristics of an American company do not remain self-evident. Further, the Cold War U.S. defense industrial base is no longer dedicated to domestic defense production, but is increasingly international in character. All this means that in the future, the U.S. military-technological advantage will derive increasingly from externally controlled sources.[16]

Following the lead of big business, organized labor is increasing its interaction across national boundaries. A recent poll of AFL–CIO unions found that two-thirds were engaged in international activity as a necessary extension of their normal organizing and bargaining, and 87 percent indicated that they need to do even more on the global scene.[17] In the 1997 United Parcel Service (UPS) strike, 185,000 teamsters forced a settlement on terms favorable to the union. The union strategy included broad international support. A year before the strike, empowered by the Internet, the teamsters formed a World Council of UPS Unions with assistance from the International Transportation Workers Federation. The group identified enough common ground to organize a World Action Day in the spring of 1997, coinciding with the final stages of negotiations. On that day, UPS was hit with more than 150 job actions or demonstrations worldwide, including work stoppages in Italy and Spain. With the trend toward privatization of military logistics, these stoppages will impact shipments of materiel to and through naval transshipment hubs like Rota, Spain, and Naples, Italy.

The halls of the U.S. judiciary do not escape this trend. In October 1995, 25 Supreme Court Justices and their designees met in Washington to inaugurate the Organization of the Supreme Courts of the Americas (OCSA [from the Spanish *Organización de Cortes Supremas de las Americas]*). The OCSA is dedicated to the principles of "promote[ing] and strengthen[ing] judicial independence and the rule of law among the members." Its charter envisages a permanent secretariat. Increasingly, judges around the world are referring to decisions made in courts outside their states. Clearly this is the case when courts from nations of the European Union refer cases up to the supernational tribunal, the European Court of Justice, in order to obtain opinions that consider the impact of European law on national law.[18]

Transnational forces do not require traditional power sources. At one extreme, the existence of "super-empowered individuals"[19] is all that is necessary to snare the policy objectives of great nations. This can be viewed as the slow erosion of American influence. Those who hold this view would not agree with international law expert Anne Slaughter, who has stated that the process of a nation-state's disaggregation harnesses the power to find, integrate, and implement solutions to global problems. For those who are concerned with national security, judging the good and bad of transnationalism is less important than understanding that the underlying process is real and ongoing, and will ultimately change the manner in which a forward, present, and engaged naval force goes about proactively shaping the international environment and responding to crisis.

This should not be a surprise to the U.S. military. For decades, it has been in the middle of transnationalism, doing more to promote its furtherance than perhaps any other organization, including the United Nations (UN). Recent successful yet painstaking efforts to include all 19 NATO member nations in the targeting processes for strikes in Kosovo and Yugoslavia are a prime example of how transnationalism works its way down to the tactical level. Evolutionary processes at the strategic level are evident in the role played by the Group of Eight (G–8) during the Kosovo crisis. NATO, in its statement on Kosovo, set forth conditions under which combat operations would cease. This in itself demonstrated new and powerful transnational cohesion. However, the prompt endorsement of the G–8 added a more significant piece, in that it meant that Russia supported the conditions.[20]

The G–8 is worth discussing in this light. A transnational organization of the world's most significant economic powers, the G–8 was established to improve cooperation in economic and financial policy. Yet it has entered into the areas of international security, crisis resolution, WMD proliferation, the Anti-Ballistic Missile Treaty, ballistic missile defense, and environmental issues. A new G–8 offshoot organization, the Group of 20 (G–20), as highlighted in the National Security Strategy (December 1999), is intended to "promote cooperation to achieve stable and sustained world economic growth."[21] It takes the G–8 transnational character even further by incorporating 12 more nations and enabling a broader consensus for G–8 ideas. Considering the potential economic power, political influence, and physical reach of the G–20, it is not difficult to imagine a changing UN role.

Privatization

The G–8 combined economic power and influence on global security and stability lifts transnationalism to new levels. The organization rides on the increasing primacy of economics and economical solutions to problems, which is reminiscent of past utilitarian practices. Utilitarians of the mid-18th century championed more economic efficiency through privatization, particularly when dealing with national security. John Rushkin, a vocal utilitarian, stated:

> If our present doctrines of political economy be just, let us trust them to the utmost . . . let us take the war business out of the governments hands and test therein the principles of supply and demand. Let our future sieges of Sebastopol be by contract—no capture no pay. Let us sell the commands of our respective battles to the lowest bidder so that we may have cheap victories.[22]

Rushkin was promoting the broader use of all the elements of British national power to achieve the most cost-effective and capable security structure for the growing and global interests of the Empire. This was reasonable during the 19th century, when expanding colonial and commercial interests spurred numerous conflicts with limited objectives. He was merely expanding government practices that had for some time required private companies to provide for their own protection. In the early 19th century, the East India Company not only deployed an army in the field but also ran a navy of 122 ships. Had Clausewitz fully recognized the extent to which private, commercial interests would both provide and apply the means of war in the 19th century, indeed into the 21st century, he might have placed commerce alongside war as extensions of policy by other means.

Utilitarian principles are again alive and well in England, where in 1983 the Adam Smith Institute called for the "civilianization" of the armed forces and the government began to privatize not only the logistics support but also front-line warfighting functions.[23] The same trend is present in the United States, primarily with regard to logistics functions.

The Chinese armed forces achieve self-sufficiency from as many as 20,000[24] People's Liberation Army businesses engaged in commercial activities, even overseas. Additionally, there are nearly 10,000 private security firms that offer services where states used to be the sole source. In South Africa, private security guards now outnumber the police. The security operations of large corporations dominate in some parts of the developing world, and the future may see these functions transcend the traditional nation-state. They provide vital security functions and pose credible asymmetrical threats. Presently, demand for their services remains "robust and fertile":[25]

> . . . at present there is no legislative prohibition or regulation which deals with private military companies [PMCs] and they are therefore . . . entitled to carry on their business within the law.[26]

Demonstrated cost-effectiveness of PMCs may prompt an expansion of services to the maritime sector. A future PMC—call it "Littoral Solutions"—subsidized through a combination of public funds and private funds from corporations exploiting off-shore resources, might very well provide security and safety services within a nation's exclusive economic zone (EEZ) or, perhaps more cost-effective, across the EEZs of multiple nations. This could be an effective way to address the growing problems of piracy and illegal exploitation of maritime resources. A transnational security organization like Littoral Solutions should have the characteristics of a responsible, multinational organization. It should observe international law and possess functional capacities that provide desired levels of interoperability. Shaping the reasonable and rational role of this growing industry can be accomplished only through an understanding of its private and transnational character.

Decline of Hierarchical Authority

Globalization brings a "decline of hierarchical authority,"[27] says Michael Mazaar. Reaction against statism in the developing world and the dissatisfaction with one-party rule are indicators of broader challenges and changes based on the rising authority of knowledge. Marshall McLuhan put it this way: "Delegated authority is lineal, visual, hierarchical. The authority of Knowledge is nonlineal, nonvisual and inclusive."[28]

Information and knowledge are putting power in the hands of more people. Small horizontally organized work groups are vesting authority and empowering their workers through direct ownership. With little to no hierarchical structure, they can have great impact. Larger, more vertically organized groups like great multinational companies may maintain hierarchical structures, but their transnational investment patterns drive authority and power downward. Now, direct foreign investment in factories, utilities, and other long-term projects bypasses the more traditional and controlled method of investment in state stocks and bonds. From 1981 to 1985, annual foreign direct investment averaged $98 billion; in 1997, the figure had risen to $440 billion.[29]

The more unseemly side of this declining trend can be seen in what John Gray calls the "Anarcho-Capitalism" of post-communist Russia. Criminal elements within the Soviet Union fused themselves to the political elite and the bosses of a clandestine economy. With the collapse of the Soviet Union, the situation remains criminal, but perhaps less clandestine. Under a growing plurality of corruption and controlled by a less hierarchical structure, the criminal organizations now reflect the diverse ethnic tapestry of Russia and they do not normally act in concert.[30]

Strict hierarchical social control has been for centuries a foundation of many Asian cultures, but this, too, is changing. Extensive research in more than a dozen Asian countries recently found that governance is a central issue everywhere in Asia. Traditional hierarchical structures hold increasingly tenuous power, while individual empowerment is on the rise. China, with the most hierarchical of governments, is experiencing declining respect for central authority among the youth and within local governments.[31]

These global trends—transnationalism, privatization, and the decline of hierarchical authorities—are sustained by the democratization of technology, finance, and information.[32] They are rooted in economics, nurtured with science, and blossom through knowledge. As stated earlier, it must be recognized that not all countries are equal participants in globalization. The countries in the stable, concentrated zones of prosperous, well-developed economies are in a race for markets in the countries that comprise the broad, unstable, and contentious zones of underdeveloped economies—zones with most of the world's population. These zones constitute that part of the globe that has yet to be fully embraced by globalization. The forces that drive a near-postmodern, developed world into interaction with the not-yet-modern or not-yet-developed world are the same forces that are driving the changes in the structure of power and influence across all sectors of a growing global economy and society.

Engagement: A Heritage

As a flexible element of national power for two and a half centuries, U.S. naval forces have made use of all possible ways of procuring, organizing, deploying, and employing ships. In the mid-19th century, they were almost entirely in support of small-scale contingencies and missions other than war.[33]

Karl Marx and Friedrich Engels commented on the era in the *Communist Manifesto*, published in 1848. They had observed the Western sensation of profit and laissez faire that provide the conditions for economic expansion. Growth had demands. Internally, women were streaming from their homes to take up work in more than 100 trades. A rigid domestic system from the Colonial Age began to crumble. Relief from labor shortages was found through immigration, which provided the additional workers for New England factories and the farmers for the western territory. Externally, political, economic, and military developments had, despite two recent wars over independence, prompted England to offer cooperation with the United States. Of this cooperation, 80-year-old Thomas Jefferson commented in 1823 that it was "the most momentous which has ever been offered . . . we should sedulously cherish a cordial friendship."[34] With these conditions, engagement began to expand. Congress was emboldened by the rapprochement of the United States and the United Kingdom, and encouraged by memorials from men interested in trade, particularly with China.

In 1815, there were only two independent nations in the New World, the United States and Haiti. By 1822, continental America had largely thrown off colonial domination. From the Great Lakes to Cape Horn, only Belize, Bolivia, and the Guianas remained under European control. The Monroe Doctrine sought to consolidate gains by declaring any further attempts to extend European political systems in the Western Hemisphere as dangerous to America's peace and safety. The doctrine went on to exempt Europe's existing colonies or dependencies, saying that, "in matters relating to themselves [European powers] we have not interfered and shall not interfere."

Key U.S. political, economic, and social trends from the mid-19th century are clearly present today. The desire to lead and consolidate democratic gains ran alongside the accelerated economic and social integration now termed globalization, albeit at a slower pace. This phenomenon is now, as it was in the 1830s and 1840s, just beginning. Pressures comparable to underdeveloped markets and labor shortages were then, and are now, relieved by influencing external factors like immigration and trade.

Of note is the fact that as the U.S. naval forces forged outward from the continent, it was empowered to act. Internal to the Navy, overseas squadrons reported directly to the Secretary of the Navy, who was a cabinet-rank political appointee; externally, the independent Department of the Navy was co-equal in status, enjoying autonomy with the Departments of War and State and other departments. In the interagency process of the time, it had equal access to the President.[35]

Not long after the War of 1812, the Navy assumed a global posture. By 1835, there were six squadrons: the Mediterranean, West India, Brazilian, Pacific, East India, and Asiatic. Often relieved on station, these squadrons and their global reach remained largely unchanged for the remainder of the century. In the 1830s, even with the administration's emphasis on continental defenses, these squadrons remained forward. The 21 ships in the Navy's registry were fully employed as the country endured the pressures and stresses that have been mentioned. However, and notwithstanding the brief but serious economic depression beginning in 1837, work continued on a special naval project, the Naval Exploring Expedition, in the planning stages for almost 2 years. Samuel Eliot Morison called the project, launched on August 18, 1838, "the most important overseas project this era."[36] The following instructions were issued by the Secretary of the Navy, James K. Paulding, to 40-year-old Lieutenant Charles Wilkes on August 11, 1838:

> Sir—The Congress of the United States, having in view the important interests of our commerce embarked in the whale-fisheries and other adventures in the great Southern Ocean, by an act of the 18th of May 1836, authorized an Expedition to be fitted out for the purpose of exploring and surveying that sea, as well to determine the existence of all doubtful islands and shoals . . . to ascertain resources and facilities for trade to teach the natives the modes of cultivation . . . to ascertain whether there is any safe route which will shorten the passage of our vessels to and from China . . . to extend the empire of commerce and science . . . to diminish the hazards of the ocean. . . .[37]

A squadron of six ships had been assembled and fitted for what would be a four-year voyage of shaping, responding, and discovering. Lieutenant Wilkes had been designated a Minister Plenipotentiary, assuming ambassadorial status for the expedition. Civilian scholars and scientists from many disciplines competed for assignment to the expedition and had formed a cadre that would "extend the bounds of science, and promote the acquisition of knowledge."[38]

Wilkes worked closely with the State Department representatives permanently stationed in the most remote places, as well as the missionaries (the early NGOs) who were often the prime sources of information. He projected the prestige and power of the United States from the sea, seeking out the centers of power in the many tribal island environments and more powerful nations of the Pacific and around the world. This formative engagement effort established cooperative relations through various agreements and, given the unprecedented access, gathered important information. Wilkes had his contingencies and had the capabilities to respond to crisis with force when it became the only alternative. He served the operative side of the engagement spectrum with his surveys and assessments of suitable coaling stations to support the Navy's pending transition from sail to steam. Additionally, his charts of the Southern Pacific were used extensively in the naval campaigns of World War II. The expedition carried many of the most important inventions of the day, as well as a unique library of scientific and academic books that would both assist the embarked scholars and scientists and astonish the people they engaged.

During preparations for the 1838 Exploring Expedition, The House of Giesse & Horckhaufs, a Philadelphia purveyor of finery, sent a letter to President Andrew Jackson asking him to consider purchasing items for the expedition. In the letter was an offer to provide the means to secure the cooperation of the natives encountered.

> The good will and friendship of rude savages are most effectively secured by gaudy presents.[39]

The ability to influence the leadership of the tribal peoples was enhanced by showy beads and trinkets that were almost worthless to the expedition. Highly valued by the natives, on occasion the gifts would even be considered by the recipients to possess certain powers and spirits. There may be a modern equivalent of these trinkets, but the spread of information has produced a broader, better sense of value. For example, in the Kayapo Indian village in a remote corner of the Amazon rain forest, the tribesmen monitor the business channel on a single satellite television set. They track the international rate for gold and then determine what to charge the gold miners who work on the tribal land.[40]

The records of the Exploring Expedition are replete with evidence of a professional acumen among its officers and men. A strong ethos of engagement and an interdisciplinary approach enabled them to set specific objectives and empower the executors. Cited as primary objectives of the expedition were the "Great Interests of commerce and navigation"—that is, increased international influence and science.[41]

Observations

Engagement appears to be an enduring imperative of the National Security Strategy. However, for the U.S. naval forces, the engagement mission is underdeveloped. Largely transfixed by the Cold War containment strategy, the capacity of naval forces to shape the international environment has yet to fully mature. Part of the U.S. naval legacy is a capacity for special utility to national interests during (relatively peaceful) periods of economic expansion and profound international change. An inspirational approach to the national imperative of engagement, one aimed at seizing opportunities and mitigating the destabilizing effects of globalization, could reaffirm this utility. If deliberate, innovative, and focused in its engagement effort, the Navy could more effectively contribute to the global goals and aspirations of the Nation while preserving its precious resources. As was the case for its warfighting doctrine, the Navy must also turn its attention from the sea in its engagement effort. In doing so it will tap into its legacy and reinvigorate the unique geostrategic perspective of the naval service (a national treasure); limit its exposure to primarily ad hoc or issues-based employment; and empower the naval force to act as a catalyst for enhanced security among a diverse set of actors and interests.

In 1993, Ambassador Linton Brooks wrote the following:

> The Navy's failure to focus on peacetime presence arises in part because the profession lacks any consensus on how such presence relates to budget and force structure decisions. A second factor is the difficulty of understanding, at more than a rudimentary level, how peacetime presence advances national goals.[42]

In 2000, budget allocation and force structure issues remain. They join with the illusive goal of transformation to consume the intellectual capital of naval force visionaries. In this time of global change, proactive and innovative strategists should implement a modest shift in mindset to a more holistic approach. This approach will send a stronger message of naval force utility in an environment of globalization, and it will better prepare the naval service for the upcoming Quadrennial Defense Review process. Important for the naval force strategy, this message will foster a solid understanding of the ends of forward presence and a full examination of the means to those ends—taking into account the entire potential of naval engagement from Har to War.

Any increase in future naval budgets and force structures will be a hollow victory without this preparation. If Congress were suddenly to allocate $100 billion more per year to the procurement budget (the current high-end budget shortfall estimate), it would be insufficient in the presence of an underdeveloped vision for employment of a larger force in a peacetime environment. Ambassador Brooks' remarks highlight the added hurdle of a rudimentary understanding of how presence works. The U.S. naval force is beginning to overcome this hurdle through experimentation and innovation at lower levels, where more than rudimentary understanding already exists.

Formative Engagement

The process of making engagement a naval presence multiplier has begun. In the mid-1990s, ship deployment patterns began to change. For example, in 1994, 97 percent of all port visits in the European area of responsibility (AOR) occurred in NATO countries (plus France and Israel). By 1997, that total had fallen to 87 percent. The shift was toward the contentious zone of the developing countries mentioned earlier, and it has continued, aiming for an informal target of 25 percent of all port visits occurring in this contentious zone. Port visits are a good indicator of operating patterns and are representative of a much wider array of engagement in a global context. Moreover, alone they represent close to 1.5 million person-days a year spent in ports of the European AOR.[43] In 1997, at the Component Commander level, there was a conscious decision to continue the modest shift toward the more unstable areas in the Black Sea region, the Maghreb, and Africa, and to begin the process of developing formative engagement—tapping the unique capabilities of naval forces and having impact at the margins of stability. What was given up in terms of decreased operative engagement with the reliable and ready navies of NATO was insignificant. The intent was to strike that symbiotic balance between operative and formative engagement. Initial priorities were determined by combining a basic understanding of instability and the forces of globalization and a fairly clear understanding of vital U.S. interests. The result was a modest shift, one that benefited both the shape and respond tenets of national strategy and that began to develop economy of force measures conducive to a greater indigenous capacity for coping with complex security conditions and contingencies.

Two developments, among others, have served to reinforce the emerging engagement balance. First was the immense contributions of those nations near the theater of conflict during Operation *Allied Force*, particularly "The Former Yugoslav Republic of Macedonia, Hungary, Bulgaria, Romania, Albania and others." The CJCS Allied Force after-action report stated that these contributions "were in large part a dividend of sustained U.S. and NATO engagement over the last few years." The report emphasized that this engagement "helped to stabilize institutions in these nations so they were better able to withstand the tremendous burden inflicted by the humanitarian crisis and the operation itself."[44] In those few years (1994–1997), formative engagement by naval forces (again measured in port visit days per year) increased 600 percent in Bulgaria and 400 percent in Romania. This was indeed a concerted effort in light of the Montreaux Convention restrictions placed on non-Black Sea naval powers using the Straits of Bosporus and Dardanelles. Increasing the quantity of port visit days does not by itself bring about the favorable conditions mentioned, however.

The second event was the sensitive evolutionary process of beginning engagement with Algeria. In 1997, when it was recognized that the internal stability of Algeria was improving, there was an effort on the part of the State Department and U.S. Naval Forces, Europe, to determine what initial steps could be taken to enhance security and signal support for reform through engagement. At the time, security conditions at the U.S. Embassy in Algiers were such that no one could leave the compound without an armed guard. However, the Algerian military was gaining against extremist factions, and the government was taking steps toward elections, political plurality, and reassurance of the outside world of its commitment to reform. It was considered by all involved that engagement by naval forces would be the least problematic. Through Algeria's long period of internal strife, its naval force remained detached from abuses and alleged abuses that occurred, and as such presented a more suitable path to strengthening relations—a recurring theme in developing countries with problematic pasts. Ultimately, engagement at multiple levels succeeded in opening doors. The initiating event, a ship port visit, included the first Algerian military exercise with a foreign military since Algeria's independence decades before. Recently, Algeria has accepted an invitation to join NATO's Mediterranean Dialogue, a significant advance toward cooperative relations across the Mediterranean and Atlantic.

These are two examples—there are more—of formative engagement as it impacts near the center left of the Har-to-War spectrum (see figure 1). More to the right on the spectrum is a promising approach being explored by naval forces in the European AOR. The Commander in Chief, U.S. Naval Forces, Europe (CINCUSNAVEUR), is seeking to strengthen formative engagement through interdisciplinary and cross-sector partnerships with nonmilitary actors and transnational organizations. A recent seminar in London entitled *Managing Instability: A Pre-Crisis Approach* brought together senior policymakers from government, NGOs, international business, academia, finance, and the naval services to determine whether a formative engagement approach was plausible and supportable. The consensus was that ongoing engagement by a wide array of national and international players does have intersecting objectives. Further, creative partnering could effectively accomplish both military and development objectives while limiting counterproductive activities. The group was against establishing any hierarchical or formalized coordinating structures and suggested that a virtual working group could begin to transform the concept into reality. The process is ongoing, with initiatives in the Caucasus and the Black Sea, and with the biennial West African Training Cruise.[45]

Efforts are being made at the unit level to enhance the quality of formative engagement. They make use of mostly organic assets to support the security-related objectives of a U.S. embassy and its country teams. A large portion of the resident expertise in a U.S. naval force unit is exportable and relevant to these country teams. Conceptually, the exportable knowledge and skills available to formative engagement are almost entirely organic to the force and incorporated in, and certified by, the basic or unit-level phase of pre-deployment training. For the many willing nations, skill sets like afloat sanitation, energy-efficient engineering plant operations, hazardous materiel control, oil spill response, shore patrol procedures, and search and rescue operations, to name a few, are relevant and desired. Other skills not traditionally organic to naval units are becoming available at higher levels. A new training program in the Navy Chaplain Corps will focus on equipping the chaplains to advise commanders on cultural and religious aspects of military decisions and to interface with local religious communities.

Military or civilian, afloat or ashore, many of the developing institutions in these countries benefit from U.S. naval force engagement that addresses functional needs, builds institutional capacity, promotes international legal norms, and highlights moral obligations. A knowledge- and skills-based approach to formative engagement has the potential to influence at levels comparable to the beads and trinkets of Lieutenant Wilkes' Exploring Expedition. A realistic agenda for this kind of engagement can be fine-tuned using the priorities and objectives articulated in the U.S. embassy Mission Performance Plans for the countries involved.

Operative Engagement

The domain of operative engagement is a prosperous developed zone of countries lashed together by alliances and interdependencies. The domain can be further reduced to the countries whose naval forces are the most reliable, ready, and capable—that is, capable of coming together with U.S. naval forces in a complex battle space, under a significant multidimensional threat, and sustaining the execution of a range of missions from surgically precise direct action to the projection of blunt force and shock from the sea. This small group should be carefully cultivated. Its combined blue-water (sea control), littoral (land attack), and space (theater ballistic missile defense) capabilities will give it unprecedented power and reach and at the same time place employment burdens on the force. Operative engagement must focus on burden sharing. Smaller yet capable partners should be encouraged to adopt (to the degree their budgets allow) critical niche competencies with plug-in interoperability. Exportable knowledge and skills available to operative engagement are almost entirely organic to a deploying naval force as subsets of the intermediate and advanced phases of pre-deployment training.

This group should be committed to a more robust and combined deployment scheme, one that occasionally slips the bonds of the now commonplace operating locations and patterns. This would require that U.S. naval forces modify the expeditionary rhythm and packaging of their presence, drawing the committed partners into a more dynamic and relevant scheme of operation. This scheme should fully recognize the realities of the new global dimension and more accurately reflect the expanding interests of the group. Conceptually, perhaps a new, syncopated rhythm could replace the standard 4/4 or 2/4 quartered rhythms that drive the Global Naval Force Presence Policy. An off-beat rhythm would demand a broader and more flexible strategic intellect, could reinforce a coalition of the committed and the ready, and would employ what Ambassador Brooks calls "constructive ambiguity," a characteristic uniquely exploited by naval forces.

Changes of this sort should be undertaken slowly but deliberately and with extensive coordination. They should involve consideration of ongoing initiatives like the

European Security and Defense Identity (ESDI). This identity will live with new command structures, institutional mechanisms like the Combined Joint Task Force, and non-Article 5 demands. The U.S. naval force should seek to integrate its processes of transformation and experimentation with the ESDI naval forces. This will be exceedingly complex with a small group of navies that are not only involved in their own naval force transformation process but also are dealing with overarching issues such as national sovereignty and institutional identity. Nevertheless, this is an essential element of operative engagement. NATO Operation *Allied Force* (Kosovo) after-action report highlighted this point by emphasizing the need for improvements: "Our experience demonstrated the urgent need to pursue the Defense Capabilities Initiative." The report went on to specify command-and-control systems, information systems, secure communications, precision strike capability, air operations support, and mobility systems as the most important deficiencies. Consolidation of European defense will happen, but its combined combat capability and readiness must improve. Operative engagement should be focused on assisting such improvement in ways that lead to a more coherent application of combined naval forces.

Operative engagement should be seeking the equivalent of Wilkes' coaling stations. Where are the coaling stations that will support future naval operations? Are they sea-based or in space, real or virtual, at home or abroad? Do they exist as a function of combined naval exercises, or are they embedded in agreements for interoperability and transfer of sensitive military technologies? Perhaps they will be formed within contractual language of international megaconglomerate mergers. Chances are there will be a mix of all these things, the complexity of which will require added organizational focus and intellectual capital.

The stresses and uncertainties of globalization are surely affecting the role of naval forces along the Har-to-War spectrum. As has been stated elsewhere in this volume (see chapter 22), to meet the challenge and adapt to new realities, it may be necessary to change the institutions, organizations, and indeed the legal basis for operating the Armed Forces of the United States. Fundamental change of this type will entail reinvigorating the unique peacetime competencies of the naval service. A from-the-sea shaping focus on the formative side of the Har-to-War spectrum has the potential to enhance the international security environment, just as does a from-the-sea response focus on the operative side of the spectrum. Achieving a symbiotic balance between formative and operative engagement amid the dynamic effects of globalization should be a national priority. This complex effort would certainly be a part of the knowledge superiority pillar of a new naval strategy.

Recommendations

After almost 10 years with a relatively consistent National Security Strategy, declining resources, increasing employment, and the impact of globalization, the time has come to fully examine the naval role in a new era. In a recent *Defense News* article, the Secretary of the Navy was quoted as saying, "There is an era for naval power in this century that is more dramatic in its reach and its capability for effecting things than we've ever seen before."[46] Noted naval analyst Wayne Hughes suggests that the 21st century can become a "maritime century" of peace and prosperity.[47]

The U.S. naval force will surely be a key factor in nurturing the kind of security conditions necessary to establish and maintain stability in the presence of profound global change. To begin the process, three actions are necessary:

- Issue an overarching U.S. naval force (Navy and Marine Corps) engagement policy that advances the operative and formative engagement construct and supports its development.
- Boost support for engagement planning and assessment from the Component Commander level (dedicated billets) to the unit level (collateral duty billets).
- Further explore and support the CINCUSNAVEUR initiative on formative engagement and adopt successful methods and approaches where appropriate.

For the future, effective engagement cannot merely rely on stronger forms of past preventive and corrective approaches. It must be deft and proactive, and it must embody the very best that the United States has to offer. It must match the goals of prosperity, security, and democracy with the enablers of leading, listening, and learning. It must combine the attributes of sense of purpose, consistency, and unity of effort with the qualities of credibility, humility, and strength. No single U.S. entity can attend to all these elements. However, the U.S. naval force can be uniquely postured in this environment of globalization, and it can serve as it has in the past as a primary catalyst for positive change and innovation.

Notes

[1] Section 108 [50USC 404a] (a) (1), National Security Act of 1947 as amended by Public Law 99–433, Department of Defense Reorganization Act of 1986, October 1, 1986, section 104(b) (3 and 4).

[2] George Bush, *National Security Strategy* (Washington, DC: Government Printing Office, January 1993), 3.

[3] Joint Staff, *Theater Engagement Planning*, *CJCSM* 3113.01 (Washington, DC: Government Printing Office, February 1998), A12, 13–14.

[4] Leenhouts interview, *OSD Strategy and Requirements*, November 16, 1999. Taken from Dirk Deverill, Brian Tarbert, Terry O'Brien, and Rick Steinke, *Global Engagement—The Shape of Things to Come* (Cambridge, MA: Harvard University, May 6, 1999), 7.

[5] Henry A. Kissinger, *Diplomacy* (New York: Touchstone, 1994), 18.

[6] The White House, *A National Security Strategy for a New Century* (Washington DC: Government Printing Office, December 1999), 3.

[7] Vanessa Houlder, "Ecowarriors Make Peace," *The Financial Times*, April 13, 1999, 14.

[8] Michael J. Mazaar, *Global Trends 2005: An Owners Manual for the Next Decade* (New York: St. Martin's Press, 1999), 4.

[9] George Gilder, *Over the Paradigm Cliff* (New York: Forbes ASAP, February 1997), 29.

[10] John Gray, *False Dawn: The Delusion of Global Capitalism* (London: Granta Books, 1999), 17.

[11] Thomas L. Friedman, *The Lexus and the Olive Tree* (New York: Farrar, Straus and Giroux, April 1999), 7.

[12] George Soros, *The Crisis of Global Capitalism* (London: Little Brown and Co., 1998), xxix.

[13] Anne-Marie Slaughter, "The Real New World Order," *Foreign Affairs* 76, no. 5 (September/October 1997), 183–184.

[14] Nicole Beauclair and Matthieu Quiret, *Military Technology* (November 1999), 73–76.

[15] Hicks and Associates, *Final Report of the Task Force on Globalization and Security* (Washington, DC: Department of Defense, December 1999), v.

[16] Ibid., 6, i.

[17] Jay Mazur, "Labor's New Internationalism," *Foreign Affairs* 79, no. 1 (January/February 2000), 86–89. Jay Mazur is the President of the Union of Needletrades, Industrial and Textile Employees, and Chair of the AFL–CIO International Affairs Committee.

[18] Slaughter, "The Real New World Order," 186.

[19] Friedman, *The Lexus and the Olive Tree*, 12.

[20] U.S. Department of Defense, *Report to Congress: Kosovo/Operation Allied Force After-Action Report* (January 2000), 8.

[21] The White House, *A National Security Strategy for a New Century*, 22.

[22] Christopher Coker, "Outsourcing War," *Cambridge Review of International Affairs* 13, no. 1 (Autumn/Winter 1999), 100.

[23] Ibid.

[24] Eric Fredland and Adrian Kendry, "The Privatisation of Military Force: Economic Virtues, Vices and Government Responsibility," *Cambridge Review of International Affairs* 13, no. 1 (Autumn/Winter 1999), 149.

[25] David Shearer, "Private Military Force and Challenges for the Future," *Cambridge Review of International Affairs* 13, no. 1 (Autumn/Winter 1999), 81, 85.

[26] Foreign Affairs Committee: Sierra Leone, second report, HC116, 1998–1999 (Washington, DC: Government Printing Office, December 1999).

[27] Mazaar, *Global Trends 2005*, 199.

[28] Marshall McLuhan, *Understanding Media: Extensions of Man* (New York: McGraw-Hill, 1964), 272.

[29] Mazaar, *Global Trends 2005*, 161.

[30] Ibid., 155.

[31] Ibid., 200.

[32] Friedman, *The Lexus and the Olive Tree*, 39–58.

[33] Peter Swartz and E.D. McGrady, *A Deep Legacy: Smaller-Scale Contingencies and the Forces that Shape the Navy* (Alexandria, VA: Center for Naval Analyses, August 1998), 3.

[34] Samuel E. Morison, *The Oxford History of the American People* (New York: Oxford Press, 1965), 413.

[35] Swartz and McGrady, *A Deep Legacy*, 24.

[36] Morison, *The Oxford History of the American People*, 443.

[37] Charles Wilkes, *Voyage Round the World: Embracing the Principal Events of the Narrative of the United States Exploring Expedition* (Philadelphia: George W. Gorton, 1849), v–viii.

[38] Ibid., viii.

[39] National Archives, records of the 1838 Naval Exploring Expedition, microfiche: M–75 057–4 (reel 1).

[40] Friedman, *The Lexus and the Olive Tree*, 31.

[41] In a letter from Secretary of the Navy, James K. Paulding, the objective of the Exploring Expedition was the "promotion of great interests of commerce and navigation." The advancement of science was to be "an object of great but comparatively secondary importance." National Archives, records of the 1838 Naval Exploring Expedition, microfiche: M–75 057–4 (reel 1).

[42] Linton F. Brooks, *Peacetime Influence Through Forward Naval Presence* (Alexandria, VA: Center for Naval Analyses, October 1993), 2.

[43] Gregory M. Swider, *Liberty Incident Analysis* (Alexandria, VA: Center for Naval Analyses, May 1999), 2.

[44] U.S. Department of Defense, *Report to Congress: Kosovo/Operation Allied Force After-Action Report*, <http://www.defenselink.mil/pubs/kaar02072000.pdf>, 5.

[45] Bradd C. Hayes and Theophilos C. Gemelas, *Managing Instability: A Pre-Crisis Approach*, DSD Report 00–4 (Newport, RI: Naval War College, September 1999).

[46] Robert Holzer, "Danzig Speeds Implementation of Strategic Shifts," *Defense News*, March 13, 2000, 4.

[47] Wayne Hughes, *United States Maritime Strategy and Naval Power in East Asia in the 21st Century*, paper delivered at the Sixth International Sea Power Symposium, Seoul, Korea, August 5, 1999, 1.

Chapter 24

The Navy and Globalization: Convergence of the Twain?

Gwyn Prins

And as the smart ship grew
In stature, grace and hue,
In shadowy silent distance grew the Iceberg too

Alien they seemed to be:
No mortal eye could see
The intimate welding of their later history

— *Thomas Hardy*
The Convergence of the Twain

Two forces stand in strong and anxious contrast at the beginning of the new millennium. This chapter is an enquiry into their likely interaction.

In retrospect, it seems that once sociologists and students of international politics were liberated from the cruel and unusual confines of the mentality created by the Cold War, one issue above others seized their imagination. A remarkable literature devoted to exploration of the dimensions of a phenomenon called "globalization" emerged in the 1990s. The quotation marks are necessary because neither the nature of the phenomenon nor its effects are easily or generally agreed.

For the purposes of this discussion, however, it can be asserted that the term *globalization* is unequivocally grounded at three points. The nature of world economic activity at the beginning of the new century, particularly the international payments system, is remarkably interactive: there are major winners and losers. Secondly, I assert that, in consequence, the relative competencies of state and nonstate actors in global politics are importantly changed. Thirdly, and in consequence again, the technological, social, and psychological empowerment of individuals and commensurate curtailment of the competencies of state power, can engender a revision of the late 18th century social contract between citizen and state (but all circumstances

---

Gwyn Prins is principal research fellow at the London School of Economics and Political Science. He also is a senior fellow in the Office of the Special Advisor on Central and Eastern European Affairs at NATO and senior visiting fellow in the Defence Evaluation and Research Agency at the Ministry of Defence. Dr. Prins was previously senior research fellow at the Royal Institute of International Affairs and taught history and politics at Cambridge.

do not necessarily have this effect). These latter insights propel that awareness of the inadequacies of both libertarian and socialist descriptions and prescriptions, and have given rise to the so-called Third Way project.

The literature on globalization is large, vigorous, often depressingly unfocused, and tends toward no single definition. But while there may not yet be a consensus on the precise shape of what is looming, there is a general sense that something lurks, which might be dangerous as much as it might be positive. In what follows, the case will be made that these empowerments and disempowerments do, indeed, force revisions of the essence of citizenship, and that whether these revisions will ultimately be supportive or destructive of global security will depend on American choices and actions. The United States is a lonely hyperpower. In particular, it will be suggested that prior and positive engagement with and fostering of a global self-consciousness, which currently is only fitfully present (in the emerging regime of human rights, for example), will be key.

The other force may be conveniently viewed by scanning its literature: the past volumes of the U.S. Naval Institute *Proceedings*. Here, if anywhere, one finds the Navy talking publicly to itself. The conversations are as vigorous as those among the globalization theorists and indeed in recent years have included excursions into aspects of operations other than war and diplomatic and military operations. But if one takes *Proceedings* in the round, these excursions are clearly that: the main focus has been and continues to be upon three other things, the first of which is astonishing improvements in the technological performance of the Navy in each of its departments. Secondly, associated with this is a continuing prime concern with maintaining readiness to engage peer competitors (Title 10 of the U.S. Code, mandating preparation for war fighting). Thirdly, linked to both is a wish to achieve these missions as automatically as possible, with the fewest personnel. A good practical indicator of this is the strengthening emphasis upon cruise missiles, both in the submarine force and as the claws of the arsenal ship.

The Ship and the Iceberg

To read these two literatures is to recollect Thomas Hardy's ominous poem about the *Titanic* and the iceberg. The great ship, in all its brilliance and warmth and technological prowess, is built and launched and celebrated, and sets out from Liverpool. Meanwhile, in the frozen Arctic wastes, the iceberg also grows, is calved, and it, too, sets out. Twins in a preordained sense, the one gaily sparkling with light and speed, the other silently gray and lurking, they come together with fatal effect in Hardy's poem.

The *Titanic* disaster is often portrayed as a morality play. The hubris of high Edwardian society ends with nemesis, and Hardy was quick with that theme. ("In the solitude of the sea; deep from human vanity, and the Pride of Life that planned her, stilly couches she.") But "The Convergence of the Twain" can also be read as a precursor to the tone in Hardy's war poems: a premonition of the calamities that war soon brought. This is a resonance that it is useful to hear again for the purposes of this chapter.

An overview of the two literatures does suggest a vivid, structural dissonance between them: the forces of globalization and the Navy may pass each other by, but, equally, they may collide. Globalization—in the form of the shadowy but vast bulk of the iceberg—faces the United States with a structurally different global reality to that which its Armed Forces were designed, or are currently configured, to face. The question that this chapter wishes to raise is what the likelihood of collision may be—what favors it—and, if it can be avoided, what the implications of a change of course might be for the Navy as it sails into the 21st century.

What, more specifically, may be seen to be newly globalized at the end of the millennium, *which bears directly upon the nature and the potential future roles of the Navy*? Three things, which together give rise to a fourth.

Accordingly, the first section suggests a view of the Navy, seen from outside (but after 20 years of interested observation). The second proposes first some general and critical observations about globalization and then suggests three generally applicable aspects of globalization that bear specifically upon the Navy's interests and responsibilities. The third section asks about the dangers of collision. What might happen under three different responses to globalization by the Navy? The conclusion reached is unexpected. Since the chapter is not merely descriptive but also openly prescriptive, the fourth section details missions: it outlines some of the suggested requirements for a course that will avoid collision. The conclusion notes that all this means that there are hard choices ahead.

What Is the United States Navy?

What is the United States Navy? The question may seem simple-minded to the point of ridicule, but that would be a mistake. The Navy is unlike other navies, even its closest and oldest partner, the Royal Navy. Therefore, four defining characteristics must be established.

The first characteristic is its shape. U.S. naval forces are not contained within a single navy. The Navy at maximal extent is, in fact, five navies: a surface navy; a sea-borne air force; a submarine navy; the Marines Corps; and the Coast Guard (the latter two less tightly associated than the first three, but associated nonetheless). Each of these is in itself larger than are the complete military assets of many other industrial countries. The Navy alone deploys more aircraft than most other national air forces. The surface fleet of gray ships is several times the size of the next largest navies: the 19th century Royal Navy principle of the "two-power standard" applies even within these subdivisions and hugely more so when the totality is added together. The U.S. Coast Guard is a force that in itself is the size of a powerful independent navy. The submarine force is *sui generis*: it is without any close analogy in scale, since the collapse of the Soviet ballistic missile submarine fleet now rotting at its moorings in Murmansk. (Announcing Russian ratification of the latest START agreement, President Vladimir Putin stated that the Russian navy currently has 23 operational submarines.) Therefore, it is the branch of the U.S. military that, in this respect, most clearly parallels the Air Force, which is also so much in a league of its own that it, too, may confidently expect not to be challenged on its own terms. Finally, the Marine Corps possesses within their own identity an inventory of ships, helicopters, airplanes, armored fighting vehicles, and marines that is, in rough approximation, of the same scale as are the entire British armed forces.

A recital of this extraordinary array of force is instructive not only by underscoring the unique nature of the U.S. maritime capability, but also in explaining why, within it, each "union" has developed such strong identity (expressed in friendly rivalry in the letters, pages, and cartoons of *Proceedings*). More importantly, one sees distinct and coherent views of the best ways to defend the U.S. national interest: views made believable by the plain fact that each of the five component navies possesses credible means to propose its own solutions. This, as will become plain in the following discussion, may be a source of strength and advantage in the face of globalization.

Secondly, the Navy as a whole is distinguished by its shared philosophy, across all unions and derived from its historical self-image. The Navy, like the country to which it belongs, inhabits the "new world," but is, in fact, much older than its birth. For the Navy is arguably the perfect expression of that view that relates together the sovereignty of the state and the sovereignty-free areas of the high seas that has been in development since Hugo Grotius gave voice to the world view of the Dutch Republic in its golden age. It was no accident that Captain Alfred Thayer Mahan, who described the Royal Navy's role in the promotion and preservation of British maritime empire, was an American; the continuing influence of his concept of sea power is to be seen to this day.

The Mahanian concept of sea power calls for different forms of maritime action in different parts of the globe: a blanking-off of areas that might be sources of threat to the independence of the sea power state, as much as it is promotion of the opposite, namely, contrôl by exclusion of others from sea areas important for the preservation of freedom of navigation and trade. This common item of self-identity in all the advanced Northern European navies was the premise with which the Navy entered the Cold War. The nuclearization of national security in general, and naval thinking in particular, after the creation of Polaris, has served, if anything, to reinforce the historical self-image of the Navy as prime defender of the State.

That this self-image crystallized so firmly in the middle of the 20th century, at a time of U.S. ascendancy from great power status to superpower status to hyperpower status since the collapse of communism (in Hubert Védrine's useful coinage), has enabled U.S. maritime thinking to escape, so far at least, the harsh lesson that Britain's economic decline forced upon the view that naval supremacy led, rather than followed, economic strength. As Paul Kennedy famously observed in his study, *The Rise and Fall of British Naval Mastery*, it is a serious mistake to invert cause and effect. The purpose of this observation is not to argue that there is much evidence that the Navy is about to learn the Royal Navy's lesson in that old harsh way: rather, it is to note that lack of such challenge has permitted the distinct shape and self-confidence of U.S. maritime strategic thought, a view to which particular reference was given just before the end of the Cold War in the publication of the quasi-official report "Discriminate Deterrence."

The third defining facet of the Navy is its growing technological uniqueness. The pages of *Proceedings* provide eloquent witness to this, as each of the unions acquires its distinctive teeth and its common access to the neural network of sensors and data processing. The latter, more perhaps than the teeth arms, set the Navy apart from any other navy, including the navies of its closest allies. In order to operate on an equal footing in other North Atlantic Treaty Organization (NATO) navies in the Standing Naval Forces Atlantic (STANAVFORLANT), for example, U.S. ships must routinely switch off data links and sensors, which are U.S.-only national assets. There is a school of thought that argues in a worried fashion that such technological prowess means that, whether it wishes it or not, the United States will be forced into the loneliness of a hyperpower, unable to operate effectively in coalition contexts.

The size, the distinct philosophy, and the massive investment that have produced the technological edge of the Navy are all products of the fourth defining characteristic: the Navy is an expression of the U.S. approach to the management of foreign affairs. From the time that President George Washington advised his countrymen to avoid the dangers of entanglement in foreign alliances, the United States has been a country wary of foreign wars. Indeed, in the history of the Republic, with the exception of the War of 1812 (which was just beating up on the British, and so a sort of family affair), the Cold War has been the only war that the United States has willingly chosen to enter. Indeed, for those attracted to geopolitical determinism, just as much might have been predicted from a reading of Professor Halford Mackinder's 1903 paper on the geographical pivot of history. At some point, the dominant sea power would have to square up to the dominant continental land power, which (after the defeat of the Third Reich) was clearly Russia. And it won, admittedly through the deployment of McDonald's, Coca-Cola, and Hollywood, rather than the 101st Airborne or the Marine Corps—except as means to outspend the Soviets on defense preparedness.

The U.S. approach to warfare is informed by the very nature of the civil settlement within the Republic at independence, when it was decided emphatically that the United States would be a civilian society. It may seem an incongruous description of the world's most awesome military superpower in all of history, the society of West Point and Annapolis; nonetheless, it is true. The Second Amendment, complete with the preamble clause that the National Rifle Association prefers to forget, gave the right to bear arms that militias might be raised so that, in turn, the dangers of standing armies might be avoided. Couple this to the high value attached to the individual in U.S. political culture and one sees without difficulty the sources of the U.S. way of war.

Two sentiments combine. War is indeed hell. General William Tecumseh Sherman meant both physical hell and moral hell (which fired his articulation of the case for massive use of force). Secondly, the lives of U.S. citizens are precious and not to be spent except in face of a clear and present danger to the Republic. Therefore, by all means engagement should be avoided, if possible. The provision and presence of the five-fold unions of the U.S. naval forces can serve powerfully to that end, and hence justify the investment. But when engagement becomes necessary, then in the interests of minimizing casualties, all the ingenuity of American know-how needs to be marshaled to the service of the most massive and the swiftest blow, the most decisively to end the circumstance of threat. Under the shadow of inter-war economic depression, U.S. engagement in foreign affairs was isolationist and introspective. But, in the context of economic well-being and the absence of any peer rival, the same views express themselves as unilateral, rather than isolationist, actions.

In this respect, the United States is a modern state that expresses the essence of its social contract with its citizens on its coinage: *e pluribus unum*. Yes, the melting pot, but yes also the continuing strength of convergent loyalty to a sharp conception of statehood. The Constitution of the United States is cosmopolitan, meaning that the rights it enshrines are not claimed for U.S. citizens alone, but for all humanity. Nonetheless, the practicality of the state after 1776 has been to become the most successful and now the oldest extant example of the French revolutionary social contract, where the moral identity of the citizen was fused with that of the state in a benign compact.

As Robert Cooper noted in his seminal essay on the postmodern state and the new world order in 1996, these characteristics are distinctive and no longer general among socially and technologically advanced nations. Particularly in Western Europe and particularly as a product of the catastrophic fratricidal wars that tore at the continent's entrails for the first half of the 20th century, a much looser form of social contract is emerging, one more easily adaptable to a world where there are multiple sources of power—a world of globalizing forces. *Prima facie*, it might seem that neither the United States nor the Navy, in its shape, philosophy, technology, and self-image, is easily a participant in these new conversations.

What, Usefully, Is Globalization?

What conversations? In what do these conversations really consist? The essay opened with a statement of the three anchors of globalization, as the term is employed here, that must now be elaborated, in order then to derive the precise aspects of the phenomena that govern the interactions of globalization with the Navy. There are three general senses of globalization in common currency.

The first sense is the most colloquial. Ours is now a world where the flows of trade, of capital, and of finance are beyond the regulation of any single state or group of states. With the sole exception of the speed of communication, however, I see nothing in modern circumstances described under the rubric of globalization that is new. The case can well be made that the best system of automatic trade and finance that was beyond sovereign control was that of the gold standard (given the important proviso that Britain exercised a self-denying ordinance of nonintervention—as it did until war broke the system apart, causing the gold to flood across the Atlantic until the United States was sheltering more gold than any country had ever had, thus destroying the system in the countries whence the gold came as well as the system in the country to which it went). The simple point at issue is that the constraints on sovereign action have probably always been rather greater than is popularly imagined. So I suggest that this convenient generalization is, paradoxically, the least revealing.

The second general sense in which modern globalization may be interpreted has a stronger claim to uniqueness. Globalization makes big winners and big losers. It has divided the human family more stringently, and more generally, into rich and poor than has ever before been the case. Roughly one-third rich and two-thirds poor. So, if, following Geoffrey Barraclough, we take the defining characteristic of contemporary affairs to be the massive and comprehensive increase in scale, then a case is more easily made for division, rather than unification, as the distinctive feature of modern globalization. Admittedly, the division in possession of wealth and access to wealth is not unprecedented as a phenomenon; in particular, the stark differences in access to *information* have been seen before. When the first undersea telegraph cable, laid by Brunel's *Great Eastern*, linked Europe to the United States in 1865 so that communication across the Atlantic became a matter of seconds rather than days or weeks, and was followed by a spurt of cable laying from 1865–1872 to India and Japan, a letter to unwired places still took 6 months to be delivered. So there is an important sense in which the one-third minority of the human family that controls the levers of the globalized world should be seen, in Anthony Giddens's memorably admonitory phrase, to be "riding the juggernaut." This world-dividing interpretation of globalization has a particular challenge within it when in the next section we consider what the Navy's responses might be.

There is, however, a third general interpretation of "globalization." This is homogenizing rather than dividing, and it is homogenizing in a particular direction. Writing recently of the groveling and divided mess of post-intervention Kosovo, Timothy Garton-Ash ended his acid observations with the pregnant thought that after a day of mutual recrimination between Kosovar Albanians and Kosovar Serbs, both parties retreated to the privacy of their homes to share in a common ambition to enjoy the fruits of American consumer materialism. In the third sense of "globalization," the world has turned American. At root, I would suggest that it is a feature to be seen less in the specifics of the marketplace (to each his Coca-Cola according to his needs), but rather in America's possession of the key determinants of revolution: possession of a common vision, a language in which to express the vision, and provision of at least some tangible evidence of what that vision might be in practice.

Therefore, in summary of these general points, it can be seen that the colloquial interpretation of globalization is inadequate and insofar as it is true that it is not particularly novel; that what is new is the scale of the material divide between the rich and poor, and that superimposed upon this deeply riven human community there is a homogenizing vision projected through the new means of information technology that is specifically and unusually American in its nature. While the second point seems to affirm the possibility that the rich may need to repel the poor (the "discriminate deterrence" thesis), and therefore to indicate maritime military roles in that direction, the third runs counter, suggesting that the model of voluntary Americanization, which was so impressively powerful during the 1989 revolutions, may be more likely the norm than the exception.

So might one conclude that the ship and the iceberg will not converge? That their courses are widely different? Three further, general aspects of globalization engage the nature, ideas, and roles of the Navy concretely.

The first of these is the growing realization that the planet and its passengers face systemic stresses arising from global environmental change. This is not a chapter to do more than signal the phenomenon, and certainly not to enter the debate about anthropogenic *versus* natural causation. Rather, I would rest the observation upon the single most authoritative accumulation of analysis, produced by the Intergovernmental Panel on Climate Change. Sir John Houghton, Chairman of Working Group 1, which focused on the science of the climate, has observed of the second review report that evidence of global climate change is now moving "out of the statistical noise." Subsequent evidence of ice thinning, sea warming, and the slowing of ocean currents in the Arctic, deriving from the transpolar research projects made possible by the ending of the Cold War, have tended to underscore that point. To what extent it is possible to ascribe recent episodes of hurricanes and other major storms to these general trends is not yet clear. But as a globalized phenomenon, the last 20 years of research on global climate change is certainly a candidate for uncontroversial status, even if we cannot yet ascribe with certainty specific events to general trends.

The second general characteristic of globalization that has specific relevance to the world of the Navy touches directly a central element of its self-image. In the 17th century, Hugo Grotius championed the notion of *mare liberum,* the sovereignty-free high seas, re-stated in Articles 87–90 of Part VIII, Section 1, of the United Nations (UN) Convention on the Law of the Seas to give it its most precise modern reference. The sovereignty-free high seas are predicated upon the existence of exclusive littoral rights in coastal waters, and thus the contrast between the realm of the high-seas fleet and the coast guard—its literal, littoral, and legal identity is in its name—is made quite precise. But the arrival of global environmental stress and the potential for global climate change mean that the transferred notions of exclusive property that give substance to the concept of the exclusive rights of sovereignty are coming under challenge in the maritime environment almost before anywhere else.

This is, perhaps, fortunate because the maritime environment is one in which issues of property and sovereignty have been, and continue to be, most intensively explored. It has been within the UN Convention on the Law of the Seas of 1982, Part IX, Section 2, Articles 136, 137.1, and 137.2, that the most revolutionary challenge to the sovereignty/property equation underpinning the international, inter-state balance of power is to be seen. "The Area (the seabed and ocean floor and subsoil thereof, beyond the limits of national jurisdiction) and its resources are the Common Heritage of mankind," declares the Convention. "No state shall claim or exercise sovereignty or sovereign rights over any part of the Area or its resources, nor shall any state or natural or juridical person appropriate any part thereof. No such claim or exercise of sovereign rights nor such appropriation shall be recognized. All rights in the resources of the Area are vested in mankind as a whole." The concept of common heritage expresses another aspect of the enlargement of scale in Professor Barraclough's terms: a globalized world is a world that cannot allow spaces to be blanked off. As Halford Mackinder observed in 1903, the opportunity to seek power and resources through horizontal expansion into imperial spaces or wilderness is now foreclosed. New power can be obtained only violently, at the expense of another, or consensually, through the construction of self-conscious common interest. This, very precisely, focuses one of the aim-points for security in a global age, and it is lineally connected to the third specific global trend that has arisen and that couples directly to the challenges and opportunities before the Navy.

On April 22, 1999, Prime Minister Tony Blair delivered an unusual speech in Chicago. In it, he sought to explain why it was in the British national interest to relieve the sufferings of the Kosovar Albanians. As has become subsequently public, in the testimony of the Chief of the Defence Staff to the House of Commons Select Committee on Defence in April 2000, Blair was prepared to commit most of the military effort of his country to that end, had it become necessary. The Chicago speech was not an isolated and unusual geyser. Rather, it was the moment when a 50-year subterranean stream surfaced.

Most attention to Blair's Chicago speech has been paid to his elaboration of the criteria that must be met before the international community can feel warranted in breaching the sovereignty of a state, even in defense of human rights. Such tests are important and necessary, of course, but what was really striking was the manner in which Blair explained how the national interest was invoked. The suffering of these people, he said, demanded the attention of the rest of the world. In that justification, he simultaneously gave contemporary grounding to the principles established at the end of World War II in the Nuremberg Tribunal and surfaced the stream that went underground in the late 18th century.

For both reasons, it was appropriate that the speech should have been given in Chicago because the United States is the country that was central both at the 50-year and at the 200-year marks in the emergence of this trend in globalization. As has been already observed, the United States is uniquely endowed with a pre-French revolutionary Constitution, which enshrines cosmopolitan rights. That tradition, expressed in the way that American individualism values the individual, puts the United States logically, as well as militarily and politically, to the fore in driving both of the dynamics that emerged from the ruins of World War II: on the one hand, creation of the United Nations, the culminating expression of the age of the balance of power, and on the other, the Nuremberg principles, the most forceful modern expression of the late 18th century cosmopolitan imperatives. Blair's speech in Chicago took both to the center of the contemporary political stage, and this is regardless of the efficiency with which the mandate may or may not have been executed. The third general aspect of globalization that touches the world of the Navy directly is, therefore, that which once again interprets national interest as a responsibility to sustain global civil society.

To be sure, particularly after the disaster of Mogadishu, there has been much greater reticence in the United States to accept the implication of this role, and, insofar as it has been accepted, strenuous efforts have been made to fulfill its mission by means that minimize the exposure of U.S. military personnel to risk (even if that may increase the risks to other parties). But the debate about public willingness to accept risk really is a diversion from the essential point, namely, that the strengthening imperative to conduct humanitarian intervention in defense of human rights is plainly a defining characteristic of globalization as well.

Therefore, in summary, the three areas of globalization that bear specifically upon the concerns and potentialities of the Navy are, in the first two cases, natural (global climate change) and social (global commons) phenomena, respectively, which have in common the fact that the maritime provides the best first lines of approach. The third case (human rights) invites vigorous development of maritime and amphibious approaches, given the demonstrated difficulties in strategies giving primacy to land or air roles.

What Could Happen?

One possibility is that, in face of the globalization challenges identified and listed in the previous section, the Navy could remain close to a narrow self-interpretation: an *introspective unilateralism*. Certainly, three of the four characteristics of the contemporary Navy mentioned in the first section of this chapter would tend toward the view that a narrow construction is to be expected. Mahanian maritime doctrine, shot through with nuclear deterrence doctrine from the Cold War, combined with a unilateral (certainly) and isolationist (possibly) interpretation of U.S. interests, would support that view. It would be in conformity with the underlying tendencies of the American way of war, and, as Edward Luttwak has recently and arrestingly observed, most Armed Forces are designed and procured precisely not in the expectation of use, but rather as contributions to so overwhelming a deterrent threat that, in that manner, the Republic is to be kept safe. However, whereas the very long design, procurement, and service cycles of naval equipment mean that it is difficult to change the basic composition of the fleet easily or swiftly, the other characteristic of naval power tends in a different direction.

Arguably, the key asset that naval power possesses, distinct from any other military form of power, is its ability to provide presence without the declaration of any explicit intention of action. Furthermore, presence combines with the well demonstrated flexibility of most forms of naval unit, with the exception of the most highly role-specialized. In action, it is the rule rather than the exception that ships find themselves undertaking types of operations for which they are not primarily designed. That, parenthetically, is a powerful argument against the trend to intense and precise role specialization that is a consequence both of technological drive and of the Cold War constraints on strategic imagination. An Aegis cruiser that is incapable of dealing with pirates or smugglers may, in the future, find that its lack of general purpose capability is more of a drawback than seemed apparent at the time that it was conceived. At present, the trend is clearly to engage the military challenges of the post-Cold War world, insofar as possible, with high precision, remotely delivered systems such as the Tomahawk land attack missile (TLAM). That was plainly to be seen in the Balkan operations and, as such, subordinates maritime to air power theory. For the purposes of the new era, this may not be prudent.

The second way in which the Navy could respond to the new circumstances of globalization would be more internationally engaged than is the introspective unilateral national model. The Navy could play its role *multilaterally*, in a traditional interpretation of alliance, principally through NATO. Such a course of action has the advantage of retaining a higher degree of international political and military engagement (if such engagement is deemed to be an advantage); the disadvantage that dogs an alliance or coalition context is that historically it is a context within which it is hard to conduct innovative thinking.

A natural tendency of alliances (and NATO is no exception) is to seek the common denominator and to find language that can be as temporizing and as inclusive as possible. In the case of the U.S. principal modern alliance, which is NATO, one consequence of its recent, fraught, physical enlargement is to exacerbate the risk aversion that is already a function of such an institution. This is a paradox. For most of the last 50 years, the political rule of thumb in the United States has been for those favoring external engagement to support U.S. participation in alliances, notably in NATO, and for those favoring isolationist or unilateral priorities to oppose engagement in international organizations, especially the United Nations.

The challenge posed by globalization calls for deep and comprehensive rethinking about where comparative risks and advantages lie. The implication of the foregoing is to suggest that the context traditionally favored by liberal engagement may not be as effective as the one traditionally associated with introspection.

The third possibility for the Navy in the face of globalization is, therefore, a different sort of unilateral action: unilateral action in support of a broad interpretation of U.S. national security interests that sees national and global security interests fused in the manner that Blair described in his Chicago speech: *extrovert unilateralism*. Unilateralism of any sort, even extrovert unilateralism, is by its nature systemically different from any form of multilateral engagement, of course, because whereas the latter depends upon acceptance of a constrained role, in certain circumstances, and an accepted part in a general international political culture, the former does not.[1] Historical analogy for the Navy taking this type of leading role is with the Royal Navy and the antislavery patrols of the 19th century. At a time when a power can take unilateral action and has the means to do so, as the Royal Navy did then, there is an opportunity to produce a far more decisive leverage upon the general direction of events than in any other way.

It is here that the five-fold nature of the Navy can become so effective an asset. Whereas many complain, in a more or less good-humored manner, of the autonomy of the different unions, in fact, the ability of certain of them to develop their own systematic approaches to maritime problems may render them especially well prepared to assume the tasks required to give the Navy its lead role in the protection of global (hence national) security. Three specific facets of globalization have been isolated as having both importance and special maritime salience. How may they be attacked by the Navy? What missions are entailed?

Avoiding the Iceberg

Mission One

The first facet identified was global environmental stress. "Soon after his accession to the throne," wrote the Lord Commissioner of the Admiralty of King George III, "having happily closed the destructive operations of war, he turned his thoughts to enterprises more humane but not less brilliant, adapted to the season of returning peace. . . . His ships, after bringing back victory and conquest from every quarter of the known world, were now employed in opening friendly communications with hitherto unexplored recesses." Thus introducing accounts of the voyages of discovery to the Pacific Ocean undertaken by Captains Cook, Clerke, and Gore in His Majesty's ships, the *Resolution* and the *Discovery,* the text is given for a similar orientation of naval efforts to other purposes in the years following the end of the Cold War.

The role of the Navy submarine force through the Science Ice Expeditions (SCICEX) program in permitting the exploration of the Arctic Ocean has been decisive. The platform of a nuclear submarine is agreed to be the best possible way in which to map and investigate the underside of the ice sheet. Therefore, it is a matter both of anxiety and regret that, with the decommissioning of the last of the Sturgeon class attack submarines in 2001, this capability may be lost. Environmental monitoring roles have been performed by other branches. Notably, the use of satellite assets in a more transparent environment has been essential to improvements in global mapping of vegetation, both natural and cultivated, of soil loss, and of meteorological and oceanographic data and the like.

Mission Two

The second precise facet of globalization is the challenge of policing the global commons. It is generally agreed that stress in fisheries is one of the most important and sensitive indicators of the general health of the oceans. Because all five of the main pelagic fisheries are now under stress, with worldwide fishery take peaking at around 100 million tons per year, there is a danger of precipitating fishery collapse. This trend increases the importance of fishery protection. Far from being a hum-drum and insignificant role, it comes rapidly to the fore. One has only to recollect the Battle of the Grand Banks to see why. Fishing boats of one NATO ally (Spain) broke all the regulations on net size and take, while warships of another NATO ally (Canada) technically committed piracy on the high seas when arresting the offending miscreant, to general applause at home. The case shows how fishery disputes provide, in not insignificant microcosm, a model of the type of global conflict over environmental resources that we may face, if we are not careful. Traditionally, it has been the role of the coast guard to protect assets within the exclusive economic zone of the country. The Grand Banks debacle was only the first of a series of deep-sea fisheries disputes that are likely to increase. In 1999, the Royal New Zealand Navy sailed to defend the fragile population of the Orange Roughy at the sea mount south of New Zealand, to protect them from predatory fishing "down the chain" by Japanese fishermen. So one sees that fishery protection is already providing a context within which the fundamental ethical and legal debates about the common heritage are being fought. Looking toward new technology applications relevant to execution both to this mission and the previous one, the rapid development in long-range, remotely guided miniature submarines, originally conceived with oil installation patrol and other fixed seabed assets in mind, offers creative possibilities.

Another, but related aspect of the global commons mission connects to an existing priority task, namely, the policing of international straits and the combating of piracy. Admiral Jacky Fisher, creator of the modern Royal Navy, once observed that a handful of "choke points" locked up the globe. Control these, he said (and at that time Britain largely did), and one controls the world oceans. The Dover Straits, the

Straits of Gibraltar, and the passage around the Cape of Good Hope are relatively well policed at present. Such is certainly not the case for the Straits of Molucca or indeed for other coastal waters in Southeast Asia, such as the South China Sea. During the Persian Gulf War, in the Strait of Hormuz, the USS *Vincennes* was harassed by small vessels that it was ill equipped to repel. Investigation of the subsequent shooting down of an Iranian Airbus suggested that tensions in the ship resulting from the prior episode may have contributed to the error in its designed task. For the purposes of this chapter, the conclusion to be drawn is simply one of the utility of general purpose frigates, combined with a willingness to explore the modalities within which best to deploy such constabulary power. A good model is the "building-block" approach to Confidence and Security-Building Measures (CSBMs) followed by the nations of Southeast Asia and expressed in the Honiara Pact. This arrangement has permitted the largest and most advanced regional maritime power, Australia, to operate in a supportive and consensual context with the much smaller forces of neighboring states in a range of antipiracy, antismuggling, and maritime asset protection roles. The Battle of the Grand Banks and the accumulating evidence of global fish stock stress tell us that we have a need for systematized presence on the high seas beyond Mahan's methods, which, if it is to be effective and legal, calls for much innovative prior effort by the Naval Judge Advocate's department. It may be that the well established practices for international straits and pirates offer a point of departure.

Mission Three

The third mission is humanitarian intervention: the one of these three missions that has been most vividly in the public eye since the end of the Cold War. While I was visiting the Adriatic city of Dubrovnik several years after it was bombarded by Serbian gunboats in 1991, a resident observed to me how in the days before the war, ships of the 6th Fleet had sometimes paid courtesy calls. "What a pity," she said, looking at me closely all the time, "that one of those ships couldn't have found the time to call on us in 1991 when we really needed it." It is easy to be wise with hindsight. But in the case of the Bosnian war, the matter is precise and was entirely clear at the time. On November 6, 1991, the assembled European foreign ministers issued a solemn declaration in which they demanded that the Slobodan Milosevic regime cease forthwith its bombardment of Dubrovnik, else unspecified consequences would follow. The bombardment did not cease, and no consequences followed. Milosevic made his judgment of the will of the West, and many tens of thousands of people lost their lives before, chastened by the horror of the massacre at Srebrenica in the summer of 1995, the international community overrode the UN effort and, acting through NATO, took decisive and expensive military action.

The Dubrovnik case is useful not simply because it is true, but also because the military task of removing the Serbian and Montenegrin mountain battery that was bombarding the city would have been so easy for carrier aircraft close to the scene to do, had they been allowed to do it. Maritime strategists never tire of observing that most of humanity lives not far from a coastline. But even so, the chastening experiences of the death of Yugoslavia, combined with the rising salience of the global concern for the observance of human rights, mean that if these tasks are to be successfully embraced, it will require a much more systematic and early deployment of amphibious capability designed for diplomatic/military operations (DMOs) than heretofore.

Since Bosnia, there have been both a greater number and a wider range of cases calling for preventative or humanitarian DMO deployments of maritime force. The regional intervention under UN auspices in East Timor (UNIFET) was an example of the former; the discoordinated relief effort for Mozambique after the epic floods, of the latter. In both cases—as indeed in most others that one can envisage—the capacity of the Navy to provide sealift logistics; communications and intelligence; a spectrum of organic maritime air power, especially helicopters; and, if necessary, amphibious assault, stands in a league of its own. In this realm, too, the United States has the unique capability to take a lead, just as in the monitoring, protection, and constabulary roles discussed earlier. Looking at new technology developments relevant to these missions, the near-term prospect of FastShip hull design that will make freighters capable of an economical, sustained transatlantic 45 knots, or a 50-knots-plus light carrier or amphibious assault ship using such a hull, serves only to heighten the relevance of a maritime approach to DMOs.

Conclusion

The previous section has linked U.S. capability to specific missions that combat potential threats with global reach, arising from facts of globalization. Of the three choices before the Navy, traditional alliance internationalism seems, on the evidence, to be too soft to take the necessarily firm imprint of new directions; the choice of introspective unilateralism might exacerbate, rather than relieve, the divisive aspect of globalization. However, extrovert unilateralism—the modernized version of the 19th century antislavery patrols—will demand important changes, not only in mission but also in the self-image and relative status ascribed to functions within the Navy.

The central commitment to maintaining the submarine leg of the strategic nuclear triad is mercifully diminished. No peer competitor now exists or is likely to emerge in the near future. The only role of the nuclear weapon is entirely passive politically. It is the *existential deterrence*, so aptly coined by the late McGeorge Bundy, where already cautious powers are made more cautious. The Navy might therefore wish to adopt another of the planning devices of the Royal Navy at its zenith, namely, the 30-year rule—that this would be the warning time for emergence of a peer competitor. If it is felt to be valid (which it could well be) a precious window of opportunity opens within which it is both safe and necessary to raise the priority of other roles that help avoid collision with the facts or consequences of globalization.

The monitoring, protection, and constabulary roles manifestly require a new form of legal entity for the new century and the global maritime stresses that it brings. The principles for policing the high seas demand the domestication of the high seas. Grotius' *mare liberum* must be replaced in legal terms by *mare nostrum*. But this cannot be done by the unilateral extension of national rights of sovereignty. Therefore, the appropriate response to globalization is the creation for the high seas of an analogue to the coast guard. Littoral states require coast guards; global security demands an ocean guard. (The legal and practical details of an ocean guard can be found in the *2000 Ocean Yearbook,* edited by Professor Mann-Borghese.) Much of the necessary thinking that would permit the extension of the coast guard concept has already been done by coast guard lawyers. What is needed now is a full political recognition of the priority that should be given to the operationalization of this task. The Navy alone is able to exert the right leverage in the right places for this to occur.

The same requirement applies to the other key emphasis that the threat of the iceberg brings. Within the vision for extrovert unilateralism by the United States, the Marine Corps could encounter arguably the most challenging and rewarding period in its history. As observed earlier, the size of the Corps gives it a structural advantage when it comes to developing both a doctrine of maritime maneuver adapted to DMOs and requests for support that it requires from other branches.

But the hard requirements are not military, and are not to be dodged. If ever substance is to be given to militarily efficient protection of human rights worldwide, then the Marine Corps, supported by the other branches, must have a pre-eminent role in the delivery of that capability to the United Nations in a larger scale and more focused version of the CSBM building-block formula devised by Professor Ball and his colleagues, which has proved to be so effective in Southeast Asia.

There are no two things about it. Such combined and joint operations can only, in a limited fashion, be conducted through NATO. In the same way that the requirements of globalization for monitoring, resource protection, and constabulary roles demand an ocean guard, so the new demands for effective worldwide protection of human rights require commensurate restructuring in response. That means, above all, finding viable ways to achieve collective political-military direction of operations that are acceptable to the United States. Of course, there are countries, notably France and the United Kingdom, that can and will happily buttress such a move. Indeed, the British have moved closer to the principle of an Article 32 allocation of force to the United Nations than ever before. But whilst they may suggest and in limited theatres may act independently, at the time of its unconstrained global influence, the United States alone has the means and the opportunity to take the lead.

While this may jar the minds of one segment of contemporary U.S. politics, the hand need not long be stayed, for, as the world faces the challenges of globalization, it is fortunate that the country best able to lead the reorientation in the political and military response is the one whose revolutionary birth, reflected in its Constitution, speaks most directly to the central values of cosmopolitan democracy.

Notes

[1] The issue is debated fully in the contributions to Gwin Prins, ed., *Understanding Unilateralism in American Foreign Relations* (RIIA, June 2000), notably in the essays by C.W. Maynes and J. Bolton.

Chapter 25

The Coast Guard: Past Catalyst, Future Tool

Timothy L. Terriberry and Scott C. Truver

The Coast Guard has been a helpful catalyst of globalization in the past, and it can provide a uniquely valuable tool for U.S. policy in the future. Nonetheless, with nontraditional threats to maritime security on the rise, the Coast Guard will need to be modernized and otherwise updated so that it will be capable of performing its future missions. Only then can it be an equal partner with the Navy in what has come to be called the "National Fleet."

Historical Background

The United States has always wanted to use the seas safely, securely, fully, and wisely—to preserve its marine resources, to ensure safe transit and passage of cargoes and people on its waters, to protect its maritime borders from intrusion, to uphold its maritime sovereignty, to rescue the distressed who ply the oceans in ships, and to prevent misuse of the oceans. In essence, the most fundamental role of the Coast Guard is to protect the freedom of Americans and promote their opportunities to compete economically by providing maritime security. But the seas have always been considered part of the global commons, belonging to all nations to freely use, except the near-shore coastal waters. Thus, any effort of the United States to protect its citizens and interests, and the interests of its friends, regarding the use of the seas, must have an impact on other nations and groups, sometimes at great distances from U.S. shores. Even before globalization became fashionable, the military, multimission, maritime U.S. Coast Guard was a key element in global issues, trends, and dynamics.

The Coast Guard and its predecessor organizations—principally the Lighthouse Service (1789), Revenue Cutter Service (1790), Steamboat Inspection Service (1838), and Lifesaving Service (1847)—have relied on a combination of regulation, enforcement activity, cooperation with other public organizations, and partnerships with private enterprise to accomplish the objectives of a safe and efficient marine operating

---

Captain Timothy L. Terriberry, USCG, coordinates participation by the Coast Guard in the Quadrennial Defense Review. He has commanded two Coast Guard cutters and also served as chief of Operational Law Enforcement at Headquarters, U.S. Coast Guard. Scott C. Truver is vice president for national security studies and director of the Center for Security Strategies and Operations in the Systems Engineering Group at Anteon Corporation. He previously held positions at Information Spectrum, Inc., and the Santa Fe Corporation.

environment for the common benefit of individuals and the security of the country. Because the Coast Guard has never enjoyed ample budgetary support, it has had to seek a "holistic" approach to accomplish the desired outcomes of its numerous and varied legislative mandates. As such, the Coast Guard has reached out around the world to create effective regimes that improve safety at sea and the operational efficiency of Coast Guard activities. Enforcement burdens have been shared when possible. Vessel carriage requirements have been standardized among maritime fleets. Merchant vessel watch-keeping and training-certification standards have been made universal by international agreement. This effort has been ongoing for more than a century.

Today's Coast Guard is dedicated to protecting the public, the environment, and U.S. economic and national security interests in the Nation's ports and waterways, along the coast, on international waters, or in any maritime region as required by U.S. national security.[1] Every day, the Coast Guard saves lives and property at sea; provides essential elements for a safe, efficient maritime transportation system; protects the marine environment; enforces laws and treaties in the maritime regions; and defends the national security interests and maritime borders of the United States. In sum, the Coast Guard exercises the sovereignty of the United States in maritime regions of vital interest, thereby establishing maritime security for the people and enterprises conducting legitimate activity.

The Coast Guard's role in providing for the national and maritime security has its origins in the first administration of this country under President George Washington. The Revenue Cutter Service was established in 1790 to provide a means to enforce the custom duties, then the young republic's primary means of paying off its $70-million debt and ensuring the solvency of the United States.[2,3] The Revenue Cutter Service was the only military, armed maritime service of the young United States at that time and the only force capable of demonstrating the sovereign power of the United States at sea. The custom duties also were structured to favor the utilization of U.S. flag shipping in coastwise trade to encourage a recovery of that industry from the losses of the Revolutionary War.[4] Thus, from its beginning, the Coast Guard protected this country's maritime sovereignty by excluding undesirable activity and promoting the development of strong economic activity.

Additionally, the ninth act of the First U.S. Congress established the public policy of assisting in promoting safety at sea by the establishment of Federally funded lighthouses and aids to navigation as a means of assisting the economic development of trade and reducing the risk to human life at sea. This was the first public works act of the United States.[5] The Lighthouse Service that grew out of this act was incorporated into the modern-day Coast Guard in July 1939.[6] This expanded the service's responsibilities on the eve of World War II, when the safe, efficient, and effective movement of cargo to support and sustain military operations would be a critical responsibility in support of U.S. national security around the world.

The December 1999 National Security Strategy outlines three core objectives: enhance U.S. security, bolster U.S. economic prosperity, and promote democracy and human rights abroad.[7] As can be seen from the first acts of the First Congress just discussed, these basic objectives have existed for more than 200 years. The predecessors of the current Coast Guard promoted and protected these objectives from the very beginning. As the United States enters a new century, the fundamental objectives of its national security will not change. As the Nation seeks to expand the acceptance of its core values worldwide, the Coast Guard, actively involved in promoting and defending those values in the beginning, must remain involved as a multimission service with an expanded role in the future.

To enhance its ability to execute its multiple responsibilities efficiently and effectively, the Coast Guard has been a catalyst for globalization. Sumner I. Kimball, head of the Lifesaving Service (merged with the Coast Guard in 1915), was a key U.S. representative to the 1899 International Maritime Conference held in Washington, DC, with the goal of promoting safety at sea. This conference standardized the "rules of the road" for sea-going traffic that are now used throughout the world.[8] By establishing an international set of rules to be followed by all mariners, conferees ensured that the safety of individual citizens would be enhanced and economic prosperity advanced by lessening the risk of collision at sea, with the attendant loss of life, property, cargo, and fouling of the environment.

In another action that further recognized the evolving international concern for safety of lives and property at sea (that is, the advancement of international concern for human rights), the International Convention for the Safety of Life at Sea, signed in London in January 1914, established the International Ice Service of Observation and Ice Patrol, directed by the United States. Convened as a direct result of the loss of the *Titanic* in 1912,[9] 14 leading maritime nations attended, and the person then serving as Captain Commandant of the Revenue Cutter Service was a member of the U.S. delegation. He became an active member of the resulting committee on safety of navigation.

Immediately after the *Titanic* tragedy, the Navy dispatched two vessels to the area south of Greenland to report on ice conditions. The following year the Navy declined to resume the patrol because it did not fall under its primary duty to be prepared to promptly defend the United States and win the Nation's wars. The Revenue Cutter Service assumed that responsibility in 1913, and the Coast Guard continues that function today. The French Ambassador to the United States in 1914 recognized the patrols as "fully effective as expected and are such as to call for the sincere gratefulness of the mariners of countries."[10]

The Coast Guard has continued to globalize the concern for safety at sea. Through the International Maritime Consultative Organization (IMCO)—now the Intergovernmental Maritime Organization (IMO)—established by the United Nations (UN) in 1958, and the 1960 Conference on Safety of Life at Sea (SOLAS), the safety of merchant ships and shipping company practices were improved and standardized. The IMCO originally had 21 member nations; in 2000, the IMO has 158 members.[11] Coast Guard-led efforts revised the standards for watertight subdivisions on vessels, set ballasting and stability standards, refined lifesaving requirements for boats and rafts to be carried on vessels, set navigation standards, and established load guidelines.[12] All of these efforts improved the seaworthiness of vessels, making them safer to operate and more likely to survive the perils of the sea. At the same time, establishing international standards that were observed by all merchant vessels and maritime shipping companies helped level the competition among international shipping companies. This kept the

U.S. merchant marine, which already had higher operating costs because of domestic laws requiring many of these safety features, in business.

The Coast Guard did not use the IMCO just to protect American economic interests. After disastrous fires on the Panamanian flag cruise ship *Yarmouth Castle* and the Norwegian cruise ship *Viking Princess*, Coast Guard efforts led the IMCO to set standards making passenger vessels "fire-safe" in 1966.[13] Several initiatives concerned standards for fire protection, including insulation and intumescent-coating barriers intended to stop the spread of shipboard fires. The Coast Guard is implementing the International Convention on Standards of Training, Certification, and Watchkeeping for Seafarers. This is the latest effort in a campaign started in the 1930s to improve the qualifications of mariners who operate vessels, reflected at that time in the Convention Concerning the Minimum Requirements of Professional Capacity for Masters and Officers on Board Merchant Ships.[14] The use of international conventions and standards has proved more effective in improving maritime safety than have efforts by individual countries acting unilaterally and without coordination.[15]

In 1870, after the departure of the Russians from Alaska, the U.S. Government attempted to prevent the wanton slaughter of seals for their skins in the Pribilof Island rookeries of the Bering Sea. The Revenue Cutter Service patrolled this region, clearing poachers from the territorial seas to protect the seals from the foreign vessels hovering in international waters.[16] The seals were easy prey when venturing outside the territorial seas. To improve the operational effectiveness of the Revenue Cutter Bering Sea Patrol in protecting the seals and to diminish the numbers of potential foreign flag sealing vessels, the United States tried for 20 years to gain the cooperation of other nations in preserving the seal population from extinction. In what was a remarkable change from the past American tradition of wasteful exploitation of natural resources, the United States successfully commenced an experiment in international cooperation by creating the Sealing Convention Treaty of 1911 between Russia, Great Britain, Japan, and the United States. This treaty prohibited pelagic sealing in the waters of the North Pacific Ocean.[17] Most unusual for that period of time was the ceding of sovereign flag state responsibility by the parties to the Revenue Cutter Service to police the agreement on all vessels of the parties to the Convention. The Revenue Cutter Service became the de facto international maritime police force for the four parties involved.[18]

Recent Missions

The Coast Guard has continued to use international conventions and treaties to expand the protection to marine resources that have been overexploited. In the 1950s, the extensive Japanese high-seas fishing fleets were taking a significant amount of American and Canadian salmon that spawned in fresh water and then traveled the oceans for three years before returning to their places of birth to start the cycle of life over again. The significant Japanese catch was rapidly reducing the number of salmon returning to generate offspring. In 1955, American and Canadian fishing interests negotiated an agreement with Japan to attempt to control the amount of fish harvested and conduct research on the migratory patterns of the salmon. Enforcement of catch quotas and authorized fishing zones was difficult. A new treaty between Japan, Canada, Russia, and the United States went into force in 1993 that banned targeting salmon fishing north of 33° north latitude in the Pacific Ocean outside the exclusive economic zones of the contracting parties.[19] Enforcement provisions were in keeping with the emerging requirements of basic responsibilities that had evolved as part of the 1982 Law of the Sea Convention, particularly enforcement by one party to the treaty on vessels belonging to other parties to the treaty.[20]

Recognition of coastal state jurisdiction over marine resources that originate in coastal and internal waters, as reflected in the creation of an exclusive economic zone, was codified in the 1982 Law of the Sea Convention. Subsequently, work has focused on defining the general obligations regarding conservation and management of fisheries by coastal states and fishing nations. This led to the development of the 1995 UN Agreement on Straddling Fish Stocks and Highly Migratory Fish Stocks, the 1995 UN Food and Agriculture Organization Code of Conduct on Responsible Fisheries, and the Agreement to Promote Compliance with International Conservation and Management Measures by Fishing Vessels on the High Seas. These important agreements set the specific rules that the international community will need to follow to move toward sustainable marine fisheries. The tightening of enforcement regimes by all of these agreements, particularly with regard to nonmember fishing nations, represents an important step forward in enabling the international community to conserve marine life.[21]

In addition to the interests of human rights, as reflected in safety concerns for mariners and passengers at sea and concern for marine life that have been advanced by the Coast Guard through global organizations, marine environmental pollution has increasingly posed regional and global challenges. Pollution of the maritime commons was becoming such a problem by the early 1970s that the Coast Guard-led U.S. delegation to the IMCO successfully gained a consensus to change the practices of tanker crews and oil shipping companies in 1973. The new international standards created were enforceable by both coastal states and flag states. The coastal states' authority was extended under certain circumstances to 50 miles off-shore, well beyond the 12-mile limit of the territorial seas.[22] The growth in the coastal states' authority was in recognition of the potential harm that could be caused to these states by the activity of tankers and hazardous material-carrying merchant vessels. Coastal states could take such measures on the high seas as may be considered necessary to prevent, mitigate, or eliminate grave and imminent danger to their coastlines.[23] Many of these merchant vessels traveled under the authority of weak flag states, but called regularly on major ports throughout the industrial world. The weak flag states were unable to enforce regulations on vessels that seldom entered their ports or came within reach of their inspection authorities. A global approach and the relinquishing of some national sovereignty evolved as the best solution to an environmental problem that was threatening common interests.

The Coast Guard has used international agreements to advance the operational effectiveness of drug law enforcement efforts in the 1980s and 1990s. Basing its actions on Article 108 of the 1982 Law of the Sea Convention, the Coast Guard has moved to take safe havens away from those who transport drugs by sea from source countries to consumption countries. Article 17 of the 1988 Vienna Convention against Illicit Traffic in Narcotic Drugs and Psychotropic Substances outlined in principle operational concepts for greater cooperation among maritime states. Through bilateral negotiations and operational engagement with training teams, cutter visits, and combined exercises and operations between the United States and member countries throughout the Caribbean, these principles are slowly becoming operational realities. The objective has been to strengthen coastal states' ability to police their own waters either independently or, when operational time lines do not allow for coastal state forces to react, to allow nearby Coast Guard forces to assist on the behalf of coastal states.

The Coast Guard and partnering nations' maritime forces have developed common operational procedures that have allowed for a more effective effort in countering drug and other smuggling activities. Excess defense articles and Coast Guard equipment have been shared with selected nations to ensure such a capability. Continuous engagement with Caribbean nations is required to reinforce training and operational procedures. This is done under ambassadorial or Commander in Chief (CINC) South sponsorship, as the circumstances require. Fifteen agreements have been concluded with maritime partners, putting into practice the cooperation called for under Article 17 of the 1988 Vienna Convention.[24] This is a real measure of the success of engagement as a tool to shape the environment, to improve friendly relations with selected countries, to improve operational effectiveness of forces for the benefit of the recipient countries and the United States, and to gain acceptance of U.S. norms in the conduct of other national law enforcement procedures.

One of the most difficult challenges facing the U.S. military today is disengaging from intervention operations, such as establishing and restoring legitimate governments in fragile nations, and engaging in peace enforcement or stabilization operations in disintegrating nations. Successful disengagement requires the establishment of legitimate local institutions that can take over the responsibilities of providing security for the population and the rule of law so that legal activity can resume for the benefit of the citizens. This is most critical where the previous governing apparatus was focused on maintaining the leadership in power over the general welfare of the population and the elements of government have no acceptably established traditions to help guide their development. When these fragile nations are coastal states, they need to develop Coast Guard-like services to provide for their maritime sovereignty, just as the United States has done. The Coast Guard is the correct service to serve as a mentor to these smaller navies.

After the overthrow of Manuel Noriega in Panama in 1991, the Coast Guard provided training teams, excess equipment, and organizational expertise to create the Panamanian National Maritime Service (SMN in its Spanish initials). This effort involved the deployment of patrol boats to help exert Panamanian sovereignty in adjacent waters while the SMN was being formed. Training team visits and the assignment of advisors in Panama lasted for 8 years. Coast Guard ship visits have been scheduled repeatedly to exercise with the SMN to develop at-sea patrol capabilities. Five Panamanian students have graduated from the U.S. Coast Guard Academy to provide long-term professional maritime leadership to the SMN and Panama. Two Coast Guard patrol boats were transferred to the SMN in 1999 to enhance its capabilities. The Coast Guard role has shifted over the last few years from providing basic skill training to providing technical operational advice and developing long-term self-support strategies for the SMN.[25] Ongoing efforts ensure that the SMN can control the activity that goes on adjacent to Panama's coastline, deterring illegal activity such as drug transshipments and smuggling of aliens through Central America and the poaching of Panamanian fishery stocks.

After the international coalition restored President Jean-Bertrand Aristide to power in Haiti in 1994, the daunting task of establishing legitimate Haitian organizations to rule over the poorest population in the Western Hemisphere remained. All Haitian civil functions had ceased to operate. Initially, U.S. Coast Guard forces provided vessel traffic control services to the capital's harbor and security patrols throughout the adjacent waters. The U.S. Coast Guard, in partnership with the Canadian Coast Guard, created from virtually nothing the Haitian Coast Guard (HCG). Starting with just 7 Haitian police personnel and no boats, the HCG has grown to 90 trained personnel, 8 operational boats, and 2 newly constructed bases. This required the long-term investment of instructors and mentors in Haiti, training team visits, ship visits, and the donation of refurbished equipment. Upon the withdrawal of U.S. in-country assistance to Haiti in the fall of 1999, the HCG, small as it might be, was one of the successful institution-building efforts. Four full-time Coast Guard trainers remain to assist the HCG.[26] For the first time, Haiti has the capability to patrol its own territorial waters outside its capital's harbor. The HCG is the only effective counterdrug trafficking unit in Haiti, having participated in 11 maritime narcotics seizures during which it captured 6 narcotics smuggling vessels through 1999.[27]

While both the Panamanian and Haitian operations were done as part of a team effort to establish a functioning country with greater respect for human rights and the rule of law, the U.S. Coast Guard benefited operationally from the existence of functioning maritime services that could help disrupt the flow of contraband in the Caribbean. The Department of State and the regional CINC supported Coast Guard efforts. Both provided funding to support these operations. Coast Guard efforts were constrained by the competing demands of other operational requirements for its limited assets.

The Coast Guard has been part of the Navy task unit conducting the CINC Atlantic's UNITAS deployments since 1959. Coast Guard participation provided a more relevant role model to the many smaller navies encountered. All have the daunting task of controlling their coastal waters from undesired activity, mostly of a nonmilitary nature (for example, fisheries encroachment, smuggling, pollution, persons and property in distress).

In 1992, the U.S. Coast Guard dispatched a vessel to the Baltic Sea to participate in exercises and professional exchanges with former Warsaw Pact members following the dissolution of the Soviet Union. This activity has continued under the sponsorship of the CINC Europe and has been extended to the Black and Mediterranean Seas. The Coast Guard organizational model represents a cost-effective way for many nations to exert the necessary maritime sovereignty within their region of interest. The Coast Guard has built an international reputation for bringing a multitude of interests together to promote the respect for law and a humanitarian concern for maritime operations. The CINC Europe stated that "the number of operations and engagement missions . . . is growing while the number of ships available is declining. . . . The Coast Guard's rich maritime heritage, unique skills, and proven expertise in crucial mission areas make it the ideal maritime operational and engagement tool for this theater."[28] The continued deployment of Coast Guard ships to the CINC Europe is needed as the size of the vessels and the day-to-day missions of the Coast Guard closely match the size and missions of host navies.[29]

Toward the Future

The President's Interagency Task Force on U.S. Coast Guard Roles and Missions for the 21st Century in 1999 concluded that, "as a multi-mission law enforcement, humanitarian, and regulatory agency, as well as a military service, the Coast Guard is well suited to perform maritime engagement roles."[30] It is likewise well suited as a "model maritime service" for emerging democratic nations. Participation in geographical CINC engagement strategies can improve mission effectiveness and efficiency.[31] Unfortunately, the demand for Coast Guard ship participation has been such that the Coast Guard has had to limit participation so as not to affect its ability to perform its other responsibilities. The CINC Central Command and the CINC Pacific have been sharing limited Coast Guard ship time because assets are just not available without having an impact on other Coast Guard missions. When U.S. vital interests are at stake, Coast Guard mission priorities shift to those most important to national security. When humanitarian and other lesser national interests are at stake in overseas regions, the chronic underfunding of the Coast Guard and the limited capital resources provided make for difficult choices. The expertise and skills of the Coast Guard may be the more appropriate response to support overseas engagement efforts with emerging democracies and military interventions, but the capacity is not available. In some of these cases, Department of Defense assets, which are more expensive and less suited for the mission, are sent; in others, the opportunities are lost.

The Office of Naval Intelligence has outlined the future threats and challenges to maritime security. They include an increased volume of illegal trade, the continuing emergence of nonstate actors who challenge sovereignty of the nation-state, organized crime (that is, smuggling goods and people), exploitation of marine and nonmarine resources, and the adoption of asymmetrical threats.[32] These are a direct result of globalization of economies, information services, and cultural clashes. Most of these threats do not lend themselves to traditional military responses. As the Coast Guard and other forces conduct operations to counter these threats, the CINC needs greater access to Coast Guard assets. Each CINC is well aware of this. Correspondence from each of the geographical CINCs to the Task Force on U.S. Coast Guard Roles and Missions has indicated an increasing opportunity to deploy Coast Guard assets and encouraged increased availability in the future.[33] The Chairman, Joint Chiefs of Staff (JCS) stated that the Coast Guard is an important international engagement resource that may be called upon more frequently in the future.[34] The Assistant Secretary of Defense for Strategy and Threat Reduction echoed the Chairman's input.[35] Unfortunately, the Task Force did not endorse the input received from these experts. The Task Force concluded that the current level of Coast Guard effort overseas should remain the same.

The term *national security* encompasses a rich and complex tapestry of economic, social, environmental, political, diplomatic, cultural, and military dimensions. Accordingly, the President's National Security Strategy has articulated a more expansive construct. The Coast Guard has broad responsibilities for ensuring maritime security—the service's singular contribution to U.S. national security posture. These capabilities help ensure homeland security, protect critical infrastructures, and safeguard U.S. maritime sovereignty.

To be sovereign at sea, the United States must control what takes place in the waters under its jurisdiction and exercise influence in the waters that it deems of high interest. Absent an organized military threat, the responsibility for upholding U.S. maritime sovereignty rests more and more upon the Coast Guard. Traditional military threats to U.S. maritime interests are now much less serious than they once were, while nontraditional criminal, operational, commercial, and environmental threats are much greater. Because of *posse comitatus* constraints and the U.S. constitutional canon, Department of Defense military services cannot and should not address these threats. Consequently, the need for the Coast Guard to ensure maritime security is a reality that makes the Coast Guard in many ways more relevant. Many of the threats and challenges to the maritime security of the United States and that of U.S. friends and allies—piracy, drug trafficking, illegal migration, Law of the Sea disputes, environmental degradation and ecoterrorism, resource wars, and the need to ensure the economic security of commercial sea-borne traffic—are the forte of the Coast Guard.

The Coast Guard may be described as the world's seventh largest navy; it is also the world's 39th oldest in terms of average platform age. The service's high- and medium-endurance cutters, patrol aircraft, and communications systems are generally old and are becoming obsolete, if they are not so already. The life cycle support challenges of severely aging cutters and aircraft also affect their effectiveness for patrols, especially for deep-water duties far from shore, as well as their ability to operate "seamlessly" with the other armed services.

Such developments bode ill for U.S. maritime security, as the Nation's economy is critically dependent on the use of the high seas and its own coastal and internal waterways. Everywhere there is an increase in pressure on marine resources and, as a result, on those charged with their protection. The pressures range from enormous increases—probably a tripling—in the volume of legitimate maritime trade by 2020 (95 percent of U.S. exports and imports still move by sea); to a boom in illegal migration; to an increase in maritime drug smuggling (at least 70 percent of the total drug flow into the United States travels part of the way by sea); to greater demands on ocean resources, such as fisheries and mineral deposits; and, finally, to a growing list of maritime security concerns.

Modernizing the Coast Guard

To hedge against tomorrow's uncertainties, the Coast Guard should be rebuilt to make it adaptable to future realities. Today's threats must be kept in mind, but tomorrow's U.S. maritime security requirements will never be precisely known. The Coast Guard of the future must have the flexibility to adapt to a wide range of maritime challenges—a fact that must be reflected in today's planning for tomorrow's forces and operations.

The recapitalization of the deep-water capability is a near-term national priority. The Coast Guard must modernize its deep-water cutter, aircraft, and command-and-control assets if it is to sustain and improve upon its current performance. This was endorsed by the findings of the Interagency Task Force on U.S. Coast Guard Roles and Missions.[36]

As the Coast Guard moves forward to resize, recapitalize, and modernize itself for the next 20-plus years, each geographical CINC should have the availability of a Coast Guard cutter full-time in his or her area of responsibility, in addition to the staff talent to maximize the benefits from this asset. Coast Guard assets conducting engagement activities deal with many nonmilitary organizations in addition to the host nation's naval forces. They provide more contact than Navy warships visiting the same nation. The Coast Guard's tradition of routinely participating in multi-agency solutions to policing, marine resource management, marine environmental protection, and marine accident prevention and mitigation operations allows it to open dialogues with a variety of host nation organizations and to build bridges among these organizations. The humanitarian nature of most Coast Guard operations makes the service acceptable in some countries where the Navy would not initially be permitted. The Chairman recognized this role in his memorandum to the Task Force on U.S. Coast Guard Roles and Missions.[37] A Coast Guard ship in each CINC theater would also be immediately available to participate in operations involving resolution of small-scale contingencies, provision of humanitarian aid, or foreign assistance where Coast Guard capabilities fit the situation.

The United States needs to take advantage of all the tools that it has available to enhance its national security. The Coast Guard provides a unique form of maritime security. It is "forward deployed" in the Caribbean and the Pacific to counter the threat of drug trafficking and illegal migration. It also operates in remote parts of the Bering Sea and the Central Pacific to protect marine resources from illegal activity. Upon request, it has operated in Europe, the Persian Gulf, and East Asia.

It was for these and other compelling reasons that in September 1998 the Chief of Naval Operations, Admiral Jay Johnson, and Commandant of the Coast Guard, Admiral James Loy, signed the National Fleet Policy Statement to ensure that, as the Navy and the Coast Guard moved to recapitalize their forces in the 21st century, they synchronized planning, training, and procurement in order to provide the highest level of maritime capability for the Nation's investment.[38] These operational needs will shape current and future designs and operational concepts for multimission naval surface warships and small, general-purpose, shallow draft cutters; these vessels can mutually support the roles, missions, functions, and tasks that will be required of both the Coast Guard and the Navy. As Admiral Loy noted in a letter to Admiral Johnson on July 31, 1998, "I envision a National Fleet . . . of surface combatants and major cutters that would be affordable, interoperable, complementary, and balanced with minimum overlaps in their capabilities."

Such a fleet would comprise highly capable multimission Navy surface combatants optimized for the full spectrum of naval operations. The Coast Guard's maritime security cutter—one element of the ongoing Deepwater Project—would be optimized for peacetime and crisis-response Coast Guard missions. But this cutter must also be able to complement its Navy counterparts in its assigned contingency and warfare tasks, filling the requirement for a small, general-purpose warship. Although not the primary purpose of the program, this cutter could provide an attractive alternative for foreign military sales, thus helping the U.S. shipbuilding base while potentially assisting future interoperability efforts with allies and friends.

The Navy and Coast Guard continue to examine closely the shared purpose and common effort focused on tailored operational integration of the two services' multimission surface platforms, with the goal of meeting the entire spectrum of U.S. maritime requirements for the 21st century. Such a partnership mandates that the Navy and Coast Guard work together to maximize their operational effectiveness across all naval and maritime missions. Furthermore, the Navy and Coast Guard should coordinate surface warship/cutter planning, information systems integration, research and development, acquisition, and life-cycle support. In addition, this cooperation could embrace joint concepts of operations, training, exercises, and deployments.

Clearly, such a joint endeavor will have broad implications for both the Navy and the Coast Guard. The likely benefits to such a coordinated and integrated approach could include the more efficient and economical meeting of operational support and upgrade requirements, coordinated acquisition strategies, standardized training and cross-training in service-specific operational specialties, improved operational planning, integrated doctrinal and tactical development, and much enhanced force and unit interoperability. The improvements in these areas will allow the United States to stretch its budget dollars to maximize the operational effectiveness of these two services. The Navy and Coast Guard have always worked well together, and the National Fleet turns tradition into policy, greatly strengthening the relationship.

Conclusion

A key element in the renaissance in the Nation's sea services will be the revolution in thinking about the shared purpose, operational integration, and common effort between the Navy and the Coast Guard that the National Fleet concept entails. The Navy-Coast Guard collective task is to build fully interoperable, multimission, naval and maritime forces for tomorrow's challenges at the best price for the U.S. citizen. To do that, the Navy and Coast Guard must work even more closely together.

Through globalization efforts, the Coast Guard has expanded its operational effectiveness by developing regional cooperation with adjacent countries' maritime forces and using international forums to standardize the approach to many common problems found in the maritime environment. The safety of life at sea has been improved. Arising awareness and concern for the health of living marine resources has led to the curtailment of harmful fishing practices. The standards to which commercial vessels are built and operated have grown safer as the nation of flag registry and the coastal states that the vessels call on have joined forces to ensure safety. The amount of petroleum and other hazardous products that have entered the maritime environment has been reduced through partnerships with private organizations and international public bodies. It has taken many years to develop the awareness, understanding, consensus building, and urgency for action to accomplish these objectives.

Notes

[1] *Coast Guard 2020 Ready Today . . . Preparing for Tomorrow* (Washington, DC: Government Printing Office, May 1998), 1.

[2] Stephen H. Evans, *The United States Coast Guard 1790–1915: A Definitive History* (Annapolis, MD: Naval Institute Press, 1949), 3–5.

[3] Bruce Stubbs and Scott C. Truver, *America's Coast Guard: Safeguarding U.S. Maritime Safety and Security in the 21st Century* (Washington, DC: U.S. Coast Guard, January 2000).

[4] Evans, *The United States Coast Guard 1790–1915*, 4.

[5] Ibid.

[6] Robert E. Johnson, *Guardians of the Sea: History of the United States Coast Guard 1915 to Present* (Annapolis, MD: Naval Institute Press, 1987), 162.

[7] The White House, *A National Security Strategy for a New Century* (Washington, DC: Government Printing Office, December 1999), iii.

[8] Evans, *The United States Coast Guard 1790–1915*, 149.

[9] Ibid., 197.

[10] Jean Jules Jusserand, letter to Secretary of State William J. Bryan, June 27, 1914.

[11] Press release, March 20, 2000, <http://www.imo.org>.

[12] Johnson, *Guardians of the Sea*, 310.

[13] Ibid., 339–340.

[14] *Coast Guard Marine Safety Manual* (Washington, DC: Government Printing Office), chapter 1.

[15] Introduction, <http://www.imo.org>.

[16] Johnson, *Guardians of the Sea*, 112.

[17] Ibid., 190.

[18] Ibid.

[19] *Convention for the Conservation of Anadromous Stocks in the North Pacific Ocean*, Article I.

[20] Ibid., Articles VI and IX.

[21] Mary Beth West, *State Department Official on Fisheries Management*, <www.usia.gov>.

[22] Johnson, *Guardians of the Sea*, 347–348.

[23] Marine pollution legislation, <http://www.amsa.gov.au>.

[24] *U.S. Coast Guard Law Enforcement Manual*, Enclosure 4.

[25] U.S. Coast Guard, *U.S. Coast Guard Involvement with Panama*, Fact Sheet, June 2000.

[26] U.S. Coast Guard, *U.S. Coast Guard Involvement with Haiti*, Fact Sheet, June 2000.

[27] U.S. Coast Guard Brief, "Haitian Coast Guard Development Plan."

[28] Wesley K. Clark, letter to Deputy Secretary of Transportation, June 24, 1999. See also *Report of the Interagency Task Force on U.S. Coast Guard Roles and Missions* (Washington, DC: Government Printing Office, December 1999), Appendix D.

[29] Wesley K. Clark, letter to Commandant, USCG, July 6, 1999. See also *Report of the Interagency Task Force.*

[30] *Report of the Interagency Task Force*, 2–33.

[31] Ibid.

[32] Office of Naval Intelligence, *Threats and Challenges to Maritime Security 2020*, Executive Summary (Washington, DC: Government Printing Office, March 1999).

[33] *Report of the Interagency Task Force.*

[34] Henry H. Shelton, memorandum to Deputy Secretary of Transportation, Chairman of Interagency Task Force, July 26, 1999. See also *Report of the Interagency Task Force.*

[35] Andrew Hoehn, letter to Executive Director of Roles and Missions Task Force, August 12, 1999. See also *Report of the Interagency Task Force.*

[36] *Report of the Interagency Task Force*, 44.

[37] Henry H. Shelton, memorandum to Deputy Secretary of Transportation, enclosure.

[38] *NATIONAL FLEET—A Joint Navy/Coast Guard Policy Statement*, September 21, 1998. See also Thomas Fargo and Ernest Riutta, "A 'National Fleet' for America," U.S. Naval Institute *Proceedings* (April 1999), 48–51.

Chapter 26

The Corporate Experience: Lessons for the Military

Solveig Spielmann

This chapter examines the corporate experience in adjusting to globalization and implications that are relevant for the Armed Forces. The analysis draws heavily on interviews with corporate executives. It examines the topic from two perspectives: how changes within multinational corporations in response to globalization may offer lessons for military departments and how government policies and globalization affect the supplier companies that are integral to a strong defense.

The business experience is directly relevant to current challenges facing the services. The U.S. military has undertaken to transform itself through a revolution in military affairs strategy that calls for new investments of about $60 billion a year to modernize equipment. In his introduction to *Mind the Gap*, former Deputy Secretary of Defense John White points out that the U.S. Congress will be reluctant to approve these new expenditures "unless DOD [Department of Defense] streamlines its support structure to yield $15 to $20 billion in annual savings. In other words, we need a revolution in business affairs (RBA) to accompany the [revolution in military affairs (RMA)]."

As the services seek appropriate paths for adjustment to globalization, they can learn important lessons from business. Business has been the front line of globalization—it has shaped and accelerated the process and, in turn, has had to reshape itself to meet the challenges created. Corporations have downsized, reorganized, combined, spun off, reinvented management, and done many other things to promote competitiveness and profitability, and to attain the overriding objective of increased shareholder value. The military services are clearly not businesses, and their mission and motivations are quite different from those driving the private sector. The services should not and cannot copy business, but they can learn some successful techniques and some pitfalls from examining the corporate experience. The pages that follow outline some of the lessons to be learned.

Equally important for defense planners is to understand how the defense industry is affected by current conditions and the magnitude of the change that it is experiencing. Because the industry is a partner of DOD and the services in protecting U.S. national security, its experiences are important for reasons beyond just the techniques of adjust-

---

Solveig Spielmann is chairman and CEO of International Business-Government Counselors, Inc. In addition, she is executive director of the Executive Council on Diplomacy, editor of Washington International Business Report, *and vice president of the German-American Business Council. She is also currently an adjunct professor at Georgetown University.*

ing to change. Its health, its ability to change and innovate, and its profitability matter to DOD because the services depend on the vitality of corporate contractors. Major defense companies are struggling to reshape their business strategies in light of changing economics and national security needs. Planners need to understand how globalization affects major DOD suppliers and contractors and to adopt policies to ensure that cooperation and partnership will be strong and effective in the future. This chapter suggests some approaches to help build that cooperation as a partnership.

Corporations and Globalization: Dynamics and Trends

Corporations have been profoundly affected by globalization, and they have adapted to meet many new challenges: the integration of the global economy, the information and communications revolutions, the new character and demands of stock and financial markets, the diversity of the labor force and the ever-changing needs for new skills, and the incessant pressure for new markets and financial results. For companies, restructuring has become a way of life. Continual organizational restructuring is demanded by the intensity of global competition, advances in communications and information technology, and changing consumer preferences. Different companies take different roads, but most successful corporations today are constantly seeking ways to improve competitiveness and corporate performance. Common elements and objectives of their programs include:

- Cut costs
- Improve productivity
- Promote flexibility
- Improve morale and motivate employees
- Build and train a skilled workforce
- Make the most of new technologies
- Improve internal communications and coordination of activities
- Encourage innovation
- Build and maintain a sense of teamwork and a meaningful corporate culture
- Adopt effective methods of management and leadership.

Approach to Restructure: Case Studies

At base, what corporations are trying to do is to retool to meet the fast-paced changes that are characteristic of globalization. They seek to become more responsive to customer needs, reduce overhead and management costs, improve organizational flexibility, simplify and accelerate decisionmaking processes, strengthen core competencies, and improve innovation. Often, this has involved decentralizing decisionmaking, developing integrated information systems, building teamwork, and finding new ways to motivate and reward personnel.

The following examples illustrate the spirit of change in three major American corporations.

IBM. In the mid-1990s, the IBM information technology management system did not support the company's strategic vision—that is, IBM found that it was not practicing what it was preaching. Its strategy was to approach the marketplace as a single, unified, global team—yet its information technology infrastructure was fragmented among hundreds of local geographies and inconsistent from one business unit to the next. IBM was not achieving the short-term cost and expense reductions needed to fund its investments in re-engineering and e-commerce. IBM—like many of its customers—had a dual challenge: managing information technology to derive maximum cost efficiencies and improving the effectiveness of application development and the speed of supporting infrastructure deployment.

Management identified an urgent need for action. A wholly new framework was developed for managing, deploying, and operating end-to-end information systems. A worldwide information technology management system was put in place to improve the effectiveness of information resources, generate a higher return on global information technology investment, and enable employees to become more productive and better able to serve customers.

The IBM transformation plan resulted in a savings of more than $12 billion over 6 years. The savings came in two areas—information technology cost avoidance and line-of-business efficiencies. IBM information technology expenditures as a percentage of total revenue decreased by almost 25 percent. This was made possible through the implementation of a common, worldwide information technology infrastructure that was acquired and deployed through an outsourcing arrangement with IBM Global Services.

Raytheon. The adjustment to globalization has not been easy for Raytheon. Changes and difficulties at this major defense contractor are illustrated in the Winter 1999/2000 issue of *Viewpoints*, the company's employee magazine. Chief Executive Officer Dan Burnham started his opening letter by saying, "I know all of us look forward to a better year for Raytheon in 2000." He went on to say, "I think there's a perception, which I certainly don't want to encourage, that we're putting cash before people. The fact is that without cash, in time there would be no business. . . . [W]e took it on the chin from Wall Street. Thank you for staying focused despite the distractions."

Burnham's direct admission of the company's problems is consistent with Raytheon's efforts to improve communications throughout the company and become "an employer of choice." In 1999, Raytheon made its businesses more efficient, streamlined reporting relationships, and refocused its commercial electronics division. It also launched "Raytheon Six Sigma," a program successfully used by Motorola and General Electric to promote a "zero defects" approach to production, excellence throughout the production process, and the elimination of inefficiencies. Raytheon invited tens of thousands of employees to awareness training about the program. It conducted its first companywide employee survey. It implemented new human resource initiatives to attract and retain talent, to improve the performance evaluation process, and to encourage and draw upon the strength of diversity.

The employee survey was used as a baseline for a continuous process of improvement. Employees now have the opportunity to participate in feedback sessions to learn about survey results, discuss strengths and areas of concern, and identify issues for action. Raytheon also planned about 200 action workshops involving more than 2,000 employees and aimed at developing specific action plans to implement recommendations for improvement. To build on the baseline survey, quarterly sample surveys are planned, followed by a comprehensive, all-employee survey every 2 years to get feedback on actions that are implemented. "We will be a great company," Burnham told his employees. "Your involvement will get us there."

Rockwell Collins. Rockwell Collins wants to be the most trusted source in the aviation electronics field. To increase its competitive advantage in the marketplace, the company has adopted an enterprisewide "Lean Electronics" concept that focuses on eliminating waste and maximizing cost efficiency and a "Best Place to Work" process that gives employees voice and feedback in establishing a "Best Place to Work" environment.

Both programs rely on employee involvement, ideas, and interaction. For the "Lean" program, each business unit has an identified "Lean" director who helps his or her unit work toward financial targets and culture changes in day-to-day work routines. Program goals are a 50 percent reduction in cycle time, a 25 percent reduction in floor space, a 50 percent reduction in inventories, and a 35 percent improvement in productivity. To help meet these goals, approximately 400 workshops were planned in 2000.

Challenges of Restructure: The Defense Industry

Corporations will continue to have experiences such as those just illustrated. The processes of globalization and change are not slowing. Competitive pressures are relentless and often unanticipated. Time horizons for technology grow shorter. Innovation and flexibility will be in demand, and adjustment to change will always be necessary and will frequently be painful. Successful companies will address the problems head-on and develop targeted programs to tackle them. Change will be constant, and the strategies for reacting to it will change, too. What worked last year may not work next year, but corporate leadership is learning that two elements must be constant: continuing reevaluation of approach and methodology, and a dedication to involvement of personnel in the change process.

The challenges of adjustment have been particularly difficult for the U.S. defense industry. The industry has shrunk, markets have shrunk, and financial health is imperiled. Former Lockheed Martin Chief Executive Norman Augustine has illustrated the problem by showing how the market value of defense firms stacks up against some of the in-vogue "new economy" companies. Calculating the market value of the seven major defense firms against that of the newly merged AOL-Time Warner, Augustine found that the defense sector was worth just one-quarter of the value of the new company—just one-eighth if Boeing were not included in the comparison.

Why has this happened? It has happened because the Cold War is over, and ever higher defense budgets are over. The industry has had to consolidate and to shrink. Unlike other industries, however, defense firms cannot "globalize" quickly. They do not operate in a pure market economy; instead, the market is controlled. Defense companies are constrained by government, laws, technology transfer restrictions, and shrinking world markets. The U.S. Government appears to want industry to globalize and to become more commercial, recognizing that this is the only way that the firms can remain competitive and innovative; however, for often understandable reasons, government policies do not always keep up with this objective.

Where there was once overcapacity in the U.S. defense sector, today the industry has been shrunk through mergers and acquisitions. The mergers have proved more difficult to manage than might have been expected, and the pressures on corporate bottom lines and raising money for investment are serious. The U.S. defense industry is severely constrained in terms of investing and growing on its own. The industry gets most of its research-and-development monies from DOD, but the private sector also needs to do its own investment. Cash is short. Management problems are many. The same management techniques that worked in a $5- to $10-billion defense corporation are not necessarily transferable to a $20-billion merged giant. Today and for the foreseeable future, the defense industry and the U.S. Government that effectively regulates it will face major business and policy challenges as the industry tries to retain its leading-edge position in the world of globalization.

Impact on International Politics and Security Affairs

The U.S. leadership position in international political and security affairs depends on this country's strength in militarily relevant technology, a superior military, a strong U.S. economy, and a healthy defense industry. All of these elements are affected by globalization and the adjustments involved. The following are relevant observations from the *1999 Final Report, Premises for Policy: Maintaining Military Superiority in the 21st Century,* produced by the Secretary of Defense Strategic Studies Group IV:

> [*On technology*] The U.S. lead in militarily relevant technology may be shrinking, or may no longer exist at all. . . . Although the U.S. does not lead in all technology areas, it has a unique ability to combine individual technologies or systems of technologies into larger systems. How well we field integrated systems ultimately will determine U.S. military advantage. Since technology diffusion cannot be prevented over time, leadership in system integration capabilities can offset a potential adversary's unique technological advantages. Attaining the primary military advantage of system integration requires cultural and educational qualities underpinning industry's—and the military's—integration ability to be identified, nurtured, and protected.

> [*On the military*] It is imperative that DOD shift its emphasis from a strategy that lost its relevance at the end of the Cold War, to one that capitalizes on the advantages and avoids the risks inherent in accelerating globalization of industry and the ongoing transformation of business practices in the Information Age, [and] people are the key to continued U.S. military superiority.

> [*On the economy*] The U.S. economy is expected to remain strong, in light of lowered trade barriers and an increasing flow of global capital to areas of greatest opportunity or least risk. U.S. businesses have adapted well to the

> rigors of a global marketplace, and remain the prime force as the engine of global economic growth.
>
> [*On the defense industry*] In the absence of an effective methodology to define clearly a short list of key military capabilities that should be developed and protected, the tendency has been to overprotect. This . . . approach limits the ability of U.S. industry to pursue market leadership in selective military and dual-use technologies. DOD strategies must evolve to account for the technology leveling that will occur as a result of globalization, and apply greater attention to the importance of U.S. economic vitality and diversity in the global marketplace. The combined impact of globalization and commercialization suggests the need for a new partnership between government and industry.

Thus, as a result of globalization, the corporate experience in building competitiveness has become highly relevant to the military establishment and to U.S. Government policies. Military planners recognize the need to change. Globalization has given the military a broader mission—peacekeeping, peacemaking, education, even government creation—and globalization means that many new and different challenges can converge at once. Technology, planning, leadership, training, and personnel recruitment and retention pose new issues for the military, as they do for corporations. At the same time, the military knows that its decisionmaking processes are different from those of the private sector. The military has no profit motive to spur efficiency and productivity, yet it must rely on an industry that is more and more driven by requirements of innovation and profitability. Two major challenges of globalization for the military are to adopt relevant features of the corporate experience and to do what it can to help its corporate partners be as strong and effective as possible.

Implications for U.S. Interests, Strategies, Policies, and Goals

To maintain the Nation's security and military strength, the U.S. armed services must seek to manage the adjustments of the globalization process with maximum efficiency and effectiveness. They must work with the private sector to share experiences, to maximize the opportunities of technology and communications, and to bring new ideas into the military system. The discussion that follows is based on interviews with business executives; students of and veterans of the U.S. military services; leaders in government, industry, and academia; and relevant studies and papers. It has two themes:

- What can the services learn from corporate experiences and techniques?
- What should the services understand about the impact of globalization on defense industries? How does the "business side" of the defense industry affect the defense mission?

Learning from Corporate Experiences and Techniques

Before looking at some lessons that may be applicable to the service experience, it is helpful to point out what to avoid. Two clear messages emerged from the interview group regarding adjustment and change:

- Do not let cost cutting overwhelm the mission.
- Do not reorganize too fast.

The corporate world has done a great deal right in the steps it has taken to become lean and mean, improve profitability and productivity, and otherwise meet the challenges of global competition. This process, however, has involved heavy costs—most notably, extreme downsizing, personnel layoffs, insecurity about continued employment, loss of loyalty to the corporation, and a general decline in motivation and morale. Some of the organizational changes have been drastic and sudden, and in some cases, they have to be reversed. For example, a company might decentralize one year and implement a new reporting hierarchy the next. The military is cautioned to move with care and deliberate speed. It is also cautioned to be open and direct about the pressures that it is facing from competing demands: how can it cut costs and be more productive at the same time that it is expected to expand its mission and take on more responsibilities? The military can "do more with less," but when the demands become too many and clearly outweigh the resources, the military has to stand up and say, "We can't do that."

As we approach the positive side of the corporate experience, it is important for the military to expect that some change in the military mindset may be necessary. As more demands are placed on military personnel, the services must do more to acknowledge how central and valuable good people are to its mission. It *is* possible to do more with less: for example, the Navy is already operating combatant ships with crews of fewer than 100 instead of 400, and the military is using force multipliers everywhere from new paints to new communications equipment. At the same time, cost cutting should not be allowed to undermine morale and overwhelm mission. One former naval officer and current business executive interviewed for this report suggested that military leaders must begin to see leadership as meaning "deal with" rather than "dictate to" (skippers are tempered today by accountability to crew, political leaders, and even the media); that the era of people as "expendable assets" is over; and that the expanded mission of the service requires its leaders to have a broader understanding of different cultures, history, and technology than ever before.

The military's interest in learning from the corporate world has been demonstrated most effectively through the establishment of the Secretary of Defense Corporate Fellows Program (SDCFP) in 1994. Under the program, the Secretary selects annually one or two military officers from each service for a 10-month assignment working with SDCFP. Corporate Fellows spend a year working with leading-edge American businesses in order to glean the best of change, innovation, and emerging business practices. They are then expected to bring that experience back and use it to help transform the services. During their fellowship year, they continually update the

Deputy Secretary on progress made and on occasion have working sessions with him. At the conclusion of the assignment, each fellow submits a final report to the Secretary of Defense, and the group as a whole provides a common report. Each member also provides a formal briefing to the Secretary, Deputy Secretary, Chairman, Joint Chiefs, service secretaries and chiefs, and other senior officials.[1]

Corporate Fellows also prepare individual reports on their experiences, and the individual presentations are aggregated to suggest general recommendations. These suggestions, made by officers in pay grades of O5 or O6 who have demonstrated high flag or general officer potential, speak directly and with great authority to the question of what the services can learn from corporate techniques and methodologies. Some of the major conclusions of the program participants from the 1997–1998 and the 1998–1999 program years are summarized in the following discussion.

SDCFP Conclusions

One objective of SDCFP is to take lessons from businesses and see how best business practices might apply to DOD, particularly infrastructure programs, which make up two-thirds of the department's budget. Those in the SDCFP see businesses outside DOD as successful in adapting to the changing global environment, exploiting the Information Revolution, structural reshaping and reorganizing, and developing innovative practices. A second program objective is to build a cadre of future leaders who understand more than the profession of arms—that is, who understand adaptive business culture, recognize organizational and operational opportunities, understand skills required to implement change, and will motivate innovative changes throughout their careers.

The 1997–1998 and 1998–1999 fellows offered observations and recommendations on a wide range of subjects, including organization and structure, planning and budgeting, human resources, and outsourcing.

Change Management

- Planning is a must. The first step is to determine actual processes.
- The second step is to educate and empower employees to effect change.
- Continuity of leadership is critical. Change is a multiyear process.
- Active top-level leadership is a must. No transformation occurs without it.

Culture

- Partnerships and teaming are important.
- Trust and sharing are objectives and motivators.
- Culture should not be adversarial; when working with partners, the goal should be to create "win-win" and long-term relationships, not a sense of constant recompetition.
- Business allies should have greater access to information.

Information Technology

- Enterprisewide architecture and protocols are a must, as are a common operating environment, authority granted to the chief information officer, and money to enforce information decisions.
- Seamless DOD-wide Intranet access is needed.
- Full implementation of information technology potential is a strategic-level leadership issue.
- DOD requires enterprise resource planning (ERP) systems.
- Lease rather than buy, when possible, to maintain state-of-the-art capability.
- Strive for paperless/deskless/virtual systems when sensible.
- Fully utilize high-technology collaboration potential throughout DOD, with "best practices" in accessible archives, video/chat meetings and decisionmaking forums, online professional news, and education.
- Use information technology more effectively for common administrative functions.
- Introduce automated shared support services (for example, pay, travel, legal, information technology) with single-point access by user.
- Professionalize DOD administration systems and not as a collateral duty.

Innovation

- Corporations take risks and expect that some experiments will fail. Such failures are not career-threatening events.

Organization and Structure

- Agility is the single most important attribute.
- Successful companies have flexible and dynamic structures.
- Collaboration and teaming are important and effective, with information technology as the enabler.
- Task-organized, rather than hierarchical, structures contribute to flexibility.
- Decisionmaking in agile firms is often decentralized.

Outsourcing

- A company must be certain of its core competencies and businesses. These should not be outsourced.
- Partnership is an alternative.

Personnel Incentives and Motivation

- Fear is not enough. Incentives are an absolute requirement for change. The benefits of change must be shared.
- There is a real workforce shortage. As a result, the military faces growing competition from the private sector for skilled employees.

- Added and high value from employees must be rewarded; a "one-size-fits-all" approach is not effective.
- DOD must rethink paradigms that limit its ability to fill gaps, rather than moving personnel only from the bottom up.
- Human resources is a profession, not a collateral duty.
- Incentives for recruitment and retention must be adapted so that DOD can compete in the marketplace. The total benefits package, not just salary, is critical.
- New incentive combinations might be considered, including compensation above basic pay for performance, flex-time, and a strong health plan.

Planning

- The time frame for fiscal planning should be 18 to 36 months or 12 to 24 months.
- Budget building and approval processes could be shortened.
- Financial reviews should be held throughout the year; at the "business-unit" level, savings should be plowed back, not taken away.
- Strategic planning should be "top down," not "bottom up."
- Strategic planning should be broad and general, with a time horizon of 1 to 5 years out. The rapid pace of change and need for agility make longer range planning outmoded.

SDCFP Recommendations

In reviewing the SDCFP conclusions and recommendations, several items stand out.

The new challenges for military leadership and the potential for learning from the private sector. There are new ways of looking at strategic planning, motivation of personnel, and technology that can perhaps help military leaders cope with their increasingly complex responsibilities.

Today's military leaders have a much broader and more subtle mandate than did their predecessors. The responsibilities of leadership are made quantitatively more difficult by the realities of globalization and the two-way communication that changes the dynamics of on-the-scene leadership. The traditional mission of the commander—"Go forth and act in the nation's best interest"—does not mean the same thing to a commander today as it did in the days before instant international communication. Then, the commander had more latitude and discretion. Today, decisions are instantly communicated to superiors, who can applaud, question, or reverse what is done by the on-site commander. A major question for leadership is, "How can we use technologies to communicate decisions and give a better picture of what is going on in the field?" Another question is, "How can leadership be made more sensitive to the complex realities of the global world, not just the military situation?" Decisionmaking today needs an informed consensus. It needs well-educated, well-rounded leaders who can "cross-fertilize" ideas and deal with different cultures (for example, in Kosovo, in Lebanon) and who are flexible enough to take on projects that have not been anticipated and that they have not been fully trained to do. Coping with these demands requires flexibility and agility—qualities that are encouraged in the private sector but that are sometimes difficult to nurture in a culture where hierarchy and rules predominate.

The need for the military to address issues of recruitment, retention, and reward of personnel. The military faces serious motivation and morale problems if more attention is not paid to recruiting good people and keeping them satisfied with their work.

The military may not be fully aware of how serious the war for talent is in this period of workforce shortages. Corporations are competing with each other for talent, and they are coming after good people from the military. Taking a "commodity approach" ("There are more people where the ones we have came from") is not satisfactory in a competitive market. Pay is not the only consideration. The military can learn from the private sector about competing for people and about the incentives and lifestyle accommodations that corporations make to keep and attract good people. Consideration should be given to relieving the pressure of long hours, long periods of time out of port, and the low ratio of money earned to hours worked. Working conditions, too, can be a major morale factor—for example, excessive bureaucracy, paperwork, insufficient personnel, lack of choice and opportunity for input for officers in the personnel selection process, and lack of spare parts. The military can also consider how the private sector rewards excellence and achievement. In the services, there is little individuality of reward, performance bonuses, or additional pay for extra skills.

The need for top-level attention to making the most of technology. Private sector corporations have learned that to maximize technology and communications, the whole company must be networked and data must be integrated to improve communications and coordination. In effective ERP systems, all functions are linked, software is integrated, and comprehensive data systems are developed. There would be significant up-front costs involved, but over time, the dollar savings and efficiencies generated would be very valuable to the services. DOD needs networked systems for traditional business applications (such as payroll and inventory) and for warfare. DOD has identified "information superiority" as the primary enabler for *Joint Vision 2020*; this demands that information be managed in a timely manner and that DOD have the correct technology mix and a top-of-the-line conceptual framework. The Department and the services should be able to obtain the same type of productivity gains and efficiencies in its overall business systems performance that the private sector is enjoying as a result of the application of networked information technology.

The need to review planning and budget cycles. Private sector firms are often criticized for being too "short-term" in their horizons, but there are advantages to a shorter planning time line: agility and flexibility are among them. Defense planners routinely look out 6 years and sometimes 20 years; businesses, by contrast, generally operate in 1- to 3-year planning periods. Long time lines mean very long research-and-development cycles. Military budgets take 2 full years to plan and have much more detail than private sector budgets do. These differences make the services less flexible than business and may hamper their ability to respond to current and future developments in technology, economics, and politics.

The need to nurture a "culture of trust" that affects internal service morale, relations with contractors, and government-industry relations. In the corporate world, the processes of "empowerment" and decentralization have included giving more responsibility to employees at every level (for example, decisionmaking responsibility, risk-taking) and more weight to the assumption that employees are basically honest and competent. Big bureaucracies in all organizations develop huge operations for audits, contract management, expense reporting, and the like. Sometimes, the costs outweigh the direct dollar savings, and the negative message of "We think you might have done something wrong" can undermine collegiality and trust in the workplace. The services might evaluate how things have changed in corporations. Says John Naland in his September 1999 *Foreign Service Journal* article "Reinventing State: Lessons from U.S. Business": "Despite a strong focus on the financial bottom line, Caterpillar does not stand over employees' shoulders when they make long-distance calls (for example, no phone logs) or travel (compare a 5x7-inch reimbursement form with a multi-page voucher)." Trust is fundamental to teamwork inside an organization, and to working with partners outside. The services and DOD should seek ways to make trust a stronger part of their management and administrative cultures.

The Impact of Globalization on Defense Industries

DOD is already sensitive to the changes in the U.S. defense industries and the resulting significant effects on the defense industrial base. The 1999 *Final Report of the Defense Science Board Task Force on Globalization and Security* says:

> Globalization affects DOD in two distinct, overlapping ways. First, it is altering the composition of DOD's supporting industrial base. In just a few short years, DOD has gone from relying almost exclusively on a captive U.S. defense industry to depending more on the commercial market, both domestic and international. Second, and perhaps more significantly, globalization is reshaping the environment in which DOD must compete. The international military-technological playing field is being leveled by a range of trends, including: an increasingly permissive and sophisticated conventional arms market, the diffusion of advanced dual-use technology, the commercialization of formerly military technology, the increasing reliance of militaries worldwide on commercially-developed technology, and the declining effectiveness of export controls. Thus, all states—not just the United States and its allies—will eventually share access to a majority of the technology underpinning the modern military.

Globalization means that the defense business world has become commercialized. This changes the way that companies do business, and it changes the pressures that they face. It means, as discussed earlier, more pressures on the bottom line, more pressures for cost cutting, for profits, and for cash. It means looking for new customers, finding new ways of doing business and of raising money, and facing a whole new set of business problems.

One of the major manifestations of globalization has been the movement away from the foreign military sales (FMS) contract approach, under which the U.S. Government sells products to the government of another country, to a direct contract approach, in which a defense company contracts directly with a foreign government.

This has been a huge change for defense firms. One major defense contractor interviewed for this report said that about a decade ago, 70 to 80 percent of his firm's international defense business was done on an FMS basis. Today, it is only 40 percent FMS, and the expectation is that this number will go down to 20 to 30 percent. This change creates a whole series of adjustments in the way that business is done. Under the FMS system, when the sale is made through the U.S. Government, the rules of business are pretty much the same, regardless of the final customer. When sales are made through direct contracts, by contrast, countries negotiate and defense firms tailor their activities to meet their requests. Some typical provisions and results:

- The foreign buyer wants the seller to work with industry in the customer country. Many teaming and joint venture arrangements come about through this request.
- The seller is often required to establish in-country operations to support the product being sold. There are complicated legal, tax, labor, and finance issues associated with establishing an off-shore operation.
- Defense firms have to deal with more than one contract and procurement system. Under the FMS system, the U.S. Government standardized these. Now, a company may have to manage 60 to 80 different systems. Some countries have vague rules. Some customers reinterpret the rules as they go along. In some countries, written contracts are the beginning of a negotiation. Getting paid can be a problem if the contracts are not clearly written and understood by both sides. The implication: a great deal of up-front analysis is being done to qualify opportunities and detail what is involved.
- Export licensing is more complex and difficult. There are frequently export-licensing questions involved in government-to-government sales, but the U.S. Government is more comfortable with these FMS transactions and more willing to cooperate.
- More work with foreign consultants and agents is required. Companies work to find honest consultants and are very strict on ethical issues.
- Offset requirements have become increasingly costly and more difficult, with countries making conditions harder to fulfill. More costly indirect offset is replacing direct offset.
- Financing can be a major problem. Many countries say, "Find us the money, and we'll buy your product." This puts the seller on the spot to arrange off-balance-sheet financing with countries that are reluctant to commit a sovereign guarantee. These same countries do not want to pay the cost of such financing.
- Foreign exchange issues are risky and difficult. Under the FMS system, contracting firms are always paid in U.S. dollars. Now, currencies come in all colors and in varying values, and sometimes there is risk around being paid at all.
- Tax planning has become more important for defense firms. Every country's tax system and rules are different, and all can cause financial troubles if business is not set up in the most advantageous way. Tax gains and losses can often overshadow the operating profits from a program.

- Accounting and bookkeeping have become very difficult. Foreign entities must be set up to collect the financial data needed for taxes and other financial matters in a manner consistent with local accounting practices. Currency issues complicate the job: for example, on some projects, a firm may buy in one currency, sell in another, and do its financial reports in a third.
- Putting people overseas and hiring local residents raise complicated and time-consuming issues. All countries have their own labor laws and employment contracts. Expatriate administration, immigration and business visas, and security clearance issues take a good deal of corporate staff time. Training of personnel is a problem, too. As the business issues change and grow more complex, it is more necessary than ever. In reality, however, training is often sacrificed to the press of time.

Two themes are consistently articulated by companies facing the challenges of globalization and commercialization in the defense field. One theme is the need for a spirit of partnership, cooperation, and support in the area of commercial sales. The second is the problems that companies face because of U.S. Government policies and procedures on technology transfer.

A Partnership Approach on Foreign Sales

There is a sense in industry that the services are so concerned about the release of technology that they are sometimes reluctant to work in partnership with American industry on commercial direct sales. The services and DOD, it is said, do not like the trend toward commercial sales and away from the FMS system; thus, they shy away from helping industry in the international arena. When defense firms do procurement in the United States, there is an arm's-length relationship with the services. At the international level, circumstances and objectives are different. Both industry and the military services are trying to help U.S. national security and the national interest. In the words of one industry representative: "It should be a team, an arm-in-arm relationship. We have to be on the team with FMS. They should be on the team for commercial."

Technology Transfer

Export control and technology transfer issues have caused problems between industry and government for many years, but industry representatives believe that these problems are more serious than ever in a world where markets are shrinking and export sales are increasingly important to corporate financial health. Some industry representatives told us that the technology transfer control is the chief inhibitor to their success in global markets. Fellows in the 1998–1999 SDCFP concluded that the technology transfer approval process is "inconsistent and glacial. A new process is needed for deciding what to protect."

Certain technologies (for example, stealth technology and sophisticated information systems) understandably need to be tightly controlled; however, many other technologies may not merit such protection. The government mentality with respect to this matter, it is believed, is still shaped by the Cold War and does not give foreign competitors their due. The result is to handicap American industry in export strategies and to slow the rate of American technological innovation. It is suggested that government undertake a significant national policy review, identifying truly "critical technologies," update the Military Critical Technologies List, and revise the International Traffic in Arms Regulations to make it a dynamic entity.

Apart from the substance of the restrictions and controls, export license processing continues to cause delays and obstacles for the defense exporters. A review of the process, as well as the substance, is highly recommended. Finally, it is suggested that somewhere in the system there should be a point of advocacy for exports, someone who looks at the technology with a different set of objectives than "Let's stop it."

The need for reform of technology transfer restrictions and export controls has been acknowledged and endorsed by recent DOD studies such as the following:

> The Department of Defense should engage the Department of State to jointly modernize the regulatory regime and associated administrative processes affecting the export of U.S. defense articles.
>
> — *Defense Science Board Task Force on Globalization and Security* (December 1999)

> In an era when: industry is globalized, the U.S. lead in militarily relevant technology may be shrinking, or may no longer exist at all; the U.S. military relies increasingly upon commercial technologies and products, and product-introduction cycles grow increasingly shorter; DOD must be selective in the technologies it chooses to protect.
>
> — *Secretary of Defense Strategic Studies Group IV, 1999 Final Report*

> Because of the continuation of outmoded export control policies and practices, defense industries in both the United States and allied European and Asian countries have attempted to remain autarkic—a self-sufficiency that is counter to the needs of coalition warfare and industrial globalization.
>
> — *Jacques Gansler, "The Defense Industrial Structure in the 21st Century," AIAA Acquisition Reform Conference* (January 21, 2000)

The difficulties in moving forward on these observations are themselves illustrative of the challenges of leadership and the problems of bureaucratic guidance in this complicated age. Industry generally welcomes the Defense Security Trade Initiative announced on May 24, 2000, but few believe this program will solve all the problems. Technology changes rapidly, and the process of evaluating technology transfer restrictions should be a constant high priority for government policymakers.

Conclusions and Key Recommendations

Globalization offers the opportunity for business, DOD, and the military services to renew and recenter their relationships, to learn from each other, and to move forward in a spirit of partnership and teamwork to meet the national security challenges of the new era. Specifically:

- The military should undertake a focused effort to analyze the corporate experience of adjustment to globalization and to assess what is and what is not relevant to the challenges that it seeks to address.
- The U.S. military should learn from the experience of corporations and try to think "out of the box." Like the private sector, the military needs to promote agility, flexibility, and creativity. Military leadership needs these attributes as it adapts to ever-changing and more complex challenges.
- The military must take steps to ensure that it has the highest class, most comprehensive, and integrated information technology systems available and that these systems are suited to its many needs.
- The military should give special attention to its personnel requirements and its corporate culture. New ideas for incentives and rewards should be encouraged, as should more traditional benefits such as significant pay increases, which would enhance recruitment and retention efforts.
- DOD and the military services should work in partnership to help the defense industry adjust to globalization. Specifically, DOD cooperation with industry commercial efforts should be encouraged, and technology transfer and export control policy and procedures should be reevaluated and reformed.
- The intensity and pace of global change demand that organizational reevaluation and restructuring be a continual process. Industry, DOD, and the services should work together in this process—promoting mutual feedback, questioning, and teamwork for change.

Notes

[1] To date, Corporate Fellows have spent time with such diverse and important businesses as Andersen Consulting, Boeing, Caterpillar, Cisco, CNN, Citicorp, Coopers and Lybrand, DirecTV, FedEx, Hewlett-Packard, Lockheed Martin, Microsoft, Mobil, Netscape, Northrup Grumman, Oracle, Raytheon Systems, Sarnoff Labs, Sears, and Southern Company.